MBLEx TEST PREP

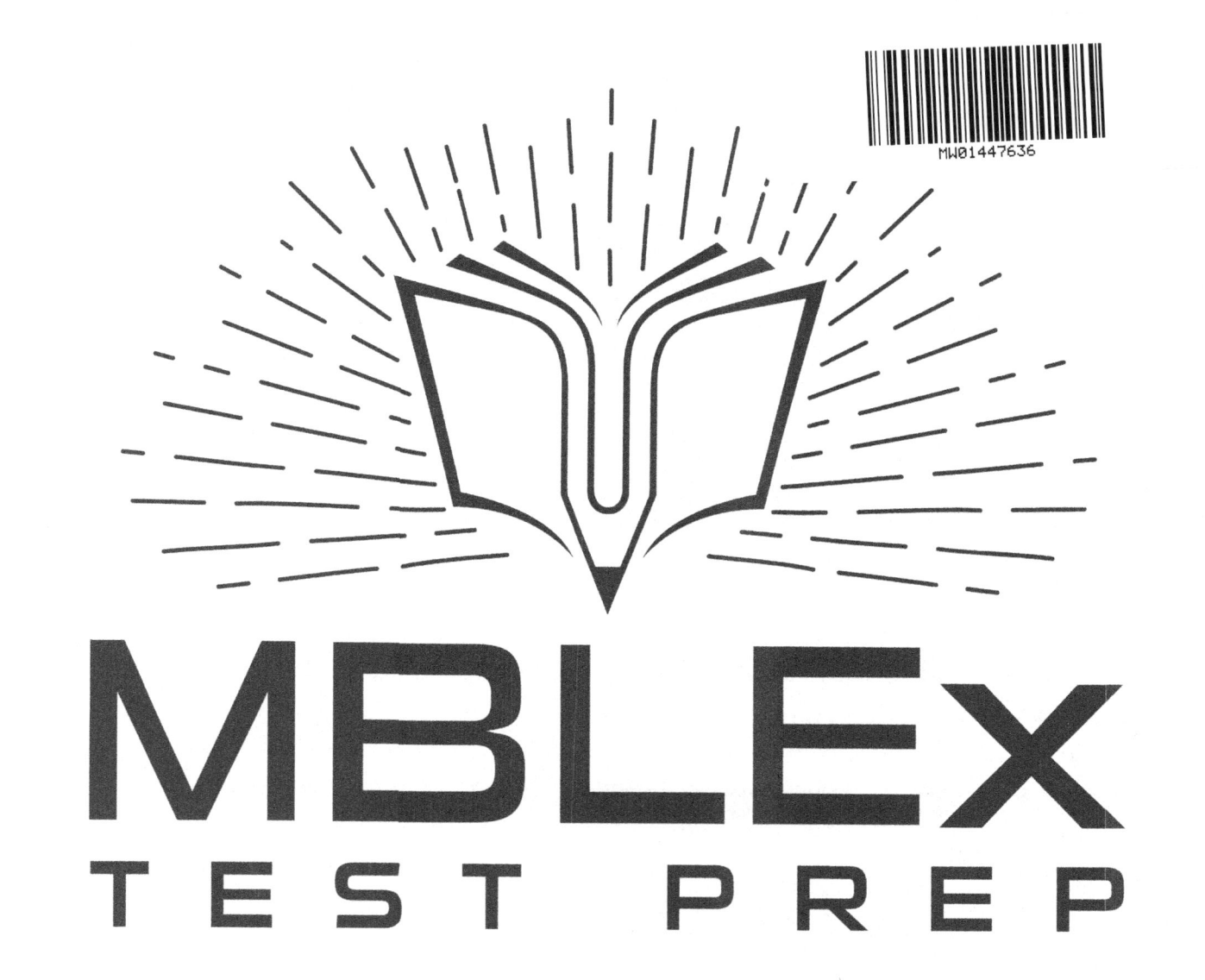

Comprehensive Study Guide and Workbook, 2021

David Merlino, LMT

MBLEX Test Prep – Comprehensive Study Guide and Workbook, 2021
Copyright © 2020, David Merlino and Wanderer Studios

Any duplication or transmission by any means, including electronic, photocopying, verbal recording, etc, of any portion of this study guide in any form without written consent is prohibited.

To obtain written permission to reproduce select portions of this study guide, email the author directly at david@mblextestprep.com.

Bulk order discounts are available for academic institutions. To obtain a written estimate or place an order, please email the author directly at david@mblextestprep.com.

Wandererstudios.us

ISBN-13: 978-1-7328356-7-2

Photo credits: Amanda Merlino, Desmond Merlino, Steven Merlino, Starrisa Reyna, Anna Owings, Ashley Capone, TJ Wilson, Andrew Briggs, Chara Lawson, Rose Matthews, Mike Escobar, Frank Butler, Robert Peterson. Stock photos via Shutterstock.

Special Contributor: Candice Merrick, BCTMB, LMT

Special Thanks: Every school and student who has used any of my guides, everyone who has supported me in my endeavors, my family, friends, Rocky McCahan, Fit Reno, Spavia Reno, Tim Ferriss, Shawn James.

PUBLISHER'S DISCLAIMER

The material presented in this study guide is for informational purposes only. Any information regarding Medications, CPR, First Aid, and Contraindications should be researched by the reader to obtain the most up-to-date requirements, as these subjects are ever-changing.

INTERNET RESOURCES

Information on how to access internet resources may be found on page 3. If these resources are not functioning properly, please email the author directly at david@mblextestprep.com to notify us of the situation.

"MBLEx" is a registered trademark of the FSMTB. This study guide bares no association with, nor is it endorsed by the FSMTB.

Table of Contents

Introduction	2	Cardiovascular System	57	Muscles of the Pelvis	268
How To Use This Study Guide	3	Digestive System	59	Muscles of the Thigh	273
Study Skills	4	Endocrine System	62	Muscles of the Leg	282
Test-Taking Techniques	4	Integumentary System	63		
Reducing Test Anxiety	5	Lymphatic System	64	Kinesiology Matching	289
		Muscular System	65	Kinesiology Crossword	290
Massage Therapy		Nervous System	69	Muscle Labeling	291
Massage Technique	7	Reproductive System	74	Kinesiology Practice Test	294
Effects of Massage Therapy	8	Respiratory System	75		
Joint Movements	8	Skeletal System	76	**Critical Thinking**	297
Stretching	9	Urinary System	88		
Assessment	11			**Answer Keys**	311
Precautions	13	A&P Matching	89	Matching Assignment Keys	312
Intake Forms	14	A&P Crossword	90	Medical Terminology Break	
SOAP Notes	17	A&P Practice Test	91	Down/Building Key	312
Massage Equipment	18			Crossword Keys	313
Draping	19	**Pathology**		Muscle Labeling Key	313
Bolsters	19	Disease	95	Individual Subject	
Body Mechanics	20	Immunity	96	Practice Test Keys	314
Personal Hygiene	21	Tissue Repair	101	Critical Thinking Answers	315
Massage Modalities	22	Medications	103		
Business	27	Medical Tests, Equipment, and	105	**Practice Tests**	329
Liability Insurance	27	Procedures	107	Complete Practice Test 1	332
Business Management	27	Cardiovascular Pathologies	112	Complete Practice Test 2	337
Types of Employment	28	Digestive Pathologies	121	Complete Practice Test 3	342
Tax Forms	28	Endocrine Pathologies	129	Complete Practice Test 4	347
Ethics	29	Integumentary Pathologies	134	Complete Practice Test 5	352
Communication	30	Lymphatic Pathologies	147	Complete Practice Tests	
Therapeutic Relationship	30	Muscular Pathologies	151	Answer Keys	358
Psychology	31	Nervous Pathologies	157		
		Respiratory Pathologies	163	References	359
Massage Therapy Matching	32	Skeletal Pathologies	168	Index	360
Massage Therapy Crossword	33	Urinary Pathologies	179		
Massage Therapy Practice Test	34	Cancers	182		
		Psychological Disorders	189		
Medical Terminology		Other Pathologies	193		
Word Roots	37	First Aid and Response			
Prefixes	39	to Emergencies	195		
Suffixes	41				
General Medical Terms	41	Pathology Matching	199		
	42	Pathology Crossword	200		
Medical Terminology Matching	44	Pathology Practice Test	201		
Medical Terminology Break					
Down/Building	45	**Kinesiology**	205		
Medical Terminology Practice Test	46	Muscle Actions	206		
		Bony Landmarks	215		
Anatomy and Physiology	49	Muscles of the Head	228		
Homeostasis	50	Muscles of the Neck	232		
Regional Anatomy	50	Muscles of the Back	237		
Body Planes	51	Muscles of the Chest	251		
Body Regions	52	Muscles of the Abdomen	255		
Cells	52	Muscles of the Arm	258		
Tissue	53	Muscles of the Forearm	264		

Introduction

Hello! My name is David Merlino, and I am the author of this study guide.

A lot of time and energy has gone in to the creation of this guide. I am extremely proud to share this guide with you, and I am honored that you have chosen my study guide to help you prepare for the MBLEx. You have a tall task ahead of you, but it isn't something you can't overcome. Trust me, I've taken and passed the MBLEx!

I've been a Licensed Massage Therapist for over 14 years, and I've learned and experienced plenty in my career. However, it all began with passing my licensing exam. I understood how to take tests, how to study, and how to give myself the best chance possible to pass the exam and advance into my career. I hope to share this knowledge with you.

In 2011, I began my new career preparing students to take their massage licensing exams at a career college in beautiful Reno, Nevada. It was here I honed my craft, helping students achieve a near-90% pass rate on the licensing exam. How did I do this? Simply put, it's called the minimum effective dose for the MBLEx. I review the information most likely to be seen on the exam, and don't review information I feel is unnecessary, or is unlikely to be seen on the exam. As Olympic pole vaulter Henk Kraaijenhof once said, "Do as little as needed, not as much as possible." This approach makes preparing for the MBLEx much easier to manage.

With this approach, my students achieved amazing success. You can too! Before you begin, however, I need to remind you of something: you will be tested on information that isn't present in this study guide. You will be tested on information you have never seen before. This happened to all of my students, and even happened to me, someone who has been teaching this information for years! Despite not seeing this information before, you can still do extremely well on these questions. Make sure you check out the Study Skills, Test-Taking Techniques, and Reducing Test Anxiety sections for information on optimizing your chances of doing well on the exam!

I've poured months of my life into the production and creation of this study guide. You are now my student. I believe in you, and I know you will do great!

If you have any questions, I am here to help. Please don't hesitate to send me an email with any questions you may have in regards to the study guide, practice tests, or the MBLEx in general.

My personal email address is **david@mblextestprep.com**. Just note, I am very much willing to help, but if your email is rude or disrespectful in any way, there will be no response from me. Just be cool!

Thank you again. I am honored that you have entrusted me with helping you pass the MBLEx. Let's get started!

Your Instructor,

David Merlino, LMT

How To Use This Study Guide

This study guide is designed to not just TELL information, but to help you LEARN information. This is achieved in many different ways, including standard study guides, assignments, and practice exams.

To get the complete, most effective and efficient experience from this study guide, I recommend the following:

Before starting, figure out the area you need to study the most: Massage Therapy, Kinesiology, Pathology, or Anatomy and Physiology. Most people tend to choose Kinesiology first. A common study routine I've helped many students implement is the following(you can change the subjects as you see fit, depending on how comfortable you are with each), with an average of six weeks of study time before the exam. For this example, we'll say the study order is Medical Terminology, Kinesiology, Pathology, Anatomy and Physiology, and Massage Therapy, with ten hours of study per week:

Week 1: Study nothing but Medical Terminology for ten hours.
Week 2: Study Medical Terminology for two hours, and Kinesiology for eight hours.
Week 3: Study Medical Terminology and Kinesiology for two hours, and Pathology for eight hours.
Week 4: Study Medical Terminology, Kinesiology, and Pathology for two hours, and Anatomy and Physiology for eight hours.
Week 5: Study Medical Terminology, Kinesiology, Pathology, and Anatomy and Physiology for two hours, and Massage Therapy for eight hours.
Week 6: Study every subject an equal amount of time, two hours per subject.

I've found that this way of studying is great for long-term memory growth in these subjects, as there is a consistent review of information every week.

While studying, be sure to finish the assignments and practice exams in the book. These are great for assessing your knowledge on the subjects you will have just covered, and help you figure out what you still need to study, and what you've learned.

I have created an enormous amount of online content for you to supplement your studying! While studying, especially in the final week before the exam, I highly recommend taking as many practice tests as possible. Watch video lectures I have created, which puts you in a class-like study session with me as your instructor. Utilize pre-made flashcards I've created for you, which cover the most important information you need to study. Go to the following website to use all the online study material:

http://www.mblextestprep.com/resources.html

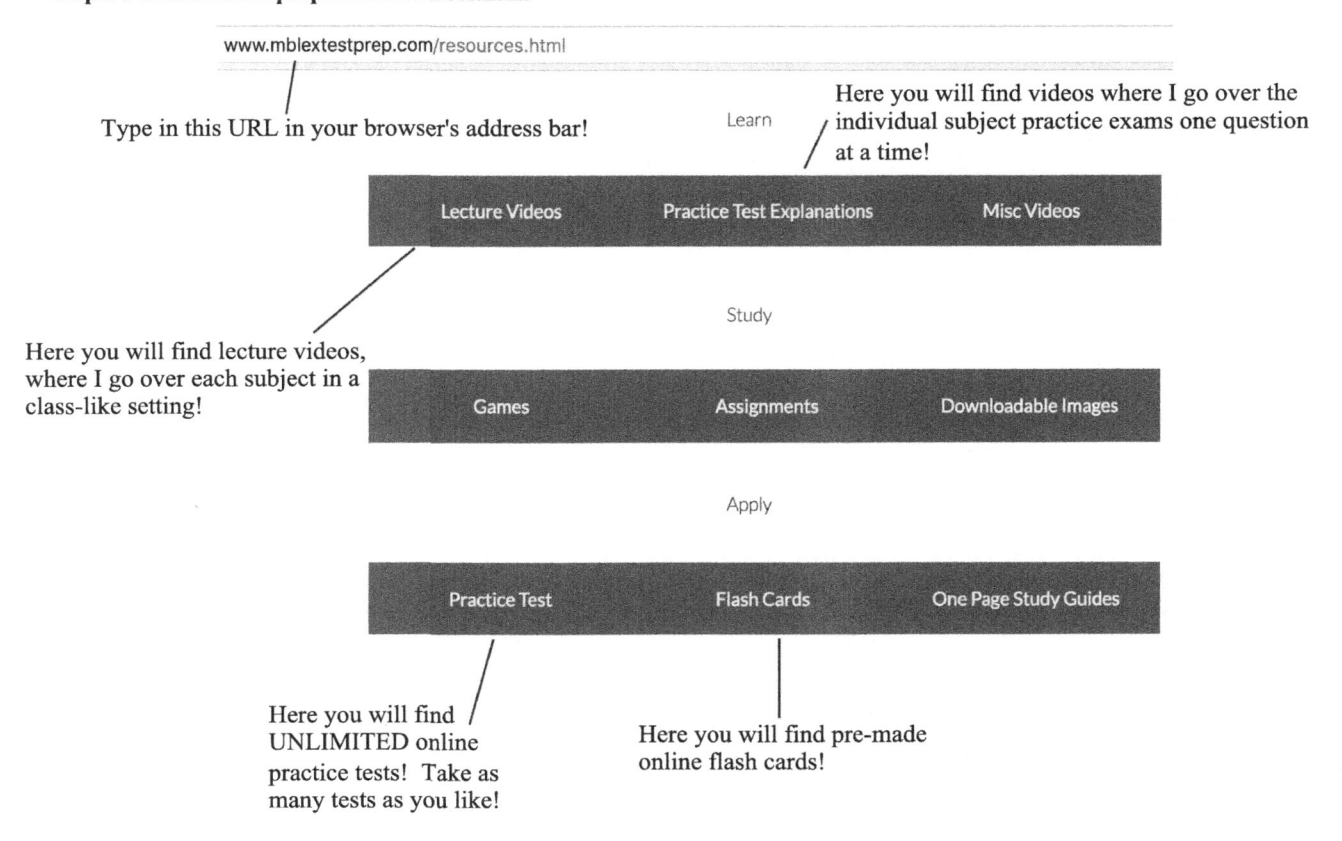

www.mblextestprep.com/resources.html

Type in this URL in your browser's address bar!

Learn

Here you will find videos where I go over the individual subject practice exams one question at a time!

| Lecture Videos | Practice Test Explanations | Misc Videos |

Here you will find lecture videos, where I go over each subject in a class-like setting!

Study

| Games | Assignments | Downloadable Images |

Apply

| Practice Test | Flash Cards | One Page Study Guides |

Here you will find UNLIMITED online practice tests! Take as many tests as you like!

Here you will find pre-made online flash cards!

Study Skills

1. Do not do all of your studying the night before or day of the test. Study consistently, up to several times per week. Cramming is good for short-term learning, but does not help with long-term learning. The more you study, the more likely you are to retain the information.

2. Use all of your class and home work as study material. The information in these assignments is information that may be seen on the exam.

3. Take many short breaks as you study. Memory retention is higher at the beginning and end of study sessions than it is in the middle. This is called the Serial Position Effect. Study for no longer than ten minutes, then take a short break, and resume studying for another ten minutes.

4. Focus on one subject at a time while studying. You don't want to confuse yourself by mixing information.

5. Study the subject you have the most difficulty with more than the subjects you are comfortable with. Studying what you aren't weak in doesn't help. If you need work on a specific subject, focus the majority of your time learning that information, even if it means taking away study time from other areas. You're better off being 80% proficient in every subject than 100% in four subjects and only 50% in the last. Not studying this information could prevent you from passing the exam.

6. While studying, take notes on important information, especially if it's information you don't recognize or remember. Use this information to study with.

7. Assign yourself tests, reports, assignments, and projects to complete. You are more likely to remember information if you write a report on it than if you just read the information.

8. Teach information you are studying to another person. If you are responsible for someone learning something, you have to know and understand the material, and be able to put that information into the simplest terms possible, so someone else can understand it. This will only help you. Trust me, from personal experience, this works extremely well.

9. Understand the material you are studying. Do not just try to memorize certain answers you think may be on the test. Certain "key words" might not be on the test. Learn everything about a subject, and you'll never get any question on that subject wrong.

Test-Taking Tips

1. Go to the restroom before taking the exam. Using the restroom beforehand ensures that you are 100% focused on the exam, and not on your bladder.

2. Read the entire question slowly and carefully. Never make assumptions about what a question is asking. Assuming you know what a question is asking may lead you to missing key words in the question that tell you exactly what the question is asking. Read every single word in every single question, multiple times if necessary.

3. Understand what the question is asking before you try answering it.

4. Identify key words in each question. Key words are words that tell you exactly what the question is asking. Identify these words easily by reading question aloud to yourself. The words you find yourself emphasizing while reading aloud are likely the key words.

Here is an example. Read this question aloud:
Q. Which of the following statements is true regarding Swedish massage?

In this question, there are two key words, which are telling you exactly what the question is asking. Which words did you find yourself putting emphasis on? Most likely, you read the question like this: "Which of the following statements is TRUE regarding SWEDISH massage?" These are the key words.

5. Do not change your answers, unless you misread the question. Changing your answers puts doubt into your mind, and leads to more changing of answers. The answer you put first is usually correct. Do not change your answers!

6. Match key words in the answers with key words in the questions. Sometimes it's as simple as matching terms, if you've exhausted all other avenues.

7. Eliminate answers you know aren't correct and justify the reason they aren't correct. If you can eliminate one answer from each question, that brings your odds of getting that question right up to 33%. If you can eliminate two answers that can't be right, that brings it up to 50%. Then it's just a coin flip!

Here's an example. Read the question, and the answers:
Q. Of the following, which is not contagious?
A. Athlete's foot
B. Herpes simplex
C. Influenza
D. Osgood-Schlatter Disease

Have you ever heard of Osgood-Schlatter Disease? Even if you haven't, you can still get this question right by eliminating the other answers. Athlete's foot is caused by a fungus, and is contagious. That leaves us with three possible answers(33% chance). Herpes simplex is caused by a virus, and is contagious. That leaves us with two possible answers(50% chance). So even if you're guessing at this point, it's only a 50/50 chance you get it right! Influenza is caused by a virus, and is contagious. This process of elimination just gave us the answer, D. Osgood-Schlatter Disease.

8. Read the entire question before looking at the answers. Again, never make assumptions about what the question is asking.

9. Come up with the answer in your head before looking at the answers. If the same answer you come up with is in the list of answers, that's most likely the right answer.

10. Read every answer given to make sure you are picking the most correct answer. Some questions have multiple right answers, and you need to make sure you're picking the most correct answer.

11. Make sure you are properly hydrated before the test. Studies have been done on the effects of proper hydration on those taking tests. People who are properly hydrated tend to score higher than those who are not.

12. Exercise for twenty minutes before the exam. Exercise has also been shown to increase test scores.

Reducing Test Anxiety

1. Study consistently. If you understand the material, you won't be as stressed out about the test. There are ways you can study without this book or your class notes as well. An example, whenever you take a bite of food, think about every structure the food passes through in the digestive tract and what each of the organs do. Another example, whenever you are massaging someone, tell yourself everything about every muscle you work on, like origin, insertion, and action.

2. Keep a positive attitude while preparing for the test and during the test. If you think you're going to fail, you will not be as motivated to study, you won't adhere to your test-taking techniques, you'll become stressed out during the exam much more easily, and you'll be more likely to fail.

3. Try to stay relaxed. Utilize deep breathing techniques to calm down if you start feeling nervous or stressed. You will have two hours to finish the exam. You can afford one or two minutes to calm yourself down if you need to.

4. Exercise consistently up until the day of the test to reduce anxiety. Exercise has been shown to significantly reduce stress, and also helps with memory retention. Try utilizing flash cards while riding an exercise bike.

5. Take your time on the test. If you find yourself rushing, slow down. Again, you have two hours to finish the exam. Do not rush through it. You may miss important information in the exam and answer questions incorrectly because of this.

I hated every minute of training, but I said "Don't quit. Suffer now and live the rest of your life as a champion."

- Muhammad Ali

Massage Therapy

Massage Therapy

Massage Technique

In western massage, there are **six** main massage strokes, which have been in a constant state of evolution since being developed.

Effleurage is the most common stroke in western massage, consisting of long, **gliding** strokes that are directed **towards the heart**. Effleurage is used to increase circulation of blood and lymph, remove waste from tissues, introduce the therapist's touch to the client, transition between strokes, and apply massage lubricant. Effleurage may be used throughout the massage, but is the main stroke used at the beginning of the treatment. The majority of the time, effleurage is performed by the therapist in the **archer(bow) stance**.

Petrissage utilizes **kneading** movements, lifting and squeezing tissue, to increase circulation, loosen adhesions that may be present in the tissue, and release metabolic waste from tissues. Petrissage is an important stroke to use in post-event sports massage, as it helps flush waste from the muscles and bring fresh oxygen-rich blood into them.

Friction consists of strokes that move **across** tissue. Friction is especially useful in breaking up adhesions and scar tissue, increasing circulation, and stretching muscles. There are many different forms of friction, such as superficial friction(rubbing the surface of the skin), parallel friction, circular friction, and cross-fiber friction.

Tapotement consists of **percussion** strokes, rhythmically affecting the tissues of the body in many different ways. Tapotement increases spindle cell activity in the muscles, which helps activate them and get them ready for use, which makes tapotement a very important stroke to use in pre-event sports massage. Tapotement may also help loosen any phlegm, or mucous, in the respiratory tract, and is very helpful in conditions such as asthma or chronic bronchitis. There are many different forms of tapotement, including hacking, cupping, tapping, and beating.

Vibration is performed by **shaking** a part of the body, using **trembling** actions. Vibration can have different effects on the body, depending on how fine the vibration is. Slow vibration is used to sedate an area(think of massage chairs that vibrate, numbing the area). Fast vibration is used to stimulate an area.

A **nerve stroke** is an **extremely light** form of **effleurage**. Like effleurage, nerve strokes, also called feather strokes, are directed towards the heart. These strokes are primarily used at the end of a massage, or at the end of work on a specific body part, to separate the therapist from the client(ending the massage session), or to transition from one part of the body to another.

Effects of Massage Therapy

Mechanical Effects

Mechanical effects of massage therapy are any physical changes in the body that are the direct result of massage being performed on a specific part of the body. For example, massage strokes such as petrissage and effleurage will forcibly move blood and lymph further through the body as the strokes are performed. This increases circulation.

Mechanical effects of the main western massage strokes include:

Effleurage: Increased blood circulation, increased lymph circulation.

Petrissage: Increased blood circulation, increased lymph circulation, removal of waste such as lactic acid from muscle, loosening of adhesions between tissues, loosening of fascia.

Friction: Break up of adhesions between tissues, temporary localized ischemia, removal of waste such as lactic acid from muscle.

Tapotement: Loosening phlegm in the respiratory tract.

Vibration: Sedation of the area, stimulation of the area.

Reflexive Effects

Reflexive effects are changes in the body that occur by stimulation of the Nervous System as a result of massage therapy. An example includes effleurage stimulating the blood vessels to dilate, which is known as vasodilation. This makes the blood vessels more permeable, and allows blood to escape the blood vessels, increasing blood concentration in an area, which is known as hyperemia. The increased blood in the area makes the area appear more red, and the temperature in the location is increased.

Another example is the activation of muscle spindle cells when tapotement is used, which causes a brief, reflexive contraction of the muscle belly to prevent the muscle from stretching too far, preventing injury.

Massage therapy has the ability to stimulate the production and release of certain hormones in the body, which can influence the sympathetic or parasympathetic nervous response. A relaxing massage would likely stimulate the release of hormones such as melatonin(page 62) and reduce cortisol levels in the body. Massaging the abdomen in a clockwise manner may stimulate peristalsis, which occurs when the parasympathetic response is activated. Massage may also help to reduce blood pressure and heart rate due to its stimulation of the parasympathetic response.

Joint Movements

Joint movements describe how a joint is, well, moved! There are four main types of joint movements, performed by the therapist on the client, the therapist and the client working together, the therapist and the client working against one another, or the client performing the action by themselves.

An **active joint movement** involves the client actively performing a movement without assistance from the massage therapist. An example would be a massage therapist asking a client to perform a range-of-motion as part of assessment. The therapist does not help with the action, as they would want to see how much movement the client can perform by themselves, and to see where any restrictions may be.

Active assistive joint movements involve the client performing a movement with assistance from the massage therapist. Active assistive joint movements are very helpful in rehabilitative settings, allowing the client to move the joint, but making sure someone is there to help move and support the joint to prevent further injury.

Passive joint movements involve the massage therapist moving the joint, with the client completely relaxed, not helping at all. Passive joint movements are helpful for performing stretches, feeling for restrictions in movements, and for assisting the client to further relax.

Resistive joint movements are when the client and massage therapist are moving a joint in opposite directions at the same time. This creates an isometric contraction(muscle tension increases, length doesn't change, see page 66), which is extremely helpful in a specific type of stretch known as Proprioceptive Neuromuscular Facilitation.

Stretching

Stretching is an exercise that is performed by **elongating** or lengthening a muscle. Stretching is extremely beneficial to a person's health.

An **unassisted stretch** is performed by the client stretching into resistance without any help from the massage therapist. It is similar to an active joint mobilization, but instead of just moving the joint through its normal range-of-motion, it moves past that point and into a stretch.

An **assisted stretch** is performed by the client with assistance from the massage therapist. Again, this is similar to an active assistive joint movement, where the massage therapist's role is to help the client move the joint into a stretch while stabilizing the joint to ensure there is no damage to the joint.

Proprioceptive Neuromuscular Facilitation(PNF) is a stretch that is very useful in loosening adhesions and scar tissue in muscles, and is very beneficial in athletes. To perform PNF, a massage therapist moves a client's joint into a stretch. Once resistance is met, the client will actively resist the movement being performed by the massage therapist. This puts the muscle into an **isometric contraction**. After holding this resisted movement for 5-10 seconds, the client **relaxes**, and the massage therapist is able to move the stretch further, until resistance is met again. The process is then repeated. PNF allows a highly noticeable increase in the amount of range-of-motion in a joint.

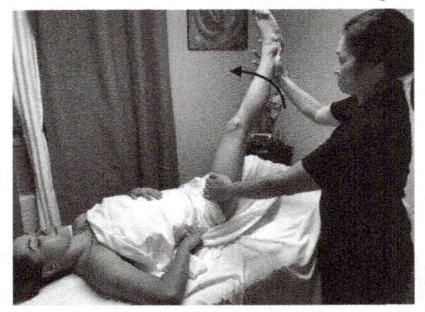

Stretch until resistance is met

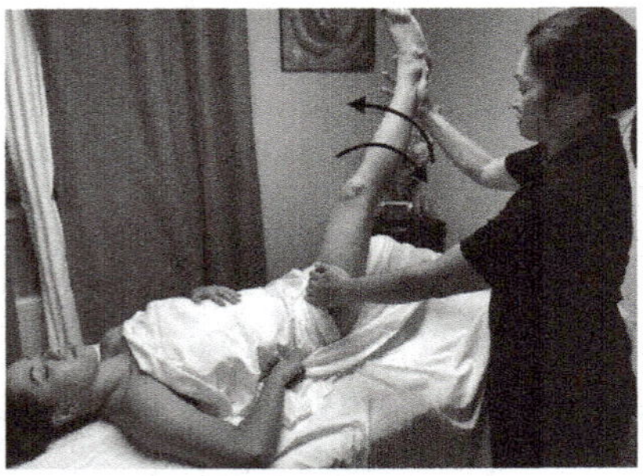

Isometric contraction

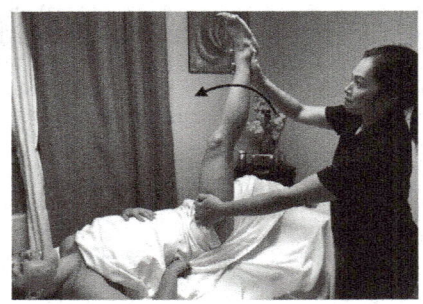

Client relaxes, then stretch moves further

During stretching and joint mobilizations, we experience **end feels**. An end feel is what causes a joint movement or stretch to not move any further.

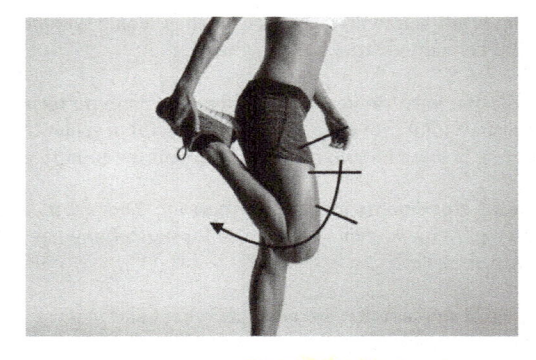

A **soft end feel** is the result of **soft tissues**, such as muscles and **tendons, pulling back on the joint, preventing any further movement**. An example is when stretching the quadriceps. The hip joint is moved into extension until resistance is met. The resistance is due to the quadriceps pulling back on the joint. If the quadriceps are loosened, the joint will move further. This is a soft end feel.

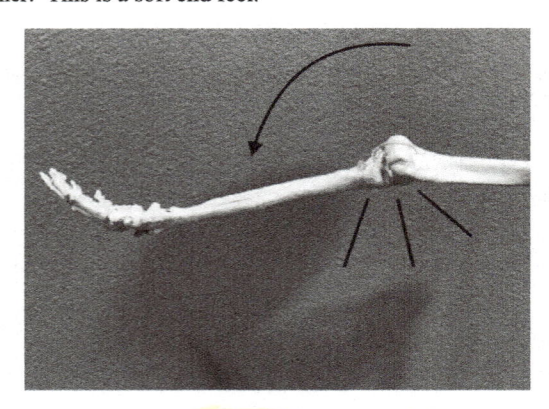

A **hard end feel** is the result of structures, primarily **bone**, preventing a joint from moving further. An example is extension of the knee or elbow. Straightening these joints can only go to a certain point. Bones will prevent these joints from extending any further. That's why hyperextension of these joints may result in broken bones. This is a hard end feel.

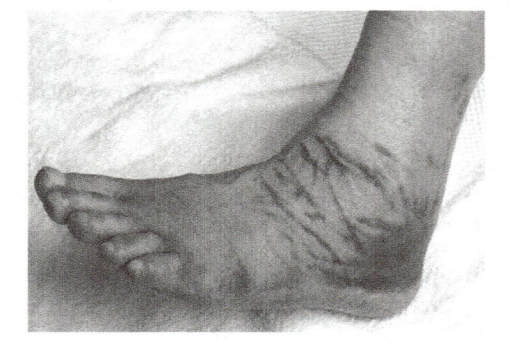

An **empty end feel** is caused by neither muscles nor bones interfering with movement. Empty end feels are the result of **trauma** to an area, which prevents movement. An example could be a sprained ankle. With a sprained ankle, bruising and inflammation may be present, which immobilizes a joint to prevent further injury. This is an empty end feel.

*Easy to Remember: A **soft end feel** is caused by **soft tissues**; a **hard end feel** is caused by **hard tissues**!*

Assessment

Assessments are a vital component of any massage treatment. Assessments are **evaluations** of the client primarily done before a massage, but the therapist is constantly assessing, even during and after a treatment.

Assessments have many different uses, from determining any contraindications the client may have, to tailoring a massage session specifically for that client and what they need. An example could be, if a client complains of low back pain, the therapist could then do visual assessment, range-of-motion exercises, and palpation to determine what the possible cause of the low back pain could be. Then, after the assessment is complete, the therapist may tailor the session to work specifically on the areas of concern(possibly the hamstrings, quadratus lumborum, iliopsoas, or rectus femoris).

Assessments may be performed in many different ways:

Subjective Information

Listening to the client and their complaints is the most effective way to determine issues a client may be experiencing. Anything the client details about themselves and their current state is considered subjective information. The way a client details areas of concern may be extremely helpful in determining the cause of their issues. An example, if a client begins stating that they have pain in the lower back, and also pain in the hamstrings, then the therapist might inquire as to activities the client is performing that may put strain on the hamstrings. Knowing that tightness in the hamstrings can lead to pain in the low back can help the therapist work with the client to alleviate the pain by working on the root cause.

Pain levels may be utilized by the therapist to determine exactly how painful an area is. A pain scale is usually based on numerical value, ranging from 1-5 or 1-10. The higher the number a client states, the more pain they are experiencing. In the scenario above, if the client were to state that their back pain was at a 6 out of 10, then the pain they are feeling is present and noticeable, but probably does not affect their ability to perform every day actions.

Some questions to consider when dealing with pain:

Is this pain acute and localized in one specific area, such as sprained ankles? Is the pain widespread and more chronic, such as with Multiple Sclerosis? Does the pain come and go, or is it persistent? What does the pain feel like? How long has the pain been present?

Objective Information

Objective information is anything that the therapist can physically see or observe. This information is measurable, and is not up to a client or therapist's interpretation of the information.

Visual assessment may be performed, focusing on alignment of specific bony landmarks to determine areas of concern. Some of these areas to compare bilaterally include the ears(possible neck tension), acromion processes(shoulder/back/chest tension), iliac crests(back/hip/thigh tension), anterior superior iliac spines(back/hip/thigh tension), and head of fibulae(back/hip/thigh tension). Visual assessment also includes how a client presents themselves while doing things as simple as talking to the therapist or walking to the massage room. A therapist may be able to tell if a client is limping, or is in some sort of pain just by interacting with them.

The therapist may be able to see certain things in a person's skin, such as inflammation or pallor. Edema and skin infections are physically observable. Scars may be a sign of past trauma that could be causing pain or discomfort. Physical disabilities can often be observed in people with conditions such as cerebral palsy or paralysis.

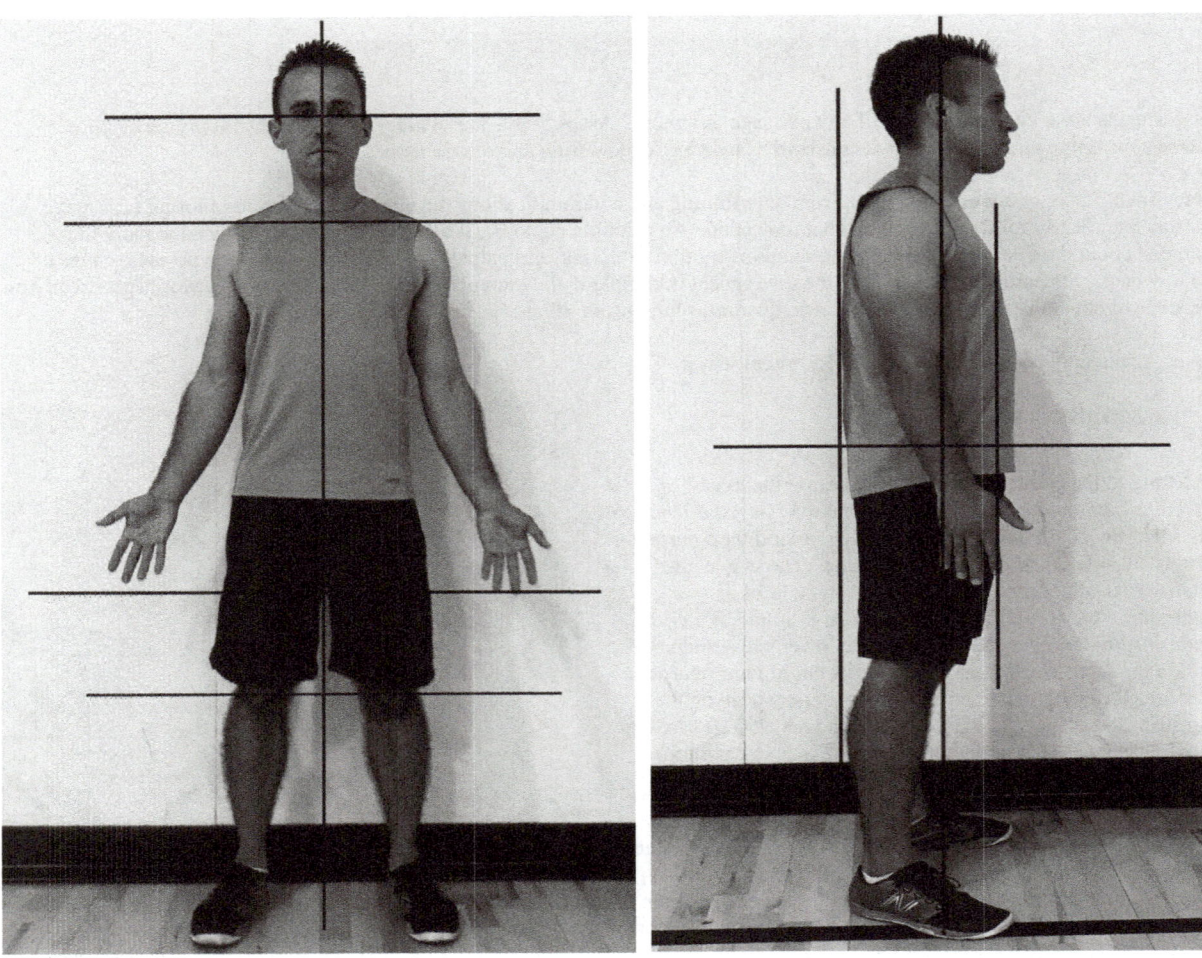

Common areas of visual assessment. These areas can be observed while standing, in addition to the client performing range-of-motion or gait analysis. This allows the therapist to observe any abnormalities between standing and performing an action.

Gait analysis may help determine hypertonic muscles unilaterally, and injuries. When observing a client walking, the therapist should pay attention to any imbalances the client has. This may indicate structural issues, pain, muscle weakness, or neurological issues. Observing the feet and their position while walking can give the therapist an idea of muscle tightness or previous injuries if the foot is over-pronated or over-supinated. Pain may be expressed on the face while walking.

Palpation is useful in feeling for adhesions or restrictions in muscles, localized ischemia, and inflammation. Ischemia, which is the lack of blood flow into an area, will feel cool to the touch. Inflammation, due to an increased amount of blood in the area, should feel warm to the touch. Assessing edema and pitting edema(page 149) requires the therapist to palpate the area.

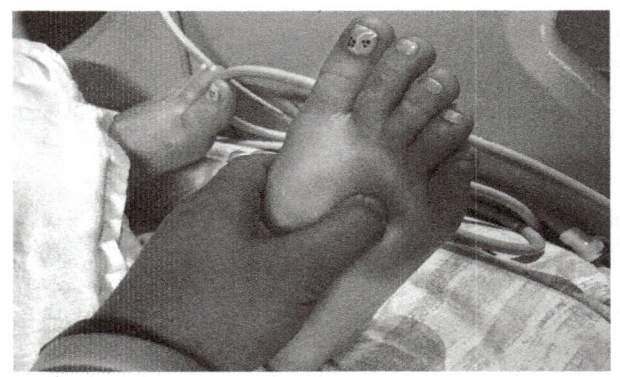

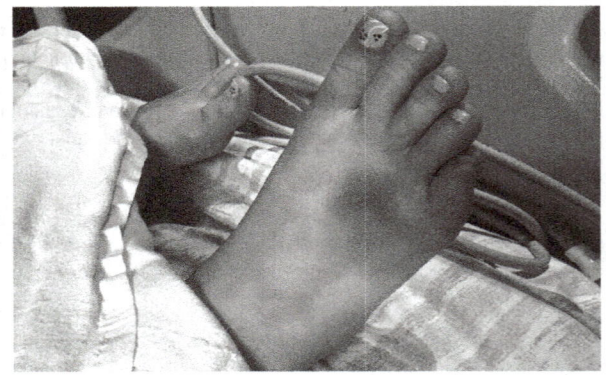

Palpation helps to assess pitting edema, seen above.

Range-of-motion may be performed by the client for the therapist to determine any restrictions of movement. Gait analysis can fall under range-of-motion. Performing any action can help determine if there is pain present during the movement, if range-of-motion is compromised in any way due to injuries or imbalances, or to determine any muscular restrictions a person may have that can be alleviated through the use of massage therapy and stretching techniques.

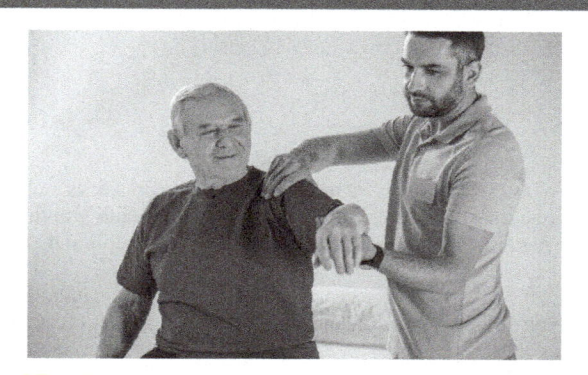

Breathing may be observed visually and by listening to the client's breathing rate and pattern. Shortness of breath may be cause for concern if there is no known cause, such as exercise. Increased respiration may be the result of the sympathetic response being activated and indicates stress. Watching a person breathe and how their body moves during respiration can help determine if there are any structural issues affecting breathing. Wheezing and coughing may indicate some sort of infection, or that the client is in the acute stage of a condition such as asthma.

Precautions

During a massage, certain precautions need to be adhered to in order to prevent injury or complications to the client.

Endangerment sites are areas of the body that, while massage may be performed on, need to be treated with **extra caution**. These are commonly due to insufficient tissues in the area to support, cushion, and protect important structures like blood vessels and nerves. Endangerment sites include the anterior triangle of the neck, the axilla, the anterior elbow, and the popliteal region.

Local contraindications are areas of the body that must be **avoided** when performing a massage. While endangerment sites allow for massage to be performed, local contraindications do not permit massage on localized areas. Reasons for a part of the body to be considered a local contraindication vary, from inflammation and trauma to infections(such as athlete's foot). The rest of the body may receive massage, but these specific areas must be avoided.

Absolute contraindications prohibit the use of massage. Massage on a person with an absolute contraindication, such as when a person is infected by a virus like influenza, can worsen the condition for the client, cause damage to the body, or even spread an infection or condition to the massage therapists. Do not perform a massage on a client with an absolute contraindication!

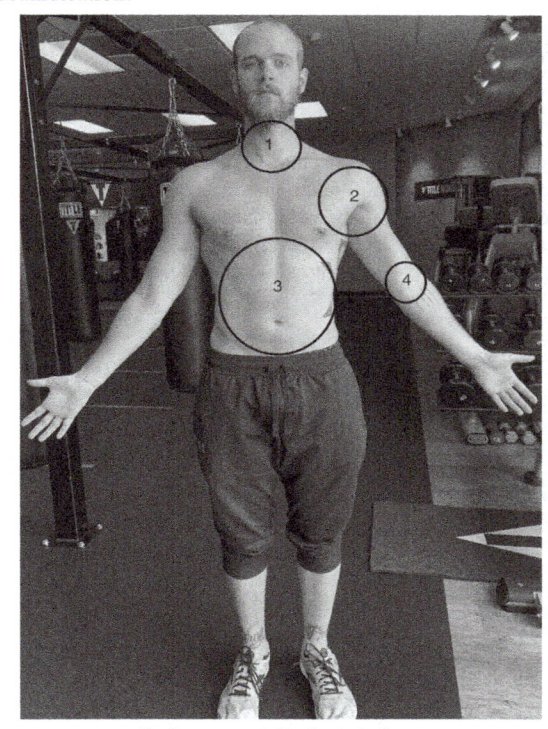

Endangerment sites(anterior):
1. Anterior Triangle of Neck
2. Axilla
3. Abdomen
4. Antecubital Region

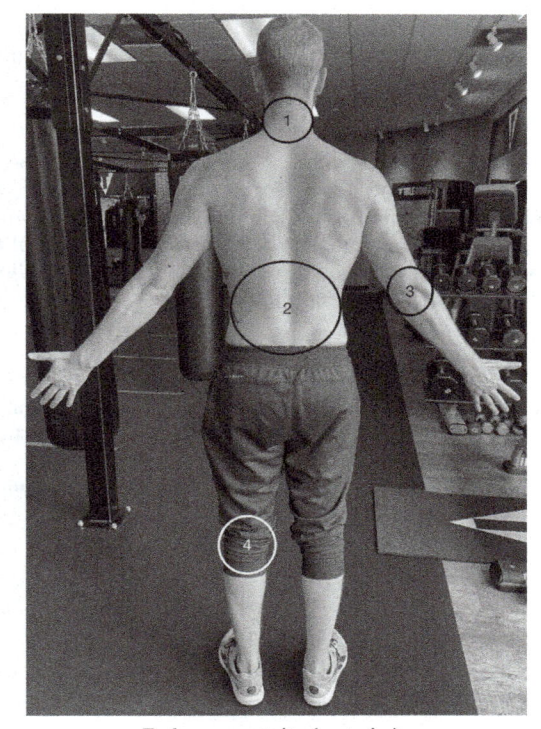

Endangerment sites(posterior):
1. Posterior Neck
2. Lower Back/Floating Ribs
3. Olecranon Process
4. Popliteal Region

Intake Forms

One of the primary ways a massage therapist can assess a client is by utilizing an intake form. These forms give the massage therapist the ability to ask numerous questions relating to the client and their well-being, which can give the therapist important insights into the client's physical and emotional states.

Intake forms should be constructed neatly, keeping similar information and questions together. This is mainly done to minimize client confusion and to speed up the time it takes for the client to fill out the form.

Medical History

Medical history is one of the primary sections detailed on an intake form. Medical history is important because it can help determine any contraindications before the massage even begins. It may also assist the therapist in developing an effective treatment plan, even if the treatment only lasts one session. The therapist needs to be aware of any past surgeries, current injuries, illnesses, and medications the client may be taking. All of these factors can determine the appropriate type of massage to perform, the appropriate session length, etc.

An intake form should always have a section to detail any allergies a client may have. Clients may be allergic to many different types of chemicals or plants which may be used during the massage treatment. Nut-based massage oils should be avoided. A hypo-allergenic massage lubricant should be sought to avoid any complications. Essential oils should not be automatically added to massage lubricant, as clients may be sensitive to them. Perfume scents should be avoided. Any allergies a client has should be documented by the client on the intake form.

Informed Consent

Informed consent refers to the client authorizing services provided by the massage therapist based on all information provided by the massage therapist regarding the services. The client agreeing to these services allows the massage therapist to perform the services. An example, if the client is booked for a hot stone massage, they need to be notified of what the treatment entails, potential benefits, and potential risks. Once the client has all of the information regarding the hot stone massage, they can either approve of the service, or deny the service and book a different type of massage.

The client also needs to be made aware of the massage therapist's training, experience, and credentials in regards to the treatment being offered. This is provided so that the client is aware of the level of training provided by the massage therapist. A client may feel uneasy with a recently licensed massage therapist performing the treatment, and may instead opt for a more experienced massage therapist. Providing training information regarding specific modalities, such as hot stone massage, helps to assure the client that the therapist is knowledgeable in that modality and able to perform the treatment.

HIPAA

The Health Insurance Portability and Accountability Act, also known as **HIPAA**, was enacted August 21st, 1996. It was created by the US Department of Health and Human Services. Inside HIPAA lies the **Privacy Rule**, which is used to **protect** all **individually identifiable** health information. The Privacy Rule ensures client/patient information is kept private. It does, however, allow this information to be transferred between healthcare providers when necessary, which allows high-quality health care. Assessments and diagnoses do not need to be re-done, as the information is already present. HIPAA should be outlined with the client intake form.

Signature and Date

Signatures and dates should always been signed by the client at the time of the intake form being filled out. This allows for a massage therapist to have added protection in case of malpractice or negligence lawsuits.

An example of a client intake form can be found on the following page.

Wanderer Studios Client Intake Form

Name: _____ Date of Birth: _____

Telephone: _____ Email: _____

Emergency Contact: _____ Relationship: _____

Emergency Contact Phone: _____

Occupation: _____ Hobbies: _____

Reason for Visit: _____

Health History

Check all that apply:

____ Allergies	____ Cancer	____ Pregnant
____ Arthritis	____ Diabetes	____ Psoriasis
____ Asthma	____ Headaches	____ Scoliosis
____ Back Pain	____ High Blood Pressure	____ Seizures
____ Blood Clots	____ Numbness/Tingling	____ Skin Conditions
____ Bruise Easily	____ Osteoporosis	____ Varicose Veins

Are you taking medications? If so, please list: _____
_____

Any past surgeries? If so, please list: _____

Do you exercise: Y/N If so, how frequently?: _____

Have you received massage therapy before: Y/N

Are there any areas you would like the massage therapist to avoid: Y/N

If so, please list: _____
_____
_____

16 Massage Therapy

Please highlight any areas on the body you would like the
massage therapist to concentrate on during the session

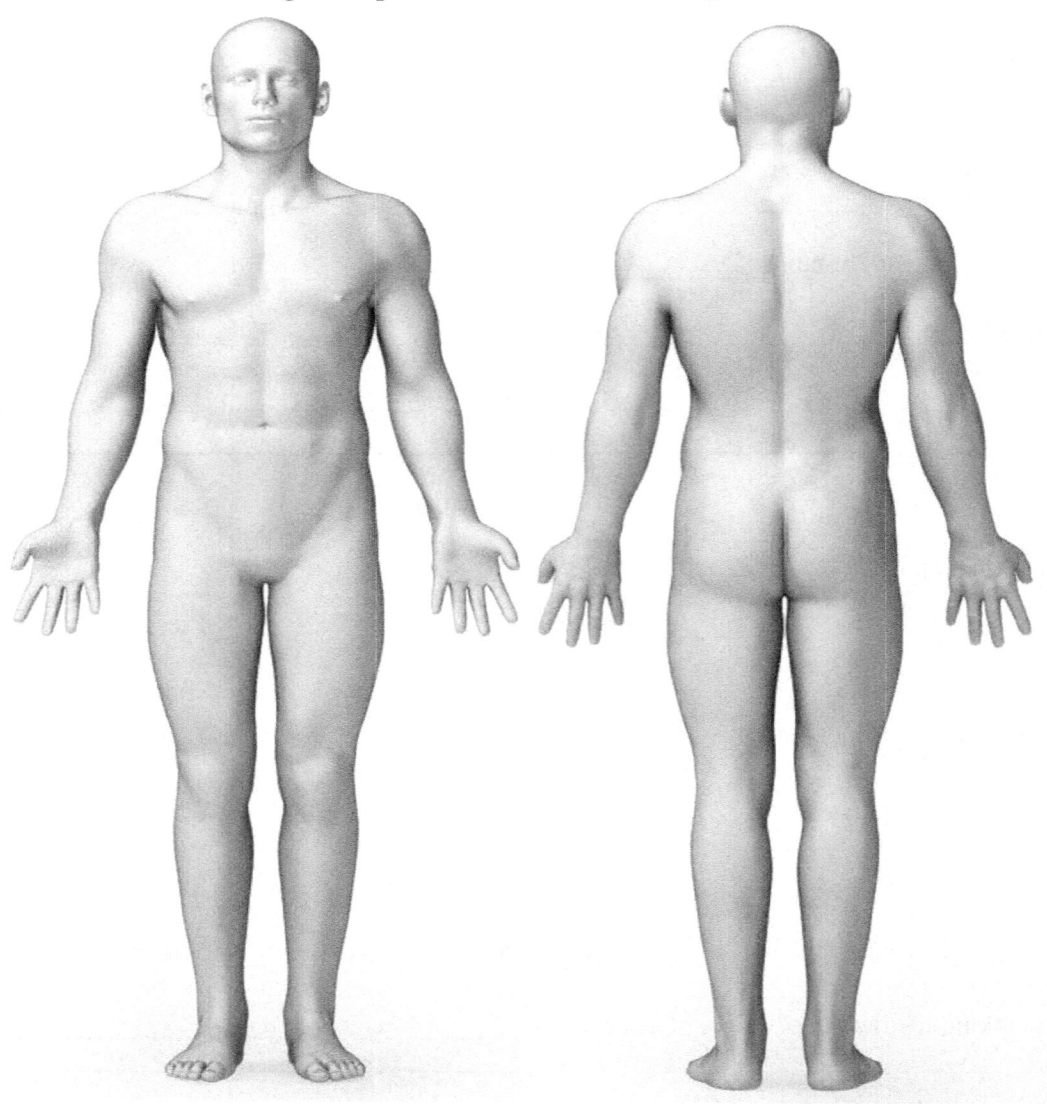

Please explain the areas highlighted: _____
_____
_____
_____

Print Name: _____

Signature: _____

Date: _____

SOAP Notes

SOAP notes are the most common form of post-massage documentation. SOAP notes help a massage therapist **document everything that happened or was said during a massage session**. Documenting this information can be helpful in many different ways, from tailoring future massage treatments to protecting the therapist from any malpractice or negligence lawsuits that may arise.

The "S" of SOAP stands for "**Subjective**". Under this section of SOAP notes, a massage therapist documents anything the client details about themselves. This can include where they experience pain, their job or hobbies, etc.

The "O" of SOAP stands for "**Objective**" or "**Observation**". Under this section of SOAP notes, a massage therapist documents the type of massage or techniques being performed(objective), and anything about the client the therapist can physically see(observe). This can include bruising, inflammation, visual assessments, and gait analysis.

The "A" of SOAP stands for "**Assessment**". Under this section of SOAP notes, a massage therapist documents any changes in the client as a result of the massage treatment. An example could be "Pre-massage, right shoulder elevated. Post-massage, right shoulder less elevated".

The "P" of SOAP stands for "**Plan**". Under this section of SOAP notes, a massage therapist documents any recommendations for future treatments, or exercises suggested for the client between sessions(such as increase stretching in a specific muscle or area, or increase water intake).

Client files, including intake forms, SOAP notes, and receipts, should be kept by the massage therapist for a minimum of **six years, per the IRS**. This allows for audits to take place by the IRS. Having all documentation stored can help prevent any possible penalties issued by the IRS.

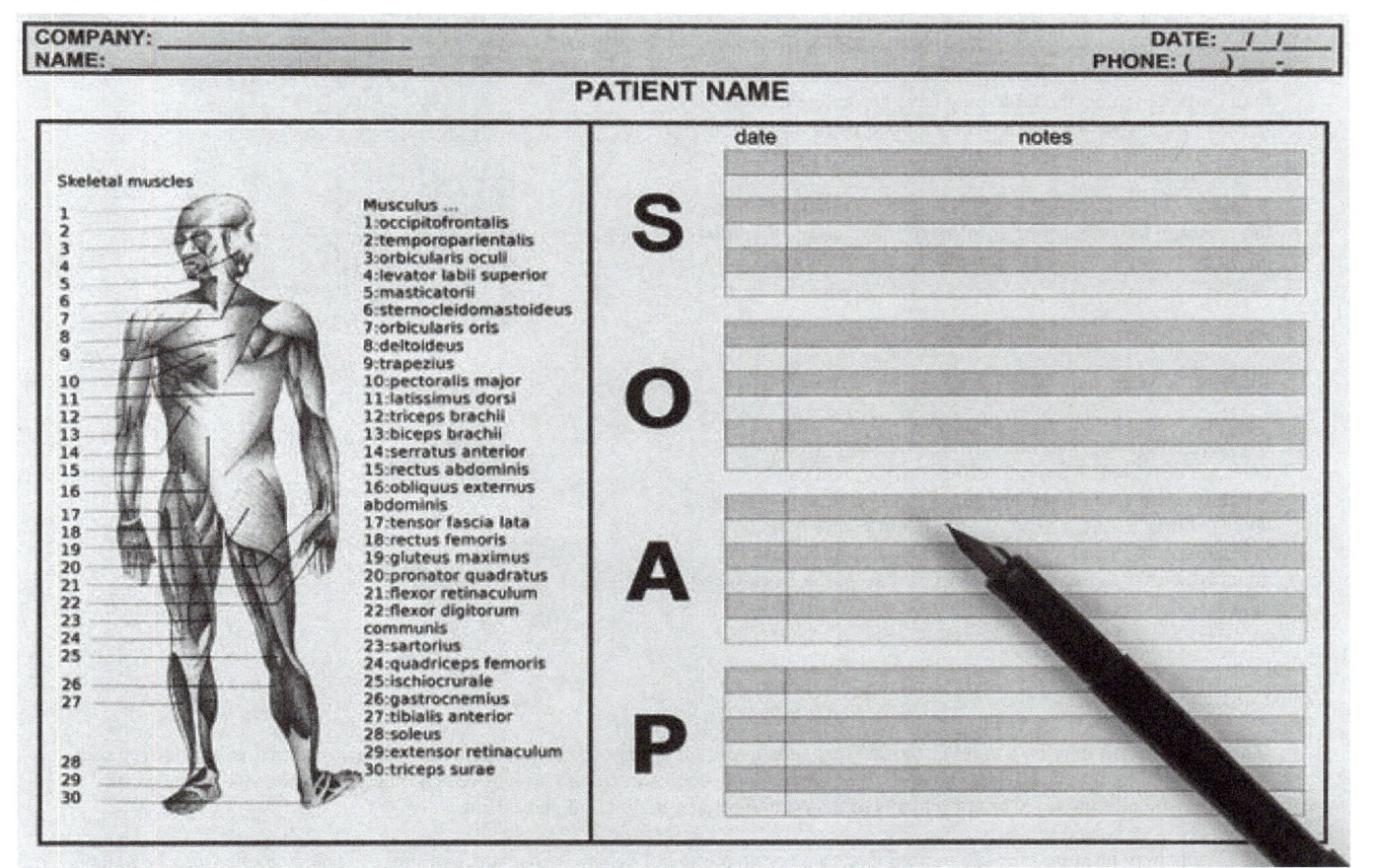

Massage Equipment

Massage equipment can enhance the massage by providing the client, and the therapist, with comfortable tables, or add other factors to the treatment that may improve the overall quality of the session.

Massage Tables

Massage tables, the primary equipment used by massage therapists, are usually the most expensive pieces of equipment a massage therapist will own. Tables may be lighter and **portable**, foldable at the center and able to be placed into a carrying case that utilizes a shoulder strap for easy transport. Other tables may be heavier and unable to be transported. These tables typically contain a motor that allows the table height to be adjusted with the use of a **foot pedal**. These types of tables are called **hydraulic tables**, and are typically much more expensive than portable tables.

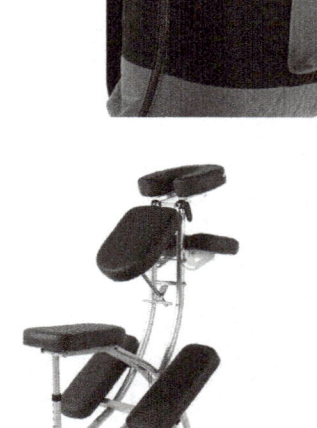

Massage tables will often include a head rest for comfortably placing a client in a prone position. Arm extenders may be added to the table to apply needed width to the table to accommodate larger clients. Bolsters are used to take pressure off certain parts of the body, depending on how a client is positioned on the table. Some massage tables may have a portion that can be removed for the face as a substitute for a head rest. Other tables may have a section that can be removed to accommodate clients with larger breasts who are lying prone. More common with hydraulic massage tables than portable tables, the table may have an incline/decline feature that allows the client to be propped up in a seated position, which may be especially helpful for pregnant clients.

Additionally, a stool may be utilized at certain points during the massage to increase the comfort of the massage therapist while performing massage on regions such as the head, neck, and face.

Massage Chairs

Massage chairs are commonly utilized when performing massage **outside the normal office setting**, and can accommodate clients who are completely clothed. A massage chair features a seat, a head rest the client places their face into, an arm rest, and leg rests. The chair position may be adjusted with the client on the chair, unlike portable massage tables, which are adjusted with the client off the table.

Lubricant

Massage lubricant may be a number of different substances. It is important that whatever substance is used is **hypoallergenic**. Allergies should always be determined before the massage begins to ensure no lubricant being used contains a substance the client may be allergic to. Common forms of massage lubricant include **oil** and **lotion**.

Lubricants may be stored for use in pourable containers, pump containers, cups, jars, and bowls. The container may be placed in specific spots around the table and moved during the course of the massage, or may be held by a **holster** wrapped around the therapist's waist. A holster allows the container to always be with the therapist no matter where they are in the room, and will almost always require the use of a pump container. After each massage, the container should be cleaned with soap and water to prevent cross-contamination.

Other Equipment

There are several other pieces of equipment that can help improve the overall quality of the massage. Several types of equipment utilize hydrotherapy in some way. **Hot towel cabinets**(also known as hot towel cabi's) are small boxes that increase internal temperature up to **170 degrees** in most models. Heating wet towels in a hot towel cabinet can give the massage therapist an effective way to remove oil from a client's feet, while also providing a relaxing experience for the client as the heated towel is wrapped around the feet. In addition, hot packs may be placed in the hot towel cabinet and sufficiently heated this way instead of using a microwave.

A **hydrocollator** is similar to a hot towel cabinet, but is specifically designed to utilize heating packs that are filled with substances such as silica, gel, or even rice. A hydrocollator will use moist heat to heat the packs, which are then placed on the client's body.

Hot stones may be heated in a **hot stone warmer**. Hot stone warmers are electric, and similar in shape and function to slow-cookers. The stones are placed in the warmer, and the warmer is filled with water. The warmer is then powered on, and the stones are heated. Temperature should be maintained at a comfortable level that will heat the stones, but not burn the client. Stones should always be checked for temperature by the massage therapist before placing the stones on the client. This can be performed by the therapist placing the stone on the anterior forearm. If the stone feels too warm in this area on the massage therapist, then the stone needs to cool before it can be used on a client.

Draping

Draping is the use of **linens** to keep a client covered during a massage session. There are many different types of linens that may be used to cover a client. Most commonly, sheets are used. Blankets and towels are other common forms of linens. Draping is a very important step in establishing **boundaries between the massage therapist and the client**. Draping the client tells the client what part of the body the therapist is, and isn't, going to work on, increasing the professionalism required of a massage therapist. Draping also helps the clients establish boundaries, telling the therapist where the client may not want massage to be performed.

Communication is key in establishing boundaries. If there is any question about a client's boundaries with regards to draping, just ask!

Top cover draping refers to the linen placed **atop** the client, which acts as the drape. As previously stated, the most common form is a sheet.

Bolsters

Bolsters are used to place the client into a comfortable position during a massage session. There are many different positions a client may be placed in during a massage, which requires the bolster to be placed in different locations to optimize comfort.

When a client is positioned **supine(face up)** on the massage table, the client may experience low back pain. A bolster should be placed **under the knees** in this case. Low back pain is likely caused by a tight psoas major, iliacus, or rectus femoris. A bolster under the knees produces slight flexion of the hip, which shortens and takes pressure off all these muscles.

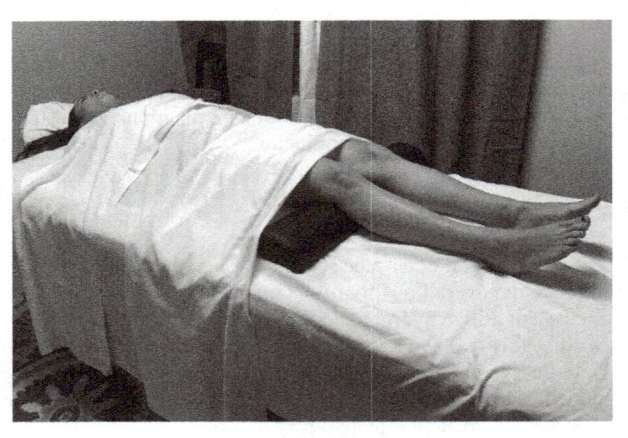

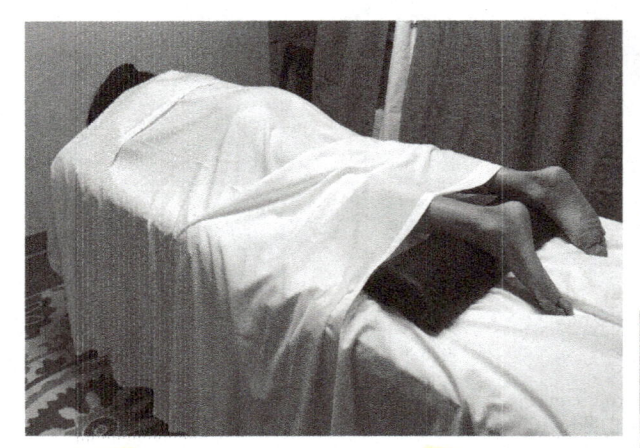

When a client is positioned **prone(face down)** on the massage table, the client may experience low back pain. A bolster should be placed **under the ankles** in this case. Low back pain is likely caused by tight hamstrings. A bolster under the ankles produces slight flexion of the knee, which shortens and takes pressure off the hamstrings.

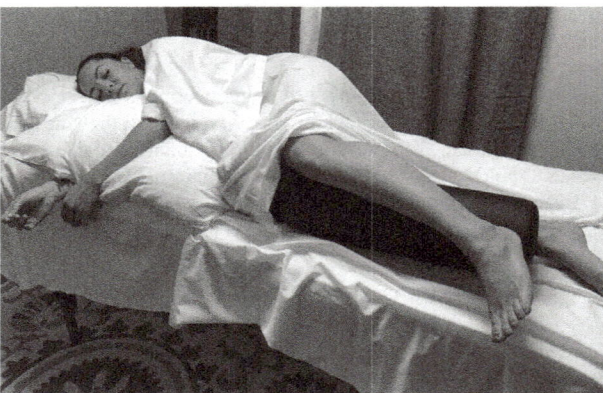

Side-lying position should be used for pregnant clients, or clients who have difficulty lying prone, such as people with kyphosis. Bolstering for side-lying clients includes placing a bolster between the **knees** to relieve pressure on the hips, under the **arms**, and under the **head**.

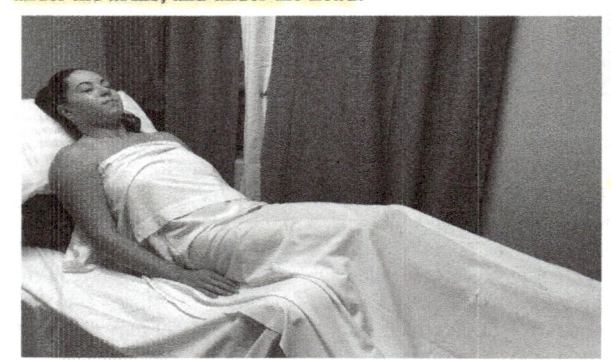

Certain clients may need to be placed in a **semi-reclined position**, such as pregnant clients who experience dizziness from lying supine(caused by the fetus placing pressure on the abdominal aorta). When a client is semi-reclined, a bolster should be placed under the **knees**, and behind the **head**.

Body Mechanics

Body mechanics are extremely important for massage therapists. Proper body mechanics prevent the therapist from **injuring** themselves during a massage, which increases the longevity of their career. It makes performing a massage less physically strenuous, and allows the therapist to perform a **better** massage by utilizing pressure and leverage more efficiently.

While performing a massage, the massage therapist's **back** should remain **straight**. **Knees** should be in a **slightly flexed** position. While performing compression, **joints** should be **stacked** to relieve pressure on one specific joint. An important factor in body mechanics that often is overlooked, however, is the **height** of a **massage table**. The table should be at the proper height for the therapist, based on the type of massage being performed. Deep tissue massages require the table to be slightly lower than Swedish massages, for example.

Body stances are very important while performing massage strokes, making them easier to perform, and makes the strokes flow and transition more smoothly.

The **bow** stance, also called the **archer** stance, is performed with the therapist's **feet** placed **parallel** to the massage table. This allows the therapist to perform long, gliding strokes, such as those seen in effleurage.

The **horse** stance, also called the **warrior** stance, is when the therapist's feet are placed **perpendicular** to the massage table. The feet will face the table, the knees will be slightly flexed. This allows short, powerful strokes to be performed, such as compression and friction.

Bow/Archer Stance   Horse/Warrior Stance

Personal Hygiene

Personal hygiene is an important aspect in massage therapy, as the massage therapist comes in to close contact with the client who may be sensitive to certain aspects of the therapist's cleanliness. A massage therapist should exhibit exceptional personal hygiene.

Hand Care

Hands should be washed constantly using soap and water, and the area being washed should extend proximally past the elbow. The fingernails should be free from dirt beneath them. The fingernails should be trimmed to avoid scratching or pinching the client. Acrylic nails and nail polish should not be applied, as dirt, debris, oil, and skin from the client can become stuck under the nail. Rings and other hand jewelry should not be worn. Calluses on the hands from activities such as weight lifting should be softened with the use of lotion.

Oral Care

Teeth should be brushed and flossed. Food that causes lingering odor after being consumed should be avoided, such as onions and garlic. Gum should not be chewed during the massage session. Breathing directly on the client, even through the nose, should be avoided. Smoking while at work, even on break, should be avoided to prevent cigarette odor from remaining on the therapist.

Bathing

The massage therapist should bathe daily. Showering helps remove any residual oil from the body. The therapist's body should be cleaned using a soap that does not contain a perfume base and is not over-bearing in scent. The therapist should avoid using perfumes or essential oils on their body to avoid complications the client or other coworkers may have with allergies. The therapist should always wear deodorant to prevent body odor.

Uniform

The massage therapist's uniform should be cleaned and washed after every shift. Any oil stains should be properly treated. Uniforms should be free of stains and holes. The uniform should be free of stray hair from the therapist, client, or pets. A lint roller may be used to remove hair on the uniform.

General Appearance

The massage therapist should have an overall professional appearance. This includes a clean uniform, longer hair tied back to prevent it from falling on the client during the massage, no obstructive jewelry, and good posture. The overall appearance of a massage therapist can influence the client's perception of the massage session.

Massage Modalities

There are many different forms of massage, and many different modalities(specialties) that may be performed by massage therapists. Some require training and certification to perform, and others require nothing aside from basic schooling. Check with your local licensing board to determine requirements to perform specific modalities.

Aromatherapy is any treatment utilizing **essential oils**, which may affect the brain's **limbic system**. Essential oils have many different effects on the body, depending on the type of oil used, and how it is administered. Examples include oils having a **stimulating effect**, such as lemon and grapefruit, having a **sedative effect**, such as eucalyptus on the respiratory tract, having **antiseptic properties**, such as tea tree on insect bites, or having **calming effects** on the brain, such as lavender. Always check with a client for any allergies before using essential oils in a treatment.

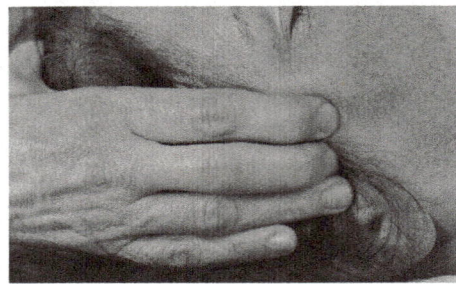

Craniosacral Therapy is a very light massage technique that helps to release **blockages** in the flow of **cerebrospinal fluid**, which runs from the **cranium** to the **sacrum**. Blockages in these fluids may cause numerous side effects, including headaches, dizziness, and difficulty processing and understanding information.

Deep Tissue massage is performed by working the **deeper** layers of tissue in the body, including **muscles and fascia**. Deep tissue may require deeper pressure to be used by the massage therapist to reach deeper structures(an example could be working deeper through the rectus femoris to reach the vastus intermedius).

Hot Stone massage is a treatment that utilizes **heated stones**. The stones may be **placed** on certain parts of the body(hands, feet, lumbar, abdomen), may be used to physically massage a client, or both. Temperature of the stones should be checked by the massage therapist on their own skin(anterior forearm) before attempting to place on the client, to ensure the client does not suffer any burns. Hot stone is used to increase circulation into muscles and tissues, and aids in relaxation.

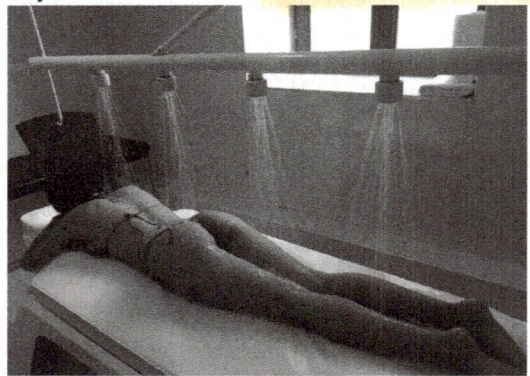

Hydrotherapy is the use of water in any treatment. There are several different types of hydrotherapy, utilizing water in solid(ice), liquid(water), or vapor(steam). **Contrast baths** utilize both a **heated** bath and a **cold** bath. Contrast baths are used to decrease systemic inflammation and increase circulation. A typical contrast bath treatment sees the client use cold water, then hot, then cold, then hot, and end with cold for inflammation relief. A **Vichy shower** is a piece of equipment that hangs over a **water-proof table**. This equipment has seven shower heads attached to it, which can pin-point specific areas of the body to be sprayed.

Vichy shower on a waterproof table

Lomi Lomi(*Hawaiian "lomi": massage*) is a **Hawaiian** massage, similar to a Swedish massage, which utilizes rhythmic gliding strokes. These strokes are used on the entire body, and can move from the feet up to the head in one fluid motion. This requires minimal draping, usually nothing more than a hand towel covering the gluteal cleft, exposing the glutes.

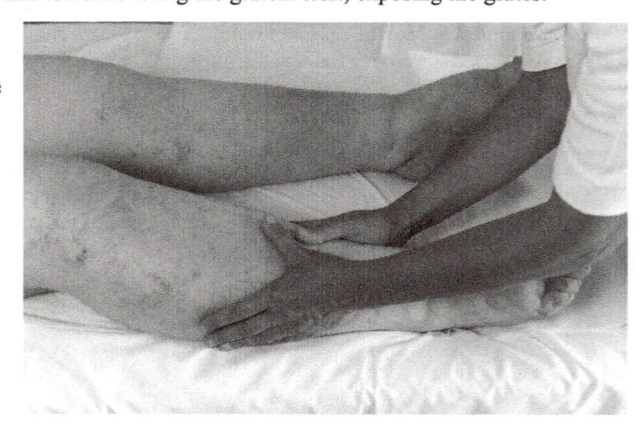

Lymphatic Drainage is a technique designed to increase the circulation of lymph utilizing very light strokes directed towards the heart. Increasing lymph circulation may help reduce swelling in areas such as the limbs or face.

Myofascial Release is a type of treatment aimed at releasing restrictions in muscles and fascia. Myofascial Release utilizes light strokes that move in the direction of the restriction, helping the muscle "unwind" on its own.

Pregnancy massage is massage for pregnant clients. As discussed earlier, pregnant clients may need to be placed into side-lying or semi-reclined position. Endangerment sites for pregnant clients include the **abdomen** and around the **ankles**.

Reflexology is used to treat **reflex points** on the hands, feet, and ears that correspond to other tissues inside the body, such as **organs**. A map of these locations can be found on page 24.

Reiki is a form of energy work, in which the therapist channels universal energy into and throughout the client. In reiki, the therapist primarily(but not always) holds their hands an inch or two **above the client**, and manipulate the client's energy to promote relaxation or other benefits.

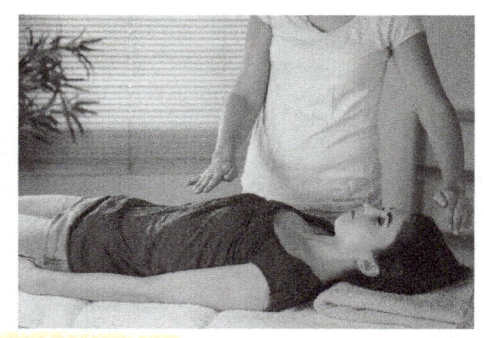

Rolfing, developed by **Ida Rolf**, is known as a **structural realignment** technique. The basic principles of Rolfing involve the body being placed back into proper vertical alignment. The Rolfer works on the **fascia** of the body. Loosening the fascia helps the body return to its natural position. Rolfing typically takes place over ten sessions, with a different part of the body worked on during each session.

Sports massage is a massage designed for athletes. Sports massage may be performed in many different ways, depending on the needs of the athlete. **Pre-event** sports massage, which may be performed up to 15 minutes before an event, will typically be **stimulating**, increasing circulation into the muscles, and using tapotement to activate spindle cells. Inter-event massage will look to achieve the same results as pre-event massage, but does not utilize tapotement. Using tapotement may result in cramping. **Post-event** massage will be much slower, rhythmic, and relaxing. The primary goal of a post-event massage is to **calm the body** down, remove metabolic waste from tissues, and increase the flow of oxygen-rich blood into the muscles to aid in recovery.

Swedish massage, the most common massage technique in western massage therapy, is mainly focused on **relaxation**. Effleurage is a stroke commonly utilized in Swedish massage, with strokes aimed towards the heart to increase circulation.

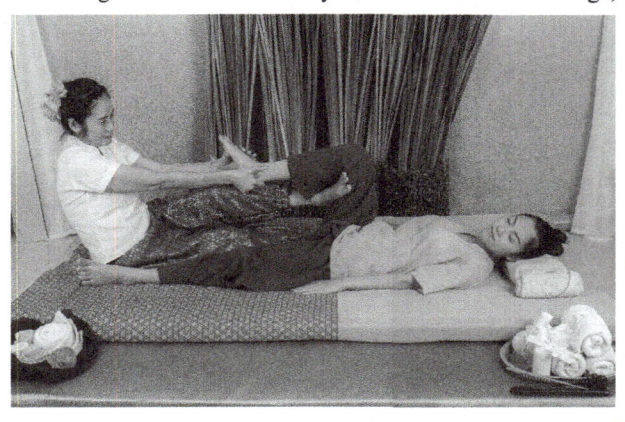

Thai massage, originating in Thailand, isn't necessarily what we consider a normal massage. Thai massage is performed with the client wearing loose-fitting clothes, on a mat, on the floor. The therapist's main goal during a Thai massage is to **stretch** the client. Massage may be incorporated into these stretching techniques.

Tuina is the name of **modern Chinese** massage. It is used to balance the eight principles of Chinese medicine. Tuina incorporates rhythmic strokes and techniques focused on specific areas of the body. The eight basic techniques utilized in Tuina are palpating, rejoining, opposing, kneading, pressing, lifting, holding, and pushing.

REFLEXOLOGY CHART

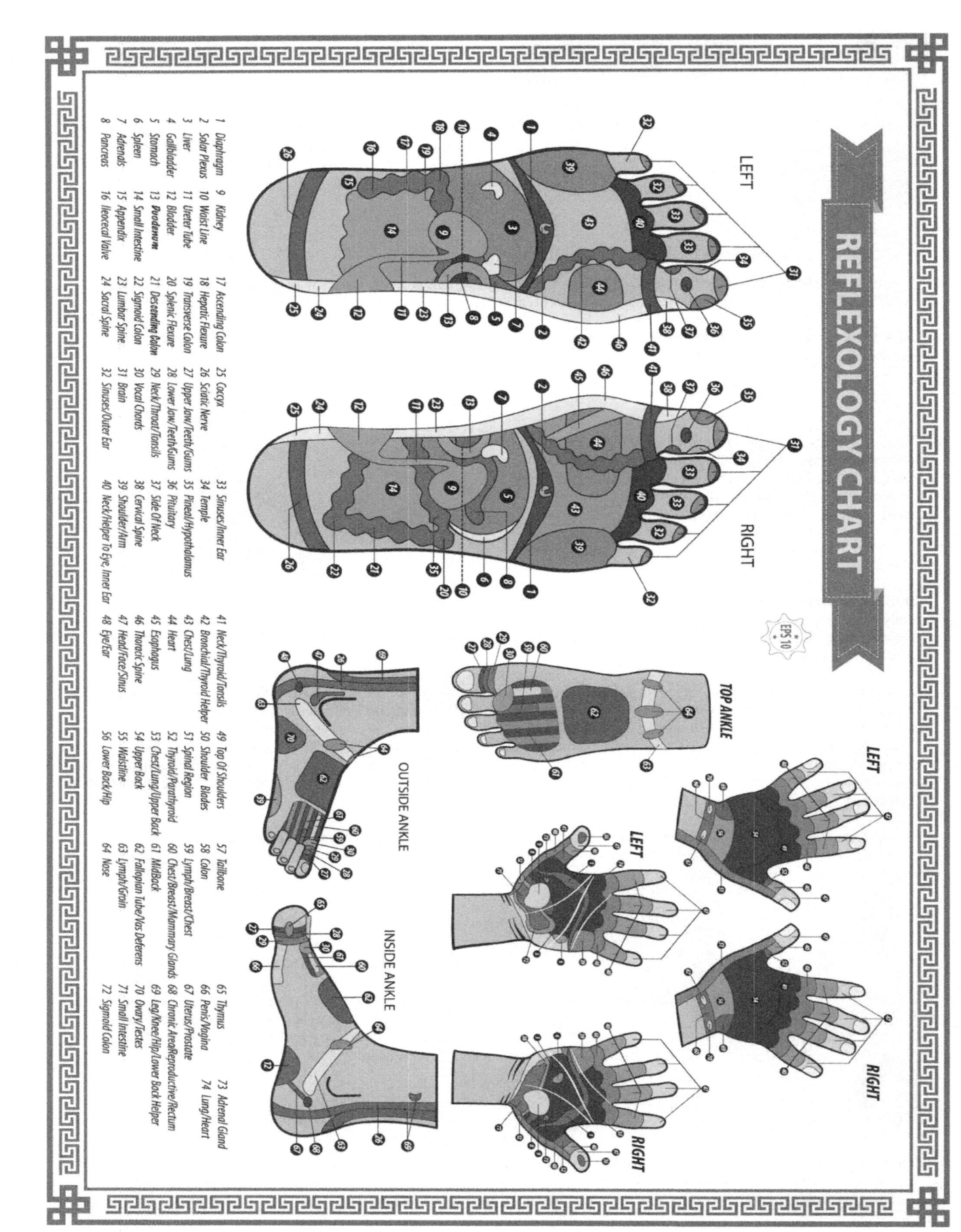

1. Diaphragm
2. Solar Plexus
3. Liver
4. Gallbladder
5. Stomach
6. Spleen
7. Adrenals
8. Pancreas
9. Kidney
10. Waist Line
11. Ureter Tube
12. Bladder
13. Duodenum
14. Small Intestine
15. Appendix
16. Ileocecal Valve
17. Ascending Colon
18. Hepatic Flexure
19. Transverse Colon
20. Splenic Flexure
21. Descending Colon
22. Sigmoid Colon
23. Lumbar Spine
24. Sacral Spine
25. Coccyx
26. Sciatic Nerve
27. Upper Jaw/Teeth/Gums
28. Lower Jaw/Teeth/Gums
29. Neck/Throat/Tonsils
30. Vocal Chords
31. Brain
32. Sinuses/Outer Ear
33. Sinuses/Inner Ear
34. Temple
35. Pineal/Hypothalamus
36. Pituitary
37. Side Of Neck
38. Cervical Spine
39. Shoulder/Arm
40. Neck/Helper to Eye, Inner Ear
41. Neck/Thyroid/Tonsils
42. Bronchial/Thyroid Helper
43. Chest/Lung
44. Heart
45. Esophagus
46. Thoracic Spine
47. Head/Face/Sinus
48. Eye/Ear
49. Top Of Shoulders
50. Shoulder Blades
51. Spinal Region
52. Thyroid/Parathyroid
53. Chest/Lung/Upper Back
54. Upper Back
55. Waistline
56. Lower Back/Hip
57. Tailbone
58. Colon
59. Lymph/Breast/Chest
60. Chest/Breast/Mammary Glands
61. Midback
62. Fallopian Tube/Vas Deferens
63. Lymph/Groin
64. Nose
65. Thymus
66. Penis/Vagina
67. Uterus/Prostate
68. Chronic Area/Reproductive/Rectum
69. Leg/Knee/Hip/Lower Back Helper
70. Ovary/Testes
71. Small Intestine
72. Sigmoid Colon
73. Adrenal Gland
74. Lung/Heart

The Body Meridians

Two Centerline Meridians:

Conception Vessel
Governing Vessel

Twelve Principal Meridians:

Stomach Meridian
Spleen Meridian

Small Intestine Meridian
Heart Meridian

Bladder Meridian
Kidney Meridian

Pericardium Meridian
Triple Warmer Meridian

Gall Bladder Meridian
Liver Meridian

Lung Meridian
Large Intestine Meridian

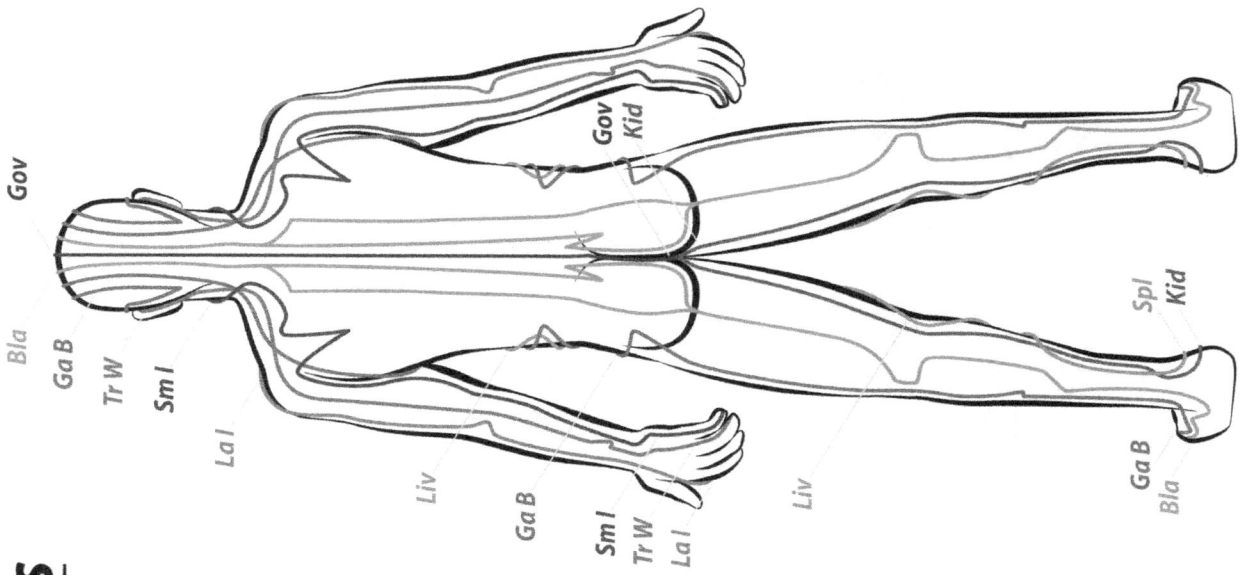

posterior view

anterior view

The Seven Major Chakras

- Crown Chakra
- Third Eye
- Throat Chakra
- Heart Chakra
- Solar Plexus
- Sacral Chakra
- Root Chakra

Business

Even if you aren't planning on becoming a business owner, understanding how businesses operate is knowledge everyone should have. It can help in retaining clientele, business relationships, and even keep you out of trouble from things like HIPAA violations.

Business for a massage therapist, in most locations, begins with a **certification**. A certification is a credential obtained by completing a certification course, usually in a school setting. It also may involve completing a certification exam. Certifications show that you have gained enough knowledge in a given subject to be able to perform that task. In this case, you gain a certificate after completing massage school.

A **license** is a jurisdictional requirement, which is used to **regulate** the practice of massage therapy. Licensing boards set rules and laws that a person is required to follow if they wish to be a licensed massage therapist. In most jurisdictions, a license allows a massage therapist to practice massage therapy and receive money as compensation.

Reciprocity refers to the ability for a massage license in one jurisdiction to be recognized as **valid** in another jurisdiction. Some jurisdictions may require a new license to be obtained, but no more schooling required. Others may require more schooling in addition to paying for a new license.

Liability Insurance

When operating a business at a physical location where there is customer exposure, liability insurance is often required. There are two types of liability insurance: General liability insurance, and Professional liability insurance.

General liability insurance protects the massage therapist in cases such as **accidental falls** by the client that result in bodily injury. **Professional liability insurance** is similar, but instead of protecting the therapist from workplace accidents, it protects the therapist from lawsuits regarding **malpractice** or **negligence**. If a massage therapist knowingly performs a service or treatment they are not authorized, licensed, or certified to perform, this is known as malpractice. If a client tells a therapist not to work on a specific part of the body(say, the feet), and the therapist forgets and works on that area, and injury results, this is considered negligence.

Subpoena

When a court requires a person to attend a hearing or trial and testify in some way, the person is issued a writ by the court known as a subpoena. Subpoena literally translates to "**under penalty**", and if the person does not appear, they will be in violation of law. There are two separate types of subpoenae. A subpoena duces tecum is a court summons in which the person being summoned is required to appear in court with documentation or other evidence used in a trial or hearing. A subpoena ad testificandum is a court summons in which the person being summoned is required to appear in court and testify.

Business Management

Business Plan

A business plan is a document prepared to state the objectives of a future business, and its means of achieving them. Business plans are often utilized to obtain a business loan as a way to show a bank how the business will operate, turn a profit, and how the loan will be repaid. Business plans often include a business objective and summary, marketing strategies and planning, financial information and planning, and a prediction of company growth over an extended period of time, often five to ten years.

A **mission statement** may be included in a business plan. A mission statement is a statement that defines the overall objective and values of the business. The mission statement often consists of the product being offered, with an over-arching vision of the business, such as the quality of service provided, who the clientele is, and what the clientele can expect to receive from the business.

Financial planning is used to state long-term objectives in regards to money. These objectives can include the amount of money expended, the amount of money saved, repayment of loans, etc. Financial planning is useful in helping to guide a business towards achieving monetary goals that they have set, without straying from the plan they have laid out. This allows for proper budgeting for products, employees, utilities, and rent.

Market analysis is utilized to assess a market, helping determine things such as customer volume, money spent in specific locations, money spent on specific products, the competition, and more. Market analysis can help determine the kind of business to launch, where to launch it, when to launch it, who to market it to, how much to price the product or service, and how to properly advertise the product or service.

When money is owed to a business, such as credit or debt from a vendor, it is known as **accounts receivable**. This money is charged to another company for services or products the charging company has performed, and the other company is responsible for paying these charges. An example of accounts receivable is a massage business shipping a crate of body scrubs to a store, who will then sell them. The store will then owe the massage business payment for the body scrubs, and is usually given a time frame in which to deliver payment. Once payment is received, accounts receivable for that transaction returns to a zero balance.

When the business owes money to another company, however, it is known as **accounts payable**. An example of accounts payable is a business accruing credit card debt. The money owed by the business to the credit card company is accounts payable. Once the credit card debt is paid off by the business, the amount in accounts payable returns to a zero balance.

Types of Employment

There are many different types of employment you may encounter as a massage therapist. These are among the most common.

An **independent contractor** is a massage therapist that works independently, for themselves, but contracts with another person or company to perform work. Independent contractors are not beholden to the same limitations as employees, however. Independent contractors may work whatever schedule they want, charge their own prices, and wear their own uniform. Independent contractors do not receive benefits from an employer.

Sole proprietors are often categorized similarly to independent contractors. Sole proprietorships are businesses owned by one person. Sole proprietors may differ from independent contractors in licensing requirements.

A **partnership** is a business owned by two or more people. Ownership may be split differently depending on variables such as money entering into a business relationship, assets, etc.

S Corporations are corporations that pass income and taxes onto the **shareholders**. This requires the shareholders to shoulder the responsibility of reporting income and taxes to the IRS.

Tax Forms

A **W2** is filed by employees, detailing earnings and money withheld for social security taxes, medicaid, state and federal income taxes. Gratuity may also be reported on the W2, if the gratuity is added to the employee's paycheck.

A **1099** is issued to an **independent contractor by the company they contract** with. This statement details the amount of income accrued by the independent contractor through the year.

	☐ CORRECTED (if checked)		
PAYER'S name, street address, city or town, province or state, country, ZIP or foreign postal code, and telephone no. Business! 890 One Two Three Street Seattle, WA 00002	1 Rents $ 3 Other income $ 5 Fishing boat proceeds $	2 Royalties $ 99,999.99 4 Federal income tax withheld $ 6 Medical & health care payments $	OMB No. 1545-0115 **2016** Form **1099-MISC** Miscellaneous Income
PAYER'S federal identification number 01-0000001	RECIPIENT'S identification number XXX-XX-5555	7 Nonemployee compensation $	8 Substitute payments in lieu of dividends or interest $	Copy B - For Recipient
RECIPIENT'S name Billy Bob 1234 Five Six Seven Street New York, NY 00001	9 Payer made direct sales of $5,000 or more of consumer products to a buyer (recipient) for resale ☐ 11 13 Excess golden parachute payments $ 15a Section 409A deferrals $	10 Crop insurance proceeds $ 12 14 Gross proceeds paid to an attorney $ 15b Section 409A income $	This is important tax information and is being furnished to the Internal Revenue Service. If you are required to file a return, a negligence penalty or other sanction may be imposed on you if this income is taxable and the IRS determines that it has not been reported.
Account number (see instructions) FATCA filing requirement ☐	16 State tax withheld $	17 State/Payer's state no.	18 State income $
Form **1099-MISC**	(keep for your records)	www.irs.gov/form1099misc	Department of the Treasury - Internal Revenue Service

A **Schedule C** is filed to the IRS by **sole proprietors**, detailing the amount of money the business made during the previous year.

A **Schedule K-1** is a form filed by individual **partnership members**. It is similar to a W-2, detailing the amount of money each partnership member made during the previous year.

Profit and Loss(income and expense) statements are forms filed by businesses that show how much money was made(**profit**) and how much money was expended(**loss**) during the year.

Gift taxes may be used as **deductions** on taxes. If a business buys a gift for a customer, no more than **$25** may be claimed as a deduction for that specific client. Other gifts for different clients may also be reported, but each gift reported cannot exceed $25.

Ethics

Ethics are **guiding moral principles**. These guiding moral principles are used to direct a massage therapist in proper course of action in ethical dilemmas. There are many different ethical dilemmas that may arise in the practice of massage therapy. Examples include becoming sexually attracted to a client(refer the client to another therapist) and attempting to sell products or merchandise to a client outside the scope of massage(don't do it).

Scope of practice is performing treatments and techniques you are **qualified to perform**. Working outside of the scope of practice can lead to malpractice lawsuits. Examples of working outside of the scope of practice include performing treatments such as acupuncture or chiropractic work without proper licensing. Stay within your scope of practice at all times!

Boundaries, as discussed earlier, are **limitations** that can be set by the massage therapist and the client. They can be verbally set, such as a client asking a massage therapist to avoid working on a specific part of the body, or non-verbal, such as a client leaving an article of clothing on, which typically means they might not want to have that part of the body worked on. The best way to identify boundaries is to communicate with the client. Ask questions, reinforce the boundaries you or the client have set.

Confidentiality, quite simply, is keeping client information **private and protected**. Client information includes anything that happens or is said during a massage session, client files, intake forms, SOAP notes, and even something as simple as names. This information needs to be kept private. Releasing this information is a violation of HIPAA.

Communication

Communication, as we've discussed, is extremely important in the client/therapist relationship. One of the main ways we communicate with clients is by asking questions.

An **open-ended question** is a question used when asking for **feedback** from clients. Often, open-ended questions are meant to extract more detail, more information. It allows the answer to be more open and abstract.

A **close-ended question** is a question used when asking for a **yes-or-no response** only. These questions are used to extract important pieces of information in a short amount of time. When time is a factor, close-ended questions are primarily used to gather the important information without sacrificing too much time.

Self disclosure is when the client shares information about **themselves**. This information, which may be documented if relevant, needs to be kept confidential.

Active listening is listening to what the client is saying, and actively interpreting the information being given. The client's statements are being paid attention to, and the client has the full focus of the massage therapist while they are speaking. This allows the massage therapist to respond to and remember what is being said.

Passive listening is listening to a client without responding. Passive listening does not require the listener to engage the talker in conversation or ask questions in response. This can result in the mind wandering, and details being provided by the client to be forgotten.

Body language is a form of **unspoken communication** in which a person is able to communicate through conscious or subconscious gestures. Facial expression can convey a person's current emotion, such as happiness. Posture can express whether a person is open and willing to engage or closed and hostile or anxious. Eye contact, avoiding eye contact, the space a person leaves between others while communicating, and crossing the arms across the chest are all other examples of body language, and can be interpreted in many different ways.

Transference and counter-transference occur when one person in the therapeutic relationship begins viewing the other as more than just their client or therapist. **Transference** is when the **client** begins viewing the massage therapist **similarly to a person** in their own personal life. They develop an emotional attachment to the massage therapist. **Counter-transference** is the opposite: a **massage therapist** develops an **emotional attachment** to a client. If either of these occur, it's best to refer the client to another massage therapist, separating the massage therapist from any possible ethical dilemmas.

Therapeutic Relationship

The relationship a massage therapist shares with a client is known as the **therapeutic relationship**. The relationship between a therapist and client has many complexities. The primary goal of the therapist in the therapeutic relationship is to help the clients achieve goals they may be seeking, whether it be physical or emotional.

In the therapeutic relationship, there exists a **power differential**. The client, while in control of the session in most aspects, gives the therapist the power to perform massage, trusting that they have obtained sufficient training and working knowledge to help achieve the client's goals. The power differential can shift back to the client if the client feels their goals aren't being met, or their boundaries are being violated, such is the drape revealing more of the client than they are comfortable with.

An extremely important part of the therapeutic relationship is communication on both ends, between the client and therapist. If the client does not properly communicate their goals, it becomes difficult for the therapist to design an effective treatment plan. On the other hand, if the therapist fails to communicate reasons for developing a treatment plan based on client goals, the client may feel as if their needs are not being met. It is incumbent on the therapist to direct the flow of communication. The therapist should not be afraid to ask questions or explain reasons for performing specific massage strokes, stretches, or techniques if the client may not understand the reasoning for them.

The therapeutic relationship is the responsibility of the therapist to guide and cultivate. Ensuring the client is happy with the service received in turn gives the therapist confidence in helping treat the client, which may increase therapist happiness and satisfaction in the job they are performing.

Psychology

A massage may leave a client in a psychologically vulnerable place, and they may exhibit defense mechanisms to help cope with their internal struggles.

Denial, a common defense mechanism, is a **refusal** to acknowledge a given situation, or acting as if something didn't happen.

Displacement is often negative. Displacement is satisfying an impulse by **substitution**. An example could be, you have a very bad day at work or school, you go home, and instead of being upset at school or work, you lash out at a significant other. Releasing your pent-up emotions at something other than what is causing the emotions.

Projection is placing one's own internal feelings onto **someone else**. An example could be my wife: when she gets hungry, she becomes easily agitated. She'll then accuse me of being in a bad mood, even though I'm feeling great. This is projection. For the record, this happens a lot.

Regression is taking a **step back** psychologically when faced with stress. An example could be quitting smoking. A person doesn't smoke for a few days, and then they are presented with a stressful situation, which causes them to regress and smoke again.

Repression is subconsciously **blocking out** unwanted emotions. Not even knowing you have something to be upset about. The mind can erase certain memories to help protect a person from stress.

Massage Therapy Matching

_____: Limitations set by the client or massage therapist

_____: Refusal to acknowledge a given situation

_____: Stoppage of range-of-motion due to tight muscles

_____: Guiding moral principles

_____: Stance with feet placed perpendicular to the table

_____: Area of the body that warrants extra caution while massaging

_____: Gliding strokes directed towards the heart

_____: Modern Chinese massage

_____: Massage therapist moving a joint without assistance from the client

_____: Protects a massage therapist from malpractice lawsuits

_____: Percussion strokes

_____: Kneading strokes

_____: Stance with feet placed parallel to the table

_____: Jurisdictional requirement used to regulate the practice of massage therapy

_____: Client moving a joint without assistance from the massage therapist

_____: Stoppage of range-of-motion due to bone

_____: Massage involving stretching performed on a mat on the floor

_____: Stoppage of range-of-motion due to trauma

_____: Client viewing a massage therapist similarly to a person in their early life

_____: Credential obtained by completing a course in a school setting

A: Tuina
B: Transference
C: Thai Massage
D: Effleurage
E: Ethics
F: Empty End Feel
G: Tapotement
H: Denial
I: Petrissage
J: Professional Liability Insurance

K: Boundaries
L: Endangerment Site
M: Soft End Feel
N: Active Joint Movement
O: Bow Stance
P: Certification
Q: Passive Joint Movement
R: Horse Stance
S: Hard End Feel
T: License

Answer Key on Page 312

Massage Therapy

Across
2. Form of massage focused primarily on relaxation
3. Utilizing essential oils in a massage treatment
6. Tax document filed by sole proprietors
9. Observing a client's walking pattern
10. Changes in the client due to the massage, SOAP notes
11. Stance in which the feet are placed parallel to the massage table
14. Percussion strokes
16. Placing one's own internal feelings onto someone else
18. Rhythmic gliding strokes directed towards the heart
19. Client viewing the massage therapist similarly to a person in their early life
20. Massage table that can be transported from one location to another

Down
1. Shaking or trembling movements
4. Statement that defines the overall objective and values of a business
5. The use of linens to keep a client covered and establish boundaries
7. Guiding moral principles
8. Stoppage of range-of-motion due to bones
12. Information that is measurable in some way, SOAP notes
13. Form used to give a detailed overview of the client's health history
15. Modern Chinese massage
17. Body position in which the client is placed face up on the table

Answer Key on Page 313

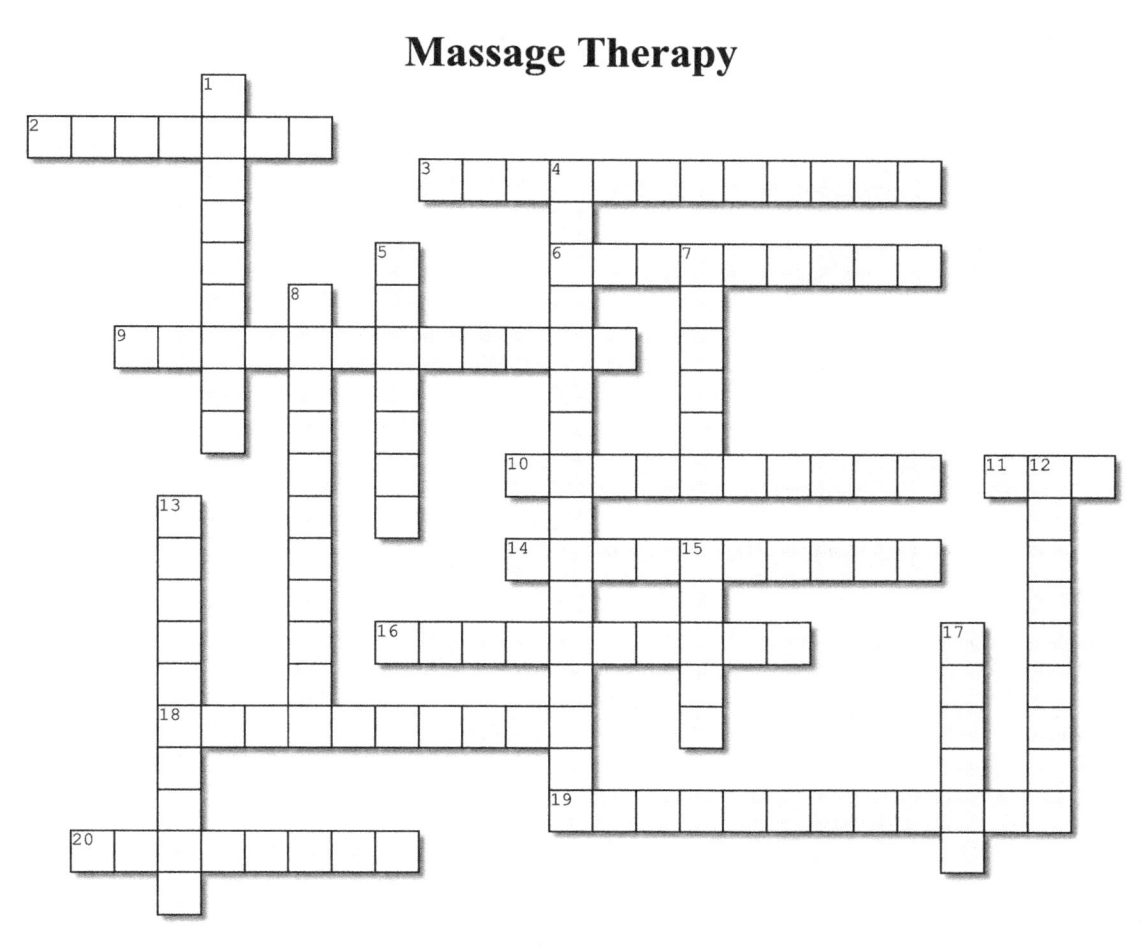

Massage Therapy Practice Exam

1. Essential oil commonly used to aid in treatment of insomnia and chronic fatigue syndrome
A. Eucalyptus
B. Sweet orange
C. Lavender
D. Rosemary

2. A massage table that is able to be folded and transported easily from one location to another
A. Hydraulic
B. Adjustable
C. Pressurized
D. Portable

3. Counter-transference
A. The client viewing a massage therapist as a significant person in their early life
B. The massage therapist bringing their own unresolved issues into the therapeutic relationship
C. Keeping a client's information private and protected
D. Relocating from one office to another

4. A client performing an action with the help of the massage therapist is an example of which joint movement
A. Active
B. Resistive
C. Passive
D. Assistive

5. Stoppage of a range of motion due to muscle and other soft tissues
A. Soft end feel
B. Hard end feel
C. Empty end feel
D. Nervous end feel

6. Gentle rhythmic massage designed to increase lymph circulation, developed by Emil Vodder
A. Lymphatic drainage
B. Swedish massage
C. Sports massage
D. Orthobionomy

7. Lomi Lomi, Craniosacral Therapy, and Rolfing are all forms of
A. Energy techniques
B. Movement techniques
C. Manipulative techniques
D. Kinesiology techniques

8. A massage room should contain all of the following except
A. A music source
B. A bathroom
C. Subdued lighting
D. Comfortable temperature

9. Stance in which the feet run perpendicular to the massage table
A. Bow
B. Archer
C. Horse
D. Swimmer

10. Petrissage
A. Light gliding strokes towards the heart, used to increase circulation and apply lubricant
B. Strokes that move across tissue, used to break up adhesions
C. Kneading strokes, used to release adhesions and increase circulation
D. Percussion strokes, used to stimulate muscle spindle cells

11. Universal precautions should be followed with
A. Clients with allergies
B. Only clients with contagious conditions
C. Every client
D. Clients with no previous medical conditions

12. Questions asked in a pre-massage interview should be
A. Forced
B. Open-ended
C. Abrupt
D. Closed-ended

13. The "A" of "SOAP" stands for
A. Alleviate
B. Assessment
C. Arrangement
D. Alignment

14. A sole proprietorship is a business that has how many owners
A. More than ten
B. Two
C. Four
D. One

15. The most common substance used in body scrubs
A. Salt
B. Sugar
C. Ground coffee
D. Powdered milk

16. A certification is obtained via
A. Passing a jurisprudence exam
B. Paying a fee to a jurisdiction licensing agency
C. Obtaining liability insurance to protect against malpractice
D. Completing educational requirements in a school setting

17. Structural realignment therapy working on muscles and fascia over the course of ten sessions
A. Rolfing
B. Trager method
C. Feldenkrais
D. Myofascial release

18. Massage results in increased production of
A. Cortisol
B. Blood cells
C. Pathogens
D. Water retention

19. Information the client shares about themselves is documented under which section of SOAP notes
A. Objective
B. Subjective
C. Assessment
D. Plan

20. Percussion strokes, used to loosen phlegm in the respiratory tract and activate muscle spindle cells
A. Petrissage
B. Effleurage
C. Friction
D. Tapotement

21. Massage may have all of the following psychological effects except
A. Increased relaxation
B. Decreased stress
C. Increased stress
D. Increased energy

22. After a massage, the massage therapist notifies the client of stretches that the therapist thinks might help with a client's range-of-motion. This information would be documented under which section of SOAP notes
A. Subjective
B. Objective
C. Assessment
D. Plan

23. The primary goal of a massage performed after a sporting event is
A. Move metabolic waste out of tissues
B. Increase circulation
C. Stimulate muscle fibers
D. Break up adhesions between tissues

24. Technique used to treat adhesions found between fascia and muscles
A. Rolfing
B. Myofascial release
C. Deep tissue
D. Osteosymmetry

25. The primary goal of Swedish massage is to
A. Decrease the formation of adhesions between muscles
B. Increase the flow of blood and lymph, and promote relaxation
C. Loosen phlegm in the respiratory tract
D. Decrease sensation in a localized area

26. Business expenses include all of the following except
A. Massages
B. Advertising
C. Electricity
D. Credit card fees

27. Slightly bent knees, straight back, and limp wrists are all examples of
A. Proper massage modalities
B. Improper body mechanics
C. Proper body mechanics
D. Improper massage modalities

28. If a client is unable to withstand any amount of pressure during a massage, a treatment the therapist might recommend would be
A. Reiki
B. Rolfing
C. Myofascial release
D. Lymphatic drainage

29. A massage license from one jurisdiction being recognized as valid in another jurisdiction
A. Reciprocity
B. Certification
C. Liability
D. Malpractice

30. A bolster is placed between the legs and arms and under the head in which position
A. Slightly elevated
B. Supine
C. Prone
D. Side-lying

31. Swedish massage is based on the Western principles of
A. Anatomy and physiology
B. Energy
C. Life force
D. Chi

32. Stretch technique in which a muscle is stretched to resistance, followed by an isometric contraction by the client, then the muscle stretched further after the contraction
A. Active static stretch
B. Proprioceptive neuromuscular facilitation
C. Strain counter-strain
D. Myofascial release

33. A set of guiding moral principles is known as
A. Regulations
B. Scope of practice
C. Ethics
D. Reputation

34. If a massage therapist begins to feel sexual attraction towards a client, what should the massage therapist do
A. Act upon these urges
B. Do nothing
C. Tell the client
D. Recommend the client see another therapist

35. Goals are
A. Measurable or attainable accomplishments
B. A generalized statement about the purpose of a business
C. The theme of a business
D. Business plans detailing projected income

36. Technique primarily used to work on trigger points
A. Wringing
B. Ischemic compression
C. Cross-fiber friction
D. Myofascial release

37. Areas of the body in which caution is advised during massage of a pregnant client include all of the following except
A. Face
B. Abdomen
C. Ankles
D. Lumbar

38. Massage stroke directed toward the heart used to increase circulation, transition between strokes, and apply massage lubricant
A. Friction
B. Petrissage
C. Effleurage
D. Vibration

39. A pre-event sports massage requires the following kinds of strokes to be performed
A. Relaxing
B. Invigorating
C. Slow
D. Sedative

40. An aura stroke is a massage stroke in which
A. The hands are pressed firmly into the body
B. The hands are touching the body very lightly
C. The hands are held just above the body
D. The hands are placed on the body without substantial pressure

41. A resistive joint movement
A. Client moves the joint without the assistance of a massage therapist
B. A client moves the joint with the assistance of a massage therapist
C. A client resists a movement being performed by a massage therapist
D. A massage therapist moves a client's joint without the help of the client

42. Essential oil commonly used to aid in relaxation of smooth muscles in the respiratory tract
A. Eucalyptus
B. Lavender
C. Lemongrass
D. Peppermint

43. Protection from malpractice lawsuits is gained by obtaining
A. Limited Liability Corporation
B. Massage certification
C. Licensure
D. Professional liability insurance

44. With a client lying supine, a bolster should be placed
A. Between the legs and arms, and under the head
B. Under the ankles and neck
C. Under the knees
D. Under the head only

45. Ability to perform services legally according to occupational standards and licensing
A. Certification
B. Scope of practice
C. Reciprocity
D. Regulations

46. Gait analysis is observation and interpretation of a person's
A. Walking pattern
B. Somatic holding pattern
C. Sitting pattern
D. Range of motion

47. Which of the following massage strokes is best in aiding lung decongestion
A. Tapotement
B. Effleurage
C. Friction
D. Petrissage

48. A client demonstrating range of motion is an example of which joint movement
A. Active
B. Assistive
C. Passive
D. Resistive

49. A 1099 should be filed quarterly by
A. S Corporations
B. Employees
C. Partnership Members
D. Independent Contractors

50. A massage therapist solicits a product to a client not related to a massage session or treatment. This could be a violation of
A. Ethics
B. Scope of Practice
C. Licensure
D. Reciprocity

Answer Key on Page 314

Medical Terminology

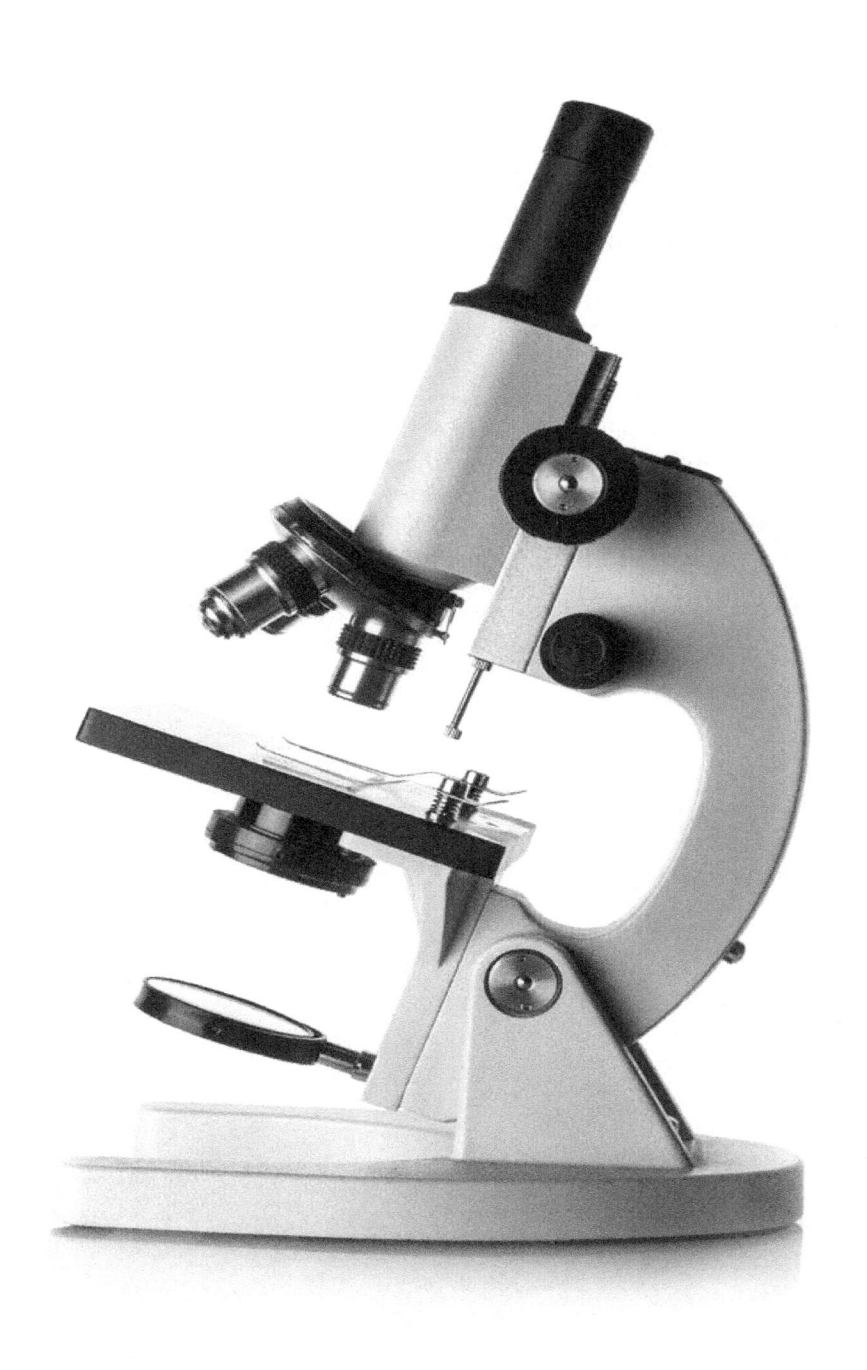

Medical Terminology

Medical terminology can be divided into three primary components: word roots, prefixes, and suffixes.

The word root of a medical term is the primary structure involved. It gives us a starting point when breaking down a word. An example is the word root "hepat/o", which means "liver".

A prefix is used to modify a word root, and is attached at the beginning of the word root. An example is "a-", which means "without". A disease that uses "a-" is "arrhythmia", which means "without rhythm".

A suffix is used to add description to, or alter, a word root, and is attached at the end of the word root. An example is "-itis", which means "inflammation". A disease that uses "-itis" is "hepatitis". As stated before, the word root "hepat/o" means "liver". If we attach "-itis", it becomes "inflammation of the liver".

Many different medical terms, prefixes, suffixes, and word roots have the same meaning. The reason for different terms having the same meaning can be traced back to the origin languages. Modern medical terminology originated in both Latin and Greek, with the majority of the words being Greek. When people like Celsus, a Roman physician, began creating medical terminology, they often used Greek terms, but conformed them to be Latin in origin. This is the reason for many terms sharing the same definition.

Medical terminology is especially useful when studying not only anatomy and physiology, but pathology as well. Knowing medical terminology can help you figure out what the general medical condition is just by looking at the name. First start by identifying the word root. We'll use the term "bursitis". The word root in "bursitis" is "burs/o", which means "bursa/bursa sac". This way, we know the condition has something to do with a bursa sac. Then we try to identify any prefixes. "Bursitis" does not contain any prefixes. Therefore, we move to suffixes. We know that "-itis" is a suffix, and it means "inflammation". We can then combine the two meanings together, and reach the conclusion that "bursitis" is inflammation of a bursa sac.

Word Roots

Cardiovascular Word Roots

angi/o:	vessel
aort/o:	aorta
arteriol/o:	arteriole
arteri/o:	artery
ather/o:	fatty plaque
atri/o:	atrium
bas/o:	alkaline
cardi/o:	heart
chrom/o:	color
eosin/o:	rose colored
erythr/o:	red
granul/o:	granule
hemangi/o:	blood vessel
hem/o:	blood
kary/o:	nucleus
leuk/o:	white
nucle/o:	nucleus
lymph/o:	lymph
morph/o:	form
phag/o:	eat
phleb/o:	vein
poikil/o:	irregular
reticul/o:	mesh
scler/o:	hard
sider/o:	iron
sphygm/o:	pulse
thromb/o:	clot
vascul/o:	vessel
ven/o:	vein
ventricul/o:	ventricle

Digestive Word Roots

append/o:	appendix
appendic/o:	appendix
bucc/o:	cheek
cheil/o:	lip
chol/e:	bile
cholangi/o:	bile vessel
cholecyst/o:	gallbladder
choledoch/o:	bile duct
col/o:	large intestine
colon/o:	large intestine
dont/o:	teeth
duoden/o:	duodenum
enter/o:	small intestine
esophag/o:	esophagus
gastr/o:	stomach
gingiv/o:	gums
gloss/o:	tongue
hepat/o:	liver
ile/o:	ileum
jejun/o:	jejunum
labi/o:	lip
lingu/o:	tongue
odont/o:	teeth
or/o:	mouth
pancreat/o:	pancreas
pharyng/o:	pharynx
proct/o:	anus
pylor/o:	pylorus
rect/o:	rectum
sial/o:	saliva
sigmoid/o:	sigmoid colon
stomat/o:	mouth

Endocrine Word Roots

aden/o:	gland
adren/o:	adrenal glands
adrenal/o:	adrenal glands
calc/o:	calcium
gluc/o:	sugar
glyc/o:	sugar
gonad/o:	gonads
home/o:	same
kal/i:	potassium
pancreat/o:	pancreas
thym/o:	thymus gland
thyr/o:	thyroid
thyroid/o:	thyroid
toxic/o:	poison
thalam/o:	thalamus

Integumentary Word Roots

adip/o:	fat
albin/o:	white
carcin/o:	cancer
cirrh/o:	yellow
cutane/o:	skin
cyan/o:	blue
derm/o:	skin
dermat/o:	skin
erythem/o:	red
erythemat/o:	red
erythr/o:	red
hidr/o:	sweat
histi/o:	tissue
hist/o:	tissue
ichthy/o:	scaly
jaund/o:	yellow
kerat/o:	hard
leuk/o:	white
lip/o:	fat
melan/o:	black
myc/o:	fungi
onych/o:	nail
pil/o:	hair
scler/o:	hard
seb/o:	sebum
squam/o:	scale
sudor/o:	sweat
trich/o:	hair
ungu/o:	nail
xanth/o:	yellow
xer/o:	dry

Lymphatic Word Roots

adenoid/o:	adenoids
immun/o:	immune
lymph/o:	lymph
lymphaden/o:	lymph gland
lymphangi/o:	lymph vessel
splen/o:	spleen
tonsill/o:	tonsils
thym/o:	thymus

Muscular Word Roots

adhes/o:	stick to
aponeur/o:	aponeurosis
duct/o:	carry
erg/o:	work
fasci/o:	fascia
fibr/o:	fiber
fibros/o:	fiber
flex/o:	bend
is/o:	same
kinesi/o:	movement
lei/o:	smooth
lev/o:	lift
levat/o:	lift
metr/o:	length
quadr/i:	four
quadr/o:	four
rect/o:	straight
rhabd/o:	rod-shaped
ten/o:	tendon
tend/o:	tendon
tendin/o:	tendon
tens/o:	strain
ton/o:	tension
tort/i:	twisted

Nervous Word Roots

astr/o:	star
ax/o:	axon
cephal/o:	head
cerebell/o:	cerebellum
clon/o:	clonus
cortic/o:	cortex
crani/o:	skull
dendr/o:	tree

dur/o:	dura mater	vas/o:	vessel	ili/o:	ilium
encephal/o:	brain	vesicul/o:	seminal vesicle	ischi/o:	ischium
esthesi/o:	sensation	vulv/o:	vulva	kyph/o:	hill
gangli/o:	ganglion			lamin/o:	lamina
gli/o:	glue	**Respiratory Word Roots**		lord/o:	curve
kinesi/o:	movement			metacarp/o:	metacarpals
lex/o:	word	alveol/o:	alveolus	metatars/o:	metatarsals
lob/o:	lobe	anthrac/o:	black	myel/o:	canal
medull/o:	medulla	atel/o:	incomplete	orth/o:	straight
mening/o:	meninges	bronch/o:	bronchus	oste/o:	bone
ment/o:	mind	bronchi/o:	bronchus	patell/o:	patella
mot/o:	move	coni/o:	dust	ped/i:	foot
myel/o:	canal	cyan/o:	blue	pelv/i:	pelvis
narc/o:	stupor	embol/o:	plug	pelv/o:	pelvis
neur/o:	nerve	emphys/o:	inflate	phalang/o:	phalanges
olig/o:	few	epiglott/o:	epiglottis	pod/o:	foot
phas/o:	speech	hem/o:	blood	pub/o:	pubis
phren/o:	mind	laryng/o:	larynx	rachi/o:	spine
psych/o:	mind	lob/o:	lobe	radi/o:	radius
spin/o:	spine	muc/o:	mucous	sacr/o:	sacrum
synapt/o:	point of contact	nas/o:	nose	scapul/o:	scapula
tax/o:	order	or/o:	mouth	scoli/o:	crooked
thalam/o:	thalamus	orth/o:	straight	spondyl/o:	vertebrae
thec/o:	sheath	ox/o:	oxygen	synov/o:	synovium
		pector/o:	chest	tal/o:	talus
Reproductive Word Roots		pharyng/o:	pharynx	tars/o:	tarsals
		phon/o:	sound	thorac/o:	chest
amni/o:	amnion	phren/o:	diaphragm	uln/o:	ulna
andr/o:	male	pleur/o:	pleura	vertebr/o:	vertebrae
cervic/o:	neck	pneum/o:	lung		
colp/o:	vagina	pneumon/o:	lung	**Urinary Word Roots**	
embry/o:	embryo	pulm/o:	lung		
epididym/o:	epididymis	rhin/o:	nose	albumin/o:	albumin
episi/o:	vulva	sinus/o:	sinus	azot/o:	nitrogenous
fet/o:	fetus	spir/o:	breathe	cyst/o:	bladder
galact/o:	milk	steth/o:	chest	glomerul/o:	glomerulus
genit/o:	genitalia	thorac/o:	chest	kal/i:	potassium
gynec/o:	woman	trache/o:	trachea	ket/o:	ketone bodies
hyster/o:	uterus			meat/o:	opening
hymen/o:	hymen	**Skeletal Word Roots**		nephr/o:	kidney
lact/o:	milk			pyel/o:	renal pelvis
leiomy/o:	smooth muscle	acr/o:	extremity	ren/o:	kidney
mamm/o:	breast	acromi/o:	acromion	trigon/o:	trigone
mast/o:	breast	ankyl/o:	crooked	ur/o:	urine
men/o:	menstruation	arthr/o:	joint	ureter/o:	ureter
metr/o:	uterus	brachi/o:	arm	urethr/o:	urethra
nat/o:	birth	calcane/o:	calcaneus	urin/o:	urine
o/o:	egg	carp/o:	carpals	vesic/o:	bladder
oophor/o:	ovary	cephal/o:	head		
orch/o:	testicle	cervic/o:	neck	**Oncology Word Roots**	
ovari/o:	ovary	chondr/o:	cartilage		
pen/o:	penis	clavicul/o:	clavicle	aden/o:	gland
perine/o:	perineum	cleid/o:	clavicle	blast/o:	germ cell
prostat/o:	prostate	condyl/o:	condyle	carcin/o:	cancer
salping/o:	fallopian tube	cost/o:	ribs	cauter/o:	burn
sperm/o:	sperm	crani/o:	cranium	chem/o:	chemical
spermat/o:	sperm	dactyl/o:	fingers/toes	cry/o:	cold
test/o:	testicle	femor/o:	femur	hist/o:	tissue
uter/o:	uterus	fibul/o:	fibula	immun/o:	immunity
vagin/o:	vagina	humer/o:	humerus	leiomy/o:	smooth muscle

leuk/o:	white	dia-:	through			**Suffixes**	
mut/a:	genetic change	dipl-:	double				
myel/o:	canal	dys-:	difficult	-ac:	referring to		
onc/o:	tumor	ec-:	out	-acusis:	hearing		
rhabdomy/o:	skeletal muscle	echo-:	repeated sound	-al:	referring to		
sarc/o:	connective tissue	ecto-:	outside	-algia:	pain		
		ef-:	away	-ar:	referring to		
	Miscellaneous Word Roots	en-:	within	-ary:	referring to		
		end-:	within	-ate:	form of		
aur/i:	ear	endo-:	within	-ation:	process		
bi/o:	life	epi-:	above	-asthenia:	weakness		
burs/o:	bursa	eso-:	inward	-blast:	germ cell		
cerat/o:	horn	eu-:	good	-capnia:	carbon dioxide		
chir/o:	hand	ex-:	outside	-cele:	hernia		
corac/o:	crow-like	exo-:	outside	-centesis:	puncture		
coron/o:	crown	extra-:	outside	-cision:	cutting		
dextr/o:	right	hemi-:	half	-clast:	break		
dors/o:	back	hetero-:	different	-crine:	secrete		
dynam/o:	power	homeo-:	same	-cusis:	hearing		
ect/o:	outside	hyper-:	excessive	-cyte:	cell		
faci/o:	face	hypo-:	below	-desis:	binding		
glauc/o:	gray	im-:	not	-derma:	skin		
hydr/o:	water	in-:	in	-duction:	bringing		
irid/o:	iris	infra-:	below	-dynia:	pain		
kerat/o:	cornea	inter-:	between	-eal:	referring to		
lacrim/o:	tear	intra-:	inside	-ectasis:	dilation		
lapar/o:	abdominal wall	iso-:	same	-ectomy:	removal		
myring/o:	eardrum	macro-:	large	-edema:	swelling		
omphal/o:	navel	mal-:	bad	-emesis:	vomiting		
ophthalam/o:	eye	meso-:	middle	-emia:	blood		
phot/o:	light	meta-:	change	-esis:	condition		
py/o:	pus	micro-:	small	-esthesia:	sensation		
pyr/o:	heat	mono-:	one	-ferent:	to carry		
therm/o:	heat	multi-:	many	-gen:	produce		
tympan/o:	eardrum	neo-:	new	-genesis:	produce		
ventr/o:	belly	nulli-:	none	-globin:	protein		
viscer/o:	internal organs	oxy-:	sharp	-gnosis:	knowing		
zo/o:	animal	pan-:	all	-gram:	record		
zym/o:	fermentation	para-:	beside	-graph:	recording		
		per-:	through	-graphy:	recording		
	Prefixes	peri-:	around	-ia:	condition		
		poly-:	many	-iasis:	abnormal condition		
a-:	without	post-:	after	-iatry:	medicine		
ab-:	away	pre-:	before	-ic:	referring to		
ad-:	towards	pro-:	before	-ical:	referring to		
af-:	towards	pseudo-:	false	-ician:	specialist		
allo-:	other	quadri-:	four	-icle:	small		
an-:	without	retro-:	behind	-ile:	referring to		
ana-:	against	semi-:	half	-ine:	referring to		
aniso-:	unequal	sub-:	under	-ism:	condition		
ante-:	before	super-:	above	-ist:	specialist		
anti-:	against	supra-:	above	-itis:	inflammation		
auto-:	self	sym-:	together	-kinesia:	movement		
bi-:	two	syn-:	together	-lalia:	speech		
brady-:	slow	tachy-:	rapid	-lampsia:	shine		
cine-:	movement	torti-:	twisted	-lepsy:	seizure		
circum-:	around	trans-:	through	-lith:	stone		
contra-:	against	tri-:	three	-logist:	specializing in		
de-:	cessation	ultra-:	excessive	-logy:	study of		
di-:	double	uni-:	one	-lucent:	clear		

Suffix	Meaning	Suffix	Meaning	Suffix	Meaning
-lysis:	dissolve	-phagia:	eat	-rrhexis:	rupture
-malacia:	soften	-phasia:	speech	-scope:	examining
-mania:	frenzy	-philia:	attraction	-spasm:	twitch
-megaly:	enlargement	-phobia:	fear	-scopy:	visual exam
-meter:	measuring	-phoria:	feeling	-stasis:	standing still
-metry:	measuring	-phylaxis:	protection	-stenosis:	narrowing
-oid:	resembling	-physis:	growth	-stomy:	opening
-ole:	little	-plasia:	formation	-tension:	stretch
-oma:	tumor	-plasm:	growth	-thorax:	chest
-orexia:	appetite	-plasty:	repair	-thymia:	emotion
-ory:	referring to	-plegia:	paralysis	-tic:	referring to
-ose:	referring to	-pnea:	breathing	-tomy:	incision
-osis:	condition	-poiesis:	formation	-toxic:	poison
-ous:	referring to	-porosis:	porous	-tripsy:	crushing
-paresis:	partial paralysis	-rrhage:	bursting forth	-trophy:	nourishment
-pathy:	disease	-rrhaphy:	suture	-uria:	urine
-penia:	deficiency	-rrhea:	discharge	-y:	condition

General Medical Terms

A

ABC: References things to check before administering resuscitation efforts, Airway, Breathing, Circulation.
Abscess: A localized collection of pus.
Acute: Sudden, severe onset of a medical condition or disease.
Adhesion: Stuck together.
Ambulant/Ambulatory: The ability to walk.
Arrest: Cessation of bodily activity or function.
Aseptic: Sterile.
Autonomy: Being self-governed.

B

Benign: Does not spread.
Biopsy: Surgically removing tissue to examine microscopically.

C

Cachexia: Loss of appetite, weight, with muscle atrophy, usually associated with a serious medical condition such as cancer.
Carcinogen: A substance that may cause cancer.
Chronic: A disease or condition that persists over a period of time.
Collis: Neck.

D

Diagnosis: Determination of the cause of a disease.

E

Edema: An excessive accumulation of fluid in an area.
Etiology: The study of the cause of a disease.
Excision: Surgically removing a structure or tissue.

F

Febrile: Presence of a fever.
Fistula: Location where an organ has developed an opening into another organ.

I

Idiopathic: An unknown cause of disease.
Incision: Cutting in to, typically with a scalpel.
Incontinence: Loss of control of the bladder and/or bowels.
In Situ: "In original place", commonly references cancer that is still in its place of origin, such as the epithelium of the skin.
Intravenous: Inside a vein, usually referencing injections.
Ischemia: Lack of blood flow to an area, which may result in necrosis.

M

Malaise: General unwell feeling or discomfort.
Malformation: A structure that is not formed properly.
Malignant: Spreading of cancer from one area to another.

N

Necrosis: Death of tissue.
Neopathy: A new disease.

P

Pallor: General paleness.
Palsy: Paralysis.
Peptic: Referring to the stomach.
Phlegm: Secretions expelled from the lungs, also known as sputum.
Phobia: Fear of a person, thing, or situation.
Prognosis: Predicted outcome of a disease and recovery rate.
Pulse: Expansion of an artery as blood passes through.
Pyrogenic: Producing fever.

S

Sepsis: An infection.
Sign: Observable indications of an illness.
Sinus: A cavity.
Sputum: Secretions expelled from the lungs, also known as phlegm.
Symptom: A physical manifestation of an illness.
Syndrome: Groups of symptoms caused by a disease.

T

Transient: Short duration.

Medical Terminology Matching

Word Roots		Prefixes		Suffixes	
____: necr/o	____: gloss/o	____: auto-	____: bi-	____: -ectomy	____: -plegia
____: leuk/o	____: my/o	____: a-	____: macro-	____: -blast	____: -gen
____: melan/o	____: nephr/o	____: hyper-	____: brady-	____: -pnea	____: -phagia
____: cost/o	____: brachi/o	____: meta-	____: micro-	____: -crine	____: -globin
____: spondyl/o	____: cardi/o	____: mal-	____: anti-	____: -cision	____: -clast
____: gastr/o	____: erythr/o	____: syn-	____: iso-	____: -trophy	____: -edema
____: derm/o	____: oste/o	____: homeo-	____: circum-	____: -algia	____: -osis
____: chondr/o	____: hem/o	____: hypo-	____: endo-	____: -stasis	____: -cyte
____: adip/o	____: pneum/o	____: inter-	____: ad-	____: -emia	____: -oid
____: hepat/o	____: phleb/o	____: dia-	____: epi-	____: -derma	____: -lysis

A. Muscle	K. Spine	A. Together	K. Large	A. Nourishment	K. Protein
B. Liver	L. Stomach	B. Change	L. Towards	B. Blood	L. Germ Cell
C. Fat	M. White	C. Without	M. Small	C. Production	M. Removal
D. Kidney	N. Vein	D. Two	N. Around	D. Swelling	N. Dissolve
E. Arm	O. Lung	E. Against	O. Bad	E. Resembling	O. Cutting
F. Blood	P. Skin	F. Above	P. Excessive	F. Condition	P. Pain
G. Black	Q. Cartilage	G. Through	Q. Inside	G. Skin	Q. Eating
H. Tongue	R. Death	H. Equal	R. Below	H. Standing Still	R. Breathing
I. Bone	S. Red	I. Slow	S. Self	I. Paralysis	S. Secrete
J. Rib	T. Heart	J. Same	T. Between	J. Break	T. Cell

Answer Key on Page 312

Medical Terminology Breaking Down/Building

Break down the following diseases by their word roots, prefixes, and suffixes, giving the definition of each part in the blank spaces.

1. Arteriosclerosis: _____/_____/_____
2. Pyelonephritis: _____/_____/_____
3. Encephalitis: _____/_____
4. Lymphedema: _____/_____
5. Hyperthyroidism: _____/_____/_____
6. Cholecystitis: _____/_____/_____
7: Hepatitis: _____/_____
8: Phlebitis: _____/_____
9. Torticollis: _____/_____
10. Dermatophytosis: _____/_____/_____
11. Acromegaly: _____/_____
12. Myocardial Infarction: _____/_____/_____
13. Insomnia: _____/_____
14. Neuralgia: _____/_____
15. Tenosynovitis: _____/_____/_____

Build the name of the following diseases just using their definition. Remember, not every disease has a prefix or suffix!

1. Without blood: _____/_____
2. Fatty plaque hard condition: _____/_____/_____
3. Stomach inflammation: _____/_____
4. Black tumor: _____/_____
5. Fiber muscle pain: _____/_____/_____
6. Bone joint inflammation: _____/_____/_____
7. Bladder inflammation: _____/_____
8: Without breath: _____/_____
9. Nail fungus condition: _____/_____/_____
10. Skin inflammation: _____/_____
11. Above tension: _____/_____
12. Without rhythm: _____/_____
13. White blood condition: _____/_____
14. Hill condition: _____/_____
15. Cell inflammation: _____/_____

Answer Key on Page 312

Medical Terminology Practice Test

1. The word root "ather/o" means
A. Fatty plaque
B. Ventricle
C. Canal
D. Artery

2. Which of the following prefixes means "without"
A. eso-
B. af-
C. iso-
D. an-

3. The term "carcinogen" is defined as
A. Study of tumors
B. Many cysts
C. Producing cancer
D. Large intestine inflammation

4. The suffix "-emia" means
A. Blood condition
B. Production
C. Inflammation
D. Death

5. The term "onychomycosis" is defined as
A. Blood vessel repair
B. Nail fungus condition
C. Skin swelling condition
D. Blood canal inflammation

6. Which of the following terms means "referring to the diaphragm"
A. Phrenic
B. Costal
C. Chondral
D. Pneumatic

7. The word root "lord/o" means
A. Hill
B. Lateral
C. Curve
D. Branch

8. Which of the following suffixes means "discharge"
A. -rrhage
B. -rrhea
C. -rrhaphy
D. -stomy

9. The word root "hist/o" means
A. Uterus
B. Smooth
C. Mouth
D. Tissue

10. The term "epinephrine" is defined as
A. Secreting into the mouth
B. Below the liver formation
C. Crooked spine condition
D. Secreting above the kidney

11. The word root "phag/o" means
A. White
B. Bile
C. Eat
D. Movement

12. Which prefix means "half"
A. semi-
B. ultra-
C. sub-
D. inter-

13. The suffix "-plegia" means
A. Deficiency
B. Nourishment
C. Paralysis
D. Vomiting

14. Which word root means "kidney"
A. Acr/o
B. Ren/o
C. Hepat/o
D. Hyster/o

15. The term "homeostasis" is defined as
A. Same standing still
B. Study of different
C. Equal formation
D. Hormone regulation

16. Which suffix means "to carry"
A. -rrhage
B. -uria
C. -ferent
D. -acusis

17. The term "encephalitis" is defined as
A. Liver inflammation
B. Skin inflammation
C. Tongue inflammation
D. Brain inflammation

18. The word root "bucc/o" means
A. Mouth
B. Teeth
C. Cheek
D. Jaw

19. The prefix "macro-" means
A. Large
B. Middle
C. Small
D. Change

20. The prefix "anti-" means
A. Around
B. Double
C. Against
D. Towards

21. "Removal of the gallbladder" is
A. Angioplasty
B. Cholecystectomy
C. Colostomy
D. Leiomyogram

22. A person diagnosed with "without rhythm" who has "slow heart" would have which conditions
A. Heart murmur and arrhythmia
B. Arrhythmia and bradycardia
C. Tachycardia and pericarditis
D. Heart murmur and tachycardia

23. A person who has a "blood tumor" would have
A. Hematoma
B. Hyperemia
C. Ischemia
D. Hematopoiesis

24. The term "endocrine" means
A. Secreting outside
B. Secreting above
C. Secreting inside
D. Secreting below

25. The word root "gluc/o" means
A. Fat
B. Protein
C. Vitamin
D. Sugar

26. "Osteomyelitis" means
A. Bone joint inflammation
B. Bone canal inflammation
C. Bone surface condition
D. Bone cartilage infection

27. The suffix "-itis" means
A. Disease
B. Growth
C. Condition
D. Inflammation

28. Which of the following describes a condition that has something to do with the kidneys
A. Pyelonephritis
B. Osteoporosis
C. Gastritis
D. Cystitis

29. Which of the following terms means "little belly"
A. Arteriole
B. Ventricle
C. Dendrite
D. Bronchiole

30. The word root "pil/o" means
A. Tongue
B. Clavicle
C. Hair
D. Potassium

31. The prefix "pan-" means
A. Above
B. Bread
C. All
D. Good

32. What form of cancer is known as "connective tissue tumor"
A. Sarcoma
B. Melanoma
C. Carcinoma
D. Leukemia

33. What form of medication works "against heat"
A. Antibiotic
B. Antihistamine
C. Antifungal
D. Antipyretic

34. Injections that are "subcutaneous" go where
A. Above the nerve
B. Under the skin
C. Into the muscle
D. Into the skin

35. A "linguist" is a person who does what
A. Specializes in the tongue
B. Specializes in the brain
C. Specializes in the skin
D. Specializes in the hand

36. Which of these word roots does not refer to a body region
A. Brachi/o
B. Inguin/o
C. Thorac/o
D. Pulm/o

37. The term "cyanosis" means
A. Red condition
B. Blue condition
C. White condition
D. Black condition

38. Which of the following word roots means "hard"
A. Dont/o
B. Scler/o
C. Xer/o
D. Ather/o

39. Which of the following terms means "crooked condition"
A. Kyphosis
B. Lordosis
C. Scoliosis
D. Osteoporosis

40. Which medication means "against life"
A. Antipyretic
B. Antibiotic
C. Antifungal
D. Antiviral

41. The term "coronoid" means
A. Head inflammation
B. Resembling a crow
C. Shoulder condition
D. Resembling a crown

42. Which term means "nerve pain"
A. Neuralgia
B. Neuritis
C. Neuroglia
D. Neuroma

43. Which term means "two head"
A. Quadricep
B. Tricep
C. Bicep
D. Unicep

44. Which of the following is "around the heart"
A. Epidural
B. Pericardium
C. Perineum
D. Epimysium

45. A person with "tinea pedis" is suffering from what
A. Virus on the face
B. Bacterial in the bone
C. Fungus on the foot
D. Parasite in the small intestine

46. Which of the following prefixes means "bad"
A. mal-
B. a-
C. sym-
D. nulli-

47. Which of the following word roots means "yellow"
A. Albin/o
B. Cirrh/o
C. Melan/o
D. Cyan/o

48. The word root "flex/o" means
A. Strain
B. Tension
C. Lift
D. Bend

49. Which of the following prefixes means "new"
A. echo-
B. exo-
C. neo-
D. di-

50. The term "thrombolytic" is defined as
A. Blood clot dissolve
B. Blood filter
C. Blood clot prevention
D. Blood clot production

Answer Key on Page 314

Anatomy and Physiology

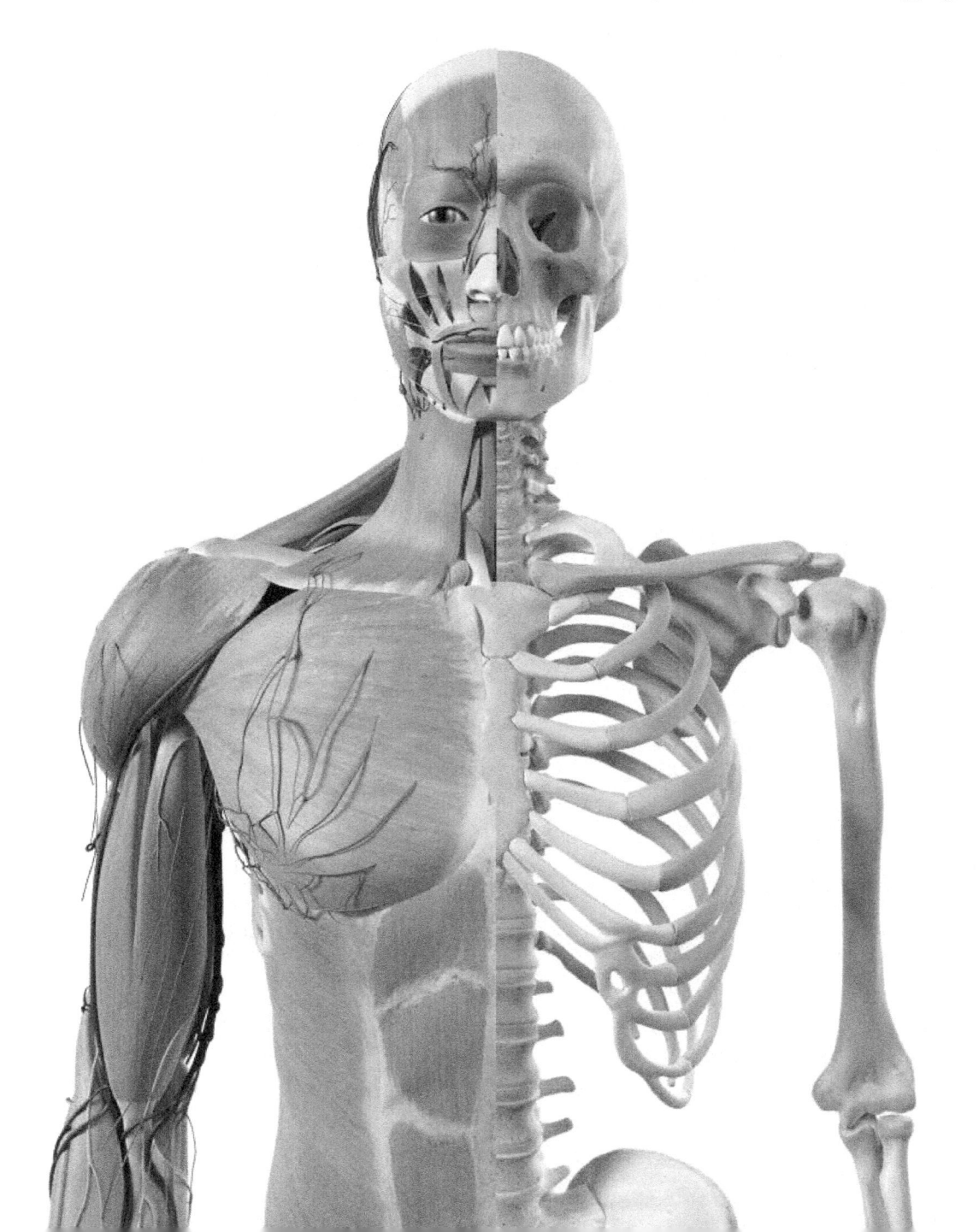

Anatomy and Physiology

Anatomy and Physiology, two extremely important aspects of the human body. **Anatomy**, simply put, is the study of the **structure** of the human body. All of the parts that make up the body constitute anatomy, from bones, muscles, and nerves, to cells, tendons, ligaments, and everything in between.

Physiology is the study of the **function** of the body. How do the parts of the body that make up the body's anatomy function? What do they do? This is physiology. Anatomy and physiology go hand-in-hand.

Homeostasis

Homeostasis is the existence and maintenance of a **constant internal environment**. The body's internal environment is constantly changing and responding to various stimuli. Examples of stimuli are temperature, hormones, diet, and the body's pH level. These stimuli that change the body's internal environment in some way are known as **homeostatic variables**. As the variables change, so too does the internal environment.

How does the body respond to these changes? Using **homeostatic mechanisms**, such as sweating and shivering. An example, when your body temperature gets too high, your body mechanically(physically) responds by sweating. Sweat evaporates off the skin, which cools the body down, lowering body temperature. When the body becomes too cold, the body responds by mechanically increasing the amount of twitching in the skeletal muscles. This increased twitching, which is normally undetectable, results in shivering, which produces body heat, raising body temperature.

The body's internal environment is constantly changing, and the body constantly adjusts certain aspects of itself to respond to these changes. If temperature is an example, the **set point**(normal range) of a body's temperature is 98.6 degrees Fahrenheit. The internal body temperature is never set right at 98.6 degrees. It is constantly fluctuating around it, maintaining a normal range of optimal body function.

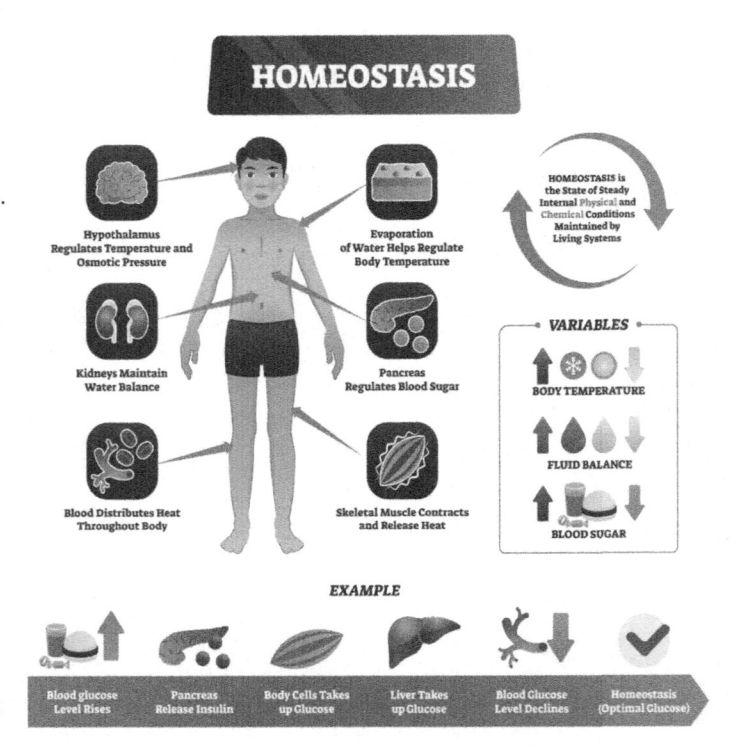

Regional Anatomy

Regional Anatomy is the study of the structures of the body, broken down into different parts. When describing the position of one structure in the body in relation to another structure or structures, we use **directional terms**. An example, using the term "medial condyle" instead of just "condyle" lets us communicate effectively which condyle is being discussed.

The main directional terms are:

- **Superior**: Above.
- **Inferior**: Below.
- **Anterior**: Front.
- **Posterior**: Back.
- **Proximal**: Closer to the midline.

- **Distal**: Further from the midline.
- **Medial**: Middle.
- **Lateral**: Side.
- **Deep**: More internal.
- **Superficial**: Towards the surface.

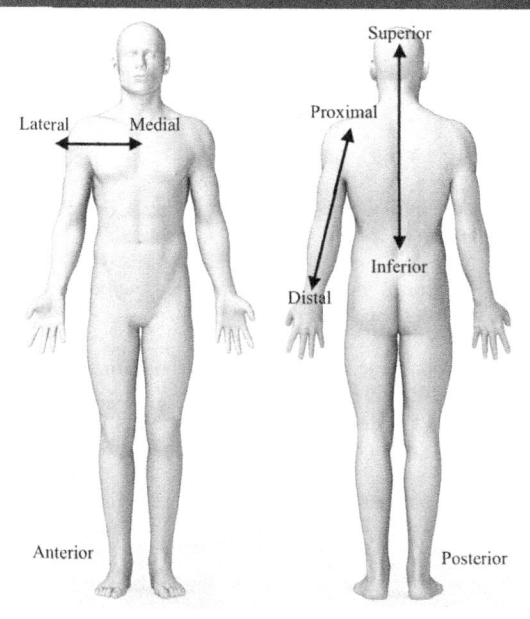

Body Planes

Body planes are important for viewing structures from different aspects. These can be used when doing simple visual assessment, or in instances such as surgery or cadaver dissection.

There are four main body planes: A **midsagittal**, or **median** plane, runs down the **midline** of the body, splitting the body into **equal left and right sides**. This is the only location for a midsagittal plane.

A **sagittal** plane also splits the body into left or right sides, but **not equally**. It can be located anywhere along the body except down the midline.

A **transverse**, or **horizontal** plane, splits the body into **superior and inferior** portions. It does not have to be at the waist. It can split the body into superior and inferior at any point along the body.

A **frontal**, or **coronal** plane, as the name suggests, splits the body into front and back, or **anterior and posterior**. If a person wanted to dissect the heart and make all four chambers visible, they would cut the heart into a frontal or coronal plane. See photo on page 57.

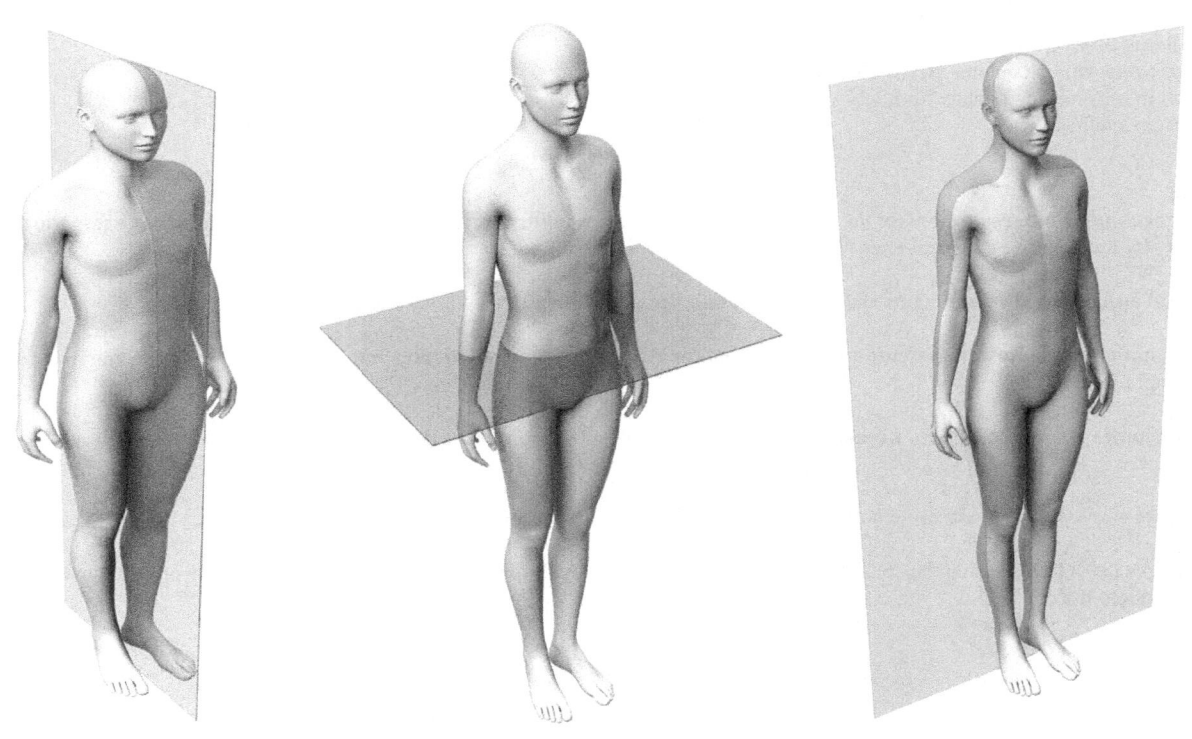

Midsagittal Plane   Transverse/Horizontal Plane   Frontal/Coronal Plane

Body Regions

The body, as stated earlier, can be broken down into different parts, or regions. There are three main body regions: the **central** body region, the **upper limb**, and the **lower limb**.

The **central** body region contains all of the structures located in the center of the body: the **head**, the **neck**, and the **trunk**. Take away the arms and legs, and you're left with the central body region.

The **trunk** can be further divided into three regions: the **thorax**, or chest, the **abdomen**, and the **pelvis**. The thorax contains the heart, lungs, esophagus, thymus, and major blood vessels connecting to the heart. The abdomen contains the majority of our digestive organs, including the stomach, liver, gallbladder, pancreas, small intestine, and large intestine. It also contains the kidneys and ureters. The pelvis contains the urinary bladder, urethra, and reproductive organs.

The **upper limb** can be broken down into four regions: the **arm**, **forearm**, **wrist**, and **hand**. The arm contains the humerus. The forearm contains the radius and ulna. The wrist contains the carpals. The hand contains the metacarpals and phalanges.

The **lower limb** can also be broken down into four regions: the **thigh**, **leg**, **ankle**, and **foot**. The thigh contains the femur. The leg contains the tibia and fibula. The ankle contains the tarsals. The foot contains the metatarsals and phalanges.

Cells

Cells are the functional **units** of all tissues. Cells are responsible for performing all essential life functions, from synthesizing nutrients to destroying pathogens and debris. Cells **divide** via a process known as **mitosis**. During mitosis, the cell splits from one single mother cell into two separate daughter cells. These daughter cells then divide further into daughter cells of their own, and the cycle repeats until enough cells are present to form a tissue.

Inside each cell are **organelles**, structures that help regulate function of the cell.

The **nucleus** regulates the **overall function** of the cell. Inside the nucleus is **DNA**(deoxyribonucleic acid), which is the building block for life. Also inside the nucleus is the **nucleolus**, which contains **RNA**(ribonucleic acid). RNA is vital in transmitting signals from DNA to ribosomes for protein synthesis.

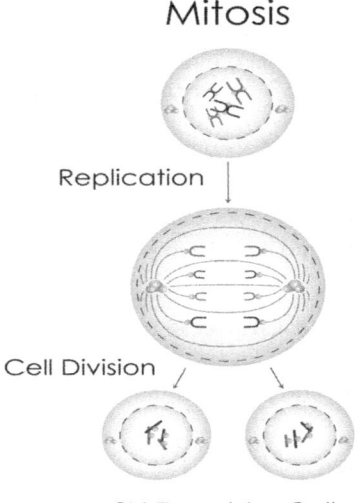

Mitosis
Replication
Cell Division
2N Daughter Cell

Mitochondria are responsible for the production of **adenosine triphosphate**(ATP), the molecule that provides **energy** to the body by transporting chemical energy to parts of the body that require it.

Golgi apparatus allows proteins and lipids to be bundled and **transported** within the cell itself.

The **smooth endoplasmic reticulum** is responsible for synthesizing **carbohydrates** and **lipids** for use in producing new cell membranes.

Lysosomes are responsible for **breaking down** several different substances inside the cell, including protein and waste products.

Ribosomes, which contain protein and RNA, are responsible for **synthesizing cell proteins**.

Cytoplasm is found inside the cell, and is a **gel-like substance**. It allows organelles, nutrients, and waste products to move throughout the cell.

Tissue

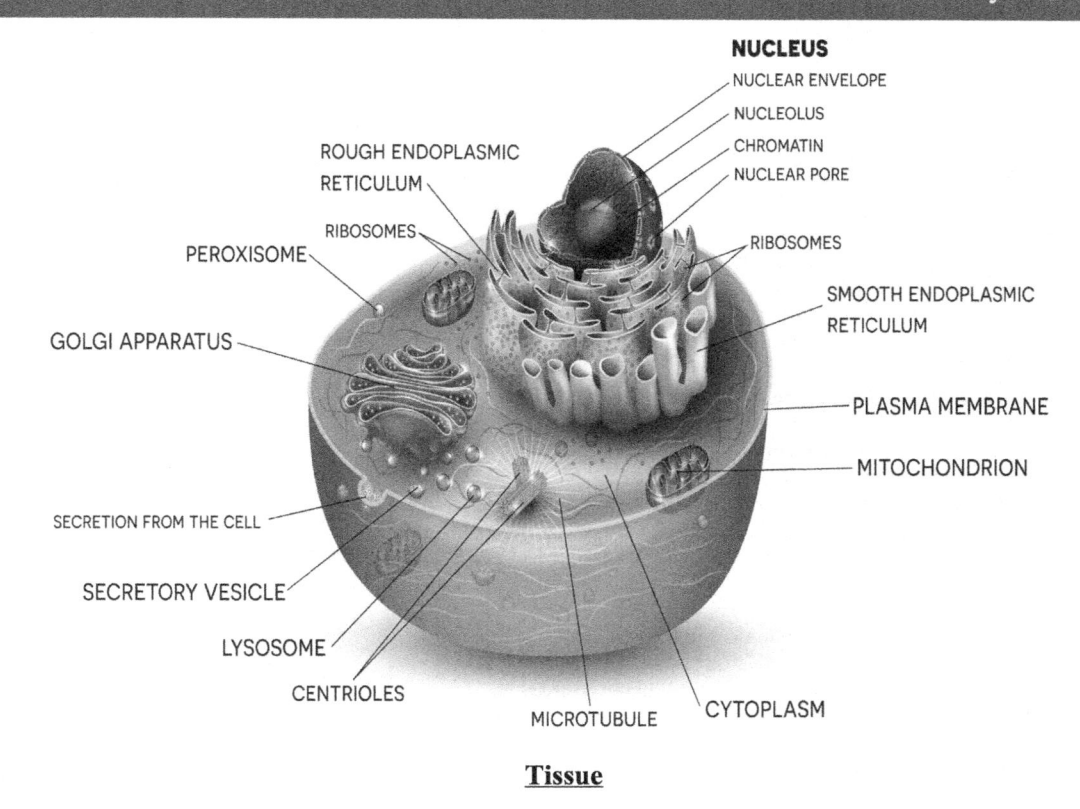

The body is constructed by smaller parts making bigger parts, until we have an organism. The organization of the body is: cells > tissues > organ > organ system > organism. A **tissue** is made of a group of **cells** with **similar function and structure**. When these cells, all formed roughly the same way, which perform the same action, come together, they form a tissue. There are **four** types of tissue in the human body: **epithelial**, **muscular**, **nervous**, and **connective**.

• **Epithelial** tissue forms most **glands,** the **digestive tract**, the **respiratory tract**, and the **epidermis**. Anywhere there is a mucous membrane, there is epithelium. Epithelial tissue is responsible for **protection**(the epidermis protects the body from pathogens and trauma), **secretion**(glands secrete substances, from hormones to mucous), and **absorption** of nutrients(the linings of the small intestine are made of epithelium, which allows nutrients to be absorbed into the blood stream). Epithelial tissue is also **avascular**, which means there is no direct blood supply to the tissue. This is what allows layers of the epidermis to be peeled away without any bleeding.

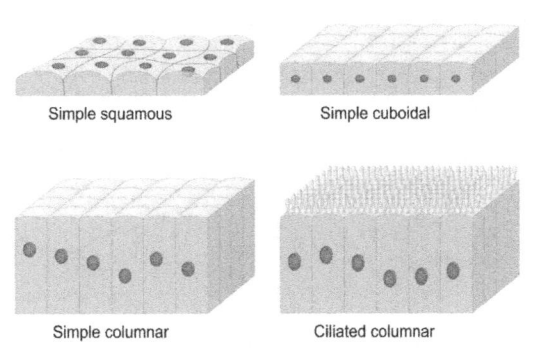

• **Muscular** tissue creates **muscles**. There are three types of muscles: **skeletal** muscles, so named because they connect to the skeleton, **cardiac** muscles, which create the heart, and **smooth** muscles, which are abundant in several locations in the body.

Skeletal muscles, as the name implies, attach to the **skeleton**. Another name for skeletal muscle is "**striated**" muscle due to its appearance under a microscope. These muscles are **voluntary**, meaning they can be controlled. When these muscles contract, they pull on the bones they attach to, which allows movement.

Skeletal muscles are always in a state of **twitching**, even if it can't be felt. It's this twitching, very fine contractions, that produces **body heat**. When body temperature drops, the skeletal muscles increase the amount of contraction, which produces high body temperature, with the twitching of the muscles becoming more apparent. This is what happens when a person shivers.

Cardiac muscle is the muscle that makes the **heart**. Another name for cardiac muscle is "**branching**" muscle due to its appearance under a microscope. Cardiac muscle is **involuntary**, meaning it cannot be controlled. Cardiac muscle is powerful, shooting **blood** out of the heart with each contraction. The only function of cardiac muscle is to send blood from one place to another.

Smooth muscle is found in several locations throughout the body. Another name for smooth muscle is "**non-striated**" muscle due to its appearance under a microscope. Smooth muscle is **involuntary**, meaning it cannot be controlled. Because smooth muscle is found in several different regions of the body, it has several different functions. Smooth muscle can be found in the **walls** of **hollow organs** such as the stomach and intestines. When these muscles contract, they force food through the Digestive System, which is known as **peristalsis**.

Other locations smooth muscle can be found are in the skin, and in the eyes. In the skin, smooth muscle attaches to hair. When these muscles contract, they stand hair up, producing goosebumps. These muscles are known as the arrector pili muscles. In the eyes, smooth muscles help to dilate the iris and pupil.

Types of Muscle Cells

skeletal muscle

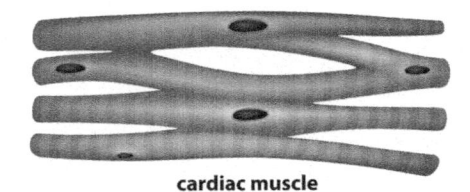

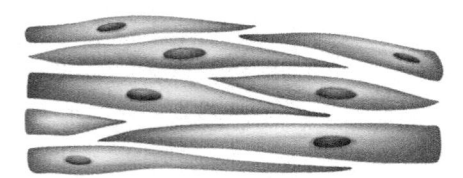

cardiac muscle

smooth muscle

- **Nervous** tissue forms the **brain**, **spinal cord**, and **nerves**. The primary cell of nervous tissue is known as a **neuron**. Neurons process nervous impulses, sending these impulses to other tissues, such as muscles, or between other neurons.

Neurons receive **action potentials** (electric impulses), which are brought into the cell by **dendrites**, branch-like projections coming off the cell body of the neuron. Once the nucleus processes the information coming into the cell, it sends the impulse out of the cell to its destination by way of the **axon**, a long projection coming off the cell body. The axons terminate at other neurons, or help innervate muscles. Surrounding the axons are sheaths of protein and fat known as **myelin**. Myelin sheaths allow efficient and rapid transmission of impulses traveling along an axon, and help provide protection for the axon. Myelin sheaths in the peripheral nervous system are produced by **Schwann cells**.

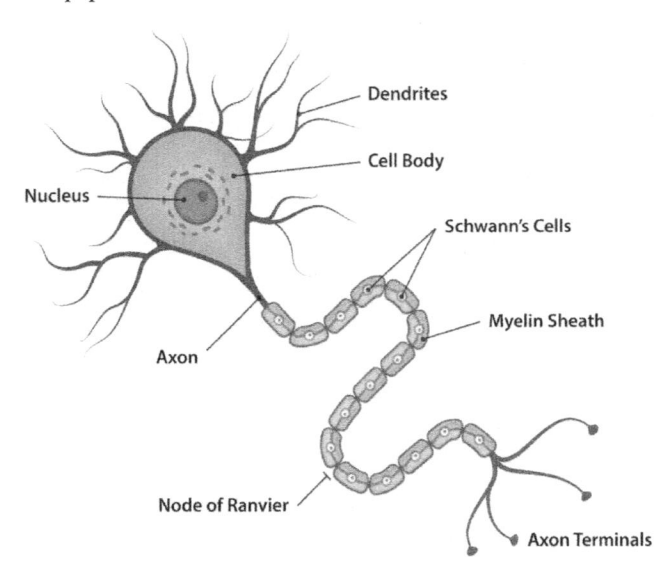

CONNECTIVE TISSUES

- **Connective** tissue is the most abundant form of tissue in the body. There are several different structures made by connective tissue, including **tendons**, **ligaments**, **fascia**, **bones**, **lymph**, **cartilage**, and **blood**. Connective tissue, as the name suggests, is responsible for **connecting** tissues. In addition to connecting tissues, it helps to **separate** tissues, as seen in serous membranes and cartilage.

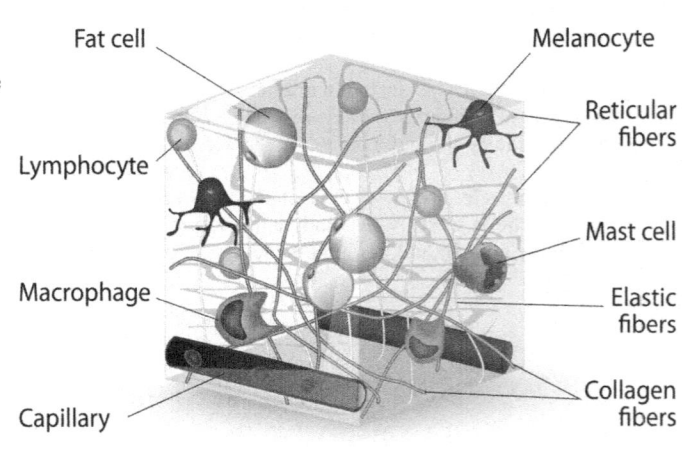

Connective tissue contains two specific types of cells known as **blast** cells and **clast** cells. These cells play a very important role in the health of connective tissue. Blast cells are germ cells that are responsible for **building** connective tissue. Blast cells divide and build tissue until the structure is complete. Once the structure is complete, the blast cells mature, and stop dividing. Clast cells are responsible for **breaking down** tissue, which is very important in keeping the tissue healthy. If a person suffers an injury such as a sprain or a fracture, clast cells will enter the area and destroy the dead tissue, cleaning the area, which allows blast cells a clean surface to build new tissue on.

Blood is the most **abundant** form of connective tissue in the body. Blood is mainly a mode of **transportation** for blood cells, hormones, nutrients, and waste products. There are four parts of blood: **erythrocytes**, **leukocytes**, **thrombocytes**, and **plasma**.

Erythrocytes, also known as red blood cells, are responsible for **transporting oxygen** and **carbon dioxide** throughout the body. The cytoplasm of erythrocytes is made of a protein known as **hemoglobin**, which is primarily made of iron. Hemoglobin is what oxygen and carbon dioxide attach to. In the lungs, when the erythrocytes are exposed to the alveoli, carbon dioxide detaches from the erythrocytes, and oxygen then attaches in its place. This is how gas exchange occurs in erythrocytes.

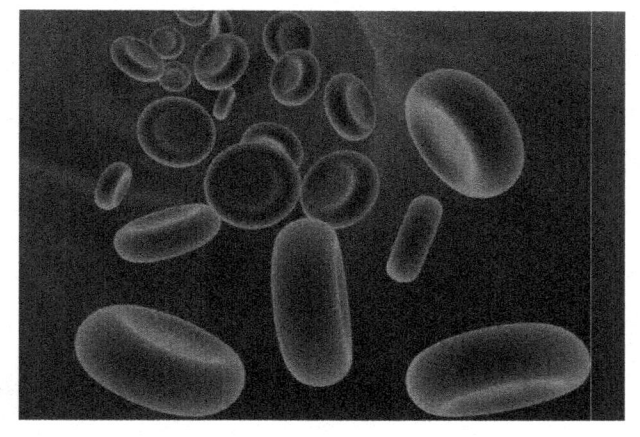

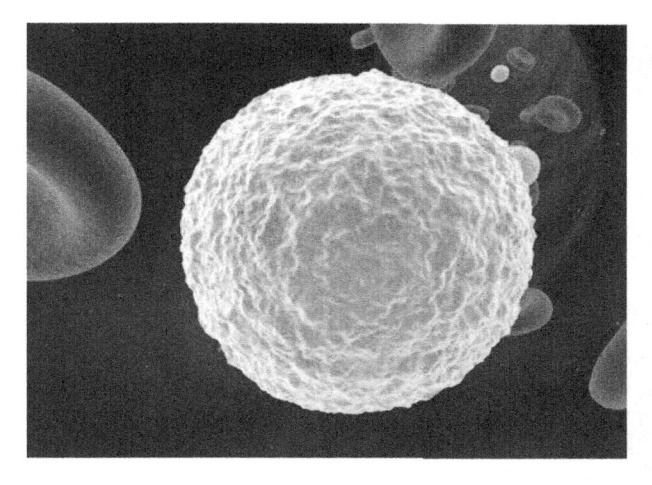

Leukocytes, also known as white blood cells, are the body's primary **defense** against **pathogens**. There are several different types of leukocytes, ranging from T-cells to basophils. These cells eat pathogens(such as bacteria), dead cells, and debris floating in the blood stream.

Thrombocytes, also known as **platelets**, have one function: to **clot the blood**. This is vitally important when a person is bleeding. If the blood does not clot, the person could continue bleeding until they lose too much blood.

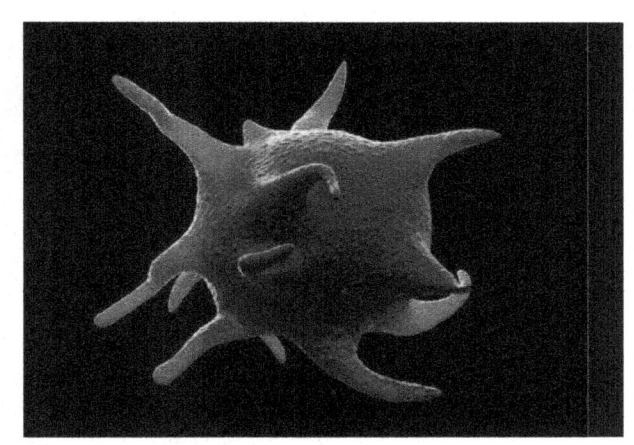

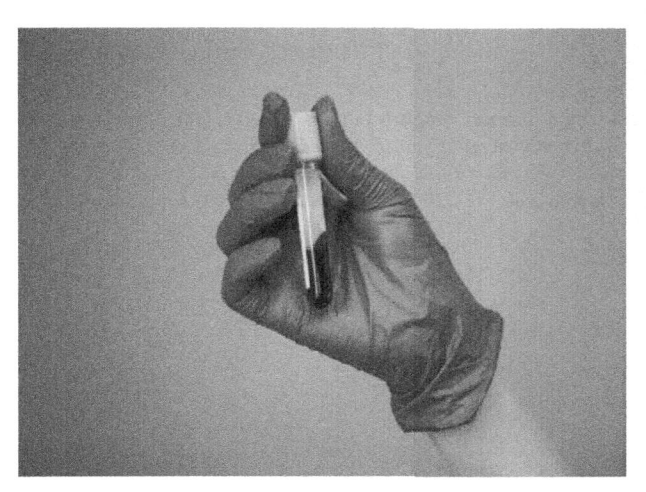

Plasma is the **fluid** portion of blood. The majority of blood, around 56%, is made of plasma. Plasma is what allows all of the blood cells, hormones, nutrients, and waste to move throughout the body. Without plasma, these substances would go nowhere!

Serous Membranes

Serous membranes are forms of connective tissue that are used to **separate** organs from one another, preventing friction. They accomplish this by **surrounding** the organ or body cavity.

Inside the thorax, there are two serous membranes: the **pericardium**, which surrounds the **heart**, and the **pleural** membranes, which surround the **lungs**. These membranes help protect these organs from injury.

Inside the abdomen and pelvis, there is one serous membrane: the **peritoneum**. This membrane keeps the organs inside the abdomen and pelvis from being injured, and provides a pathway for many blood vessels, lymph vessels, and nerves to travel. The peritoneum is commonly utilized to filter waste from the body in a person with kidney failure, a procedure known as peritoneal dialysis(page 108).

Inside of a serous membrane is a thick fluid, known as **serous fluid**. This fluid helps the membranes absorb shock. Holding the fluid in place are two walls. The inner wall, which comes into contact with the organs, is known as the **visceral serous membrane**. The outer wall, which comes into contact with other structures such as bones or other organs, is known as the **parietal serous membrane**.

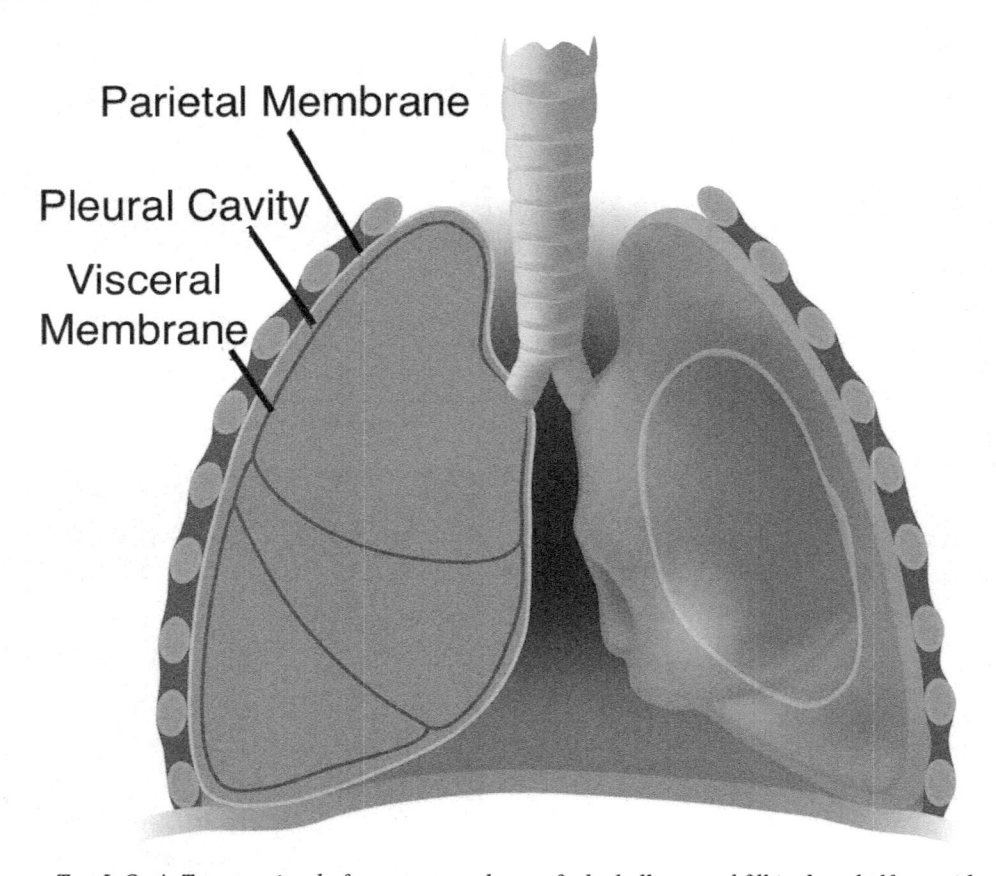

Test It Out!: To get a visual of a serous membrane, find a balloon, and fill it about halfway with some sort of oil, tying it off. Gently push a finger into the balloon, so it wraps around your finger. The part of the balloon that is pressed up against your finger would be the visceral serous membrane. Inside the balloon is the serous fluid. The outside of the balloon would be the parietal serous membrane. NOTE: Do this over a sink, in case the balloon accidentally breaks!

Cardiovascular System

The Cardiovascular System is one of the most important organ systems in the body, responsible for **transportation** of nutrients such as oxygen and hormones to tissues. It also allows for waste to be moved to areas of the body where it can be eliminated, such as the lungs, liver, and kidneys. Wastes include carbon dioxide and urea.

Heart

The primary organ of the Cardiovascular System is the **heart**. The heart, a large, powerful muscle, has one function: to **pump blood** throughout the body.

Blood is sent to the body to exchange oxygen and carbon dioxide. When gas exchange occurs, oxygen detaches from the erythrocytes, and carbon dioxide takes its place. Deoxygenated blood is returned to the heart via the **largest veins** in the body, the vena cavae. The **superior vena cava** returns blood to the heart from the head and upper limbs, while the **inferior vena cava** returns blood to the heart from the trunk and lower limbs. When blood first enters the heart, it is deoxygenated, and enters into the **right atrium**. It then passes through the **tricuspid valve** (which separates the right atrium from the right ventricle), into the **right ventricle**. The cardiac muscle in the right ventricle contracts, and it sends the deoxygenated blood out of the heart to the lungs through the **pulmonary arteries**. Despite carrying deoxygenated blood, these vessels are still called arteries because they carry blood away from the heart. After blood cycles through the lungs, exchanging oxygen and carbon dioxide, the blood returns back to the heart through the **pulmonary veins**. Again, despite carrying oxygenated blood, these vessels are called veins because they carry blood towards the heart. The blood re-enters the heart into the **left atrium**. It passes through the **bicuspid/mitral valve** (which separates the left atrium and left ventricle), into the **left ventricle**. An extremely powerful contraction occurs in the left ventricle, which shoots blood out of the heart to the rest of the body through the **aorta**, the **largest artery** in the body.

The pathway of blood flow through the heart

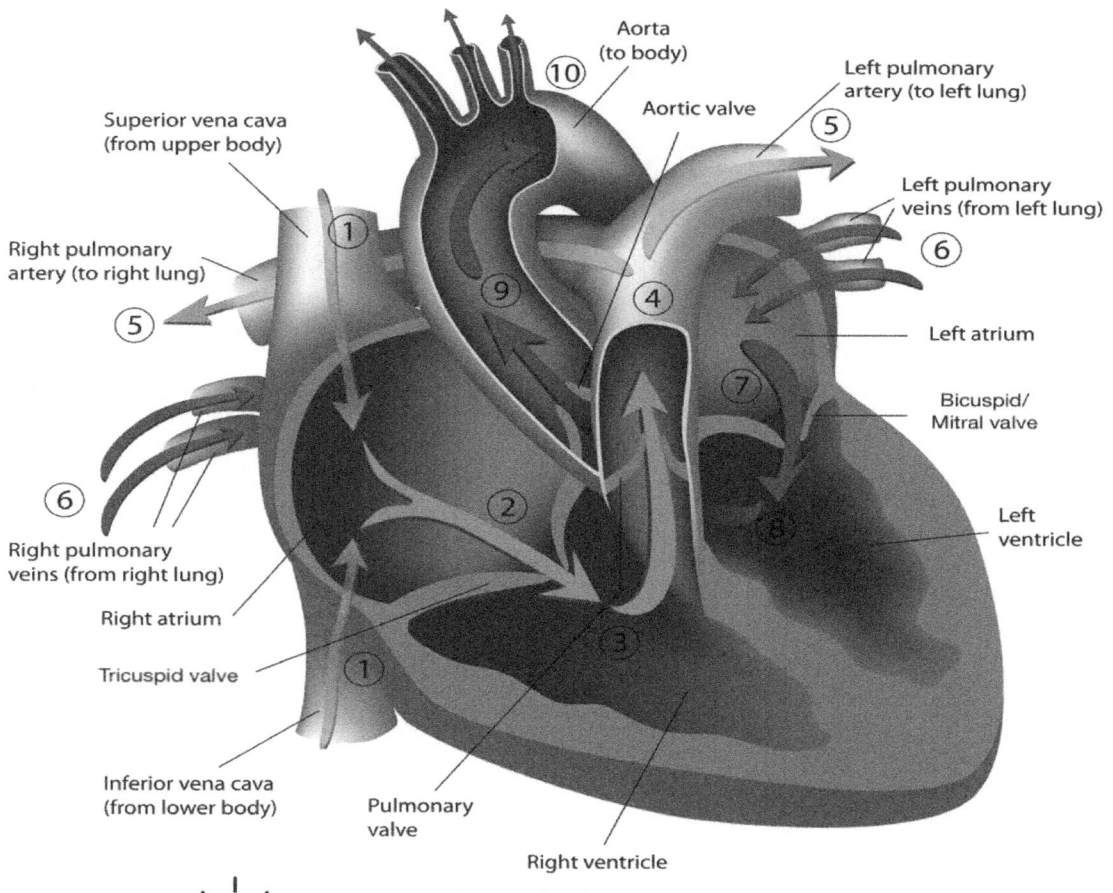

Easy to Remember: Each side of the heart is made of the same structures, just with different names!
Remember "VAVVA": Vein, Atrium, Valve, Ventricle, Artery!

Blood Vessels

Blood vessels are the main mode of transportation for not only blood, but other substances, such as hormones. These substances are carried throughout the body in blood vessels. The largest types of blood vessels are known as **arteries**. Arteries primarily carry oxygenated blood away from the heart, to tissues. Arteries are the deepest blood vessels due to their size and importance. Tissues surrounding the arteries help to protect them from damage, which could result in severe bleeding and loss of oxygen.

Veins are blood vessels that primarily carry deoxygenated blood towards the heart, where it can replace carbon dioxide with oxygen. Veins are much more superficial than arteries, often visible under the skin, whereas most arteries cannot be seen.

Capillaries are microscopic arteries, and are where gas exchange takes place between blood vessels and tissues.

Major arteries and veins are often named after their location in the body, such as the brachial artery/vein(in the arm), femoral artery/vein(in the thigh), abdominal aorta(in the abdomen), etc.

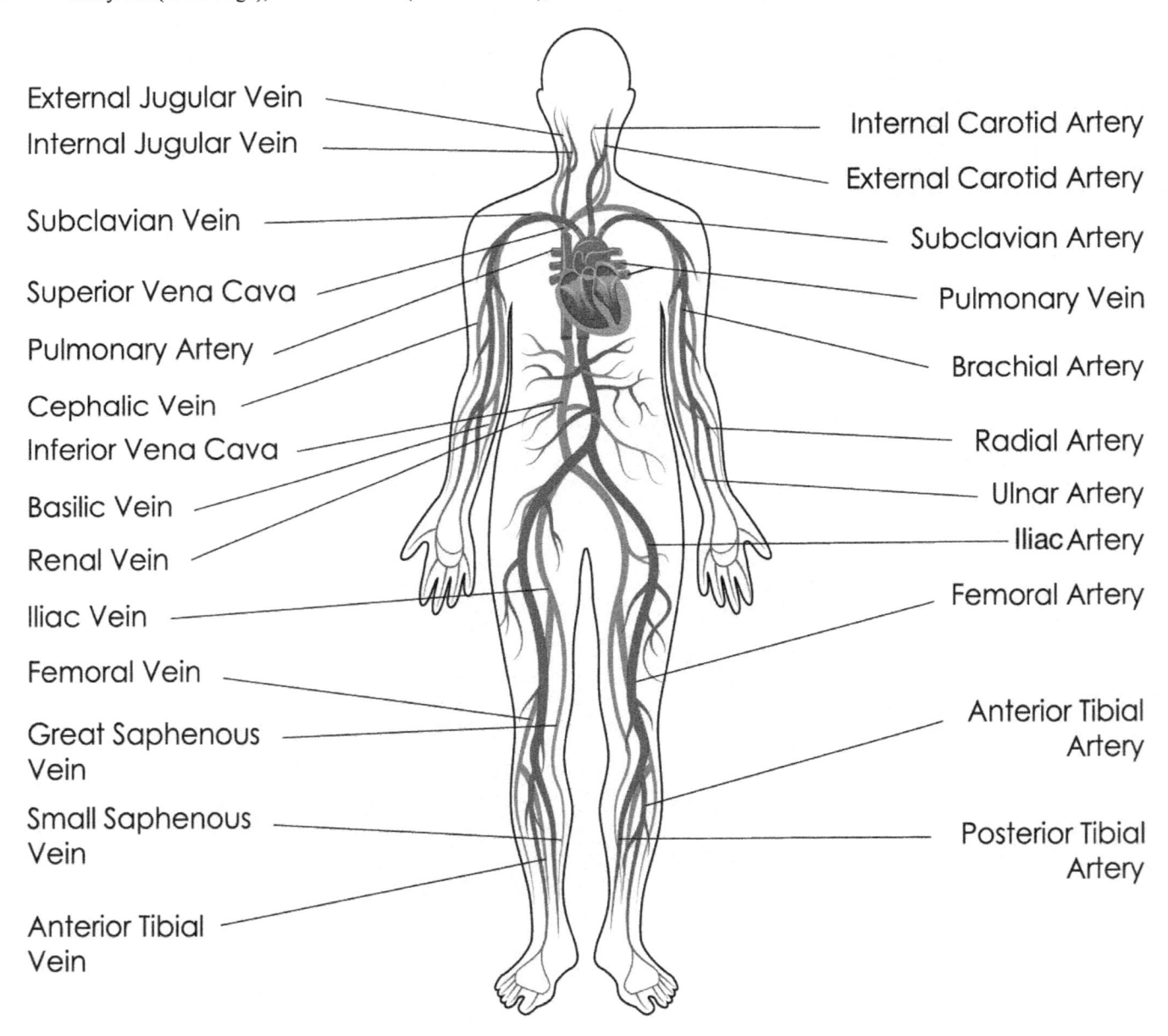

Left labels (veins):
- External Jugular Vein
- Internal Jugular Vein
- Subclavian Vein
- Superior Vena Cava
- Pulmonary Artery
- Cephalic Vein
- Inferior Vena Cava
- Basilic Vein
- Renal Vein
- Iliac Vein
- Femoral Vein
- Great Saphenous Vein
- Small Saphenous Vein
- Anterior Tibial Vein

Right labels (arteries):
- Internal Carotid Artery
- External Carotid Artery
- Subclavian Artery
- Pulmonary Vein
- Brachial Artery
- Radial Artery
- Ulnar Artery
- Iliac Artery
- Femoral Artery
- Anterior Tibial Artery
- Posterior Tibial Artery

Digestive System

The Digestive System has many structures, organs, and functions. It is one of the most important systems in the body, responsible for bringing nutrients **into** the body, **digestion** of food, **absorption** of nutrients into the body's tissues, and **elimination** of waste products.

Structures of the Digestive System include the **mouth, pharynx, esophagus, stomach, liver, gallbladder, pancreas, small intestine**, and **large intestine**.

Digestion

The **mouth**, also known as the **oral cavity**, is the first place digestion begins taking place. The **teeth** manually break down food by **chewing,** or **mastication**. The food mixes with **saliva**, which contains digestive enzymes such as **amylase**, that help to break down carbohydrates. The **tongue** assists with mastication by pressing food against the teeth. Once food has been properly chewed, it is swallowed.

After food is swallowed, it moves from the mouth into the **pharynx**, also known as the **throat**. The pharynx is simply a passageway for food, water, and air on the way to their respective destinations. Food leaves the pharynx and enters the esophagus.

The **esophagus** is a long tube that runs from the pharynx inferiorly, passes through the diaphragm, and connects to the **stomach**. The esophagus, much like the pharynx, has one function: transporting food. The esophagus, like every hollow organ of the Digestive System, is lined with smooth muscle. When the smooth muscle rhythmically contracts, it forces food further along in the organ. This is known as **peristalsis**.

Once food reaches the **stomach**, both ends of the stomach close off, and the stomach begins **digesting** the food. Powerfully, it churns the food, breaking it down manually. Stomach acids like hydrochloric acid and pepsin mix with the food inside the stomach and further help to break down the food. Once food is properly digested, the stomach opens at the pylorus, the bottom of the stomach, and food exits the stomach and enters into the small intestine.

The **small intestine** is where the majority of **absorption** of nutrients occurs. **Accessory organs** produce substances that help aid the small intestine in digestion. These accessory organs are the liver, gallbladder, and pancreas.

The **liver** mainly acts as a **blood detoxifier**. It filters harmful substances from the blood. However, it aids in digestion by producing **bile**, a yellowish substance that aids in the emulsification of fats. Connecting to the liver is the gallbladder. Once the liver produces bile, it empties the bile into the gallbladder, where it is stored until it is needed.

The **gallbladder** simply has one function: to **store bile** and empty bile into the small intestine through the bile duct, which connects to the duodenum, the first section of the small intestine.

The **pancreas** creates **pancreatic juice,** which aids in the digestion of proteins, lipids, and carbohydrates. These substances empty into the small intestine through the same path as bile, the bile duct.

Food moves from the stomach into the **small intestine**. The first section of the small intestine is known as the **duodenum**. The duodenum is the last section of the Digestive System that digestion of food takes place. Bile and pancreatic juice mix with food in the duodenum and further break down substances. Peristalsis forces the food from the duodenum further into the small intestine, into the middle portion, known as the **jejunum**. The jejunum is where the majority of nutrient absorption takes place in the small intestine. As the food is forced through the small intestine, it moves into the final section, known as the **ileum**. Final absorption occurs in the ileum. Food moves through the ileum and into the large intestine.

The **large intestine** has two primary functions: **absorption** of **water**, and **elimination** of **waste**. As feces moves through the large intestine, water is absorbed. If too much water is absorbed, constipation may result. If not enough water is absorbed, diarrhea may result. The large intestine has four sections: the **ascending colon**, the **transverse colon**, the **descending colon**, and the **sigmoid colon**. As the feces leaves the sigmoid colon, it enters the rectum, where it is ready to be eliminated from the body.

DID YOU KNOW? *The liver is the heaviest internal organ!*

The Digestive System

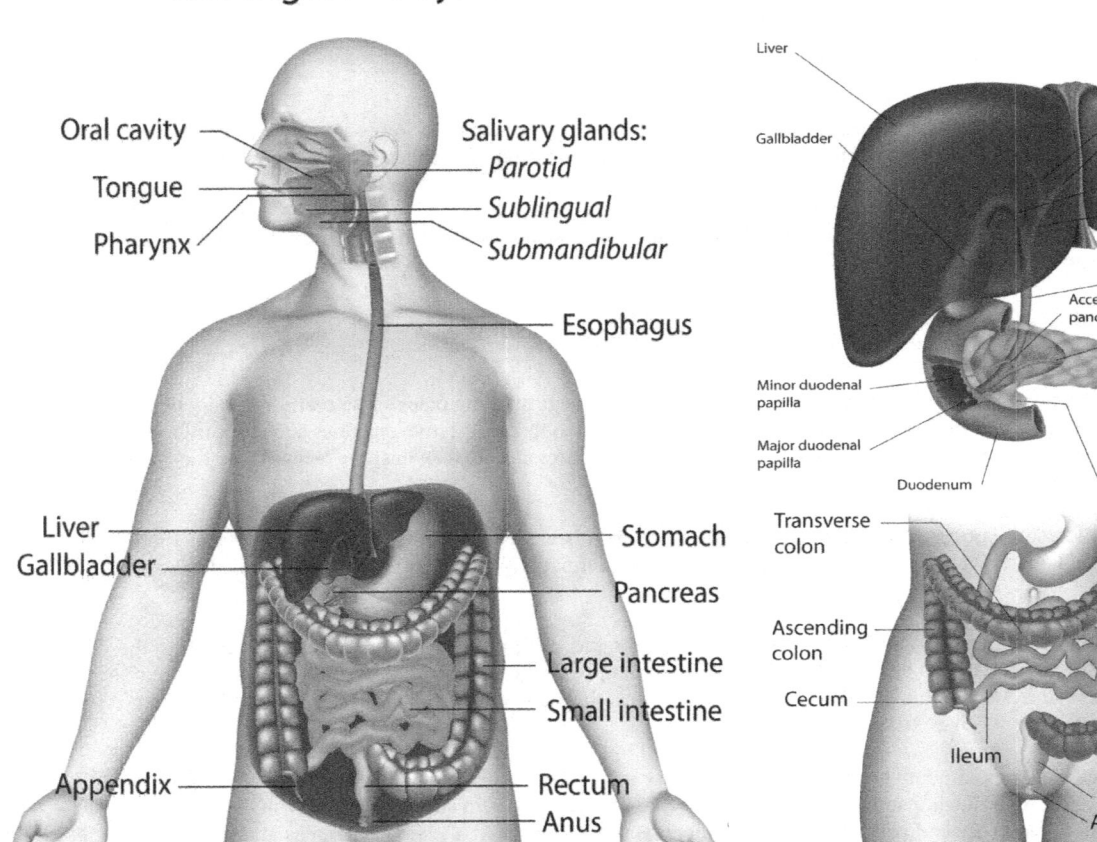

- Oral cavity
- Tongue
- Pharynx
- Salivary glands:
  - Parotid
  - Sublingual
  - Submandibular
- Esophagus
- Liver
- Gallbladder
- Stomach
- Pancreas
- Large intestine
- Small intestine
- Appendix
- Rectum
- Anus

Liver, Gallbladder, Pancreas and Bile Passage

- Liver
- Gallbladder
- Right and left hepatic ducts
- Cystic duct
- Common hepatic duct
- Bile duct
- Accessory pancreatic duct
- Pancreatic duct
- Minor duodenal papilla
- Major duodenal papilla
- Duodenum
- Tail of pancreas
- Body of pancreas
- Head of pancreas
- Transverse colon
- Ascending colon
- Descending colon
- Cecum
- Ileum
- Sigmoid colon
- Rectum
- Anus

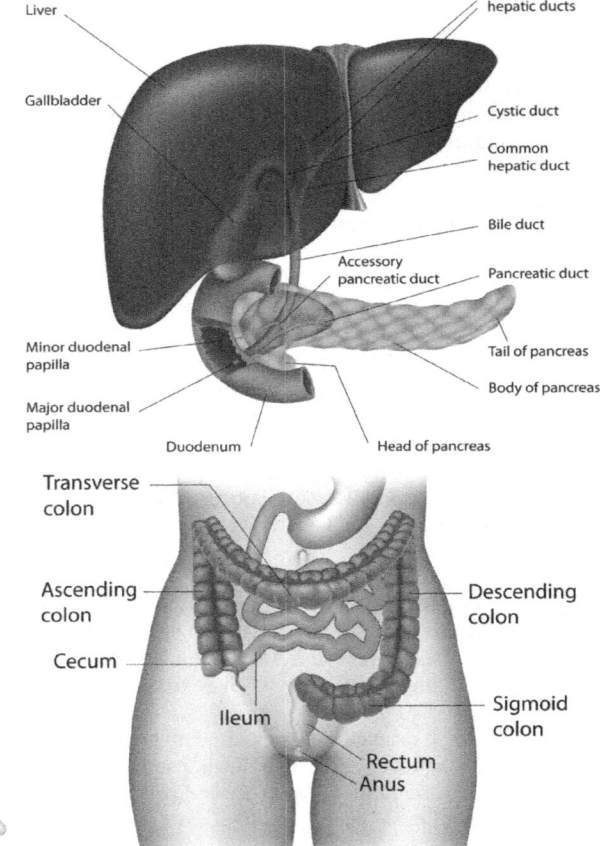

Mesentery

The mesentery is a fan-shaped extension of the peritoneum that **suspends** the **small and large intestines** from the posterior abdominal wall, holding them in place. The point of attachment where the mesentery attaches to the posterior abdominal wall is known as the **mesenteric root**. The mesentery additionally allows a **conduit** for blood vessels, nerves, and lymphatic channels to pass in the abdomen.

Several blood vessels use the mesentery as a conduit. Arteries found in the mesentery include the superior mesenteric artery and inferior mesenteric artery. Veins found in the mesentery include the superior mesenteric vein and inferior mesenteric vein.

In a person with Crohn's disease, the mesentery often presents with an increased amount of fat. This fat is thicker than the fat of a person without Crohn's disease, and this may lead to future treatments for Crohn's disease that specifically target the mesentery. In addition, these fat cells produce a type of protein known as **C-reactive protein**, which is normally produced by the liver. C-reactive protein(CRP) levels typically increase when there is some sort of inflammation in the body. High levels of CRP in the blood may indicate infection, inflammation, and other conditions such as heart disease or cancer.

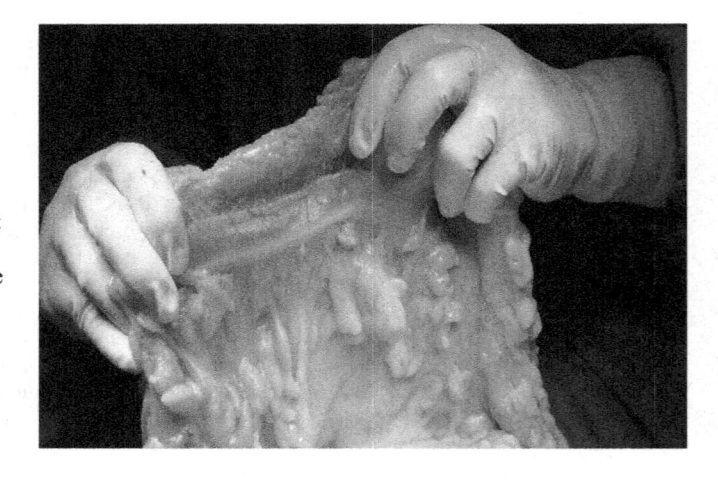

Sphincters

In the Digestive System, there are **ring-like** bands of **muscle** between digestive organs, known as **sphincters**. Sphincters function to allow food to enter into an organ, or to keep food from moving backwards.

There are four primary sphincters in the Digestive System:

The **esophageal** sphincter is located between the **pharynx** and the **esophagus**. It opens and allows food to move down into the esophagus. Another name for this sphincter is the upper esophageal sphincter.

The **cardiac** sphincter is located between the **esophagus** and the **stomach**. It is named after the region of the stomach it connects to, which is known as the cardia. When food enters the stomach, the cardiac sphincter closes, preventing food and stomach acid from ascending into the esophagus. Another name for this sphincter is the lower esophageal sphincter.

The **pyloric** sphincter is located between the **stomach** and the **small intestine**. It is named after the region of the stomach it connects to, which is known as the pylorus. When food enters the stomach, the pyloric sphincter closes, preventing food from leaving the stomach before digestion has taken place. When food has been properly digested, the pyloric sphincter opens, and food leaves the stomach and enters the small intestine.

The **ileocecal** sphincter is located between the **small intestine** and the **large intestine**. It is named after the parts of the two organs that come together, the ileum(small intestine) and cecum(large intestine).

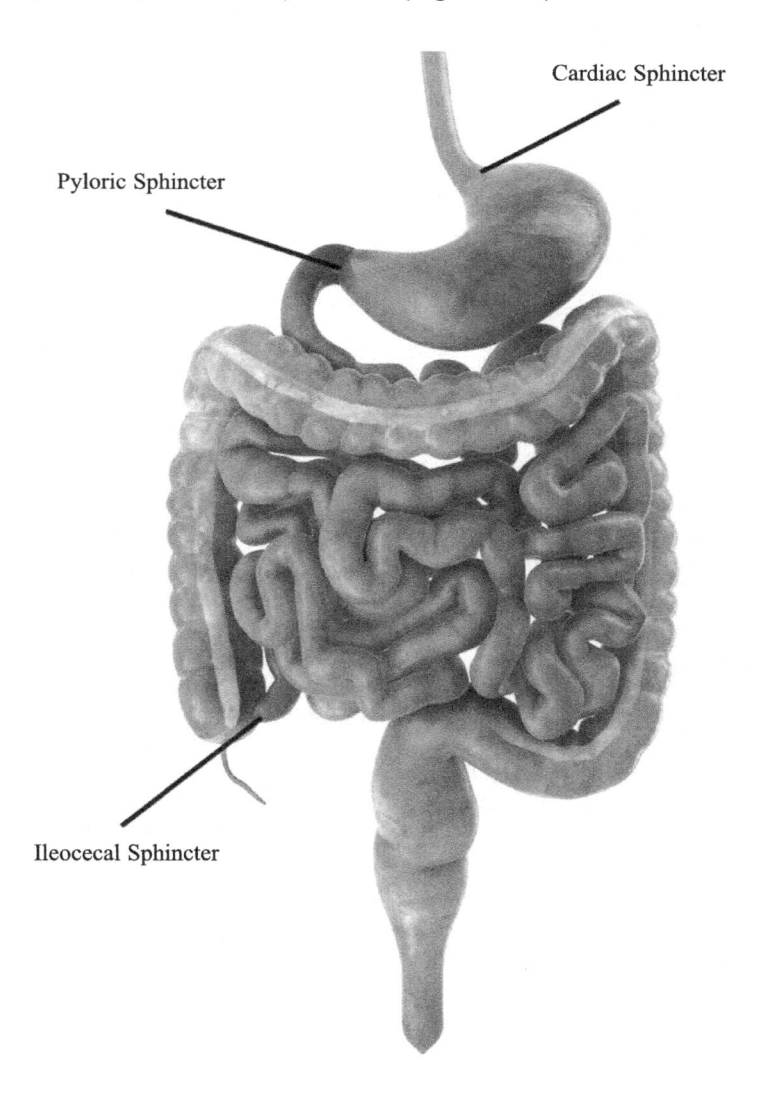

Cardiac Sphincter

Pyloric Sphincter

Ileocecal Sphincter

Endocrine System

The Endocrine System is responsible for coordinating specific activities of cells and tissues by releasing **hormones** into the body. Endocrine glands differ from exocrine glands in two specific ways: endocrine glands create and secrete hormones, while exocrine glands create and secrete things like sweat, saliva, and oil. Endocrine glands secrete hormones directly into the **blood stream**, while exocrine glands secrete their substances onto a **surface**(such as the surface of the mouth or skin).

Endocrine glands have many different functions that help regulate body function and homeostasis.

Glands

The **adrenal** glands, located atop the kidneys(*ad-:* towards; *renal:* kidney), secrete **epinephrine** and **norepinephrine**. These hormones help to elevate blood pressure, heart rate, and blood sugar. They are considered stress hormones, and are secreted when the body is under stress, or in the sympathetic nervous response.

The **hypothalamus** produces **dopamine**, an important hormone that increases blood pressure and heart rate. It is considered the reward center hormone. If you win at a game or contest, your hypothalamus may release dopamine, which gives a sensation of excitement.

The **ovaries** are the female gonads. They create **estrogen** and **progesterone**, two hormones important to female development and bone growth.

Pancreatic Islets are the parts of the pancreas that create **glucagon**, which increases blood sugar levels, and **insulin**, which decreases blood sugar levels. Glucagon is created by **alpha cells**, and insulin is created by **beta cells**.

The **pineal** gland is responsible for the production of **melatonin**, the hormone that regulates the body's wake/sleep cycle, also known as the **circadian rhythm**.

The **pituitary** gland, which many consider the "master gland", secretes **growth hormone**, which regulates the amount of growth a person may experience. It also secretes **prolactin**, which stimulates milk production, and **follicle-stimulating hormone**, which influences production of female egg cells and male sperm cells.

The **testes** are the male gonads. The testes secrete **testosterone**, the primary male hormone, responsible for increasing bone and muscle mass.

The **thyroid** is a gland in the neck that produces **calcitonin**, which aids in decreasing the levels of calcium in the blood stream. Too much calcium in the blood may weaken the bones and cause kidney stones.

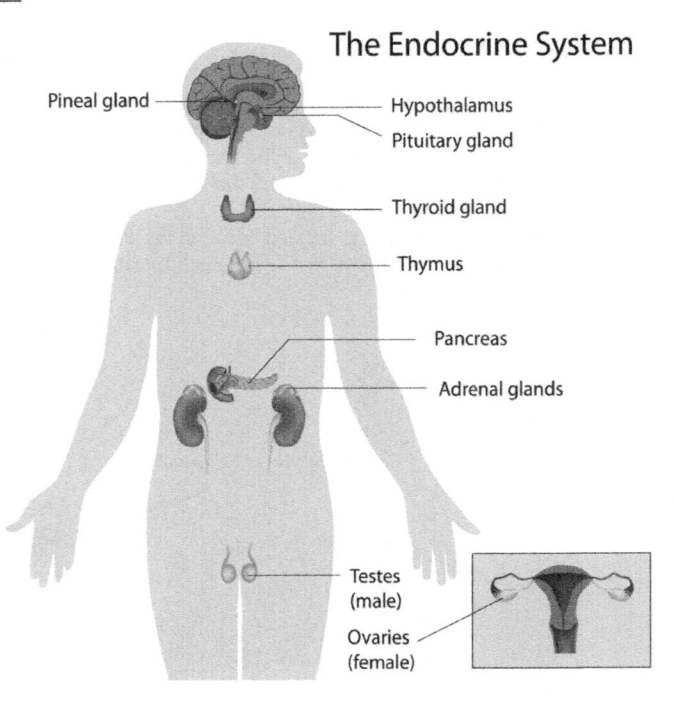

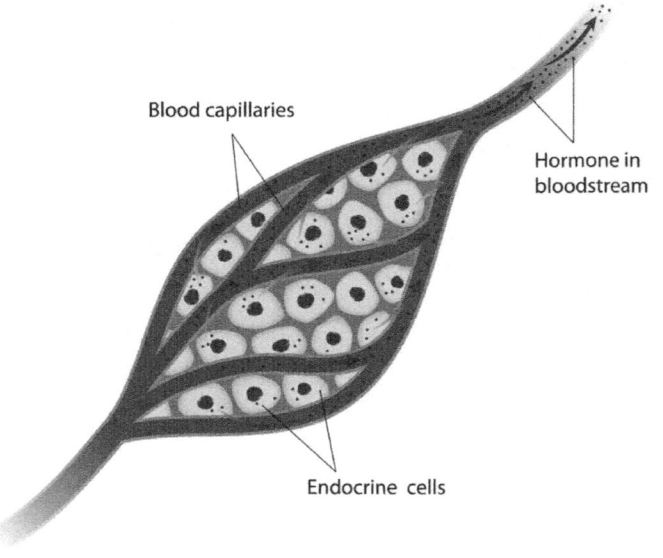

Integumentary System

The Integumentary System is the body's first line of defense against pathogens and trauma. Its primary function is to protect the body. It also secretes substances, may absorb certain substances, and even eliminates waste.

Skin

The skin, which is the body's **largest organ**, is the main structure of the Integumentary System. The skin **protects** the body by creating a thick barrier that prevents pathogens from entering, and helps to cushion the body from blunt trauma.

Aiding the skin in protection are the **nails**. Finger and toe nails are made of **keratin**, the same cells that create thick layers in the skin called calluses. The nails prevent damage to the distal phalanges.

Hair also aids in protection, but in a different way. Hair is used to regulate temperature. When body temperature drops, smooth muscle that attaches to each hair, known as **arrector pili**, contract, forcing the hair to stand up. This creates an insulating layer, which is meant to trap warmth underneath the hair, much like a blanket. This does little for humans, but is utilized by animals to retain heat in cold environments.

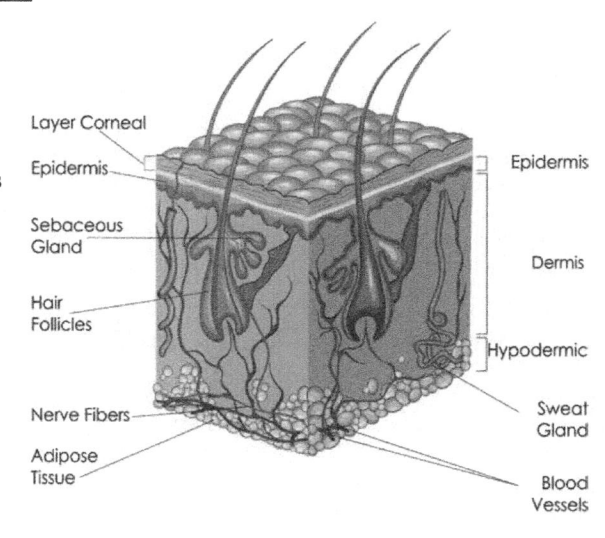

Glands

Inside the skin are glands, which also aid in protection. **Sudoriferous** glands emerge from deep in the skin to the surface directly through tubes. Sudoriferous glands create and secrete **sweat**. Sweat is mostly made of water, but may also contain salt and waste products such as ammonia. Sweat is used to lower body temperature by evaporating off the surface of the skin. The evaporation cools the skin, which helps lower the internal body temperature.

Sebaceous glands are glands that connect to hair, and produce **oil(sebum)**. Oil helps to protect the body from pathogens and debris in the air. Blockage of a sebaceous gland, however, may lead to a bacterial infection, and acne.

Sensory Receptors

Inside the skin, there are many types of receptors that detect certain sensations, relaying the information to the brain. Sensory receptors aren't exclusive to the skin, but there are an abundance of them in the skin.

Nociceptors are a type of sensory receptor that detects the sensation of **pain**. Pain, while unpleasant, is actually vital in protection of the body. The term "*noci-*" is Latin for "*hurt*".

Easy to Remember: Nociceptors detect pain.
Remember the old saying "No pain, No gain".

Meissner's Corpuscles are sensory receptors that are very superficial in the skin, and detect **light pressure**. Massage strokes such as effleurage and feather strokes are detected by Meissner's Corpuscles.

Pacinian Corpuscles are sensory receptors that are very deep in the skin, and detect **deep pressure**. Deep massage strokes, such as compression, are detected by Pacinian Corpuscles.

Easy to Remember: Pacinian Corpuscles detect deep pressure.
Match up "Paci" of Pacinian with "Paci" of Pacific Ocean.
The Pacific Ocean is deep.

Lymphatic System

The Lymphatic System is vital in the body's **defense** against pathogens and disease. Not only are leukocytes abundant in lymph, but antibodies are created in the Lymphatic System. The Lymphatic System contains **lymph, lymph nodes, lymph vessels**, and **lymph organs**.

Lymph, the primary structure of the Lymphatic System, is a fluid composed of **water**, protein, leukocytes, urea, salts, and glucose. Lymph allows **transport** of all of these substances through the body, ultimately dumping into the blood stream. Lymph is made of **interstitial fluid**, fluid found between cells.

Lymph travels throughout the body through **lymph vessels**. Lymph vessels are similar to blood vessels, but only flow in one direction, towards the heart. Lymph vessels absorb foreign bodies and nutrients from tissues, bringing them into the lymph to be transported to the blood stream or lymph nodes. The **largest lymph vessel** in the body is located in the trunk. It is known as the **Thoracic Duct**. The Thoracic Duct drains lymph into the **left subclavian vein**, where it joins with blood.

Lymph nodes are large **masses** of lymphatic tissue. They are responsible for production of **antibodies**, and help destroy any foreign objects that enter the lymph. During an infection, lymph nodes may become tender and swollen.

The **thymus**, located in the chest, is responsible for production of **T-lymphocytes**, or T-cells. T-cells are vital in regulation of the body's immune system. If a person contracts HIV, the virus destroys the T-cells, which essentially disables the immune system.

The **spleen** is an organ of the Lymphatic System responsible for **destroying** dead or dying **red blood cells** from the blood stream, in addition to destroying pathogens and debris.

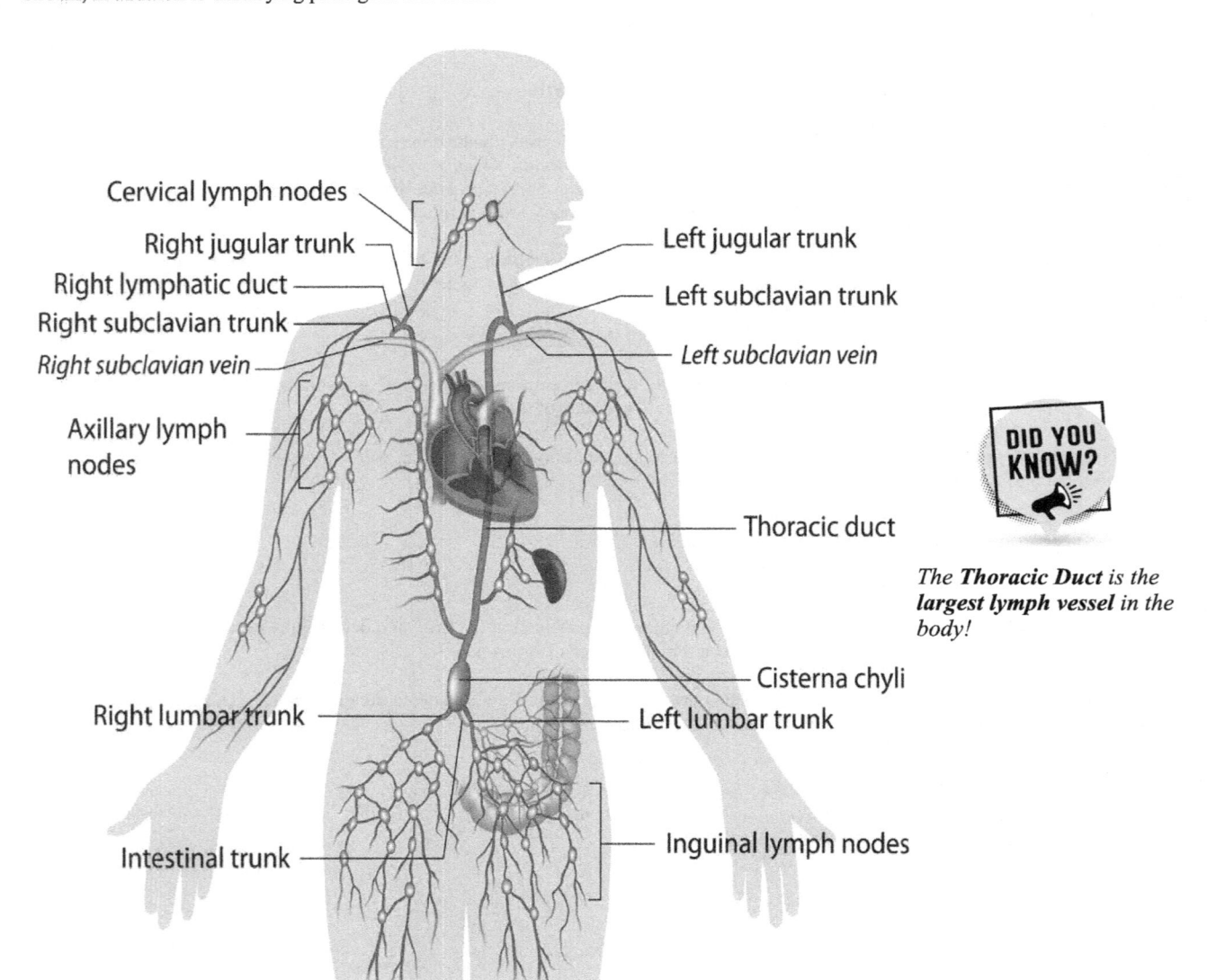

DID YOU KNOW?

The **Thoracic Duct** is the **largest lymph vessel** in the body!

Muscular System

Muscles have numerous actions in the body, primarily **producing body heat**, contracting to allow **movements**, and constricting **organs** and **blood vessels**.

Muscle Structure

Skeletal muscles are broken down into the following components:

- **Sarcomeres** are the functional units of skeletal muscle. When they shorten, the muscle contracts.
- **Actin** is part of a sarcomere, known as the **thin** filament. Actin is what myosin attaches to during a muscle contraction. Actin anchors to the **Z-Line** in a sarcomere.
- **Myosin** is part of a sarcomere, known as the **thick** filament. Myosin resembles a golf club head, and attaches to actin during a muscle contraction. The entire span of the thick filaments in one sarcomere is known as the **A-Band**.
- **Tropomyosin** is a protein that **covers** the attachment sites where myosin attaches to actin during a contraction. **Calcium ions** are responsible for removing the tropomyosin from the actin, allowing the myosin to attach to the actin and initiate a contraction.

Muscle contractions begin with **action potentials** sent from the brain. Action potentials terminate at the **neuromuscular junction**, releasing **acetylcholine**(aCh) into the synapse. This results in the aCh binding to certain receptors in the muscle fiber, which in turn allows sodium ions to enter the muscle fiber. The sodium ions come into contact with the sarcoplasmic reticulum, which causes a release of **calcium ions**. The calcium ions enter into the working unit of muscles, known as sarcomeres. A sarcomere contains thick filaments, known as myosin, and thin filaments, known as actin. When a muscle isn't in a state of contraction, the myosin and actin do not interact due to the presence of tropomyosin preventing myosin from attaching to actin. When the body wants to allow the muscle to contract, calcium ions bind to tropomyosin, causing them to reveal the attachment sites on the actin for the myosin. Once the tropomyosin is removed, the myosin attaches to the actin, pulling the Z-lines closer together. This causes the sarcomere to shorten. The shortening of all the sarcomeres in a muscle fiber result in the entire muscle contracting.

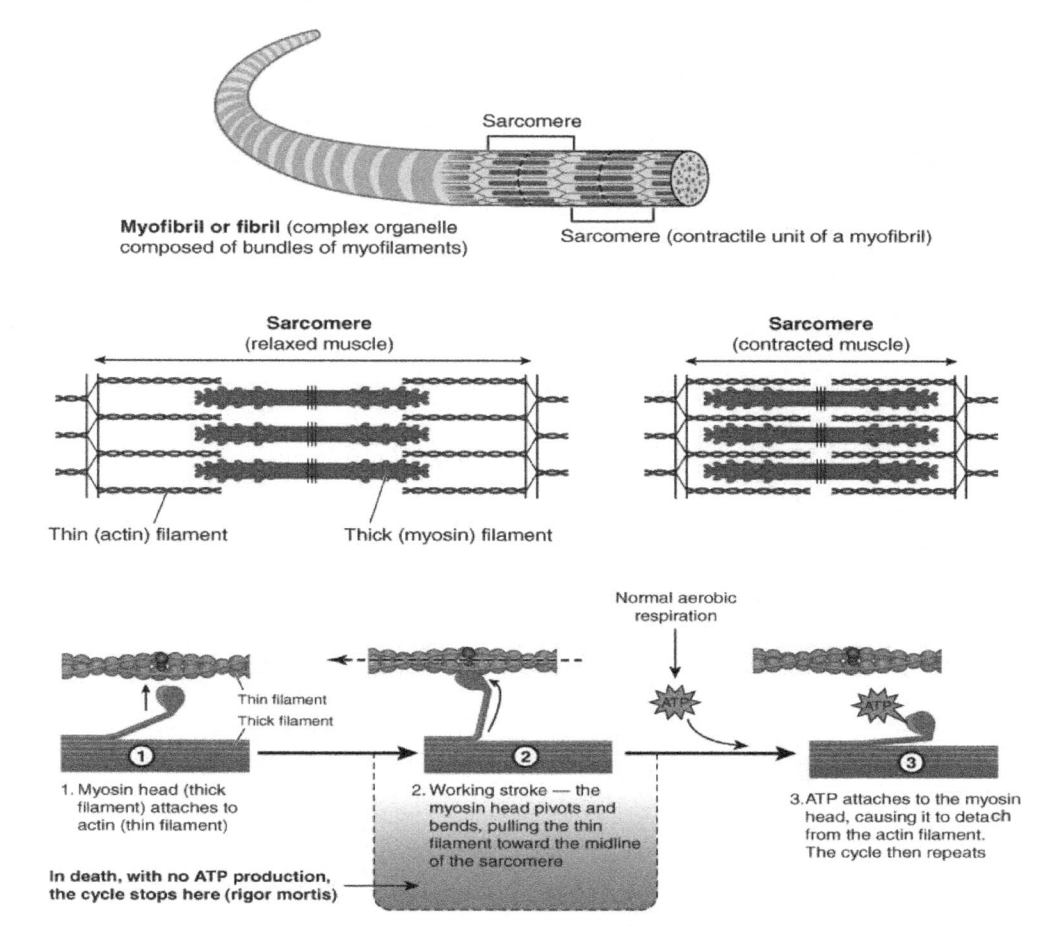

Myofibril or fibril (complex organelle composed of bundles of myofilaments)

Sarcomere (contractile unit of a myofibril)

Sarcomere (relaxed muscle)

Sarcomere (contracted muscle)

Thin (actin) filament   Thick (myosin) filament

Normal aerobic respiration

Thin filament
Thick filament

1. Myosin head (thick filament) attaches to actin (thin filament)

2. Working stroke — the myosin head pivots and bends, pulling the thin filament toward the midline of the sarcomere

3. ATP attaches to the myosin head, causing it to detach from the actin filament. The cycle then repeats.

In death, with no ATP production, the cycle stops here (rigor mortis)

Muscle Shapes

Muscles have several different shapes. These include:

Circular: Circular muscles are arranged in a **circular** manner. Examples include orbicularis oris and orbicularis oculi.

Convergent: Convergent muscles are **spread out** on one end and **merge** together at another end. An example is pectoralis major.

Fusiform: Fusiform muscles are **thin** at the **attachment sites** and **wider** in the **middle**. An example is biceps brachii.

Parallel: Parallel muscles have muscle fibers that all run in the **same direction**. Examples include sartorius and coracobrachialis.

Pennate: Pennate muscles have an appearance resembling a **feather**. These muscles can be **unipennate**(one feather), **bipennate**(two feathers), or **multipennate**(multiple feathers). Examples include flexor pollicis longus(unipennate), rectus femoris(bipennate), and deltoid(multipennate).

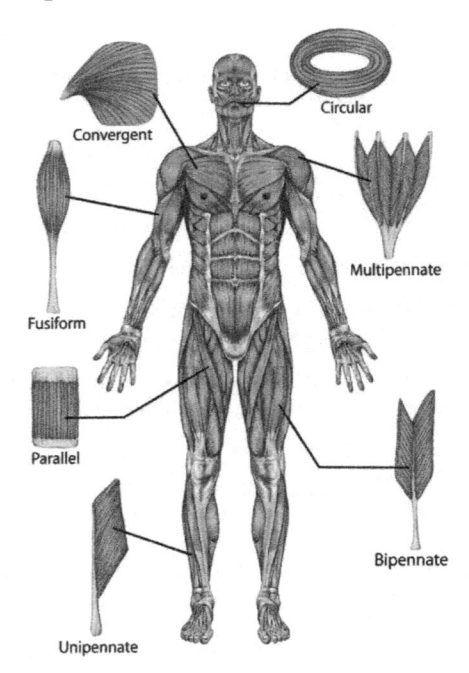

Muscle Contractions

When there is **tension** in a muscle, it is **contracting**. A muscle can contract without causing movement, though. There are four types of muscle contractions.

Isometric Contraction: Iso means "**same**" or "**equal**". Metric means "**length**". When an isometric contraction occurs, as the name implies, the length of the muscle **stays the same**, but tension in the muscle **changes**. An example: imagine trying to lift something that is too heavy for you to lift. The muscles required to lift the object increase in tension, but because the muscles aren't strong enough, the length of the muscles doesn't change.

Isotonic Contraction: Iso means "**same**" or "**equal**". Tonic means "**tension**". When an isotonic contraction occurs, as the name implies, the tension in the muscle **stays the same**, but the muscle length **changes**. There are two separate types of isotonic contractions:

Concentric Contraction: When a concentric contraction occurs, several things take place. The tension in the muscle **initially increases** until the amount of tension required to perform the action is reached, then the tension **remains constant**. While the tension remains constant, the muscle **length decreases**. An example is performing a biceps curl.

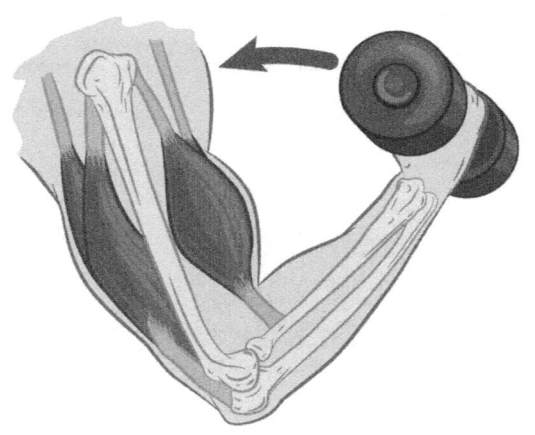

Eccentric Contraction: When an eccentric contraction occurs, several things take place. The tension in the muscle **initially decreases** until the amount of tension required to perform the action is reached, then the tension **remains constant**. While the tension remains constant, the muscle length **increases**. An example is extending the elbow and lowering the weight down after the biceps curl in a concentric contraction.

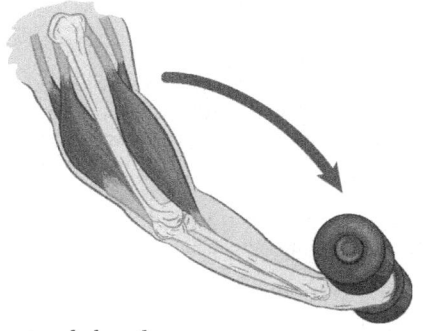

👍 *General Rule of Thumb: With concentric contractions, the muscle length decreases. With eccentric contractions, the muscle length increases.*

Proprioceptors

Proprioceptors are structures in the body that are responsible for detection of the body's **position in space**. Proprioceptors allow the location of the parts of the body, the body's weight, and center of gravity to be known even on a subconscious level. Proprioceptors can be found in several locations in the body, such as the skin, muscles, tendons, and ears. The two main types of proprioceptors are **muscle spindles**, and **Golgi tendon organs**.

Muscle spindles, also known as **stretch receptors**, are able to detect when a muscle is stretching or elongating. When muscle spindles detect the muscle is stretching too far, they send a sensory impulse to the spinal cord, which responds by sending a motor impulse to the muscle that stimulates the muscle to **produce tension**. This counteracts the stretch and prevents damage to the muscle.

Golgi tendon organs are able to detect the amount of tension in a muscle. They are located at the origin and insertion of muscle fibers and tendons, also known as the musculotendinous junction. Golgi tendon organs detect when the muscle is producing tension, and if the tension is too great, Golgi tendon organs will **prevent the muscle from producing additional force**. This is done to prevent injury to muscles. An example is during weight lifting, when performing repetitions at the end of a set. The muscle may become more difficult to contract when lifting the weight due to the Golgi tendon organ preventing further force from being exerted by the muscle.

Muscle Actions

Muscles perform numerous actions on the body, depending on which muscle is contracting. To see examples of all of these actions, refer to page 206. Muscle actions include the following:

Flexion: **Decreasing** the **angle** of a joint.

Extension: **Increasing** the **angle** of a joint.

Adduction: Moving a structure **towards** the **midline**.

Abduction: Moving a structure **away** from the **midline**.

Protraction: Moving a structure **anteriorly**.

Retraction: Moving a structure **posteriorly**.

Inversion: Turning the **sole** of the foot **in** towards the **midline**.

Eversion: Turning the **sole** of the foot **out** away from the **midline**.

Elevation: Moving a structure **superiorly**.

Depression: Moving a structure **inferiorly**.

Supination: Rotating the **palm** so it is facing **upwards**.

Pronation: Rotating the **palm** so it is facing **downwards**.

Rotation: **Turning** a structure around its **long axis**.

Circumduction: **Turning** a structure around the **circumference** of a joint.

Opposition: Moving structures in **opposite** directions.

Lateral Deviation: Moving a structure from **side-to-side**.

Plantarflexion: Pointing toes **down**.

Dorsiflexion: Pointing toes **up**.

When a muscle performs an action, other muscles associate with the muscle in different ways.

A **Prime Mover/Agonist** is the muscle that primarily performs a specific action. An example: when plantarflexion is performed, the **strongest** muscle performing it is the gastrocnemius. That means gastrocnemius is the prime mover/agonist.

A **Synergist** is the muscle that **assists** the prime mover/agonist in performing the action. Synergists are not as strong as prime movers. An example: when plantarflexion is performed, soleus contracts to allow more strength, assisting gastrocnemius in performing the action. That means soleus is the synergist.

An **Antagonist** is a muscle that performs the **opposite** action of the prime mover/agonist. Every muscle has an antagonist. An example: gastrocnemius contracts, performing plantarflexion. To return the foot to the starting position, gastrocnemius relaxes, and tibialis anterior contracts, which performs dorsiflexion. This makes tibialis anterior the antagonist to gastrocnemius.

A **Fixator** is a muscle that **stabilizes** an area or joint while an action is being performed. Stabilizing the joint prevents things like injury and allows optimal movement to occur. An example: supraspinatus stabilizes the head of the humerus in the glenoid fossa, keeping the joint together during the numerous movements the glenohumeral joint performs.

Easy to Remember: Just think of it like this: Batman is the Agonist, the main character. Robin is the Synergist, the helper. The Joker is the Antagonist, who does the opposite of Batman. Alfred is the Fixator, who helps hold the situation together.

Davis's Law states that when going through periods of **unuse**, muscle and tendon strength will **decrease**!

Nervous System

Nerves are structures in the **Nervous System**, made of nervous tissue. Nerves have many functions, from regulating vital functions within the body, to controlling muscles.

There are two divisions of the Nervous System: the **Central Nervous System**, and the **Peripheral Nervous System**. The Central Nervous System consists of the **brain** and **spinal cord**. The Central Nervous System is under involuntary control, responsible for interpretation of sensations and mental activity.

Nerve impulses are categorized as **sensory** or **motor**. Sensory impulses are detected by sensory receptors throughout the body(such as nociceptors, olfactory receptors, etc), and travel **to the brain** and/or spinal cord for processing. These impulses are called **afferent** impulses. In the case of reflexes, these impulses only reach the spinal cord, due to the immediacy of the required response. This is why reflexes are involuntary! Once the impulse reaches the brain and/or spinal cord, the brain and/or spinal cord interpret the sensation, and send a **motor** impulse back down the body to tell the body **how to respond** to the stimulus. These impulses are called **efferent** impulses.

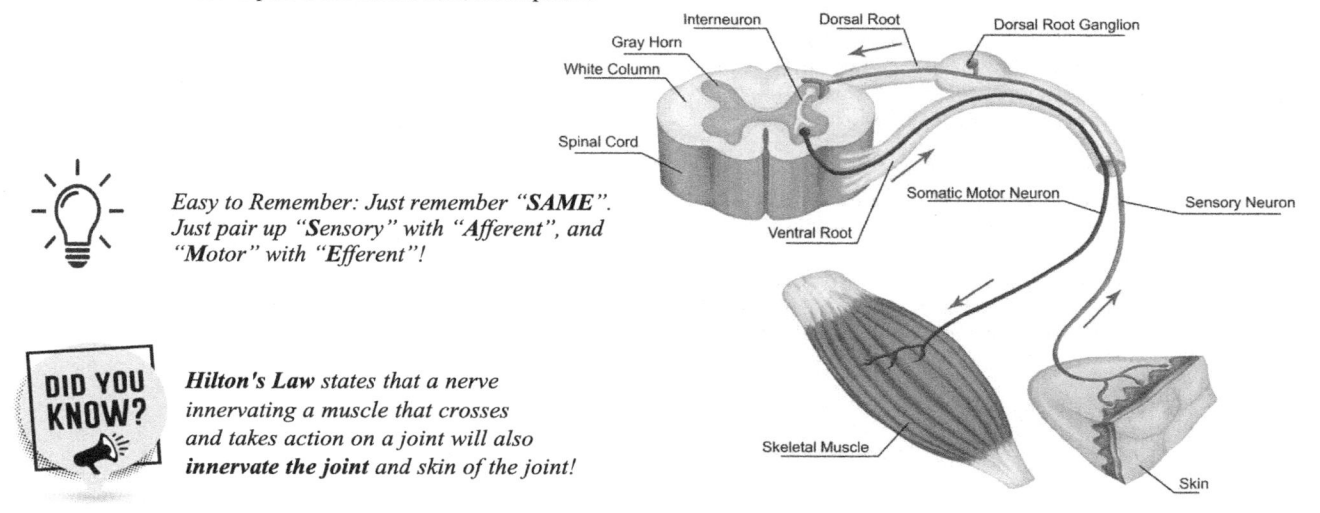

Easy to Remember: Just remember "SAME". Just pair up "Sensory" with "Afferent", and "Motor" with "Efferent"!

Hilton's Law states that a nerve innervating a muscle that crosses and takes action on a joint will also **innervate the joint** and skin of the joint!

Central Nervous System

The brain consists of three parts: the **cerebrum**, which is the largest part of the brain and split into left and right hemispheres, the **cerebellum**, located at the back and bottom of the brain, and the **brain stem**, which connects the brain to the spinal cord.

Each side of the **cerebrum** is divided into **lobes**, named after the bones atop them: **frontal** lobe(processes motivation, aggression, mood), **temporal** lobe(processes memory, hearing, and smell), **parietal** lobe(processes most sensory information), and **occipital** lobe(processes vision).

The cerebellum is responsible for regulation of **muscle tone**, **balance**, **coordination**, and control of **general body movements**.

The **brain stem**, which consists of(in descending order) the **midbrain**, the **pons**, and the **medulla oblongata**, controls the **vital functions** of the body, such as breathing, heart rate, coughing, sneezing, vomiting, and blood vessel diameter.

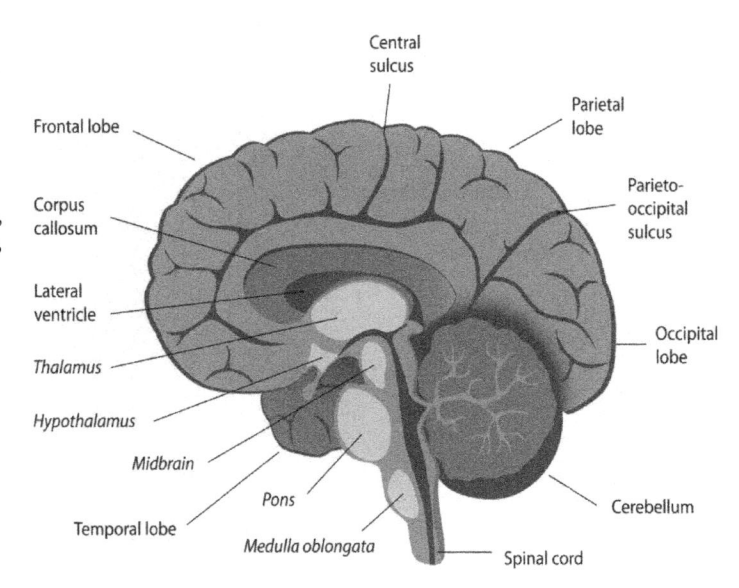

Meninges

Surrounding the brain and spinal cord are three layers of connective tissue known as the **meninges**. The deepest layer that comes into contact with the brain is known as the pia mater. The intermediate layer is known as the arachnoid. The most superficial layer, which comes into contact with the bones of the cranium, is known as the dura mater.

The **pia mater**(tender mother) is responsible for helping to protect the brain and spinal cord by containing cerebrospinal fluid. This fluid provides a cushion for the brain and spinal cord to help prevent injury. The pia mater is very delicate, and covers the brain completely by extending into the folds.

The **arachnoid**, which is the intermediate layer of the meninges, is separated from the pia mater by subarachnoid space. The subarachnoid space contains cerebrospinal fluid, which helps to cushion and protect the brain and spinal cord. The arachnoid resembles cob webs or spider webs, which is where it gets its name. It is made of fibrous material that fluid is easily able to pass through. Unlike the pia mater, the arachnoid does not extend into the folds of the brain. The arachnoid is wrapped loosely around the brain.

The **dura mater**(tough mother) is the most superficial and strongest layer of the meninges. The dura mater is responsible for protecting the brain by providing a thick padding around it. The dura mater is made of fibrous tissue, giving it the ability to properly protect the brain and spinal cord. It contains large blood vessels than branch off into capillaries that go into the pia mater.

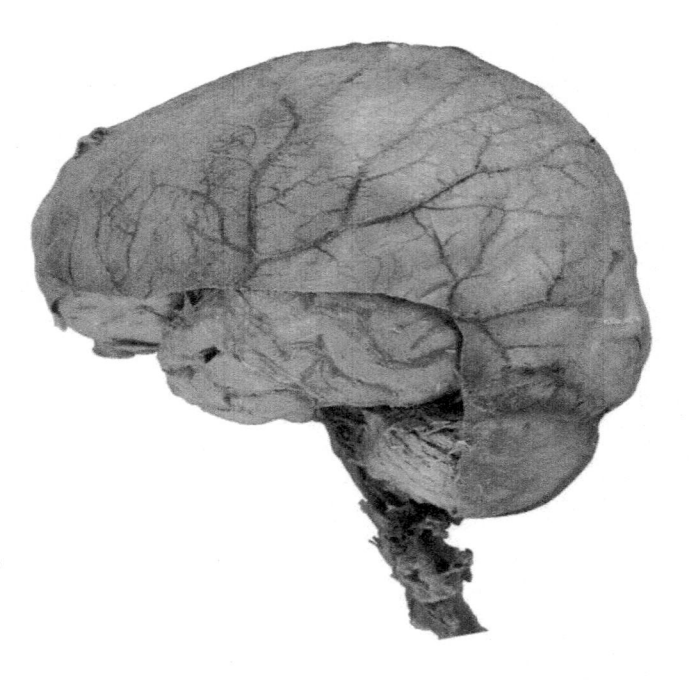

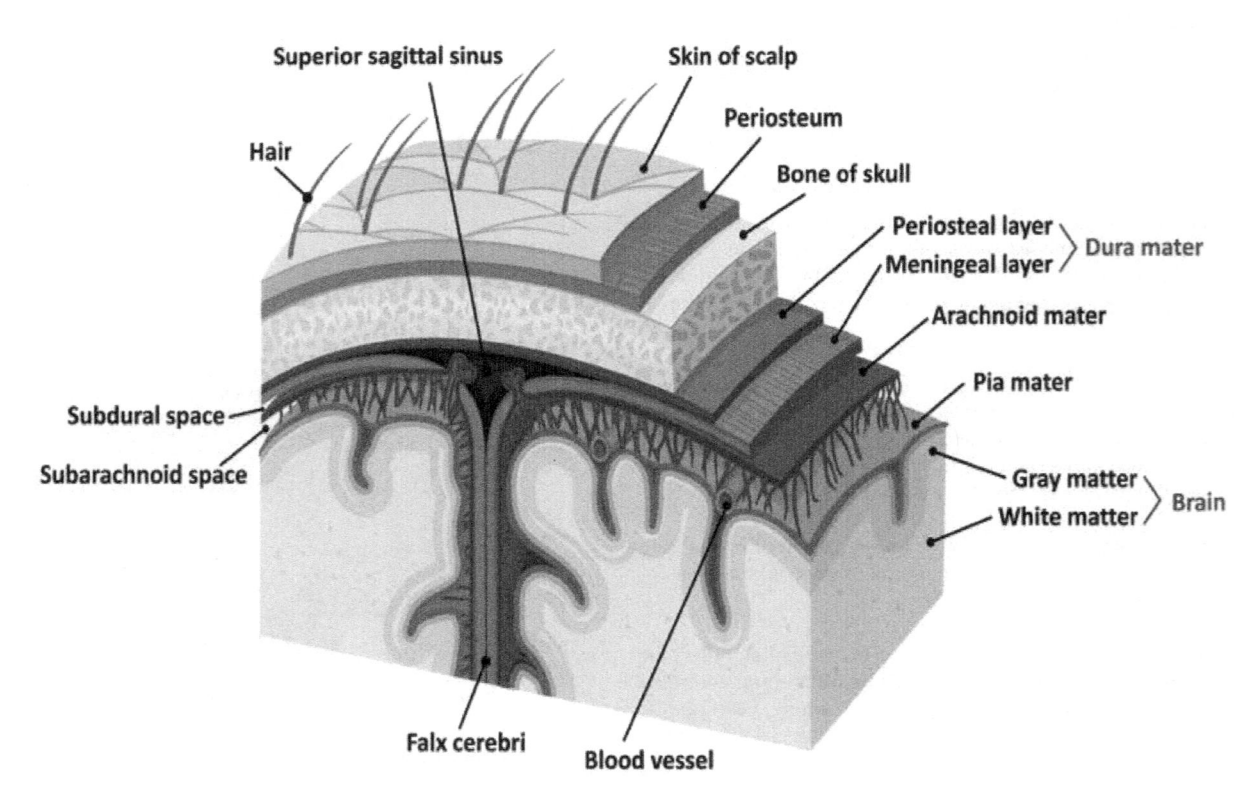

Peripheral Nervous System

The Peripheral Nervous System consists of the body's **nerves**. There are two divisions of the Peripheral Nervous System: **Cranial Nerves** and **Spinal Nerves**. Cranial Nerves, as the name suggests, emerge from the brain, and help to regulate the functions of the head and face. There are **twelve pairs** of Cranial Nerves, each numbered in Roman Numerals:

- Olfactory(I)
- Optic(II)
- Oculomotor(III)
- Trochlear(IV)
- Trigeminal(V)
- Abducens(VI)//
- Facial(VII)
- Vestibulocochlear(VIII)
- Glossopharyngeal(IX)
- Vagus(X)
- Accessory(XI)
- Hypoglossal(XII)

The Cranial Nerves

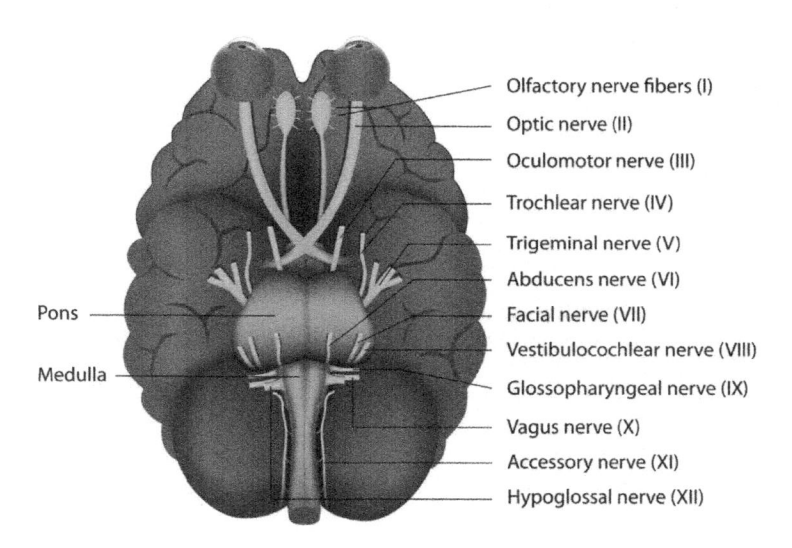

- Olfactory nerve fibers (I)
- Optic nerve (II)
- Oculomotor nerve (III)
- Trochlear nerve (IV)
- Trigeminal nerve (V)
- Abducens nerve (VI)
- Facial nerve (VII)
- Vestibulocochlear nerve (VIII)
- Glossopharyngeal nerve (IX)
- Vagus nerve (X)
- Accessory nerve (XI)
- Hypoglossal nerve (XII)

Pons
Medulla

Spinal Nerves are much more numerous than Cranial Nerves. There are **31 pairs** of Spinal Nerves. The Spinal Nerves, as the name suggests, emerge from the spinal cord, and are responsible for controlling skeletal muscle.

A bundle of Spinal Nerves that emerge from the spinal cord is known as a **Plexus**. There are three plexi in the body: **Cervical Plexus**, **Brachial Plexus**, **Lumbosacral Plexus**. The Cervical Plexus emerges from the spinal cord in the range of **C1-C4**. The primary nerve of the Cervical Plexus is known as the **Phrenic Nerve**.

The Phrenic Nerve descends inferiorly from the cervical vertebrae and innervates(provides nervous stimulation to) the **diaphragm**.

The Brachial Plexus emerges from the spinal cord at **C5-T1**. As the name suggests, the nerves of the Brachial Plexus move distally, controlling the muscles of the **upper limb**. There are five primary nerves of the Brachial Plexus:

- Radial
- Musculocutaneous
- Axillary
- Median
- Ulnar

The Brachial Plexus

The **Radial Nerve** is located on the posterior arm and forearm, and innervates the triceps brachii, anconeus, brachioradialis, and wrist extensors.

The **Musculocutaneous Nerve** is located in the anterior arm, and innervates the biceps brachii, brachialis, and coracobrachialis.

The **Axillary Nerve** is primarily located in the armpit, and innervates the teres minor and deltoid.

The **Median Nerve** is located in the anterior arm, forearm, and hand, and innervates the wrist flexors, and most muscles on the lateral side of the hand.

The **Ulnar Nerve** is located on the anterior arm, medial forearm, and medial hand, and innervates the wrist flexors and most muscles on the medial side of the hand.

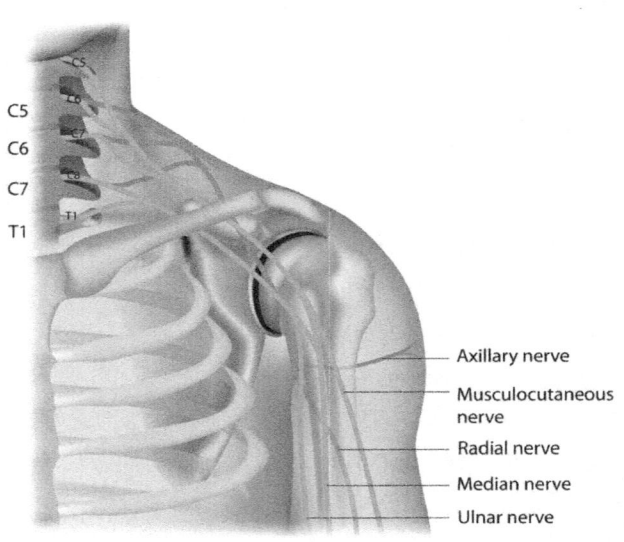

The Lumbosacral Plexus, as the name suggests, emerges from the **entire span** of the Lumbar and Sacral vertebrae. The major nerves of the Lumbosacral Plexus include:

- Sciatic
- Femoral
- Obturator
- Tibial
- Common Peroneal
- Deep Peroneal
- Superficial Peroneal

The **Sciatic Nerve** is a large nerve located on the posterior thigh. The Sciatic Nerve is actually both the Tibial Nerve and the Common Peroneal Nerve bundled together. Once the Sciatic Nerve reaches the back of the knee, it branches off into two separate nerves. The Sciatic Nerve innervates the Hamstring muscle group.

The **Femoral Nerve** is located on the anterior thigh, and innervates the quadriceps muscle group, iliacus, sartorius, and pectineus.

The **Obturator Nerve** is located on the medial portion of the thigh, and innervates the adductor muscle group.

The **Tibial Nerve**, after branching off the Sciatic nerve, runs down the posterior leg, and innervates the gastrocnemius, soleus, tibialis posterior, and plantaris.

The **Common Peroneal Nerve**, after branching off the Sciatic Nerve, actually branches off into two other nerves of its own: The Deep Peroneal and Superficial Peroneal Nerves.

The **Deep Peroneal Nerve** is located on the anterior leg, and innervates the tibialis anterior.

The **Superficial Peroneal Nerve** is located on the lateral portion of the leg, running along the fibula, and innervates the peroneus longus and peroneus brevis.

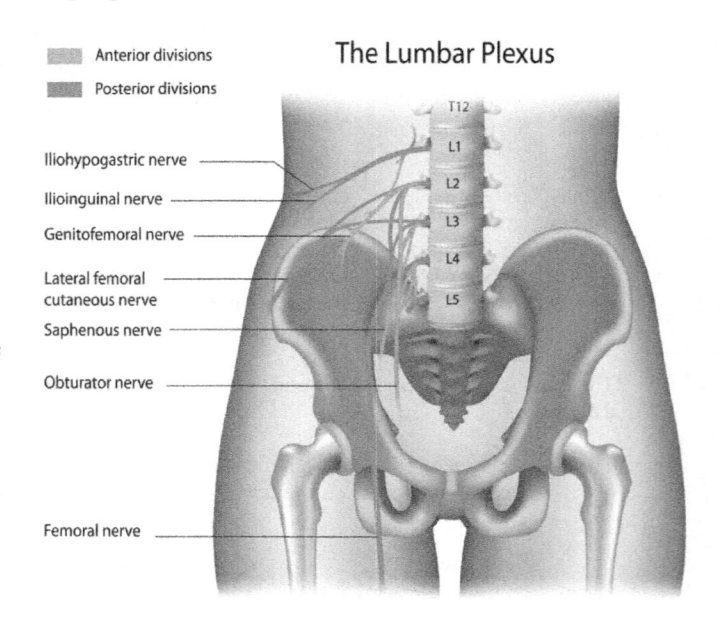

Autonomic Nervous System

The autonomic nervous system helps to regulate **homeostasis** by release of hormones, controlling heart rate, breathing rate, and other bodily functions. There are two divisions of the autonomic nervous system: the **Sympathetic Nervous System**, and the **Parasympathetic Nervous System**.

The Sympathetic Nervous System is also known as "**fight-or-flight**". When the body is in a state of **stress**, the Sympathetic Nervous System helps the body respond by releasing **norepinephrine** into the blood stream, which increases heart rate and blood sugar. The digestive organs will also shut down, and blood will be pulled from these organs and supplied to the muscles for use.

The Parasympathetic Nervous System is also known as "**rest-and-digest**". When the body is in a state of **relaxation**, the Parasympathetic Nervous System helps the body to calm itself. It decreases the body's heart rate, and increases blood flow to the digestive organs to increase **peristalsis**. The Parasympathetic Nervous System, decreasing heart rate, and peristalsis are all controlled by Cranial Nerve X, the **Vagus Nerve**.

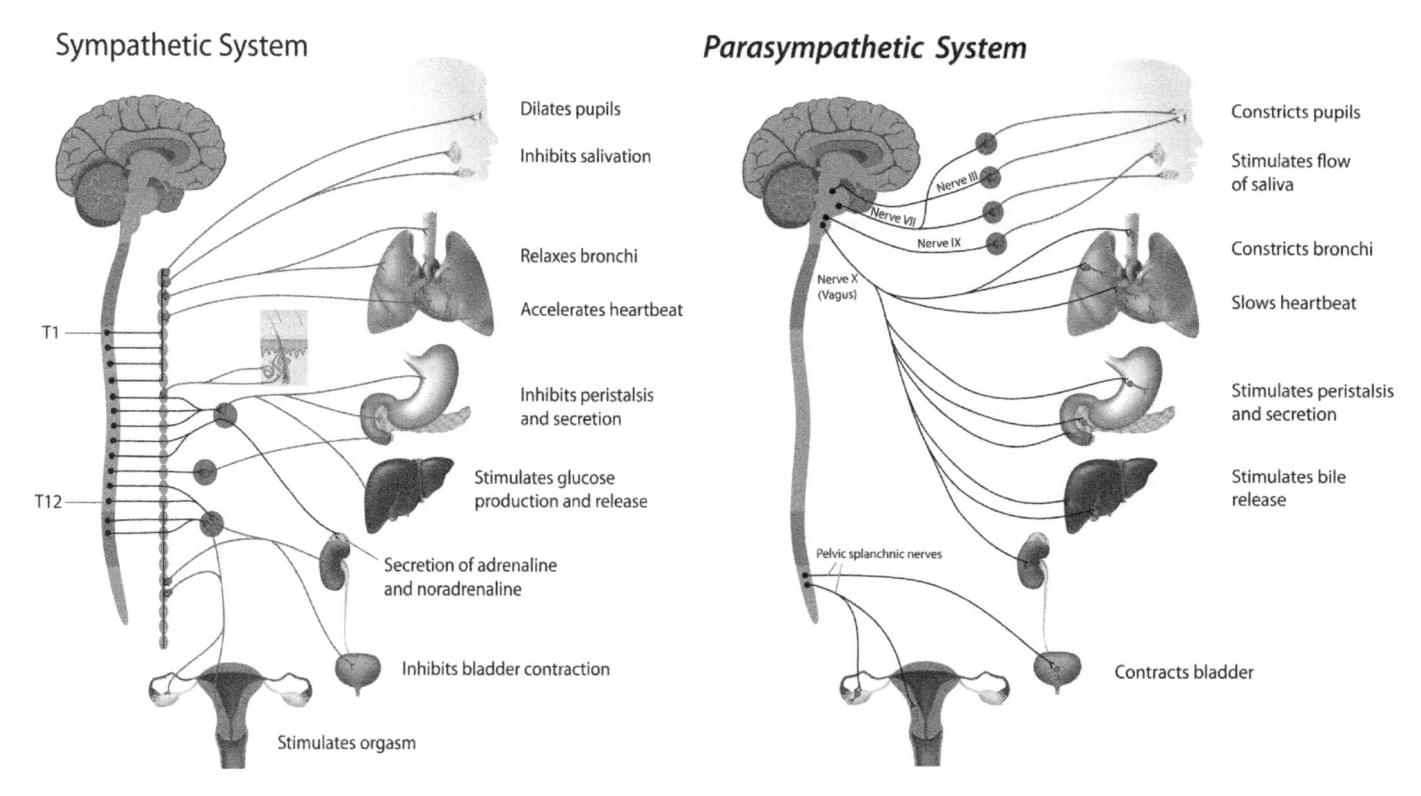

Sympathetic System

- Dilates pupils
- Inhibits salivation
- Relaxes bronchi
- Accelerates heartbeat
- Inhibits peristalsis and secretion
- Stimulates glucose production and release
- Secretion of adrenaline and noradrenaline
- Inhibits bladder contraction
- Stimulates orgasm

T1 – T12

Parasympathetic System

Nerve III, Nerve VII, Nerve IX, Nerve X (Vagus), Pelvic splanchnic nerves

- Constricts pupils
- Stimulates flow of saliva
- Constricts bronchi
- Slows heartbeat
- Stimulates peristalsis and secretion
- Stimulates bile release
- Contracts bladder

Reproductive System

The Reproductive System is responsible for **reproduction,** or the creation of offspring. Many organs and structures in the Reproductive System are shared with other body systems, such as the urethra, testes, and ovaries. The two divisions are the **Male Reproductive System** and **Female Reproductive System**, which vary in structures and function.

Male Reproductive System

The **Male Reproductive System** is responsible for the production of **spermatozoa**(sperm) and male hormones, such as testosterone. Major structures of the Male Reproductive System include the penis, testes, scrotum, and ducts that carry sperm.

The **penis** is the primary organ of the Male Reproductive System, responsible for **sexual intercourse**, which allows passage of sperm outside the body through the urethra. The penis also allows urine to leave the body. During sexual arousal, nerves cause blood vessels in the penis to dilate, which then causes the penis to fill with blood. This results in an erection.

The **testes**, as discussed in the Endocrine System, are responsible for the production of **testosterone**. They are also responsible for **spermatogenesis**, or sperm production. After the testes produce sperm, it is stored in a tube located atop each testicle known as the **epididymis**. Upon ejaculation, the sperm leaves the epididymis and enters the vas deferens.

The **vas deferens** are tubes that connect the epididymis to the **urethra**. During ejaculation, smooth muscle in the walls of the vas deferens contract rhythmically(known as peristalsis), forcing sperm into the urethra. The sperm mixes with secretions from structures such as the prostate, which creates semen.

The **prostate** is a gland located near the bladder that produces secretions that join with sperm to create **semen**.

Female Reproductive System

The **Female Reproductive System** is responsible for the production of **egg cells**, estrogen, progesterone, and **fetal development**. Major structures of the Female Reproductive System include the vagina, ovaries, fallopian tubes, uterus, and cervix.

The **vagina** is the **passageway** located between the cervix and the opening to the outside of the body. The vagina is often confused with the outer, visible portion, known as the vulva. The vagina allows a passageway for the penis during sexual intercourse.

The **ovaries**, as discussed in the Endocrine System, are responsible for the production of **estrogen** and **progesterone**. The ovaries are also the structures that produce and release **egg cells**(oocytes) in women. Eggs are typically released once a month from one ovary.

The **fallopian tubes** allow **passage** of oocytes from the ovaries to the uterus. Fertilization most commonly occurs in the fallopian tubes.

The **uterus** is an inverted pear-shaped organ responsible for the **development of a fetus**. Upon fertilization, the embryo attaches to the wall of the uterus. The placenta develops, which connects to the embryo, providing it with blood flow and nutrients to help it grow. During childbirth, the placenta detaches from the uterus and exits through the cervix and vagina.

The **cervix** is a narrow, circular passage that connects the **vagina to the uterus**. During pregnancy, the cervix is closed by a thick layer of mucous. During childbirth, the cervix dilates widely, which allows a passage for the child to pass through.

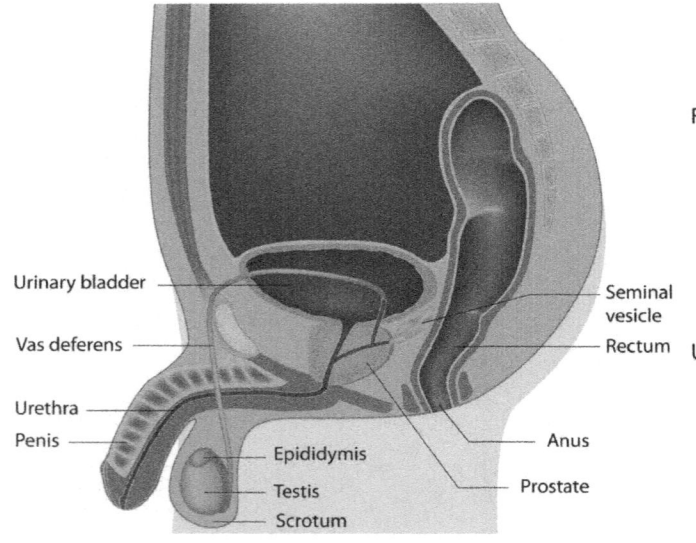

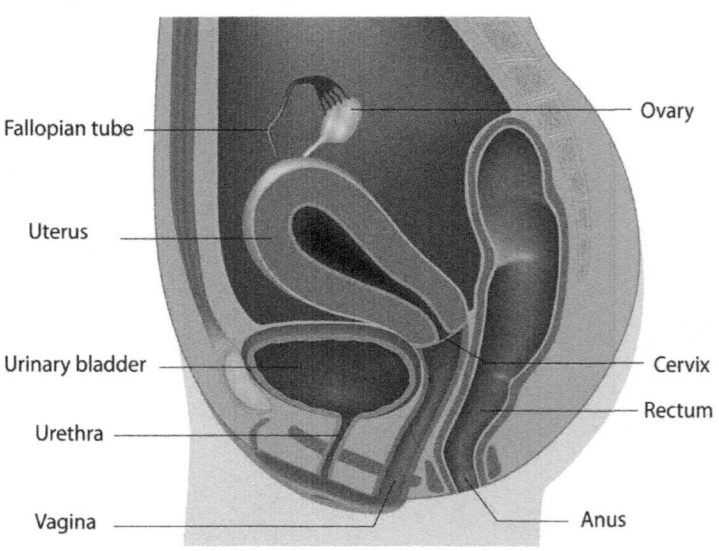

Respiratory System

The Respiratory System has one essential function: to bring **oxygen** into the body, and eliminate wastes such as **carbon dioxide** from the body. The main organs of the Respiratory System are the **lungs**. The left lung has two lobes and is smaller than the right lung, which has three lobes. This is due to the presence of the heart on the left side of the chest.

Conduction of air is controlled by the **nose**. Air enters the body through the nose, and is filtered by **hair** and **mucous**. The nose also warms the air as it enters the body.

The **larynx**, also known as the voice box, is a short tube located inferior to the pharynx. As air passes over the vocal cords in the larynx, the vocal cords vibrate, which produces **sound** used with the tongue to create **speech**.

Sitting atop the larynx is a flap of tissue known as the **epiglottis**. Upon swallowing, the epiglottis lies on top of the larynx, blocking any food or fluid from entering the larynx, which **prevents choking**.

Connecting to the larynx inferiorly is a tube of cartilage known as the **trachea**, or the wind pipe. The trachea is the primary passageway for air to enter into the lungs.

Once air enters the lungs, it goes into each lung through **bronchial tubes**, which branch off of the trachea. These tubes branch into smaller tubes called bronchioles. Bronchial tubes secrete **mucous**, which helps to trap any dirt or debris that have made it into the lungs.

At the end of the bronchioles are tiny **air sacs**, known as **alveoli**. The alveoli resemble a cluster of grapes. Capillaries attach to the alveoli and move blood across the surface of the alveoli. This allows carbon dioxide to detach from the erythrocytes and exit the blood stream, and also allows oxygen to enter the blood stream and attach to erythrocytes. Alveoli are where **gas exchange** occurs in the Respiratory System.

Respiration is accomplished by contraction of the **diaphragm**, a large muscle connected to the rib cage that separates the chest from the abdomen. The diaphragm creates a **vacuum** inside the chest. When it contracts, it descends, pulling the chest down. This allows air to enter into the lungs. When the diaphragm relaxes, it ascends up into the chest, which forces air out of the lungs.

The Respiratory System

Nasal cavity
Nostril
Epiglottis
Pharynx
Larynx
Trachea
Primary bronchus
Pleural cavity
Right lung
Left lung
Diaphragm

Human Lung Anatomy and Function

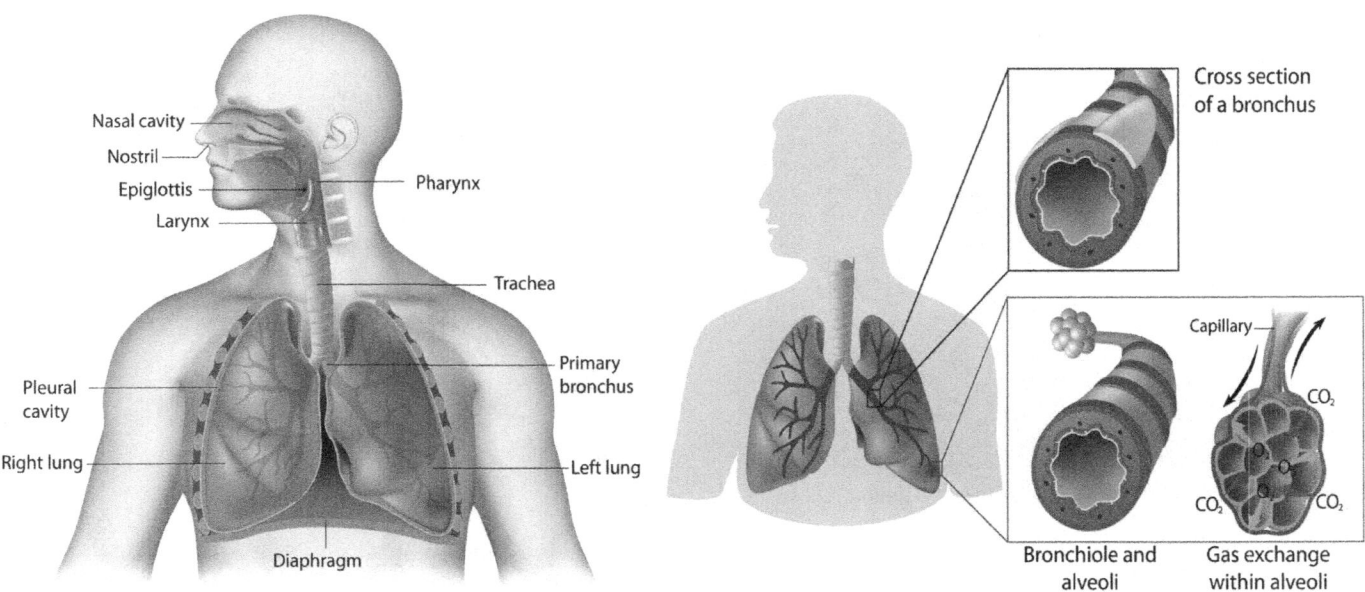

Cross section of a bronchus
Capillary
CO₂
Bronchiole and alveoli
Gas exchange within alveoli

DID YOU KNOW? *There are four major structures that pass through the diaphragm: the **aorta**, the **inferior vena cava**, the **thoracic duct**, and the **esophagus**!*

Skeletal System

The Skeletal System is a vital component of movement. We wouldn't be able to move if we didn't have bones! Muscles attach to bones, and when a muscle contracts, it pulls on a bone(or bones), which performs an action. Bones also produce blood cells, provide stability for the body, and protect structures and organs in the body. Needless to say, bones are extremely important!

There are **206** bones in the human body. Each bone can be classified as one of the following: **Long** bone, **Short** bone, **Irregular** bone, **Flat** bone, **Sesamoid** bone.

Long bones appear longer than they are wide. There are numerous long bones in the body, including, but not limited to, the clavicle, humerus, femur, metatarsals, and phalanges.

Short bones are **as long** as they are **wide**. Examples include the carpals and tarsals.

Irregular bones are bones that have generally **unusual shapes**. Examples include the mandible, vertebrae, and pubis.

Flat bones are named after how they look: **flat**. They are typically thin and flat. Examples include the scapula, ribs, and cranial bones.

Sesamoid bones are bones embedded **inside tendons**, and named after what they look like. They are rounded, and resemble **sesame seeds**. The primary examples are the patella and pisiform.

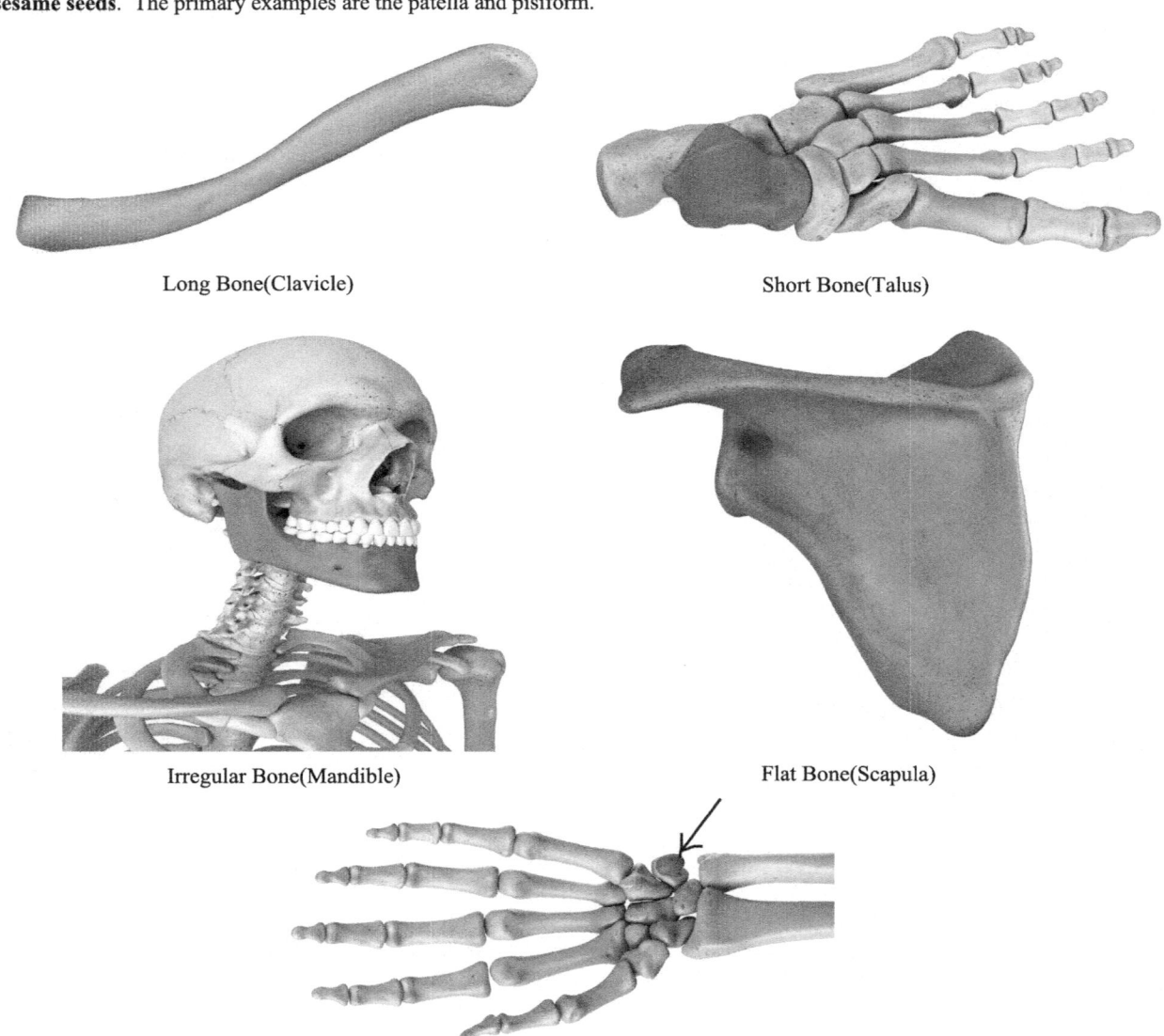

Long Bone(Clavicle)

Short Bone(Talus)

Irregular Bone(Mandible)

Flat Bone(Scapula)

Sesamoid Bone(Pisiform)

Long bones consist of three main parts: the **epiphyses**, the **metaphyses**, and the **diaphysis**. The epiphyses can be found on the **ends** of the long bone, where the bone articulates with other bones. The epiphyses are covered with cartilage to prevent friction between the articulating bone surfaces. The epiphyses are primarily made of spongy bone, which allows certain bones to withstand extreme pressure without fracturing.

The **metaphyses** are the sections between the epiphyses and the diaphysis. Inside the metaphyses, there is a line of cartilage called the **epiphyseal plate/line**, and it is where **growth** in the bone takes place during childhood and adolescence. As a person grows, eventually the cartilage ossifies and becomes part of the bone, and growth in the bone no longer occurs.

The **diaphysis** is the **shaft** of the bone. Inside the shaft of the bone is the medullary cavity. The medullary cavity contains **red bone marrow** during childhood, which is the site of **red blood cell formation**. When the child ages, the red bone marrow is converted into yellow bone marrow, which is mainly just fat. The diaphysis is made of compact bone to provide as much strength as possible around the medullary cavity, while still giving enough space for the cavity itself to fill with marrow.

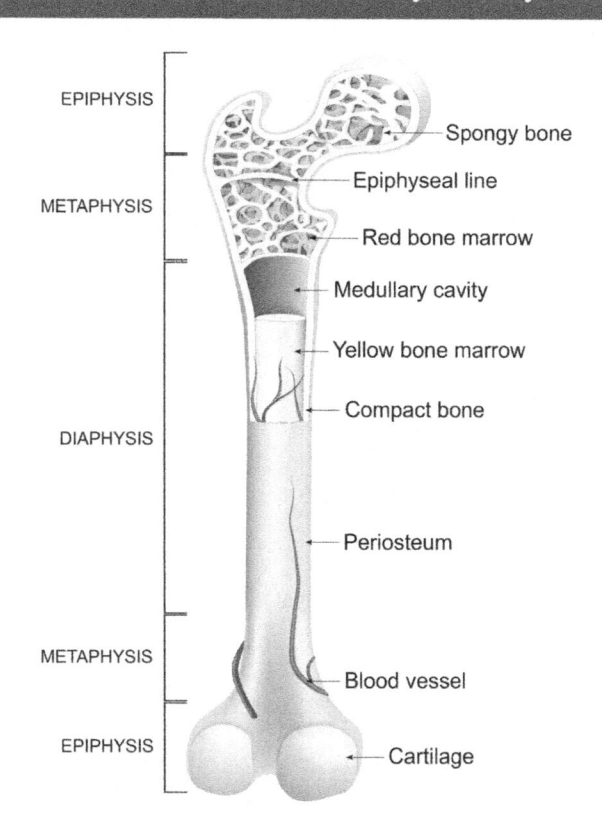

Joints

Where bones come together is known as an **articulation**. Another name for articulation is "**joint**". Joints are where **movements** occur. We don't flex muscles, we flex joints!

All joints are classified as one of the following: **Synarthrotic**, **Amphiarthrotic**, or **Diarthrotic**. Synarthrotic joints are joints with little to **no movement** in them, such as the sutures in the skull. Amphiarthrotic joints are joints that are **slightly movable**, such as the intervertebral joints. Diarthrotic joints are **freely movable** joints, and have no real movement restrictions, such as in the shoulder or hip.

Easy to Remember: To remember the joint classifications, just think of "**SAD**". This tells you the joint classifications in order from least movable joint to most movable joint. **Synarthrosis, Amphiarthrosis, Diarthrosis**.

Joints have several structures that help create and support them. Between bones that articulate, on the **epiphyses**, there is **articular cartilage**. This type of cartilage is known as **hyaline** cartilage. It is a dense form of cartilage, very thick, and is a shock-absorber. Hyaline cartilage also **prevents friction** between the articulating bones, so bones don't rub against each other during movement.

Certain joints have a specific type of cartilage in them known as a **labrum**. The labrum, found in the glenohumeral joint and iliofemoral joint, is used to **deepen** the joint, providing a deeper socket for these ball-and-socket joints. This provides more **strength** and **stability** for the joint.

Bones are held together by **ligaments**. Ligaments are avascular, meaning they are not supplied with blood by blood vessels. Ligaments are strong, but do not stretch very far before injury can occur. Tearing of ligaments such as the Anterior Cruciate Ligament is common in activities such as sports, or in car accidents.

Four of the most important joints joined together by ligaments are located in the skull, between the cranial bones. These synarthrotic joints are called **sutures**. The **sagittal** suture runs along a sagittal plane on the top of the head, connecting the two **parietal bones**. The **coronal** suture runs on a coronal plane, connecting the **frontal** bone to the **parietal** bones. The **squamous** suture runs on a sagittal plane, but is located on the side of the skull, connecting the **parietal** and **temporal** bones together. Finally, the **lambdoid** suture, named for its resemblance to the Greek letter "lambda", connects the **occipital** bone to the **parietal** bones.

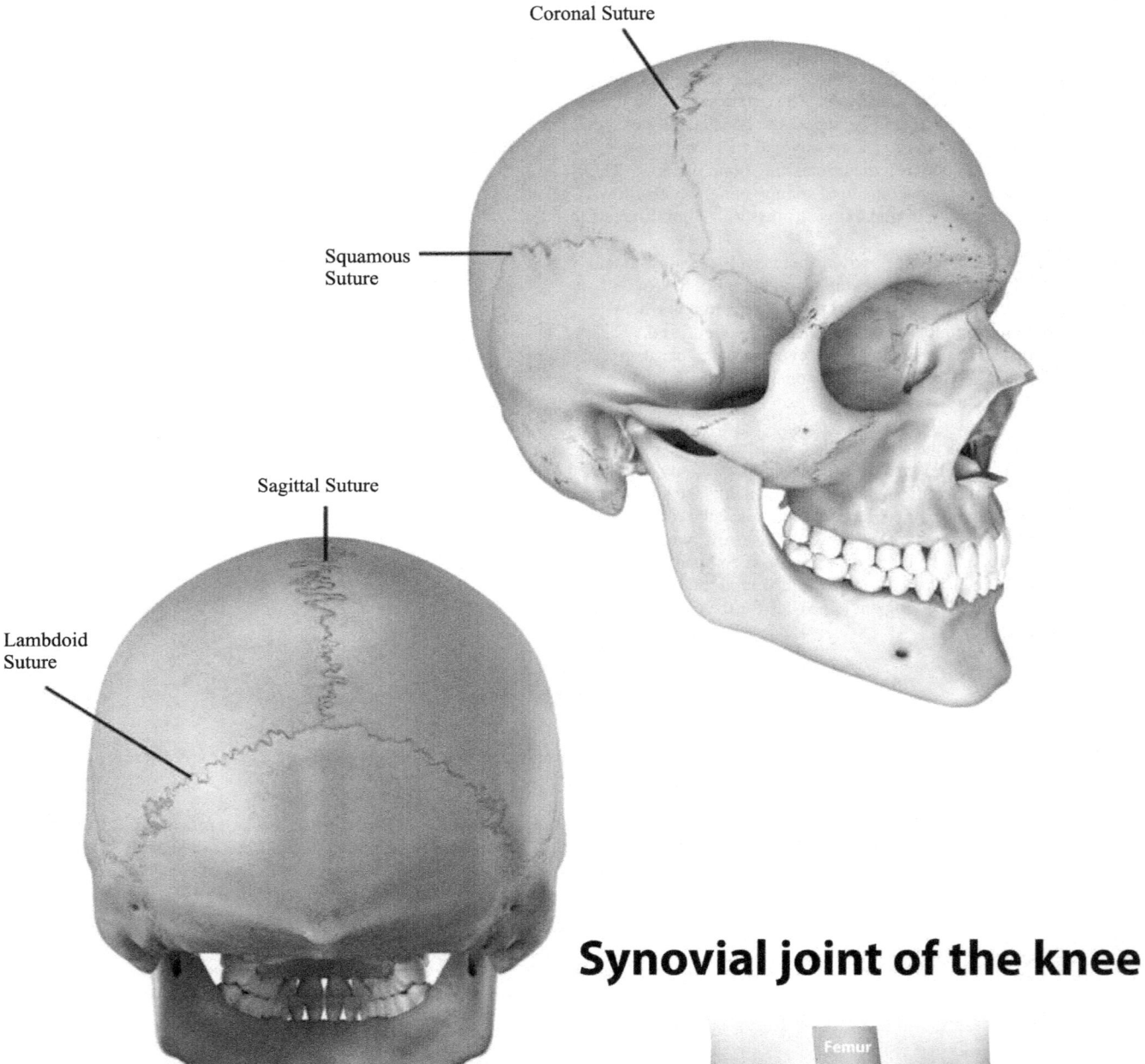

Coronal Suture

Squamous Suture

Sagittal Suture

Lambdoid Suture

Synovial joint of the knee

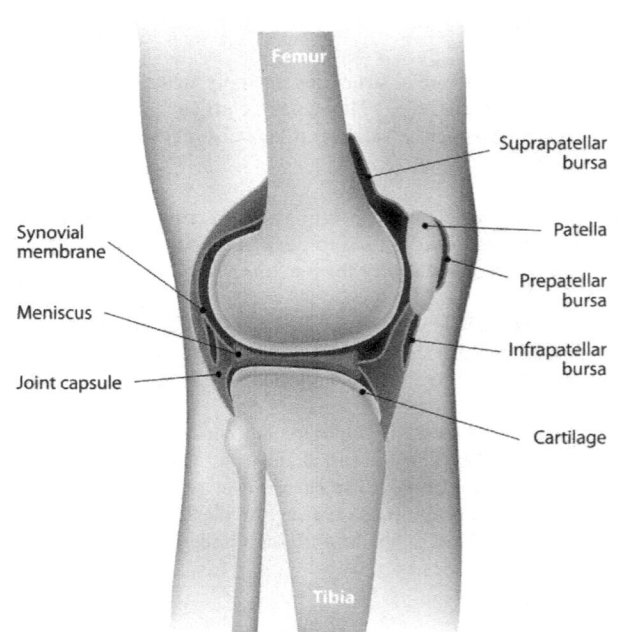

Muscles are held to bones via **tendons**. Tendons are similar to ligaments, but have a much more rich blood supply, and are able to stretch further before injury occurs.

Inside the joint itself, a membrane is present, known as the **synovial membrane**. The synovial membrane produces a fluid that helps to **lubricate** the joint, known as the **synovial fluid**. Lubrication of the joint is key in keeping the joint functioning optimally. Surrounding the entire joint is thick, dense connective tissue known as the **joint capsule**. The joint capsule keeps everything inside the joint, such as the synovial fluid, and provides even more strength and support for the joint.

Types of Synovial Joints

There are **six** different types of synovial joints.

Ball-and-Socket joints feature one bone with a **ball** at the epiphysis, and another bone with a **socket**. The ball fits in the socket, creating a ball-and-socket joint. Examples include the shoulder and hip joints. Ball-and-socket joints have the most amount of movement, able to move the joint in really any direction.

Hinge joints act much like the hinge on a door, only opening and closing. Hinge joints only allow movement in **one plane**, allowing only **flexion** and **extension**. Examples include the elbow and knee joints.

Pivot joints allow only one type of movement: **rotation**. All they do is allow structures to turn. An example is the atlantoaxial joint, which lets us shake our head "no". This is rotation.

Plane/gliding joints are produced when the articulating bones have **flat** surfaces, and there is a **disc of cartilage** between the bones. This allows the joint to move, or glide, in any direction, although with slight movement. Examples include the joints between the carpals and tarsals.

Saddle joints are only located in one part of the body: the **carpometacarpal joint** of the **thumb**. Saddle joints are named after the appearance of the articulating bones. The articulating surfaces are both shaped like saddles. The two bones that create the saddle joint are the **first metacarpal** and the **trapezium**.

Ellipsoid/condyloid joints are extremely similar to ball-and-socket joints. On one bone, there is a **condyle**, which resembles a ball, but isn't as pronounced. This condyle fits into an **elliptical cavity** on another bone, which is similar to a socket, but not as deep. This allows movements such as flexion, extension, adduction, abduction, and circumduction. An example is the radiocarpal joint.

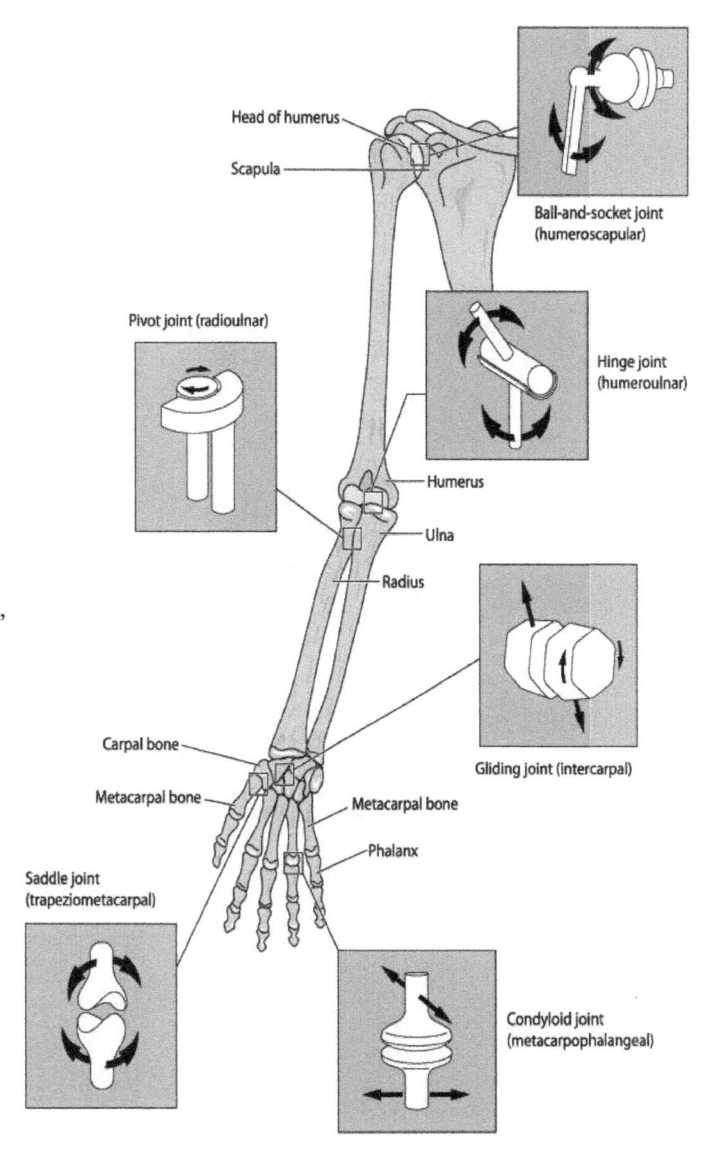

Skeleton Divisions

There are two divisions of the skeleton: the **Axial Skeleton** and the **Appendicular Skeleton**.

The Axial Skeleton contains all of the bones that do not correspond to any appendages: the **skull**, **vertebral column**, and **thoracic cage**. These bones make up the trunk.

The Appendicular Skeleton contains all of the bones that correspond to the appendages: the **humerus, radius, ulna, carpals, metacarpals, phalanges, femur, tibia, fibula, metatarsals, phalanges**, the **pectoral girdle**(clavicles and scapulae) and **pelvic girdle**(ilium, ischium, pubis, and sacrum).

Bones of the Axial Skeleton

Skull

The skull's primary function is to **protect the brain**. The bones that create the skull are:

Parietal	Mandible
Frontal	Vomer
Temporal	Ethmoid
Occipital	Sphenoid
Zygomatic	Nasal
Maxilla	Lacrimal

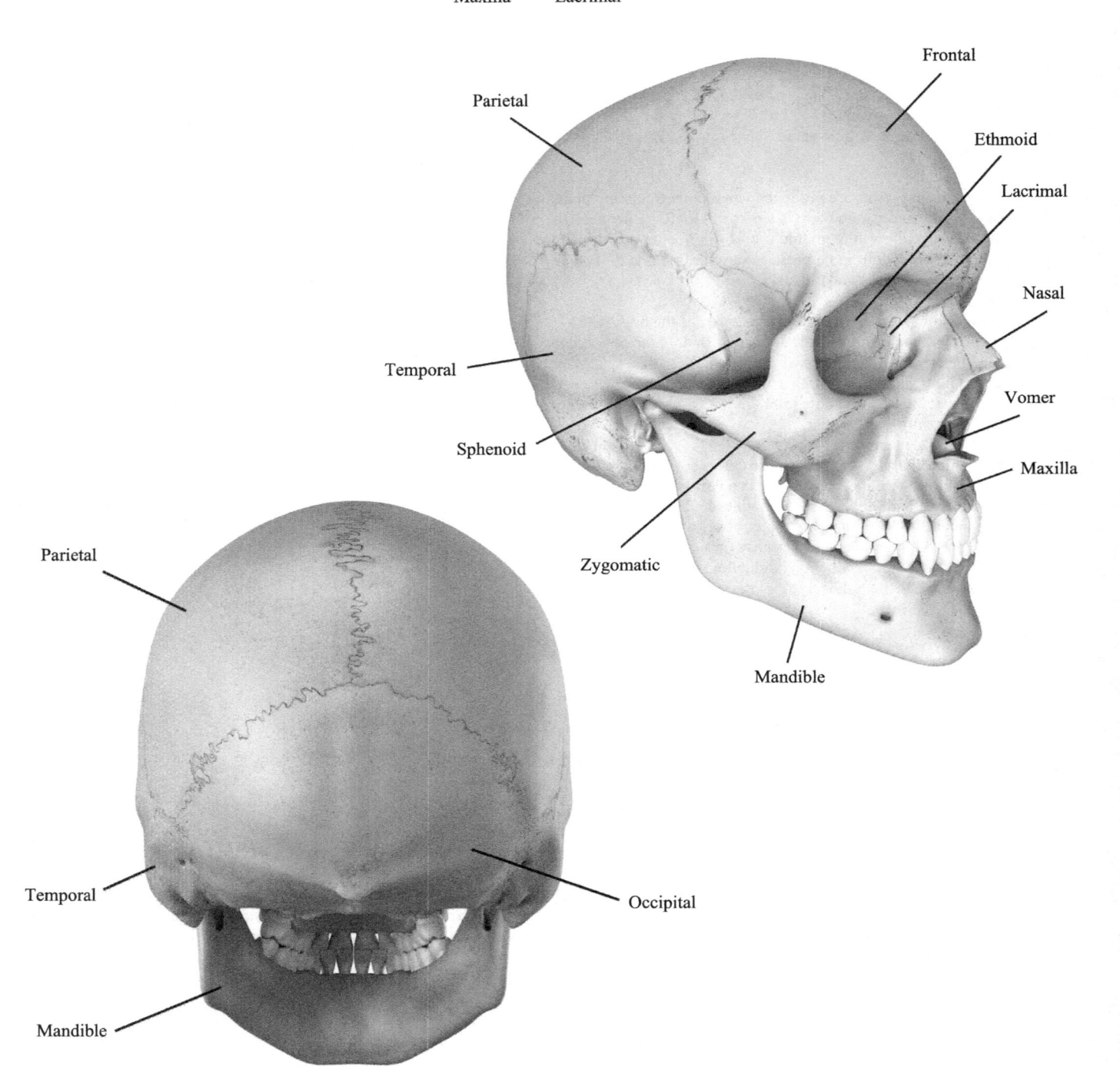

Vertebral Column

The vertebral column consists of **26 individual bones**. Its primary function is to **protect the spinal cord**, which runs through it. There are five different regions of the vertebral column. They are:

Cervical(7 vertebrae)
Thoracic(12 vertebrae)
Lumbar(5 vertebrae)
Sacral(1 vertebrae)
Coccygeal(1 vertebrae)

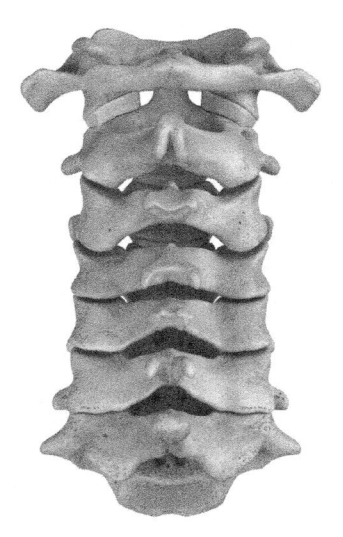

Cervical Vertebrae

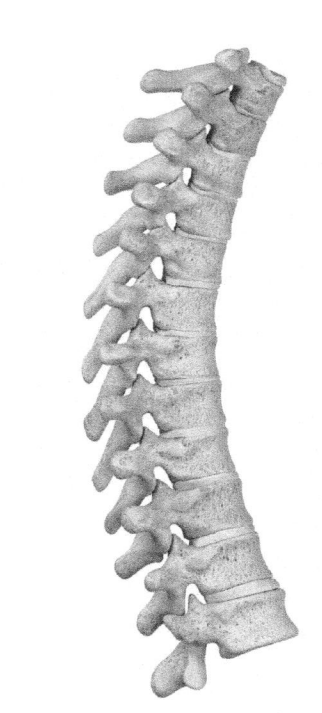

Thoracic Vertebrae

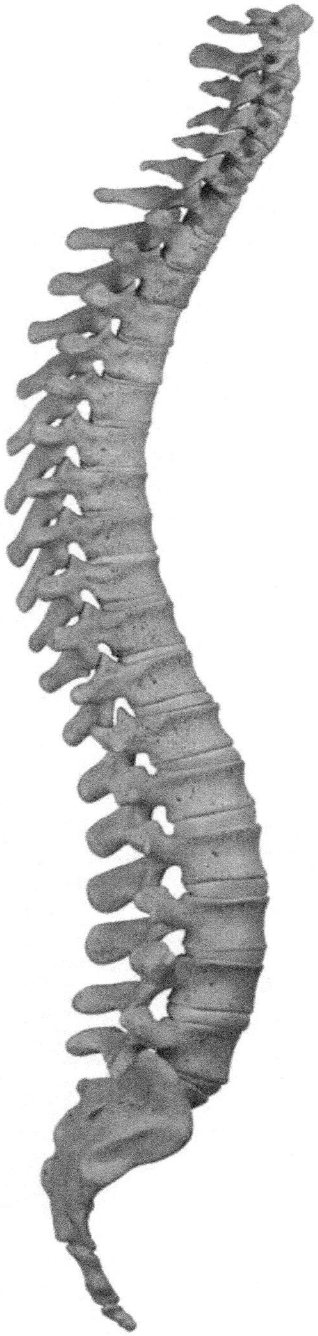

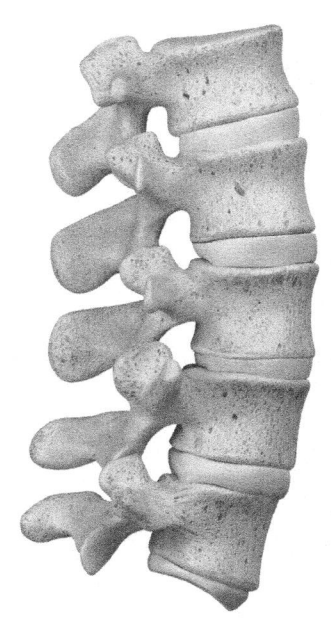

Lumbar Vertebrae

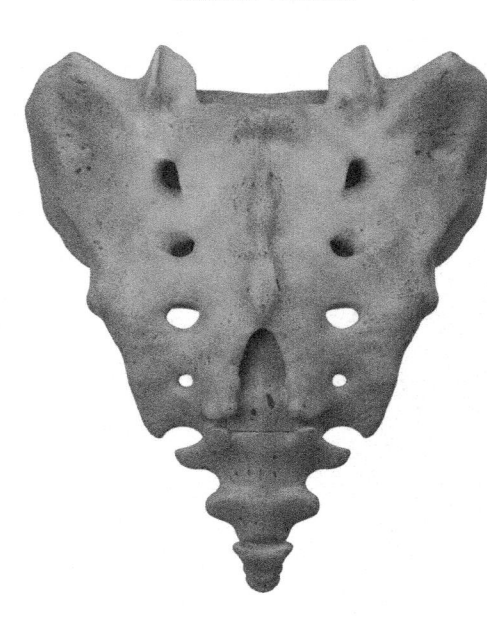

Sacral Vertebrae

*Easy to Remember: To remember how many vertebrae are in the cervical, thoracic, and lumbar regions, just think of **breakfast, lunch, and dinner**. Breakfast(cervical) at **7**, lunch(thoracic) at **12**, dinner(lumbar) at **5**!*

Chest

The chest consists of the **rib cage**. The primary function of the rib cage is to **protect vital organs** inside the thorax, and assist in breathing by giving the diaphragm a place to attach. The rib cage consists of:

True ribs(superior seven ribs)
False ribs(inferior five ribs)
Floating ribs(ribs 11 and 12)

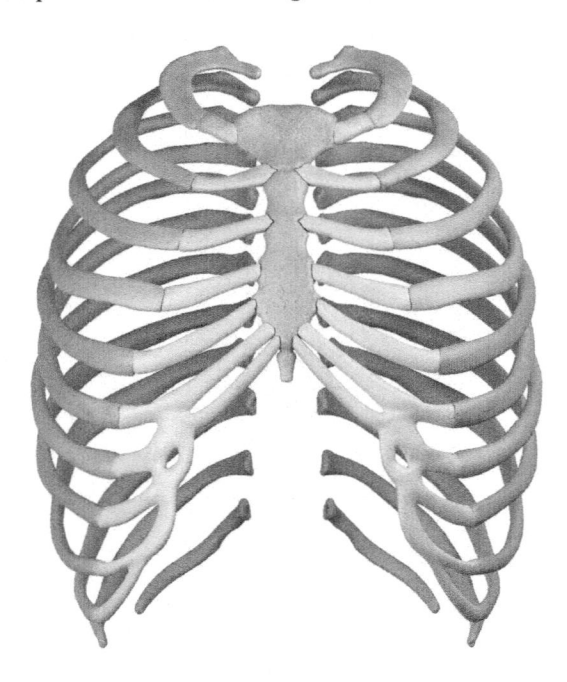

Bones of the Appendicular Skeleton

Pectoral Girdle

The pectoral girdle is responsible for holding the upper limbs to the body. The pectoral girdle consists of four bones:

Scapulae(two bones)
Clavicles(two bones)

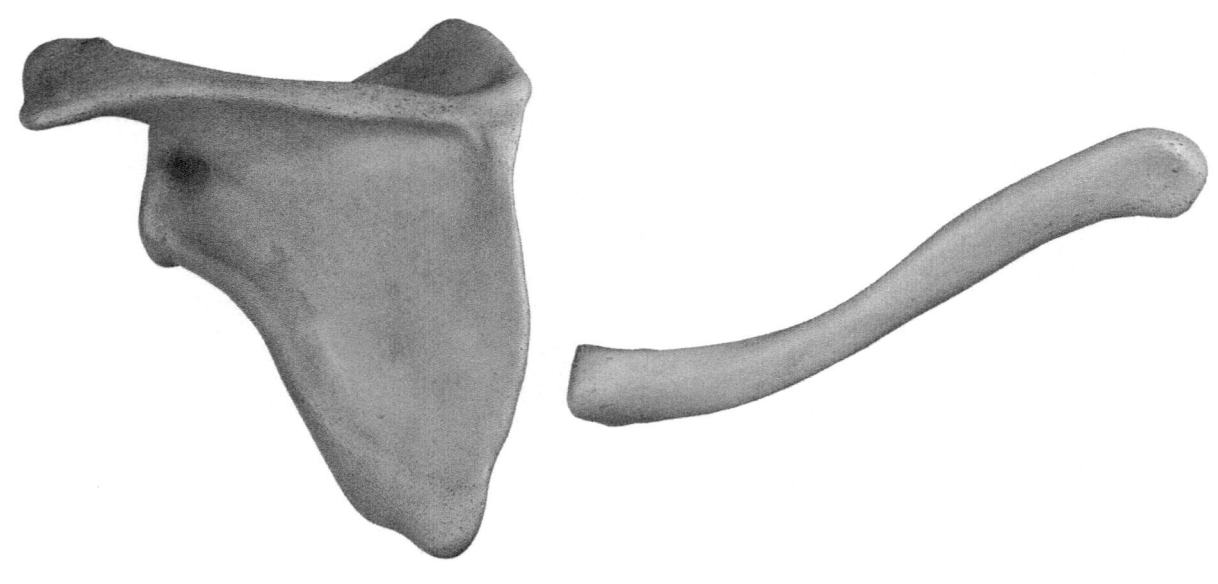

Scapula   Clavicle

Pelvic Girdle

The pelvic girdle is primarily responsible for holding the lower limbs to the body. The pelvic girdle contains:

Ilium(two bones)
Ischium(two bones)
Pubis(two bones)
Sacrum(one bone)

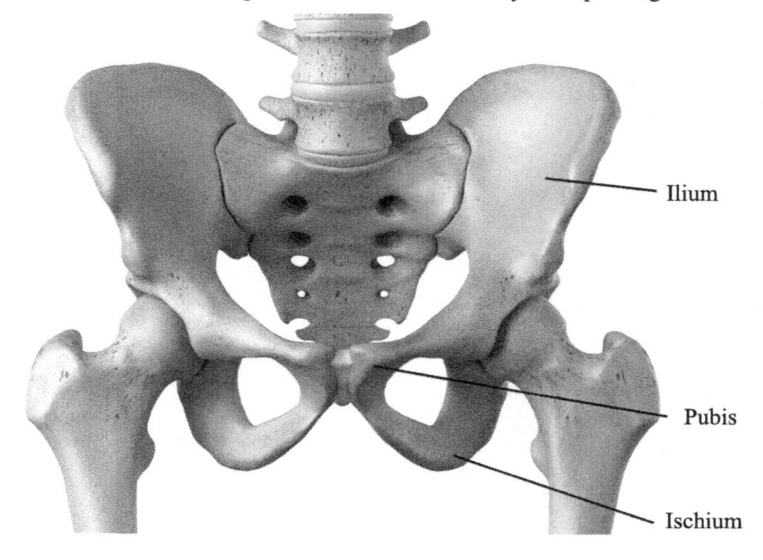

- Ilium
- Pubis
- Ischium

Arm

The arm contains one bone:

Humerus

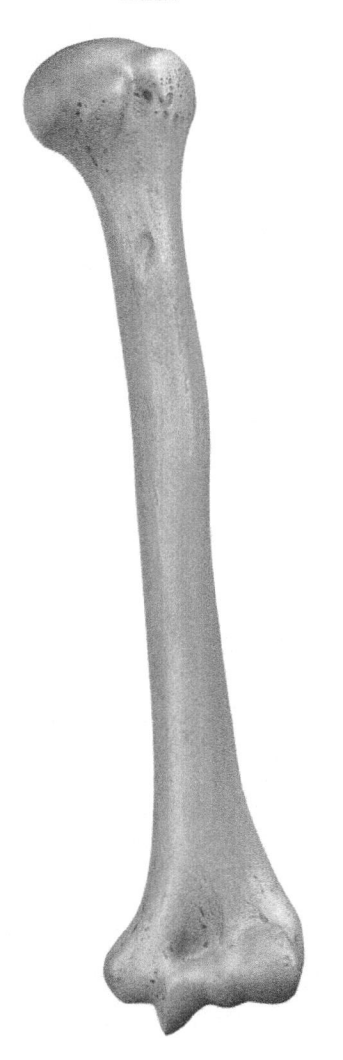

DID YOU KNOW?

*The humerus is the **funniest** bone in the body! Get it? Humerus?*

Forearm

The forearm contains two bones:

Radius
Ulna

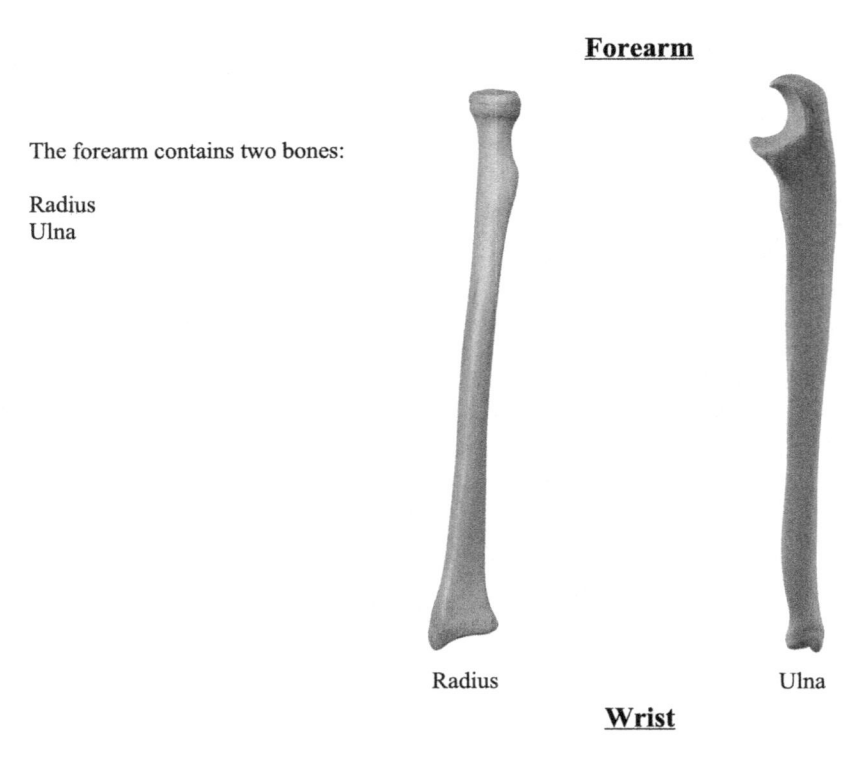

Radius   Ulna

Wrist

The wrist is located distally to the forearm, and it contains the **carpal bones**. The carpal bones are divided into two separate lines, each containing four bones. The proximal line is listed first, then the distal line:

Proximal Line: **Distal Line:**
Scaphoid   Trapezium
Lunate   Trapezoid
Triquetrum   Capitate
Pisiform   Hamate

DID YOU KNOW?

*The **carpometacarpal joint of the thumb**, made by the **trapezium** and **first metacarpal**, is the only place in the body you find a **saddle joint**!*

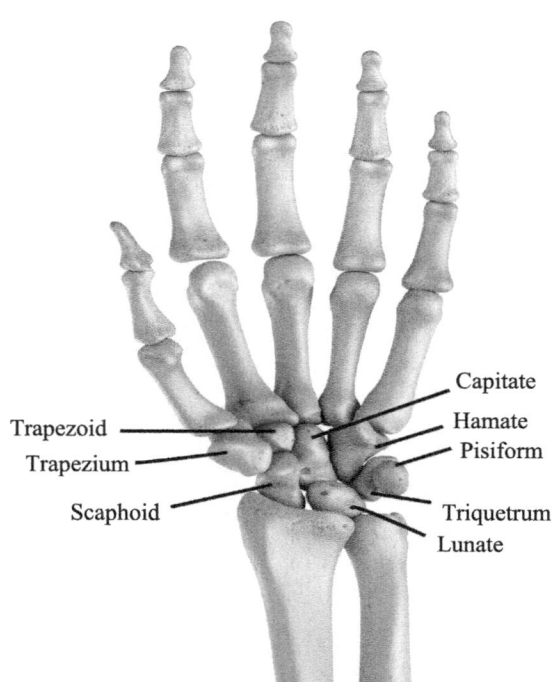

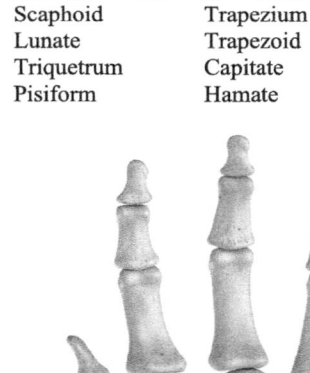

Capitate
Hamate
Trapezoid
Pisiform
Trapezium
Triquetrum
Scaphoid
Lunate

Easy to Remember: To remember the order of the carpals, think of this old saying: Some Lovers Try Positions That They Can't Handle(Scaphoid, Lunate, Triquetrum, Pisiform, Trapezium, Trapezoid, Capitate, Hamate)!

Anatomy and Physiology 85

Hand

There are **19 bones** in each hand:

Metacarpals(5 bones)
Phalanges(14 bones)

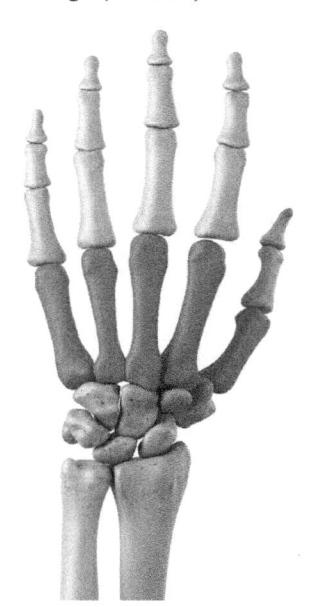

Metacarpals 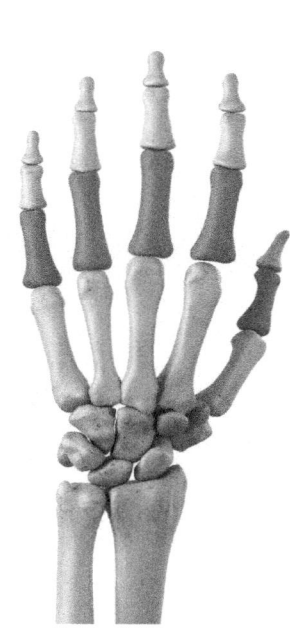   Proximal Phalanges 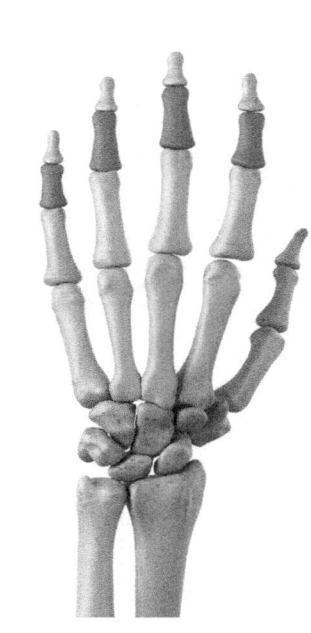   Middle Phalanges 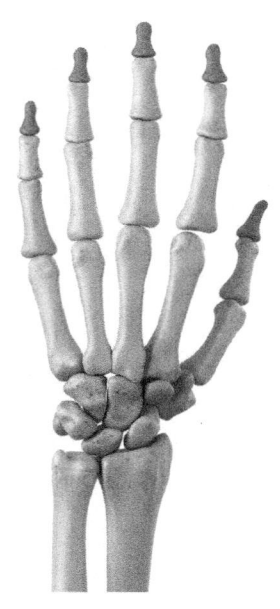   Distal Phalanges

Thigh

The thigh contains one bone:

Femur

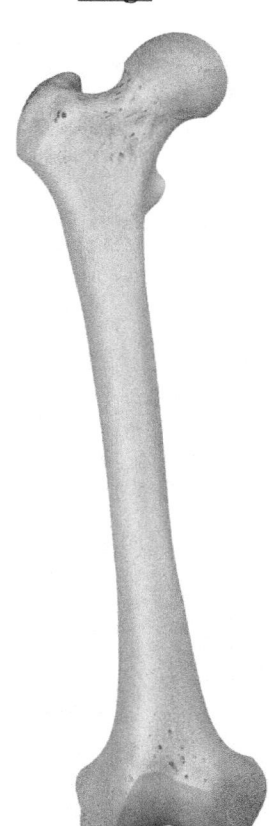

DID YOU KNOW?

*The femur is the **longest** and **strongest** bone in the body!*

86 Anatomy and Physiology

Leg

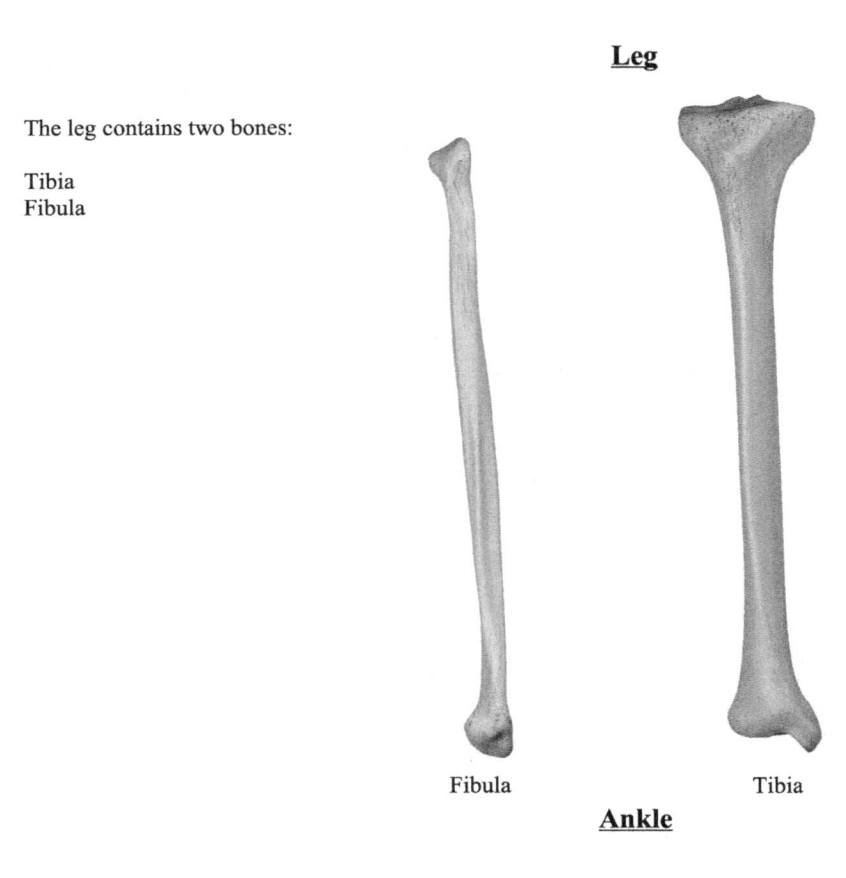

The leg contains two bones:

Tibia
Fibula

Fibula   Tibia

Did You Know?

*Wolff's Law states that when placed under significant pressure and load, bone **strength** and **density** will **increase**! So go hit the squat rack!*

Ankle

The ankle is located distally to the leg, and it consists of the bones of the **tarsals**:

Calcaneus   Cuneiform I
Talus   Cuneiform II
Navicular   Cuneiform III
Cuboid

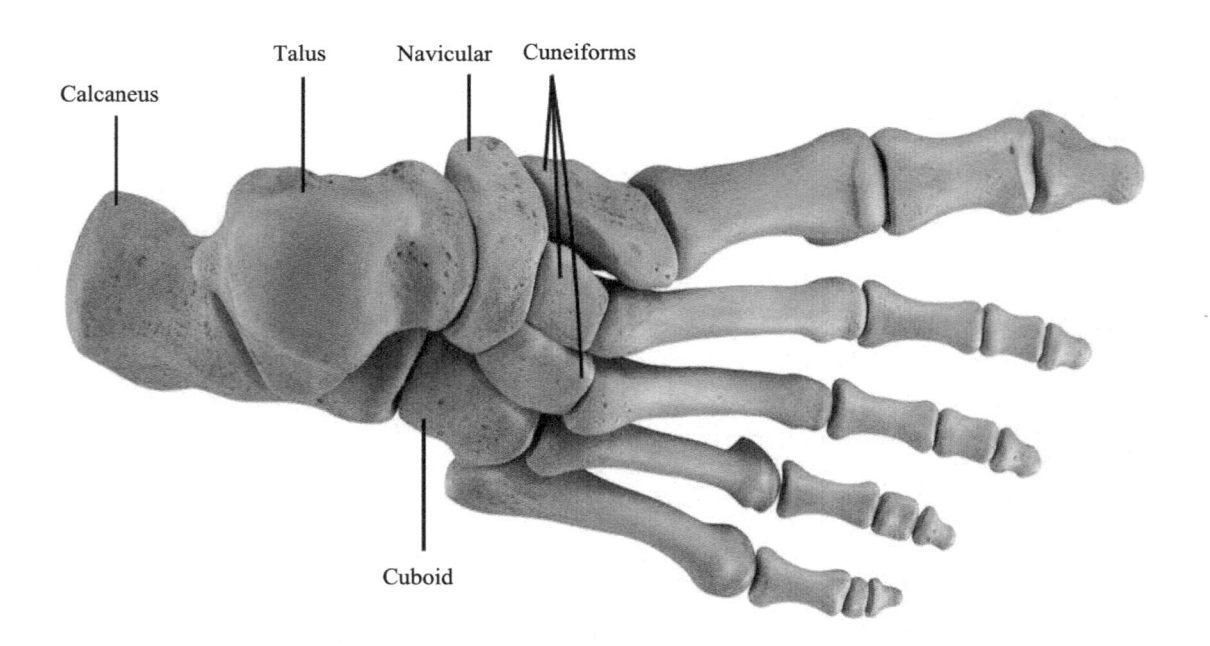

Calcaneus   Talus   Navicular   Cuneiforms

Cuboid

Foot

The foot contains **19 bones**:

Metatarsals(5 bones)
Phalanges(14 bones)

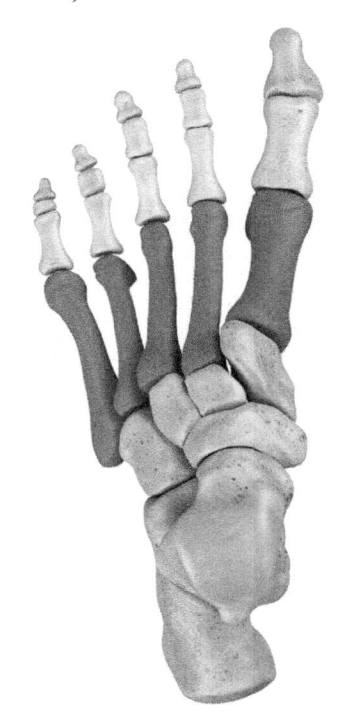

Metatarsals

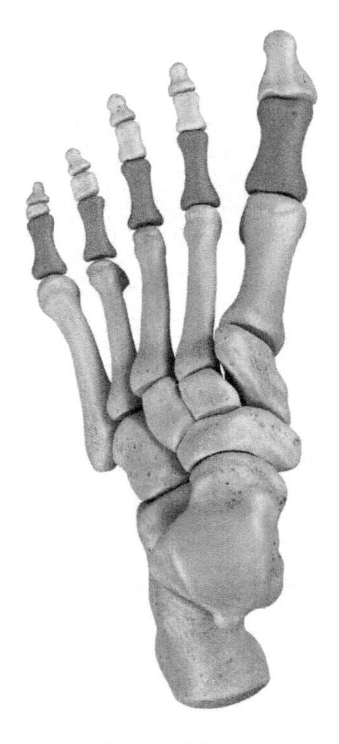

Proximal Phalanges

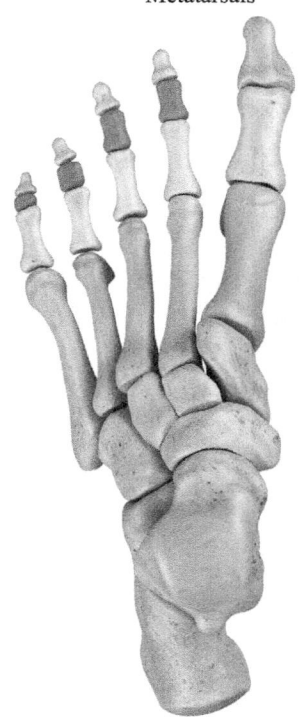

Middle Phalanges

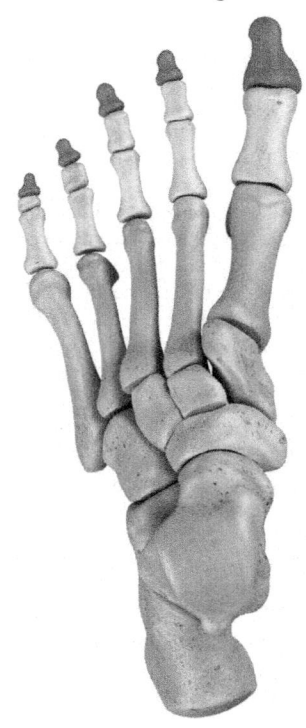

Distal Phalanges

Urinary System

The Urinary System is primarily responsible for **elimination** of **waste** from the body. It also assists in regulating the **pH level** of the body, and may also assist in reabsorption of substances back into the body. The four main structures of the Urinary System are(in descending order) the **kidneys, ureters, urinary bladder,** and **urethra**.

pH Scale

A **pH scale** is used to determine the **acidity** or **alkalinity** of a substance. If a substance reads between **7-14** on a pH scale, it is base, or **alkaline**. The higher the number, the more alkaline a substance is. An example, bleach is highly basic, and comes in at 12.6. Blood is slightly basic, and comes in at 7.4. On the other hand, if a substance comes in between **0-7** on a pH scale, it is **acidic**. The lower the number, the more acidic a substance is. An example, hydrochloric acid(the kind of acid in the stomach that helps digest food) comes in at 2.0, so it is highly acidic. Black coffee registers at about 5.0, so it is slightly acidic. The kidneys help regulate substances in the body that make the body's fluids either too acidic or too basic by filtration.

The pH Scale

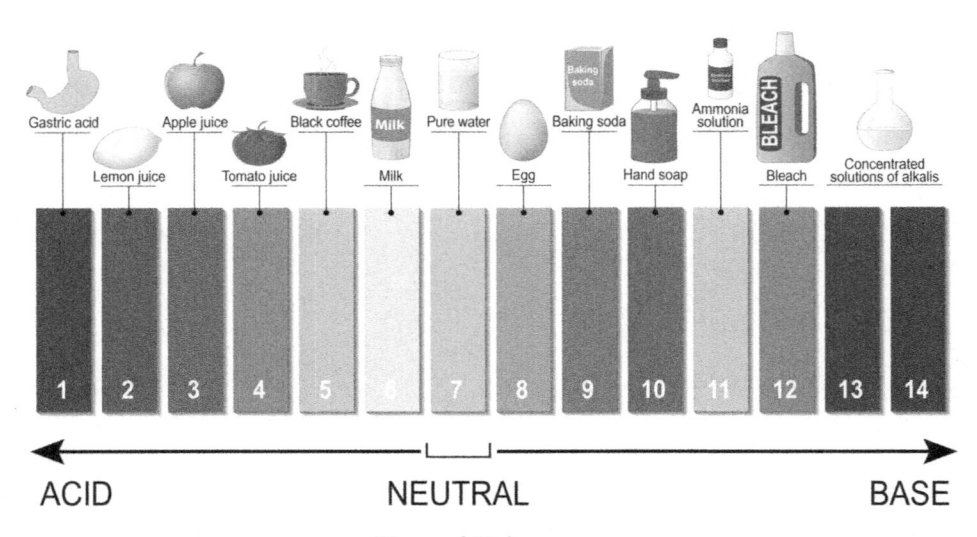

Flow of Urine

Blood enters the kidneys through the renal arteries. Inside the kidneys, blood is **filtered** through the **nephrons**, which extract waste products such as **urea** out of the blood. Inside each kidney, there are over one million nephrons. The waste products filtered out of the blood by the nephrons become **urine**. The nephrons also allow nutrients and water to be reabsorbed back into the blood stream.

Once urine has been created, it is sent from the kidneys to the urinary bladder through two small tubes known as ureters. The ureters only function as a **passageway** for urine.

Urine **collects** in the urinary bladder, until it is ready to be eliminated from the body. The urinary bladder expands as more urine is added to it. The urinary bladder can typically hold between 300-500 ml of fluid. Once urine is released from the urinary bladder, it passes through the urethra.

The urethra, much like the ureters, is a small tube that has one function: **transporting urine** from the urinary bladder **out of the body**.

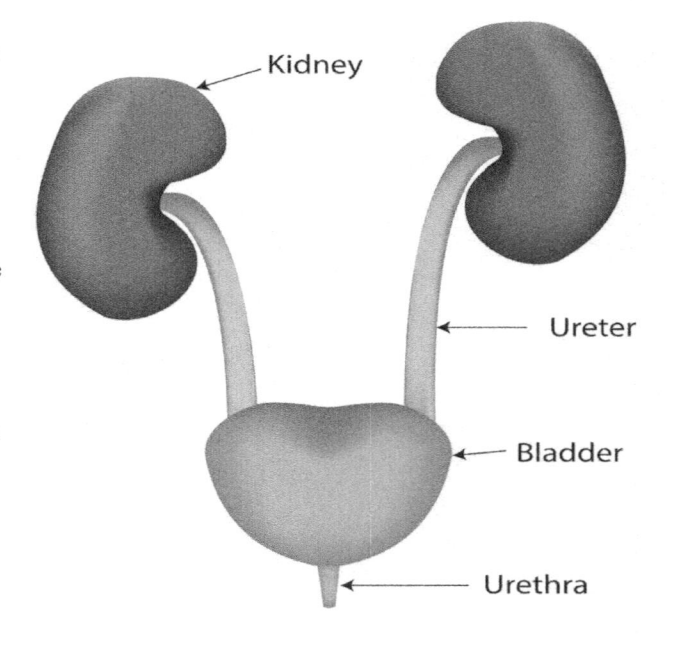

Anatomy and Physiology Matching

_____: Constant internal environment

_____: Suture connecting the two parietal bones

_____: Organ that creates bile and detoxifies blood

_____: Tissue responsible for separating structures

_____: Sensory receptor that detects pain

_____: Organ that filters blood and creates urine

_____: "Rest-and-digest" response

_____: Muscle contraction with constant tension and decreasing muscle length

_____: Gland responsible for the creation of T-cells

_____: Muscle contraction with constant tension and increasing muscle length

_____: Region of vertebral column with five bones

_____: Suture connecting the occipital bone and parietal bones

_____: Cell responsible for transporting oxygen and carbon dioxide

_____: Tissue responsible for protection, secretion, and absorption

_____: "Fight-or-flight" response

_____: Glands responsible for production of estrogen and progesterone

_____: Region of the vertebral column with seven bones

_____: Body plane that splits the body into superior and inferior

_____: Largest lymph vessel in the body

_____: Body plane that splits the body into anterior and posterior

A: Erythrocytes
B: Thymus
C: Homeostasis
D: Kidneys
E: Liver
F: Cervical Vertebrae
G: Transverse Plane
H: Epithelial Tissue
I: Thoracic Duct
J: Ovaries

K: Sagittal Suture
L: Concentric Contraction
M: Parasympathetic Response
N: Lambdoid Suture
O: Nociceptor
P: Lumbar Vertebrae
Q: Eccentric Contraction
R: Frontal Plane
S: Sympathetic Response
T: Connective Tissue

Answer Key on Page 312

Anatomy and Physiology

Across
2. Most common form of cartilage in the body
3. Contraction resulting in muscle tension increasing and muscle length remaining constant
7. Carpal that is a sesamoid bone
8. Carpal articulating with the radius
9. Largest lymph vessel in the body
11. Valve located between the right atrium and right ventricle
12. Study of the function of the body
14. Cell that carries oxygen and carbon dioxide
15. Maintaining a relatively constant internal environment
16. Part of the brain regulating muscle tone and coordination
18. Tissue that forms the brain, spinal cord, and nerves
19. Air sacs where oxygen and carbon dioxide are exchanged

Down
1. Sphincter located between the esophagus and stomach
4. Hormone produced by the thyroid
5. Structure that holds the intestines in place and gives blood vessels a place to travel through
6. Largest artery in the body
7. Hormone produced by the ovaries
10. Tissue that forms glands and epidermis
13. Cell that destroys pathogens
17. Organ that produces bile

Answer Key on Page 313

Anatomy and Physiology Practice Exam

1. The sympathetic nervous response is also referred to as
A. Housekeeping
B. Rest and digest
C. Fight or flight
D. Central

2. A sudoriferous gland is a type of exocrine gland that produces what substance
A. Oil
B. Sweat
C. Testosterone
D. Milk

3. The longest vein in the body, located on the medial aspect of the leg and thigh
A. Great saphenous
B. Femoral
C. External iliac
D. Brachial

4. The pituitary gland produces all of the following hormones except
A. Growth hormone
B. Testosterone
C. Follicle-stimulating hormone
D. Prolactin

5. Perirenal fat surrounds the
A. Rectum
B. Bladder
C. Liver
D. Kidneys

6. Primary function of a gland
A. Secretion
B. Protection
C. Absorption
D. Contraction

7. Branching muscle tissue is also called
A. Smooth
B. Skeletal
C. Cardiac
D. Striated

8. What aspect of the body is being studied in anatomy
A. Structure
B. Function
C. Diseases
D. Movement

9. Mastication is more commonly known as
A. Chewing
B. Swallowing
C. Sneezing
D. Defecating

10. The pulmonary arteries carry blood from the right ventricle to
A. Left atrium
B. Rest of the body
C. Aorta
D. Lungs

11. Beta cells produce
A. Bile
B. Glucagon
C. Somatostatin
D. Insulin

12. Where two bones come together
A. Fracture
B. Articulation
C. Contracture
D. Ellipsoid

13. T-lymphocytes are produced by which gland
A. Thymus
B. Thalamus
C. Pituitary
D. Pineal

14. Light pressure is detected by
A. Nociceptors
B. Pacinian corpuscles
C. Merkel discs
D. Meissner's corpuscles

15. The phrenic nerve emerges from the
A. Neck
B. Chest
C. Lumbar
D. Brain

16. Another name for a leukocyte is
A. Thrombocyte
B. Red blood cell
C. Platelet
D. White blood cell

17. The cervical plexus emerges from which sets of vertebrae
A. C1-C7
B. C1-C4
C. T1-T6
D. L1-S4

18. There are seven vertebrae in which region of the vertebral column
A. Thoracic
B. Cervical
C. Lumbar
D. Coccygeal

19. Erythrocytes
A. Carry oxygen and carbon dioxide throughout the body
B. Are also called neutrophils and perform phagocytosis
C. Produce thrombi at an area of trauma
D. Allow transport of blood cells throughout the body

20. Storage of bile is controlled by the
A. Gallbladder
B. Liver
C. Small intestine
D. Stomach

21. Absorption of nutrients primarily takes place in what part of the small intestine
A. Jejunum
B. Ileum
C. Duodenum
D. Cecum

22. The superior seven pairs of ribs are also called
A. Inferior ribs
B. False ribs
C. Superior ribs
D. True ribs

23. Waste moves through the large intestine in the following order
A. Transverse colon, ascending colon, sigmoid colon, descending colon
B. Sigmoid colon, descending colon, transverse colon, ascending colon
C. Ascending colon, transverse colon, descending colon, sigmoid colon
D. Descending colon, ascending colon, transverse colon, sigmoid colon

24. Peristalsis is controlled by which of the following types of muscle
A. Cardiac
B. Skeletal
C. Smooth
D. Striated

25. Vitamin D is produced in the following organ
A. Liver
B. Skin
C. Pancreas
D. Spleen

26. Glucagon is produced by
A. Delta cells
B. Beta cells
C. Alpha cells
D. Theta cells

27. Part of the respiratory passage that divides into the left and right bronchus
A. Larynx
B. Pharynx
C. Trachea
D. Epiglottis

28. Which of the following is not one of the four types of tissue
A. Nervous
B. Connective
C. Epithelial
D. Skeletal

29. The largest internal organ in the body
A. Liver
B. Stomach
C. Brain
D. Spleen

30. Enzyme located in the saliva which aids in digestion of carbohydrates
A. Epinephrine
B. Prolactin
C. Amylase
D. Parotid

31. The esophagus passes through the following structure on its way to the stomach
A. Peritoneum
B. Liver
C. Pericardium
D. Diaphragm

32. Heat creation is produced by which type of muscle tissue
A. Smooth
B. Cardiac
C. Skeletal
D. Adipose

33. The functional unit of tissue is called
A. Cell
B. Nerve
C. Blood
D. Muscle

34. Most superior portion of the sternum
A. Costal cartilage
B. Body
C. Xiphoid process
D. Manubrium

35. Which of the following molecules attaches to hemoglobin
A. Nitrogen
B. Oxygen
C. Helium
D. Argon

36. Breaking down food, absorption of nutrients, and elimination of waste is the function of which body system
A. Urinary
B. Digestive
C. Cardiovascular
D. Lymphatic

37. Non-striated muscle is
A. Involuntary
B. Voluntary
C. Controlled easily
D. Controlled by concentration

38. Connective tissue connecting bone to bone
A. Fascia
B. Tendon
C. Ligament
D. Dermis

39. There are how many pairs of spinal nerves in the peripheral nervous system
A. 24
B. 12
C. 18
D. 31

40. All of the following carry blood away from the heart except
A. Capillaries
B. Arteries
C. Arterioles
D. Veins

41. The ovaries and testes are examples of
A. Exocrine glands
B. Digestive organs
C. Endocrine glands
D. Cardiovascular vessels

42. Chyme moves from the stomach into the small intestine through which sphincter
A. Ileocecal
B. Cardiac
C. Pyloric
D. Esophageal

43. Epithelial tissue
A. Holds tissue together and separates tissues
B. Provides protection, secretes substances, and absorbs substances
C. Is found inside joints and helps to lubricate joints
D. Allows nerve impulses to be transmitted from the brain to muscles

44. The adrenal glands are located atop which organs
A. Large intestine
B. Small intestine
C. Kidneys
D. Ureters

45. Dopamine is an example of a
A. Hormone
B. Synapse
C. Neuron
D. Dendrite

46. The largest veins in the body, responsible for returning deoxygenated blood to the heart
A. Aorta
B. Vena Cava
C. Pulmonary arteries
D. Pulmonary veins

47. Function of serous membranes
A. Secreting sebum
B. Connect organs
C. Creating blood
D. Separate organs

48. Which of the following is not a structure in the Digestive System
A. Gallbladder
B. Spleen
C. Liver
D. Pancreas

49. The first cervical vertebrae is also called the
A. Occiput
B. Axis
C. Atlas
D. Dens

50. Pepsin is located in the
A. Stomach
B. Small intestine
C. Pancreas
D. Gallbladder

Answer Key on Page 314

Do as little as needed, not as much as possible.

- Henk Kraaijenhof

Pathology

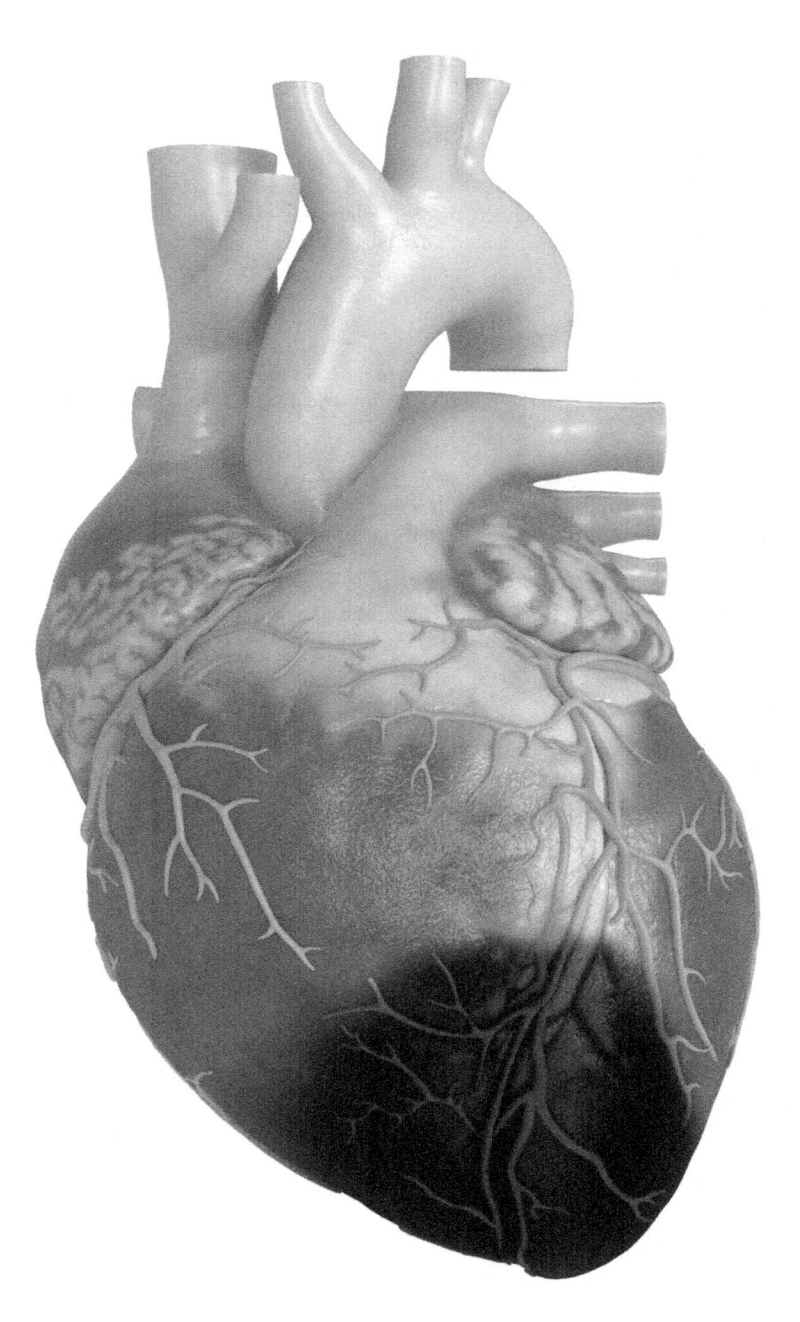

Disease

A disease is a condition affecting certain functions or structures in the human body, which can usually be associated with signs or symptoms. Diseases most commonly affect a specific location in the body, and aren't the result of physical trauma. Diseases range in severity from mild to severe, and in length from acute to chronic. These factors are determined by the type of disease, and the ability to treat the disease.

An **acute** disease or disorder has a **sudden onset**, which lasts for a **short period** of time. Acute conditions can be seen often with infections or trauma, and as the body's immune system fights off the infection, the acute condition dissipates. However, if the condition is severe enough, it may result in death. It is in this way that acute conditions are typically more dangerous in the short term than chronic conditions.

Chronic diseases or disorders are present for **long periods**, usually over three months. Examples of chronic diseases include asthma and hepatitis C. Chronic diseases may have periods of exacerbation and remission. The period where the disease is not actively showing signs or symptoms is the remission period, while the period where the disease is affecting a person's health is the exacerbation period. Other forms of chronic diseases, such as cancer or diabetes, are always present, and can make a person continuously ill.

Acquired Diseases

An acquired disease is a disease a person has obtained at some point **after birth**. Commonly thought of as some sort of infection, it actually just means the disease has appeared after birth. If a person has a disease that was not congenital, then it is referred to as an acquired disease.

Autoimmune Diseases

Autoimmune diseases are the result of the body's **immune system attacking cells and structures in the body** that it **cannot differentiate** from pathogens that have entered the body. Autoimmune diseases can attack different parts of the body with differing levels of severity.

In a person with an autoimmune disease, the body releases proteins known as **autoantibodies**. Autoantibodies are the cells that cannot tell the difference between normal tissue and foreign substances. Autoantibodies may attack only one specific structure, such as Graves' disease where the thyroid is the only structure attacked, or they may attack structures throughout the entire body, such as in lupus.

Autoimmune diseases may be hereditary, such as multiple sclerosis. If one person in a family has an autoimmune disorder, it may increase the likelihood of another family remember having it as well.

Congenital Diseases

A congenital disease is a disease that is **present at birth**. These diseases may be inherited, or may be the result of certain environmental factors. Common examples of congenital diseases include heart defects, cleft lip, Down syndrome, HIV infection, and spina bifida.

Causes for these diseases vary, but many are likely due to lack of maternal nutrition intake, alcohol use, drug use, and the fetus not receiving adequate nutrients.

Deficiency Diseases

Deficiency diseases are the result of the body not receiving **adequate nutrients**, vitamins, and/or minerals in the diet. Examples of nutrients include iron, vitamin C, zinc, calcium, and iodine. When a person does not receive these nutrients in adequate amounts, it can cause organs and structures in the body to function improperly, or not at all. For example, if a person lacks sufficient vitamin C in the diet, they may develop scurvy. If a person does not consume enough calcium, they may develop osteoporosis(page 175). Other examples of diseases caused by a nutrient deficiency include anemia(page 112), goiter (page 131), and rickets.

Hereditary Diseases

A hereditary disease, also known as a genetic disease, is the result of some sort of **abnormality** in a person's **genome**. These abnormalities vary in severity, and in turn, may cause differing levels of difficulty in normal function.

Genetic disorders are commonly passed down from the parents, but some genetic disorders may be the result of mutations in the genes due to environmental factors. Other times, the mutation in the gene may be completely random.

There are differing types of gene inheritance that contribute to the development of hereditary diseases.

Single gene inheritances are the result of mutations occurring in one single gene. This leaves the majority of the body operating normally, but can change one specific aspect of the body. An example is cystic fibrosis, where the mutated gene causes the respiratory passages to produce an extremely excessive amount of mucous.

Multifactoral gene inheritances are the result of a mutation in multiple genes, in association with environmental factors. The gene may be present that can cause the disease, but it may lie dormant unless it is activated by environmental factors. Examples include cancers, hypertension, and cardiovascular disease. If the person avoids the environmental factors, they see less of a chance of developing the disease associated with the mutated gene.

Abnormal chromosomes are often caused by problems during cell division, known as **nondisjunction**, which can damage the chromosomes in the cell's DNA. An example of an abnormal chromosome disease is Down syndrome. This is caused by having an extra copy of chromosome 21. This gives the person 47 total chromosomes, instead of the standard 46.

Idiopathic Diseases

An idiopathic disease is a disease that has an **unknown origin or cause**. These diseases show no obvious sign of origin, and spontaneously appear. There may be theories about why a disease occurs, but the exact reason is unknown. Examples of idiopathic diseases include ankylosing spondylitis(page 168), chronic fatigue syndrome, and fibromyalgia(page 152).

Infectious Diseases

An infection is an **invasion** of a **microorganism** inside the body in some way, which can be localized and less serious, to systemic and life-threatening. These microorganisms are usually not inside the body, and therefore, the body does not have a knowledge of how to exactly combat the infection when first exposed. When there is an infection, the body develops antibodies, and these are used to destroy the invading microorganism.

There are four primary types of infections: bacterial, viral, fungal, and parasitic.

Bacterial Infections

Bacteria are single-celled organisms that can only be seen under a microscope. They have a membrane surrounding the cell, and are able to freely reproduce via cell mitosis.

Bacterial infections are caused by an invasion of certain types of bacteria, such as H. pylori, staphylococcus, streptococcus, and salmonella. Bacteria come different shapes and sizes, some looking like rods(bacillus), and others looking like balls(borrelia) or spirals(spirilla). Bacterial infections make a person sick by releasing toxic substances in their waste. An overabundance of these toxins cause a person to become ill, depending on the severity. Bacteria are known to reproduce quickly, and treatment should be sought for serious bacterial infections such as pneumonia and strep throat. Treatment for bacterial infections involves taking a course of antibiotics, such as penicillin, which destroy the bacteria. Any course of antibiotics should be completed fully, as ceasing taking the prescribed dosage could result in any remaining bacteria becoming resistant to the antibiotics. It's in these cases where infections such as MRSA(methicillin-resistant staphylococcus aureus) may appear and become extremely difficult to treat, which may be life-threatening.

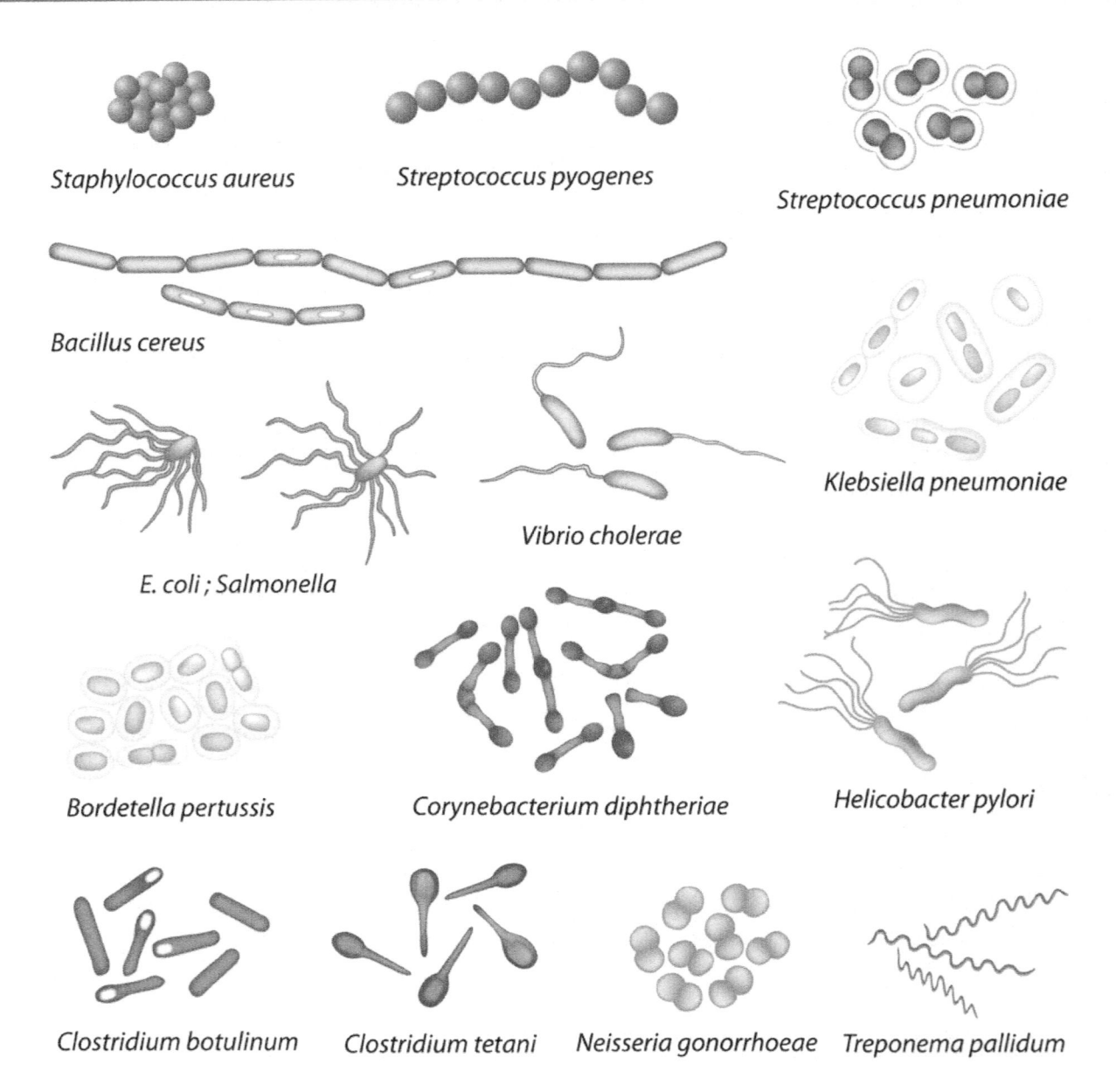

Staphylococcus aureus   *Streptococcus pyogenes*   *Streptococcus pneumoniae*

Bacillus cereus

E. coli ; Salmonella   *Vibrio cholerae*   *Klebsiella pneumoniae*

Bordetella pertussis   *Corynebacterium diphtheriae*   *Helicobacter pylori*

Clostridium botulinum   *Clostridium tetani*   *Neisseria gonorrhoeae*   *Treponema pallidum*

Viral Infections

Viral infections are caused by viruses, structures smaller than bacteria, that contain RNA or DNA in their core. They attach to healthy cells and insert code into the cell that changes the behavior in the cell and causes the infected cell to create more virus particles. These particles come together in the cell, creating new viruses. When too many of these viruses have formed, they break through the host cell and enter the body, infecting more healthy cells. This process is known as the **lytic cycle**.

When the body detects a viral infection, it releases chemicals known as **pyrogens** into the body, which elevate body temperature. This increased body temperature, known as a fever, does not give the viruses an environment to thrive in, and ultimately the viruses die or fail to reproduce due to the extreme temperature change. Treatments for viral infections typically are used to treat the symptoms, as there is no way to destroy the virus itself. Vaccines can be used to introduce dead or weakened viruses into the body, which allow the body's immune system to develop antibodies for them, preventing future infections. Antiviral medications can be used to prevent a virus from reproducing, but cannot kill the virus.

Some viruses never leave a person's body and become dormant, not always causing problems. Others never leave the body and actively affect the body, such as HIV. Most of the time, in instances such as influenza, the body's immune system naturally fights off the virus over the course of a week or two.

HIV   Hepatitis B   Ebola Virus

Adenovirus   Influenza   Rabies Virus   Bacteriophage

Papillomavirus   Rotavirus   Herpes Virus

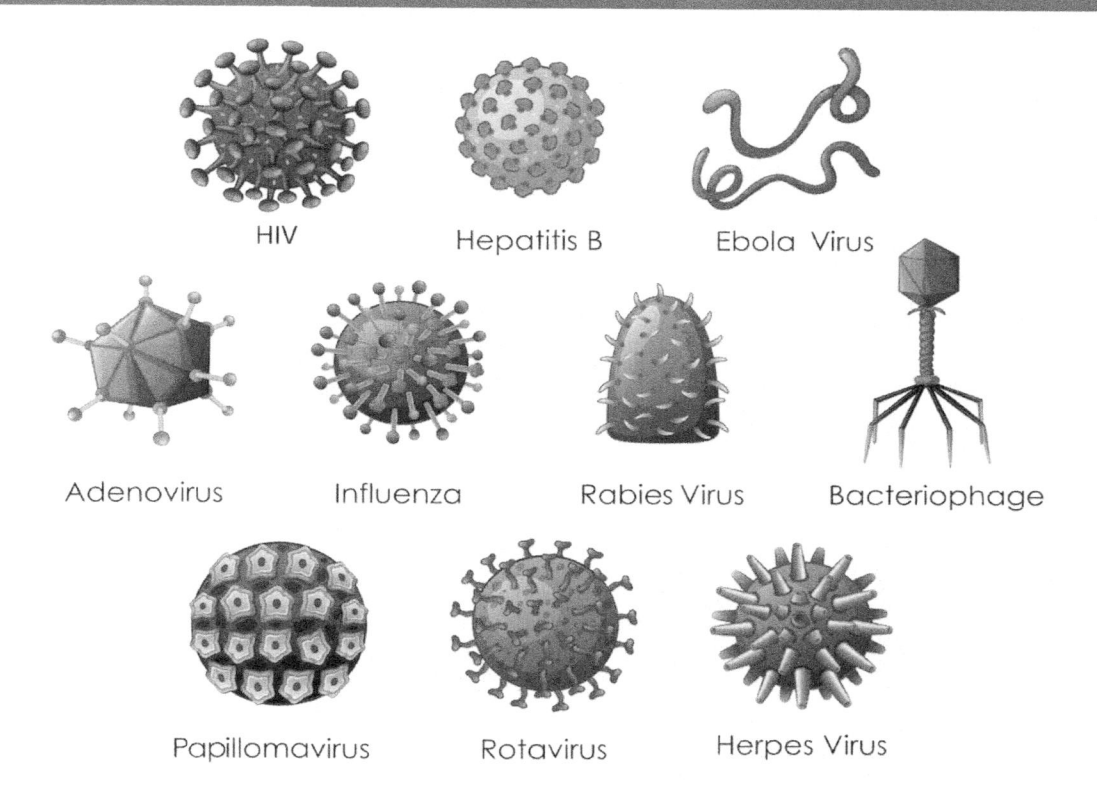

Fungal Infections

Fungal infections are caused by a fungus coming into contact with the skin or entering into the body via means such as inhalation. Certain fungi thrive in specific environments that are dark, warm, and humid. Examples of these include athlete's foot and jock itch. Other fungi may attach to dead tissues, such as the nails or skin. Examples of these include ringworm and onychomycosis.

Common forms of fungi that result in infection include candidiasis, aspergillosis, sporothrix, talaromyces, and histoplasma. These fungi can be found in various parts of the world, and can affect people differently depending on the strength of their immune system. Some fungi thrive in extremely moist environments, while other fungi may not need as much moisture to grow.

Fungal infections are treated with medications known as antifungals, which are designed to destroy fungus. These can be used directly on the skin as ointments or shampoos, orally in gel or liquid form, or inserted into a part of the body such as the vagina in cases such as yeast infections. Serious fungal infections may need to be treated with antifungals injected into the body.

Parasitic Infections

Parasitic infections are caused by small organisms that use a host in order to survive. These parasites may affect their host in some way, or they may not, depending on the type of parasite. The three types of parasites are protozoa, helminths, and ectoparasites.

Protozoa are single-celled organisms, and they live inside the host's body, multiplying beyond safe levels. A protozoa infection is considered serious, most commonly the result of drinking water that may contain the parasite.

Helminths are also known as **worms**, such as tapeworms, flukes, and roundworms. Worms most commonly enter the host's body through consuming a food or drink that contains the worm or worm larvae.

Ectoparasites are parasites that attach to the surface of the host, often feeding off the blood of the host to survive. Examples include mosquitoes, leeches, and ticks.

Some parasitic infections do not require treatment. If symptoms or infection appears, treatment should be sought. Common parasitic infection treatments include anti-parasitic medications used to destroy any parasites, and removal of the parasite if medication does not work.

HELMINTHS

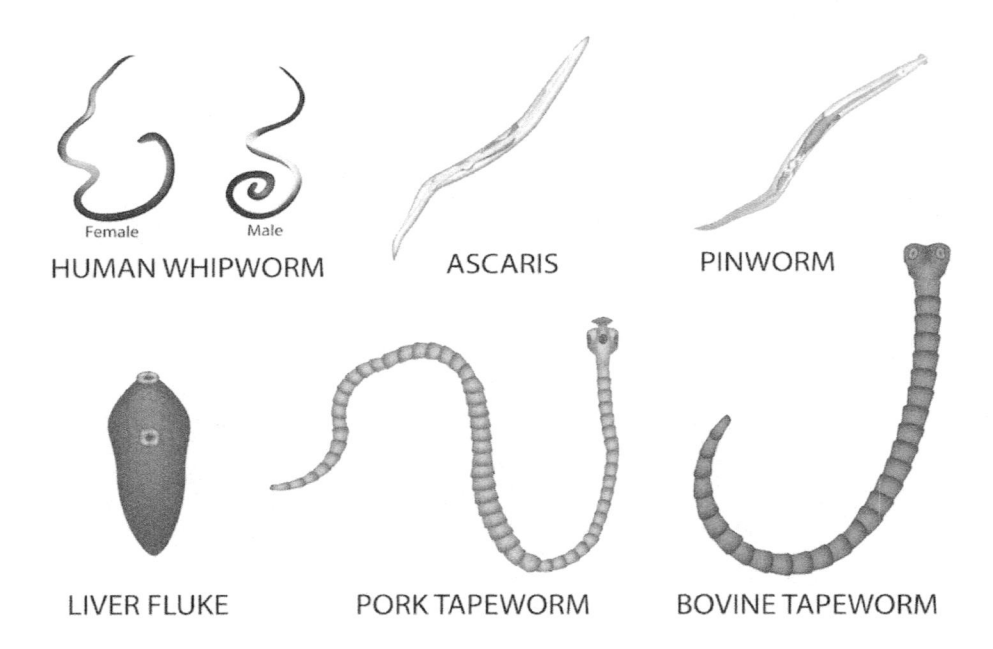

HUMAN WHIPWORM (Female, Male) ASCARIS PINWORM

LIVER FLUKE PORK TAPEWORM BOVINE TAPEWORM

Psychological Diseases

Psychological diseases, often referred to as **mental disorders**, are often associated with problems a person may experience with their mood or thoughts. Causes are hard to pin-point, and may vary from person to person. These mental disorders can have an extremely adverse affect on the overall well-being of the person. Treatment via medications and psychotherapy may be available.

Mental disorders commonly seen in children include autism, ADHD(Attention Deficit/Hyperactivity Disorder), attachment disorder, and stuttering. Disorders commonly seen in adults may include addiction, depression, bipolar disorder, eating disorders, PTSD, and panic disorder.

Personality disorders are disorders that may influence how a person acts or responds to certain situations. Examples of personality disorders include Antisocial Personality Disorder, Dissociative Identity Disorder, and Obsessive-Compulsive Personality Disorder.

Immunity

Immunity refers to the ability of the body to protect itself from disease and pathogens. Immunity is the responsibility of the **immune system**, which destroys foreign objects that enter the body that may produce infection or disease. The process through which these substances are destroyed is known as the **immune response**.

The **humoral immune system** is the part of the immune system that takes place in the body's **fluids**, known as the **humors**. This results in the production of **antibodies** when a foreign substance is observed in the body. Antibodies react by neutralizing the pathogen, or allowing the pathogen to be destroyed easier by other cells.

T-cell activation

The **cell-mediated immune system** involves **T lymphocytes**, also known as **T cells**. These cells vary in type, depending on the kind of pathogen involved. The T lymphocytes are responsible for **destroying** the pathogen, and do not utilize antibodies. Types of T cells include effector, helper, cytotoxic, natural killer, memory, and regulatory, each responsible for a different aspect of immune support.

B-cell activation

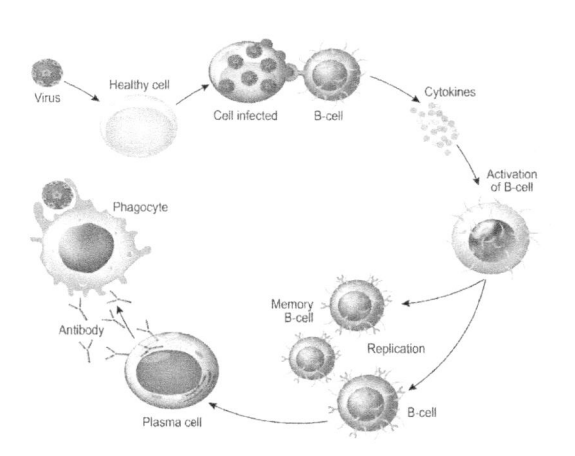

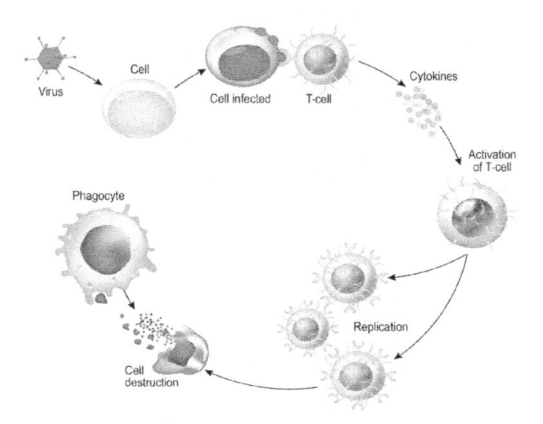

When a pathogen is detected in the body, a B cell or T cell will bind to the pathogen, and release **cytokines**. Cytokines are proteins responsible for allowing **communication between cells**. Cytokines will send a message to the immune system, which will then bring more B cells or T cells into the area to combat the pathogen.

Phagocytes

Phagocytes, which are certain types of white blood cells, are responsible for "**eating**" pathogens or debris in a process known as **phagocytosis**. Debris can include foreign objects or substances that have entered the body, or dead or dying cells that need to be removed from the body. An example is the fading of tattoos. Over time, tattoo ink is broken down by the body's phagocytes, because the body senses it is a foreign substance that should not be present. When enough ink is broken down by phagocytes, the tattoo fades. Laser tattoo removal works by breaking the ink into smaller pieces, which the phagocytes can then absorb and eliminate from the body easier.

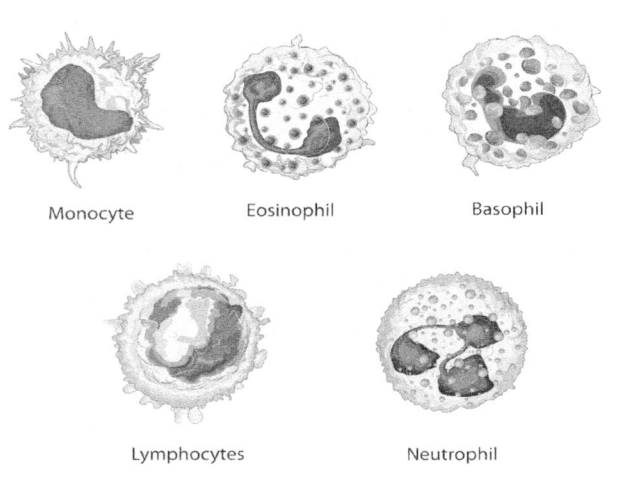

White Blood Cells

Monocyte Eosinophil Basophil

Lymphocytes Neutrophil

Examples of phagocytes include neutrophils, monocytes, macrophages, and dendritic cells. Neutrophils are typically the first phagocyte into the area. **Neutrophils** release enzymes that **destroy bacteria**, and perform phagocytosis. **Monocytes** move from the blood into the area, where they are then known as **macrophages**. Much like neutrophils, they perform **phagocytosis** to eliminate the debris or infection. **Dendritic cells** are located on **surfaces** of the body such as the skin and gastrointestinal tract. Dendritic cells act by performing phagocytosis on a pathogen to retrieve its specific **antigen**. Once this information has been obtained, it is **passed on** to T cells via cytokines produced by the dendritic cells.

Phagocytosis

Phagocytosis is the process of a cell "**eating**" an object or substance, a process known as **endocytosis**. The phagocyte envelops the debris or pathogen in a vesicle known as a **phagosome**. A phagosome is produced when the cell wraps the cell membrane around the structure and the cell membrane fuses together. The phagosome is introduced into the cell, holding the substance, where the substance is broken down by granules that produce toxic or acidic matter to dissolve the substances. Once the substance has been destroyed, the waste is removed from the cell in a process that is essentially the opposite of bringing the substance into the cell. The phagosome fuses back with the cell membrane, and the waste product is expelled into the extracellular fluid. This process is known as **exocytosis**.

Antibodies

An **antibody**, also known as **immunoglobulin**, is a protein produced by **plasma cells** to neutralize pathogens in the body such as viruses and certain bacteria. Antibodies are **Y shaped**. The tips of the antibodies that produce the Y shape contain what's known as a **paratope**, which binds together with the **epitope**, the substance found in antigens that the body's immune system recognizes. **Antigens** are molecules the pathogen contains that the antibodies recognize and attach to, similar to a key fitting into a lock.

Antibodies are produced and secreted by **B cells**, in two different forms. The first form is **soluble** and moves freely throughout the body. These types of B cells are known as **plasma cells**. The second is a **membrane-bound form**, and it attaches to the surface of B cells. These types are known as **B cell receptors**. B cell receptors bind to the surface of B cells and are able to quickly identify pathogens seen before in the body. This allows the B cells to produce sufficient antibodies to attack the pathogen with a faster response time.

Antibodies vary depending on the type of pathogen detected. For each different pathogen, a different type of antibody is produced. The amount of pathogens exposed to the body determines the amount of different antibodies being produced. If a person has been exposed to the pathogen before, **memory cells** may be produced, which **store information** on how the immune system is to destroy the pathogen. It is when this happens that a person is considered **immune** to a certain disease.

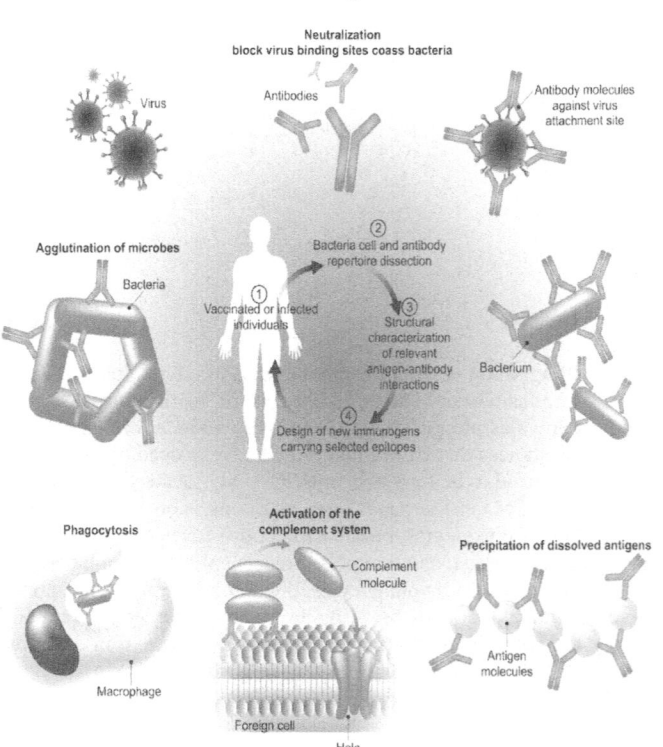

Tissue Repair

When a part of the body is injured or damaged, the damaged tissue must go through repair to allow proper functioning of the structure once again. The amount of repair correlates to the amount of tissue damage that has occurred. Some tissue may not be able to be repaired effectively, and may require scar tissue to complete the repair.

Inflammation

Upon damage to tissue, the tissue will experience **inflammation**. Inflammation starts with **dilation** of **capillaries** in the area of the trauma. Damaged tissues release **histamines** into the area, which stimulates the capillaries to dilate. When the capillaries dilate, the walls of the capillaries become thinner and more **permeable**. This allows **leukocytes** and **plasma** from the blood to enter the extracellular fluid in the damaged area, which is what produces inflammation. Because there is an increase in blood in the area, the inflamed area will feel **warmer** to the touch, and have a **reddish** appearance. The leukocytes release chemicals into the area, such as bradykinin, which causes **pain** by stimulating the nerve endings in the area. The four markers of inflammation are **pain**, **swelling**, **redness**, and **heat**.

As more leukocytes enter the area, they destroy any tissue that is damaged and any foreign objects or organisms that are present. Once the area is clear of damaged tissue and other organisms, the inflammation resolves. The capillary walls constrict, and the excess fluid in the area is removed through **lymphatic ducts**. As the blood and fluid is removed from the area, the swelling, redness, and heat subside.

Healing

Most tissue in the body can regenerate and create more tissue to replace any damaged tissue. Some tissue, such as nerve tissue and brain tissue, usually cannot. If a large portion of the body has experienced damage, the tissue may need to be removed to prevent the area from becoming gangrenous.

If a person has suffered a wound(page 145), and the damaged areas are close together, the body will heal itself through a process known as **primary intention**. Examples of wounds that are healed via primary intention are small cuts, scratches, and surgical incisions. These wounds allow for **blood clots** to form that hold the tissues together and stop bleeding. Beneath the clot, which is known as a **scab**, new tissue is formed, and the two sides of the wound join together. Once the new tissue is formed, the scab sloughs off, revealing the new tissue.

If a person suffers a wound that requires healing via **secondary intention**, the edges of the wound cannot be approximated. The edges are uneven, do not properly align, and may be far apart. This type of healing requires **granulated tissue** to form at the base and sides of the wound. As the healing progresses, the granulated tissue fills in the area missing tissue. This type of healing often takes far longer than primary intention healing, and will leave the area with scar tissue to help fill the damaged area. An example of secondary intention healing is seen with decubitus ulcers(page 137).

When a person experiences a wound that requires medical intervention, delayed primary closure may be utilized. With delayed primary closure, the **wound** is **left open** to ensure it is properly cleaned and free of bacteria or other pathogens before being closed. This is also known as **tertiary intention healing**. Once it is determined that there is no infection present, the wound is then surgically closed. An example of wounds that often require tertiary intention healing is animal bites(page 198).

Bone Healing

Damage to bones, such as fractures(page 170), requires the use of **osteoclasts** and **osteoblasts** to help repair the structure. These cells continuously maintain the bone matrix, but if the bone is injured, they are the primary cells responsible for healing. After a bone is fractured, **osteoclasts** will begin **breaking down** the damaged bone tissue. This leaves the bone with a clean surface in which to build new bone tissue. It is similar to demolishing a building and erecting another building in its place. The rubble from the demolished building needs to be removed before another building can be constructed.

After the damaged surface has been cleared by the osteoclasts, **osteoblasts** begin forming **new bone matrix** to replace the matrix that has been lost. The material produced by osteoblasts is known as **callus**, and it binds the two sides of the fracture together, similar to scar tissue in the skin. The bone will absorb the callus, and the callus is then replaced by bone tissue. These cells are known as **osteocytes**. The bone is then remodeled into essentially its original shape, and osteoblasts stop producing osteocytes to replace the damaged bone.

Scar

A scar, also known as **cicatrix**, is a fibrous tissue formed to help a wound heal. Scar tissue acts as a bandage, holding the damaged tissue together when it cannot be effectively replaced on its own. Scarring depends on the size, location, and depth of the wound suffered. Other factors that may play a role in scar development is a person's age, genes, and overall health of the person and the part of the body involved.

Different types of scars include acne scars, keloid scars, contracture scars, and hypertrophic scars.

Acne scars may occur in a person with severe acne. These scars can leave **deep pits** in the skin, usually the result of a follicle wall being broken by an excessive accumulation of oil, bacteria, or fluid.

Keloid scars are more commonly seen in people with darker skin tone. These scars are the result of over-healing in the area. Keloid scars are often **raised** off the skin, extending beyond the area of damage. If large enough, these may be uncomfortable, cause pain, or reduce movement.

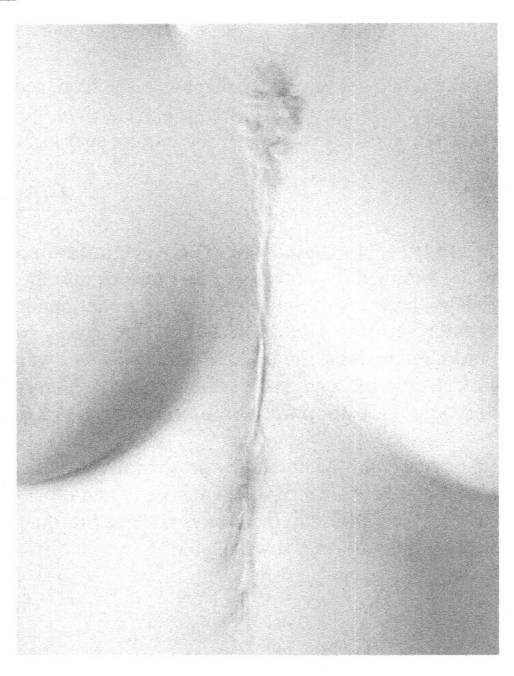

Contracture scars are usually seen in people who have suffered **burns**. These scars are spread out, and may extend deeper into the skin and affect muscles and nerves. The larger the burn, the more likely it is contracture scars may affect the ability to move certain parts of the body, depending on the location. If a person develops a contracture scar early in life, the scar may become mixed with healthy tissue.

Hypertrophic scars are similar to keloid scars, but they do not extend past the area of damage. These scars often appear **red**, and may be tender or painful. Hypertrophic scars are the result of a **collagen imbalance** at the site of injury, which does not allow the scar to form properly. **Excessive tension** on the area may also lead to the development of hypertrophic scars.

Striae, also known as **stretch marks**, are scars that form in the skin when the body experiences a **rapid growth**, such as during pregnancy, puberty, or during activities such as weight lifting. These scars generally have a different color than the surrounding skin. As the area grows, the skin is stretched and pulled apart. In response, the skin develops fibrous tissue to hold the expanding area together, which produces scarring.

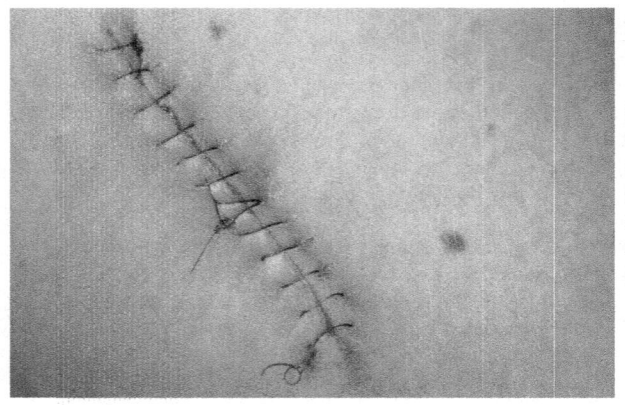

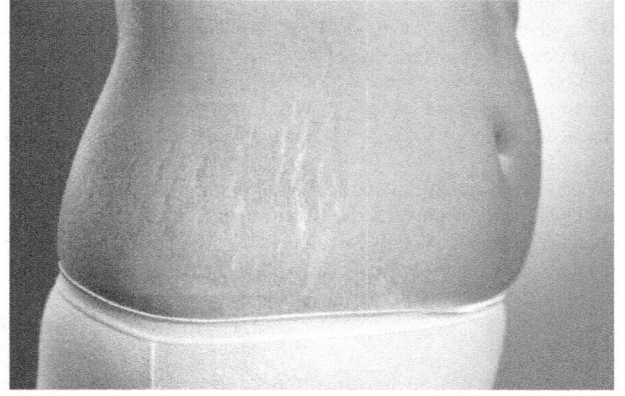

Sutures are used to **close wounds** produced through damage to tissues or surgery. Suturing a wound closed allows the damaged tissue to join together and produce a scar. There are many types of sutures, but all are either absorbable or non-absorbable. Absorbable sutures will be absorbed by the body and will not require surgical removal, while non-absorbable sutures require a doctor to surgically remove them.

Medications

There are many different types of medications used to treat many types of illnesses, diseases, and infections. Among the most common are:

Analgesics, which help to **relieve pain**. Examples include acetaminophen and non-steroidal anti-inflammatory drugs. These help treat symptoms of conditions that cause pain, such as cancer.

Antacids, which reduce the activity of **acids** in the stomach. These help treat conditions such as Gastroesophageal Reflux Disease.

Antibiotics, which are used to combat **bacterial** growth. Examples include penicillin, amoxicillin, and erythromycin. These are used to treat infections in the body, such as cellulitis, impetigo, and strep throat.

Anticoagulants, which are used to reduce the formation of **blood clots**. Examples include aspirin, heparin, and warfarin. These are used to treat conditions such as deep vein thrombosis and phlebitis.

Antidepressants, which are used to **combat depression**. Common forms include selective serotonin reuptake inhibitors(SSRIs), serotonin and norepinephrine reuptake inhibitors(SNRIs), and tricyclic antidepressants.

Antidotes, which are used to counteract the effects of **poison** on the body. These are used when too much of a substance has entered the body that can result in harmful, or even fatal effects.

Antifungals, which aid in destroying **fungus**. Examples include terbinafine and fluconazole. These are used to treat any type of fungal infection, such as Tinea Pedis(Athlete's Foot) or Tinea Capitis.

Antihistamines, which reduce the effects of **histamines** on the body, including runny nose and itching. These are used to treat allergic reactions.

Anti-inflammatory agents, which help to reduce **inflammation**. Examples include non-steroidal anti-inflammatory drugs such as ibuprofen. These are used to help treat inflammation in conditions such as bronchitis, and potentially Alzheimer's Disease.

Antipyretics, which help to reduce **fever**. Examples include ibuprofen and aspirin. These are used to treat symptoms of fever and other systemic infections.

Antivirals, which aid in preventing **virus** reproduction. Examples include amantadine and rimantadine. These are used to combat virus reproduction in conditions such as encephalitis.

Beta blockers, which help to reduce **blood pressure**. Examples include acebutolol, nadolol, and nebivolol. These are used to treat conditions such as hypertension, arrhythmia, and myocardial infarction.

Bronchodilators, which aid in **dilation** of the **bronchial tubes**. Examples include albuterol and salmeterol. These are used to treat conditions such as asthma and bronchitis.

Decongestants, which reduce **inflammation** in the **nasal cavity**. Examples include pseudoephedrine and phenylephrine. These are used to treat congestion caused by allergies.

Diuretics, which increase the production of **urine**. Examples include bumetanide, amiloride, and mannitol. These are used to treat conditions such as edema and hypertension.

Expectorants, which are used to help a person **expectorate**, or cough/spit mucous from the lungs. Common forms include over-the-counter brand names such as Mucinex and Robitussin. These are commonly used to treat chest congestion.

General anesthetics, which are used to **numb** the **entire body**. Examples include propofol, ketamine, and etomidate. General anesthetics are primarily used when a person is having surgery performed that requires them to be in an unconscious state. These can be administered via needle injection or may be inhaled.

Insulin, which **lowers** the amount of **sugar** in the blood stream. Insulin is primarily used to treat diabetes.

Laxatives, also known as stool softeners, which are used to help **loosen** and eliminate **feces** from the digestive tract. Common forms include mineral oil and milk of magnesia. These are used to treat constipation.

Local anesthetics, which are used to **numb** an area. They are most commonly administered via **needle injection**. Examples include lidocaine and nitracaine. These are typically used before performing a surgical procedure around the area of incision.

Sedatives, which are used to **calm** and **relax** the body. Examples include diazepam and clonazepam. These are typically used to calm a person before a painful or uncomfortable procedure is performed, such as a colonoscopy.

Statins, which aid in **lowering cholesterol** levels in the blood stream. Examples include atorvastatin, rosuvastatin, and lovastatin. These are used to treat and/or prevent heart disease and its various symptoms, including **hypertension** and stroke.

Steroids, which are primarily used to combat **inflammation** in specific areas. Common forms include corticosteroids and anabolic steroids. Corticosteroids are useful in treating conditions such as asthma, arthritis, and lupus.

Suppositories, which are used in cases where a person may have difficulty orally consuming a medication. The most common type of suppository is a rectal suppository, but vaginal and urethral suppositories are also used. Suppositories are often used to treat constipation, hemorrhoids, fever, bacterial infections, and fungal infections.

Vaccines, which are used to **prevent** a contagious disease from developing in a person. Common vaccines include MMR(Measles-Mumps-Rubella), DTaP(Diphtheria, Tetanus, and Pertussis), influenza, and human papilloma virus. Vaccines are commonly administered via intramuscular needle injection.

Medical Tests, Equipment, and Procedures

AED(Automated External Defibrillator): An AED is a portable defibrillator, used to send electric shocks to the heart in a person who is suffering from sudden cardiac arrest. The person will have two sticky pads attached to their skin that connect to the AED, one pad placed on the chest and one on the left side of the trunk. The AED sends a shock to the person through the pads, directly into the heart, which can help return the heart to its normal rhythm.

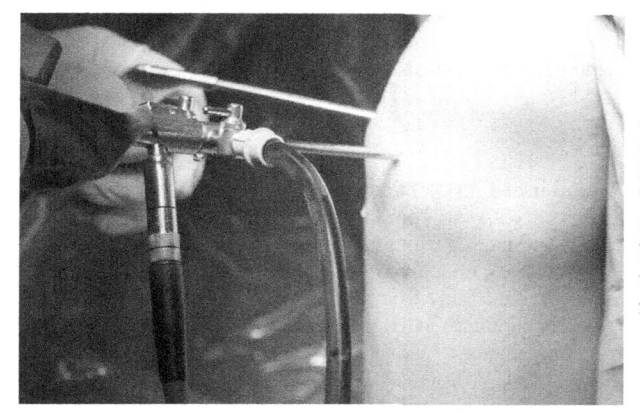

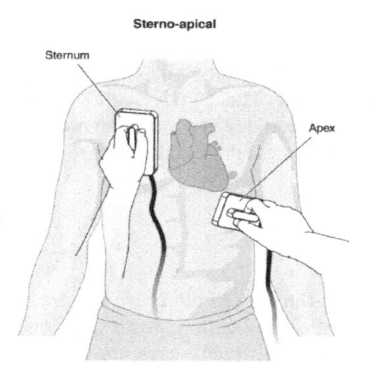

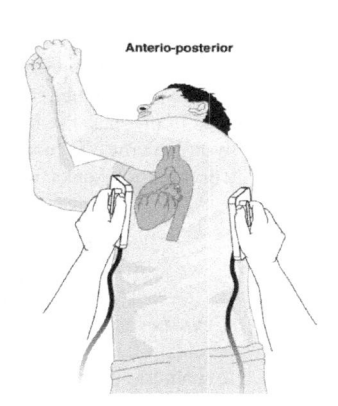

Arthroscopy: Arthroscopy is used to view the inner structures of a joint. It is performed by making a small incision, and inserting a tube with a camera attached directly into the joint. This allows a view of any structural damage that may occur, such as torn ligaments. If surgery is being performed, it may be performed arthroscopically, where all the instruments being used are inserted into the joint through small holes, without making a large incision.

Bone Graft: A bone graft, similar to a skin graft, is the removal of a small amount of bone tissue from one part of the body, placing the removed tissue on another bone that may be lacking in sufficient tissue. This can be done if part of a bone is removed during surgery, or in cases such as joint replacements to help the new structures anchor in to the bone more securely. The new bone sets, and the area where the graft is located becomes stronger.

Catheter: A catheter is a small tube inserted in to a part of the body to help fluid drain. The most common form is a urinary catheter. These are inserted into the urethra and into the urinary bladder. From there, fluid is able to drain freely from the bladder.

Centrifuge: A centrifuge is a medical device used to separate solids from liquids. This is especially useful in separating plasma from the blood cells in blood. Centrifuges accomplish this by spinning in circles extremely fast, forcing the solids in a substance to move to the bottom of the vial, and the liquids move to the top.

Chemotherapy: Chemotherapy is the use of certain chemicals to destroy cancerous cells and tumors in the body. Chemotherapy may be administered at different times and different ways, depending on the cause of the cancer. It may be used to destroy some cancer cells and shrink a tumor to aid with pain relief, or to make surgery on the tumor more successful. After a tumor is removed, chemotherapy may be used to destroy any remaining cancerous cells in the body and prevent it from recurring or spreading elsewhere. Chemotherapy is usually given intravenously, but may also be given orally or topically.

Compression Devices: Compression devices are used to mimic the Lymphatic System, and rhythmically compress the legs to increase the flow of lymph. This can decrease lymphedema. Typical compression devices may also include compression socks, and cuffs that wrap around the legs.

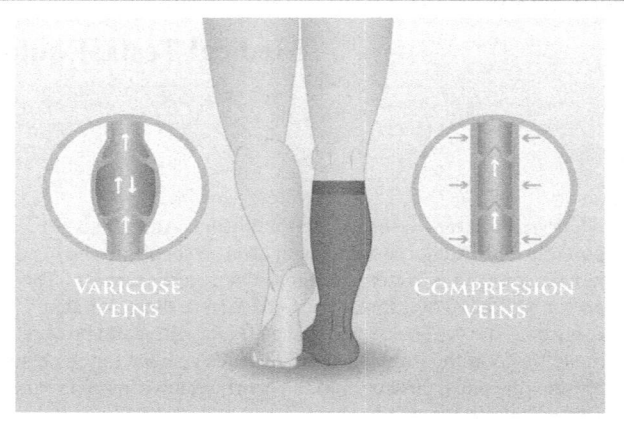

Cryotherapy: Cryotherapy is the use of cold or ice in a treatment. Cryotherapy can be used to reduce inflammation, increase circulation after a short period of application, destroy tissues such as warts, or even destroy nerves that may be causing pain. Cryotherapy can be applied many different ways, from the use of cold packs, to ice baths.

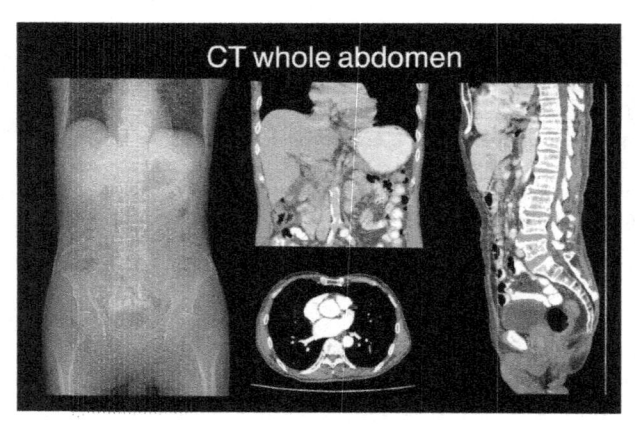

Computerized Axial Tomography(CT/CAT Scan): Computerized Axial Tomography, also known as CT or CAT Scan, is an imaging technique in which a snapshot is taken of a part of the body on a given body plane. This allows viewing of structures in the body from differing points of view. CT is extremely similar to MRI, but uses X-ray to produce images instead of magnetic fields.

Dialysis: Dialysis is used when the kidneys are no longer able to properly function and filter waste products from the blood. Dialysis is meant to mimic the kidneys, pulling waste from the blood and filtering blood back into the body. There are two types of dialysis: hemodialysis and peritoneal dialysis. Hemodialysis is performed by drawing blood from the body, which is cycled through a machine. The dialysis machine contains a permeable membrane that filters the blood, known as a dialyzer. When the waste from the blood has been filtered, the blood is returned to the body. Peritoneal dialysis is performed by administering a catheter into the peritoneum. Dialysate, a fluid, is placed in the body, and it's this fluid that draws waste from the blood. The peritoneum acts as the filter. The waste is removed from the body, and blood never leaves the body like it does with hemodialysis.

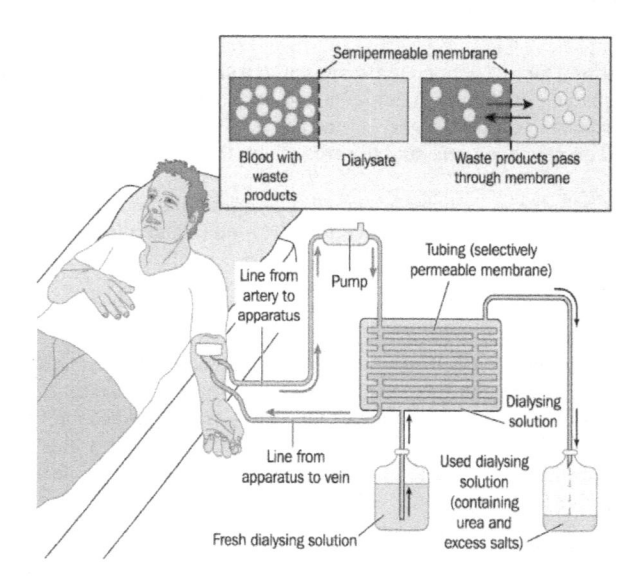

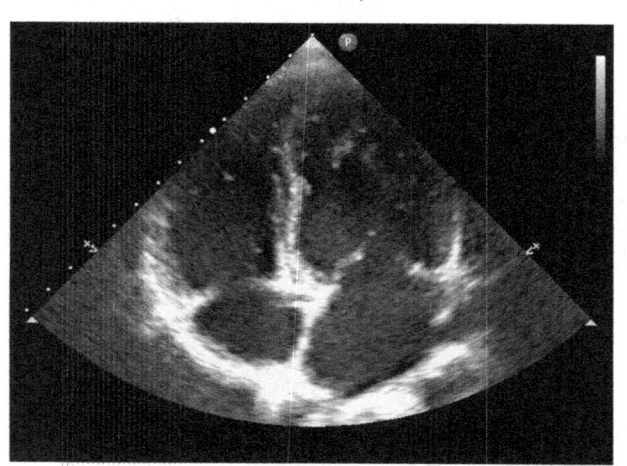

Echocardiogram: An echocardiogram is a type of ultrasound performed on the heart in order to view all the structures and chambers of the heart. This can be used to determine if there are any issues with the heart, such as valve defects, how strong the heart muscle is, or if there are any abnormal holes in the heart.

Electrocardiogram(ECG/EKG): If a doctor feels as if a patient needs to have their heart rhythm monitored, they may administer and ECG/EKG. During this procedure, ten pads attached to electrodes are attached to the patient's bare skin on specific points around the trunk. The ECG/EKG picks up the electrical activity of the heart, and produces a visualization that shows each wave of electrical activity. The first wave seen is known as the P wave, and shows the contraction of the atria. Next is the QRS wave, which shows the depolarization and contraction of the ventricles. Following that is the T wave, which represents re-polarization of the ventricles.

In some cases, a person may need to have heart activity recorded over 24-48 hours. In these cases, a Holter Monitor is used. These are portable machines that remain attached to a patient, continuously recording heart activity. These can be used if a person has irregular heart rhythms that come and go, and aren't present during an initial ECG reading.

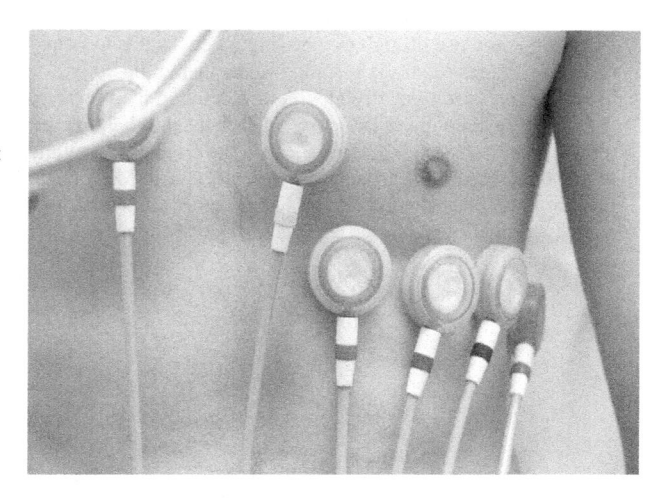

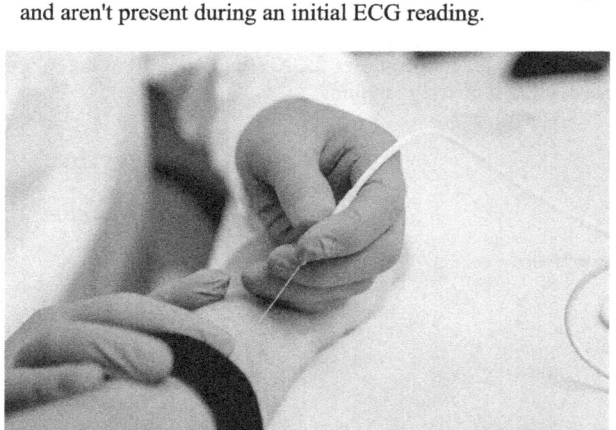

Electromyography(EMG): Electromyography is a test used to detect the proper functioning of muscles and the nerves that innervate the muscles. This is done to assess any nerve or muscle damage that may be present, or if communication between the nerve and muscle has been impaired. Electromyography is performed by several different means. A needle may be placed directly into the muscle to read electrical activity. Adhesive pads may be placed on the skin above the muscle to detect nervous conduction as well.

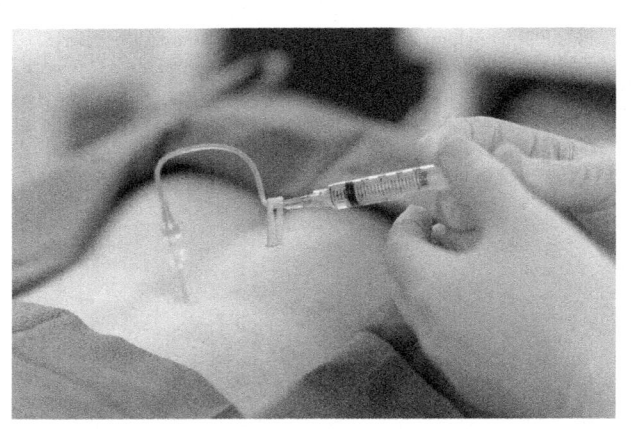

Epidural: An epidural is a medical procedure used to block pain and sensation in the lower body. It is performed by injecting analgesics and anesthetics around the spinal cord in the lumbar region. The medications are delivered via a catheter inserted into the site of injection. Epidurals are commonly used during labor to eliminate pain associated with child birth.

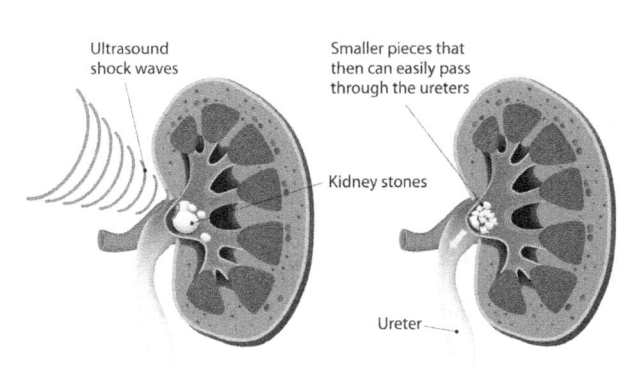

LITHOTRIPSY

Lithotripsy: Lithotripsy is the use of sound waves administered via ultrasound to break up or destroy deposits building up in the body, such as kidney stones and gallstones. Lithotripsy is typically only performed if one of these deposits is too large to pass from the body on its own. The sound waves produced break up the deposit, and allow it to be passed normally. These sound waves are produced by a machine known as a lithotripter.

Magnetic Resonance Imaging(MRI): Magnetic Resonance Imaging is the use of high powered magnetic fields to help produce images of structures and organs inside the body. These images are typically much more detailed than X-rays, especially when viewing organs. MRI is used to help diagnose conditions such as tumors, issues with the Digestive System, and issues with the heart and blood vessels. The MRI machine is a large tube in which a person lies for an extended period of time, which allows a thorough image to be produced.

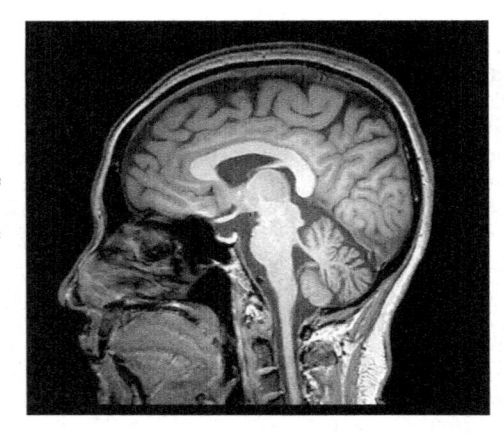

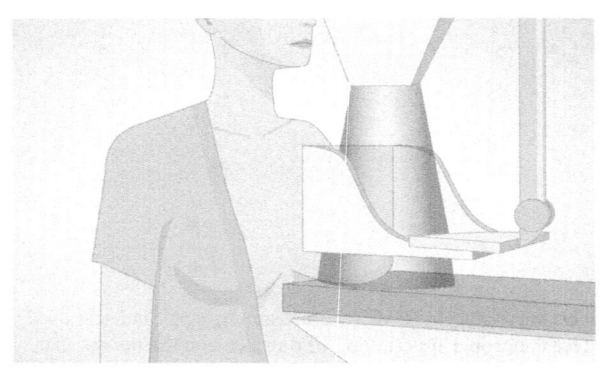

Mammogram: A mammogram is a procedure used to detect breast cancer in patients who are not showing any symptoms. It uses an X-ray to view the internal breast tissue. A mammogram is typically performed by placing the breast between two glass plates that compress the tissue. Compressing the tissue allows the X-ray to view all of the breast without missing anything.

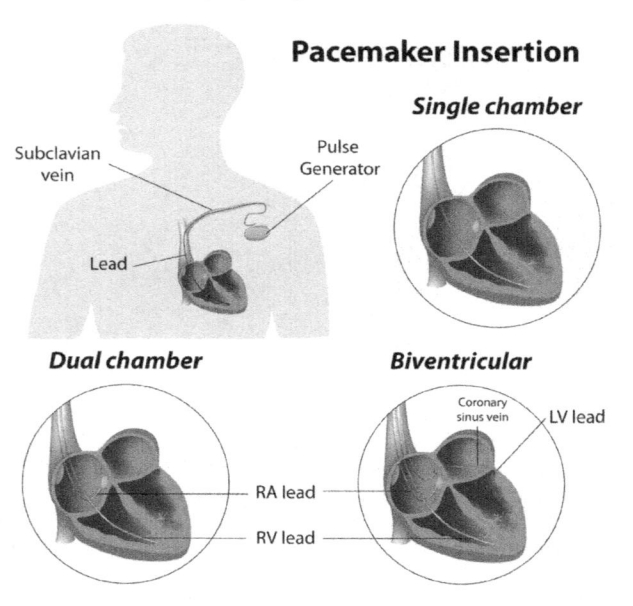

Pacemaker: If a patient suffers from severe arrhythmia, a pacemaker may be implanted into the body to help regulate heart rhythm. The pacemaker is usually placed under the skin on the upper left side of the chest, just inferior to the clavicle. A pacemaker is a small metal device with a battery inside that sends electric shocks to the heart when it detects the heart rhythm is not functioning properly. It accomplishes this with the use of leads that travel through the superior vena cava directly into the heart. The leads go into the atrium, ventricle, or both, depending on the type of arrhythmia a person has. The battery in a pacemaker typically lasts between five and ten years, and can be replaced.

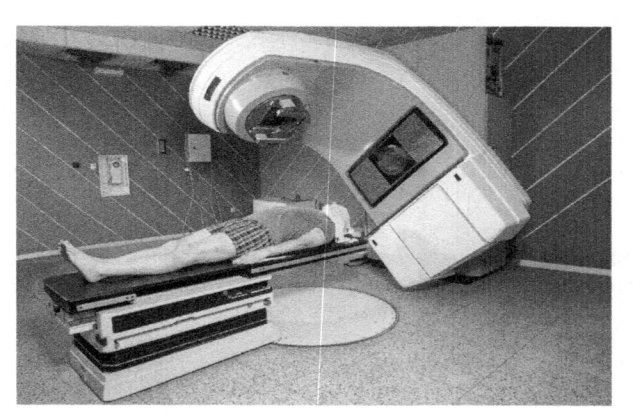

Radiation Therapy: Radiation therapy is a type of treatment used to destroy cancerous tissue. It is performed by exposing the affected portion of the body to a highly concentrated beam of radiation. The machine responsible for administering the radiation is pointed directly at the spot to be treated, and uses X-rays to destroy cancerous cells. It may also destroy healthy tissue, however. Radiation therapy may also be used to make tumors smaller and prevent a tumor from growing or spreading before surgery may be performed.

Skin Graft: A skin graft is transplanting skin from one location on the body to another where skin has been lost, commonly from burns or injuries. A thin layer of epidermis is removed using a shaver(similar to a potato peeler), then placed on the area where skin is needed. The area is covered in bandages to allow healing. Over time, the skin adheres to the injured area and becomes new skin for the area.

Sphygmomanometer: When measuring blood pressure, a sphygmomanometer is wrapped around a person's arm. The cuff around the arm inflates, and the pressure of the blood passing through the arteries can be felt. The sphygmomanometer produces two numbers: the systolic number and diastolic number. The systolic number reads systolic pressure, which is the pressure felt as blood is pumped from the heart and passes through the arteries. The diastolic number reads diastolic pressure, which is the pressure felt when the heart is at rest and blood is not passing through that portion of the arteries at that time. A normal blood pressure is 120/80 mmHg, in which the systolic pressure is 120 mmHg, and the diastolic pressure is 80 mmHg.

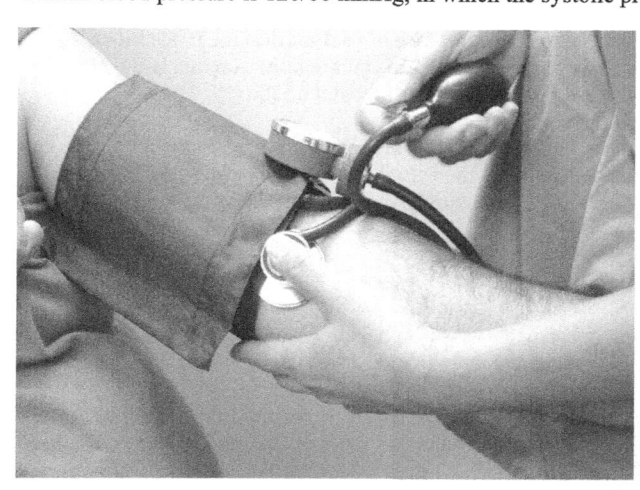

Ultrasound: An ultrasound, also known as sonography, is an imaging technique utilizing sound waves to produce pictures of structures inside the body. Commonly, ultrasound is used to view the development of a fetus during pregnancy, but may also be used to examine infections inside the body, liver and gallbladder function, and heart conditions. The part of the machine that is used to perform the scanning is known as the transducer.

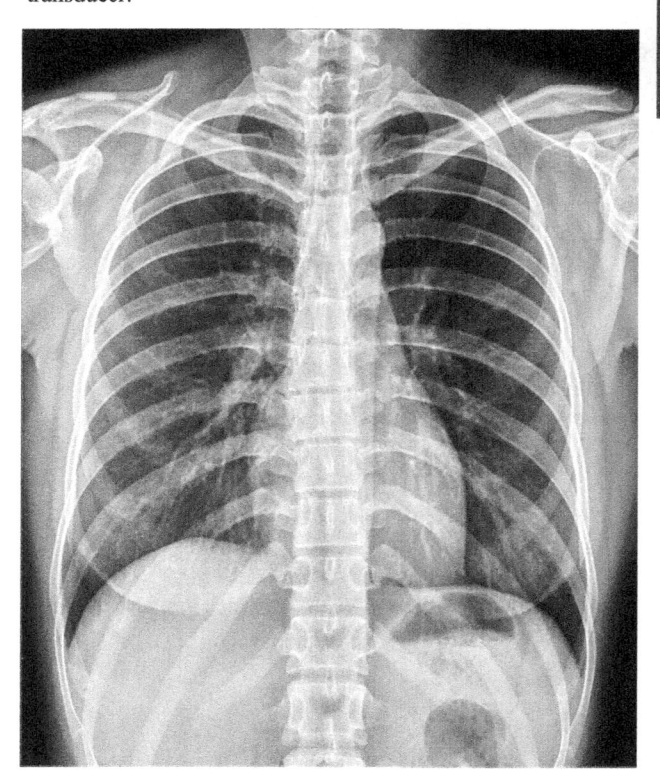

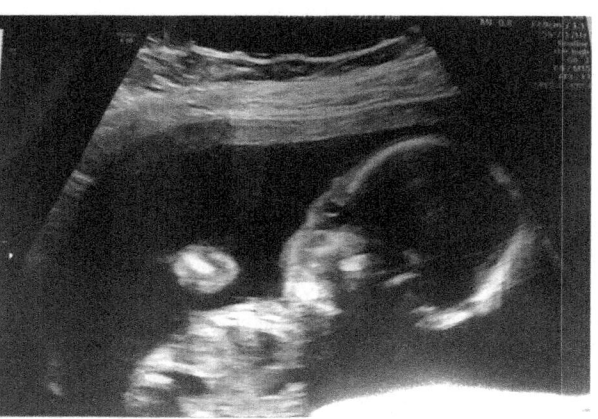

X-Ray: An X-ray is an imaging technique using radiation to view structures that light typically does not pass through. Structures most commonly seen using X-rays are bones and metals. X-rays allow visual examination of structures that may be broken, damaged, or infected.

Cardiovascular System Pathologies

Anemia
(an-: without; -emia: blood)

Anemia is a disease of the blood, resulting in a **lack of oxygen** and an **over-abundance of carbon dioxide** in the blood. There are many different types of anemia, ranging from **iron-deficient anemia** to **sickle cell anemia**. Anemia is the most common blood condition in the United States, with an estimated 3.5-4 million people afflicted with it.

Iron-deficient anemia is the most common form of anemia. The cells in the blood that are responsible for carrying oxygen and carbon dioxide throughout the body are the erythrocytes, or red blood cells. In the cytoplasm of erythrocytes, there is a protein present known as hemoglobin, which is made of iron. The hemoglobin attracts oxygen and carbon dioxide, allowing these molecules to attach to the erythrocytes.

Causes

In iron-deficient anemia, the primary cause is a lack of iron being consumed. Less iron being consumed results in less **hemoglobin** in the erythrocytes, which in turn causes a lack of oxygen and carbon dioxide attaching to the red blood cells.

Sickle cell anemia is an inherited form of anemia, in which the erythrocytes have a sickle shape, as opposed to a normal erythrocyte, which is circular. This shape can cause the erythrocytes to become stuck in blood vessels, and reduce adequate blood flow to tissues.

Symptoms

People with anemia may feel sluggish, tired, have an increased heart rate, may show paleness in the skin, shortness of breath, and experience dizziness, all due to a lack of sufficient oxygen reaching tissues.

Sickle cell anemia may also result in the further development of infections due to damage caused to the spleen, pain in the thorax and abdomen(known as crises) due to blockage of blood vessels in these locations, and a lack of nutrients to the body, which can stunt growth.

People whose diet lacks proper amounts of iron or vitamin B-12 may develop anemia. Pregnancy, and a lack of folic acid, may result in anemia in pregnant women. Sickle cell anemia is primarily seen in African-Americans, resulting from a genetic defect.

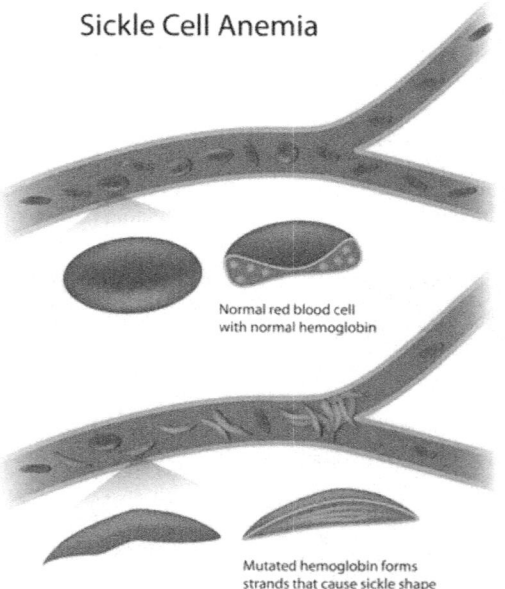

Treatments

Treatments for anemia vary depending on the type, but may include increasing iron intake, bone marrow transplants, or blood transfusions. Pregnant women may require an increased intake of folic acid. People with sickle cell anemia face less treatment options. The only potential cure is through a bone marrow transplant. Often times, the only treatment is trying to minimize the number of crises a person may experience. Antibiotics and pain relievers may help in preventing infections in younger patients and reducing pain experienced during crises.

Contraindications

Massage is indicated for a client with anemia. Massage helps increase circulation and oxygen intake, which provides the body with needed nutrients.

Aneurysm
(Greek "aneurysma": a widening)

An aneurysm is a condition of the arteries, resulting in a **bulge in the wall of an artery**. There are several different forms and causes of aneurysms. Different types of aneurysms include Aortic(bulge in the wall of the aorta), Cerebral(bulge in an artery supplying blood to the brain), and Ventricular(bulge in the wall of the heart).

Causes

Aneurysms are the result of a part of an arterial wall becoming weakened. When the wall of the artery becomes weakened, it forces the wall out, creating a pouch or bubble. Most commonly, aneurysms are the result of hypertension putting too much pressure or strain on the artery. Ventricular aneurysms are most commonly caused by myocardial infarction, which can weaken the heart muscle.

When the arterial wall stretches due to weakness, it makes it much easier for the artery to rupture. Because the artery carries oxygen-rich blood, this makes aneurysms very dangerous, as any rupture will severely cut off blood flow to the structure supplied with blood by the artery.

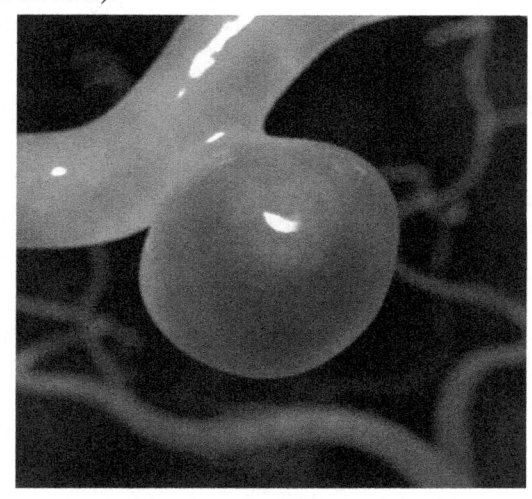

Berry aneurysm

Symptoms

Unfortunately, aneurysms that have not ruptured are asymptomatic. In fact, aneurysms themselves, unless very large, cause no symptoms at all. When an aneurysm ruptures, however, a person may experience severe chest or back pain, low blood pressure, severe headache, tachycardia, and lightheadedness.

People may develop aneurysms for many different reasons, including obesity, hypertension, diabetes, advanced age, and alcoholism. Some people develop aneurysms for no apparent reason at all.

Treatments

Common locations for aneurysms include the abdominal aorta and the brain. Aneurysms may be treated surgically before rupture to prevent major medical emergencies in the future. Beta blockers are commonly used as medications before surgery is required.

Contraindications

Massage is indicated with a doctor's note. Any massage that increases blood pressure should be avoided, such as deep tissue, because it can put pressure on arteries, which may lead to bursting of an aneurysm.

Arrhythmia
(a-: without; rhythm: rhythm)

Arrhythmia is a condition of the heart, which results in the heart's natural **rhythm being altered**. There are several different forms of arrhythmia. Some of the most common forms of arrhythmia are Atrial Fibrillation, Bradycardia, and Tachycardia.

Causes

Atrial fibrillation, the most common form of arrhythmia, results when the atria, the heart's upper chambers, contract irregularly, which sends blood into the ventricles at uncoordinated times. This is caused by an electrical signal from the SA Node not firing correctly, which disrupts the timing of the atria contracting. This can affect the ability of the heart to consistently deliver oxygenated blood to the body.

Bradycardia*(brady-: slow; -cardia: heart)* results in the heart rate being reduced to a rate of contraction that is considered too slow to deliver substantial oxygen to the body.

Tachycardia *(tachy-: rapid; -cardia: heart)* results in the heart rate being increased to a rate of contraction that is considered too rapid. In tachycardia, the ventricles of the heart are contracting too rapidly, which may cause a lack of oxygen-rich blood from reaching the body, as the quick contractions do not allow the ventricles to properly fill with blood before being pumped out to the rest of the body. Older adults, those over age 60, are more likely to develop arrhythmia than younger adults and children. Heart diseases are a main contributing factor towards older adults developing arrhythmia. Other diseases may also play a role in the development of arrhythmia, so people who have had myocardial infarction may be more prone to developing the disease. Diabetes, sleep apnea, and hypertension all have contributed to the development of arrhythmia.

Symptoms

There are many different symptoms seen with arrhythmia. Symptoms include dizziness, fatigue, shortness of breath, pain in the chest, lightheadedness, and fainting. In severe cases, arrhythmia may result in cardiac arrest.

Treatments

Treatments vary, depending on the type of arrhythmia a person suffers from. Medical devices such as pacemakers may be implanted into the body to help regulate and control heart rhythm(IE, if a person's heart rate drops too low, the pacemaker will stimulate the heart muscle and cause it to contract, increasing heart rate back to safe levels). Alternative methods to controlling arrhythmia, such as massage therapy and yoga, may be applied in some cases.

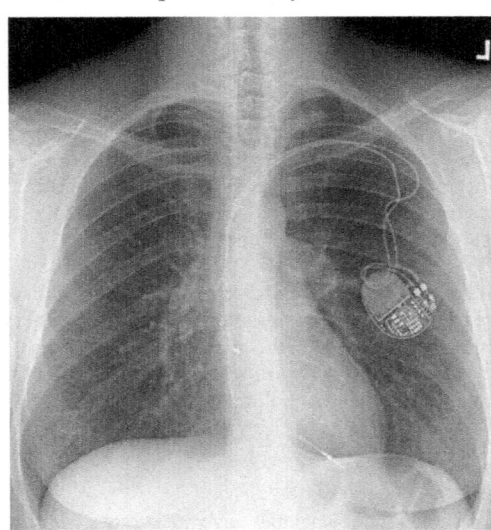

Contraindications

X-ray showing pacemaker with leads

Untreated arrhythmia is an absolute contraindication for massage therapy. If a client has a pacemaker, massage may be performed. A client may have discomfort while lying prone due to pressure on the pacemaker, which may call for side-lying massage to be performed, or pillows to be used to take pressure off the area. Avoid massaging the site of the pacemaker(upper left chest just below clavicle).

Arteriosclerosis/Atherosclerosis
(arterio: artery; scler-: hard; -osis: condition);
(athero: fatty plaque; scler-: hard; -osis: condition)

Arteriosclerosis is a **hardening of the walls of arteries**, a condition that progresses slowly over time. Atherosclerosis is a **build-up of fatty plaque** inside the arteries. These two conditions are commonly caused by one another, and are often interchangeable.

STAGES OF ATHEROSCLEROSIS

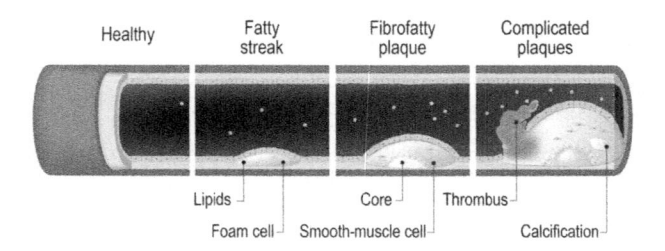

Healthy | Fatty streak | Fibrofatty plaque | Complicated plaques

Lipids | Core | Thrombus
Foam cell | Smooth-muscle cell | Calcification

Causes

Arteriosclerosis has many different contributing factors, including hypertension, high cholesterol, and smoking. Each of these can damage an artery. The body's response to this damage is to increase the thickness of the artery to prevent further damage. When this occurs, the artery becomes much harder and unable to move and stretch normally. This may also lead to increased deposits of plaque in the arteries, a condition known as atherosclerosis. This increased plaque, along with the hardening of the artery, may restrict blood flow and lead to conditions such as angina pectoris and myocardial infarction.

Symptoms

Symptoms include angina pectoris, shortness of breath, fatigue, and pain in any area of the body that may have any sort of restriction in the arteries.

Treatments

Medications are effective treatments for arteriosclerosis/atherosclerosis, including beta-blockers, statins, calcium channel blockers, and diuretics. If an increased plaque buildup is severe, an angioplasty may be performed, or a stent may be placed inside the artery to increase blood flow. Plaque may be surgically removed, or a bypass surgery may be performed to increase circulation into areas that may be experiencing ischemia.

Contraindications

Massage for atherosclerosis/arteriosclerosis may be performed. Certain medications may require a lighter massage to be performed, because they may thin the blood and damage to a blood vessel can lead to increased bleeding internally.

Deep Vein Thrombosis
(thromb/o: clot; -osis; condition)

Deep Vein Thrombosis(DVT) is a condition in which **blood clots(thrombi)** form in the **veins** deep in the body, typically the **legs**. These blood clots can **block blood flow** in the veins, which can lead to several serious issues.

Causes

There are various causes for DVT. Primary causes are injury to a vein, surgery, impaired or limited mobility, and certain medications. An injury to a vein can result in blood clots, especially if there is significant damage to the vein. Surgery, which can result in cutting through veins, can also lead to blood clots. Post-surgery, if a patient is immobilized for extended periods, circulation starts to decrease in efficiency, which can lead to blood pooling in the veins of the legs. This pooling of blood can result in clots. It is this same reason people who have paralysis may develop blood clots as well.

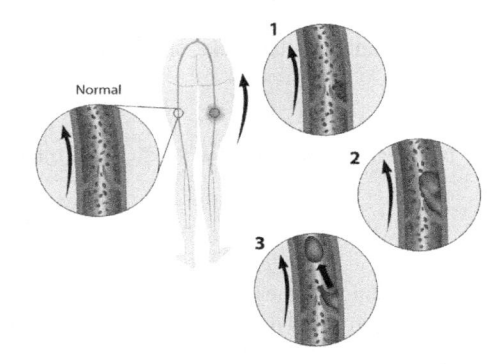

Symptoms

Although symptoms may not be present in someone with DVT, others do show symptoms, which include a warm sensation in the affected area, pain in the affected area that can increase in intensity, and discoloration in the affected area. Most commonly, DVT affects the lower limb, so this is where a person will most likely experience these symptoms.

Treatments

The primary treatment for DVT is medication. Certain medications can help reduce the chance of developing DVT in the future, or even remove the blood clot from the body. Intravenous anticoagulants such as heparin help to thin the blood. Other anticoagulants, such as warfarin, work extremely well in conjunction with injectable anticoagulants.

If the blood clot is severe, the patient might be given a thrombolytic, a type of medication that destroys blood clots. These are typically only given in serious cases of blood clots, such as those that result in pulmonary embolism.

Compression socks, which compress the leg up to the knee, can help reduce the amount of swelling a patient might experience with DVT.

Contraindications

Deep vein thrombosis is typically a local contraindication. Avoid the site of the thrombus, as dislodging the clot may lead to circulation being cut off in organs such as the lungs, brain, or heart. Massage that increases blood pressure may be contraindicated, and deeper massages may be contraindicated due to the use of anticoagulants and thrombolytics.

Heart Murmur
(murmur: to mutter)

A heart murmur is a condition of the heart, which results in **blood flowing backwards** in the heart. A "murmur" refers to the sound of blood flowing through the heart. There are two types of heart murmurs: Innocent and Abnormal. Innocent heart murmurs are seen in children and infants, usually the result of congenital heart disease. Abnormal heart murmurs are much more serious, most likely due to the development of heart disease or valve malfunction.

Causes

Heart murmurs may not require any medical attention, depending on the cause. Other times, medical attention may be needed. Most commonly, heart murmurs are the result of a **bicuspid/mitral valve** prolapse, where the valve is pulled backwards into the left atrium. This allows blood to flow backwards in the heart, which may reduce the ability of the heart to pump enough oxygen-rich blood to the body.

People who have developed endocarditis or Rheumatic fever often develop heart murmurs due to damage to the valves in the heart.

Symptoms

While most heart murmurs aren't serious, abnormal heart murmurs may present with symptoms such as cyanosis on the fingers, chest pain, dizziness, shortness of breath, and fainting.

Treatments

Heart murmurs may require the person to take anticoagulants to prevent the formation of blood clots, may be treated for hypertension if it is resulting in heart murmurs, or may need surgery to repair or replace the malfunctioning valve.

Contraindications

Massage may be performed on a client with a heart murmur.

Hypertension
(hyper-: above; -tension: tension)

Hypertension is a condition of the Cardiovascular System, resulting in **elevated blood pressure**. There are numerous factors that may contribute to the development of hypertension. For an average healthy adult, systolic blood pressure(pressure felt in arteries when the heart beats) is around 120 mmHg, and diastolic pressure(pressure felt in arteries when the heart is at rest) is around 80 mmHg. To be diagnosed with hypertension, a person's systolic pressure would be 140 mmHg and diastolic pressure would be 90 mmHg.

Causes

Hypertension may have no underlying cause, or may be the result of factors such as dysfunction of the adrenal glands or thyroid, dietary issues such as obesity or high sodium intake, kidney disease, and alcohol consumption.

Hypertension is most commonly associated with people who smoke, drink excessive amounts of alcohol, are overweight, are older in age, consume excessive salt, and more.

Symptoms

Unfortunately, hypertension is largely asymptomatic. Only in extreme cases, where the heart's blood pressure spikes extremely high, will someone experience symptoms, such as dizziness and headaches. Most symptoms people associate with hypertension are actually side effects of medications.

Treatments

Untreated, hypertension may lead to numerous serious medical conditions, such as myocardial infarction, stroke, atherosclerosis, and aneurysm. Luckily, hypertension is very easy to detect, and very treatable. Often times, treatment is as simple as making lifestyle or dietary changes, such as consuming less sodium and increasing exercise. Other times, hypertension may require the use of medications such as beta blockers, statins, and diuretics.

Contraindications

Hypertension is generally not contraindicated for massage. Massage that increases blood pressure, such as deep tissue or hot stone, may be contraindicated if the client is not taking medication to control hypertension. Light massage, which promotes lowering blood pressure, should be performed.

Migraine Headaches

Migraine Headaches are a type of headache that affect the brain, which results in most side effects experienced.

Migraines have been referred to as "**vascular headaches**", due to the involvement of **blood vessels**. In migraines, when the brain is stimulated by a trigger, neurons rapidly send impulses which affects the blood vessels surrounding the meninges, three layers of connective tissue that surround and protect the brain(page 70). At first, the blood vessels constrict, which does not result in pain. A short time after constricting, the blood vessels will dilate, which places immense pressure on the meninges, which results in severe pain.

Causes

Migraines have numerous causes, which may be from exposure to substances like tyramine(a naturally occurring chemical found in foods such as aged cheese, alcoholic beverages, and cured meats), caffeine, stress, or even hormonal imbalance during stages such as menstruation. Migraines may even be considered hereditary.

Symptoms

Symptoms include nausea, fatigue, extreme pain, loss of sight, blurred vision, sensitivity to sound, and pain on one side of the head. Not everyone that experiences a migraine experiences all of the symptoms detailed, as each migraine is different.

Treatments

If a migraine is in the beginning stages, taking pain medication such as aspirin or ibuprofen can help reduce the symptoms of mild migraines. Other medications, called triptans, can help to constrict blood vessels, which can help reduce the effects of migraines.

Preventative drugs may be taken to reduce the chances of developing a migraine in the future. These medications include beta blockers, non-steroidal anti-inflammatory drugs, and even antidepressants.

Contraindications

Migraine headaches are generally not contraindicated for massage.

Myocardial Infarction
(myo-: muscle; -cardia: heart; infarct: obstruction of blood flow)

A Myocardial Infarction, or **heart attack**, is a condition that affects the heart muscle, reducing blood flow throughout the body.

An infarction is an **obstruction of blood flow** to a specific part of the body. In this case, blood flow to the heart is obstructed. The two arteries that supply blood to the heart muscle are known as the **coronary arteries**. When an abundance of substances such as **plaque** build up inside these arteries, it restricts blood flow to the heart muscle. When blood flow is restricted, the tissue does not receive adequate oxygen, which results in **necrosis** of the affected tissue. When too much cardiac muscle dies, the body experiences a myocardial infarction, or heart attack.

Causes

Myocardial infarctions may be the result of atherosclerosis(page 114), a condition which causes the artery walls to harden and thicken due to a build-up of plaque in the arteries. Hypertension, smoking, and obesity may also contribute to the development of atherosclerosis.

Symptoms

Symptoms of myocardial infarction may be acute, or build up over a period of days leading up to the myocardial infarction. In the preceding days, a person may experience malaise, fatigue, and discomfort in the chest. Acute stages of myocardial infarction include intense chest pain, pain in the neck and left arm, and increased heart rate.

Treatments

A person who has suffered from a myocardial infarction may have a coronary bypass surgery performed, an angioplasty or stent placed in the affected artery, or may not need any surgery and only require medications such as aspirin, beta blockers, and statins.

Contraindications

Massage is an absolute contraindication during a myocardial infarction. After a myocardial infarction has occurred and a client has been treated, it is a good idea to get a note from a doctor before proceeding. Depending on the severity of the infarct and treatment, certain massages should not be performed due to strain they may place on the heart when increasing blood pressure.

Phlebitis
(phleb-: vein; -itis: inflammation)

Phlebitis is a condition of the Cardiovascular System, affecting the **veins**, causing them to become **inflamed**. **Blood clots** may form in these veins.

Causes

Phlebitis may have numerous causes, including **trauma to a vein**, and **immobility**. Trauma to a vein results in what is known as superficial phlebitis, usually the result of IV catheters being placed into a vein via needles.

Deep vein thrombosis is another type of phlebitis, taking place deeper in the body. Deep vein thrombosis(DVT) is most commonly caused by immobility of a limb. The body's veins move and stretch with the rest of the body during movement. If the veins are immobilized, they will become irritated, due to blood pooling in the veins. The blood pooling may result in blood clot formation. If a blood clot dislodges from its location and flows freely in the blood stream, it is known as an embolus, which could become lodged in other blood vessels throughout the body, cutting off blood flow and resulting in ischemia. Depending on the part of the body this takes place, it could even lead to possible death.

Symptoms

Symptoms of superficial phlebitis include tenderness and swelling around the injured vein, often with the affected vein presenting with a red line in the skin following the vein. The vein may feel hard to the touch due to inflammation.

Deep vein thrombosis may present with pain in the entire affected limb(usually the leg), along with swelling. If infection results, people may have fever.

Treatments

Treatments of phlebitis include anticoagulants for deep vein thrombosis such as heparin, ibuprofen, and antibiotics for superficial phlebitis.

Deep vein thrombosis requires immediate medical attention, as it may result in embolism, which could potentially be fatal.

Contraindications

Phlebitis should be treated as a local contraindication. Because medications may be prescribed that thin the blood, lighter massage should be performed to prevent internal bleeding from damaged blood vessels. Massaging the site of phlebitis may dislodge a clot, which can result in an embolism.

Raynaud's Syndrome

Raynaud's Syndrome is a condition that results in **constriction** of the **blood vessels** in the **fingers** and **toes**, **reducing circulation** to these areas. This constriction is known as "vasospasm". Primary Raynaud's Syndrome occurs independently, while Secondary Raynaud's Syndrome is typically associated with other conditions.

Causes

The primary contributors to Raynaud's Syndrome are **cold temperatures, stress, and cigarette smoking**. Raynaud's Syndrome is typically not a debilitating disease. During a flare-up, the skin typically turns pale, the person may experience numbness or pain, and the affected areas become very cold.

Secondary Raynaud's Syndrome may be associated with conditions such as lupus or scleroderma, and develops later in life than Primary Raynaud's Syndrome.

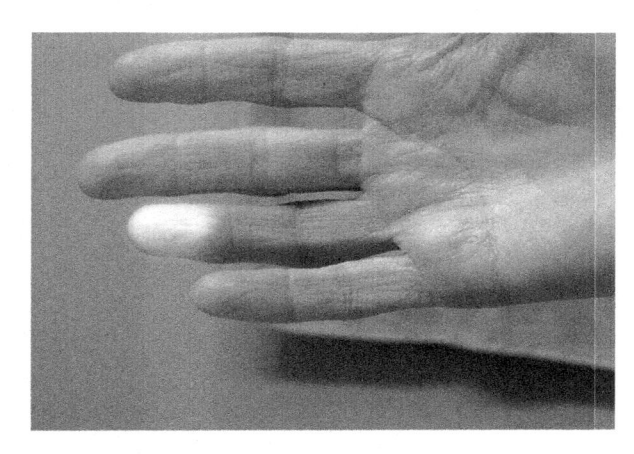

Symptoms

Symptoms of Raynaud's Syndrome include discoloration of the skin in affected areas, cold fingers and/or toes, numbness, and stinging pain upon warming of the area.

Treatments

Treatments for Raynaud's Syndrome include exercise, reducing stress, not smoking, and avoiding cold temperatures whenever possible. Secondary Raynaud's Syndrome may require medications such as statins to help regulate blood pressure and cholesterol.

Contraindications

Raynaud's Syndrome is indicated for massage. Using heat should be avoided, as sensation in the affected area may be decreased and tissue damage may result. Massaging the area can help dilate blood vessels and bring blood back into the fingers and toes. Increasing the temperature of the massage room may also help dilate blood vessels.

Varicose Veins
(varicose: abnormally swollen)

Varicose veins are the **abnormal swelling of veins** in the body, most commonly seen in the **legs**, but may be present in any vein. There are many different types, ranging from regular varicose veins, to spider veins, and even hemorrhoids.

Causes

Inside the veins, there are valves that push deoxygenated blood back up to the heart. Typically, as a person ages, the valves stop working as efficiently, which allows blood to pool **backwards** in the veins. This added pressure causes irritation and swelling of the veins. Blood pooling in the veins may also lead to complications such as the development of blood clots.

Because veins are much more superficial than arteries, when a vein becomes swollen, it is often visible. Varicose veins often present with a purple color, may look cord-like, and may even cause pain and discomfort. Causes of varicose veins include sitting or standing for prolonged periods, age, and even pregnancy.

Symptoms

Often times, varicose veins occur with no symptoms other than visual symptoms, such as discoloration of veins. If a varicose vein becomes painful, a person may experience burning, itching, edema, and cramping in the legs around the site of the varicose vein.

Treatments

Treatment is often unnecessary, outside of self-care. Self-care may include wearing compression socks, exercise, diet, and elevating the legs to help circulation. If treatment is required, there are a number of different things that can be done, such as sclerotherapy, laser therapy, and removing the varicose vein from the body.

Contraindications

Varicose veins are a type of phlebitis, and are considered a local contraindication. Massaging a swollen vein may dislodge a clot, which could become an embolism.

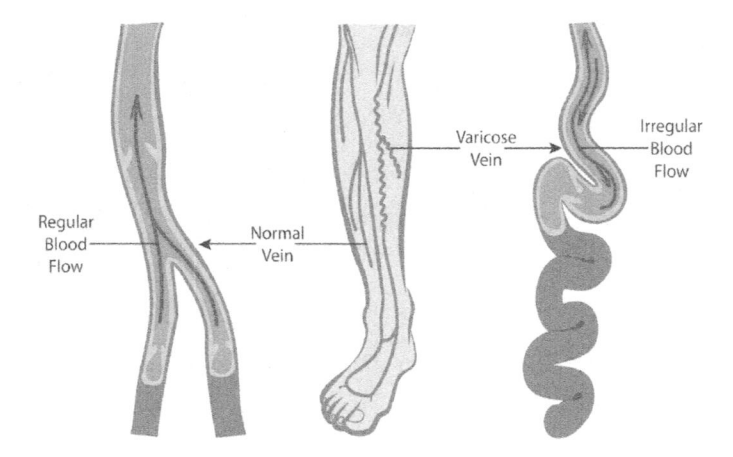

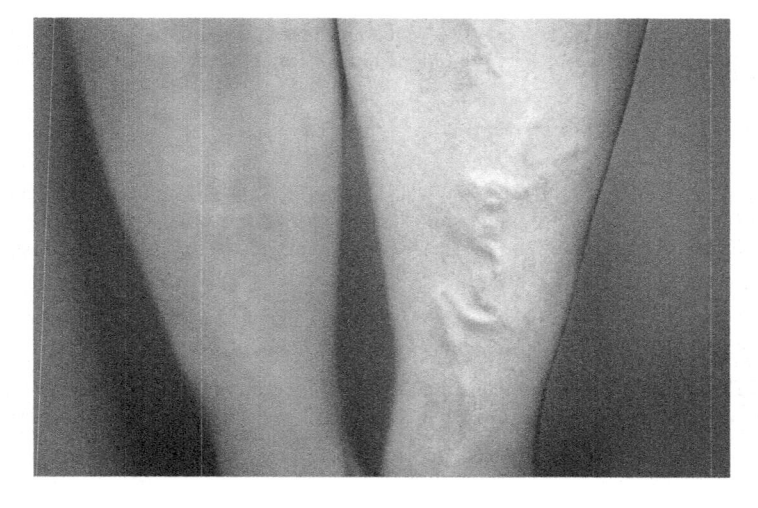

Digestive System Pathologies

Cholecystitis
(chole-: bile; cyst-: bladder; -itis: inflammation)

Cholecystitis is **inflammation** of the **gallbladder**. If untreated, cholecystitis may lead to extremely serious conditions such as rupture of the gallbladder.

Causes

Most commonly, cholecystitis is the result of formation of **gallstones**. Gallstones can block the cystic duct, which connects the gallbladder to the bile duct on its way to the duodenum, causing inflammation of the gallbladder as bile backs up in the organ.

There is no consensus on what causes gallstones to form. Some theories state gallstones form because the bile contains too much cholesterol, too much bilirubin, or the gallbladder doesn't properly empty bile into the duodenum.

Symptoms

Symptoms of cholecystitis include severe abdominal pain in the upper right quadrant near the liver, nausea, vomiting, fever, and pain in the right shoulder/back. These symptoms often occur after ingesting large meals.

Treatments

A diagnosis of cholecystitis almost always results in a hospital stay. Treatments may include antibiotics to fight off any associated infection, pain medication to reduce discomfort, and fasting to let the gallbladder rest and reduce inflammation.

Cholecystitis often recurs, and therefore most people who are diagnosed with cholecystitis require surgery to completely remove the gallbladder. The liver is then connected directly to the duodenum, allowing bile to enter into the small intestine.

Contraindications

Cholecystitis is considered an absolute contraindication in the acute stage. After the underlying cause has been determined, medications may be prescribed to help deal with the formation of gallstones and infection, or the gallbladder may be removed completely. This will require a hospital stay, in which massage will not be performed.

Cirrhosis
(Greek "kirrhos": yellowish; -osis: condition)

Cirrhosis is **scarring of the liver**, due to other conditions such as **hepatitis**(page 125). Each time the liver is damaged, it repairs itself. During this repair process, scar tissue is formed. As the liver is damaged over time, more scar tissue forms, which makes liver function difficult. Cirrhosis gives the liver a cobble-stone, yellow-orange appearance.

Causes

Most commonly, cirrhosis is the result of chronic hepatitis and alcohol abuse. Every time there is a flare-up of chronic hepatitis(HBV and HCV), it damages the liver, resulting in scar formation. Nonalcoholic fatty liver disease may also contribute to the development of cirrhosis.

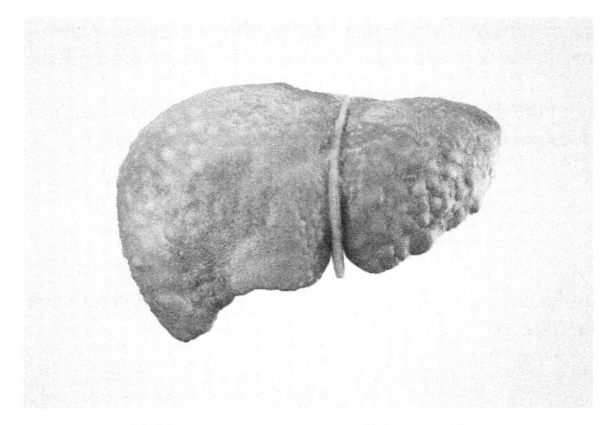

Cobble-stone appearance of damaged liver

Symptoms

Cirrhosis often does not present with symptoms until the damage caused is excessive. Symptoms may include nausea, weight loss, jaundice, bleeding and bruising easily, fatigue, edema in the legs, and an accumulation of fluid in the abdomen.

Treatments

Early stages of cirrhosis are treated by addressing the underlying cause, not the scarring itself, as the scarring is irreversible. A patient with early stages of cirrhosis may seek treatment for alcohol dependency to reduce the intake of alcohol, look into weight loss to reduce nonalcoholic fatty liver disease, and medications to help control HBV and HCV, which can substantially damage the liver.

Advanced stages of cirrhosis may require liver transplantation to provide the body with a liver that functions properly.

Contraindications

Massage should be avoided in a client with cirrhosis, due to increased waste products being filtered through the liver.

Crohn's Disease

Crohn's Disease is an **inflammatory bowel disease**, which causes **inflammation of the digestive tract**. Crohn's has periods of exacerbation and remission, where the disease is actively causing inflammation, then periods where it is not. Crohn's disease typically appears in younger people, people who are of East European Jewish descent, people who have relatives with the disease, and people who smoke cigarettes.

Damage to the digestive tract, including ulcerations and scarring, may result. Depending on the location of ulceration and scarring, abscesses and constipation may result.

Causes

The exact cause of Crohn's disease is unknown. The leading theory is that heredity and an immune system that does not function properly are the main causes of Crohn's.

Symptoms

In acute stages of Crohn's, symptoms may include diarrhea, abdominal pain, cramping, fatigue, fever, and bloody stool. Depending on the severity of these symptoms, a person may need to visit a doctor.

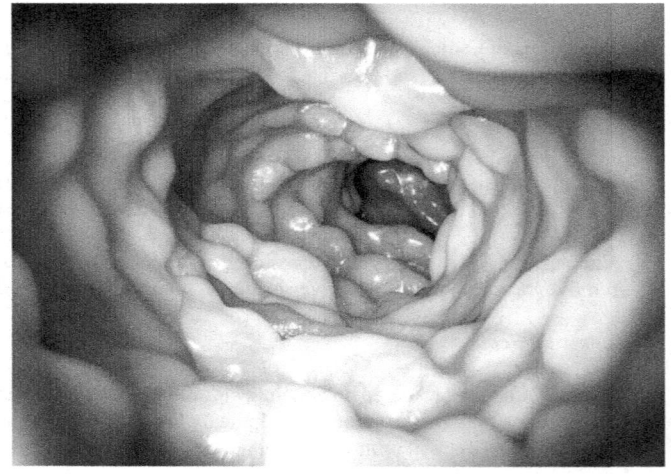

Treatments

Inflamed digestive tract

A variety of medications may be prescribed for a patient with Crohn's, including anti-inflammatory drugs such as corticosteroids to reduce inflammation in the digestive tract, immunosuppresors to help regulate the effects of the immune system on the digestive tract, and antibiotics to reduce any abscesses that may result. Pain relievers may also be prescribed.

In serious cases, surgery may be required. During Crohn's, scarring in the ileum or large intestine may result. In this surgery, the damaged portion of the digestive tract may be removed. This does not cure Crohn's, but can make it easier to manage.

Changes in diet, especially in acute stages, may be beneficial.

Contraindications

Massage in the acute stage of Crohn's disease should be avoided, as the client may be in pain and experience symptoms such as diarrhea. In the post-acute stage, massage is indicated for Crohn's disease.

Diverticulitis
(diverticula: tubular sac branching off a cavity; -itis: inflammation)

Diverticulitis is a condition affecting the large intestine, but may also affect other structures such as the abdomen, or the entire Cardiovascular System. If a person is affected by diverticulosis, they have small pouches that develop in the large intestine. In certain cases, these pouches may become **inflamed** and/or **infected**, which then becomes diverticulitis.

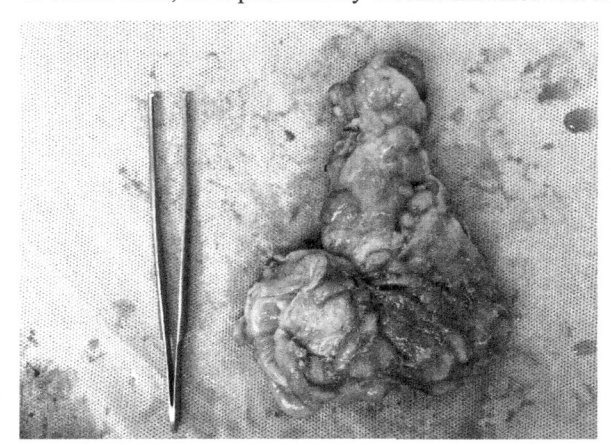

Causes

Because diverticulitis puts strain on sections of the large intestine that are already weakened, ulcerations or open sores may result. These open sores may lead to infection, and leaking of feces into the abdomen, which results in peritonitis(inflammation of the peritoneum, a very serious condition that requires medical attention).

Symptoms

Symptoms of diverticulitis include fever, nausea, vomiting, pain in the lower left abdomen, and constipation. Tenderness in the abdomen may also be present.

Treatments

Diverticulitis may be treated in several different ways, depending on the severity. Pain medication may help with discomfort in less severe cases. In recurring diverticulitis, scarring may be present, which could lead to backing up of fecal content in the large intestine. Infections will require antibiotics.

If scarring is severe due to ulceration, surgery to remove the damaged part of the large intestine may be required.

Contraindications

Diverticulitis is considered an absolute contraindication to massage.

Diverticulosis
(diverticula: tubular sac branching off a cavity; -osis: condition)

Diverticulosis is a condition affecting the large intestine, which presents with **pouches** forming in the walls of the large intestine, typically in the descending and/or sigmoid colons. It is a common condition seen in roughly half of people over the age of 65.

Causes

During peristalsis, the smooth muscle located in the walls of the large intestine contract, forcing food to move further through the organ and eventually out of the body. If the large intestine does not contain enough fecal matter, as in the case of a low-fiber diet, the contractions may result in weakening of the wall of the large intestine. As a result, small pouches may develop.

If a person develops diverticulosis, small pieces of feces, nuts, seeds, etc, may become stuck inside the pouches. If feces becomes trapped in a pouch, the large intestine will absorb all of the water from it, and it will become very solid and extremely hard to remove. This may result in pain in the abdomen.

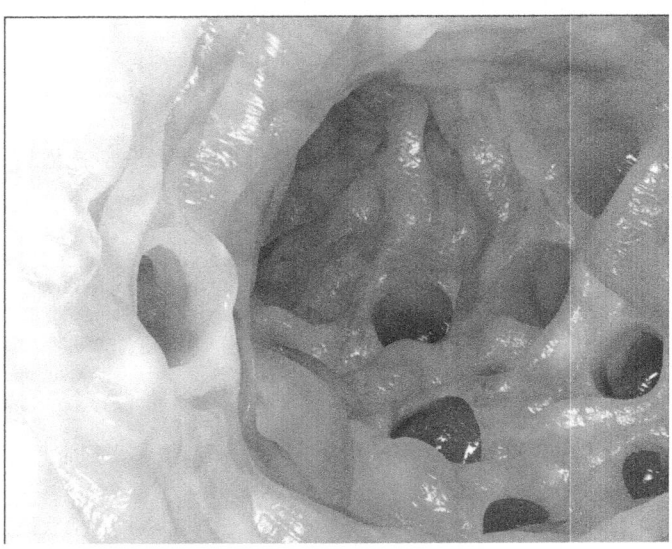

Pouches formed in the large intestine

Symptoms

Typically, people with diverticulosis don't exhibit symptoms. When they do, however, symptoms may include diarrhea, abdominal cramping, or fever. These are typically the result of infection, which may lead to diverticulitis.

Treatments

Treatment primarily includes increasing intake of fiber via fruits and vegetables, and increasing fluid intake to make passing of stool easier to manage.

Contraindications

Diverticulosis is not contraindicated for massage. If pain is present, massage of the lower back and abdomen should be avoided, but may be performed elsewhere.

Gastritis
(gastr/o: stomach; -itis: inflammation)

Gastritis is **inflammation of the stomach**, specifically the **lining** of the stomach. Gastritis may occur suddenly or slowly over time.

Causes

Some primary causes of gastritis include infection by **H. pylori bacterium**, excessive use of **alcohol**, use of **anti-inflammatory drugs**, **vomiting**, and **stress**. Gastritis should be treated, as it may lead to more serious conditions such as stomach cancer.

Symptoms

Some people with gastritis actually don't exhibit any symptoms. Those that do, however, may present with nausea, vomiting, loss of appetite, pain in the abdomen, and bloating in the abdomen.

Treatments

Treatment often consists of dietary changes, such as avoiding spicy food and dairy, taking antacids to reduce the amount of stomach acid present, and possibly even a round of antibiotics to combat infection by the H. pylori bacterium.

Contraindications

Massage on a client with gastritis is dependent on the cause and severity. If gastritis is causing nausea and vomiting, massage should not be performed.

Gastroenteritis
(gastr/o: stomach; enter/o: small intestine; -itis: inflammation)

Gastroenteritis is **inflammation** of the **stomach** and **small intestine**, commonly known as the "**stomach flu**".

Causes

The primary cause of gastroenteritis is a **viral** or **bacterial infection**. These infections can be spread by coming into contact with someone who has it, or consuming contaminated food or water that contains the virus or bacterium. The main types of virus that cause gastroenteritis are **rotavirus** and **norovirus**. The main types of bacterium that cause gastroenteritis are **E. coli** and **salmonella**.

Symptoms

Symptoms of gastroenteritis include diarrhea, vomiting, fever, abdominal pain, and body chills.

Treatments

Most people recover from gastroenteritis without requiring any treatment. The primary goal of treatment for gastroenteritis is to prevent dehydration. Therefore, drinking plenty of fluids is advised. Over-the-counter medications that help with nausea and vomiting may also help.

Contraindications

Gastroenteritis is often caused by a viral infection, and is contagious. Therefore, gastroenteritis is an absolute contraindication to massage.

Gastroesophageal Reflux Disease
(gastr/o: stomach; esophag/o: esophagus; reflux: flowing back)

Gastroesophageal Reflux Disease(GERD) is a condition in which **stomach acid**, or food from the stomach, comes **back up** into the **esophagus**, causing **irritation and burning** in the lining of the esophagus.

Causes

GERD is the result of acid flowing backwards into the esophagus. This is primarily caused by the lower gastroesophageal sphincter(also known as the cardiac sphincter) relaxing when it normally is contracted and tightened. This can happen abnormally, or be caused by the sphincter weakening over time.

Symptoms

Symptoms include burning in the chest, pain in the chest, a dry cough, a sour taste in the mouth, and a sore throat. It is advisable to seek medical attention if chest pain is present, because symptoms are very similar to those seen in myocardial infarction.

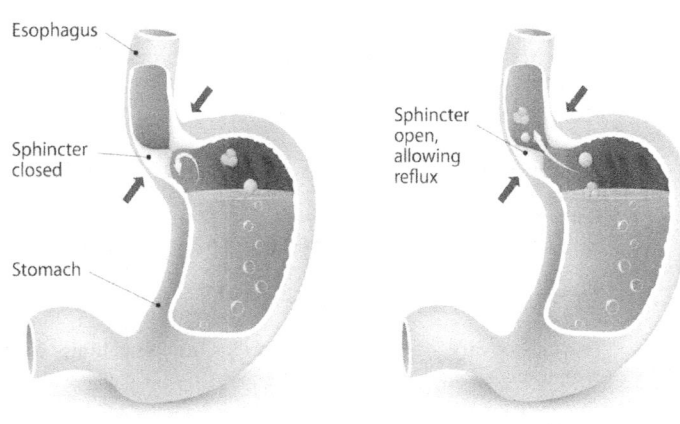

Treatments

Over-the-counter medications, such as antacids, are the primary treatment for GERD. Other medications may be prescribed by a doctor if the GERD is not helped by antacids, such as H-2-receptor blockers, which reduce stomach acid production, and proton pump inhibitors, which completely block the production of stomach acid and give the lining of the esophagus time to heal.

Contraindications

Unless chest pain is present, massage is indicated for Gastroesophageal Reflux Disease. Semi-reclined position may help reduce acid from moving into the esophagus.

Hepatitis
(hepat-: liver; -itis: inflammation)

Hepatitis is a condition that results in **inflammation of the liver**.

Causes

There are numerous causes of hepatitis, which affect numerous different organ systems. Most commonly, hepatitis is the result of a **viral infection**, but may also result from **toxic substances** entering into the body, such as **alcohol**. Short-term symptoms of hepatitis include jaundice(yellowing of the skin due to increased bilirubin in the blood stream), fever, and nausea. Long-term symptoms include cirrhosis(destruction of healthy liver cells), scarring of the liver, liver cancer, and liver failure.

There are five known hepatitis viruses: Hepatitis A, B, C, D, and E. Each varies in mode of contraction, and severity of symptoms.

Hepatitis A is the most common form, and is typically transmitted through ingestion of fecal matter(most commonly seen in parts of the world with low sanitation standards). People infected with Hepatitis A most frequently make a full recovery, and develop an immunity to the virus.

Hepatitis B is typically transmitted through exposure to body fluids such as blood. The virus produces symptoms for a period greater than Hepatitis A, but most people will develop an immunity to it after about four weeks. A small percentage of people who contract Hepatitis B will become chronically affected by it. Vaccines for Hepatitis B are available.

Hepatitis C, much like Hepatitis B, is contracted through exposure to body fluids such as blood. Hepatitis C is a chronic condition which damages the liver even further each time the person's symptoms are in the acute stage. Hepatitis C is one of the leading causes of liver failure.

Hepatitis D is an infection that only results in symptoms if the person is also infected with the Hepatitis B virus. When this occurs, major complications may arise. Because Hepatitis D is only activated by the Hepatitis B virus, the Hepatitis B vaccine may contribute to the prevention of Hepatitis D.

Hepatitis E, like Hepatitis A, is contracted through exposure to fecal matter. It is most commonly seen in developing countries, where sanitation standards may not be high. Hepatitis E, if severe, may lead to liver failure, despite being an acute infection.

Symptoms

Hepatitis often results in no symptoms. More severe cases of hepatitis may result in a person presenting with nausea, fatigue, mild fever, loss of appetite, abdominal tenderness, and jaundice, among others.

Treatments

Treatments vary, depending on severity. Immunizations are available for Hepatitis B, and medications may help reduce the symptoms.

Contraindications

In the acute stage, massage is an absolute contraindication for hepatitis. In the post-acute stage, massage is indicated.

Hernia
(hernia: a rupture)

A hernia is a rupture in a muscle or connective tissue, allowing an organ or other tissue to **protrude** through its normal location. There are many different types of herniae in the Digestive System, including **hiatal**, **umbilical**, and **inguinal**.

Causes

A hernia is caused by a weakness in the affected tissue, and/or straining of the tissue. When the tissue tears, the organ, usually the small intestine, protrudes through it. This can lead to many complications, such as organ strangulation, constipation, pain, or even trauma to other structures, such as the testes.

A hiatal hernia results from part of the stomach protruding upwards through the diaphragm, into the chest. Gastroesophageal Reflux Disease may result from this type of hernia, where stomach acids leak from the stomach backwards into the esophagus.

An umbilical hernia, most commonly seen in infants, is caused by the small intestine protruding through the abdominal wall and into the umbilicus. This condition usually resolves on its own.

An inguinal hernia, most commonly seen in men, is caused by the small intestine protruding through the wall of the abdomen, which typically descends into the scrotum. This may cause trauma to the testes. Sometimes, the small intestine may even drop farther down the body, into the thigh.

Symptoms

Symptoms vary depending on the type of hernia suffered. Examples include swelling beneath the skin in the abdomen or groin in an inguinal or umbilical hernia, and heart burn and pain in the upper abdomen in hiatal herniae.

Treatments

Treatments may include dietary changes in cases such as a hiatal hernia, weight loss, medication such as antacids, or even surgery to repair the hernia.

Contraindications

Massage of a hernia is locally contraindicated.

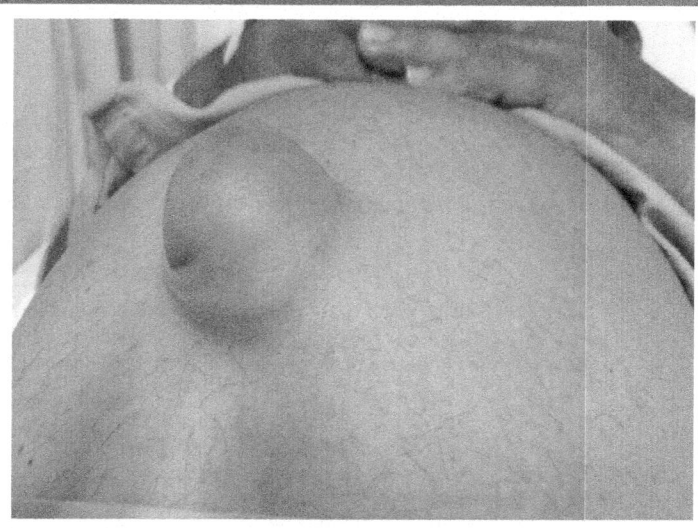

Umbilical hernia

Pancreatitis
(pancreat/o: pancreas; -itis: inflammation)

Pancreatitis is **inflammation of the pancreas**. Pancreatitis may be either acute or chronic, each presenting with differing levels of severity.

ACUTE PANCREATITIS

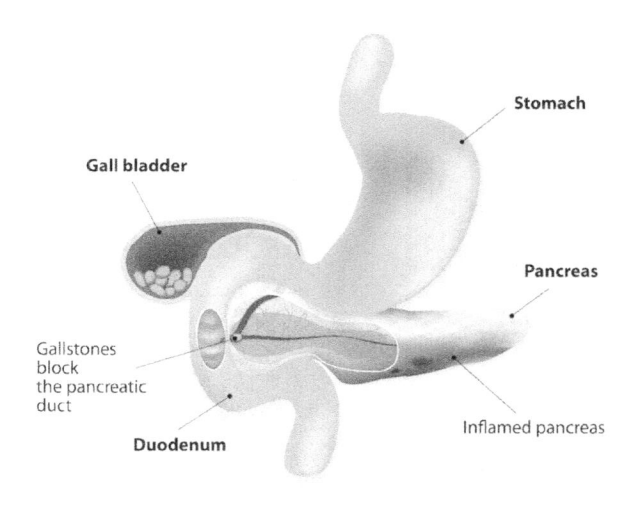

Causes

Pancreatitis results when **enzymes** produced by the pancreas, **insulin** and **glucagon**, **become active in the pancreas** before entering into the digestive tract or blood stream. This causes the pancreas to become irritated and inflamed. Things that may contribute to pancreatitis include blockage of the bile duct by gallstones, alcoholism, pancreatic cancer, infection, and cystic fibrosis.

Symptoms

Acute pancreatitis presents with fever, nausea, vomiting, pain in the upper abdomen, abdominal tenderness, and pain radiating to the back. Chronic pancreatitis may also present with the same symptoms in the acute stage, but weight loss may also occur.

Pancreatitis may lead to the development of other serious conditions such as diabetes, pancreatic cancer, and kidney failure.

Treatments

Upon admission to a hospital, a patient with pancreatitis will be prescribed pain medication. Fasting reduces the production of insulin and glucagon, and is therefore beneficial to decrease irritation. Other treatments that treat the underlying causes of pancreatitis can include removal of the gallbladder or gallstones, and treatment for alcohol dependency.

Contraindications

In the acute stage, pancreatitis is considered an absolute contraindication. In a client with chronic pancreatitis, massage may be performed in the post-acute stage.

Pharyngitis
(pharyng/o: pharynx; -itis: inflammation)

Pharyngitis is **inflammation of the pharynx**, or the throat. A **sore throat** is considered pharyngitis.

Causes

Pharyngitis is usually the result of a **viral infection** from the **common cold or the flu**. Bacterial infections may also result in pharyngitis, such as **strep throat**. Non-exudative pharyngitis, the kind usually caused by a virus, does not produce increased mucous, while exudative pharyngitis, the kind usually caused by bacteria, does produce mucous. Both types of pharyngitis are contagious.

Symptoms

Pain in the throat is one of the main symptoms of pharyngitis. Speaking and swallowing food may be painful. A person may develop a fever, and the tonsils and lymph nodes in the neck may enlarge. Excessive mucous may be produced if it is caused by bacterial infection.

Treatments

Antiviral medications may prevent the condition from worsening. If the condition is caused by bacterial infection, antibiotics can help combat the infection and improve the condition.

Contraindications

Pharyngitis is commonly considered an absolute contraindication to massage during the acute stage. After the infection has cleared, massage may be performed.

Strep Throat

Strep throat is a **bacterial infection**, resulting in **sore throat**. Typically, a throat culture is performed in order to diagnose strep throat.

Causes

Strep throat is caused by an infection of the **streptococcal bacteria**, which is contagious. Children are most at risk of contracting strep throat, but it can occur in people of all ages.

Symptoms

In addition to sore throat, a person with strep throat may exhibit red spots on the roof of the mouth, white patches on the tonsils, swollen lymph nodes in the neck, pain upon swallowing, and fever, amongst others. If left untreated, strep throat may contribute to the development of rheumatic fever, which can cause damage to heart valves.

Treatments

Because strep throat is caused by bacteria, antibiotics are the primary treatment. Acetaminophen is useful in treating any pain that may be present due to the infection. After starting a course of antibiotics, a person should begin feeling better within a couple days. Taking all the medication prescribed is required to prevent the infection from returning and becoming resistant to the antibiotics.

Contraindications

Because strep throat is highly contagious, it is considered an absolute contraindication until the condition has resolved.

Endocrine System Pathologies

Acromegaly
(acro-: extremity; -megaly: irregular enlargement)

Acromegaly is **abnormal growth** during **adulthood**, resulting from the release of **excessive amounts** of **growth hormone** by the **pituitary gland**. This can cause bones to keep growing, increasing a person's size and changing their appearance.

Acromegaly can result in numerous severe complications, such as cardiovascular issues, hypertension, sleep apnea, and arthritis.

Causes

Acromegaly is caused by increased amounts of growth hormone being produced by the pituitary gland. The most common reason for this to occur is a tumor growing on the pituitary gland. The tumor produces growth hormone and secretes it into the blood stream, increasing the growth hormone levels in the body. Rarely, a tumor elsewhere in the body, such as the adrenal glands, may produce growth hormone. This can also increase growth hormone levels in the body.

Symptoms

Symptoms of acromegaly generally take some time to appear as the disease slowly progresses. Enlarged hands and feet are an extremely common symptom. Enlargement of facial features, including the jaw and brow lines, can typically be seen in advanced stages. Skin can become thickened and the voice can deepen.

Treatments

If acromegaly is the result of a tumor, surgery may be performed to remove the tumor. Removing the tumor should stabilize the growth hormone levels in the body. After surgery, radiation therapy may be performed to destroy any remaining tumor cells in the body. This can help ensure the tumor does not return. Medications may help reduce the effects of growth hormone in the body.

Contraindications

Massage is indicated for acromegaly.

Addison's Disease

Addison's Disease is an **autoimmune** disorder affecting the **adrenal glands**, which results in a lack of cortisol and/or aldosterone production.

Causes

Addison's Disease is caused by **damage** to the **adrenal cortex** by the body's **immune system**. Damage to these glands results in an inability to produce cortisol, which regulates stress levels in the body by helping control blood sugar, blood pressure, and metabolism, and aldosterone, which aids in reabsorption of water and sodium back into the blood stream.

Symptoms

Addison's Disease may result in fatigue, weight loss, low blood pressure, hair loss, hyperpigmentation of the skin, and nausea. It may become life-threatening if not treated.

Acute adrenal failure, also known as Addisonian Crisis, may result in severe vomiting and diarrhea, dehydration, low blood pressure, and pain in the low back, abdomen, and/or legs.

Treatments

Treatment primarily consists of hormone replacements, which may be taken orally or injected.

Contraindications

Massage is indicated for a client with Addison's Disease. However, the type and length of massage varies depending on how a client is feeling and their stamina. Clients with low stamina should receive shorter, lighter massages, while clients with increased stamina may receive longer and stimulating massages.

Cushing's Disease

Cushing's Disease is a disease of the pituitary gland, which results in **hyper-production** of **adrenocorticotropic hormone(ACTH)**.

Causes

Cushing's Disease is the result of hyperplasia(excessive growth) of the pituitary gland, or development of a tumor. This causes too much ACTH to be released in the body, which stimulates **hyper-production** of **cortisol**.

Symptoms

Cushing's Disease may result in weight gain around the face and torso, weakening of bone, thinning of skin, fatigue, and acne, amongst other complications.

Treatments

Treatments for Cushing's Disease include surgery to remove a tumor, and hormone therapy to reduce the amount of cortisol being produced.

Contraindications

Massage is indicated for Cushing's Disease, but precautions may be taken in clients with weakened bones. Lighter massage is recommended for these clients to prevent damaging bone.

SYMPTOMS of Cushing's syndrome

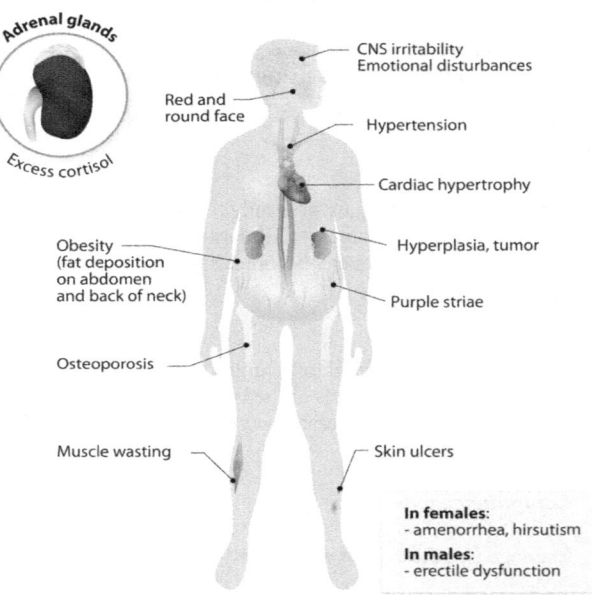

- Adrenal glands
- Excess cortisol
- Red and round face
- CNS irritability, Emotional disturbances
- Hypertension
- Cardiac hypertrophy
- Obesity (fat deposition on abdomen and back of neck)
- Hyperplasia, tumor
- Purple striae
- Osteoporosis
- Muscle wasting
- Skin ulcers

In females:
- amenorrhea, hirsutism

In males:
- erectile dysfunction

Diabetes Mellitus
(diabetes: to pass through; mellitus: sweet)

Diabetes Mellitus is a condition of the Endocrine System that affects **insulin** function in the body.

There are three types of diabetes: Diabetes Type I, Diabetes Type II, and Gestational Diabetes.

Causes

Diabetes Type I is often known as **juvenile diabetes**, as it begins in childhood. In Type I, the body's immune system attacks the pancreas, the organ that produces insulin. This results in the body not producing enough insulin, which the body needs in order to convert glucose to energy.

Diabetes Type II, the most common form of diabetes, is caused by the body having an **insulin resistance**. The insulin in the body is unable to break down glucose, which causes high levels of sugar in the blood stream. Obesity is a common cause of Diabetes Type II.

Gestational Diabetes is only present during **pregnancy**. Gestational Diabetes affects less than 10% of all pregnant women, and typically resolves after pregnancy ends.

Symptoms

Symptoms of diabetes include frequent urination, fatigue, weight loss, pain and/or numbness in the hands or feet, extreme thirst, and extreme hunger.

Treatments

Treatment for Diabetes Type I is primarily insulin injections. Treatment for Diabetes Type II includes medications, but exercise and dietary changes are most common. Treatment for Gestational Diabetes includes exercise, regulating weight gain during pregnancy, and insulin medication depending on the severity.

Contraindications

Massage is indicated for a client with diabetes. If neuropathy is present, lighter massage in the affected area should be performed. If ulcers are present in areas afflicted with neuropathy, ulcers should be treated as local contraindications. If a client injects insulin, the injection site should also be avoided.

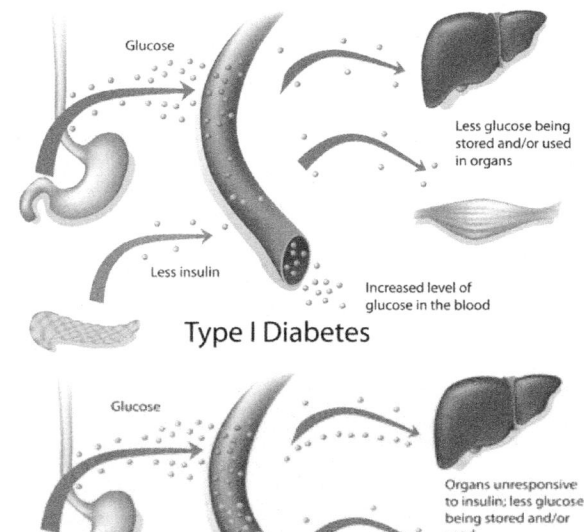

Goiter
(Latin "guttur": throat)

A goiter is an **enlargement of the thyroid gland**, located at the base of the neck.

Causes

The primary cause of a goiter is a **lack of iodine** in the diet. If a person does not consume enough iodine, the body is unable to produce sufficient thyroid hormones. Other conditions, such as Graves' disease or Hashimoto's disease, can affect the levels of thyroid hormone being produced. Too much thyroid hormone or too little thyroid hormone being produced can have negative effects on the thyroid and could produce a goiter.

Symptoms

Goiters produce a bulge in the throat, which may place pressure on other structures such as the esophagus or trachea, making it difficult to eat or breathe.

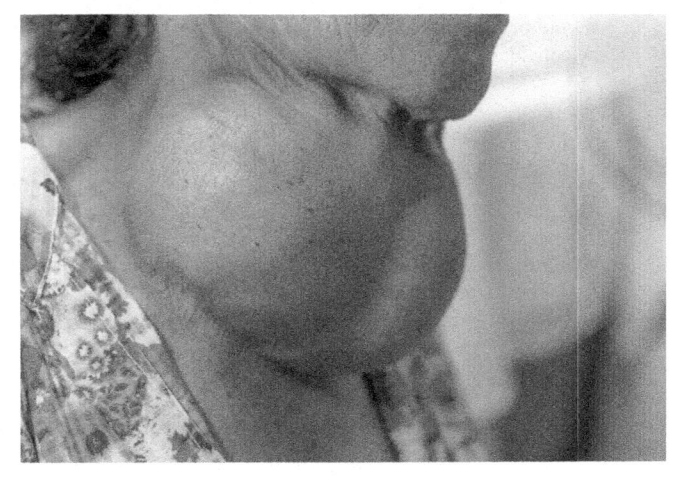

Treatments

Treatment of a goiter typically depends on the cause. If it is caused by low levels of thyroid hormones, thyroid hormone replacement medications may be prescribed. If the thyroid is producing too much thyroid hormone, medications may be prescribed to stabilize the levels of thyroid hormone in the body. Surgery to remove the thyroid may be an option if the goiter causes any difficulty in breathing or swallowing, or causes discomfort.

Increasing iodine consumption may be all it takes to reduce the goiter. Iodized salt may be added to the diet, along with other foods high in iodine such as seafood.

Contraindications

A goiter is considered a local contraindication.

Graves' Disease

Graves' Disease is an autoimmune disorder, in which the body's **immune system** attacks the **thyroid gland**, causing an increase in thyroid hormone production(**hyperthyroidism**).

Causes

The exact cause of Graves' disease is unknown.

Symptoms

Graves' disease can affect numerous parts of the body, resulting in sensitivity to heat, weight loss, the development of a goiter(enlargement of the thyroid), bulging of the eyes, and irregular heart rhythm. Women are more likely to develop Graves' disease, as well as people under the age of 40.

Treatments

Treatment for Graves' disease include medications such as beta blockers and anti-thyroid medications. If medication isn't helpful, surgical removal of the thyroid may be an option.

Contraindications

Graves' disease is generally considered not contraindicated. However, a client with Graves' disease may be sensitive to heat, so anything that uses heat in the massage treatment should be avoided. A goiter may also be present, which would be considered a local contraindication.

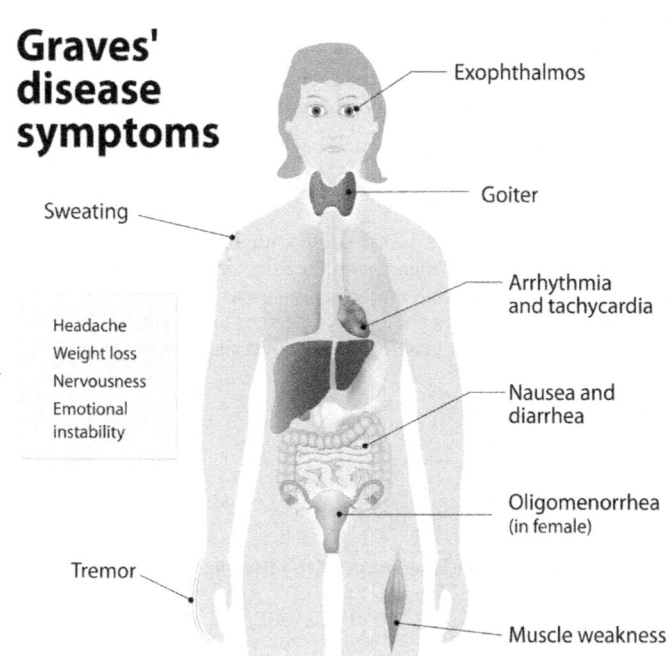

Hyperthyroidism
(hyper-: excessive; thyroid: thyroid gland; -ism: condition)

Hyperthyroidism is an **increase in production of thyroxine**, a hormone secreted by the thyroid gland. Thyroxine is primarily responsible for **stimulating tissues to consume oxygen**. Excessive amounts of thyroxine can significantly increase the body's metabolism, which can have numerous effects.

Causes

Hyperthyroidism is often caused by other conditions such as Graves' disease. Tumors may grow in or on the thyroid, which can increase production of thyroxine.

Symptoms

Symptoms of hyperthyroidism are vast, and may be confused with other medical conditions. The main symptom of hyperthyroidism is sudden, rapid weight loss due to an increased metabolism. This may even cause an increase in appetite,

Symptoms of HYPERTHYROIDISM

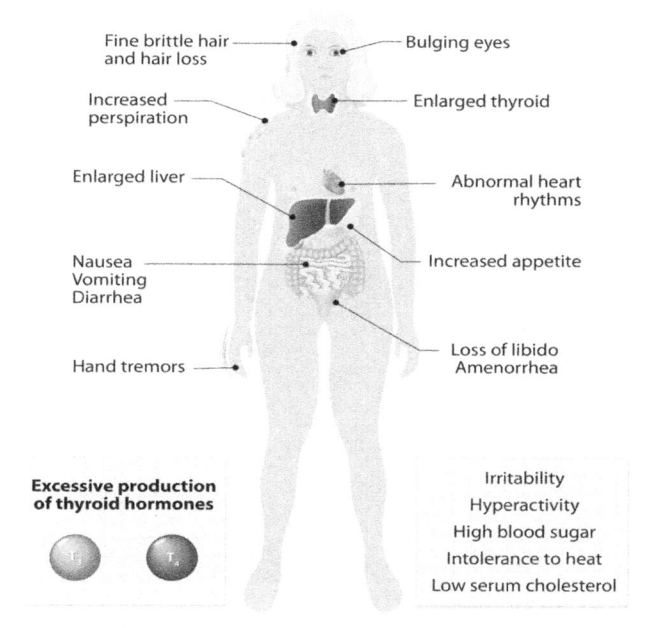

- Fine brittle hair and hair loss
- Bulging eyes
- Increased perspiration
- Enlarged thyroid
- Enlarged liver
- Abnormal heart rhythms
- Nausea, Vomiting, Diarrhea
- Increased appetite
- Hand tremors
- Loss of libido, Amenorrhea

Excessive production of thyroid hormones
T_3 T_4

- Irritability
- Hyperactivity
- High blood sugar
- Intolerance to heat
- Low serum cholesterol

despite the lost weight. Arrhythmia, specifically tachycardia, may also result. Heat sensitivity and sweating are other symptoms to be aware of.

Treatments

Treatments are often the same as those seen with Graves' disease, including a prescription of oral radioactive iodine. Other medications may help lower the amount of hormone being produced by the thyroid. If a person has tachycardia as a result of hyperthyroidism, beta blockers may also be prescribed. In cases where these treatments aren't helpful, surgical removal of the thyroid may be performed.

Contraindications

Generally, hyperthyroidism is not contraindicated. However, conditions such as arrhythmia that can be caused by hyperthyroidism may be contraindicated if uncontrolled.

Integumentary System Pathologies

Acne

Acne is an infection of the skin, resulting from numerous factors. Acne may result in whiteheads, blackheads, or even cysts if left untreated.

Causes

Acne is caused by an increased production of sebum on the skin, which results in blocked pores. These blocked pores may become **infected**, which may develop into pustules. There are several contributing factors that lead to the development of acne, including **testosterone** production, stress, hormonal imbalances, and poor personal hygiene.

Symptoms

Acne may result in the development of whiteheads, blackheads, pimples, or even cystic lesions beneath the skin. These are often painful to the touch and may present with infection and inflammation.

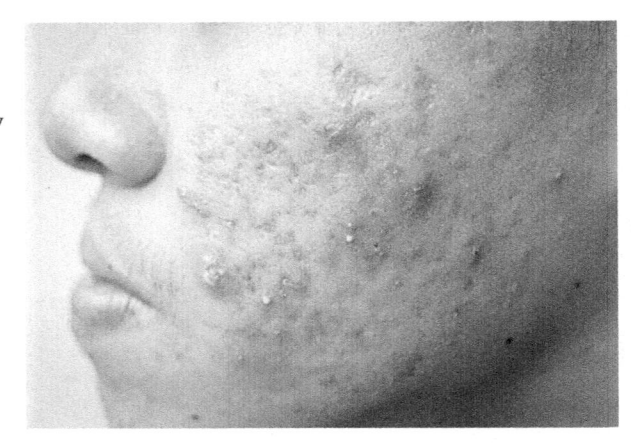

Treatments

Treatment includes over-the-counter skin care products for mild acne, or in the case of severe acne, medications such as birth control pills to regulate hormone levels in women, and antibiotics to eliminate bacterial growth. Other treatments include light therapy and chemical peels.

Contraindications

Whiteheads are considered local contraindications. Any part of the body experiencing inflammation from acne should also be considered a local contraindication.

Athlete's Foot
(tinea: fungus; pedis: foot)

Athlete's Foot (also known as Tinea Pedis) is a **fungal infection of the foot**. Despite the name, anyone may develop athlete's foot, not just athletes. Athlete's foot, like other fungal infections such as ringworm and jock itch, is highly contagious.

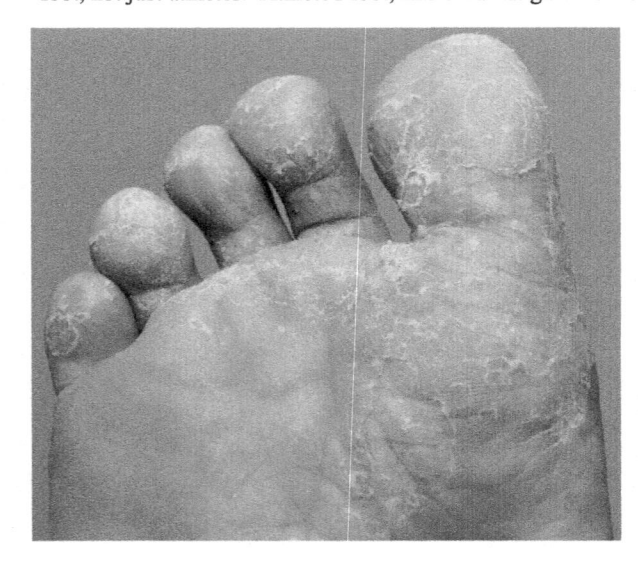

Causes

Athlete's foot is caused by exposure to fungus on the foot. When a person wears tight-fitting shoes, it provides an environment for the fungus to thrive: a warm, humid, dark space. The fungus spreads, growing between the toes, then expanding across the foot. The infection causes the skin to become dry and scaly, which may result in breaking of the skin and bacterial infection.

Symptoms

Symptoms of athlete's foot are typically the development of a red, scaly rash between the toes, which may spread proximally. Blisters and ulcers may be present in the area. Itching of the affected area is common.

Treatments

Treatment of athlete's foot primarily consists of over-the-counter medications, in addition to self-care, such as ensuring the foot and footwear are dry as much as possible, wearing shower shoes in public bathing areas, etc.

Contraindications

Because athlete's foot is contagious, it is considered a local contraindication. The feet should be avoided, and any linens the feet have come in contact with should be treated as contaminated.

Boil

A boil is a **bacterial infection of a hair follicle**, also known as a **furuncle**. A group of these infections together in one localized area is known as a carbuncle.

Causes

A boil typically results from small cuts in the skin(caused by things like shaving), allowing staphylococci bacterium to enter the body and reproduce. Boils can be red, inflamed, and painful to the touch. The lump initially produced by the infection begins to soften over a few days, and becomes much more painful. Pus develops on the affected area.

Symptoms

A boil may result in pain around the boil, the development of a fever, and swelling of lymph nodes. More boils may develop around the site of the original boil.

Treatments

Boils are treated by lancing(draining) the area with application of antibacterial soap and water, or in more severe cases, prescription of antibiotics to combat the bacterial infection.

Contraindications

A boil is considered a local contraindication for massage.

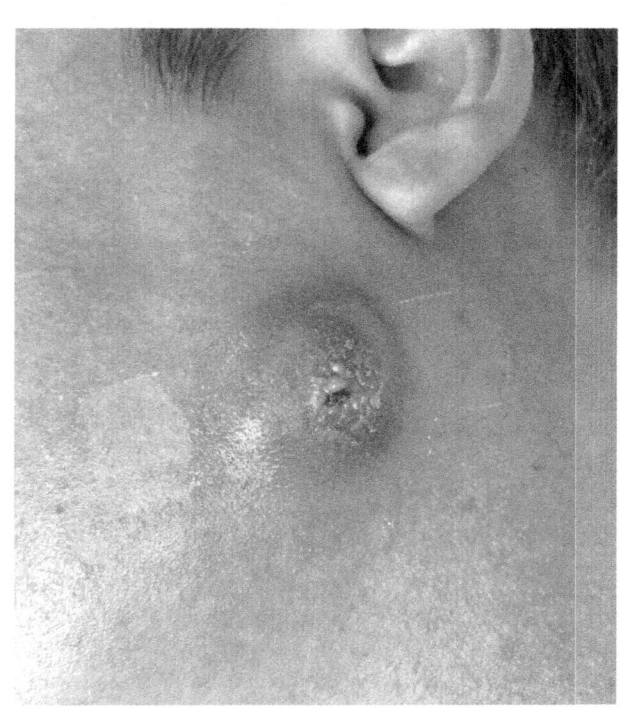

Burns

Burns are a skin condition in which the skin is **damaged** due to exposure to **heat, chemicals,** or other means. This may result in inflammation, blister formation, or necrosis, depending on the severity of the burn.

Burns of the skin can be categorized as first, second, third, or fourth degree, with first being the least severe.

A **first degree burn** only affects the **epidermis**. It may lead to pain and inflammation of the skin, but nothing more. A common first degree burn is a sun burn. The pain and inflammation subsides in a day or two, and the skin returns to normal.

A **second degree burn** is more severe. In a second degree burn, the burn moves through the epidermis and into the **dermis**. Because the burn goes deeper into the skin, it causes more damage, which can be seen by **blistering**. Blisters form to help repair the damage done by the burn. Second degree burns may result in scarring if they are too severe.

Third degree burns move even deeper into the skin, reaching the **subcutaneous layer** of the skin. Third degree burns often cause **severe tissue damage and necrosis**. Skin grafts may be needed to help repair an area damaged by a third degree burn.

While first, second, and third degree burns are most common, a **fourth degree burn** moves completely through all layers of the skin, and goes deeper into tissues beneath the skin, such as tendons, ligaments, muscles, and bones.

Causes

As stated, burns may be caused by many different factors, including heat(thermal burns), chemicals, electricity, radiation(such as sunburns), friction(rug burns), and even extreme cold temperatures.

Symptoms

Burn symptoms vary based on severity. First degree burns often present with inflammation and pain. Second degree burns present with pain, blistering, and discoloration of the skin as the body repairs the damaged tissue. Third degree burns may present with blackened, charred tissue, with the skin having a waxy appearance. Because tissue is destroyed in third and fourth degree burns, loss of sensation may occur resulting from nerves being destroyed.

Treatments

Treatment for burns often depends on the severity of the burn. Application of aloe vera may help reduce the pain in first degree burns. Second degree burns may require bandages with topical antibiotic cream to prevent infection. Third degree burns may require surgery and skin grafts to repair the affected areas.

Contraindications

Burns are considered local contraindications for massage. Avoid any area experiencing inflammation, blistering, or has suffered necrosis.

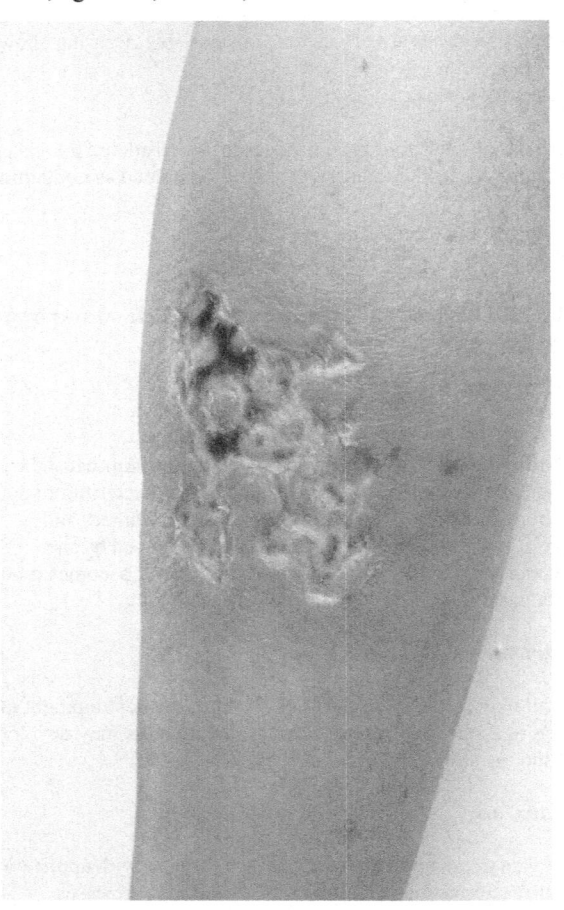

Third degree scald burn

Cellulitis
(cell: cell; -itis: inflammation)

Cellulitis is a **bacterial infection** of the **skin**, causing symptoms such as inflammation of the infected area, fever, pain, and blisters.

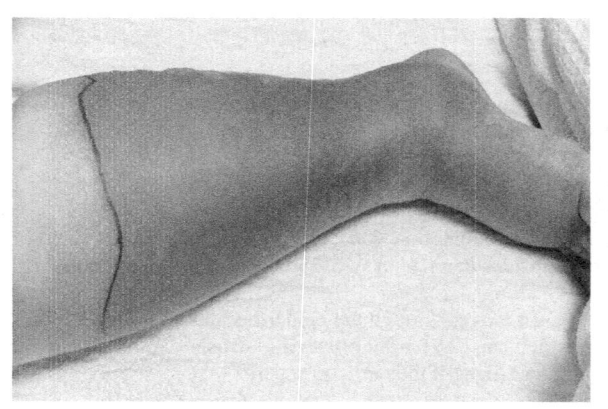

Causes

Cellulitis is caused by **staphylococci bacterium** entering the body through exposure to **wounds**, most commonly on the legs. The infection typically stays localized, but continues to spread to surrounding tissues as the bacteria grows. The infection can present with well-defined borders of infection. If the infection enters the blood stream, it may result in septicemia, a potentially life-threatening condition.

Spider or insect bites may also introduce the bacterium into the body. Any insect bite should be cleaned thoroughly to prevent infection.

Cellulitis presenting with defined border of infection

Symptoms

Cellulitis may present with many symptoms, including a red area of skin that spreads and increases in size over time, swelling, pain, fever, and blisters on the infected area.

Treatments

Treatment for cellulitis includes antibiotic medication, taken orally. Cellulitis is not typically contagious.

Contraindications

Cellulitis is considered a local contraindication. Any open wounds should be avoided.

Contusion

A contusion, also known as a **bruise**, is **damage to blood vessels** in the skin, resulting in **bleeding**. The bleeding usually stops quickly due to thrombocytes clotting the blood, but blood remains in a localized area until it can be slowly removed by the body over time.

Causes

Contusions are caused by trauma to an area damaging and breaking open capillaries in the skin. The trauma is usually caused by a direct blow to the skin.

Symptoms

In the acute stage, pain may be present in the area, as there is trauma. Inflammation may occur as a result to tissue damage. After the contusion has stopped bleeding, the inflammation usually subsides. There may be a dull ache in the contusion as the tissue is being repaired internally.

Contusions leave discoloration in the skin until they are healed and the blood has been removed from the area. The closer to the time trauma occurs, the darker the bruise is. The contusion lightens over time as the blood is removed from the area.

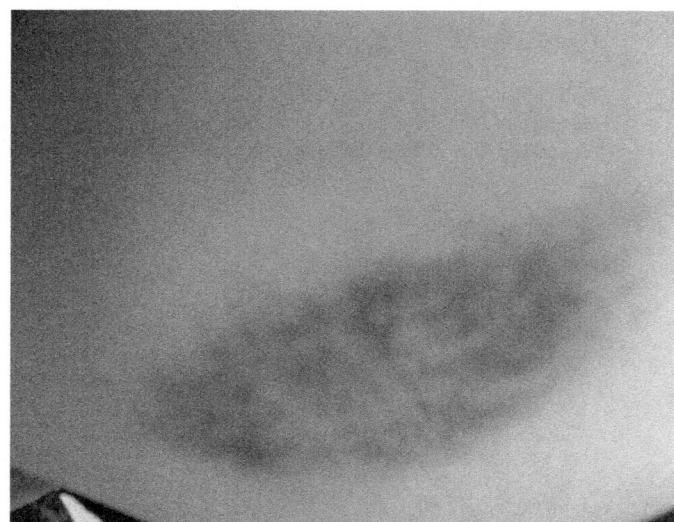

Contusion caused by a baseball that I threw

Treatments

PRICE is the best method of treating a bruise: protect the area from further damage, rest the area, ice the area to reduce pain and inflammation, compress the area to further decrease inflammation, and elevate the area to promote effective blood flow and limit inflammation. Over-the-counter pain medication may be used if the area is painful.

Contraindications

A contusion is considered a local contraindication to massage, due to the potential presence of blood clots in the contusion.

Decubitus Ulcer
(decubitus: the act of lying down; ulcer: open sore)

A decubitus ulcer is a condition affecting the skin, resulting in the development of open sores.

Causes

Decubitus ulcers are also known as **bed sores** or **pressure ulcers**. When the body is in a static position for an extended period of time, such as when lying down, the parts of the body coming in contact with the bed, floor, or chair experience **ischemia**, a reduction of blood flow to the tissues due to pressure. When ischemia is present for too long, the tissue experiences **necrosis** due to a lack of oxygen. The dead tissue becomes ulcerated, and bacterial infection may occur.

People who are prone to decubitus ulcers are the elderly, disabled people, and people confined to a bed or wheelchair.

Symptoms

Symptoms of decubitus ulcers include discoloration of the skin, tenderness in the affected area, temperature variation in the affected area, and swelling. In severe cases, infection may result after ulceration has occurred.

Treatments

Treatments for decubitus ulcers vary, depending on the severity of the ulceration. If an infection is present, antibiotics may be prescribed. If there is an abundance of necrotic tissue, cleaning of the area (debridement) may be performed. If there is ischemia, but no ulcer, massage and application of heat may help bring blood back into the area.

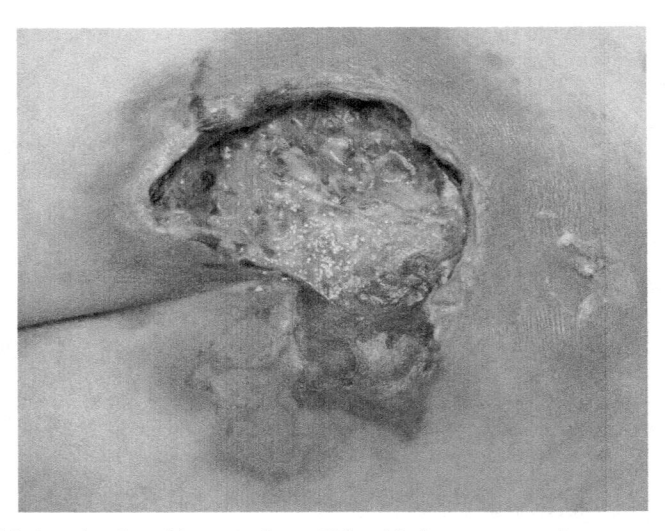

Contraindications

A decubitus ulcer is considered a local contraindication if the skin has developed into an ulcer. If the skin has not opened, massage in the area is indicated to increase blood flow into the affected tissue. If the sore is present, massage up to two inches around the area is indicated to increase circulation and prevent further necrosis.

Dermatitis
(dermat/o: skin; -itis: inflammation)

Dermatitis is **inflammation** of the **skin**. There are several types of dermatitis, including **contact** dermatitis, **atopic** dermatitis, and **seborrheic** dermatitis. Each has different causes, but each presents with some sort of inflammation of the skin.

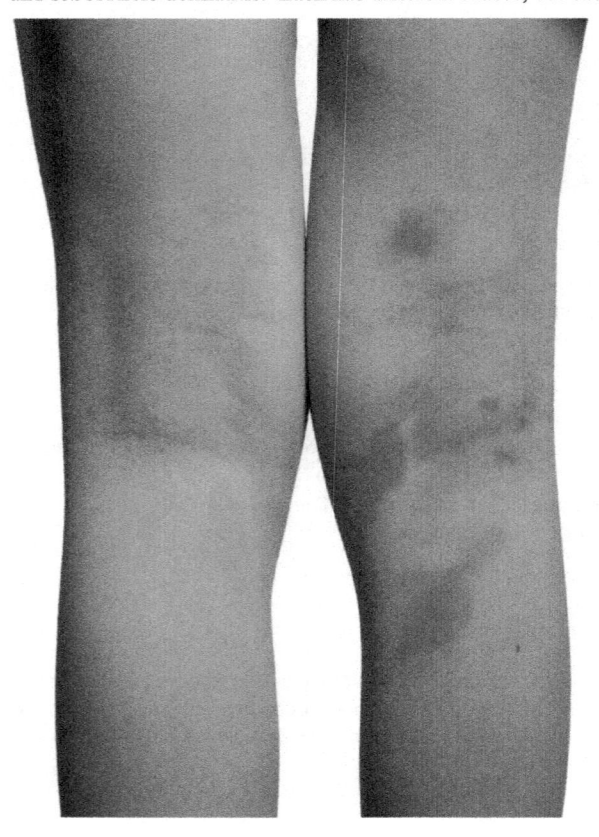

Causes

Contact dermatitis results when the skin comes in to contact with some sort of irritant or allergen, causing the skin to become inflamed. Atopic dermatitis, also known as **eczema**, can be caused by numerous factors, including an improperly functioning immune system, bacteria, dry skin, and the environment. Eczema usually begins in infancy. Seborrheic dermatitis is typically the result of a fungus growing on the skin, usually in regions that are more oily than others such as the scalp.

Symptoms

Contact dermatitis presents with inflammation and possible blistering where the skin has come into contact with an irritant. This is usually an acute condition, and will improve after the irritant has been cleaned or removed from the body. Atopic dermatitis presents with red, itchy patches on the body, usually near joints that flex and extend. This can be a chronic condition, and the patches may go away and come back later depending on factors such as the weather. Seborrheic dermatitis can cause itchy patches around the face, cheeks, nose, back, and chest.

Treatments

Often times, application of an over-the-counter corticosteroid cream is all that's needed to alleviate dermatitis symptoms. If over-the-counter creams are ineffective, prescription strength corticosteroid creams may be administered, which usually take care of the dermatitis. Other treatments can even include exposure to sunlight.

Contraindications

Dermatitis is considered a local contraindication, as massage to the affected area will increase inflammation.

Eczema

See: Dermatitis, Atopic.

Herpes Simplex
(herpein: to creep; simplex: simple)

Herpes Simplex is a **viral infection** of the skin. There are two types of herpes simplex: Herpes Simplex I, which causes sores around the mouth, and Herpes Simplex II, which causes sores around the genitals.

Causes

Herpes simplex is highly contagious, passing between people via direct contact. During an acute outbreak, a sore may appear on the skin, most commonly the mouth, face, or genitals. This sore disappears after a short time. Despite not having any sores present, a person may still be able to transmit the virus to another asymptomatically.

Symptoms

Symptoms vary depending on the type of herpes simplex a person has. Herpes simplex I primarily presents with sores around the mouth, while herpes simplex II may cause painful urination. Both forms, however, may result in fever, headache, and swollen lymph nodes.

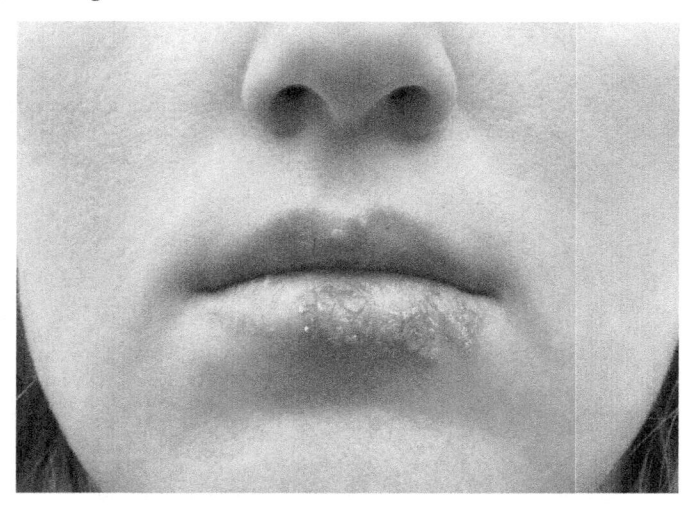

Treatments

While there is no cure for herpes simplex, medications may be prescribed to reduce the chance of spreading the infection to others.

Contraindications

In the acute stage, any sore caused by the herpes simplex virus is considered a local contraindication. In the post-acute stage, massage is indicated.

Impetigo
(impetere: to attack)

Impetigo is a **bacterial infection** of the skin, most commonly seen in **children**. Impetigo is often confused with Hand, Foot, and Mouth Disease, which is a viral infection.

Causes

Impetigo is a highly contagious infection, caused by staphylococci or streptococci, which most commonly enter the body through already damaged skin, but may affect healthy skin as well. When the bacteria enters the skin, it produces sores that blister and leak a yellow, crust-like fluid. These sores typically develop around the mouth, nose, and ears.

Symptoms

Symptoms of impetigo include red sores that may pop and leave a yellowish crust, swollen lymph nodes, and fluid-filled blisters. The affected areas may also itch.

Treatments

Depending on the severity of the infection, impetigo may be treated with topical antibiotic cream for less severe cases, or with oral antibiotics for more severe cases. Recovery time is typically around one week with the use of medication.

Contraindications

Impetigo is a highly contagious bacterial infection, and therefore, is an absolute contraindication.

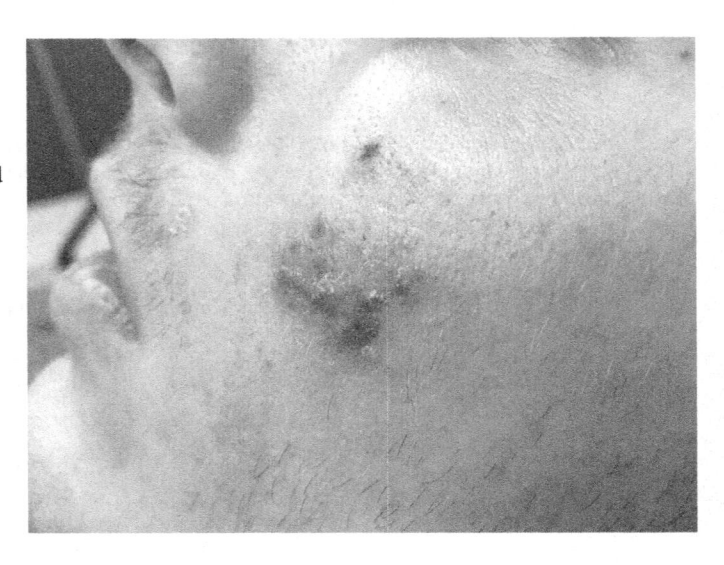

Lice

Lice, plural for a head louse, are small **parasites** that live on the **head** that feed on **human blood**. They primarily live on the scalp. Children are most likely to contract a lice infestation, also known as **pediculosis capitis**.

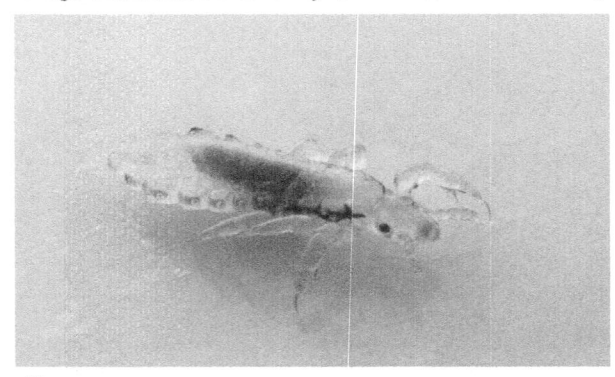

Causes

Lice are spread via direct contact. Lice do not jump or fly, and therefore must physically come into contact with a person to transfer to them. After lice have attached to a new host, they lay eggs on hair shafts. Once the eggs hatch, more lice are present.

Symptoms

The main symptom of lice is itching, caused by an allergy to the saliva of the lice.

Treatments

Over-the-counter or prescription medications may be prescribed to help kill the lice. Shampoos specifically designed to eliminate lice are often used.

Contraindications

Lice is a highly contagious parasitic infection, and is therefore an absolute contraindication.

Onychomycosis
(onycho-: nails; myc-: fungus; -osis: condition)

Onychomycosis is a **fungal infection of the nails**, most commonly the result of an infection by the **dermatophyte fungi**.

Causes

Onychomycosis is caused by fungi entering a nail, typically more common in older people due to the natural drying and cracking of nails that happens with age. The fungus enters into these cracks and begins growing, infecting the nail. Athlete's foot may also spread in to the area and infect the nail.

Symptoms

Symptoms of onychomycosis include thickening of the infected nail, change in the nail shape, discoloration of the nail turning it yellow or brown, and the nail becoming brittle.

Treatments

If symptoms are mild, treatment may not be necessary. When treatment is required, however, antifungal medications are the main form of treatment. Oral antifungals are used more often than topical creams, as they can work quicker. If the infection is severe, the nail may need to be surgically removed to allow antifungal cream to be applied directly to the nail bed.

Contraindications

Onychomycosis is a contagious fungal infection, and is considered a local contraindication.

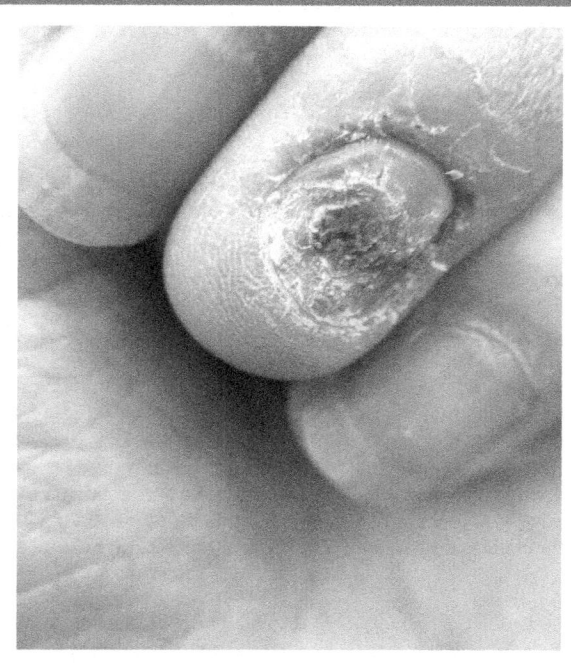

Psoriasis
(psora-: to itch; -iasis: condition)

Psoriasis is an **autoimmune** disorder of the skin, resulting in the production of **thick, dry, scaly patches**. Psoriasis has periods of exacerbation and remission, where the patches appear and then may resolve themselves.

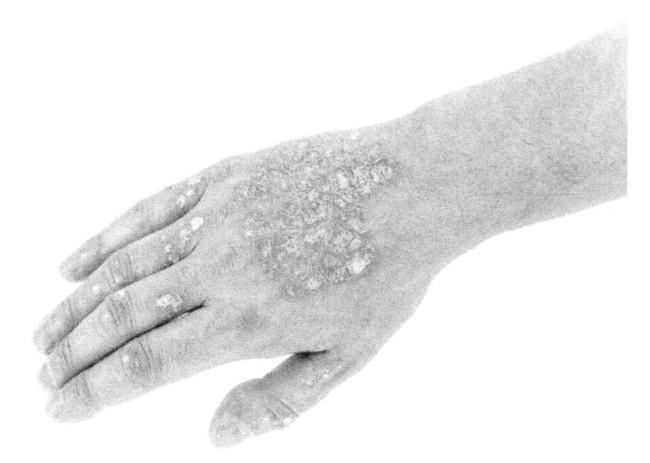

Causes

The exact cause of psoriasis is unknown. Certain triggers, such as stress, may cause the body's immune system to attack the skin. Normally, skin cells have a life span of 3-4 weeks, and ultimately flake off the body. When the immune system attacks the skin, the body responds by increasing production of epithelial cells at an extremely rapid pace, which is much faster than the cells are being destroyed. This rapid pace of cell production is what produces the patches on the skin.

Symptoms

Symptoms of psoriasis differ based on each person, but may include red, patchy skin covered in thick, silvery scales, dry skin that may crack and bleed, thickened finger and toe nails, and itchy skin.

Treatments

There is no cure for psoriasis, but treatments are available to help manage the condition. Treatments include topical creams(which may contain steroids), exposure to sunlight, and application of aloe vera.

Contraindications

Psoriasis is not contraindicated for massage. Massage may be altered if the patches are painful or are scabbing, but otherwise, the patches may be massaged.

Ringworm
(dermato-: skin; phyt-: plant; -osis: condition)

Ringworm(also known as dermatophytosis) is a **fungal** infection of the skin, similar to athlete's foot. Despite the name, it is not a parasitic infection. It results in a **ring-like** area of infection.

Causes

Fungus, like the kind found in ringworm, live on the dead cells of the body, such as the epidermis. When ringworm is contracted, it forms red blisters and a ring of infection begins to show, which then spreads as the infection grows through the skin.

Ringworm is contagious, and may be spread from person to person. It is especially common in athletes, whose bodies come in close contact with one another, such as wrestlers.

Symptoms

Ringworm typically presents with well-defined circular patches of infection on the skin, usually more red on the outer edges than inside. These patches can be itchy and develop blisters.

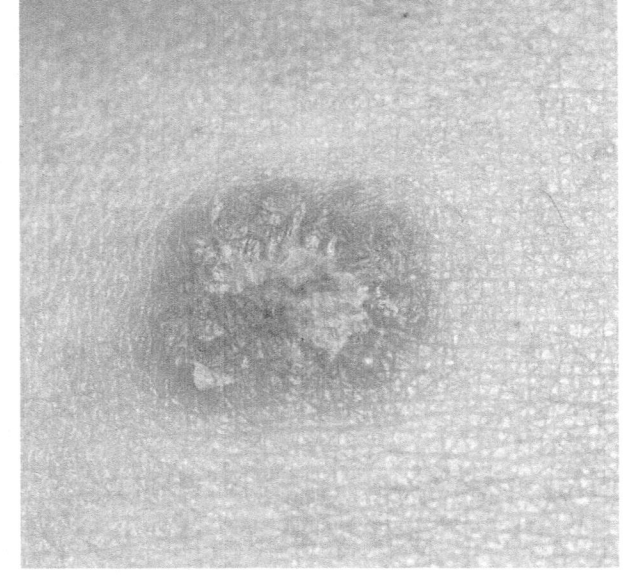

Treatments

Treatment includes good personal hygiene, and most commonly application of antifungal ointment to the affected area. More severe cases may require oral antifungal medication.

Contraindications

Ringworm is a highly contagious fungal infection, and is considered a local contraindication. Linens should be treated as contaminated.

Scabies

Scabies is a **parasitic infection** caused by a **mite**, known as **Sacroptes scabiei**. This mite **burrows under the skin** and **lays eggs**, causing intense **itching**. The tunnels the mite creates are visible in the skin. Scratching due to a scabies infection may lead to an infection, and is not recommended.

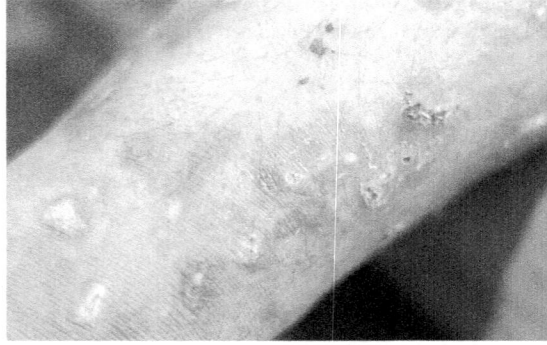

Causes

Scabies are extremely contagious, transmitting easily from one person to the next via physical contact, or sharing clothing or other linens.

Symptoms

The main symptoms of a scabies infection are severe itching and visible burrows in the skin where the mite has worked its way in to the body.

Treatments

Topical creams that are specifically designed to kill mites are prescribed to treat scabies. They kill the mites quickly, but itching may persist for some time after treatment begins.

Contraindications

Scabies is a contagious parasitic infection, and is considered an absolute contraindication.

Sebaceous Cyst

A sebaceous cyst is a condition affecting the skin, but may affect other tissues as well. These are typically the result of a **blockage** in a **sebaceous gland** that causes a backup of sebum, which is then surrounded by a **membrane** to keep it or an infection from harming the rest of the body.

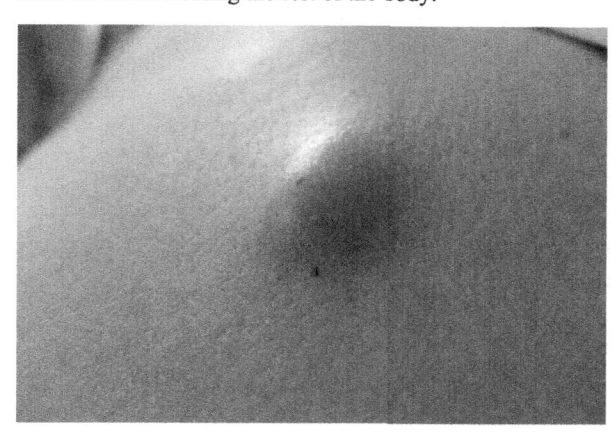

Causes

A sebaceous gland produces oil, and secretes oil onto the surface of the skin. If a blockage of a sebaceous gland occurs, oil cannot escape the gland, and bacteria may infect the area. If too much bacteria is present, the body may develop connective tissue that surrounds the infected sebaceous gland, trapping it inside. This is a sebaceous cyst.

Sebaceous cysts may be large or small. They may be painful to the touch, or may lead to localized infections known as abscesses. Cysts may need to be removed surgically. If the entire cyst membrane is not removed, there may be a chance of the cyst returning in the future.

Symptoms

Some cysts show no symptoms, but symptoms are more likely to appear the larger the cyst is. Small cysts usually do not cause pain, but large cysts may cause pain and discomfort in the surrounding area.

Treatments

Treatment, if necessary, includes moist compresses on the area to help drain the cyst, or possible surgery if there is a risk of infection. Surgical removal may be required if the cyst is large, causes pain, or may be cancerous.

Contraindications

Sebaceous cysts are considered local contraindications, and should be avoided to prevent damaging the cyst and allowing the fluid inside to harm the body. The area may also be painful.

Shingles

Shingles, also known as **herpes zoster**, is a **viral infection** that results in a **painful skin rash**. The rash most commonly occurs on one side of the torso, although it can appear anywhere. The strain of herpes is not the same strain that causes cold sores or genital herpes(herpes simplex, page 139), but the same strain that causes chickenpox.

Causes

Shingles is the result of an infection of the varicella-zoster virus, the virus that causes chickenpox. Shingles occurs when the virus lies dormant in the Nervous System after a chickenpox infection. The virus reactivates, but instead of causing chickenpox again, it causes a rash to appear in the skin. Not every person infected with chickenpox will have the virus reactivate and get shingles. Older adults and people with immune systems that may be weakened tend to develop shingles more commonly than others.

Symptoms

Painful, burning rashes appear on the skin, usually on one side of the body. These rashes may contain blisters that can break open.

Treatments

Although there is no cure for shingles, treatments are available to help with symptoms. These treatments include antiviral medications to prevent the virus from reproducing, and medications that relieve pain that may be associated with the infection. The condition should resolve after no longer than six weeks.

Contraindications

Much like chickenpox, shingles should be treated as an absolute contraindication until the condition resolves.

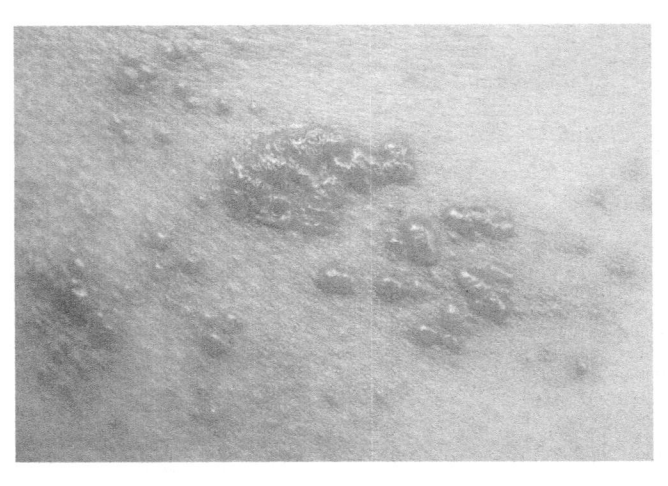

Urticaria

Urticaria, also known as **hives**, is a condition that results in **welts**, known as **wheals**, appearing on the skin. Wheals are raised areas that typically itch. Wheals can appear anywhere on the body.

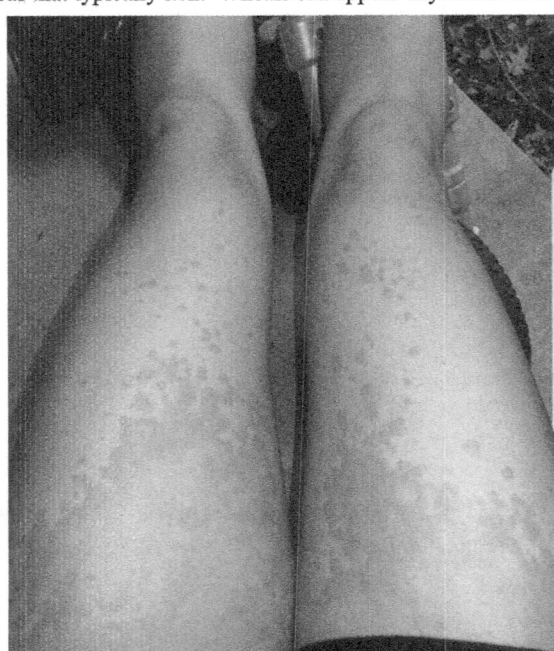

Causes

Urticaria is caused by the release of **histamines** into the blood. The body may release histamines in response to the body coming in to contact with a substance it is allergic to, in response to insect or bug bites/stings, scratches, and even certain infections. Histamines dilate blood vessels, which bring leukocytes and plasma in to the area to help destroy any substance that may be causing the reaction.

Symptoms

Typically seen in the skin, wheals form that are usually itchy. These can be raised off the skin, discolored, and possibly painful.

Treatments

Over-the-counter antihistamines are likely the first treatment recommended. If the condition does not resolve, prescription antihistamines may be given. Immunosuppressants, anti-inflammatory medication, and even oral corticosteroids such as prednisone may also be given to help with the reaction.

Contraindications

In the acute stage, the cause of the hives should be determined before massage can be performed. Once the cause is determined, massage on the area should be avoided, or if it's a more serious reason for hives, massage should be avoided completely.

Wart

Warts(also known as verrucae), are small **benign growths** on the **skin**, caused by the **human papilloma virus(HPV)**.

Causes

Warts are contagious, and may be spread by direct skin contact. The human papilloma virus stimulates the skin to produce more keratin, which causes a hard, thick overgrowth on a small localized area.

Warts may be located in numerous locations on the body, including the hands, feet(plantar warts), and genitals(genital warts).

Symptoms

Warts are typically rough, grainy bumps, which may be a range of colors, from the color of the person's skin to white, tan, or even pink. Often, warts may have black spots in them, which is nothing more than blood clots.

Depending on the location of the wart, such as plantar warts, the wart may be painful due to calluses forming over them, pushing them deeper into the skin.

Treatments

Warts often go into remission on their own, and treatment is not necessary. Treatment options include cryotherapy to freeze the wart, excising(cutting out) the wart, or electrosurgery to burn the wart.

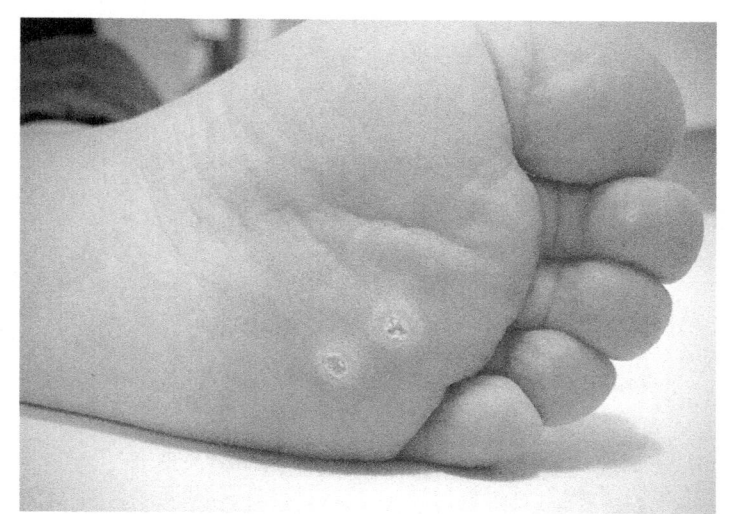

Contraindications

Plantar warts

Warts are contagious, and should be treated as a local contraindication.

Wounds

Wounds are the result of a **breakage** in the **skin**, which exposes underlying tissues. There are several different types of open wounds.

An **abrasion** is a scraping off of layers of the skin, such as a skinned knee from falling. An **avulsion** is when the skin or another structure, such as a finger or toe nail, is pulled and ripped. An **incision**, such as produced during surgery, is a **clean cut** through tissue. A **laceration** is a cut that produces **jagged edges**. A **puncture** is caused by an object **piercing** the skin, producing a **hole**.

Causes

Wounds can be caused by many different factors. Ischemia may cause wounds in cases such as decubitus ulcers(page 137). Infections may cause wounds to appear in the skin as well. Damage to blood vessels, like those seen in diabetes mellitus (page 130) can result in wounds.

Trauma is usually the main cause of wounds, however. These include abrasions, lacerations, incisions, and punctures.

Symptoms

Wounds in the acute stage often present with bleeding, pain, and redness in the area. These symptoms usually resolve with the healing process. If a wound is not properly treated, infection may occur, along with fever if the infection becomes systemic. A wound that becomes infected and results in necrosis is known as gangrene, caused by a severe lack of blood flow in the area.

Treatments

Wounds should be cleansed with soap and water, and a sterile bandage should be applied to stop bleeding. If a wound is caused by a bite from an animal or insect, medical attention may(and probably should) be recommended.

Contraindications

Wounds should be treated as local contraindications until healed.

Abrasion

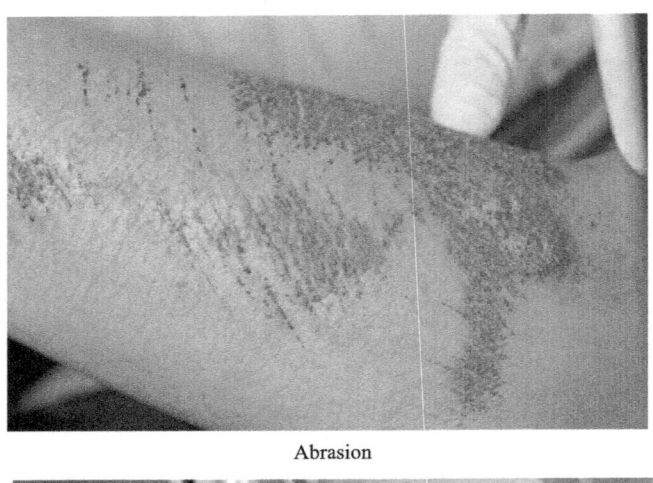

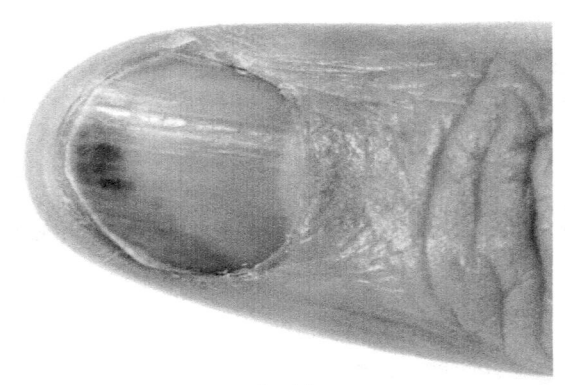

Avulsion

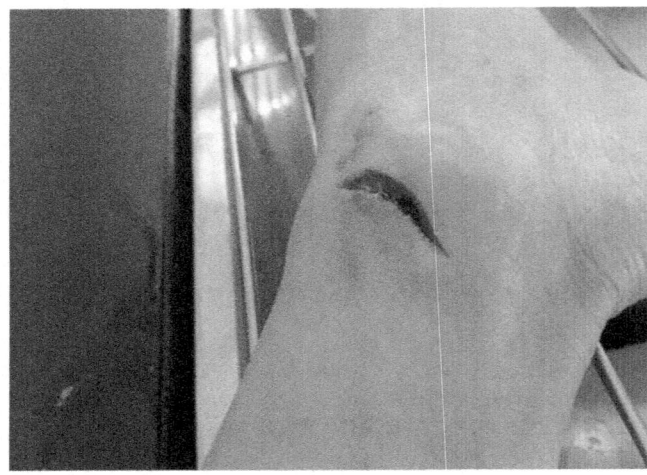

Laceration

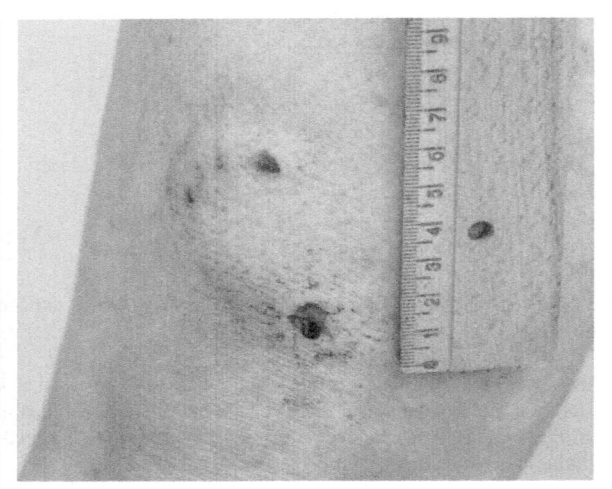

Puncture

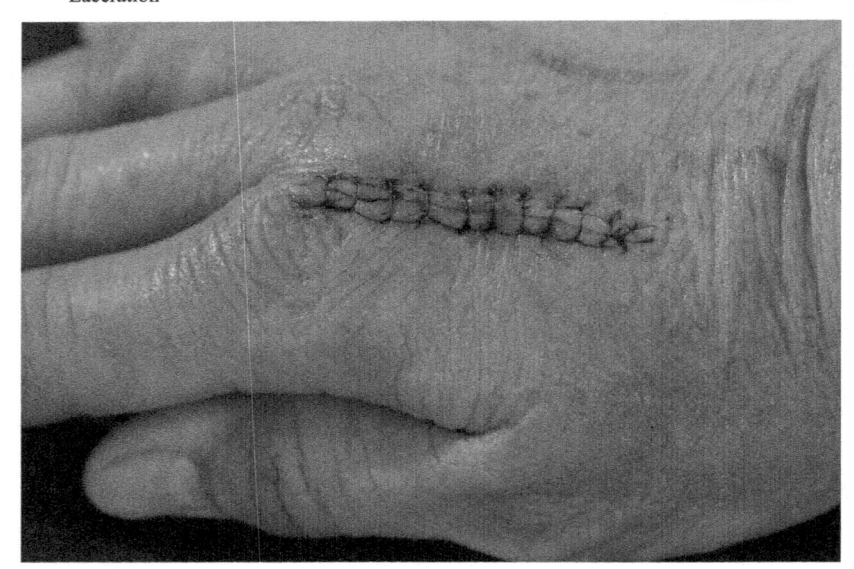

Incision closed with sutures

Lymphatic System Pathologies

Acquired Immunodeficiency Syndrome

Acquired Immunodeficiency Syndrome, also known as **AIDS**, is a chronic condition caused by **HIV** infection, or the human immunodeficiency virus. Once in the body, HIV **destroys** the body's **T-cells**, which function to regulate the response of the body's immune system to antigens. When HIV destroys too many of the body's T-cells, the immune system is considered compromised, and a person is then diagnosed with AIDS. While most people who are infected with HIV in the United States are properly treated and don't develop AIDS, a small portion of people do gets AIDS after HIV infection, typically around ten years after initial infection.

Causes

HIV is spread though unprotected sex, through needles that have been shared by an infected person, as a result of a mother passing HIV on to their unborn child, or even through blood transfusions if the blood has not been properly screened beforehand. HIV cannot be spread through skin contact, water contact, through the bites of insects such as mosquitoes, or breathing in the air of an infected person.

Symptoms

Close after the initial infection has occurred, a person may experience fever, fatigue, body aches, headache, and swollen lymph nodes. As the infection spreads, symptoms emerge such as diarrhea and weight loss in conjunction with previously mentioned symptoms.

Complications caused by infection by HIV include being more prone to infection of other conditions such as pneumonia. A type of cancer known as Kaposi's Sarcoma may develop. Severe wasting of the body may occur, in which a person loses at least ten percent of their total body weight.

Treatments

A person infected with HIV should be prescribed antiretroviral therapy to help prevent the virus from further replicating.

Contraindications

AIDS is not a contraindication to massage. Any open sores should be treated as a local contraindication. If the client isn't feeling well, massage should be rescheduled.

Allergy

An allergy is a reaction of the body's immune system in response to substances that normally **do not affect people**. Common substances people may be allergic to include dust, pollen, mold, certain foods, pet dander, and medication.

Causes

Allergies occur when a substance enters the body that the body's immune system thinks is dangerous. The body produces **antibodies** for that specific substance. When the substance enters the body, the body releases the antibodies and other substances such as **histamines** to attack the substance. The release of histamines is what gives people allergy symptoms.

Symptoms

Allergies may be mild, or may be severe and result in serious conditions such as anaphylactic shock. Anaphylactic shock requires the use of an epinephrine shot to reverse the effects of the allergen. Less severe allergies may result in a runny nose, itchy eyes or skin, and hives.

Treatments

Typical treatments of allergens include the use of antihistamines, decongestants, and steroid nasal sprays. Avoiding the allergen is advised.

Contraindications

Allergies should be determined prior to massage to avoid using any allergens in massage lubricant. If a client develops any signs of contact with an allergen during the massage, massage should be stopped. If essential oils are the cause of the allergic reaction, effects can be managed with the application of vegetable oil.

Lupus Erythematosus
(lupus: wolf; erythemat-: red skin; -osus: pertaining to)

Lupus Erythematosus is an autoimmune disorder affecting the **connective tissues** of the entire body, but can be physically seen in the skin by the formation of a **butterfly rash** that appears on the face during flare-ups. This rash is similar in shape to the markings found on the face of a wolf, which is where lupus gets its name.

Causes

The exact cause of lupus is unknown. Some experts believe it is a genetic disorder that influences the immune system's function. Lupus may also be triggered by smoking, sunlight, infections, and medications.

Symptoms

Symptoms of lupus erythematosus include fever, the formation of a butterfly rash, joint pain, discomfort, fatigue, and sensitivity to sunlight. It may also contribute to the development of other medical conditions, such as Raynaud's Syndrome.

Treatments

There is no cure for lupus erythematosus, but treatment is available to help manage the condition. Non-steroidal anti-inflammatory drugs may help with systemic inflammation in non-severe cases. Topical corticosteroid creams may help alleviate rashes. Blood thinners may also be used in more severe cases.

Contraindications

During flare-ups, lupus may cause extensive pain over the body, and massage would likely be postponed until the condition has gone into remission. If there are no symptoms, lupus is not contraindicated.

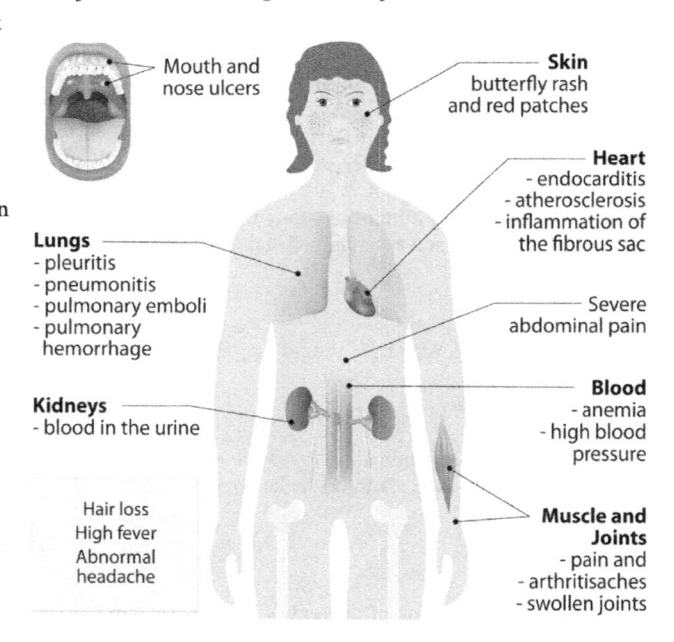

Systemic lupus erythematosus

- Mouth and nose ulcers
- Skin: butterfly rash and red patches
- Heart: endocarditis, atherosclerosis, inflammation of the fibrous sac
- Lungs: pleuritis, pneumonitis, pulmonary emboli, pulmonary hemorrhage
- Severe abdominal pain
- Kidneys: blood in the urine
- Blood: anemia, high blood pressure
- Hair loss, High fever, Abnormal headache
- Muscle and Joints: pain and arthritisaches, swollen joints

Lymphedema
(lymph: lymph; -edema: swelling)

Lymphedema is a condition of the Lymphatic System that results in increased **interstitial fluid** in a limb, which causes **swelling**.

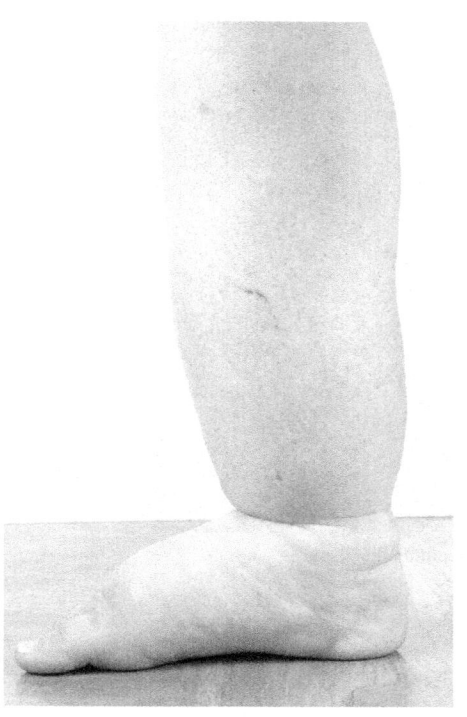

Causes

Causes of lymphedema vary. Most commonly, it results from damage to the lymph nodes and vessels during treatment for cancer(such as a mastectomy, where breast tissue and lymph channels may be completely removed). This results in lymph not draining properly. Other causes include obesity and advanced age.

Symptoms

Symptoms of lymphedema include swelling in the limbs, restricted range-of-motion, discomfort in the affected area, and thickening of the skin.

Treatments

While there is no cure for lymphedema, treatments may help reduce the amount of fluid in the area by stimulating lymph circulation. Massage therapy is highly effective at increasing lymph circulation. Compression clothing may help move lymph. Exercise is also extremely helpful in increasing lymph flow.

Contraindications

Lymphedema is not contraindicated for massage. Lymphatic drainage may help move lymph out of the area. When performing lymphatic drainage, light strokes moving towards the trunk should be performed on the proximal end of the affected limb, then distal areas may be worked on, again with strokes moving towards the trunk.

Pitting Edema
(edema: swelling)

Pitting edema is a form of lymphedema that produces **pits** in the skin after **pressure** is applied and released. Lymphedema does not leave pits, and the skin rebounds immediately due to the amount of fluid in the area.

Causes

Pitting edema may be non-serious, or may have severe underlying causes. A common cause of pitting edema is pregnancy, due to the body creating much more fluid than it normally has. This increases fluid retention. Other more serious causes include heart failure, liver failure, or most commonly amongst these, **renal** failure. If these organs are not functioning properly, fluid is not effectively drained from the body, which increases swelling.

Symptoms

Pitting edema results in pits left in the skin after applying pressure. Other symptoms may include swelling, pain, numbness, and cramping in the area. If the swelling is near a joint, movement of the joint may become difficult.

Treatments

For serious cases of pitting edema, it is recommended to visit a doctor to find the underlying cause. Once the cause is determined, a proper treatment plan may be developed. Typically, if a person is suffering from organ failure, diuretics may be prescribed to help drain excess fluid from the body. Keeping limbs such as the legs elevated may also help reduce swelling.

Contraindications

Massage on a client with pitting edema should not be performed until the cause of pitting edema is established. If the cause is something such as pregnancy and not organ failure, massage of the limb may be performed as it would be done with lymphedema.

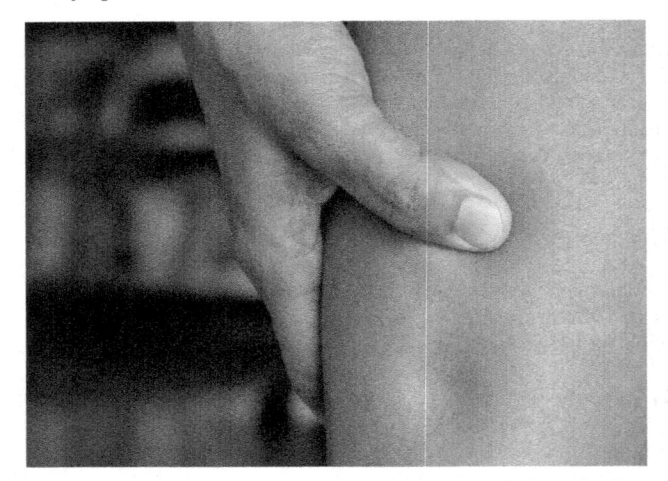

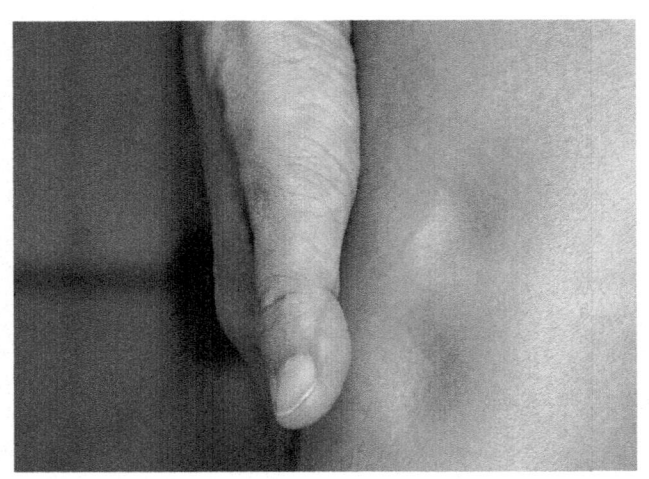

Applying pressure then releasing, showing pitting due to excessive fluid

Muscular System Pathologies

Adhesive Capsulitis
(capsul-: capsule; -itis: inflammation)

Adhesive capsulitis is a condition resulting in **restricted range-of-motion** at the **shoulder joint**. Another name for adhesive capsulitis is **"Frozen Shoulder"**.

Causes

Surrounding the glenohumeral joint is connective tissue known as the joint capsule. This joint capsule holds everything in the joint in place, such as the bones themselves, synovial membrane, synovial fluid, etc. If there is irritation or over-use of the shoulder joint, **adhesions** may form between the joint capsule and the head of the humerus. These adhesions can decrease range-of-motion in the joint, and make movement in the joint uncomfortable.

The **subscapularis** muscle is often called the "Frozen Shoulder Muscle", due to its possible role in adhesive capsulitis. If the subscapularis is hypertonic, it may pull back on the humerus, which can restrict range-of-motion.

Symptoms

As adhesive capsulitis progresses, symptoms vary. In beginning stages, pain may be present, with a gradual decrease in the range-of-motion. As the condition advances, pain may subside, with a severely reduced range-of-motion.

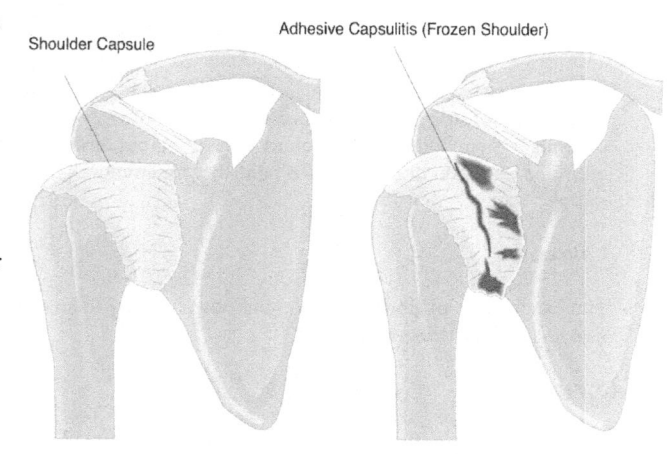

Treatments

Treatments include stretching exercises and massage therapy to help break up the adhesions restricting range-of-motion, or to relax the subscapularis.

Contraindications

Adhesive capsulitis is not a contraindication. Massage may help loosen adhesions and increase range-of-motion. Stretching should be performed, as well as compression in the joint.

De Quervain's Tenosynovitis
(teno-: tendon; synov-: synovial; -itis: inflammation)

De Quervain's Tenosynovitis is a form of tenosynovitis(page 155) that specifically affects the **thumb**.

Causes

De Quervain's Tenosynovitis is caused by **over-use of the thumb**, which contributes to straining of the tendons around the thumb and their protective sheaths. This may cause pain around the thumb, inflammation, and difficulty in moving the area.

Symptoms

Symptoms include pain and inflammation at the base of the thumb, loss of sensation in the posterior thumb, and difficulty moving the thumb and/or wrist while performing certain actions. Pain may gradually increase and radiate to other areas, such as the posterior forearm.

Treatments

Treatments primarily consist of rest and ice to reduce pain and inflammation in the area. Any repetitive actions that are causing the inflammation should be stopped to allow irritation to subside.

Contraindications

Massage is a local contraindication for De Quervain's Tenosynovitis, as it may increase inflammation and pain. Application of cold may be performed to decrease inflammation around the thumb.

Fibromyalgia
(fibro-: fibrous; my-: muscle; -algia: pain)

Fibromyalgia is a condition causing **pain throughout the body**, in conjunction with **fatigue**. Trouble with memory may also be present. Fibromyalgia may occur suddenly, or may worsen over time. Fibromyalgia typically affects women much more often than men. Diagnosis involves first ruling out other conditions that may be causing symptoms. If these other conditions are ruled out, then the duration of pain(over three months) and location of pain(using the **Widespread Pain Index**) are taken into account.

Causes

The exact cause of fibromyalgia is unknown. Many theories state the cause could range from hereditary to environmental factors, such as stress or trauma.

Symptoms

Symptoms of fibromyalgia primarily include widespread pain, usually a dull ache, in specific regions of the body for longer than three months, general fatigue, and issues with memory.

Treatments

Medications are important in the treatment of fibromyalgia. Pain relievers help to reduce the pain a person may be experiencing, while antidepressants can help treat depression that may result due to the fatigue a person can experience.

Contraindications

Fibromyalgia is indicated for massage, working within the client's pain tolerance.

Golfer's Elbow

Golfer's Elbow is a form of tendonitis that affects and weakens the **flexors** of the wrist. Golfer's Elbow is also known as Medial Epicondylitis, inflammation of the **medial epicondyle**.

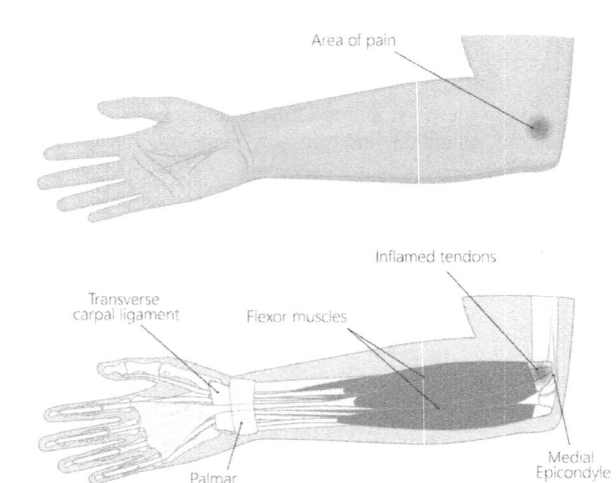

Causes

Golfer's Elbow is caused by repetitive motions such as elbow flexion, which put strain on the tendons connecting the flexors of the wrist to the humerus, at the medial epicondyle.

Symptoms

Golfer's Elbow may present with pain and inflammation at the medial epicondyle of the humerus, weakness in the elbow joint, and numbness in digits four and five.

Treatments

Treatment typically involves rest, and ice on the medial epicondyle to reduce inflammation. Any repetitive actions that are causing the inflammation should be stopped to allow irritation to subside.

Contraindications

Golfer's Elbow should be treated as a local contraindication. Application of cold may help reduce pain and inflammation at the medial epicondyle of the humerus.

Muscle Cramp

Muscle cramps are **involuntary contractions** of a muscle, and are usually **painful**.

Causes

Dehydration and **overuse** of a muscle are prime causes of muscle cramps. However, a cramp may develop due to other factors, including a low supply of blood which reduces oxygen intake in the muscle, or compression of nerves. Loss of electrolytes, such as sodium or potassium, may also lead the muscle cramping.

Symptoms

Pain in the location of the cramp is the prime symptom of muscle cramps. A person may also be able to visibly see the muscle cramping under the skin.

Treatments

Cramps are typically not serious, and only require minimal treatment to fix. Stretching and utilizing reciprocal inhibition(contracting the opposing muscle of the muscle cramping) can help calm the cramping in the acute stage. Keeping hydrated and providing the body with nutrients such as potassium may help prevent muscle cramping.

Contraindications

Muscle cramps in the acute stage should be considered a local contraindication. Reciprocal inhibition should be performed to stop the cramp. After a cramp has subsided, massage may be performed on the area, bringing fresh blood and nutrients into the area. The client should increase water intake after the massage as a preventative measure.

Strain

A strain is an injury to a **tendon** or **muscle**, usually caused by over-exertion or over-use.

Causes

Activities such as exercise are a common cause of strains. Much like burns, there are three grades of strains: grade 1, grade 2, and grade 3. The less severe the strain, the lower the grade.

A **grade 1 strain** results in **slight tearing** of a tendon or muscle. An example could be a person's muscles being sore after exercise. The muscles have experienced slight tears during exercise, but will heal after a day or two.

A **grade 2 strain** results in more tearing of a muscle or tendon. Grade 2 strains may require surgery to repair, or may heal on their own with rest. There may be accompanying **bruising and inflammation** around the strain.

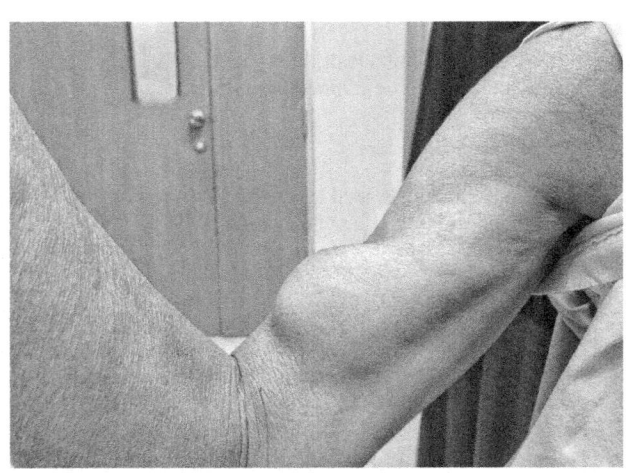

Torn tendon of the long head of the biceps brachii, grade 3 strain

A **grade 3 strain** results in **complete tearing** of a muscle, or more commonly, a tendon. Surgery is required to repair a grade 3 strain. The quadriceps and biceps brachii are two muscles prone to grade 3 strains more than others. Grade 3 strains will inhibit movement involved with the muscle involved, due to its inability to pull on the bone.

Symptoms

Strains may result in pain, inflammation, and an inability to move the injured muscle or tendon.

Treatments

Treatment varies depending on the severity of the strain. Grade 1 strains should be able to receive massage and heat therapy after 24-48 hours to increase circulation and promote healing. Grade 2 strains may need to rest longer before treatment. Grade 3 strains would require surgery to repair.

Contraindications

Acute strains are considered a local contraindication, and should be avoided to prevent increasing pain and inflammation in the area. Contrast therapy, utilizing alternating cold and heat, ending with cold, may be performed to decrease inflammation and bring fresh blood to the area.

Easy to Remember: To remember the difference between a strain and sprain, look for the "t" in "strain"! "T" for "tendon"!

Tendonitis
(tendon-: tendon; -itis: inflammation)

Tendonitis is an injury that results in **inflammation of a tendon**.

Causes

Tendonitis is a mostly repetitive strain injury, caused by repeated use of one specific muscle, which can over-exert the tendon. When the tendon is over-exerted, it may tear slightly, which causes pain and inflammation.

There are several different types of tendonitis, including Golfer's Elbow(inflammation of the tendon at the medial epicondyle of the humerus), Tennis Elbow(inflammation of the tendon at the lateral epicondyle of the humerus), and Jumper's Knee(inflammation of the patellar tendon). All these conditions are caused by repetitive movements.

Symptoms

Symptoms may include pain upon moving a muscle connected to an affected tendon, and inflammation.

Treatments

Treatment for tendonitis is primarily rest and application of ice to reduce any inflammation. Repetitive actions causing the inflammation should be stopped until the irritation subsides.

Contraindications

Tendonitis should be treated as a local contraindication. Alternating application of cold and heat, ending with cold, can assist in decreasing inflammation and associated pain.

Tennis Elbow

Tennis Elbow is a form of tendonitis that affects and weakens the **extensors** of the wrist. Tennis Elbow is also known as Lateral Epicondylitis, inflammation of the **lateral epicondyle**.

Causes

Tennis Elbow is caused by repetitive motions such as elbow extension, which put strain on the tendons connecting the extensors of the wrist to the humerus, at the lateral epicondyle.

Tennis Elbow
Right arm, lateral (outside) side

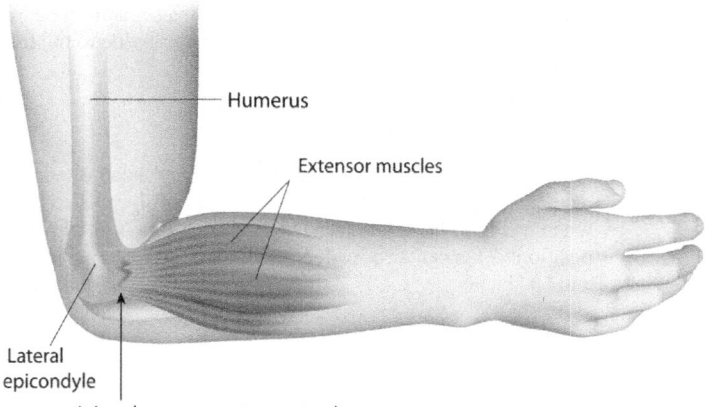

Symptoms

Tennis Elbow commonly presents with pain that radiates distally to the posterior forearm. Weakness may result, especially when performing actions that require grasping.

Treatments

Treatment typically involves rest, and ice on the lateral epicondyle to reduce inflammation. Any repetitive actions that are causing the inflammation should be stopped to allow irritation to subside.

Contraindications

Tennis Elbow should be treated as a local contraindication. Alternating application of cold and heat, ending with cold, can assist in decreasing inflammation and associated pain at the lateral epicondyle of the humerus.

Tenosynovitis
(teno-: tendon; synov-: synovial; -itis: inflammation)

Tenosynovitis is a repetitive strain injury that results in **inflammation of a tendon** and its **protective sheath**.

Causes

Tenosynovitis primarily affects the hands, wrists, and feet due to the length of the tendons in these areas. The longer the tendon is, the easier it becomes to strain. Because there may be inflammation, pain may be present, and it may be difficult to move the affected area.

A common type of tenosynovitis is known as De Quervain's Tenosynovitis, which causes inflammation around the thumb due to over-use.

Symptoms

Tenosynovitis may produce pain and inflammation in affected joints, making it painful to move these joints. The area of the inflamed tendon may also be red.

Treatments

Tenosynovitis is typically treated the same as any strain, with rest and ice to reduce pain. Less commonly, tenosynovitis may be the result of bacterial infection, which may produce a fever. If a fever is present, medications such as antibiotics and antipyretics may be prescribed to combat bacterial growth and fever.

Contraindications

Massage is a local contraindication for tenosynovitis, as it may increase inflammation and pain. Application of cold may be performed to decrease inflammation in the tendon and reduce pain.

Torticollis
(torti-: twisted; collis: neck)

Torticollis, also known as **wry neck**, is a condition causing the neck to **twist to one side**, which **tilts the head**.

Causes

Trauma to the cervical region may cause torticollis. An injury to the **sternocleidomastoid** is often the prime cause. Spasms of the sternocleidomastoid may cause a type of torticollis known as spasmodic torticollis, and is usually a chronic condition. An injury to the trochlear nerve may cause a separate type of torticollis known as trochlear torticollis, in which a person must adjust the position of their head to see properly due to the trochlear nerve, which provides stimulation to muscles controlling the eye, no longer functioning as effectively.

Symptoms

A person affected by torticollis will have their head tilted to one side. This can be uncomfortable or painful, especially when trying to move the neck or head back to a normal position. This can also lead to pain in the back and shoulders, and headaches.

Treatments

Because torticollis is the result of a spasm or contraction of neck muscles, treatments aim to relax the affected muscles. These treatments may include physical therapy, prescribing muscle relaxants, or possible surgery to correct any structural issues that may arise. Torticollis usually resolves itself within a few days, unless there is a more severe cause.

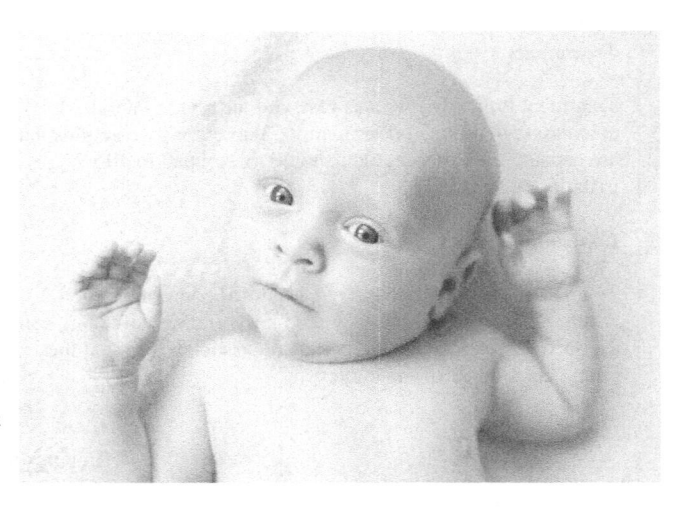

Contraindications

Torticollis is generally not considered a contraindication, but precautions should be taken if damage to a muscle or nerve is the cause.

Nervous System Pathologies

Alzheimer's Disease

Alzheimer's Disease, the most common form of **dementia**, is an over-arching term for **memory loss**, **confusion**, and a **general loss of intellectual abilities**. Alzheimer's is a result of brain tissue gradually dying over time. Increased age is a risk factor of developing Alzheimer's, and becomes much more common after the age of 65 in those affected.

Causes

While the exact cause of Alzheimer's is unknown, environmental factors are the most likely culprit. Few people with Alzheimer's disease develop the disease due to genetic factors.

Two factors strongly contribute to the death of nervous tissue: plaque and tangles. Plaque is the formation of deposits of a protein known as beta-amyloid, which develops in the space between nerves, restricting communication between nerve cells. Tangles are the development of another protein known as tau inside the nerve cells, which can cut off the natural flow of nutrients through cells.

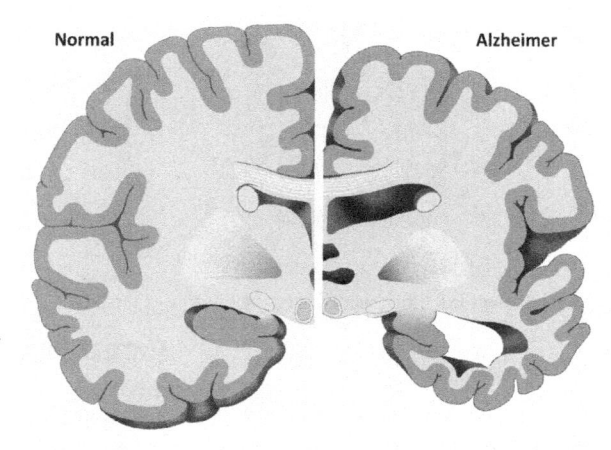

Symptoms

Symptoms begin with difficulty remembering information, such as locations of items or things just learned. As the condition progresses, more brain tissue is lost, and a person may have difficulty making decisions, identifying people or places, and become more irritable or aggressive. Later stages of Alzheimer's may see the loss of the ability to read, write, dance, sing, and other activities learned early in life.

Treatments

There is no cure for Alzheimer's, but there are treatments available that can help manage the condition. Medications may be prescribed that can help with memory loss and other cognitive symptoms. In later stages, other medications may be prescribed that can help with memory, speech, and the ability to perform simpler tasks.

Contraindications

Alzheimer's Disease is not contraindicated for massage, although precautions may be taken in advanced stages of the disease. A person the client knows and is familiar with may stay in the room to assist with the client if the client becomes forgetful regarding their location.

Bell's Palsy
(palsy: paralysis)

Bell's Palsy is a condition affecting the **facial nerve**, causing **paralysis** on **one side of the face**.

Causes

The exact cause of Bell's Palsy is unknown, but is likely the result of an attack to the facial nerve (cranial nerve VII) by the herpes simplex virus. The inflammation damages the nerve, causing the muscles of the side of the face controlled by the facial nerve to become paralyzed or severely weakened. The side of the face affected may also become numb.

Bell's Palsy is mostly a temporary condition, and should resolve over the course of a month or two. In some cases, it can become permanent.

Pathology

Symptoms

Symptoms, which are usually only present on one side of the face, include the inability to close the eye, difficulty chewing, twitching of muscles in the face, and watery eyes. These symptoms typically resolve within three weeks at the earliest, but may persist for several months, or even become permanent.

Treatments

A person with Bell's Palsy may take corticosteroids to help treat the muscle weakness. Self care, including facial exercises, are recommended.

Contraindications

Bell's Palsy is indicated for massage. The side of the face that is paralyzed should be massaged lightly to avoid damaging any tissue. The client may not be able to tell the therapist if the massage is too deep around facial structures, so lighter massage on the affected area should be performed.

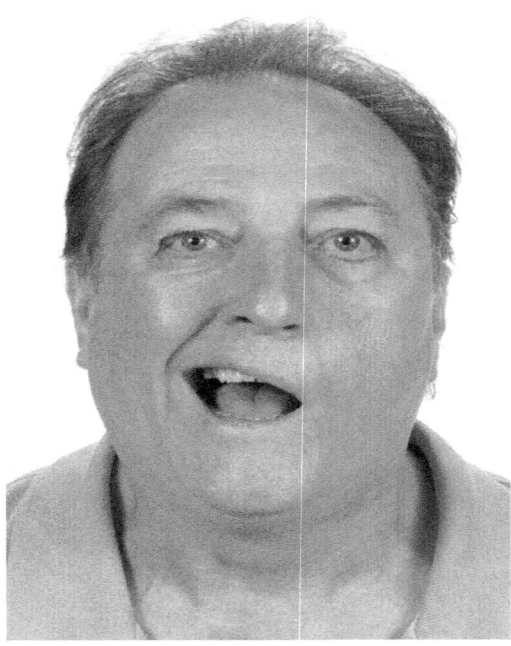

Patient exhibiting paralysis on the left side of the face

Carpal Tunnel Syndrome

Carpal Tunnel Syndrome is a condition caused by compression of the **median nerve** between the carpals and the **transverse carpal ligament**.

Causes

Several factors may contribute to the development of carpal tunnel syndrome, although the most common cause is **repetitive movements**. These repetitive movements can cause straining of the tendons that run through the carpal canal, which can place pressure on the median nerve. If the transverse carpal ligament tightens, it can also place pressure on the median nerve. When pressure is placed on the median nerve, numbness, pain, or tingling sensations may be experienced in the thumb, index, ring, and lateral side of the ring finger.

Symptoms

Carpal tunnel syndrome often results in pain, numbness, and tingling sensations in the hand and wrist. Atrophy of the hand muscles may result due to lack of use.

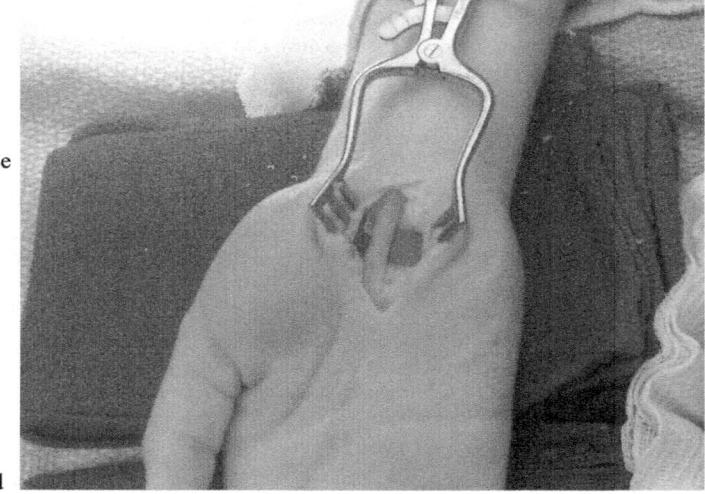

Carpal tunnel release surgery with median nerve visible

Treatments

Several treatments are available for carpal tunnel syndrome. Self-care is recommended, including stretching the forearm and wrist flexors, massaging the transverse carpal ligament and hand muscles, and icing the area. Because carpal tunnel syndrome is often caused by repetitive actions, ceasing these actions is recommended. Non-steroidal anti-inflammatory medications may be prescribed. Surgery to remove the transverse carpal ligament may also be an option if the condition is severe.

Contraindications

Massage is indicated for carpal tunnel syndrome. Cross-fiber and circular friction on the transverse carpal ligament should be performed to help loosen adhesions in the area. Application of heat can help soften the ligament, and allow more space in the carpal canal.

Encephalitis
(encephal-: brain; -itis: inflammation)

Encephalitis is primarily a **viral infection** that results in **inflammation** of the **brain**.

Causes

Causes of encephalitis vary, but may include **mosquito-borne viruses**, such as West Nile, the Herpes Simplex virus, and the Rabies virus. Symptoms of encephalitis are usually mild, with the infected person suffering no more than flu-like symptoms, but severe cases may result in brain damage or death.

Symptoms

Symptoms of encephalitis vary depending on severity. Mild cases result in flu-like symptoms, such as fever, headache, general body ache, and fatigue. More severe cases may result in unconsciousness, seizures, weakness, and difficulty speaking or hearing.

Treatments

Because most cases of encephalitis are mild, treatment often consists of bed rest, and letting the virus work through its course. Antiviral medications may also be administered via an IV if the infection is more severe.

Contraindications

Because encephalitis is contagious and a serious medical condition, it is an absolute contraindication. Massage may be performed after the condition has completely resolved.

Meningitis
(mening-: meninges; -itis: inflammation)

Meningitis is **inflammation of the meninges**, the protective connective tissue surrounding the brain and spinal cord. In the US, meningitis is most commonly caused by **viral infection**. However, certain **bacterial** and **fungal infections** may also cause meningitis. Bacterial meningitis is the most severe form of meningitis, usually preceded by a sinus or ear infection.

Causes

Being exposed to a pathogen, such as streptococci bacterium, or West Nile virus, are the causes of meningitis. Exposure to these may differ, and contracting them does not necessarily mean a person will develop meningitis. West Nile virus, which also may cause encephalitis, is often transmitted by mosquitoes.

Rarely, meningitis may be caused by things that are not infectious, such as medications or allergies to certain chemicals.

Symptoms

Symptoms vary depending on the underlying cause. Viral meningitis may present with symptoms extremely similar to influenza, and will likely clear up on their own within a couple weeks. Fever, headache, nausea, vomiting, and an unusually stiff neck are symptoms to watch for. Meningitis is considered a medical emergency, and a person with suspected meningitis should be seen by a medical professional right away.

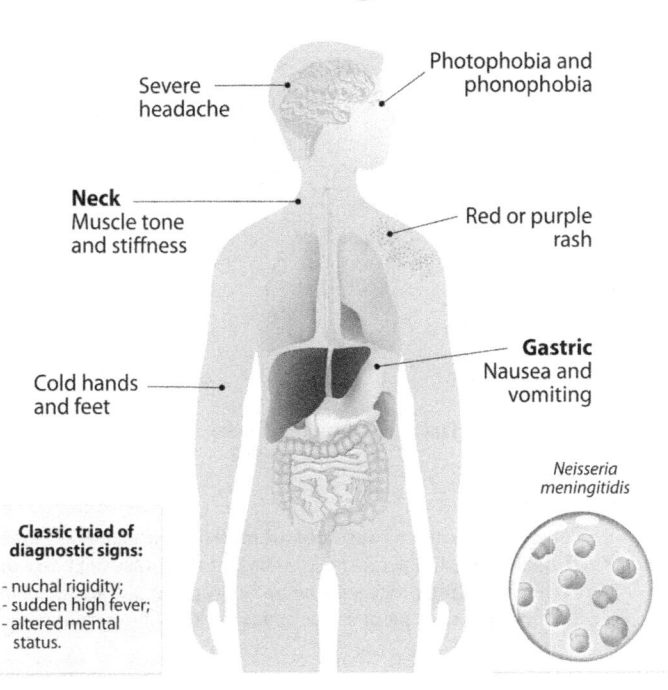

Meningitis

- Severe headache
- Photophobia and phonophobia
- **Neck** Muscle tone and stiffness
- Red or purple rash
- Cold hands and feet
- **Gastric** Nausea and vomiting

Neisseria meningitidis

Classic triad of diagnostic signs:
- nuchal rigidity;
- sudden high fever;
- altered mental status.

Treatments

Bacterial meningitis is treated with intravenous antibiotics to combat the infection, and a course of corticosteroids to prevent inflammation in the brain. Draining the infection from the sinuses may be helpful. Viral meningitis, however, is far less serious, and often clears up after a couple weeks. Treatment for viral meningitis is simply rest and increasing fluid intake. Pain relievers may also help if a person has general body aches or is suffering from mild fever.

Contraindications

Because meningitis is a contagious condition, it is an absolute contraindication to massage. Massage may be performed after the condition has completely resolved.

Multiple Sclerosis
(scler-: hard; -osis: condition)

Multiple Sclerosis is an **autoimmune** disorder, affecting the **myelin sheaths** that protect the axons of the Nervous System.

Causes

The cause of Multiple Sclerosis is unknown, but may be hereditary, and even environmental factors have been linked to the development of the disease. The disease begins with the body's immune system attacking the myelin sheaths, the protective fatty layers surrounding axons. These sheaths help to insulate the axons and prevent damage to the axons. When the myelin sheath is attacked and destroyed, it exposes the axons, which can have many different effects. Impulses traveling along an axon may terminate at the site of myelin degeneration, which may cause loss of functions. Scar tissue may form over the axons, which leads to extreme pain.

Symptoms

Symptoms of Multiple Sclerosis in acute stages include pain, weakness, fatigue, numbness(usually in the face), tingling sensation, blurry vision, and difficulty walking.

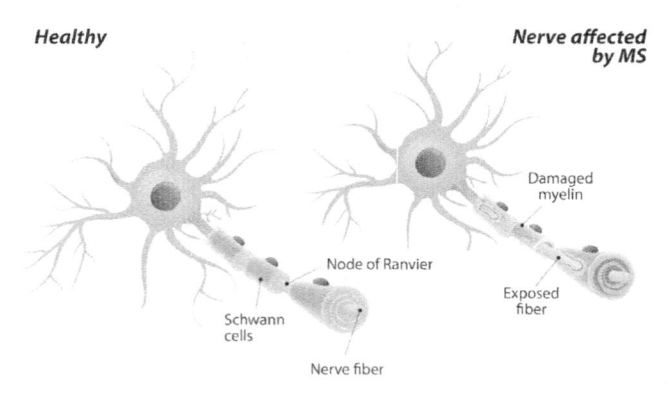

Treatments

There is no cure for Multiple Sclerosis. People may be prescribed disease-altering drugs that suppress the functions of the immune system. People may seek other means of managing Multiple Sclerosis and the accompanying pain and fatigue, including massage therapy, yoga, and meditation.

Contraindications

Massage in the acute stage of Multiple Sclerosis may be performed, but it is unlikely a client will seek massage because of the pain involved. Modalities that do not involve touching, such as Reiki, may be recommended and performed in these instances. In the post-acute stage, massage may be performed.

Parkinson's Disease

Parkinson's Disease is a motor disease that results in **trembling** due to a loss of the neurotransmitter **dopamine**.

Causes

There is no known cause of Parkinson's Disease. Neurons in the brain that produce dopamine are gradually destroyed. Dopamine is the neurotransmitter that stabilizes the body during motor movements, especially fine movements like writing. When dopamine levels in the body drop, trembling and shaking increases. Over time, as dopamine levels drop, the trembling increases. As dopamine continues to drop, larger movements become affected, like walking and talking.

Symptoms

Symptoms of Parkinson's Disease include tremors, which usually begin in the hands and fingers and advance to larger body areas, difficulty writing, slower movement, difficulty in speech, and the loss of movements such as blinking.

Treatments

While there is no cure for Parkinson's Disease, treatments are available to help manage the condition, including dopamine replacement medications.

Contraindications

Massage is indicated for clients with Parkinson's Disease. In advanced stages, when a client is unable to lie on a table without the entire body trembling, a doctor's note may be requested. In these advanced stages, the therapist may need to help the client on and off the table.

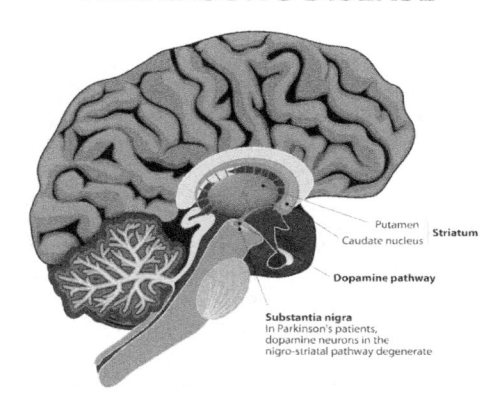

Sciatica

Sciatica is a condition causing pain radiating down the buttocks, posterior thigh, and leg.

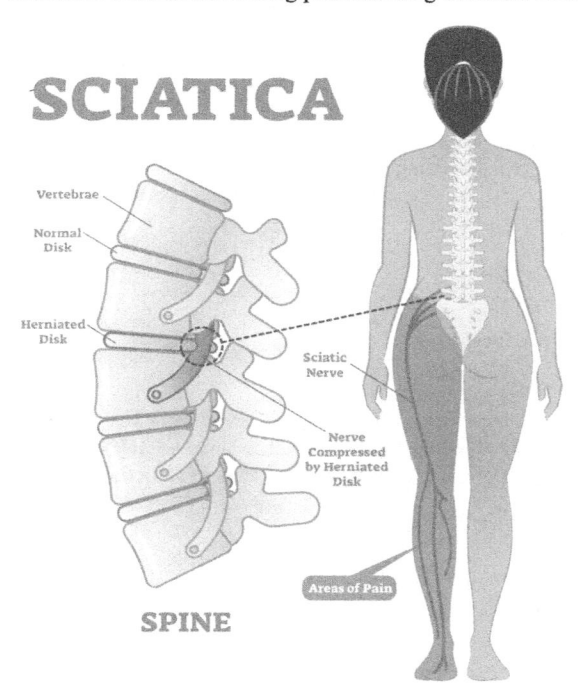

Causes

Sciatica is most commonly caused by a **herniated disc** in the lumbar vertebrae, which puts compression on the nerves that comprise the **sciatic nerve**. Bone spurs may also place pressure on the nerves.

Piriformis Syndrome is often confused with sciatica. Piriformis syndrome is caused by tightness in the piriformis muscle, which may place substantial pressure on the sciatic nerve.

Symptoms

The primary symptom of sciatica is pain in the posterior leg, thigh, and glutes, usually only on one side of the body. There may also be numbness and tingling in the affected area.

Treatments

Treatment for sciatica may include physical therapy, anti-inflammatory medications, or surgery if the condition is severe enough.

Contraindications

Massage is indicated for sciatica. However, if sciatica is the result of a herniated disc, the site of disc herniation should be considered a local contraindication. Stretching techniques, especially in the glutes, may help ease some pain associated with sciatica.

Thoracic Outlet Syndrome

Thoracic Outlet Syndrome is a condition caused by **compression** of **nerves** and **blood vessels** passing through the **thoracic outlet**.

Causes

Thoracic outlet syndrome may be caused by tight muscles, including **pectoralis minor** and **scalenes**, obesity, and tumors in the neck, such as those seen in Non-Hodgkin's Lymphoma.

Symptoms

Pressure placed on the nerves and blood vessels may cause pain, numbness, and weakness in the upper limb. If a blood vessel is compressed, it may cause the hand to become a bluish color due to lack of circulation, cause pain and fatigue in the arm, and coldness in the hands and fingers. If a nerve is compressed, numbness in the limb and atrophy of the muscles innervated by the nerve may result.

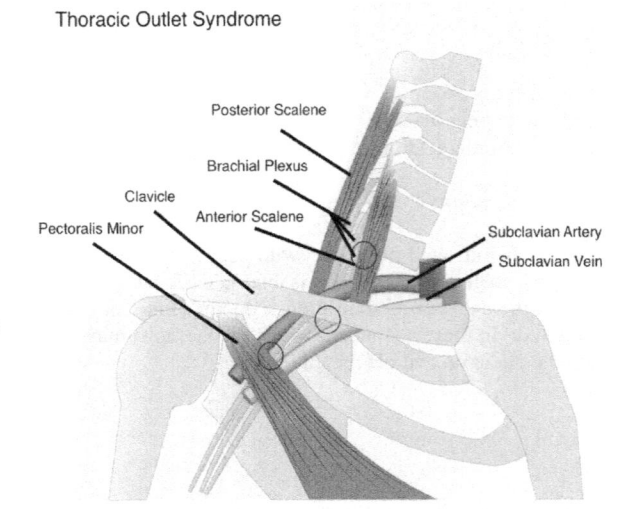

Treatments

Treatments primarily consist of stretching of the tight muscles to release pressure on the nerves and blood vessels. In the case of a tumor, surgery to remove the tumor may be required.

Contraindications

Massage is generally indicated for thoracic outlet syndrome. Massaging the scalenes and pectoralis minor may assist in releasing pressure on the area, returning sufficient blood supply to the area. Sensation may return to the upper limb as a result. If thoracic outlet syndrome is the result of tumors, the area should be avoided, and massage would be a local contraindication.

Trigeminal Neuralgia
(neur-: nerve; -algia: pain)

Trigeminal Neuralgia is a chronic condition causing **extreme pain in the face**.

Causes

The **trigeminal nerve** (cranial nerve V) sends sensory information from the face to the brain. When a blood vessel comes into contact with the trigeminal nerve at the brain stem, it results in dysfunction of the trigeminal nerve. This dysfunction results in hyper-sensitivity of the face, making even light touch extremely painful.

Symptoms

Extreme pain in the face, which may last from days to weeks, is the primary symptom of trigeminal neuralgia. This pain is typically only felt in one side of the face, but may worsen over time.

Treatments

Treatments for trigeminal neuralgia include medications to reduce pain, botox injections, or possible surgery to reduce pressure on the trigeminal nerve caused by blood vessels.

Contraindications

Massage for trigeminal neuralgia is generally not contraindicated, but everything is dependent on the severity of pain experienced by the client. If pain is severe, massage may be considered a local contraindication, or the client may not want to be massaged at all and the appointment would need to be rescheduled. If massage is able to be performed, the therapist should not use a face rest, instead opting to use a pillow for the client to rest their head upon while prone.

Respiratory System Pathologies

Apnea
(a-: without; -pnea: breathing)

Apnea, commonly referred to as sleep apnea, is a **temporary cessation of breathing** during sleep. Apnea may be a serious condition, depending on the patient. There are three types of sleep apnea: central sleep apnea, obstructive sleep apnea, and complex sleep apnea syndrome.

People who are overweight have a much higher rate of occurrence than others. Advanced age and being male are also common demographics for the development of sleep apnea.

Causes

Central sleep apnea is the result of the brain not stimulating muscles responsible for breathing. A patient may experience shortness of breath due to lack of oxygen intake. This form of sleep apnea is not common.

Obstructive sleep apnea is the result of throat muscles relaxing, which causes the air passages to narrow or completely close upon inhalation. This reduces the amount of oxygen getting into the body. As a result, the brain may force the patient awake momentarily to unblock the airways. People with obstructive sleep apnea often snore, and may even sound as if they are choking.

Complex sleep apnea syndrome is diagnosed when a person experiences both common and obstructive sleep apnea.

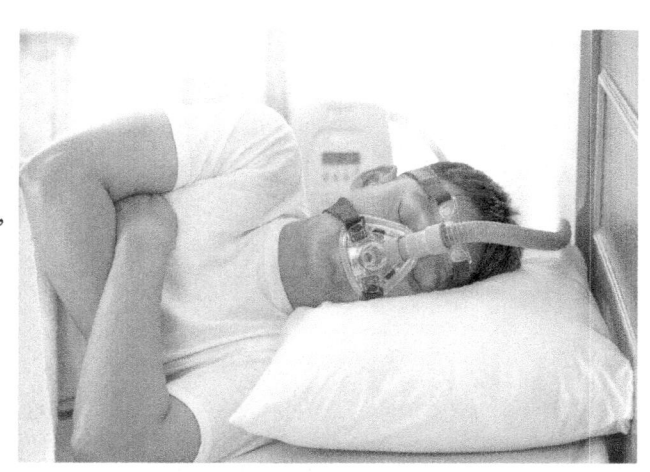

Patient utilizing CPAP machine

Symptoms

Symptoms of apnea include snoring, shortness of breath upon waking, fatigue, and briefly waking at night. Another person may see the cessation of breathing and report it to the patient.

Treatments

Less severe forms of apnea may require less drastic forms of treatment, such as losing weight. In more severe forms, a person may be instructed to wear a CPAP(continuous positive airway pressure) machine during sleep, which increases air pressure in the airway, keeping the airways open enough for adequate oxygen intake to occur.

If other treatments are ineffective, surgery may be performed to remove tissue in and around the airway, which can increase the passageway for air to travel through.

Contraindications

Apnea is not contraindicated for massage.

Asthma

Asthma is a chronic respiratory disease that causes **constriction** of the **airways**, restricting oxygen intake. Asthma usually begins in childhood, but may disappear with age. Other times, it remains a chronic condition. Other factors such as smoking or obesity may lead to the development of asthma.

Causes

Asthma affects the **smooth muscle** in the **walls of the bronchial tubes**. Typically, when a person inhales an irritant(such as dust or smoke), the smooth muscle spasms and constricts in an effort to reduce the irritant moving further into the lungs. The bronchi will also produce an **excessive amount of mucous**, which further restricts the flow of oxygen into the lungs.

Symptoms

Symptoms include wheezing, chest tightness, and shortness of breath. Treatment varies depending on the severity in acute stages. If it is mild, medication may not be required. If symptoms are more severe, bronchodilators may be required to calm and open the airways. In extreme cases, where regular bronchodilators do not work, medical attention should be sought. A nebulizer, with inhalable steroids, should be used with asthma attacks.

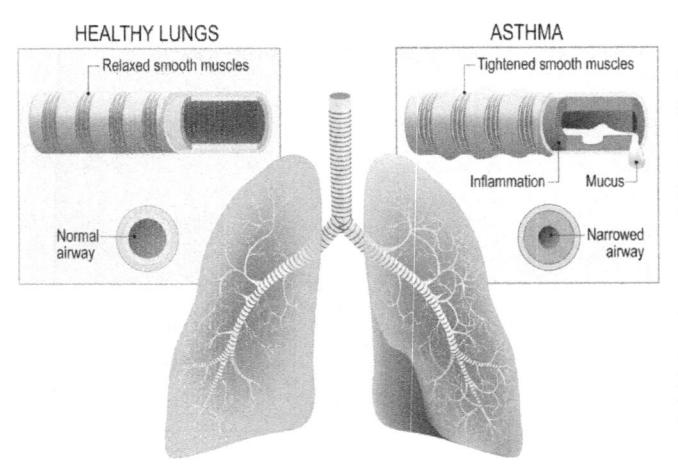

Treatments

Treatment for asthma primarily consists of the use of steroids and bronchodilators administered directly to the lungs via inhalers. If a person suffers from an asthma attack or has more severe forms of asthma, a nebulizer(which turns medication into a mist) may be required. Corticosteroids may also be used to lessen the chances of having an asthma attack.

Contraindications

In the acute stage, asthma is considered an absolute contraindication. Once breathing has returned to normal, massage may be performed. Tapotement may be performed on the back and chest to help loosen any excess phlegm that may be present.

Bronchitis
(bronch-: bronchi; -itis: inflammation)

Bronchitis is an inflammatory disease of the Respiratory System, restricting oxygen intake.

Causes

There are two different types of bronchitis: acute bronchitis and chronic bronchitis. **Acute bronchitis** is the result of a **primary** infection of the Respiratory System, such as influenza or pneumonia. These diseases affect the bronchial tubes, causing them to become irritated and inflamed. When these diseases resolve, the bronchitis will also resolve. **Chronic bronchitis** is the result of **constant irritation** to the bronchial tubes, caused by exposure to things such as **cigarette smoke** or **dust**. When exposure to the irritant ceases, the bronchitis will also cease.

Symptoms

With both forms of bronchitis, there is an increased amount of mucous produced in the lungs, which makes breathing difficult. Increased coughing may be a side effect of the increase in mucous.

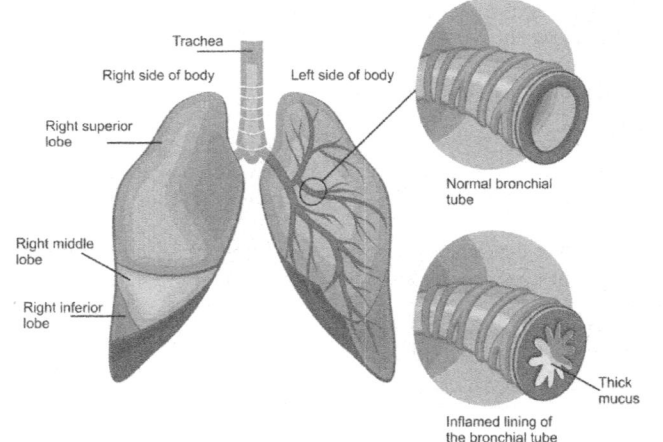

Treatments

Treatments vary depending on which type of bronchitis is involved. Acute bronchitis may require nothing more than a bronchodilator or cough suppressant. Because acute bronchitis is usually caused by a viral infection, antivirals may be prescribed to stop the advancement of the virus. Chronic bronchitis often requires the use of a bronchodilator, but not much else.

Contraindications

Acute bronchitis is considered an absolute contraindication, because it only appears as a secondary condition with another infection that is an absolute contraindication, such as influenza or pneumonia. Once these conditions resolve, the bronchitis will also resolve, and massage may be performed. Chronic bronchitis is indicated for massage. Tapotement may help loosen any excess phlegm as a result of the bronchitis, which can help breathing.

Emphysema
(emphyso: inflate)

Emphysema is a chronic condition of the lungs, resulting in difficulty bringing oxygen into the body and eliminating carbon dioxide from the body.

Causes

Emphysema is caused by over-exposure to substances such as **cigarette smoke**. Constant irritation of the lungs by smoke can lead to degeneration of the **alveoli**, air sacs at the end of bronchial tubes where gas exchange takes place. When the alveoli degenerate, they lose surface area, which is what capillaries move across to eliminate carbon dioxide from the body and bring oxygen into the body. Lack of sufficient alveoli surface area makes gas exchange extremely difficult.

Symptoms

Emphysema causes shortness of breath. A person with emphysema may be much more likely to develop a collapsed lung due to damage to the lungs.

Treatments

Breathing exercises and oxygen supplementation may help control emphysema. If needed, bronchodilators can help relax the airways. If infections such as pneumonia occur, antibiotics may help.

Contraindications

Massage is indicated for emphysema.

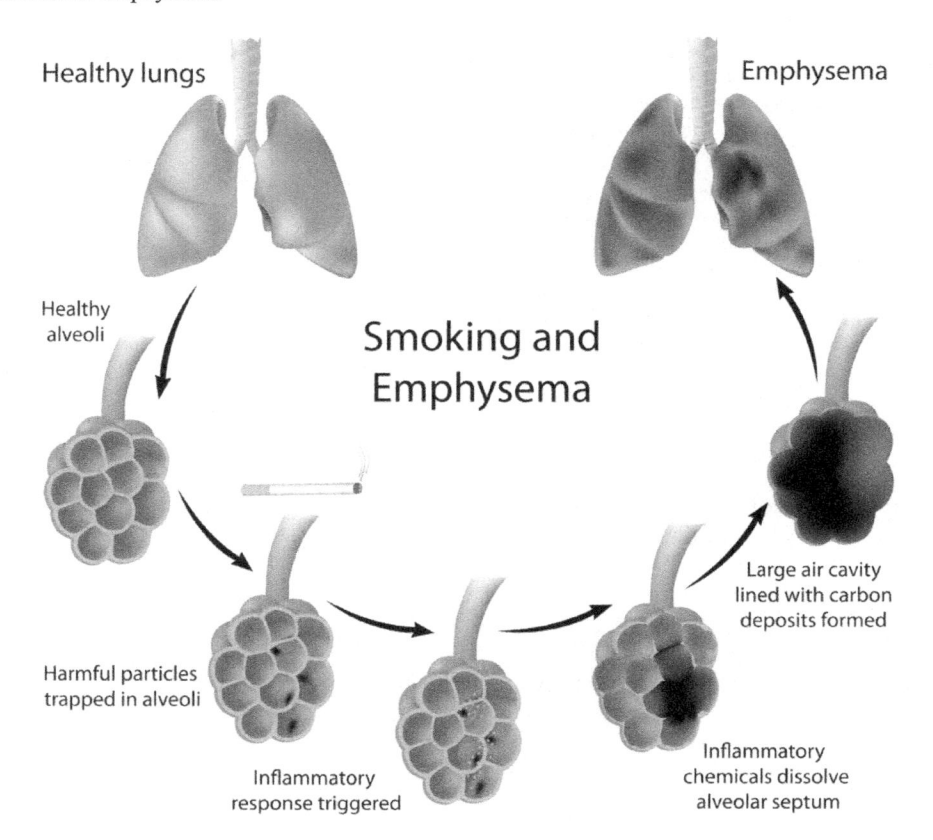

Healthy lungs

Emphysema

Smoking and Emphysema

Healthy alveoli

Harmful particles trapped in alveoli

Inflammatory response triggered

Inflammatory chemicals dissolve alveolar septum

Large air cavity lined with carbon deposits formed

Influenza
(Italian "influenza": influence)

Influenza is a highly contagious **viral infection** that primarily affects the **lungs**.

Causes

There are many different strains of the flu virus. It is constantly mutating, so treatment can be difficult. **Vaccinations** are the primary form of prevention for influenza.

Influenza, during acute stages, results in fever, general malaise, body aches, runny nose, and cough. Symptoms generally last no more than a week. Depending on the person involved, it can be a moderate infection, or can be life-threatening. Children and the elderly are much more likely to have serious cases of influenza than the general population.

Symptoms

Influenza typically has a sudden onset of symptoms, including fever, body ache, fatigue, sore throat, nasal congestion, body chills, and sweating.

Treatments

Treatment for influenza is usually nothing more than rest and increased fluid intake. Antiviral medication may be prescribed, and may help reduce the length of the infection. Influenza usually clears up on its own.

Contraindications

Influenza is highly contagious, and is considered an absolute contraindication.

Pneumonia
(pneumo: lung)

Pneumonia is a highly contagious infection of the lungs, resulting in a buildup of **fluid in the alveoli**.

Causes

The primary cause of pneumonia is **bacterial infection**(staphylococci), but may also be caused by a virus or fungi. The bacterium enters the body through breathing, which then infects the lungs.

Symptoms

Mild cases of pneumonia usually present with symptoms similar to those of influenza. Other symptoms may include pain in the chest upon breathing, coughing which may produce phlegm, fever, nausea, and shortness of breath. Symptoms can range from mild to severe, and even life threatening, based on the overall health and age of the person infected.

Treatments

Pneumonia is typically treated with antibiotics. Cough medicine and antipyretics may be prescribed to aid with coughing and to lower fever.

Contraindications

Pneumonia is a highly contagious condition, and is therefore an absolute contraindication.

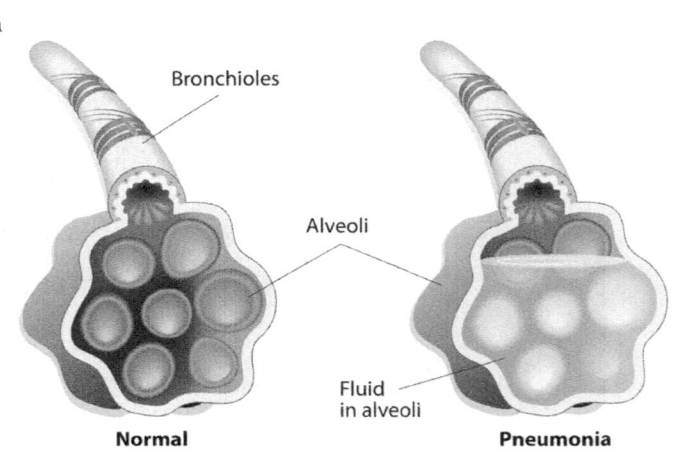

Sinusitis
(sinus: sinus; -itis: inflammation)

Sinusitis is an acute condition causing **inflammation and swelling in the nasal sinuses**, which can result in **excessive mucous production**. It can also prevent mucous from properly draining from the sinuses, causing a person to feel a lot of pressure in the face around the nose and eyes. Bacterial infection may result, which can increase the amount of fluid present in the sinuses.

Causes

The most common cause of sinusitis is an acute viral infection, such as the common cold, which may in turn cause bacterial infection to take place.

Symptoms

A person with sinusitis may experience pressure in the face around the nose, eyes, and ears, headache, a thick mucous produced by the nose usually presenting with a yellow or green color, and congestion in the nasal cavity.

Treatments

Decongestants are effective at helping to drain the nasal cavities, which can help ease pressure in the area. Nasal sprays can help alleviate inflammation and clean out the nasal cavity, further helping to reduce pressure. If bacterial infection is present, antibiotics may be prescribed.

Contraindications

During the acute stage, and due to being caused by a contagious viral infection, sinusitis is considered an absolute contraindication. Once the condition has resolved, a client may receive massage.

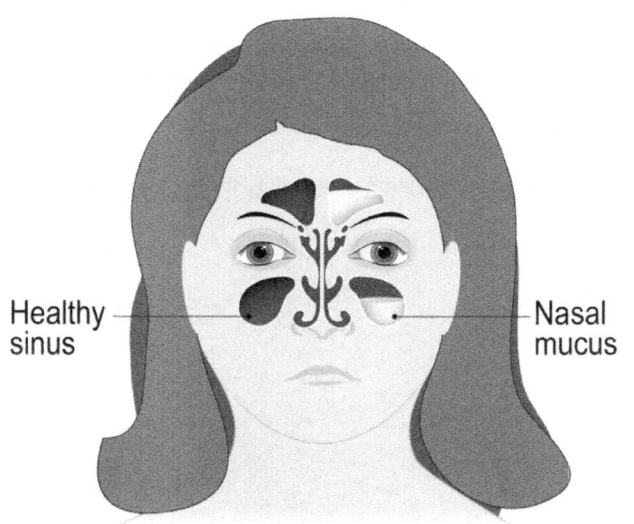

Skeletal System Pathologies

Ankylosing Spondylitis
(ankyl/o: crooked; spondyl-: spine; -itis: inflammation)

Ankylosing Spondylitis is an **autoimmune disorder**, similar to rheumatoid arthritis(page 176), in which the body's immune system attacks and destroys the **annulus fibrosus** of the **intervertebral discs**. Over time, the curvature in the vertebrae is lost. Because the intervertebral discs are destroyed, the space between vertebral bodies lessens, eventually allowing the vertebral bones to sit directly atop one another. Movement between these bones is severely reduced, and eventually the bones can fuse together, which eliminates any movement between the bones at all.

A person with ankylosing spondylitis may appear to be hunched forward, and may present with kyphosis(page 172) as a result. Another name for ankylosing spondylitis is "Bamboo Spine" because after fusion, the vertebrae resembles a bamboo stalk.

Causes

Ankylosing spondylitis is caused by the body's immune system attacking the intervertebral discs for unknown reasons.

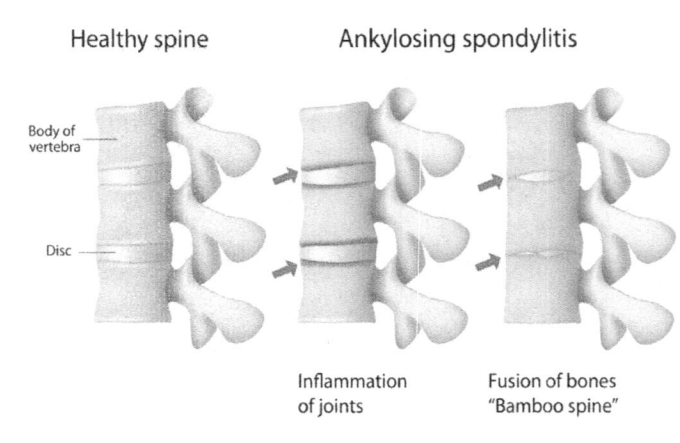

Symptoms

Pain is an extremely common symptom of ankylosing spondylitis, especially in the neck, base of the skull, and lumbar region. Lack of mobility is a secondary symptom, usually the result of pain.

Treatments

Non-steroidal anti-inflammatory medications may be prescribed to help reduce pain and inflammation in affected areas. Physical therapy, massage therapy, stretching, and range-of-motion exercises are all helpful in maintaining mobility in the vertebral joints and preventing bones from fusing together.

If the condition is severe, surgery may be performed to remove fused bone, or to insert metal rods to correct posture.

Contraindications

Massage is indicated for ankylosing spondylitis. Stretching and range-of-motion exercises should be performed within the client's pain tolerance. If the client has difficulty lying supine due to kyphosis, side-lying position may be needed.

Bunion

A Bunion is a **subluxation of the big toe**, the result of the toe pushing back against the first metatarsal. Excessive force against this bone causes the big toe to subluxate medially, creating a **large bump**.

Causes

Tight fitting shoes may contribute to the development of bunions. Rheumatoid arthritis(page 176) may also contribute. Foot injuries may also play a role.

Symptoms

Pain and swelling may present in the area of the bunion. With bunions, the big toe may cross under the second toe. This may cause calluses or corns to form on the area where these toes rub together. Movement in the big toe may reduce.

Treatments

How severe the bunion is determines the treatment. Less severe bunions may require only changing shoes or applying a splint to help reset the toe. More severe forms of a bunion may require surgery to correct the placement of the toe.

Contraindications

Massage is generally not contraindicated for a bunion. However, if the client is experiencing pain as a result of the bunion, massage in the area should be avoided.

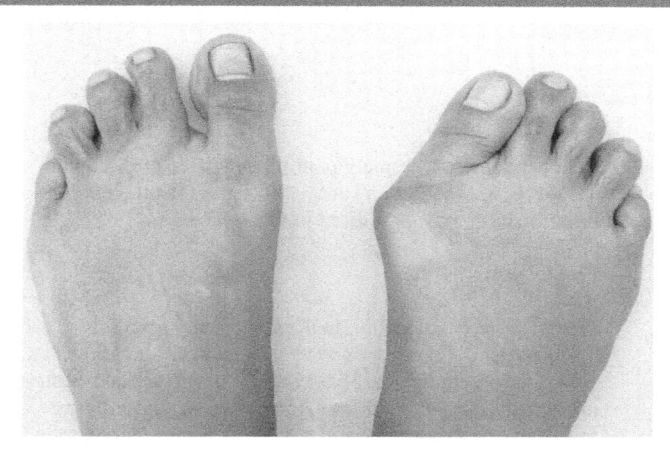

Bursitis
(burs-: bursa; -itis: inflammation)

Bursitis is a condition that results in **inflammation** of a **bursa**, a small sac filled with synovial fluid.

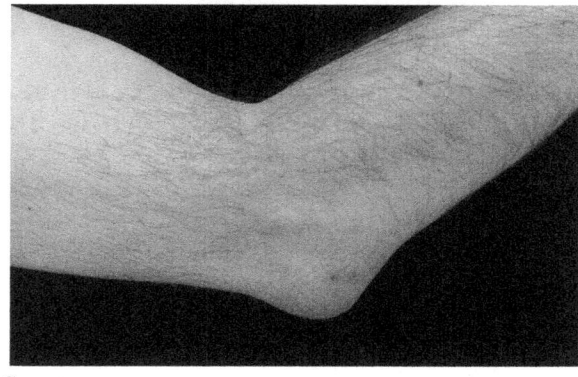

Causes

Bursae are located all over the body, typically between a tendon and bone to prevent friction and irritation. When there is repeated stress placed on the bursa, it can become inflamed. Bursitis may affect many different joints, including the knee, shoulder, elbow, hip, and ankle.

Bursitis is most often caused by repetitive motions in the affected joint, which may irritate the bursa. Trauma may also result in bursitis, such as fractures or tendonitis.

Symptoms

Typically, a joint affected with bursitis will be inflamed and painful to move. The inflammation may be moderate or severe.

Treatments

Bursitis is easily treatable, primarily with rest and ice. Depending on the severity, the bursa may also need to be surgically drained or removed, or injected with corticosteroids to reduce the inflammation.

Contraindications

Bursitis is considered a local contraindication for massage. Cold packs may be used to help decrease inflammation in the area.

Dislocation

A dislocation is when a bone at an articulation becomes **displaced** from its normal location. A dislocation, in the acute stage, results in immobilization of the joint and temporary deformation. It may also be painful and result in inflammation around the joint.

Causes

Dislocations are most commonly the result of trauma to the joint, which pushes a bone out of place. The most common areas for dislocations are the fingers and shoulder, but dislocations may occur in many other joints as well, such as the knee or hip.

Dislocations may result in tearing of tendons, ligaments, muscles, or in the case of the shoulder or hip, the labrum (circular cartilage surrounding the joint). The dislocated joint, while most commonly returns to normal strength and function after being relocated, may become prone to dislocations in the future. This may cause arthritis to develop.

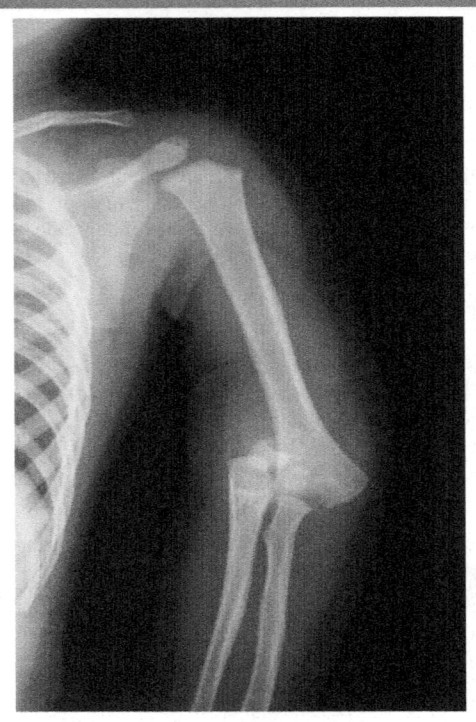

170 Pathology

Symptoms

Dislocations are extremely painful, and often present with deformity of the joint and an inability to move the joint. Inflammation may be present in some cases.

Treatments

Treatment of a dislocation in the acute stage primarily involves trying to get the bone back to its normal position, known as reduction. After the joint has returned to its normal position, it is typically immobilized for a number of weeks to reduce recurrence of dislocation and to help the tissues around the joint to heal. If the dislocation is severe and unable to be returned to position, surgery may be required.

Contraindications

In the acute stage, a dislocation is considered a local contraindication. If the joint has healed, massage may be performed on the area with caution. Stretching and range-of-motion should be avoided because the joint is much weaker after a dislocation.

Dislocated elbow presenting with fracture

Fracture

A fracture is a **break in a bone**. There are several different types of fractures, including transverse, greenstick, oblique, and spiral.

Causes

Fractures are the result of trauma to a bone. Despite many different types of fractures, every fracture is categorized as one of the following: Simple or Compound. A **simple** fracture is a fracture that **does not break through** the skin, and does not damage any surrounding tissue. A **compound** fracture, which is much more severe, **breaks through** the skin and damages surrounding tissues. Compound fractures are much more prone to infection due to exposure to the outside environment.

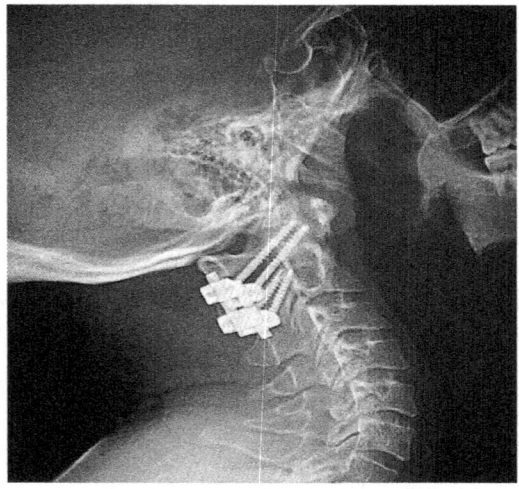

Symptoms

Fractures result in deformity of the affected bone, pain, immobilization of the area, and inflammation. In the case of compound fractures, external bleeding may also occur.

Despite most fractures being the result of blunt trauma, certain diseases that weaken the bones may also cause fractures, such as osteoporosis.

Treatments

Fractures should be treated immediately. A cast or splint may be applied, depending on which bone is fractured. Other fractures, such as vertebrae fractures, may need more extensive treatment, including metal plates or bone grafts.

Cervical fusion surgery after fracture of C1-C2

Contraindications

In the acute stage, a fracture should be considered a local contraindication. After the fracture has healed, massage may be performed on the area. If metal plates, rods, screws, or pins have been placed in the bone, caution should be taken in the area, but massage may still be performed.

Gout

Gout is a form of arthritis, mostly seen around the base of the **big toe**, but may also affect other joints in the body, such as the hands and fingers.

Causes

Gout is the result of an over-abundance of **uric acid crystals** in the body. Gravity pulls the uric acid crystals down the body, where they collect in the most distal points in the limbs, the big toes, hands and fingers. Gout is typically the result of the kidneys not excreting enough uric acid, or the body producing too much uric acid.

Symptoms

Gout may be extremely painful in the acute stage as the crystals collect in the joints. Inflammation may set in, which can increase the pressure and pain in the joint. Loss of range-of-motion may also occur. Untreated, gout may result in kidney stones.

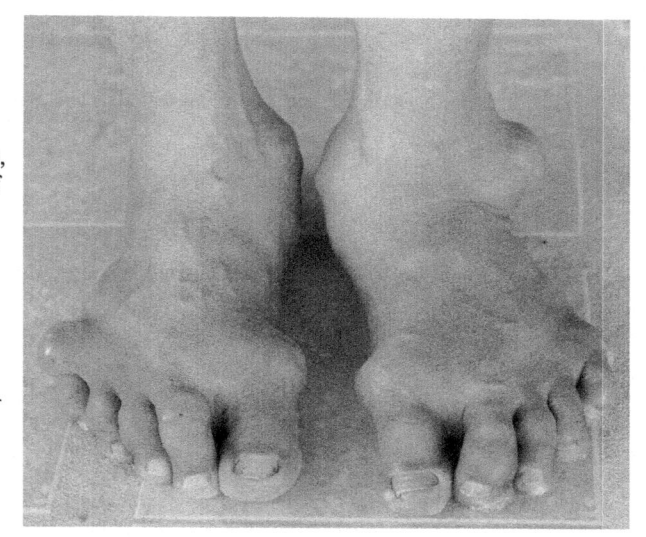

Treatments

Treatments for gout include non-steroidal anti-inflammatory drugs and/or corticosteroids to reduce pain and inflammation. Gout may also require the use of certain medications that prevent the creation of uric acid in the body.

Contraindications

Gout is considered a local contraindication.

Herniated Disc

A herniated disc is a condition affecting the vertebral column, which may cause intense pain and numbness.

Causes

An intervertebral disc, located between two vertebrae, is made of two parts: the nucleus pulposus, and the annulus fibrosus. The nucleus pulposus is a gelatinous substance located in the center of the disc. The annulus fibrosus is the part of the disc made of thick cartilage. If a tear occurs in the **annulus fibrosus**, the **nucleus pulposus** may **protrude** through the torn section, which may place pressure on spinal nerves emerging from the spinal cord. This is a herniated disc.

A herniated disc is primarily caused by degeneration of a disc, which takes place gradually. This makes injury of the disc much easier in actions such as lifting and twisting. Other times, trauma may cause a herniated disc, such as in car accidents.

Symptoms

Herniated discs may result in pain and/or numbness due to the disc placing pressure on the spinal nerves. Because numbness may occur, weakness in the muscles innervated by the nerves may also set in due to impaired function.

Treatments

Treatment for a herniated disc varies depending on the severity. Pain medication may help control pain. Muscle relaxers may help take pressure off the area of the herniation. Physical therapy may also contribute to lessening the effects of the herniated disc. Very rarely, surgery may be required.

Contraindications

Herniated discs are considered local contraindications. The area around the hernia may be massaged, but the disc itself should be avoided.

Kyphosis
(kyph-: hill; -osis: condition)

Kyphosis is a condition affecting the **thoracic** vertebrae, resulting in **hyper-curvature**. Another name for kyphosis is "Dowager's Hump".

Causes

A kyphotic curvature in the vertebrae is a curvature that moves posteriorly. If the curvature is exaggerated, it is known as kyphosis. Kyphosis has many different causes. Kyphosis may be caused by extremely tight muscles(such as **pectoralis minor** and **serratus anterior**) pulling the scapulae anteriorly, which rounds the back. It may also be the result of bone degeneration(osteoporosis), disc degeneration(ankylosing spondylitis), or even birth defects.

Symptoms

Kyphosis may cause pain in the back, and difficulty in movement and breathing as a result. It may also result in the lumbar vertebrae losing its curvature, a condition known as **flat back**.

Treatments

Kyphosis may vary from mild to severe, depending on the cause. Treatments include exercises that strengthen the muscles of the back, stretching of tight muscles that may contribute to kyphosis, braces to keep the vertebrae properly aligned, and possibly even surgery if it's warranted.

Contraindications

Kyphosis is not contraindicated for massage. A person with kyphosis may be uncomfortable lying supine, and may need to be placed into side-lying position for comfort. Massage of the pectoralis minor and serratus anterior muscles may help the scapulae return to their normal locations, which can help straighten the vertebrae.

Lordosis
(lord-: curve; -osis: condition)

Lordosis is a condition affecting the **lumbar** vertebrae, resulting in **hyper-curvature**. Another name for lordosis is "Swayback".

Causes

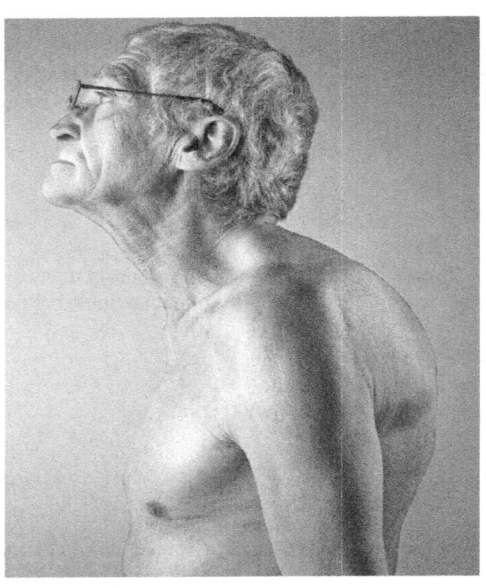

A lordotic curvature in the vertebrae is a curvature that moves anteriorly. If the curvature is exaggerated, it is known as lordosis. Lordosis has many different causes. Lordosis may be caused by tight muscles(such as **psoas major**, **iliacus**, **quadratus lumborum**, and **rectus femoris**), weak muscles(such as **rectus abdominis** and the **hamstrings**), obesity, or bone diseases(such as osteoporosis). Pregnancy is also a common cause of lordosis, but the condition typically subsides post-pregnancy.

Symptoms

Lordosis may place excessive pressure on the vertebrae, and alter a person's stance and gait. Lordosis may result in pain in the back, and cause difficulty moving.

Treatments

Treatment primarily includes strengthening weak muscles, stretching tight muscles, and lifestyle changes such as adjusting posture, diet, and exercise.

Contraindications

Lordosis is not contraindicated for massage. Stretching exercises on the psoas major, iliacus, and quadratus lumborum muscles may help return the lumbar spine back to its normal curvature.

Lyme Disease

Lyme Disease is a **bacterial infection** spread by **deer ticks**, and contracting the infection is much more common in grassy or wooded areas where deer ticks are found. The condition may affect a person for months, and lead to symptoms that may last for years afterwards.

Causes

The bacteria responsible for Lyme Disease is spread through a bite from deer ticks. The bacteria is usually only transmitted if the bite lasts longer than **36 hours**.

Symptoms

Symptoms of Lyme Disease vary depending on the stage of infection. In the early stages, a bump may appear where the person has been bitten. Sometime later, within 30 days, a rash may appear that forms a bullseye pattern. It may spread outward from that area over a few days. A person may experience flu-like symptoms when the rash appears. In advanced stages, conditions may begin occurring such as pain and inflammation in joints, meningitis, and paralysis in different parts of the body such as the face.

Treatments

Bullseye pattern seen around the area of the tick bite

Lyme Disease is a bacterial infection, and therefore is treated with antibiotics. Advanced stages of Lyme Disease, where there may be some sort of paralysis, require the use of intravenous antibiotics. Otherwise, oral antibiotics may be taken. The course of treatment usually lasts up to three weeks to completely destroy all bacteria.

Contraindications

Massage largely depends on the symptoms a client is experiencing. Lesser symptoms, such as aches and joint inflammation, may allow for massage while avoiding general local contraindications. If a client is experiencing flu-like symptoms, the massage should be postponed until the client is feeling better.

Osgood-Schlatter Disease

Osgood-Schlatter Disease is a repetitive strain injury, caused by **over-use of the patellar tendon**.

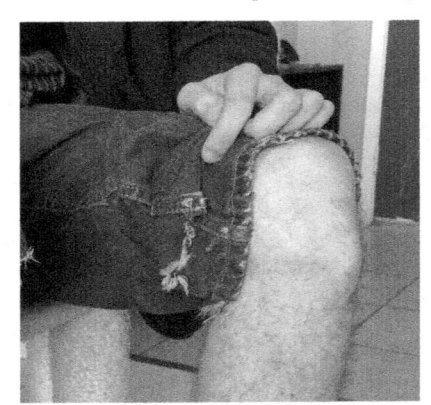

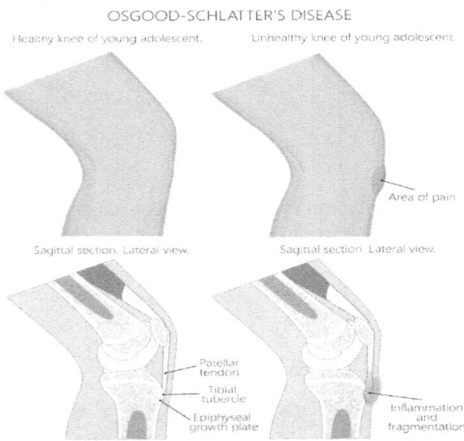

Causes

Osgood-Schlatter Disease primarily affects adolescents, particularly those involved in sports. Over-use of the **quadriceps** during activities such as running and jumping can cause tightness in the patellar tendon. When the patellar tendon tightens, it pulls proximally on the tibial tuberosity. Because the bone is still growing, the force of the patellar tendon on the tibial tuberosity can cause an **over-growth of bone**, resulting in a bony lump. Males are more likely to develop this condition than females, but instances in females are increasing as participation in sports by females increases.

Symptoms

Osgood-Schlatter Disease may cause pain, but it varies from person-to-person. The pain may be mild, or it may be more intense, making movement of the knee difficult.

Despite complications from Osgood-Schlatter Disease being rare, inflammation of the area may persist over time. The bony lump produced by increased bone production may also remain.

Treatments

Treatment is mild, usually nothing more than pain relievers, rest, and ice. Exercises that stretch the quadriceps are recommended.

Contraindications

In the acute stage, massage of the tibial tuberosity is a local contraindication. If the client is beyond the age of 21, and bone is no longer being produced at the tibial tuberosity, massage on the area may be performed.

In the acute stage, massage and stretching techniques should be performed on the quadriceps to loosen the muscles and take pressure off the patellar tendon, which can reduce the excessive development of bone at the tibial tuberosity.

Osteoarthritis
(osteo-: bone; arthr-: joint; -itis: inflammation)

Osteoarthritis is the most common form of arthritis, which is **inflammation** of a **joint**.

Causes

Osteoarthritis, also known as **"wear-and-tear arthritis"**, is caused by damage to the **hyaline cartilage** separating one bone from another. The cartilage between bones reduces friction between the bones, and absorbs shock in the joint. Over time, the articular cartilage may begin to break down and wear away. This causes irritation in the joint and increases friction between the bones, which causes inflammation. As this persists, damage to the bone may take place. The most common location of osteoarthritis is the knee, but in massage therapists, it may also affect the carpometacarpal joint of the thumb(saddle joint).

Symptoms

Osteoarthritis may cause pain, difficulty moving the affected joint, and bone spurs in the joint due to increased friction between the bones. When the condition advances to the point of the joint being mostly unusable, joint replacement surgery may be recommended.

Treatments

Treatment includes non-steroidal anti-inflammatory drugs, lifestyle and dietary changes if caused by obesity, and alternative methods such as yoga.

Contraindications

In the acute stage, massage is considered a local contraindication for any form of arthritis because it can bring more blood into the area and increase inflammation. In the post-acute stage, massage should be performed on the area usually affected to bring fresh blood and nutrients into the area, and to increase production of synovial fluid in the joint. This can help reduce irritation in the joint and lessen the effects of arthritis.

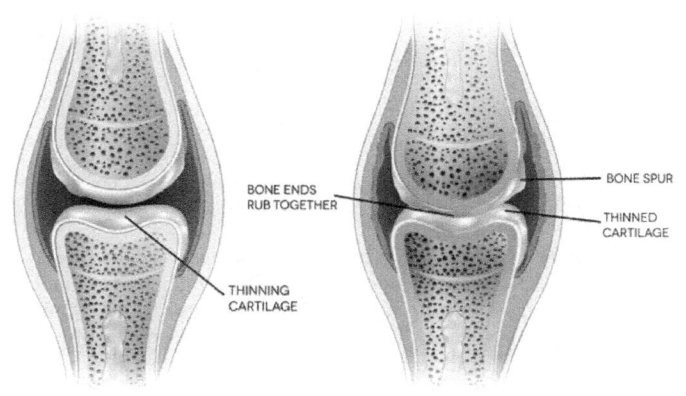

Osteoporosis
(osteo-: bone; por-: porous; -osis: condition)

Osteoporosis is a condition that causes **weakness and degeneration in the bones**.

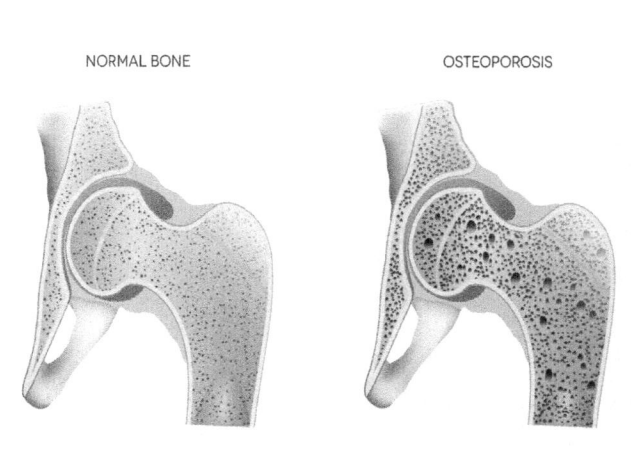

Causes

Osteoporosis mainly affects post-menopausal women. After menopause, a woman's body produces less **estrogen**. Estrogen, during growth stages of a person's life, helps the bones grow and mature. When estrogen levels drop post-menopause, osteoclast levels increase and more bone is destroyed than is created. When this occurs, the bones become brittle, weak, and prone to fracture.

Osteoporosis, in addition to making bones brittle, may also contribute to the development of kyphosis and back pain. One of the most common places for fracture to occur is in the neck of the femur. The femur, which is normally the strongest bone in the body, should be able to support roughly 2,000 pounds of pressure per square inch. When the femur becomes weakened, it makes it incredibly easy to break. If a fracture takes place around the hip joint, joint replacement surgery is often required.

Symptoms

In the early stages of osteoporosis, there are usually no symptoms. As bone loss increases over time, a person may experience back pain, hunched posture(kyphosis), and bones that fracture easier than usual. These symptoms often become worse as the disease progresses and more bone tissue is lost.

Treatments

Treatments for osteoporosis include estrogen replacement therapy, and weight-bearing exercise earlier in life before any symptoms of osteoporosis surface. Weight-bearing exercise, such as squats and dead-lifts, helps to strengthen the bones, which substantially reduces the risk of developing osteoporosis in older age.

Contraindications

Massage is indicated for osteoporosis. However, precautions should be taken, such as performing a lighter massage, and not performing techniques such as tapotement to avoid damaging bone.

Rheumatoid Arthritis

Rheumatoid Arthritis is an **autoimmune** disorder, resulting in **inflammation**, **pain**, and **deformity of the joints** around the **hands and wrists**.

Causes

Around synovial joints, there is a membrane called the synovial membrane, which supplies joints with synovial fluid. In rheumatoid arthritis, the body's immune systems attacks the **synovial membranes**, destroying them. This is especially common in the metacarpophalangeal joints. After the synovial membranes have been destroyed, extremely thick, fibrous material replaces them, which not only makes movement painful and difficult, but can also cause deformity, turning the fingers into an adducted position.

Symptoms

Rheumatoid arthritis can produce pain and discomfort in the affected joints, as well as cause pain and stiffness after long periods of inactivity in the joints. Fever and fatigue may also be symptoms of general rheumatoid arthritis. Less commonly, some people may experience symptoms in structures completely unrelated to the affected joints, such as the eyes, heart, lungs, and kidneys.

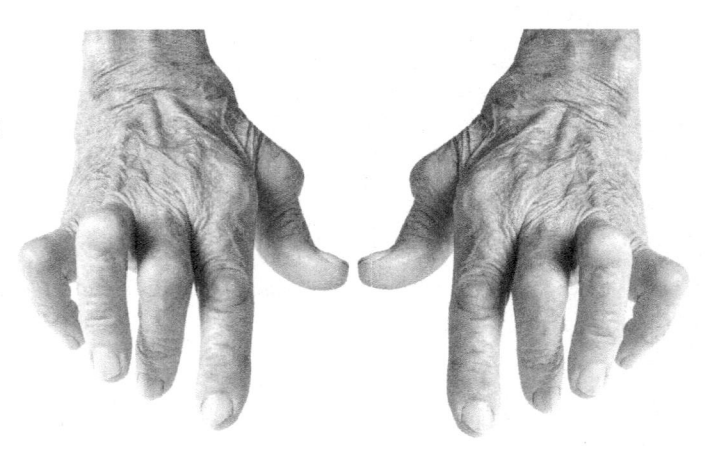

Treatments

There is no cure for rheumatoid arthritis, but treatments include non-steroidal anti-inflammatory drugs, corticosteroids, and physical therapy.

Contraindications

In the acute stage, rheumatoid arthritis is considered a local contraindication, as the pain may be too intense for the client to receive massage on the affected area. In general, however, a client with rheumatoid arthritis may receive massage to help ease pain associated with inflammation if the body can tolerate a light-to-medium pressured massage.

Scoliosis
(scoli-: crooked; -osis: condition)

Scoliosis is a condition causing the vertebral column, usually in the thoracic region, to be pulled into a **lateral** position.

Causes

The causes of scoliosis are unknown, but there may be a hereditary link. Scoliosis typically develops around the beginning stages of puberty. Scoliosis is mostly mild in severity, but can become much more prominent, which can put incredible strain on the ribs, vertebrae, and hips. With scoliosis, one hip may be higher than the other, which causes a discrepancy in gait. Tight muscles may also contribute to the development of scoliosis, as seen in cases such as a hypertonic rhomboid major and minor unilaterally, which pulls the vertebrae to one side.

Symptoms

If scoliosis is severe, damage to the heart or lungs may occur, due to the deformity of the rib cage. Back pain may also persist.

Treatments

Treatment, while commonly unnecessary, may include the use of braces to correct posture, the use of chiropractic therapy, massage therapy, or in severe cases, surgery with metal rod implantation.

Contraindications

Scoliosis is indicated for massage. In instances where scoliosis is caused by hypertonic muscles, such as the rhomboids unilaterally, massage may help loosen the muscles and allow the bones to realign themselves. If surgery has been performed and metal rods have been placed in the back, massage should be performed lighter on the area, and the use of cold packs should be avoided.

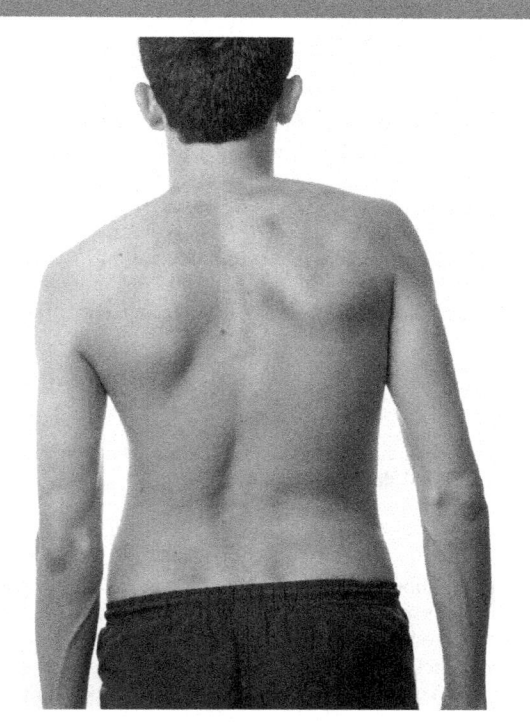

Sprain

A sprain is an **injury to a ligament**.

Causes

Sprains are much less likely to be caused by repetitive motions, unlike strains. Sprains typically occur quickly, causing tears in a ligament. Like strains, sprains may be broken down in severity by using grades: grade 1, grade 2, and grade 3.

A **grade 1 sprain** is caused by **stretching of a ligament**, but does not cause major tearing. Common grade 1 sprains may be caused by activities such as running. After 24-48 hours, the ligament should return to normal, and any pain and/or inflammation should subside.

A **grade 2 sprain**, such as a high ankle sprain, causes **tearing of a ligament** and presents with **bruising and inflammation**. Grade 2 sprains may require surgery to repair, or they may heal on their own, depending on the severity of the tear.

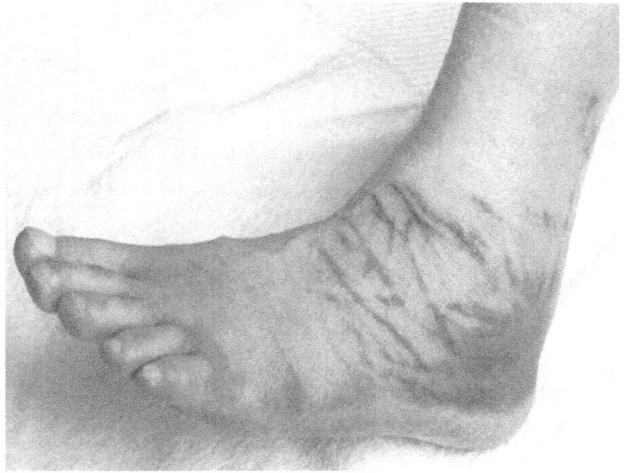

Bruising and inflammation commonly seen with second grade sprains

A **grade 3 sprain** is a **complete rupture of a ligament**, and much like a grade 3 strain, does **require surgery** to repair. The most common form of grade 3 sprain is a torn anterior cruciate ligament(ACL, the ligament holding the femur and tibia together), most commonly caused by sports or automobile accidents.

Symptoms

Symptoms of sprains are very similar to symptoms of strains, including inflammation, pain, and potential bruising depending on the grade of sprain. If the sprain is severe, a pop in the joint may be heard or felt at the time of injury.

Treatments

Sprains take much longer to heal than strains, due to ligaments being avascular, compared to muscles and tendons, which have a rich blood supply. Treatment for sprains vary depending on the severity of the sprain. The less severe, the more likely it is that rest, ice, and elevation will suffice. Surgery is only required when there is no chance of the ligament repairing itself.

Contraindications

In the acute stage, sprains are local contraindications. If inflammation has subsided from a first degree sprain, gentle massage in the area may be performed to bring fresh blood and nutrients into the area and speed healing. Contrast therapy may be performed in addition to gentle massage to reduce any inflammation that may occur due to the massage.

Temporomandibular Joint Dysfunction

Temporomandibular Joint Dysfunction(TMJD) is a condition affecting the mandible, causing simple tasks such as **chewing** to become **painful** and **difficult**.

Causes

The temporomandibular joint is the joint that connects the mandible to the temporal bone. Between the bones, there is a small disc of cartilage, used to prevent friction between the bones and to make movement smooth. If there is arthritis in the joint, or the disc is damaged, it can result in temporomandibular joint dysfunction. This can cause pain, difficulty in moving the jaw, and produce a clicking sensation when the jaw opens. Often times, the muscles that connect to the mandible(temporalis, lateral pterygoid) may tighten and pull the mandible out of place.

Symptoms

Temporomandibular joint dysfunction can produce pain in the face, a clicking or popping sound when closing the mouth, and difficulty in opening the mouth. The jaw may become locked while open.

Treatments

Treatments vary depending on the primary cause, ranging from prescription muscle relaxants and pain relievers, to physical and massage therapy.

Contraindications

Massage is indicated for temporomandibular joint dysfunction. Massage of the temporalis may help the jaw realign and reduce the pain and clicking.

Urinary System Pathologies

Cystitis
(cyst-: bladder; -itis: inflammation)

Cystitis is a **bacterial infection** resulting in **inflammation of the bladder**. It can often involve the entire Urinary System, and is then known as a Urinary Tract Infection(UTI). Cystitis is most common in women, as the female urethra is shorter than the male urethra, giving bacteria a shorter passage to the bladder.

Causes

Cystitis is caused most commonly by E. Coli entering the urethra, then reproducing. The increased amount of bacterium in the urethra causes the infection to spread upwards into the bladder. Cystitis can cause numerous symptoms, including blood in the urine, burning sensations while urinating, and a frequent urge to urinate. If untreated, the infection may spread to the kidneys. When this happens, it is known as pyelonephritis.

Symptoms

Symptoms of cystitis include a frequent urge to urinate, a painful burning sensation upon urination, urinating small amounts at a time, fever, and blood in the urine.

Treatments

Because cystitis is a bacterial infection, it is treated with antibiotics.

Contraindications

In the acute stage of infection, massage is contraindication for cystitis. Once the infection has cleared, massage may be performed.

Kidney Stones

Kidney Stones, also known as Nephroliathiasis, are **deposits** of **salts and minerals** created inside the kidney, which are hard and rough. Stones vary in size, and may cause many differing health complications.

Kidney stones are more common in people who are obese or have a family history of kidney stone development. Diet may play a role as well.

Causes

Kidney stones may be caused by numerous factors. Most commonly, they are caused by increased amounts of calcium oxalate, which is found in many types of food. Excessive amounts of calcium oxalate can cause stones to develop. Uric acid may also produce stones if a person does not drink enough fluids. A high protein diet may contribute to the development of uric acid stones.

Less commonly, struvite stones may form, which are the result of bacterial infections of the urinary tract.

Symptoms

Kidney stones are largely asymptomatic until they leave the kidney and enter the ureter. When this occurs, pain may be felt around the abdomen, groin, back, and sides. Painful urination may take place as the stone blocks the ureter. The urine may have a pink or brown appearance due to blood in the urine. An inadequate amount of urine may be produced due to blockages.

Treatments

Many treatment options are available. In less severe cases, increasing water intake can help flush the kidneys of the increased calcium and help move the stones out of the body. To aid in moving the stone out of the body, a doctor may prescribe medications that help to relax the smooth muscle in the ureter, known as alpha blockers.

In more severe cases, stones may be destroyed while still inside the body using a treatment known as **extracorporeal shock wave lithotripsy**. The stones are broken down using sound waves, and then are able to be passed out of the body easier. If the stones are too big to be destroyed using sound waves, they may be removed surgically.

Contraindications

Kidney stones are not considered a contraindication for massage therapy.

Pyelonephritis
(pyel/o: renal pelvis; nephr/o: kidney; -itis: inflammation)

Pyelonephritis is a **bacterial infection** of the kidney, usually beginning in the urethra or bladder. The infection spreads upwards through the ureters and **into the kidneys**. Pyelonephritis is considered a serious condition, and if suspected, should be seen by a doctor immediately for treatment.

Causes

Bacteria enters the urethra. Usually, urinating cleans out the urethra. Rarely, it does not, and bacteria can reproduce in the urethra. The bacteria then can spread upwards into the bladder, then move further up into the ureters and kidneys. Women are more likely than men to develop urinary tract infections due to a shorter urethra.

Symptoms

Symptoms of an acute infection in the kidneys include pain in the back, groin, or abdomen, nausea, vomiting, fever, blood in the urine, burning during urination, and an urge to constantly urinate. Cloudy urine may also be a sign of an infection, especially if there is a foul odor.

Treatments

Antibiotics are used to combat pyelonephritis. They are typically administered orally, but in more severe cases that require hospitalization, they may be administered via IV. Pain relievers may be used to aid with associated pain.

Contraindications

Pyelonephritis is considered an absolute contraindication. A client who suspects a kidney infection should seek medical treatment.

Renal Failure

Renal Failure is **kidney failure**, where the kidneys stop functioning properly. This can lead to the body being **unable to eliminate waste**, electrolytes, and excessive fluid. This can lead to dangerous, even fatal levels of these substances in the body.

Causes

Renal failure is commonly the result of another condition damaging the kidney enough to impair function. Examples are hypertension, glomerulonephritis, pyelonephritis, diabetes, and polycystic kidney disease.

Symptoms

Usually, renal failure occurs gradually, and symptoms become more known as the kidney begins to lose function. Fatigue, nausea, vomiting, hypertension, increased fluid accumulation in the lower limbs, and loss of appetite are common symptoms.

Treatments

As the kidneys begin failing, treatment usually revolves around treating the symptoms to try and slow the disease. Once the kidneys have experienced too much damage and the body is unable to eliminate waste and fluid effectively, dialysis may be performed to remove these substances, either through the blood or through the peritoneum.

Kidney transplants may be performed. Instead of removing the damaged kidneys, a doctor will leave the damaged kidneys in the body and attach another kidney. Despite not functioning optimally, the damaged kidneys can still assist the new kidney in filtering waste and fluid, even though it may only be a small amount.

Contraindications

Because massage may increase the load on kidneys by helping rid the body of waste, massage is considered an absolute contraindication in clients with renal failure. There is debate amongst kidney specialists on this matter, though, and some believe massage therapy does not do harm in people with renal failure.

Urethritis
(urethr/o: urethra; -itis: inflammation)

Urethritis is **inflammation** of the **urethra**, usually caused by a **bacterial** infection. It is extremely treatable.

Causes

Urethritis is caused by a bacterial infection. Bacteria enters the urethra and reproduces, resulting in an infection. The infection may spread up the urinary tract, and may lead to cystitis or pyelonephritis if left untreated.

Less commonly, urethritis may be caused by herpes simplex.

Symptoms

Pain upon urination is the primary symptom of urethritis. A less common symptom is inability to effectively urinate, known as dysuria. Discharge from the vagina may present, and the urine may contain blood.

Treatments

Because urethritis is most commonly caused by bacterial infection, antibiotics are prescribed to destroy the bacteria and prevent the infection from moving further into the Urinary System.

Contraindications

Massage is indicated for clients with urethritis.

Cancer

When the body produces an **abnormal amount** of a **specific tissue**, it develops what is known as a **tumor**. Tumors are also known as neoplasms. Tumors may be either benign or malignant. **Benign** tumors are considered **noncancerous**, and do not spread to other areas of the body. **Malignant** tumors are considered **cancerous**, and will spread to other areas of the body. The most common type of cancer is skin cancer.

Benign tumors typically grow **slowly**. These tumors do not invade other tissues or structures in the body. Benign tumors may cause harm, however, by placing pressure on regions of the body that contain major blood vessels, lymph vessels, or nerves. Benign tumors are often removed before they get to this point if there is a risk of damaging other structures. Other benign tumors may be left alone if they do not cause problems.

Malignant tumors **spread** through the body and affect other tissues and structures through a process known as **metastasis**. Cancerous cells spread through the body by entering into the **blood stream** and **lymph vessels**, allowing the cells to easily transport to another region. Once these cells settle in another region or structure, they continue to reproduce at a rapid, uncontrolled rate. The **original site** of the tumor is known as the **primary tumor**, while the tumor that has **developed elsewhere** is known as a **secondary tumor**. Some cancers, such as leukemia, do not result in any tumor growing. Malignant cancers commonly spread through the Lymphatic System and can result in tumors in major lymph nodes. This is especially common in areas like the breasts and neck.

There are three main classifications for cancer: carcinoma, sarcoma, and cancers of the blood stream/Lymphatic System. **Carcinoma** is cancer that occurs in the **epithelial tissue**, which can be found in the skin, digestive tract, and respiratory tract. A common form of carcinoma is basal cell carcinoma. **Sarcoma** is cancer that occurs in the body's **connective tissues**, such as bone and cartilage. Examples include bone cancer and Kaposi's Sarcoma. Examples of cancers that involve the blood stream and Lymphatic System include leukemia and Non-Hodgkin's Lymphoma.

Tumor in situ

Growth and intravasation

Diffusion via blood stream

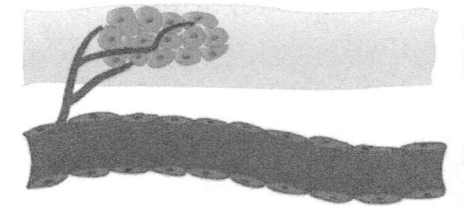

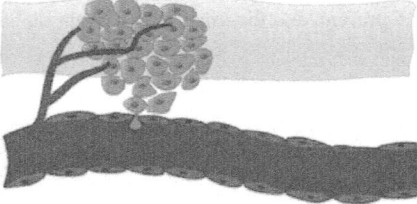

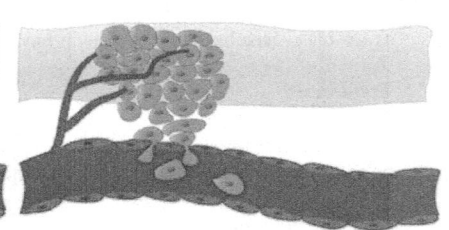

Adhesion and extravasation

Invasion of a new distant tissue

Growth and angiogenesis

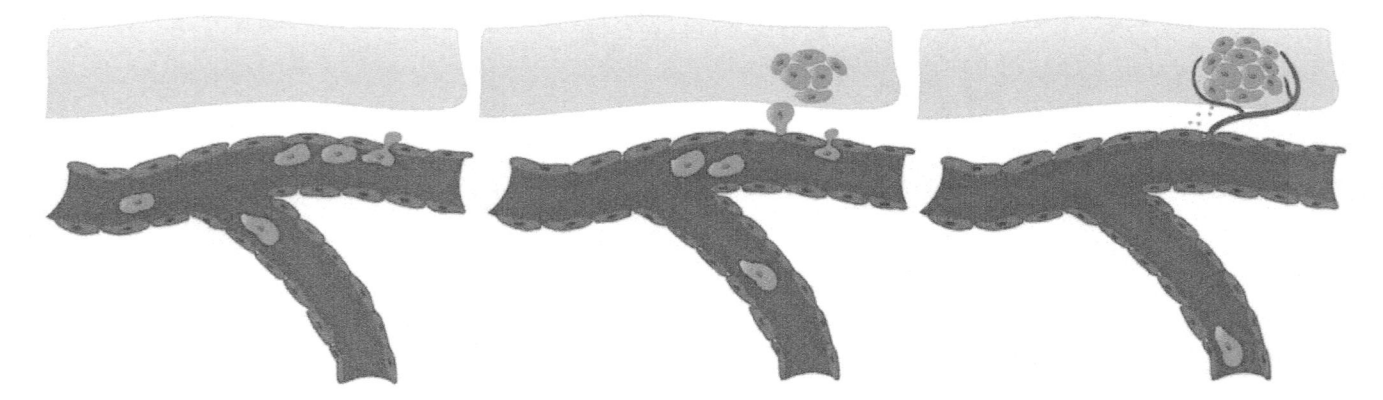

Cancers

Basal Cell Carcinoma
(carcin-: cancer; -oma: tumor)

Basal Cell Carcinoma is a type of **skin cancer** typically seen around the **face, head, neck, and arms**.

Causes

Basal cell carcinoma is the most common form of skin cancer, caused by exposure to **ultraviolet light**. The tumor grows **extremely slowly**, which makes basal cell carcinoma much more treatable than other types of skin cancer. Because it is much more treatable, it is considered the **least serious** form of skin cancer.

Basal cell carcinoma is considered a malignant form of cancer, due to its ability to spread to the tissues immediately surrounding it. It will very rarely spread to other organs, however.

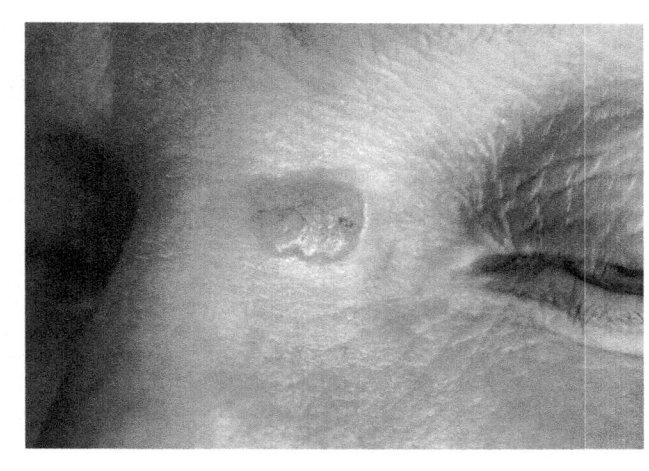

Symptoms

Basal cell carcinoma tumors may appear to have blood vessels in them, and vary in color from black to brown to pink. These growths may bleed easily.

Treatments

Treatment for basal cell carcinoma includes surgical excision of the tumor, freezing the tumor, or in more serious cases, medications that prevent the cancerous cells from spreading to other tissues.

Contraindications

Massage is indicated for a client with basal cell carcinoma. However, the tumor is a local contraindication, and massage around the area should be avoided to prevent spreading of cancerous tissue through increased blood and lymph flow.

Breast Cancer

Breast cancer is cancer of **breast tissue**, including **lymph nodes and vessels** in the **breast and axillary region**. Breast cancer is the second most common form of cancer diagnosed in women, behind skin cancer. Breast cancer is much more common in women, but it can also occur in men.

Breast cancer can spread throughout the breast and to other regions of the body, and is considered a malignant form of cancer.

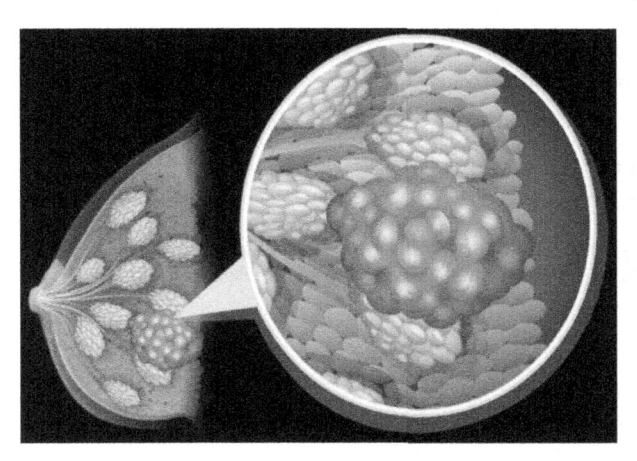

Causes

Breast cancer occurs when breast tissue begins growing abnormally, forming a tumor that feels like a lump under the skin. Breast cancer may be a genetic disorder, or may be the cause of unspecified environmental factors. Women who are older in age tend to develop breast cancer more often than younger women.

Symptoms

Symptoms include a lump in the breast that does not feel the same as tissue surrounding it, a nipple that has recently become inverted, change in size or appearance of the breast, dimpling of the skin of the breast, the skin of the breast and/or areola becoming scaly or flaky, and the skin of the breast becoming red. If any of these symptoms occur, a person should be seen by a medical professional.

Treatments

Treatment is based on the severity of the tumor growth. Surgery to remove the tumor will likely be performed after locating it via mammogram and ultrasound. If a large amount of breast tissue is involved, the breast may be completely removed, known as a mastectomy. Lymph nodes may also be removed to prevent any cancerous tissue from spreading to other parts of the body. Chemotherapy and radiation therapy are performed to kill the remaining cancerous cells.

Contraindications

A massage therapist should obtain a doctor's note approving massage. Afterwards, massage may be performed, avoiding any tumors, lymph nodes, or other areas affected.

Hodgkin's Lymphoma
(lymph-: lymph; -oma: tumor)

Hodgkin's Lymphoma is a malignant cancer affecting the Lymphatic System, specifically the **lymph nodes** in the **upper limb, chest, and neck**. Hodgkin's Lymphoma usually follows lymph channels in a predictable manner, moving from one lymph node to the next.

Causes

Hodgkin's Lymphoma is caused by an excessive amount of B-cells being produced. These cells, known as **Reed-Sternberg cells**, are larger than normal and contain multiple nuclei, as opposed to non-cancerous B-cells, which are smaller and only contain one nucleus.

Symptoms

Symptoms of Hodgkin's Lymphoma include swelling of lymph nodes in the neck, upper limb, and axilla that may be painless, weight loss, fever, and fatigue. A person may also experience sensitivity to alcohol.

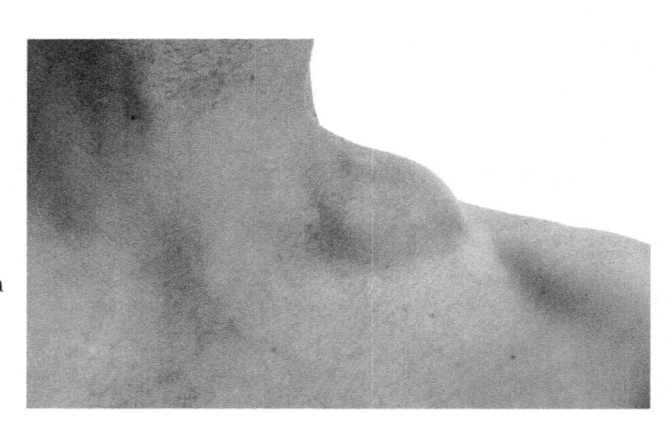

Treatments

Surgery isn't usually performed for a patient with Hodgkin's Lymphoma. Instead, chemotherapy and radiation therapy are used to destroy the cancerous lymphocytes. Bone marrow transplants may also be performed to stimulate the production of non-cancerous cells.

Contraindications

A massage therapist should obtain a doctor's note approving massage. Afterwards, massage may be performed, avoiding any tumors, lymph nodes, or other areas affected.

Leukemia
(leuk/o: white; -emia: blood condition)

Leukemia is a cancer of the **bone and lymph** involving **excessive production of non-functioning leukocytes**. These leukocytes do not function the way normal leukocytes should, leaving the body with a compromised immune system. These cancerous cells may spread to other parts of the body such as the liver and brain.

Symptoms of leukemia

- **Lungs** (shortness breath)
- **Skin** (tiny red spots)
- **Bone and joints** (pain or tenderness)
- **Chronic fatigue** (weakness and low energy)
- **Lymph node** (swelling)
- **Liver and spleen** (swelling)
- **Muscle aches**

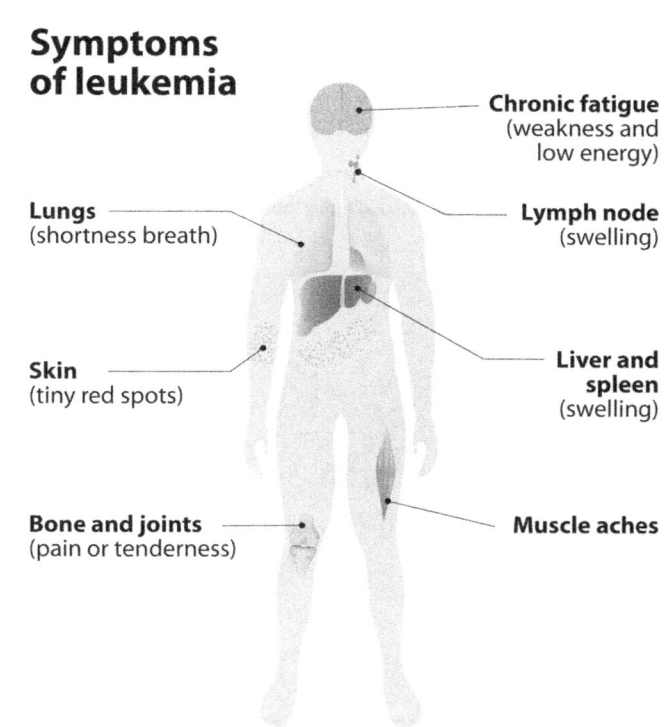

Causes

There is no known cause for the development of leukemia.

Symptoms

Common symptoms of leukemia include pain in the bone, swollen lymph nodes, fatigue, fever, chills, increased likelihood of developing infections, the appearance of small red spots in the skin, and bruising or bleeding easily. A doctor should be seen if any of these symptoms persist.

Treatments

Treatment for leukemia largely depends on the advancement of the condition. If the cancer has metastasized to other parts of the body, treatment would be performed on those areas in conjunction with treating the leukemia. Chemotherapy and radiation therapy are used to target and destroy cancerous cells throughout the body. After chemotherapy and/or radiation therapy, stem cell transplant may be performed to supply the bone with stem cells that grow healthy marrow, which produces functioning leukocytes. Bone marrow itself may also be transplanted into the patient to accomplish the same goal.

Contraindications

A massage therapist should obtain a doctor's note approving massage. Afterwards, massage may be performed, avoiding any tumors, lymph nodes, or other areas affected.

Lung Cancer

Lung cancer is the development of **tumors in the lung**. People who **smoke cigarettes** are at a much higher risk to develop lung cancer than anyone else. Lung cancer is the leading cause of cancerous death in the United States.

Causes

Lung cancer is primarily caused by exposure to carcinogens being inhaled. Carcinogens that cause lung cancer may be found in cigarette smoke. Other carcinogens may include radon and asbestos. These substances damage the tissue of the lungs, which in turn may begin reproducing unnaturally, causing cancer.

Lung cancer may spread to other areas and organs of the body, including the liver and brain.

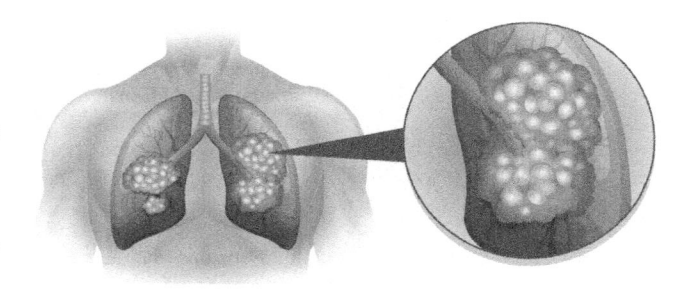

Symptoms

Lung cancer is usually asymptomatic in early stages. As the condition progresses, however, symptoms may begin to appear and worsen over time. Symptoms include coughing that may produce blood, shortness of breath, and chest pain. Hoarseness may occur due to excessive coughing.

Treatments

Treatment largely depends on the stage of the cancer. The earlier stages of cancer may only require surgical removal of a small portion of the lung to take out the tumor. Advanced stages involving larger tumors may require an entire lobe of a lung to be removed, or in extreme cases, having the entire lung removed.

After the tumor is removed, radiation and chemotherapy may be performed to destroy any remaining cancerous cells.

Contraindications

A massage therapist should obtain a doctor's note approving massage. Afterwards, massage may be performed, avoiding any tumors, lymph nodes, or other areas affected.

Malignant Melanoma
(melan-: black; -oma: tumor)

Malignant Melanoma is a type of **skin** cancer that may affect any part of the skin, and can also affect other tissues such as the eyes and internal organs.

Causes

Malignant melanoma is the **least common** form of skin cancer, but it is the **most serious**. It is caused by exposure to **ultraviolet light**. The cells in the body that produce skin pigment, **melanocytes**, become stimulated by exposure to ultraviolet light and reproduce, causing darker skin. In malignant melanoma, the melanocytes reproduce uncontrolled. This uncontrolled reproduction results in a tumor, and these cancerous cells can easily spread throughout the body and damage other organs and tissues.

Dermatologists use the ABCDE method to diagnose malignant melanoma:

A: Asymmetrical; moles are typically symmetrical, but melanoma tumors have an unusual shape, and the sides don't match.

B: Borders; the borders of the growth change over time and are uneven. This is a sign of significantly increased melanin production.

C: Color; moles are typically some shade of brown. If there are multiple shades or colors, or if the tumor is black, this may be a sign of increased melanin production.

D: Diameter; if a growth is 6mm or greater in diameter(the distance through it), this may be a sign of melanoma.

E: Evolving; moles typically look the same over time. If a mole or growth begins to evolve or change in any way, this may be a sign of melanoma.

Malignant melanoma most commonly begins to appear on a part of the body that doesn't have any prior lesions, like moles. If a new growth appears where there was nothing prior, this may be a sign of melanoma. Less commonly, moles may become cancerous.

Symptoms

Symptoms of melanoma are all included in the ABCDE's.

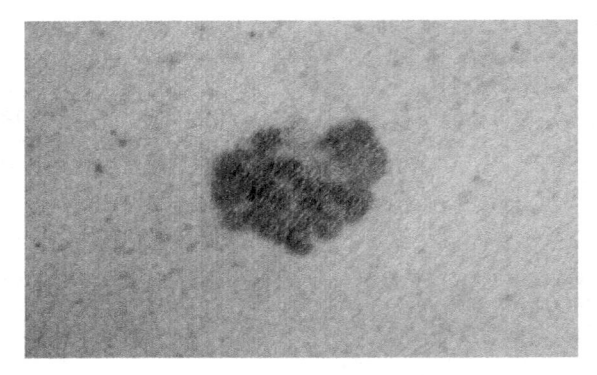

Treatments

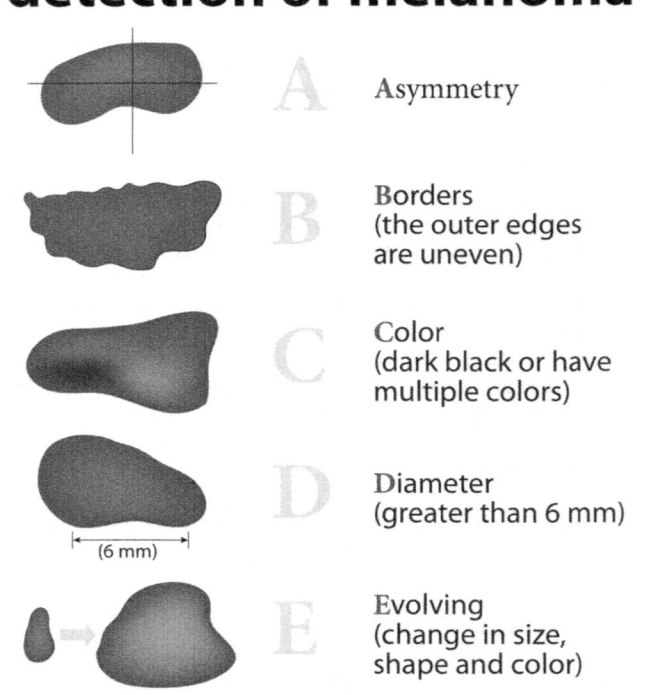

Malignant melanoma, if caught early enough, is easily treatable. Later stages, where it has grown beyond the skin, need more advanced treatments, including surgery to remove any tumors or cancerous lymph nodes, chemotherapy, and radiation therapy.

Contraindications

A client with malignant melanoma should obtain permission from a doctor before proceeding with any type of massage, because the cancerous cells are easily spread throughout the body through the blood and lymph. The site of tumor growth should be avoided.

Non-Hodgkin's Lymphoma
(lymph-: lymph; -oma: tumor)

Non-Hodgkin's Lymphoma is a type of cancer of the Lymphatic System, caused by the development of tumors by **lymphocytes**.

Causes

In the body, lymphocytes, like every cell, go through their normal life cycle, and die when they are supposed to. In Non-Hodgkin's Lymphoma, the **lymphocytes don't die**, but **continue reproducing**. This causes an **excessive amount** of **lymphocytes** to build up in the lymph nodes.

Symptoms

People with Non-Hodgkin's Lymphoma may experience swollen lymph nodes around the neck, groin, and axilla, fatigue, weight loss, and fever.

Treatments

Often times, Non-Hodgkin's Lymphoma isn't serious, and treatment is only required when it becomes advanced. Advanced Non-Hodgkin's Lymphoma is treated with chemotherapy and radiation therapy to destroy the cancerous cells.

Contraindications

A massage therapist should obtain a doctor's note approving massage. Afterwards, massage may be performed, avoiding any tumors, lymph nodes, or other areas affected.

Squamous Cell Carcinoma

Squamous Cell Carcinoma is a form of **skin** cancer that in many cases is not serious, but has the ability to spread to other parts of the body. Squamous cell carcinoma is **more serious** and **less common** than **basal cell carcinoma**, but **not as serious** and **more common** than **malignant melanoma**.

Causes

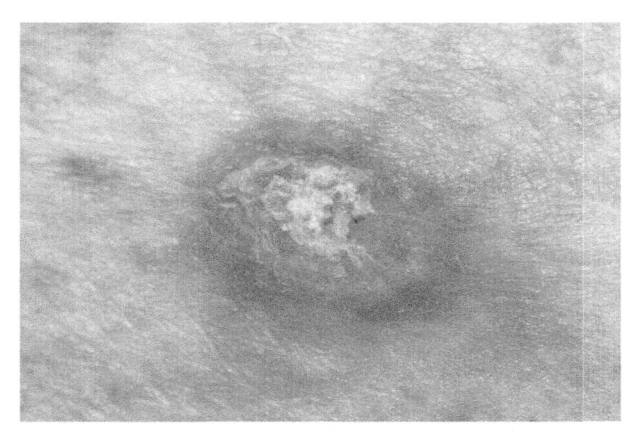

Squamous cell carcinoma, much like basal cell carcinoma and malignant melanoma, is most often caused by exposure to ultraviolet light. Tumors most commonly develop on areas of the body commonly exposed to sunlight, such as the head, neck, arms, and hands. Tumors may be flat, scaly, and firm, and appear around the mouth, in the mouth, and on the lips.

Symptoms

Squamous cell carcinoma tumors are typically shaped like a dome, and tend to bleed easily. They appear red and scaly, with a rough texture. If the tumor is large, pain may be present around the area.

Treatments

Much like basal cell carcinoma, treatment for squamous cell carcinoma is relatively easy, with several different methods, from surgical excision and freezing of the tumor, to radiation therapy for more advanced tumors.

Contraindications

A client with squamous cell carcinoma may receive massage, but the site of the tumor should be avoided due to possible spreading of cancerous tissue.

Psychological Disorders

Anorexia Nervosa

Anorexia nervosa is a condition marked by **severe weight loss** resulting from an **unhealthy restricting of caloric intake**. In conjunction with eating an inadequate amount of food, a person with anorexia may also try losing weight by taking diuretics, laxatives, and vomiting after eating. This can cause a severe lack of nutrition, resulting in the body thinning far beyond a healthy level.

Causes

Anorexia is a psychological disorder in which a person's perception of their weight is distorted. Contributing factors towards the development of anorexia include environmental influences that put an over-emphasis on being thin, and psychological issues such as obsessive compulsive disorder that make it easier to not eat by sticking to set goals.

Symptoms

Symptoms are wide-ranging, from severe thinness and weight loss, to problems with tooth decay from excessive vomiting.

A lack of proper nutrition can lead to fatigue, weakness, thinning hair, and dehydration. A person with anorexia may develop anemia, osteoporosis, abnormalities in hormone production and regulation, issues with kidney function, and muscle atrophy.

Psychologically, a person may withdraw socially, and try to hide their anorexia by wearing clothing to hide their weight loss. A person may become irritable and skip meals. When confronted, a person may deny skipping meals or lie about how much food they have eaten.

Treatments

Treatment for anorexia may include hospitalization in severe cases, where the body is not receiving adequate nutrition over a long period of time. While in the hospital, a person will be given fluids to balance dehydration and electrolyte levels, and be treated for issues possibly relating to the heart, liver, and kidneys. A feeding tube may be inserted to ensure a person is receiving enough nutrients.

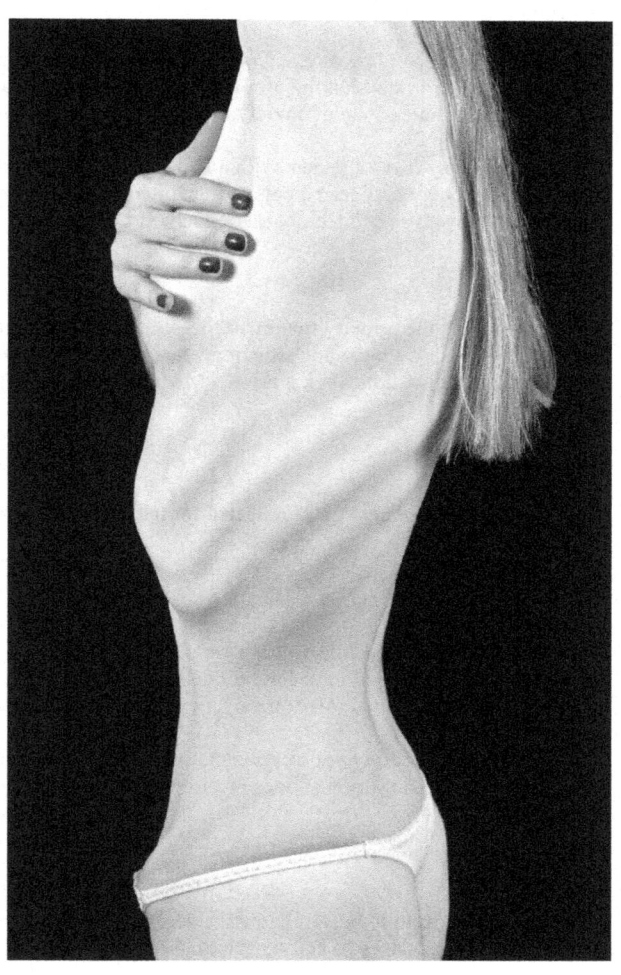

Aside from a stay in the hospital, a person may be seen by a mental health professional to deal with underlying causes of anorexia. A person may work closely with a dietician to maintain a healthy diet.

Contraindications

Massage therapy is not contraindicated in clients with anorexia. A lighter massage should be performed to prevent damage to bones and other structures in the body.

Anxiety Disorders

Anxiety disorders are a group of disorders in where a person experiences an **increased amount of anxiety**, often at a level where the person feels they are in a **life-or-death situation**. These anxious moments can adversely affect a person's daily life and relationships. Different types of anxiety disorders include panic disorder, social anxiety disorder, and general anxiety disorder.

A person with an anxiety disorder may also suffer from addiction, depression, chronic pain, or even attempt suicide.

Causes

Often times, underlying medical issues may be the cause of anxiety disorders. Some examples include cardiovascular diseases, substance withdrawal, asthma, and hyperthyroidism. Medications may also induce anxiety.

Symptoms

Symptoms vary depending on the type of anxiety a person suffers from. General symptoms include nervousness, increased breathing and heart rate, shaking, trembling, digestive issues, and the inability to stop thinking about whatever it is that is putting a person into a state of anxiety.

Panic anxiety may leave a person with a feeling of fear or terror, and lead to chest pain, shortness of breath, and a rapid heart beat. Social anxiety may lead a person to avoid contact with others as a means to protect themselves from situations they might find themselves being embarrassed or self-conscious in.

Treatments

Psychotherapy is the primary treatment for anxiety disorders. Cognitive Behavioral Therapy is used to help treat social anxiety by exposing a person to situations they may experience in real life, giving them exposure and helping them learn how to cope with the situation when it arises. Medications may be prescribed, such as antidepressants, that can help a person from feeling anxious.

Contraindications

Anxiety disorders are not contraindicated for massage therapy.

Bulimia
(Greek "boulimia": ravenous hunger)

Bulimia is a psychological disorder in which a person ingests abnormally **large portions of food**, followed by **purging** of the food ingested. Purging of food can be caused by **self-induced vomiting**, by consuming **laxatives or diuretics**, and/or **excessive exercise**. This is all done in an effort to avoid weight gain.

The use of self-induced vomiting and laxatives/diuretics is known as Purging Bulimia. These involve ridding the body of the ingested food in some way that doesn't allow it to be properly digested. The use of excessive exercise is known as Non-Purging Bulimia.

Causes

The exact cause of bulimia is unknown, although there are several contributing factors that may lead to the development of the condition. Stress, history of abuse, trauma, low self-esteem, and having a negative image of one's body can all be contributing factors.

Symptoms

Common symptoms may include dehydration, imbalances in electrolyte levels, fluctuating weight, lesions in the mouth due to excessive vomiting, chronic heart burn, and infertility.

People with bulimia may exhibit some of the following traits and behaviors: frequent bathroom usage after eating, eating privately, smelling of vomit, and lacking control when eating.

Treatments

Bulimia is most commonly caused by low self-esteem and negative body image. Therefore, the primary treatment is therapy to help the patient overcome these psychological issues.

Contraindications

Bulimia is not contraindicated for massage. Massage may help psychologically and improve self esteem and body image. A lighter massage may be indicated, as the client may have atrophied muscles and a weakened body due to lack of nutrients.

Dementia

Dementia is a general term for symptoms that involve **memory loss**, loss of **social skills**, and diminished **critical thinking skills**. These skills may be impaired to the point where it affects a person's ability to function effectively on a daily basis. Dementia is caused by damage to neurons in the brain. There are numerous reasons for neurons to be damaged that can contribute to dementia.

Causes

Dementia may be permanent, or may be reversed, depending on the cause. Causes of dementia that involve permanent damage to the brain include progressive disorders such as Alzheimer's disease. Strokes may permanently damage the brain. Similar to strokes, injuries to the brain such as concussions may lead to brain damage.

Cases where dementia may be reversed include certain infections that cause high fever, autoimmune disorders such as multiple sclerosis, tumors in the brain, hypoxia, inadequate fluid intake, and hormonal problems such as having too much calcium in the body. As these conditions are treated, the dementia should go away.

Symptoms

Dementia is most commonly associated with memory loss. This can lead to problems communicating, focusing, using the body properly, and problem solving. A person may become depressed, develop anxiety or paranoia, and become easily irritated.

Treatments

Dementia itself can't be cured. Treating the underlying cause is the best way to treat dementia. This can include medications to help brain function, and physical therapy to help with any motor skills that may be affected.

Contraindications

Dementia is not contraindicated for massage therapy.

Depression

Depression is a disorder affecting **mood**, causing a person to feel **sad**, usually over a **prolonged period of time**. A person may become disinterested in normal daily activities, and become more distant.

Depression usually develops during teenage years, but may occur at any time. If a person is experiencing depression, they should seek help from a mental health professional.

Causes

There are many different causes for depression, and no one person is the same as another. Causes include a change in the body's hormone levels, such as during and after pregnancy, changes in the function of neurotransmitters in the brain, and even may be genetically passed down.

Symptoms

Symptoms are wide-ranging, and people experience depression differently. Symptoms may include a feeling of sadness, fatigue, disinterest in eating, anxiety, insomnia, irritability, and consistently thinking about death and suicide. A person with depression may attempt suicide.

Treatments

If a person is diagnosed with depression, antidepressants known as selective serotonin reuptake inhibitors, or SSRIs, are usually prescribed to help manage hormone levels and increase serotonin levels in the blood. Talking with a mental health professional may help a person feel better. Exercise and a healthy diet may help with hormone imbalances and increase a person's self esteem, which can aid in lowering depression. Other relaxation techniques, such as massage therapy and yoga, may be sought.

Contraindications

Depression is not contraindicated for massage therapy. Massage may help relax a person with depression, increase self-esteem and body image, and help manage hormone levels in the body.

The National Suicide Prevention Lifeline is 1-800-273-8255

Insomnia
(in-: not; somnus: sleep)

Insomnia is a disorder causing a **lack of sufficient sleep**. This may be the result of a person having difficulty falling asleep, staying asleep, or waking too early. This can lead to many health complications.

Causes

There are many reasons a person's sleep may be affected. Stress is the most common cause of insomnia, making it difficult to "turn off" thoughts when it's time to sleep. Having an irregular sleep schedule may make it difficult for the body to adjust when it's time to sleep. Jet lag may also cause insomnia.

Certain medications may interfere with normal sleep. Pain associated with medical conditions may also keep a person from sleeping.

Symptoms

Common symptoms include trouble falling asleep, trouble staying asleep, waking too early, general fatigue, irritability, increased stress and anxiety, and depression. A person with insomnia may develop other health conditions as a result of not getting enough sleep, such as hypertension.

Treatments

Determining and treating the root cause of the insomnia is the primary treatment for insomnia. Reducing stress, getting a person on a set sleep schedule, increasing exercise, meditation, yoga, and massage therapy can all aid in eliminating insomnia. If these methods do not accomplish the goal, medications to help a person sleep may be prescribed. Over-the-counter sleep aids may help a person sleep, but should not be used long-term as a person may develop a dependency on them.

Contraindications

Insomnia is not a contraindication for massage. Massage therapy may aid a person in reducing stress and helping them obtain a normal sleep cycle.

Other Pathologies

Conjunctivitis
(conjunctiv/o: conjunctiva; -itis: inflammation)

Conjunctivitis is **inflammation** and/or **infection of the conjunctiva**, the clear membrane that lines the inner eyelid and covers the sclera of the eye. Conjunctivitis is also known as **pinkeye**, due to the appearance of the conjunctiva when the blood vessels inside become irritated and inflamed.

Causes

The most common cause of conjunctivitis is a bacterial or viral infection. In infants, conjunctivitis may occur if tear ducts become blocked. Allergens may also cause conjunctivitis.

Symptoms

The affected eye may appear red, producing a discharge. This discharge may crust over and make it difficult to open the eye in the morning after sleep. The eye may feel itchy. Vision is not affected by conjunctivitis, but an increased amount of tears may be produced.

Treatments

Treating conjunctivitis is dependent on the cause. If it is caused by bacteria, antibiotic eye drops are prescribed. Antiviral medications may be prescribed in certain cases, such as a herpes simplex outbreak.

If conjunctivitis is caused by an irritant such as contact lenses, a person will stop using contacts until the conjunctivitis clears up.

Contraindications

Conjunctivitis is generally not a contraindication, unless it is caused by bacteria or a virus. If this is the case, massage is considered an absolute contraindication, and should be rescheduled until after the condition has resolved.

Tinnitus
(Latin "tinnire": to ring like a bell)

Tinnitus is the presence of a **sound in the ear**, typically **ringing**, without an external auditory source. Tinnitus is usually related to another cause, such as an injury to the ear or hearing loss. It is usually not serious, but may be somewhat irritating. Tinnitus may always be present, or may come and go. The volume and pitch of the sound may be low or high, and may be loud enough to interfere with a person's ability to hear properly.

Causes

Common causes of tinnitus include exposure to loud noises, such as music, machinery, and firearms, hearing loss related to aging, and Meniere's disease. Less commonly, conditions that affect the Cardiovascular System may contribute to tinnitus, such as atherosclerosis and hypertension. With these conditions, more pressure is being placed on the blood vessels, which can harm the blood vessels in the ears, making them more susceptible to developing tinnitus.

Symptoms

The main symptom is a sound in the ear that only the person can hear. This sound can be a ringing, clicking, humming, roaring, or buzzing sound. Depending on the cause, it may be heard in one or both ears.

Treatments

Treatment for tinnitus is often treating the underlying cause, which should alleviate the ringing in the ear. If a cardiovascular issue is suspected, medications may be prescribed to help treat these, which can eliminate the tinnitus. Less commonly, excessive ear wax may produce tinnitus. If this is the case, impacted ear wax may be removed. Avoiding loud noises will also help alleviate tinnitus.

Contraindications

Tinnitus is not contraindicated for massage therapy. However, if a client complains of ringing in the ear, other conditions should be assessed for contraindications.

Vertigo

Vertigo is the sensation that a person's **surroundings** are **moving or spinning**, which may cause **dizziness**. This can be especially prevalent if a person is looking down from a tall height.

Causes

Commonly, vertigo is the result of a problem with the **inner ear**. Meniere's disease, which causes fluid buildup that changes pressure inside the ear, is a common cause. A buildup of calcium deposits in the inner ear can alter balance. Viral infections, such as vestibular neuritis, may also cause vertigo. Less commonly, tumors in the ear may cause vertigo.

Symptoms

Vertigo presents with a feeling of the environment around a person spinning, moving, swaying, or tilting. A person may become unbalanced, become nauseated, vomit, or develop headaches.

Treatments

Treatment for vertigo is usually dependent on the cause. If calcium is present in the inner ear, certain head and neck movements may be performed to aid the calcium in leaving the inner ear, allowing it to be broken down by the body. Medications may be prescribed to aid with nausea and fluid build up associated with Meniere's disease. Surgery may be performed if there is a tumor present.

Often times, no treatment is necessary, as the brain becomes acclimated to vertigo and the symptoms lessen or disappear.

Contraindications

Vertigo is not contraindicated for massage. The massage therapist may need to help the client on and off the table to avoid accidental falls due to dizziness.

First Aid and Response to Emergencies

First Aid

There are many different ways to care for a person with a medical emergency, depending on the type of injury and the severity. When using first aid, **universal precautions** should be administered. Universal precautions are treating every person and fluid as if they were **contaminated** or **infectious**. Universal precautions are extremely important in containing blood-borne pathogens. Any time there is exposure to any type of bodily fluid, **gloves** and other **personal protective equipment** should be worn, and contact with blood should be avoided at all costs.

CAB refers to the initial assessment steps that should be taken when coming into contact with an unconscious person. **Circulation** should be checked using pulse points. If no circulation is detected, the **airway** should be checked to determine if there is an obstruction that is causing the person to be unable to **breathe**. If there is an obstruction, it should try to be removed using a gentle finger swipe. If there is no circulation, the airway is not blocked, and the person is not breathing, CPR should be performed and EMS should be notified.

Good Samaritan laws, instituted in numerous states in the US, are designed to provide good samaritans with **legal protections** arising from any unforeseen circumstances that occur while caring for a person who is injured or in danger.

Responding to Emergencies

Bleeding

If a person is bleeding, a sterile bandage should be placed on the wound to promote blood clotting, which stops bleeding. If the bleeding is severe, a tourniquet may be applied, which should significantly reduce the bleeding. The person should lie down and be kept warm using a blanket, if available.

Cardiac and Respiratory Arrest

If a person is suspected of suffering from cardiac arrest, CPR should be performed immediately. CPR, which stands for **Cardiopulmonary Resuscitation**, is extremely important to know and understand how to perform. Refer to REMSA guidelines for appropriate instruction. CPR consists of alternating **chest** compressions and **breathing** support in cases where cardiac arrest has occurred. Refer to REMSA for up-to-date CPR techniques and requirements.

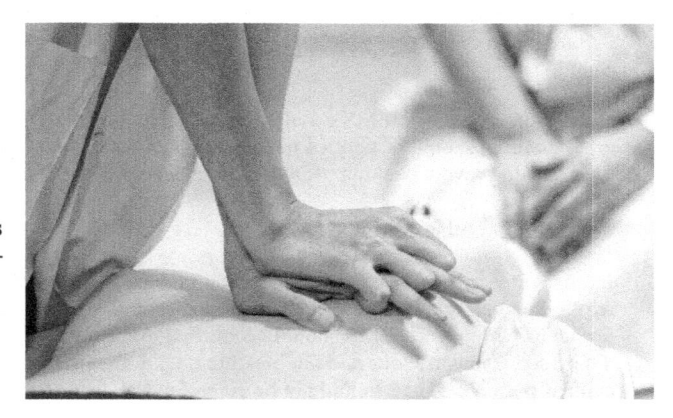

Choking

If a swallowed object or piece of food enters the larynx or trachea, choking will occur. A person who is choking may have extreme difficulty in coughing or talking, and may place their hands to their throat to indicate they are choking. This person should be treated immediately, utilizing five blows to the back, followed by five abdominal thrusts. This process should be repeated until the object is dislodged. If the person becomes unconscious, they should be placed on the ground, and the throat should be checked for blockages. If the blockage is able to be removed without pushing it further into the respiratory tract, a finger sweep should be utilized. If not, CPR should be performed until paramedics arrive.

Diabetic Ketoacidosis

Diabetic ketoacidosis occurs when a diabetic person has too many ketones in the body, caused by hyperglycemia. A person may have problems breathing, be fatigued, exhibit pain in the abdomen, and experience nausea and vomiting. If this person is unconscious as a result, EMS should be notified immediately. If they are not breathing, CPR should be administered until paramedics arrive.

Insulin Shock

If a person has diabetes, they need to take insulin to help manage their body's blood sugar. If blood sugar levels fall too far, it is known as hypoglycemia, and may result in insulin shock. A person may develop insulin shock for several reasons, such as injecting too much insulin, not increasing blood sugar levels, not eating, or exercising without increasing carbohydrate consumption. Mild drops in blood sugar levels can be treated quickly by ingesting high carbohydrate food or liquid. Severe hypoglycemia may result in insulin shock, however, and a person may develop seizures, muscle tremors, or they may become unconscious. If a person becomes unconscious, EMS should be notified immediately. If a shot of glucose is available, it should be administered immediately.

Fractures

Tending to a broken bone depends on the severity of the fracture. All fractures should be seen by a medical professional right away. If a fracture breaks through the skin, bleeding should be stopped. The area of the fracture should be immobilized, as movement in the area may cause damage to other structures in the body. The person may develop shock, and wrapping them in an insulating blanket may help. An ice pack may help reduce inflammation and pain in the area. The person should be taken to a hospital to have the bone reset, and the ensure there isn't major damage to other structures such as blood vessels inside the body that may cause internal hemorrhaging.

Seizures

If a person is having a seizure, the seizure should be allowed to run its course. Afterwards, the patient should be placed into a seated position, where they can rest and recover. If the seizure lasts for five minutes or longer, it is the person's first seizure, or the person is unable to effectively walk or breathe afterwards, EMS should be contacted.

Shock

If a person is in shock, EMS should be notified immediately. The person should lie down, keeping the head flat. A blanket or other clothing should be applied to keep the person's body temperature up. If the person is vomiting, they should be placed on their side to prevent choking. If any injuries are apparent, they should be treated.

Cerebral Vascular Accident

If a person is suspected of suffering a cerebral vascular accident, they may be exhibiting symptoms commonly seen with strokes, including drooping face, difficulty speaking, weakness in the arms that occurs suddenly, sudden headache, and sudden problems with vision. EMS should be notified immediately, as a cerebral vascular accident is a life-threatening condition. If the person is unconscious and not breathing, CPR should be performed. If the person is still conscious, they should be kept as calm as possible. They should not be given food or drink, to avoid vomiting.

Syncope

Syncope, also known as fainting, is usually not a serious condition. It is caused by the brain very temporarily losing blood flow. However, injuries caused by falling may occur. If a person has fainted, any restrictive clothing should be removed, and the legs should be elevated at least one foot above the heart. If the person is unconscious and not breathing, EMS should be notified, and CPR should be performed. If the person has not regained consciousness after one minute, EMS should be notified. Injuries sustained during a fall should also be treated, such as bleeding.

Vertigo

Vertigo is dizziness a person may experience for many different reasons, but commonly a problem with the inner ear. If a person becomes dizzy, they should be seated, or lie down. Preventing movement is the most important step in treating vertigo. If vertigo lasts for an extended period, EMS should be notified.

Asthma Attack

During an asthma attack, a person may have extreme difficulty breathing due to constriction of the bronchial tubes. The person may be unable to effectively speak, and the lips and fingers may turn a blueish color. Constrictive clothing should be removed or loosened. If the person has an inhaler, it should be utilized. The person should be taken to a hospital for treatment, as an asthma attack may actually worsen despite symptoms seemingly disappearing, such as wheezing.

Hyperventilation

Hyperventilation is a psychological disorder that causes a person to breathe extremely rapidly or deeply. This creates a surplus of carbon dioxide in the body, as the person is not effectively exhaling. Because it is a psychological disorder, a common symptom of panic attacks, helping the person calm down is the primary treatment. Using a calm, reassuring tone can help a person regain proper breathing. The person should try holding their breath, as this may help reset the breathing pattern. If hyperventilation persists, EMS should be notified.

Concussion

A concussion occurs when there is a blow to the head that causes an injury to the brain. While a concussion is not always obvious, if a person suffers a head injury, assuming a concussion has occurred is recommended. The person should keep the head and neck immobilized, and simple questions should be asked to determine cognitive function. These questions can include asking the person their name, their age, and their location.

If the person is unconscious, CAB should be checked. If the person is not breathing, the throat should be checked for an obstruction. If there is an obstruction, it should try to be removed using a gentle finger swipe. If there is no obstruction, CPR should be performed and EMS should be notified.

Heat Injuries

There are three main types of heat injuries, that don't involve burns: heat exhaustion, heat cramps, and heat stroke. **Heat exhaustion** is caused by a person having a **high body temperature** with **excessive sweating**. Sweating is a product of homeostasis, which is trying to cool the body. If the person continues to sweat, it means the body isn't properly cooling down. This can lead to **heat cramps**, which cause tightening and involuntary **spasms** of the **muscles** due to dehydration and loss of electrolytes, such as sodium and potassium. **Heat stroke** is when a person has an **extremely high body temperature**, with a **lack of sweating**. This occurs when a person is severely dehydrated, and has no more fluid to use as sweat to try cooling the body down. This can be potentially fatal.

Cold Injuries

There are two main types of cold injuries: **hypothermia** and **frostbite**. Hypothermia is caused by the body temperature dropping below 90 degrees. This can be potentially fatal. Frostbite is caused by a formation of ice crystals in soft tissues, typically the fingers, toes, and parts of the face such as the nose and ears. If the tissues are frozen for too long, they experience necrosis.

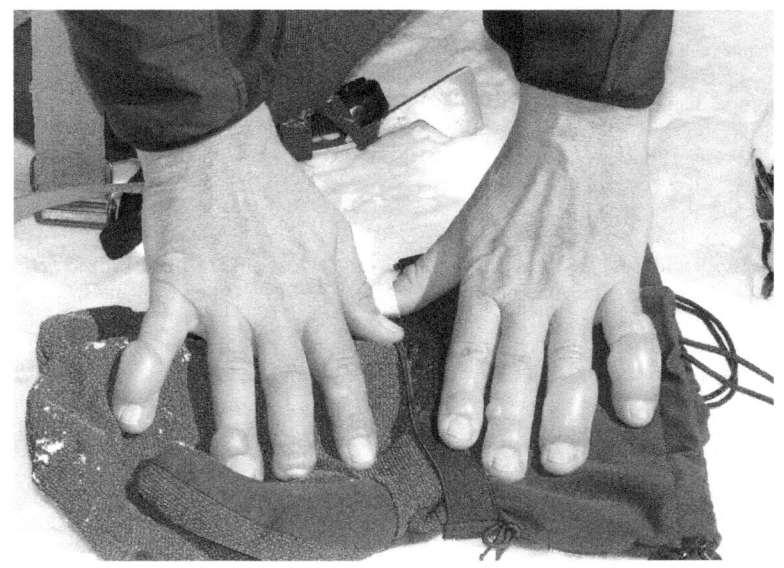

Blistering caused by frostbite

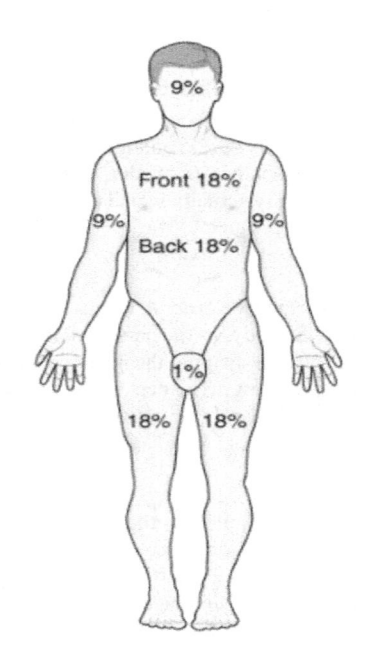

The Rule of 9's

The **Rule of 9's** is used to determine the extent of **burns** by the total body area involved. Each percentage represents the percentage of the body damaged by burns:

- Head and Neck: 9%
- Right Arm : 9%
- Left Arm: 9%
- Right Leg: 18%
- Left Leg: 18%
- Thorax: 18%
- Abdomen: 9%
- Lower Back: 9%
- Groin: 1%

Orthopedic Injuries

Strains, sprains, and dislocations are all forms of **orthopedic injuries**. Strains and sprains are primarily treated with the use of **PRICE: Protect, Rest, Ice, Compression, Elevation**. The damaged area should be protected from further injury, rested to allow proper healing, iced to reduce inflammation, compressed to help further reduce inflammation, and elevated to assist in proper circulation and reduce inflammation. If a bone is dislocated, it should be relocated if possible. If not, the area should be stabilized and protected. If a fracture has taken place in conjunction with the dislocation, the fracture should be treated as normal, and the person should be taken to a hospital for treatment.

Poisoning

Poisoning may occur in several different ways. Poisoning via **inhalation**, such as carbon monoxide poisoning, may require the person be given an **antidote**, or require breathing support by way of an **oxygen mask**. **Injection** poisoning introduces harmful substances into the body via **needles**, **insect stings**, **sharp objects**, or **bites**. The poison usually requires the use of an **antidote** to treat. **Absorption** of poison typically includes exposure to substances such as **pesticides**. The area affected should be cleansed thoroughly with water.

Ingestion is introducing harmful substances through **swallowing**. Depending on the substance ingested, the person may be required to induce **vomiting**, or need to drink milk or water.

Bites and Stings

If an animal bite occurs that results in a puncture, bleeding should be forced from the wound to try clearing out as much bacteria as possible. The area should be cleansed with soap and water, and a sterile dressing should be applied to control bleeding and allow for proper healing.

Insect stings, such as from bees, should be scraped with a sharp flat surface to remove any stinger left behind that may be in the skin. The area should be cleansed with soap and water. If asphyxiation is suspected, EMS should be contacted immediately.

Snake bites should be cleansed with soap and water. The area of the bite should be immobilized below the heart to decrease the ease of blood flow to the heart from the area that contains venom. EMS should be notified.

Spider bites should be cleansed with soap and water. The area of the bite should be immobilized below the heart. The patient should be advised to seek medical attention.

Scorpion stings should be cleansed with soap and water. The area of the sting should be immobilized below the heart. The patient should be advised to seek medical attention.

Pathology Matching

_____: Hyper-curvature of the thoracic vertebrae caused by tight pectoralis minor and serratus anterior

_____: Protrusion of the nucleus pulposus through the annulus fibrosus

_____: Inflammation of the liver

_____: Erosion of the articular cartilage, causing inflammation in a joint

_____: Swelling of veins due to malfunctioning valves

_____: Injury to a ligament caused by over-stretching

_____: Lack of cortisol production caused by damage to the adrenal cortex

_____: Epidermal growth caused by the human papilloma virus

_____: Fungal infection of the skin causing a circular rash

_____: Autoimmune disorder causing dry, scaly patches to form on the skin

_____: Swelling of a limb due to excessive interstitial fluid in an area

_____: Degeneration of alveoli, reducing gas exchange

_____: Constriction of blood vessels in the hands and feet, reducing blood flow

_____: Bacterial infection causing inflammation of the bladder

_____: Paralysis of one side of the face due to damage to the facial nerve

_____: Necrosis of heart tissue

_____: Compression of the brachial plexus and blood vessels caused by tight scalenes and pectoralis minor

_____: Bacterial infection of a hair follicle, also known as a furuncle

_____: Form of tendonitis causing inflammation at the lateral epicondyle of the humerus

_____: Highly contagious viral infection of the respiratory tract

A: Varicose Veins
B: Emphysema
C: Thoracic Outlet Syndrome
D: Kyphosis
E: Psoriasis
F: Boil
G: Hepatitis
H: Myocardial Infarction
I: Raynaud's Disease
J: Wart

K: Tennis Elbow
L: Bell's Palsy
M: Cystitis
N: Sprain
O: Osteoarthritis
P: Herniated Disc
Q: Influenza
R: Lymphedema
S: Ringworm
T: Addison's Disease

Answer Key on Page 312

Pathology

Across
6. Destruction of lung alveoli
7. Hyper-curvature of the thoracic vertebrae
8. Tendonitis affecting the lateral epicondyle of the humerus
14. Autoimmune disorder that attacks epithelial cells in the skin
16. Autoimmune disorder that attacks myelin sheaths in the CNS
17. Injury to a ligament
18. Injury to a muscle or tendon
19. Increased amounts of interstitial fluid in a limb

Down
1. Inflammation of the liver most commonly due to a viral infection
2. Inflammation of bronchial tubes
3. Least serious, most common, slowest growing form of skin cancer
4. Constriction of blood vessels in the hands
5. Bladder infection
9. Inflammation of the brain
10. Blood pressure reading of 140/90 or higher
11. Paralysis of one side of the face
12. Lateral curvature of the vertebrae
13. Hyper-curvature of the lumbar vertebrae
14. Inflammation of a vein
15. Bulging of an artery wall due to weakness in the wall

Answer Key on Page 313

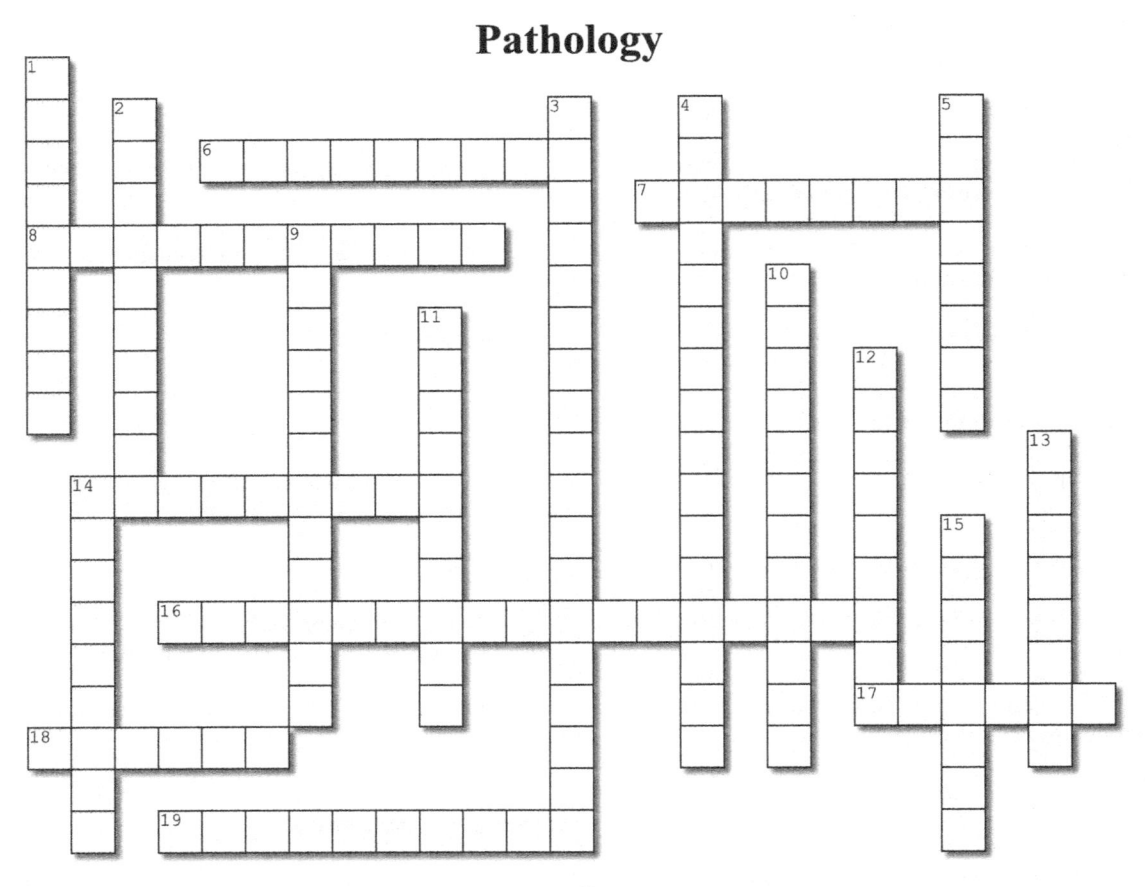

Pathology Practice Exam

1. Most common form of arthritis
A. Rheumatoid arthritis
B. Gouty arthritis
C. Osteoarthritis
D. Periostitis

2. Loss of density in bone, caused by a decrease in the hormone estrogen in the body
A. Osteomyelitis
B. Menopause
C. Osteoporosis
D. Scoliosis

3. Cellulitis
A. Bacterial infection producing yellow scabs around the nose
B. Viral infection resulting in yellow scabs around the mouth
C. Bacterial infection involving the skin and surrounding tissues
D. Viral infection causing cold sores to appear around the mouth

4. Aneurysm
A. Bulge in an artery wall, usually caused by a weakened artery due to a condition such as hypertension
B. Inflammation of a vein due to trauma, resulting in blood clot formation
C. Blood clot in the blood stream becoming lodged in the heart, lungs, or brain, resulting in death of tissue
D. Ischemia in the myocardium due to a blockage in the coronary arteries, resulting in myocardial infarction

5. Pain felt at the medial epicondyle of the humerus is associated with
A. Tennis elbow
B. Golfer's elbow
C. Carpal tunnel syndrome
D. Synovitis

6. Bradycardia is a form of
A. Aneurysm
B. Heart murmur
C. Infarction
D. Arrhythmia

7. Bacterial infection resulting in honeycomb sores around the mouth and nose
A. Boil
B. Impetigo
C. Psoriasis
D. Meningitis

8. Lordosis is also known as
A. Swayback
B. Dowager's hump
C. Scoliosis
D. Bamboo spine

9. Decrease in oxygen traveling throughout the body
A. Hypoplasia
B. Hypoglycemia
C. Hypoxia
D. Hyperplasia

10. Achilles tendonitis can be caused by a strain to the
A. Pes anserinus
B. Patellar tendon
C. Calcaneal tendon
D. Ischial tuberosity tendon

11. While at work, Chris falls and lands on his back, injuring it. The next day, he calls to make a massage appointment, hoping the massage will help with his pain. The appropriate response would be
A. Reschedule the massage and refer the client to a physician
B. Perform the massage and do compression onto the back
C. Perform the massage and apply heat to the affected area
D. Perform the massage and do passive joint mobilization on the vertebrae

12. The most common site of sprain
A. Shoulder
B. Knee
C. Elbow
D. Ankle

13. Nausea, vomiting, and fatigue with yellowing of the skin may be the result of
A. Hepatitis
B. Food poisoning
C. Diarrhea
D. Meningitis

14. Spasm of capillaries in the fingers and toes, restricting circulation
A. Cyanosis
B. Raynaud's syndrome
C. Emphysema
D. Diabetes mellitus

15. Signs of inflammation include
A. Heat, pain, redness, coldness
B. Pain, edema, swelling, redness
C. Swelling, heat, redness, pain
D. Redness, pain, heat, dehydration

16. Squamous cell carcinoma is what type of tumor
A. Benign
B. Malignant
C. Idiopathic
D. Lymphatic

17. A client who suffers from pitting edema would be referred to which doctor
A. Dermatologist
B. Nephrologist
C. Cardiologist
D. Gastroenterologist

18. Ischemia may ultimately result in
A. Phlebitis
B. Arteriosclerosis
C. Necrosis
D. Varicose veins

19. Anticoagulants are medications that prevent
A. Blood vessel dilation
B. Inflammation
C. Mucous production
D. Blood clotting

20. All of the following are contagious conditions except
A. Mononucleosis
B. Herpes Simplex
C. Psoriasis
D. Osteomyelitis

21. Encephalitis
A. Inflammation of the brain caused by a viral infection
B. Aneurysm in the cerebrum causing brain damage
C. Blockage of a coronary artery, resulting in necrosis of myocardium
D. Inflammation of the meninges, leading to migraine headaches

22. Inflammation of a bursa sac, usually present due to trauma
A. Synovitis
B. Bursitis
C. Osteoarthritis
D. Bruxism

23. Medication prescribed to fight off bacterial infections
A. Anti-inflammatory
B. Antivenoms
C. Antipyretics
D. Antibiotics

24. Pacemakers are commonly implanted in patients who suffer from
A. Arrhythmia
B. Emphysema
C. Angina pectoris
D. Heart murmur

25. Virus resulting in the development of warts
A. Herpes simplex
B. Human papilloma virus
C. Epstein-Barr virus
D. Urticaria

26. Excessive death of myocardium results in
A. Arrhythmia
B. Stroke
C. Myocardial infarction
D. Heart murmur

27. Grade 3 sprain
A. Complete rupture of a ligament
B. Partial tearing of a tendon
C. Complete rupture of a tendon
D. Partial tearing of a ligament

28. A lack of hemoglobin in erythrocytes may result in
A. Decreased immune response
B. Raynaud's syndrome
C. Myocardial infarction
D. Anemia

29. Due to having a shorter urethra, women are more prone to developing the following condition than men
A. Prostatitis
B. Nephritis
C. Cystitis
D. Cholecystitis

30. In a client with lordosis, the following muscle might be weakened, resulting in an exaggerated anterior tilt of the pelvis
A. Psoas major
B. Latissimus dorsi
C. Quadratus lumborum
D. Rectus abdominis

31. Viral or bacterial infection resulting in severe increases of fluids in the lungs
A. Pneumonia
B. Asthma
C. Bronchitis
D. Emphysema

32. Dopamine is a neurotransmitter which helps to stabilize the body in specific movements. A lack of dopamine in the body would result in
A. Anemia
B. Alzheimer's disease
C. Parkinson's disease
D. Sleep apnea

33. A cardiologist is a doctor who specializes in the
A. Lungs
B. Heart
C. Liver
D. Bladder

34. A blood pressure reading of 140/90 results in a person being diagnosed with
A. Hypertension
B. Hypotension
C. Hyperemia
D. Myocardial infarction

35. The most common type of diabetes
A. Insulin-dependent diabetes
B. Diabetes type I
C. Juvenile diabetes
D. Diabetes type II

36. Emphysema
A. Spasm of smooth muscle surrounding bronchial tubes, reducing inhalation
B. Inflammation of bronchial tubes due to inhalation of smoke from cigarette smoking
C. Destruction of alveoli, resulting in decreased oxygen intake
D. Bacterial infection of the lungs, reducing carbon dioxide output

37. Paralysis of one half of the face, caused by stimulation of the Herpes Simplex virus, which affects the Facial nerve
A. Graves' disease
B. Cerebral palsy
C. Trigeminal neuralgia
D. Bell's palsy

38. Chronic inflammation located at the tibial tuberosity, caused by overuse of the quadriceps
A. Osgood-Schlatter disease
B. Graves' disease
C. Raynaud's disease
D. Knock-knee

39. Viral infection resulting in inflammation of the liver
A. Nephritis
B. Hepatitis
C. Mononucleosis
D. Encephalitis

40. Varicose veins most often occur in
A. Legs
B. Arms
C. Thighs
D. Ankles

41. Portion of an intervertebral disc that protrudes through the annulus fibrosis during a disc herniation
A. Spinal cord
B. Annulus pulposus
C. Facet cartilage
D. Nucleus pulposus

42. Autoimmune disorder affecting myelin sheaths in the central nervous system
A. Multiple sclerosis
B. Myasthenia gravis
C. Parkinson's disease
D. Alzheimer's disease

43. Paralysis of the lower limbs
A. Quadriplegia
B. Hemiplegia
C. Paraplegia
D. Triplegia

44. Fungal infection affecting the epidermis, resulting in a circular rash
A. Cordyceps
B. Athlete's foot
C. Ringworm
D. Whitlow

45. A common treatment for bursitis
A. Lymphatic drainage
B. Heat and compression
C. Rest and ice
D. Cold compress and friction

46. Chris has recently been diagnosed with pneumonia. What type of medication would be prescribed in this case
A. General anesthetics
B. Antivirals
C. Antibiotics
D. Antipyretics

47. Analgesics are used to combat
A. Pain
B. Obesity
C. Inflammation
D. Gout

48. Benign tumors
A. Spread to other parts of the body through lymph
B. Do not spread to other locations in the body
C. Spread to other parts of the body through blood
D. Spread to other parts of the body through interstitial fluid

49. Overproduction in melanocytes results in a tumor known as
A. Sarcoma
B. Carcinoma
C. Melanoma
D. Lymphoma

50. Lice, scabies, and ticks are all types of
A. Parasites
B. Bacterium
C. Fungi
D. Viruses

Answer Key on Page 314

Today I will do what others won't, so tomorrow I can accomplish what others can't.

- Jerry Rice

Kinesiology

Muscle Actions

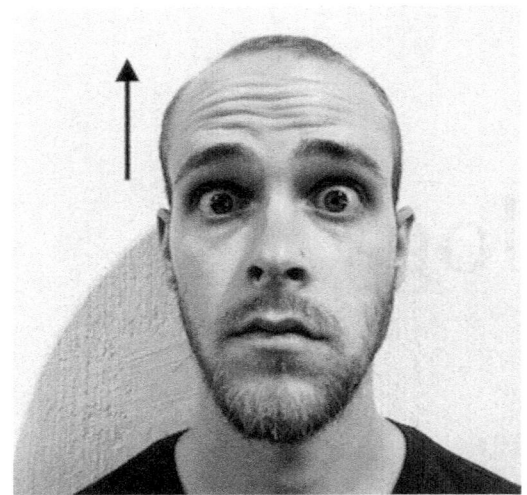

Eyebrow Elevation

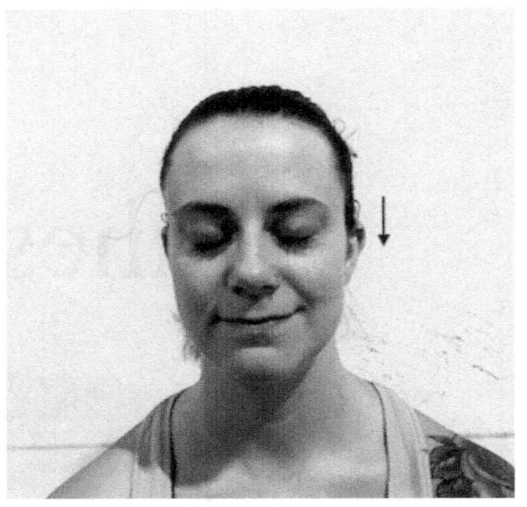

Eyelid Depression

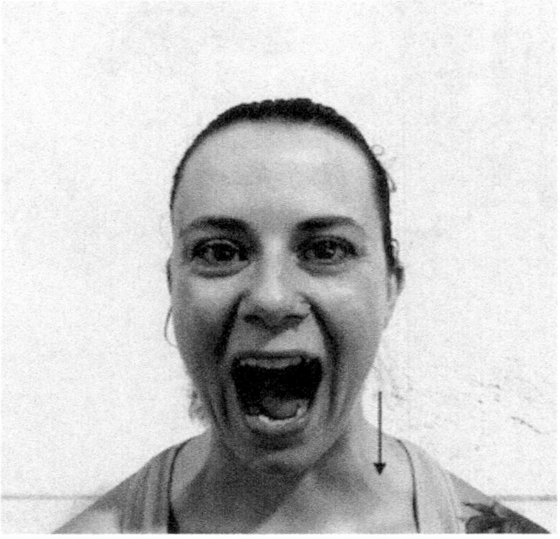

Jaw Depression

Jaw Elevation

Smiling

Lips Puckering

Kinesiology

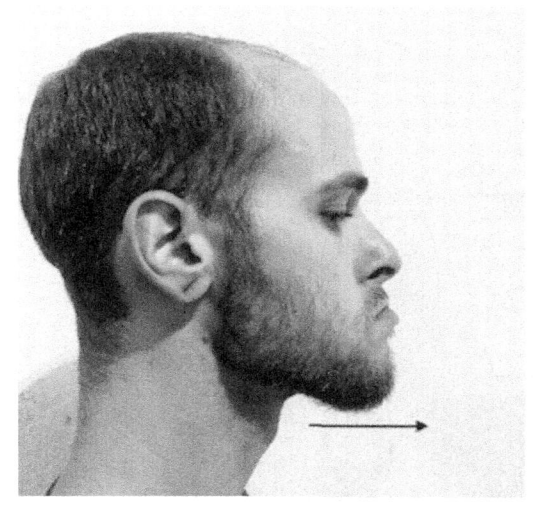

Jaw Protraction

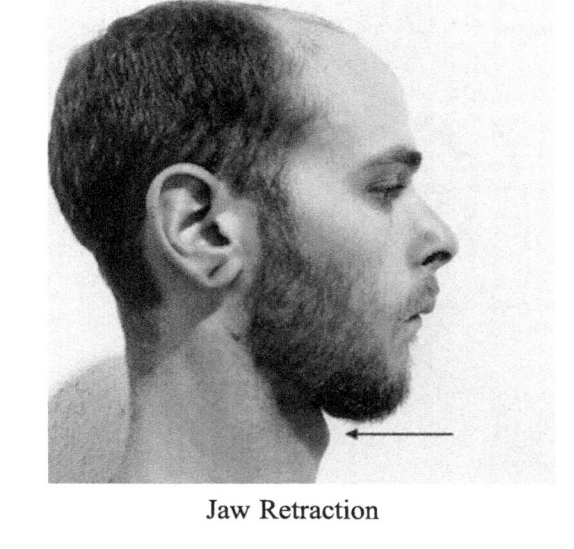

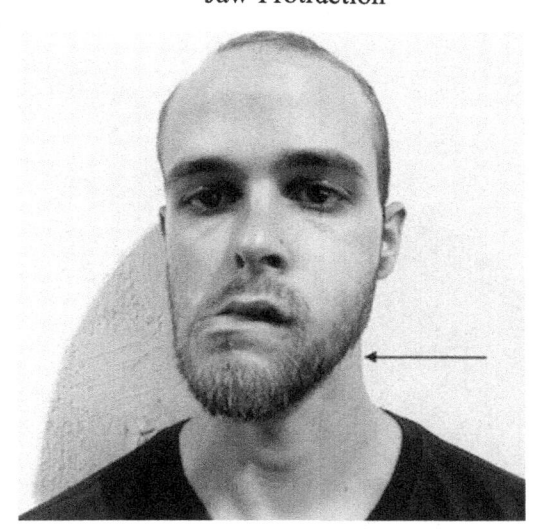

Jaw Retraction

Jaw Lateral Deviation

Neck Rotation

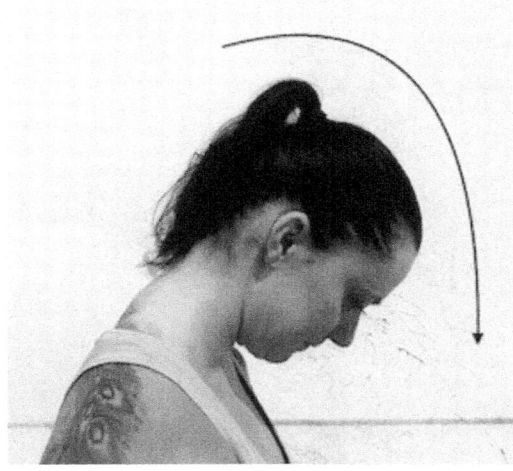

Neck Flexion

Neck Extension

208 Kinesiology

Neck Lateral Flexion

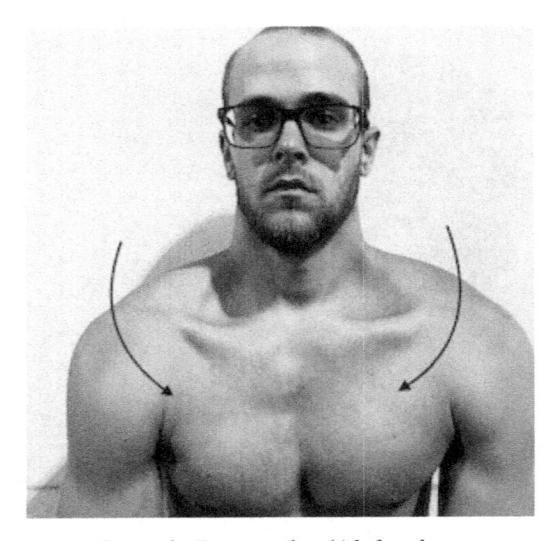

Scapula Protraction/Abduction

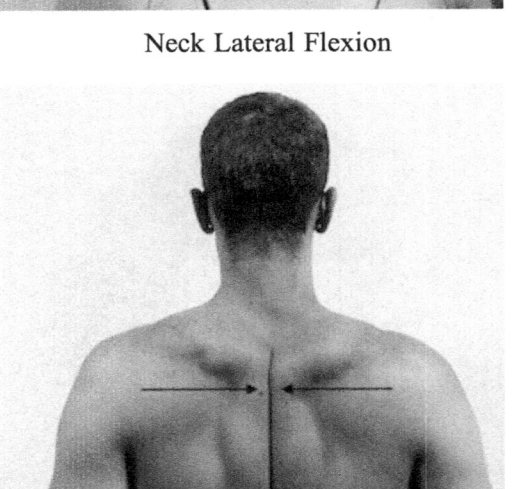

Scapula Retraction/Adduction

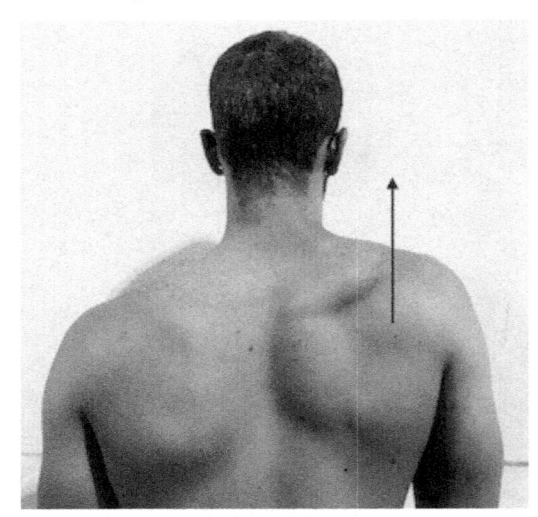

Scapula Elevation

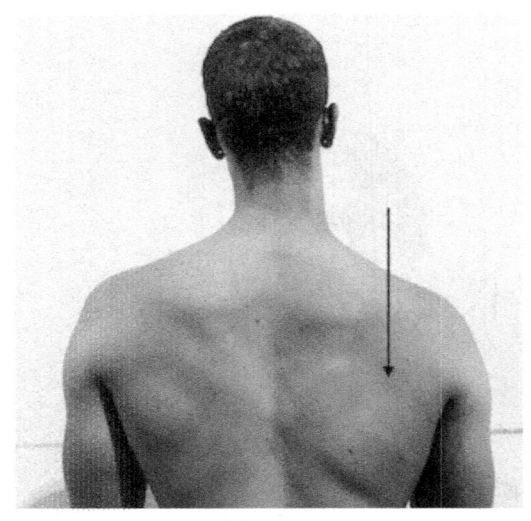

Scapula Depression

Shoulder Flexion

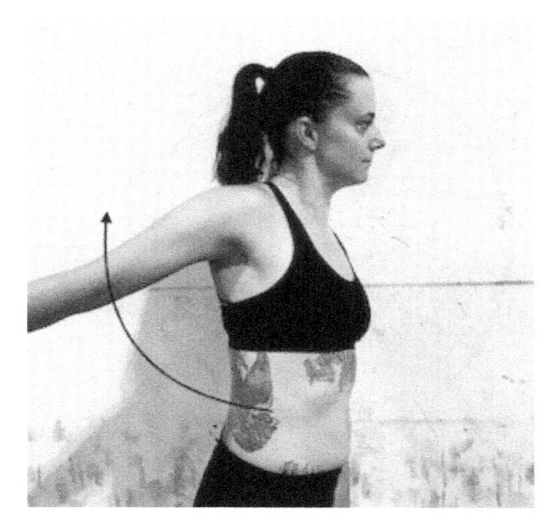

Kinesiology 209

Shoulder Extension

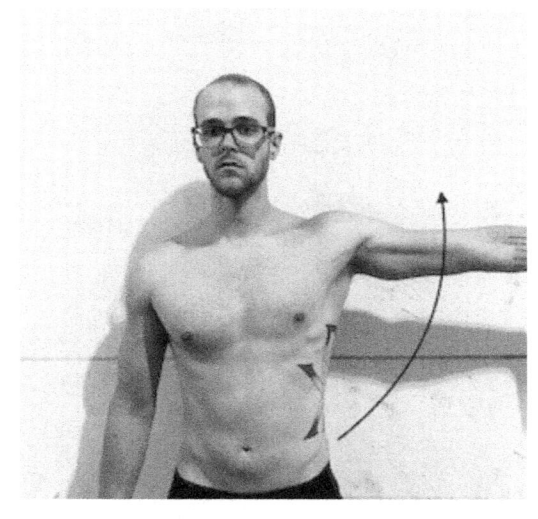

Shoulder Abduction

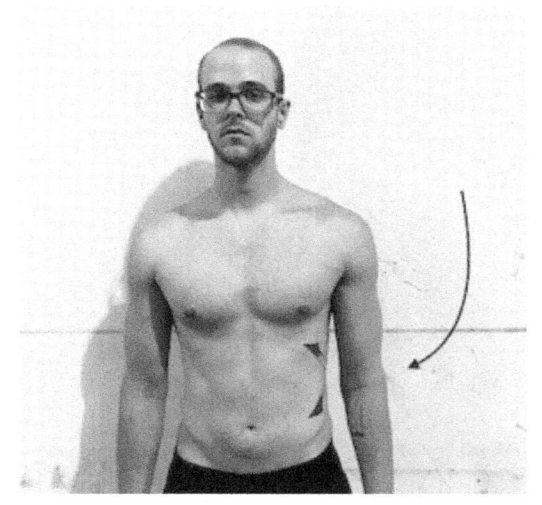

Shoulder Adduction

Shoulder Medial Rotation

Shoulder Lateral Rotation

Shoulder Horizontal Adduction

Shoulder Horizontal Abduction

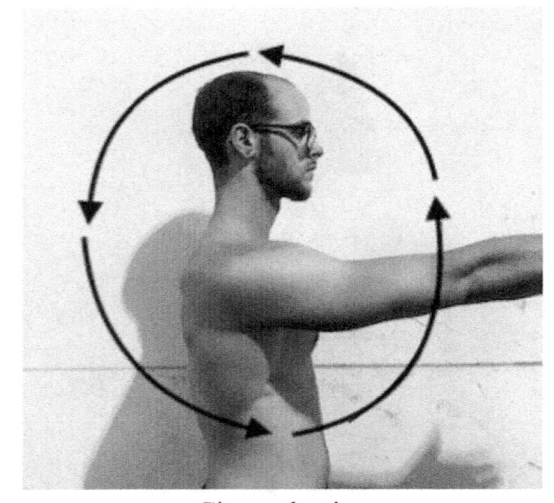

Circumduction

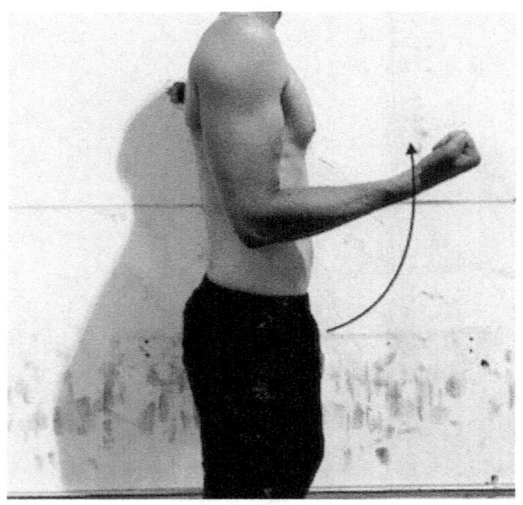

Elbow Flexion

Elbow Extension

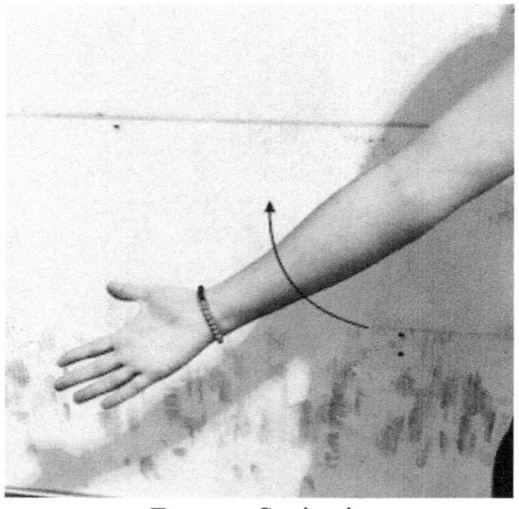

Forearm Supination

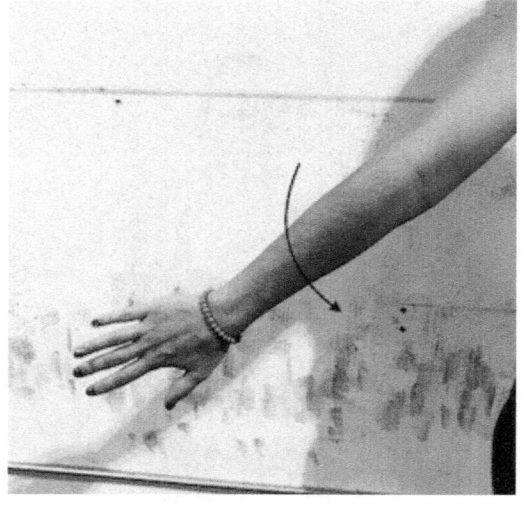

Forearm Pronation

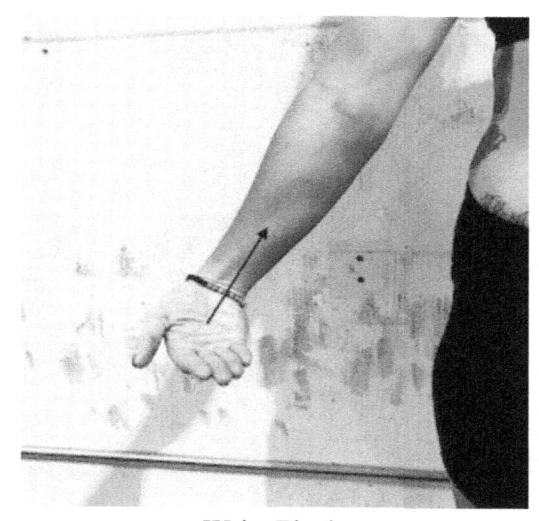

Kinesiology 211

Wrist Flexion

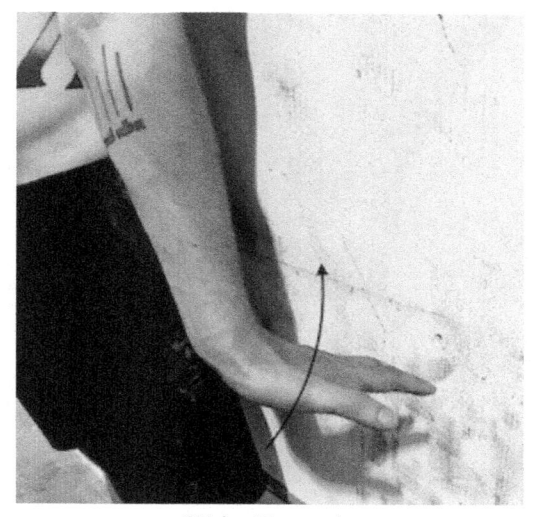

Wrist Extension

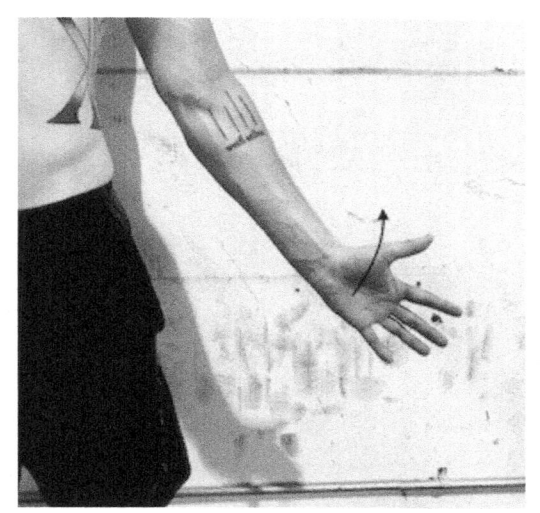

Wrist Abduction

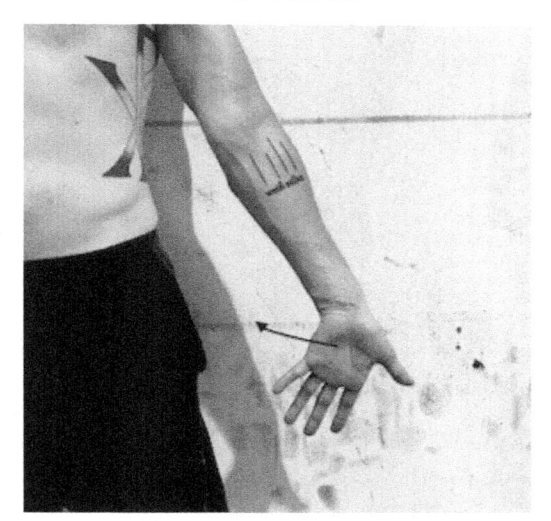

Wrist Adduction

Digit Flexion

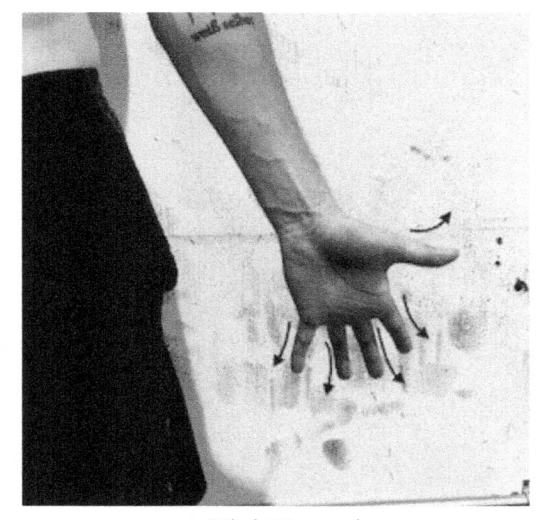

Digit Extension

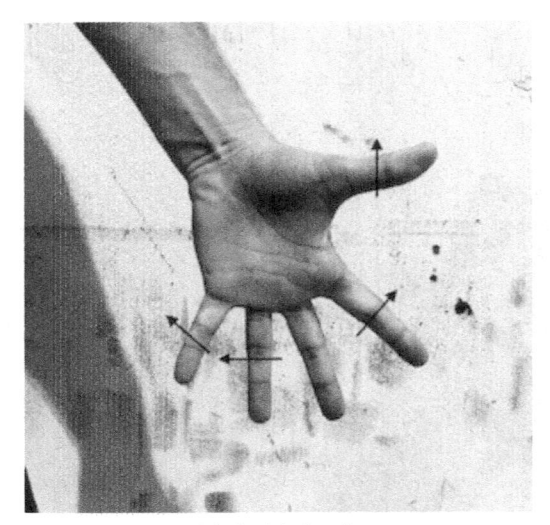

212 Kinesiology

Digit Abduction

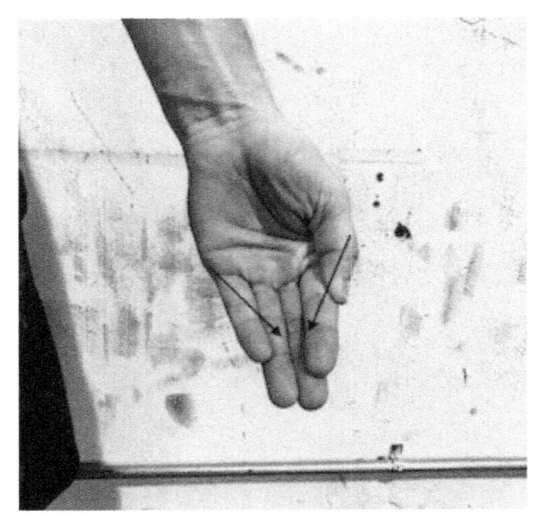

Digit Adduction

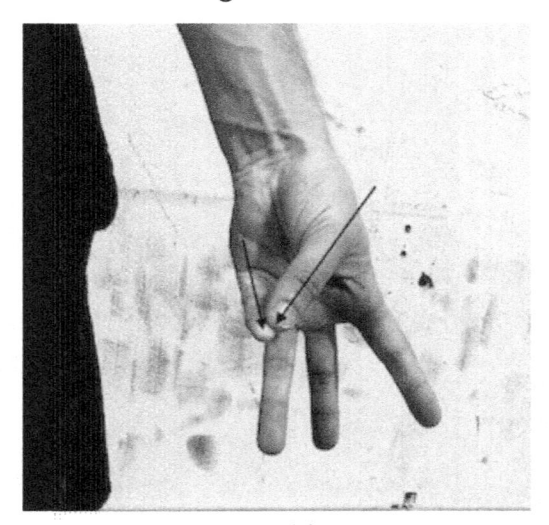

Opposition

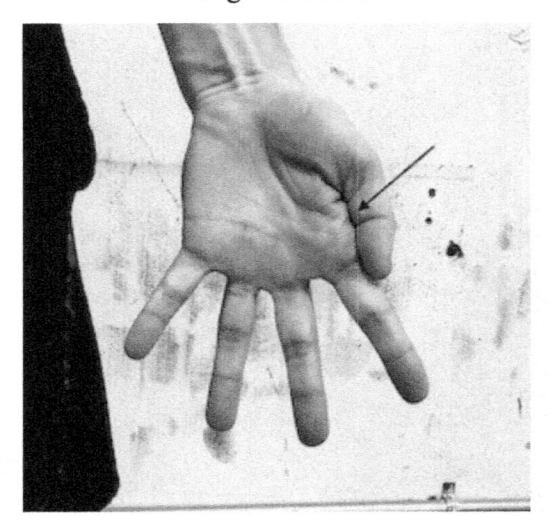

Thumb Adduction

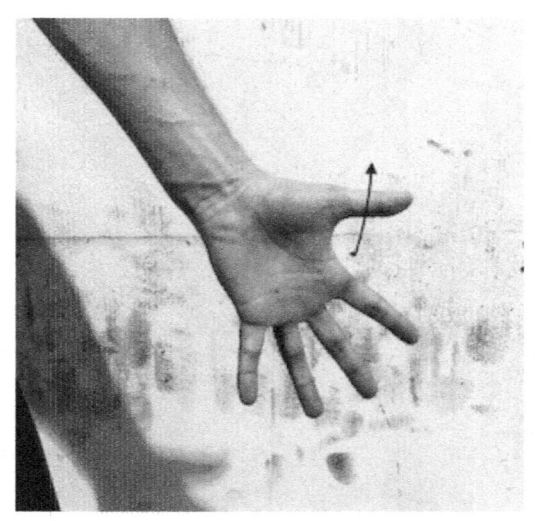

Thumb Abduction

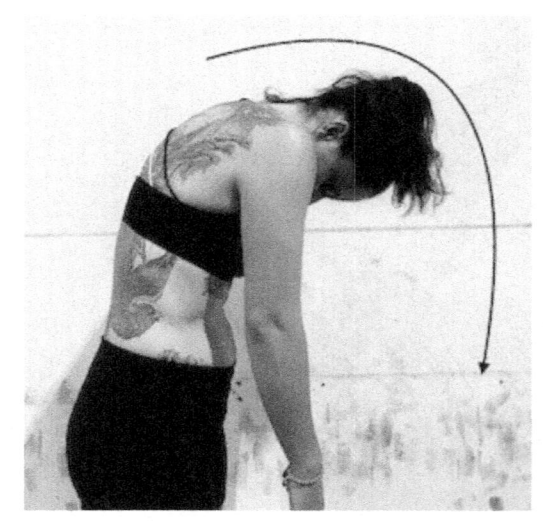

Trunk Flexion

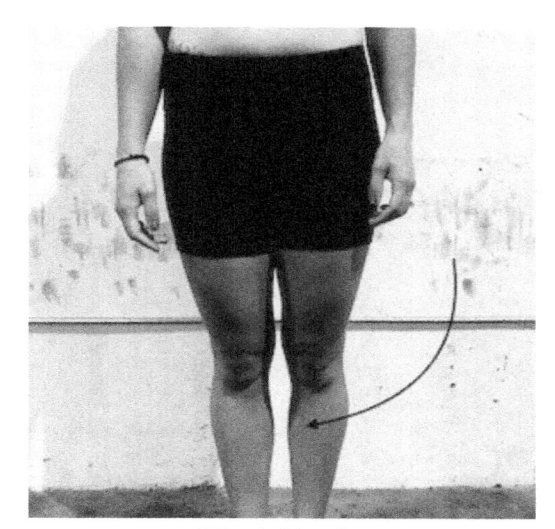

Kinesiology 213

Hip Adduction

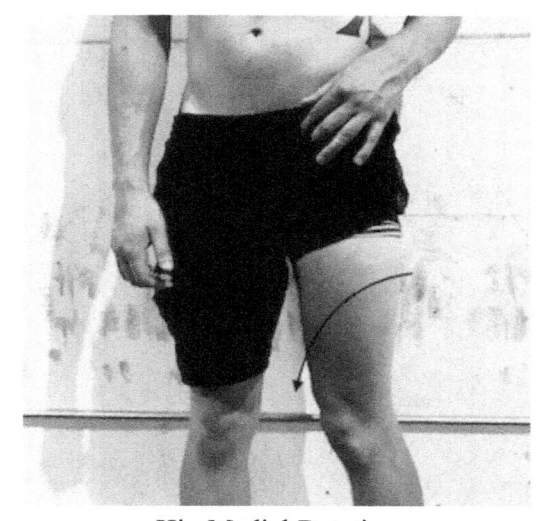

Hip Medial Rotation

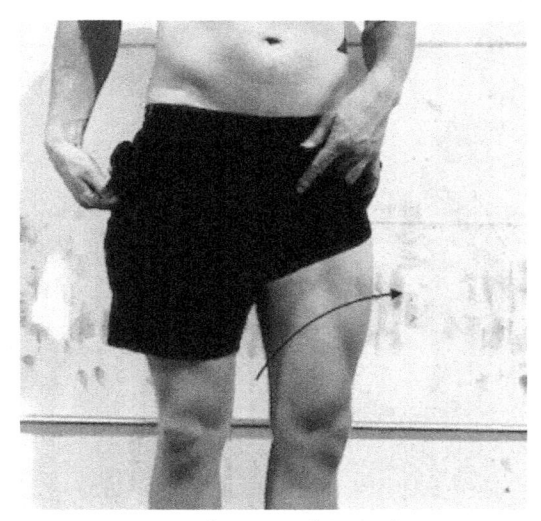

Hip Lateral Rotation

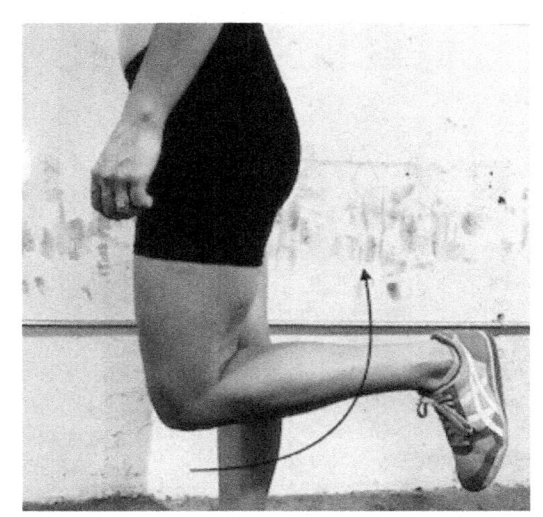

Knee Flexion

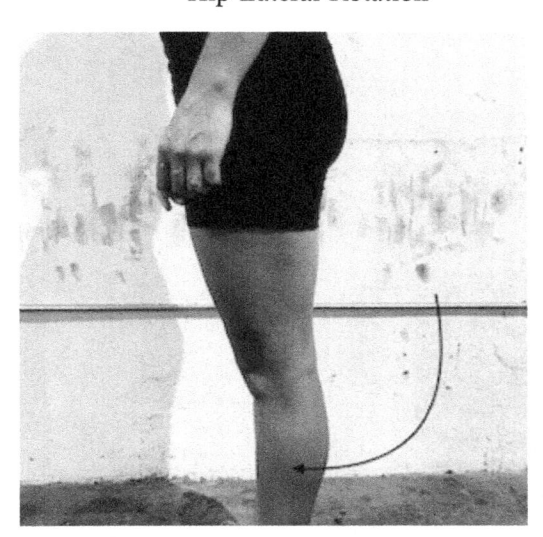

Knee Extension

Dorsiflexion

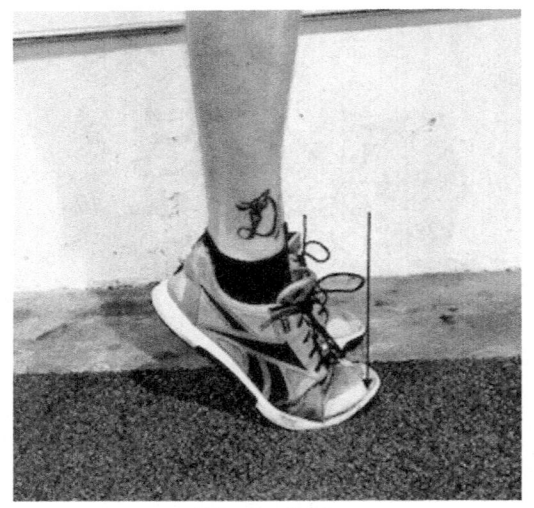

214　Kinesiology

Plantarflexion

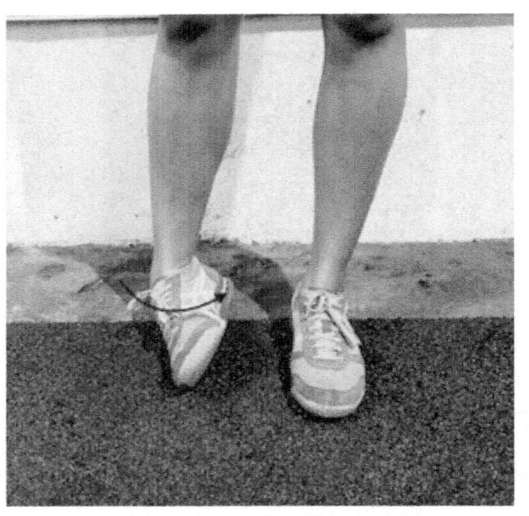

Foot Inversion/Supination

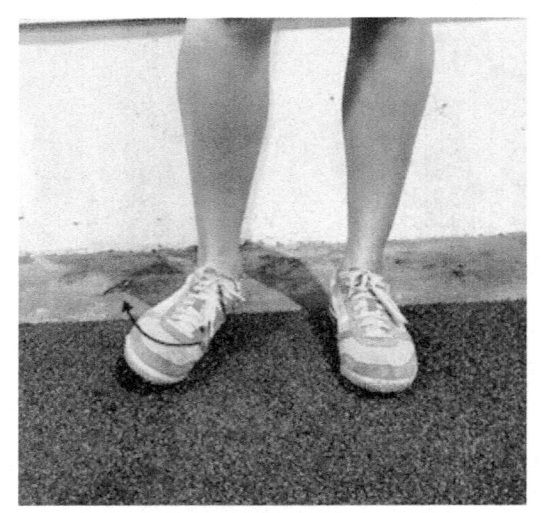

Foot Eversion/Pronation

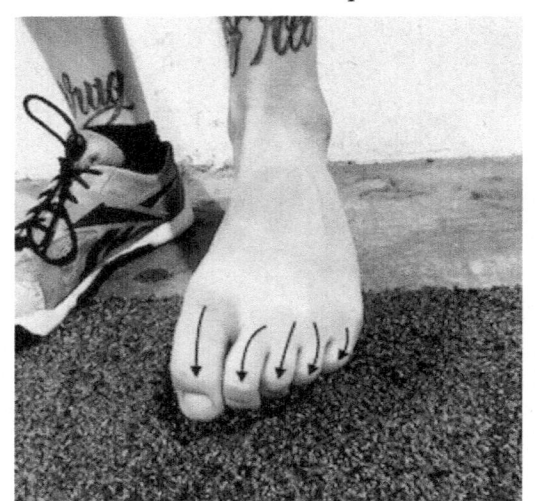

Digit Flexion

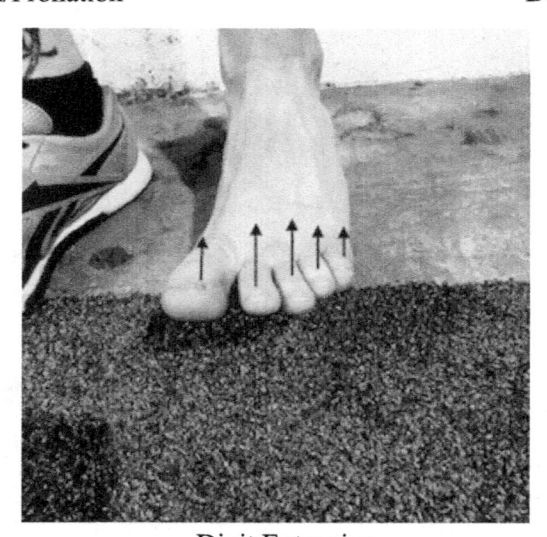

Digit Extension

Bony Landmarks

Bony landmarks are specific locations on bones where muscles attach. There are many different kinds of landmarks, from tubercles and tuberosities, to condyles and epicondyles.

A condyle is a rounded projection coming off a bone at an articulation.
An epicondyle is the part of the bone located superior to the condyle.
A crest is a thin ridge of a bone.
A facet is a smooth articular surface of a bone.
A fissure is a narrow opening, resembling a crack.
A foramina(foramen) is a hole or opening in a bone.
A fossa is a shallow depression in a bone.
A linea is a narrow ridge, less pronounced than a crest.
A meatus is a canal-like passage.
A process is a prominent structure on a bone.
A ramus is an elongated, seemingly stretched-out part of a bone.
A sinus is a cavity created by bones.
A suture is a type of synarthrotic joint that doesn't allow movement.
A trochanter is a very large process, only found on the femur.
A tubercle is a small, rounded projection.
A tuberosity is a large, rounded, often rough projection.

Bones have numerous different types of landmarks. Landmarks are not only named after their type (above), but often times what they look like(example, "coracoid" means "resembling a crow's beak"), what muscles attach to them(example, deltoid tuberosity), or even where they're located in the body(example, anterior superior iliac spine).

Head

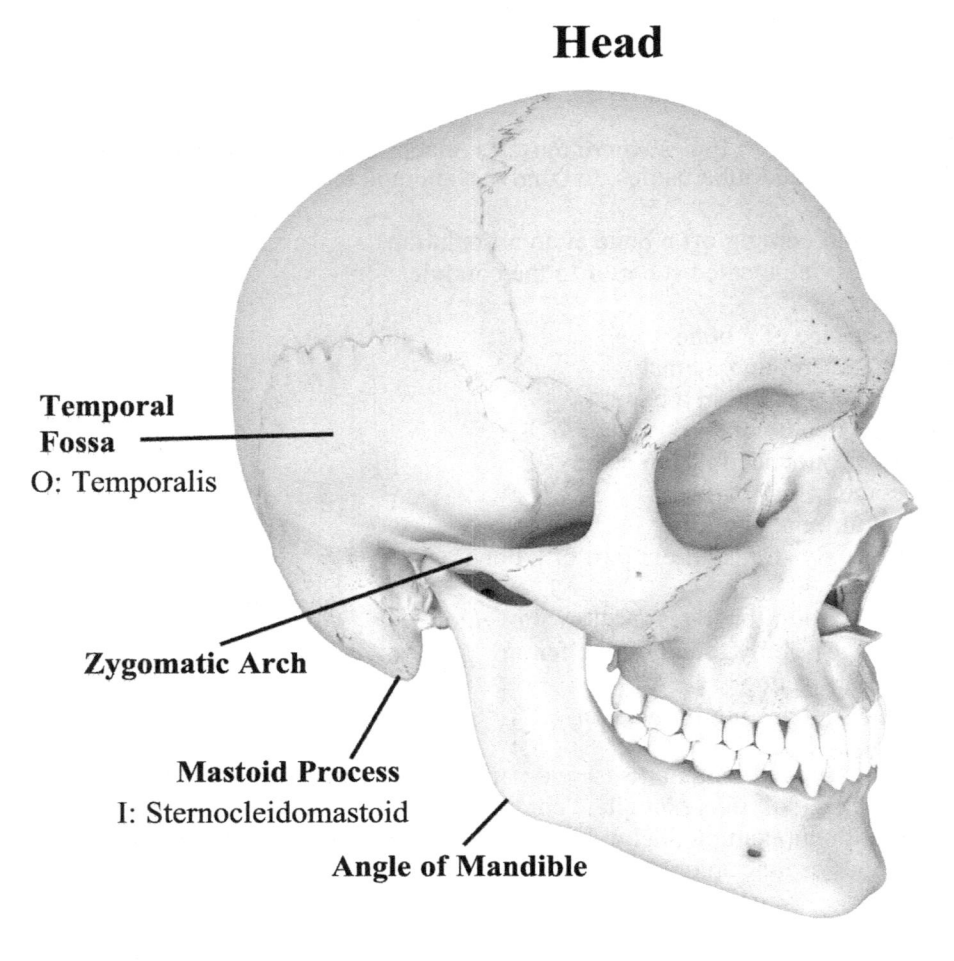

Temporal Fossa
O: Temporalis

Zygomatic Arch

Mastoid Process
I: Sternocleidomastoid

Angle of Mandible

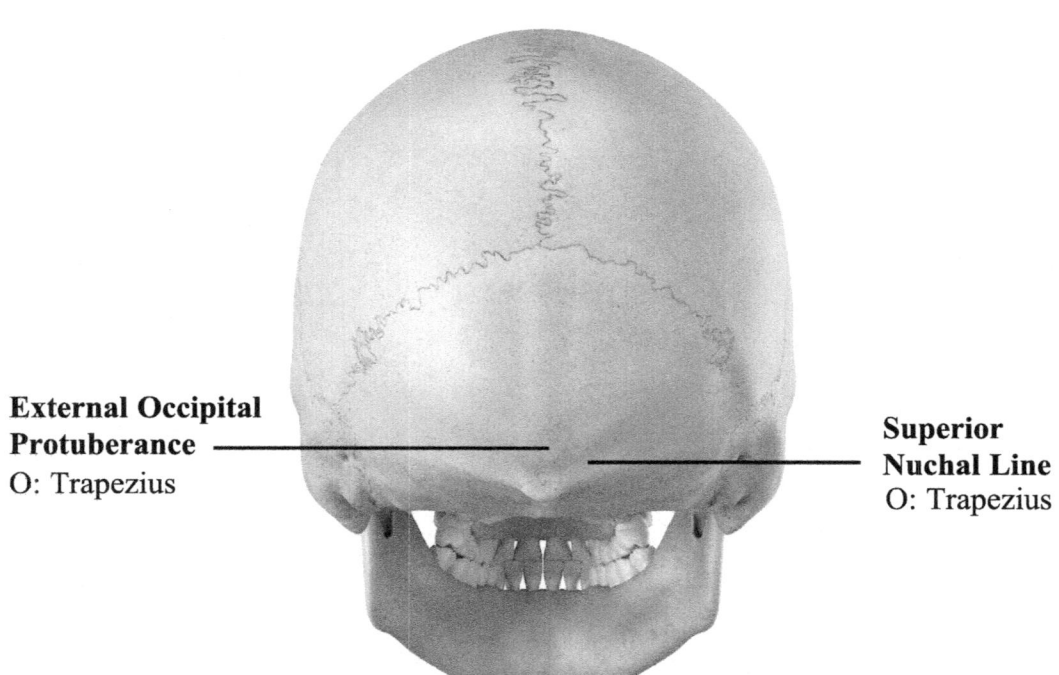

External Occipital Protuberance
O: Trapezius

Superior Nuchal Line
O: Trapezius

Vertebrae

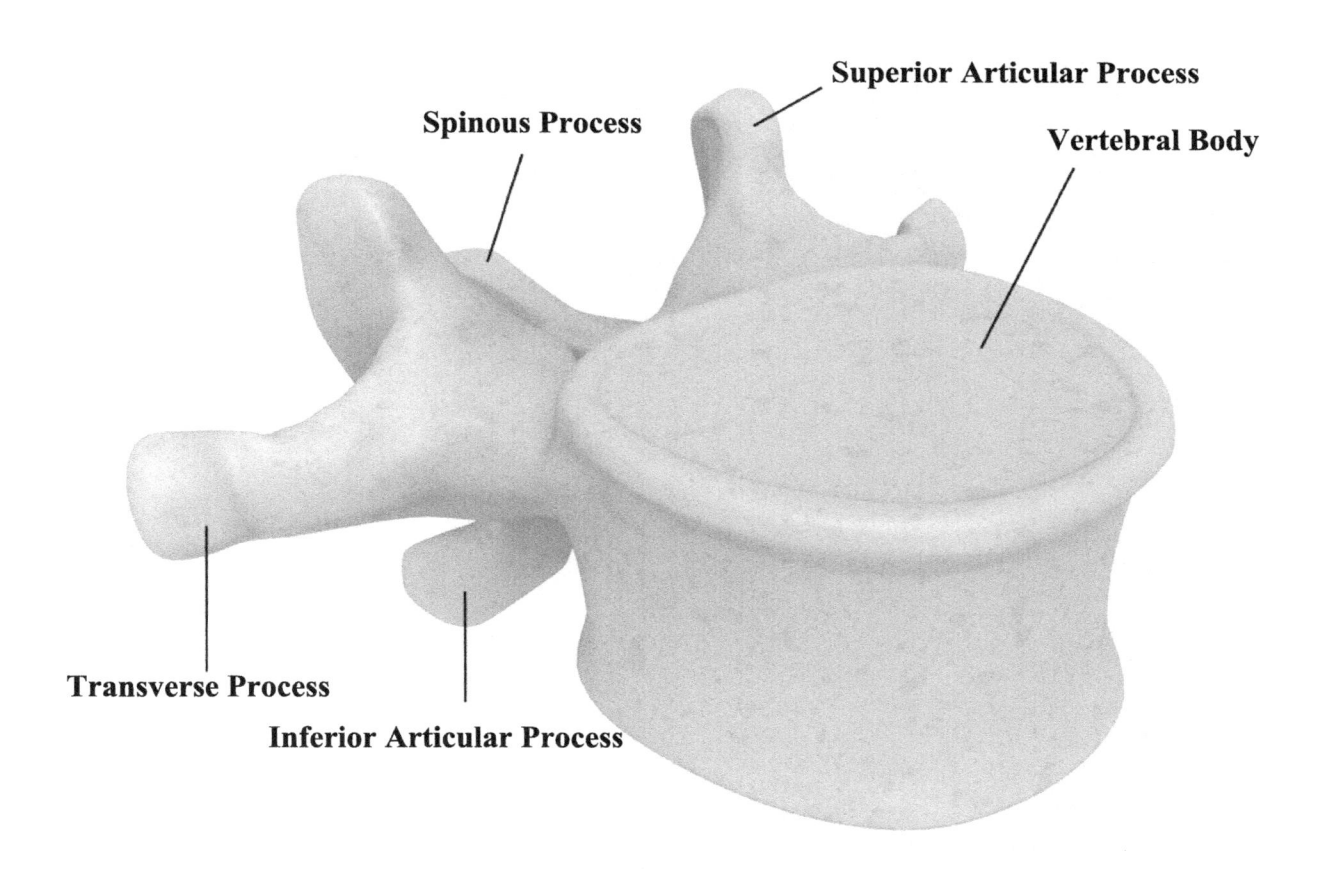

- Spinous Process
- Superior Articular Process
- Vertebral Body
- Transverse Process
- Inferior Articular Process

Back
Anterior Scapula

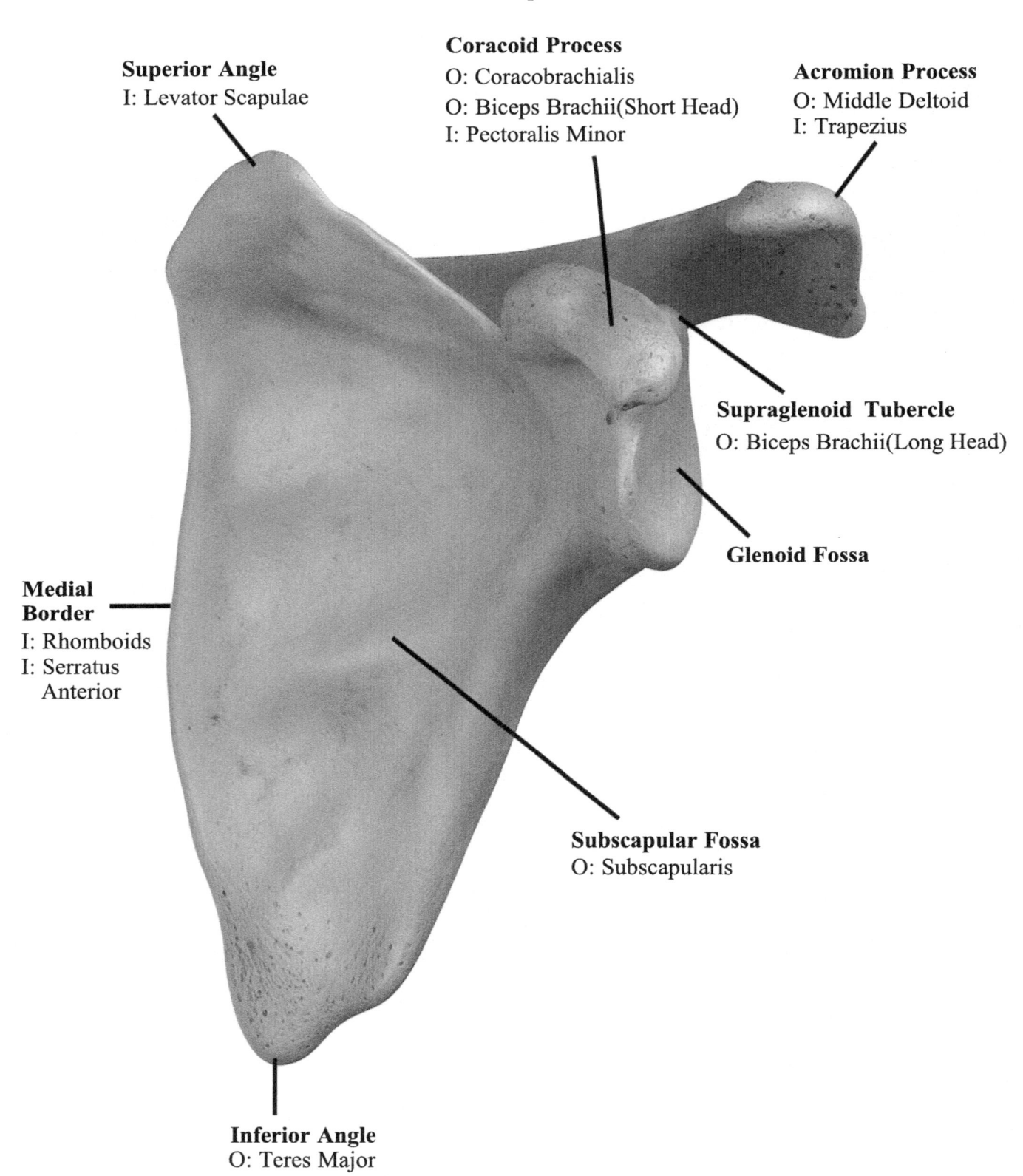

Superior Angle
I: Levator Scapulae

Coracoid Process
O: Coracobrachialis
O: Biceps Brachii(Short Head)
I: Pectoralis Minor

Acromion Process
O: Middle Deltoid
I: Trapezius

Supraglenoid Tubercle
O: Biceps Brachii(Long Head)

Glenoid Fossa

Medial Border
I: Rhomboids
I: Serratus Anterior

Subscapular Fossa
O: Subscapularis

Inferior Angle
O: Teres Major

Kinesiology 219

Posterior Scapula

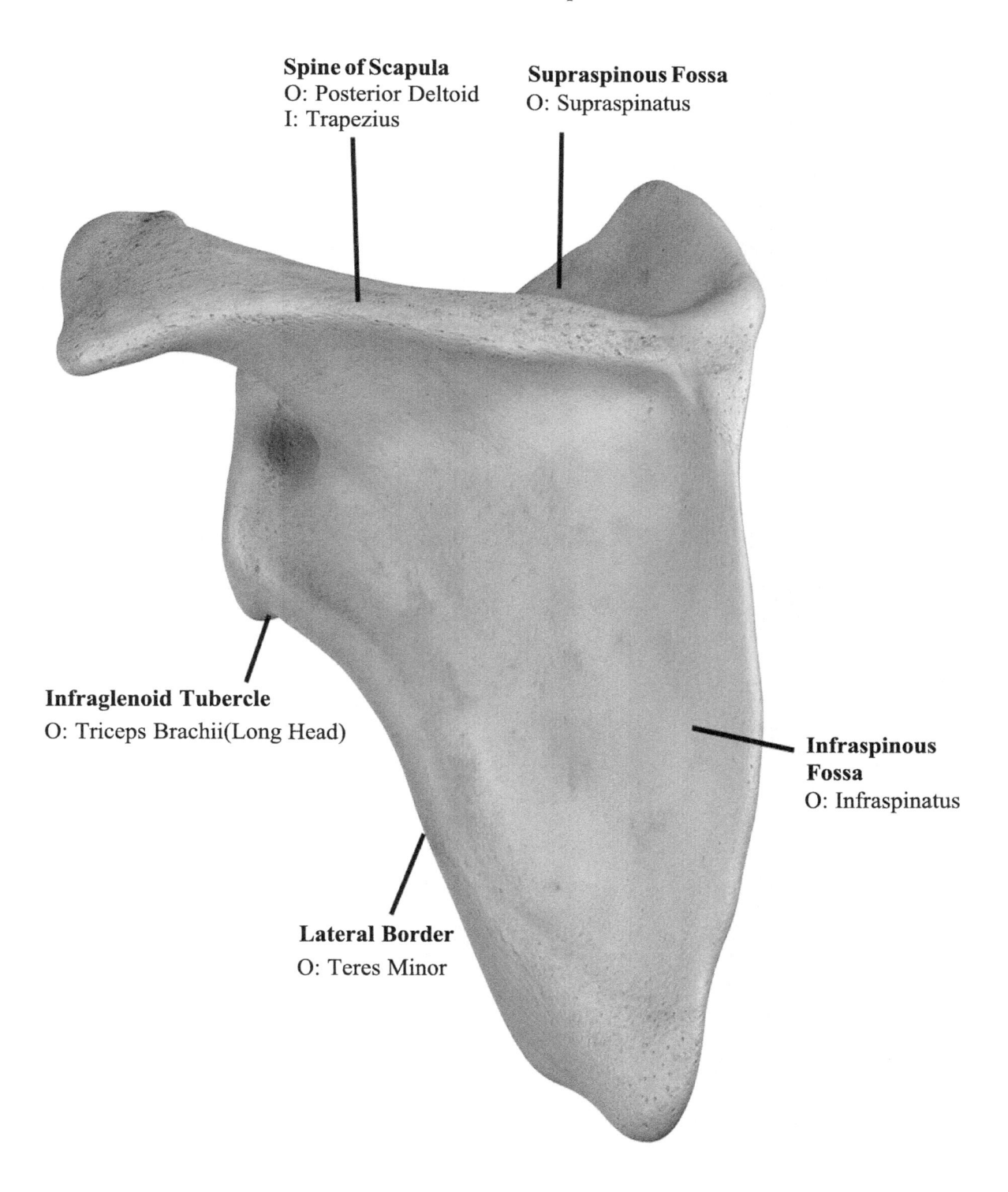

Spine of Scapula
O: Posterior Deltoid
I: Trapezius

Supraspinous Fossa
O: Supraspinatus

Infraglenoid Tubercle
O: Triceps Brachii(Long Head)

Infraspinous Fossa
O: Infraspinatus

Lateral Border
O: Teres Minor

Chest

Clavicle

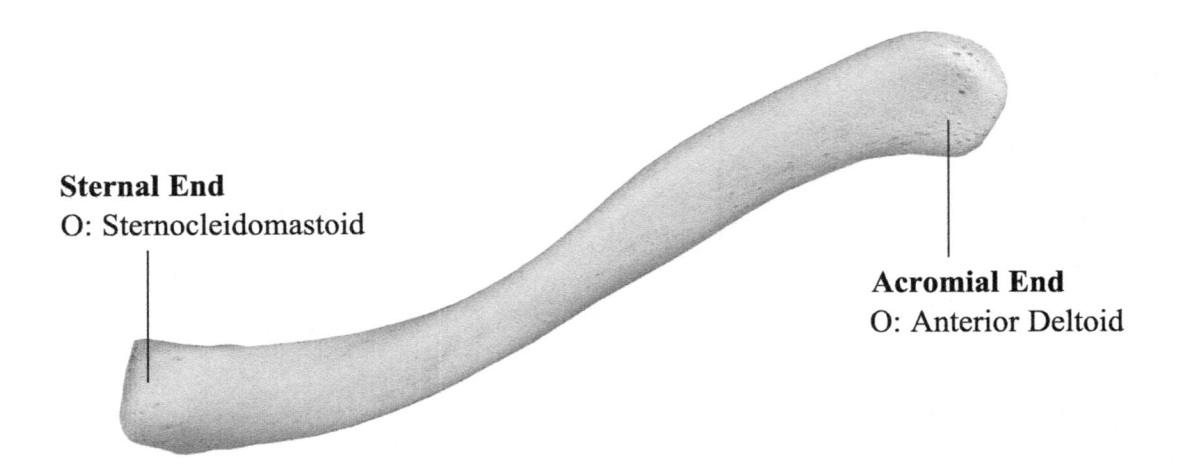

Sternal End
O: Sternocleidomastoid

Acromial End
O: Anterior Deltoid

Sternum

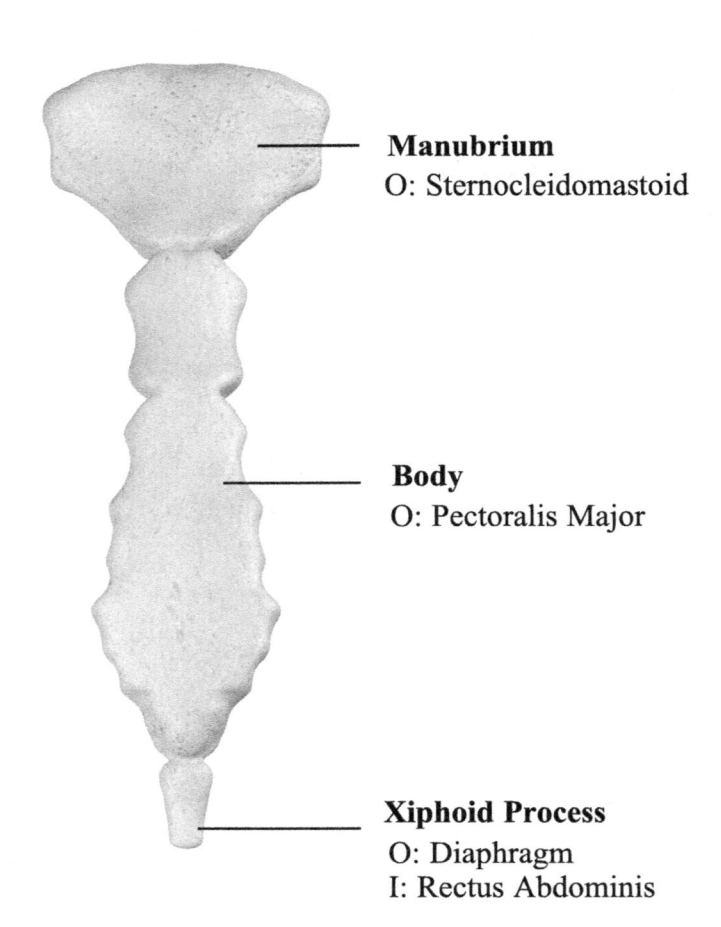

Manubrium
O: Sternocleidomastoid

Body
O: Pectoralis Major

Xiphoid Process
O: Diaphragm
I: Rectus Abdominis

Arm

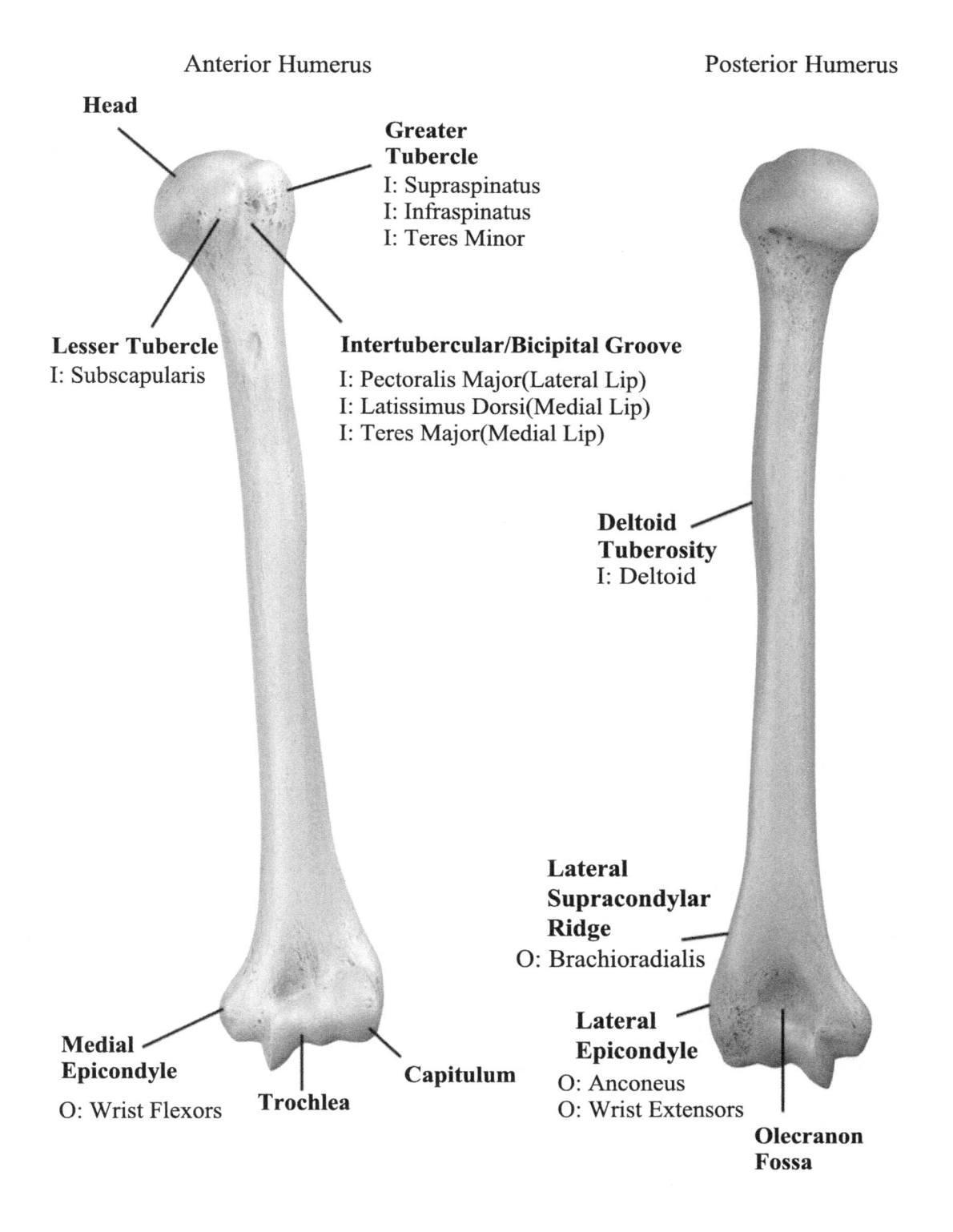

Anterior Humerus

- **Head**
- **Greater Tubercle**
  I: Supraspinatus
  I: Infraspinatus
  I: Teres Minor
- **Lesser Tubercle**
  I: Subscapularis
- **Intertubercular/Bicipital Groove**
  I: Pectoralis Major (Lateral Lip)
  I: Latissimus Dorsi (Medial Lip)
  I: Teres Major (Medial Lip)
- **Medial Epicondyle**
  O: Wrist Flexors
- **Trochlea**
- **Capitulum**

Posterior Humerus

- **Deltoid Tuberosity**
  I: Deltoid
- **Lateral Supracondylar Ridge**
  O: Brachioradialis
- **Lateral Epicondyle**
  O: Anconeus
  O: Wrist Extensors
- **Olecranon Fossa**

Forearm

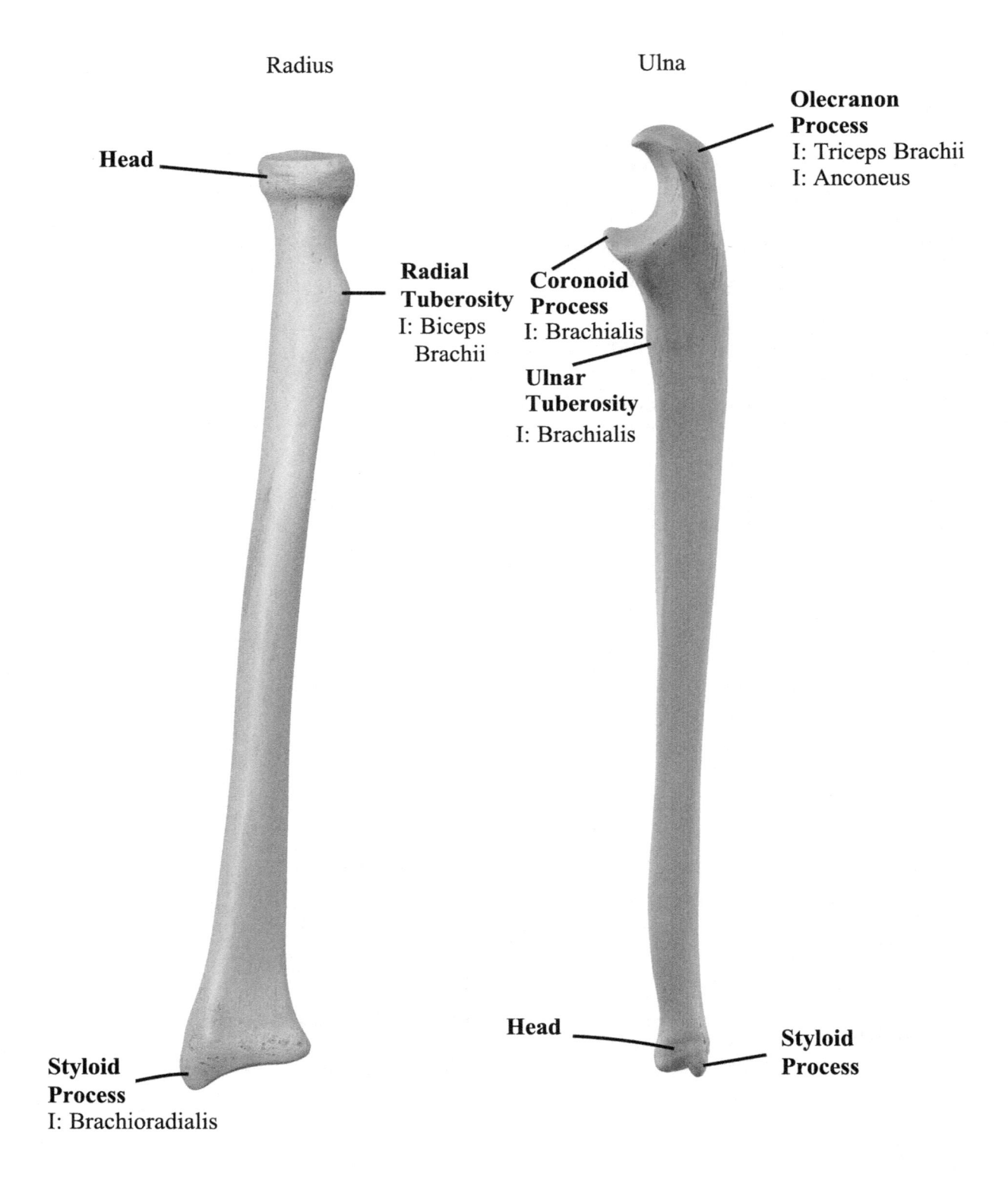

Radius

Head

Radial Tuberosity
I: Biceps Brachii

Styloid Process
I: Brachioradialis

Ulna

Olecranon Process
I: Triceps Brachii
I: Anconeus

Coronoid Process
I: Brachialis

Ulnar Tuberosity
I: Brachialis

Head

Styloid Process

Wrist

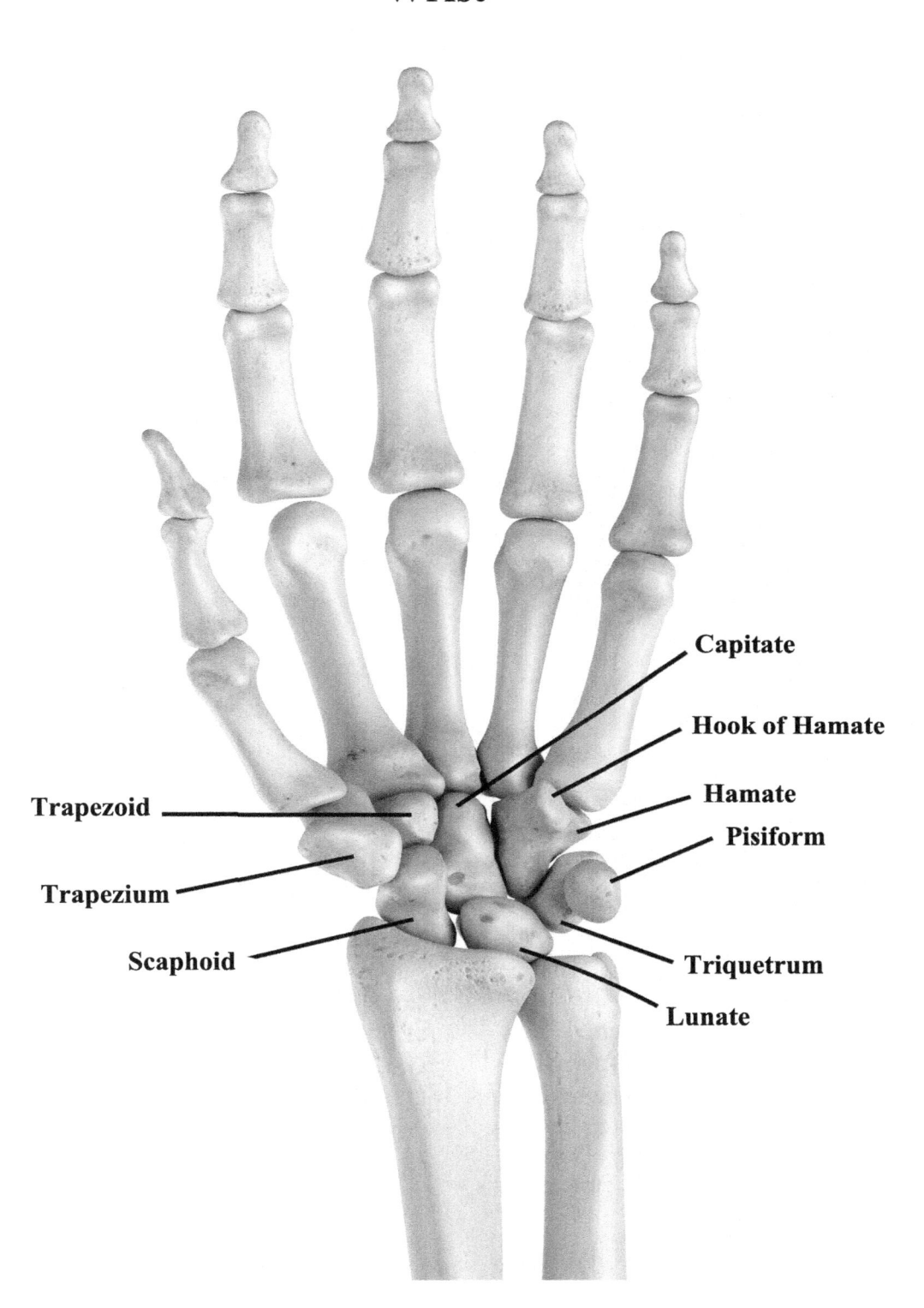

- Capitate
- Hook of Hamate
- Hamate
- Pisiform
- Triquetrum
- Lunate
- Scaphoid
- Trapezium
- Trapezoid

Pelvis

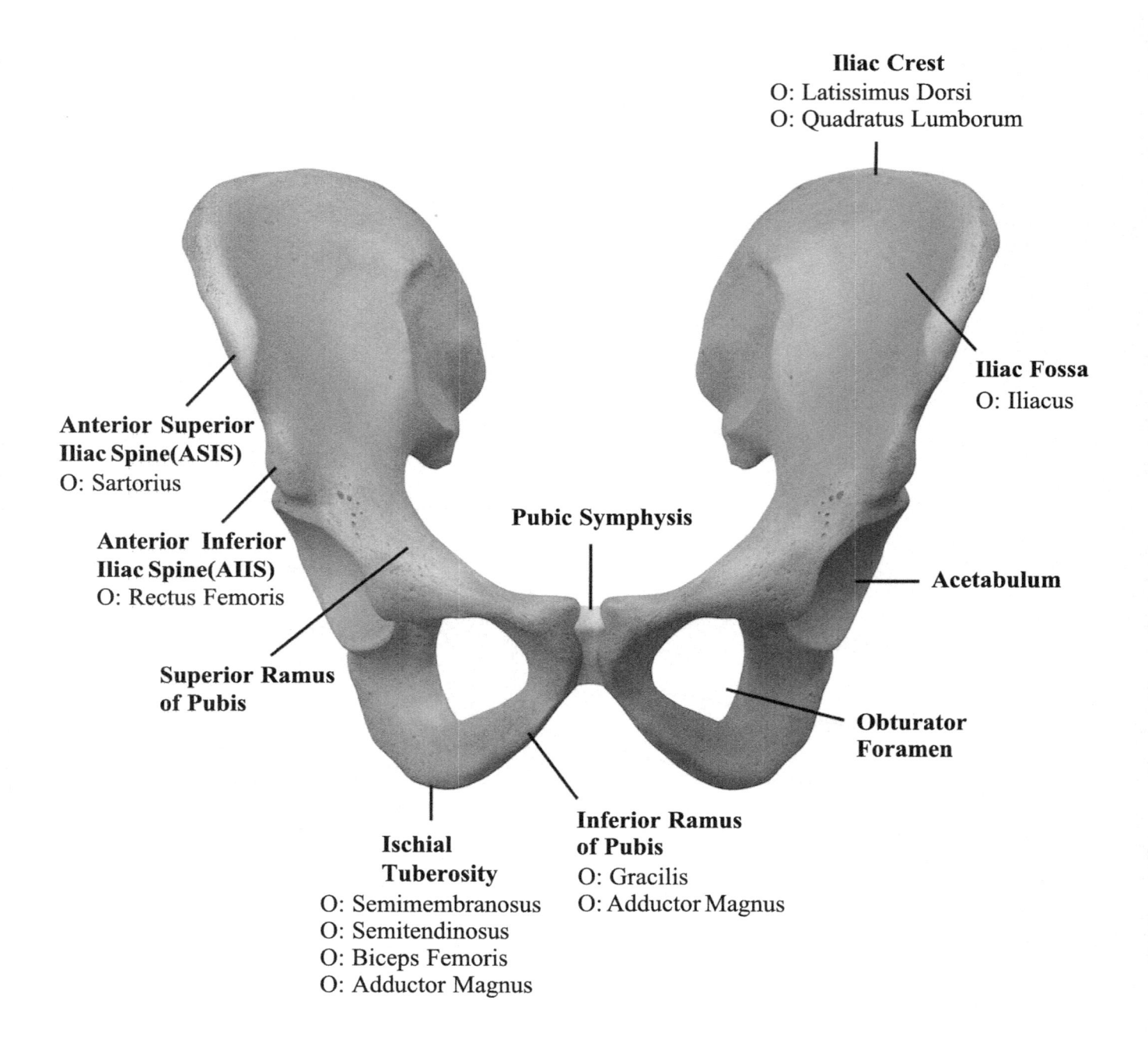

Iliac Crest
O: Latissimus Dorsi
O: Quadratus Lumborum

Iliac Fossa
O: Iliacus

Anterior Superior Iliac Spine(ASIS)
O: Sartorius

Pubic Symphysis

Anterior Inferior Iliac Spine(AIIS)
O: Rectus Femoris

Acetabulum

Superior Ramus of Pubis

Obturator Foramen

Inferior Ramus of Pubis
O: Gracilis
O: Adductor Magnus

Ischial Tuberosity
O: Semimembranosus
O: Semitendinosus
O: Biceps Femoris
O: Adductor Magnus

Thigh

Anterior Femur

Posterior Femur

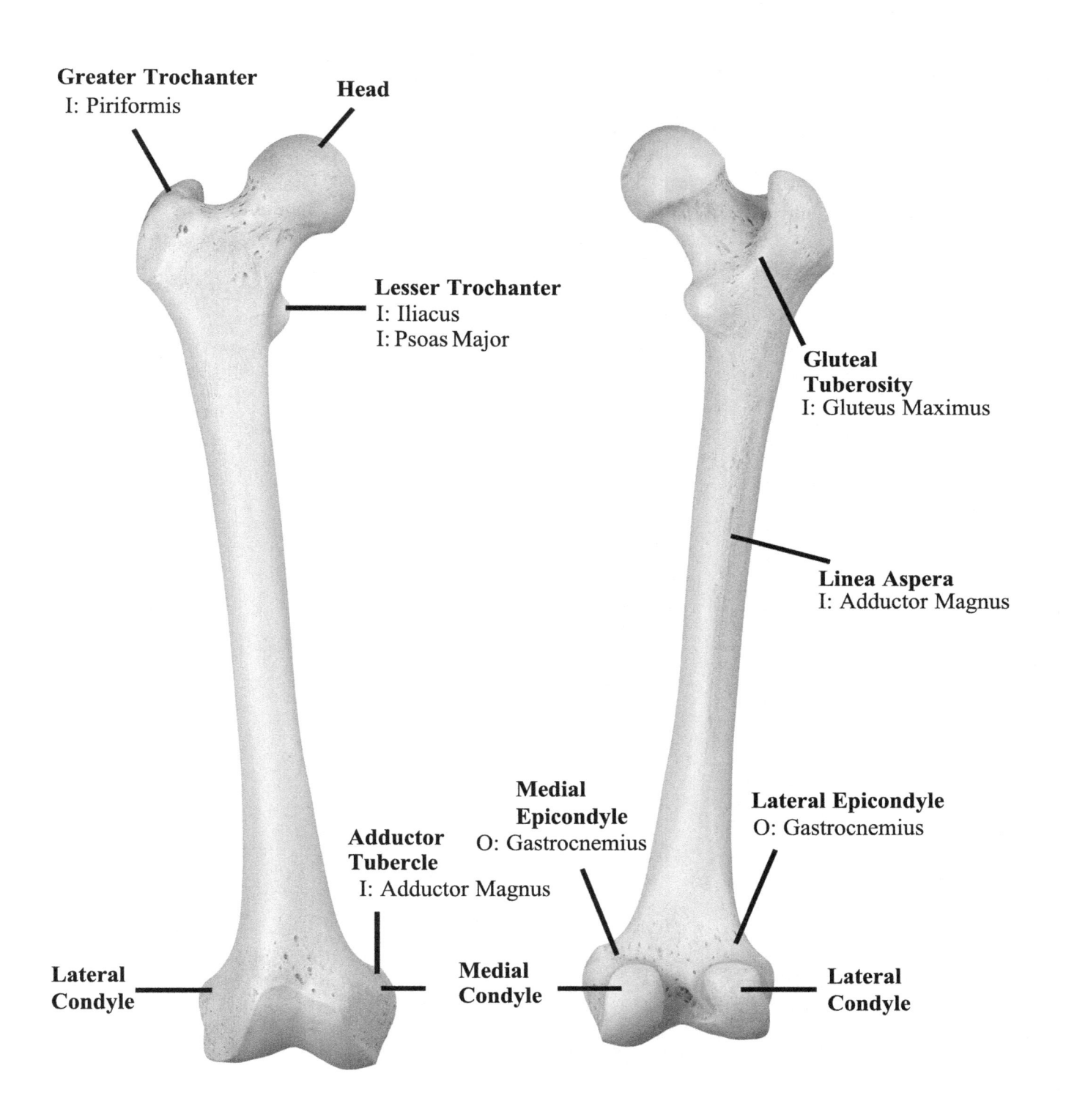

Greater Trochanter
I: Piriformis

Head

Lesser Trochanter
I: Iliacus
I: Psoas Major

Gluteal Tuberosity
I: Gluteus Maximus

Linea Aspera
I: Adductor Magnus

Medial Epicondyle
O: Gastrocnemius

Lateral Epicondyle
O: Gastrocnemius

Adductor Tubercle
I: Adductor Magnus

Lateral Condyle

Medial Condyle

Lateral Condyle

Leg

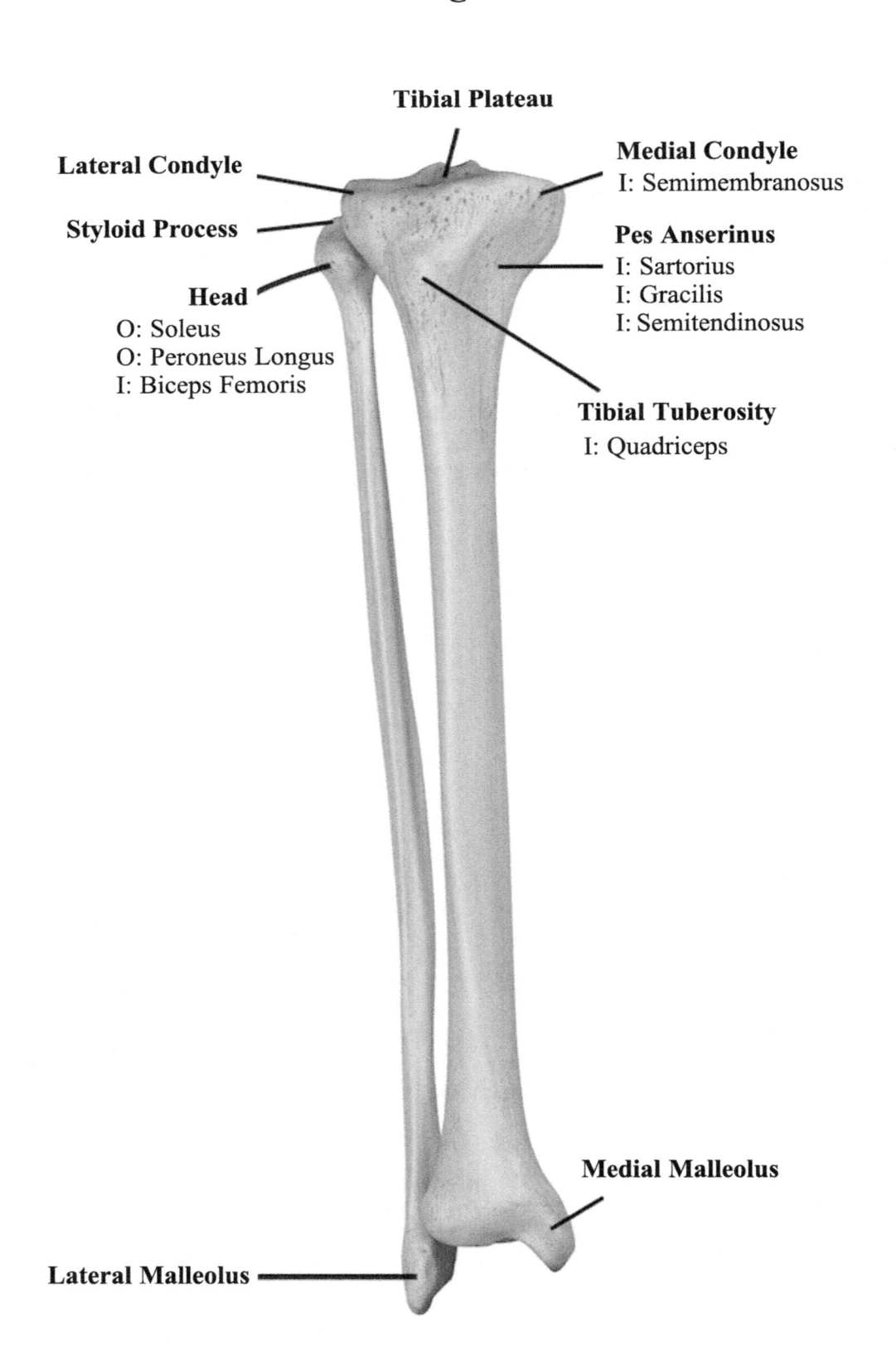

Tibial Plateau

Lateral Condyle

Medial Condyle
I: Semimembranosus

Styloid Process

Pes Anserinus
I: Sartorius
I: Gracilis
I: Semitendinosus

Head
O: Soleus
O: Peroneus Longus
I: Biceps Femoris

Tibial Tuberosity
I: Quadriceps

Medial Malleolus

Lateral Malleolus

Ankle

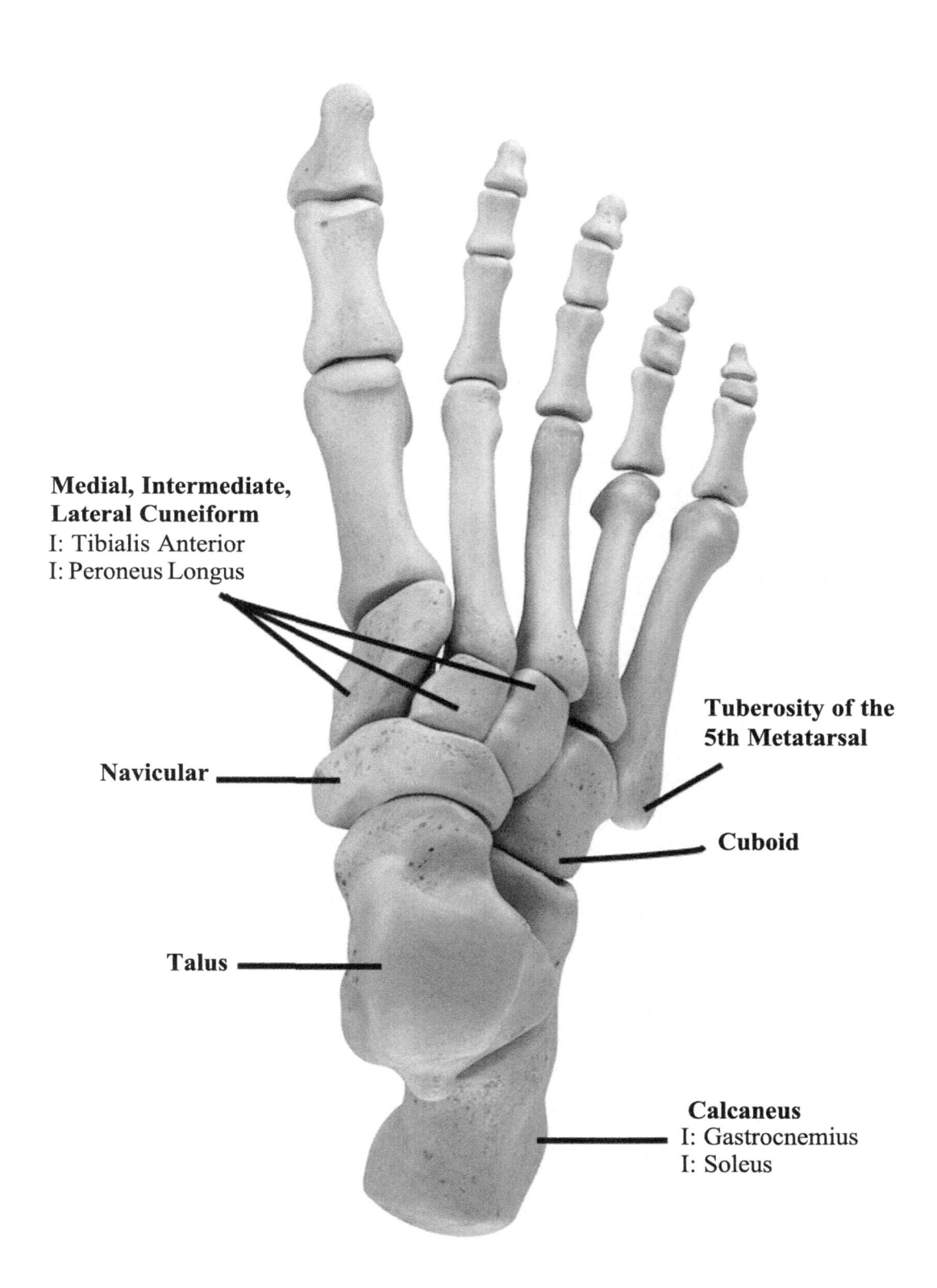

Medial, Intermediate, Lateral Cuneiform
I: Tibialis Anterior
I: Peroneus Longus

Navicular

Talus

Tuberosity of the 5th Metatarsal

Cuboid

Calcaneus
I: Gastrocnemius
I: Soleus

Muscles of the Head

Muscles to Know:

Buccinator
Masseter
Temporalis

Terms to Know:

Bucc/o: Cheek

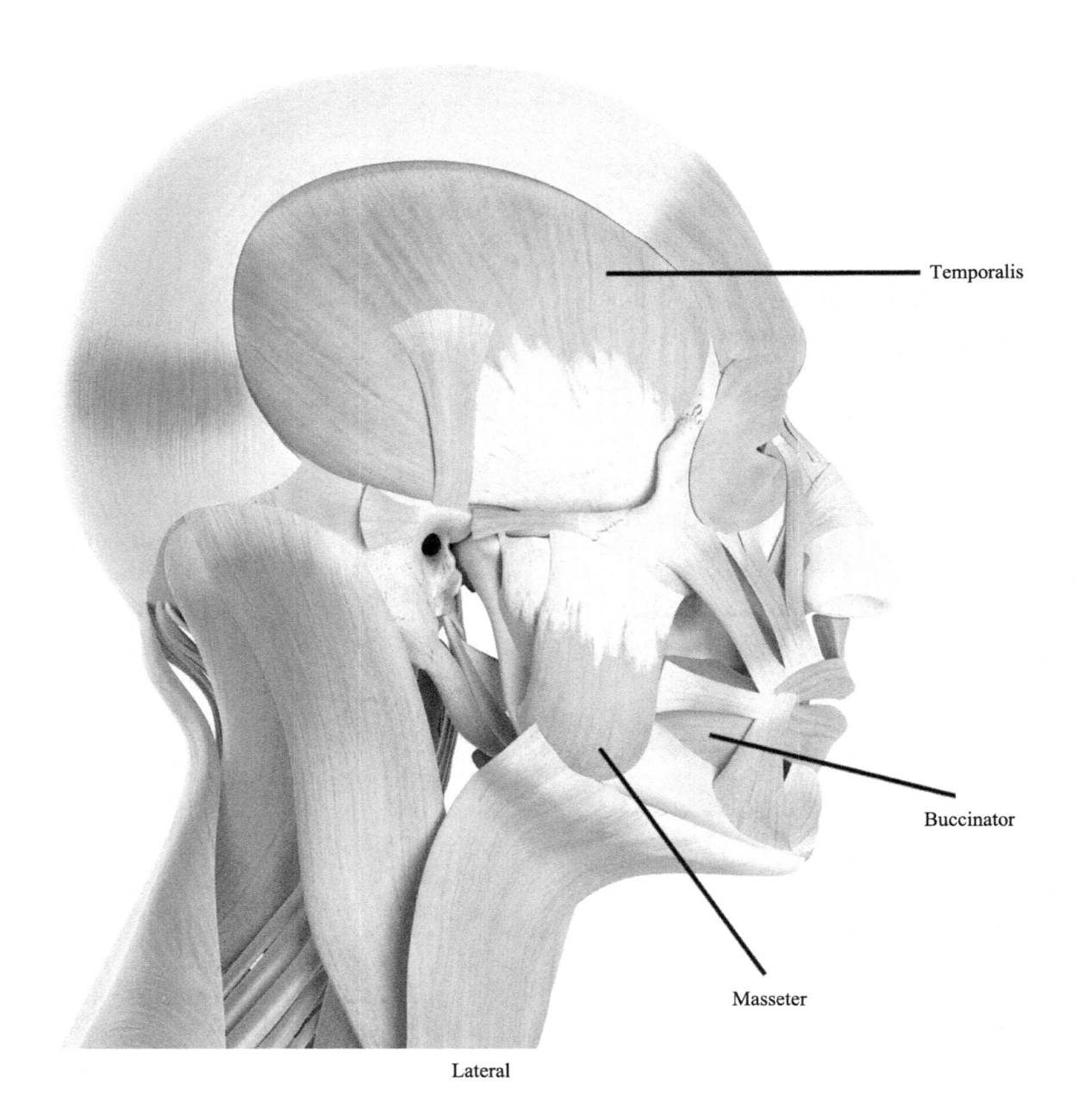

— Temporalis

— Buccinator

— Masseter

Lateral

Buccinator

Buccinator is a muscle of the face located in the area of the cheek, also known as the "buccal" region. The term "bucc/o" means "cheek".

Buccinator originates on the Alveolar Processes of the Mandible and Maxilla, and inserts onto the angle of the mouth and the Orbicularis Oris muscle.

Buccinator primarily assists in chewing by squeezing the cheeks closer together while the jaw is depressed. This forces the food back in towards the teeth, allowing proper mastication to take place upon elevation of the mandible. Buccinator is also the muscle primarily used for whistling, again by squeezing the cheeks together, and it also assists in smiling.

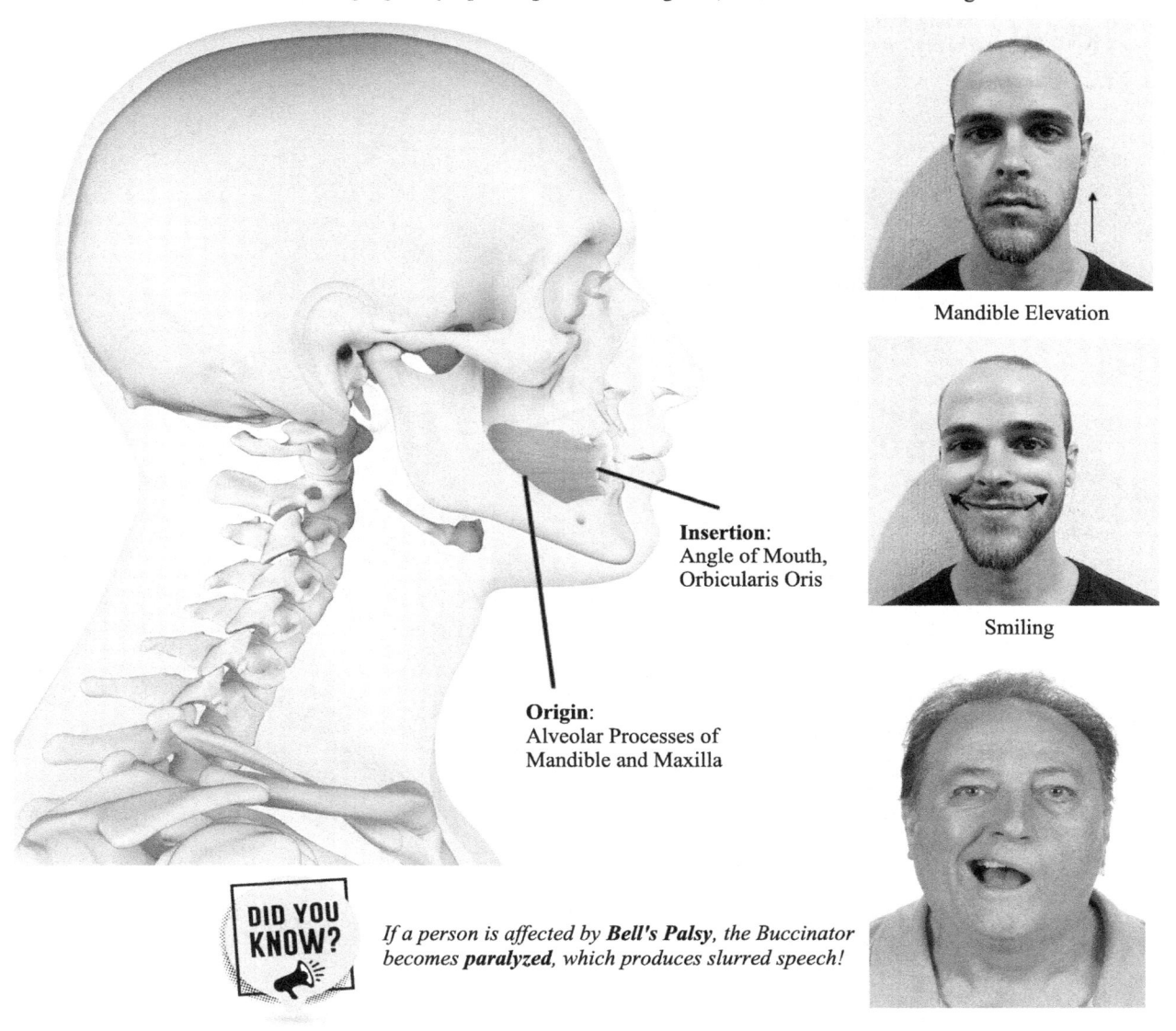

Mandible Elevation

Smiling

Insertion: Angle of Mouth, Orbicularis Oris

Origin: Alveolar Processes of Mandible and Maxilla

DID YOU KNOW? *If a person is affected by **Bell's Palsy**, the Buccinator becomes **paralyzed**, which produces slurred speech!*

Origin: Alveolar Processes of Mandible and Maxilla
Insertion: Angle of the mouth, Orbicularis Oris
Action(s): Elevation of Mandible, Compresses Cheeks against Teeth
Innervation: Buccal Branch of Facial Nerve
Synergist: Masseter
Antagonist: Lateral Pterygoid

Masseter

Masseter, named after its primary action of mastication, is a muscle of the face that attaches to the mandible. When it contracts, it allows chewing to take place. It works with other muscles, such as Buccinator, to perform mastication.

Masseter originates on the zygomatic arch and maxilla, and inserts onto the coronoid process and ramus of the mandible.

Masseter is one muscle primarily involved in TMJ(Temporomandibular Joint) Dysfunction, along with Temporalis and Pterygoid.

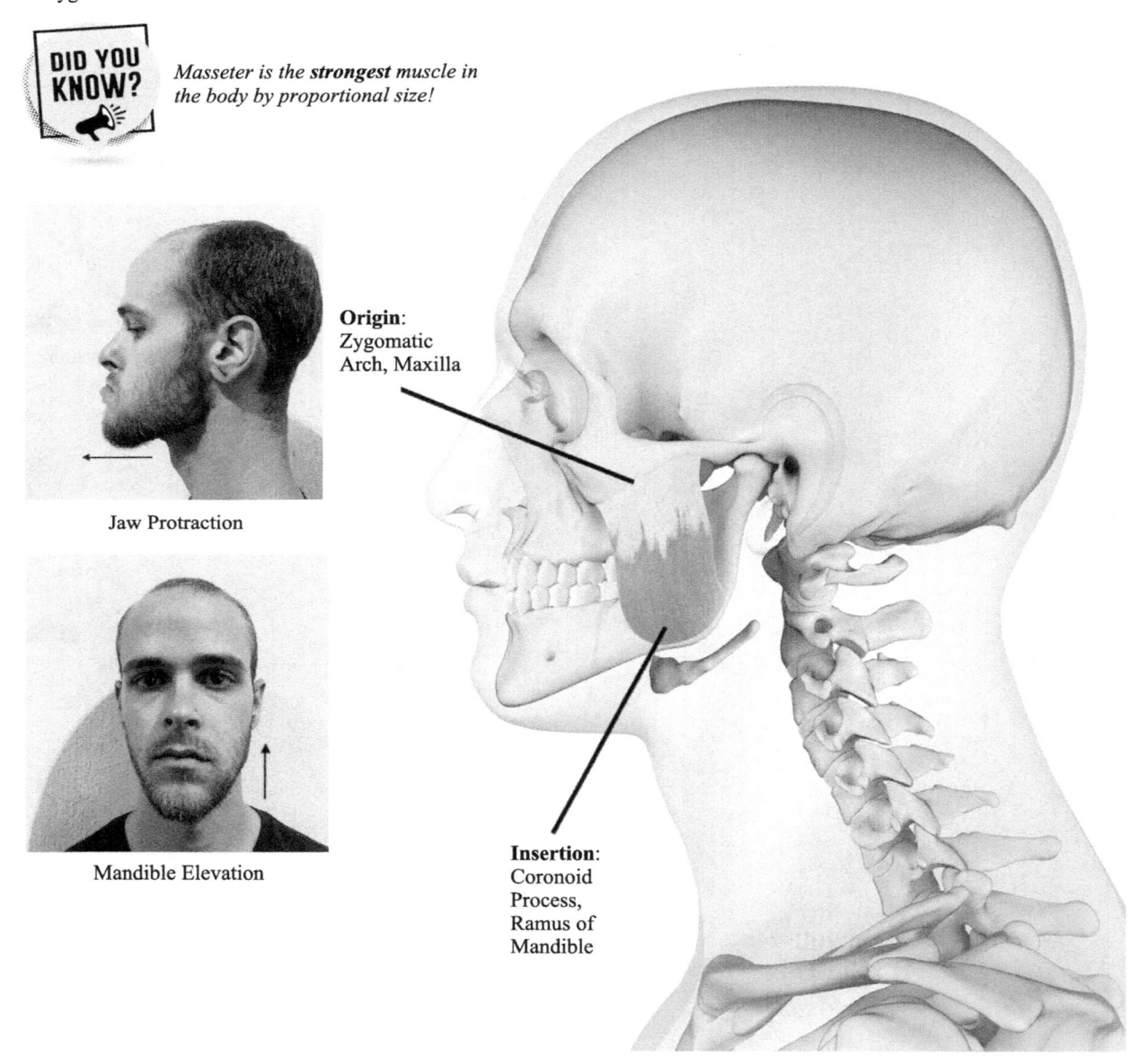

DID YOU KNOW? *Masseter is the **strongest** muscle in the body by proportional size!*

Jaw Protraction

Mandible Elevation

Origin: Zygomatic Arch, Maxilla

Insertion: Coronoid Process, Ramus of Mandible

Origin: Zygomatic Arch, Maxilla
Insertion: Coronoid Process and Ramus of Mandible
Action(s): Elevation, Protraction of Mandible
Innervation: Mandibular Nerve
Synergist: Buccinator
Antagonist: Lateral Pterygoid

Temporalis

Temporalis is a muscle of the cranium, named after the Temporal bone, which is its origin.

Temporalis inserts onto the Coronoid Process of the Mandible. "Coronoid" means "resembling a crown". Inserting onto the Mandible allows the Temporalis to assist in mastication, along with Masseter.

If a person is affected by TMJ(Temporomandibular Joint) Dysfunction, Temporalis may be involved.

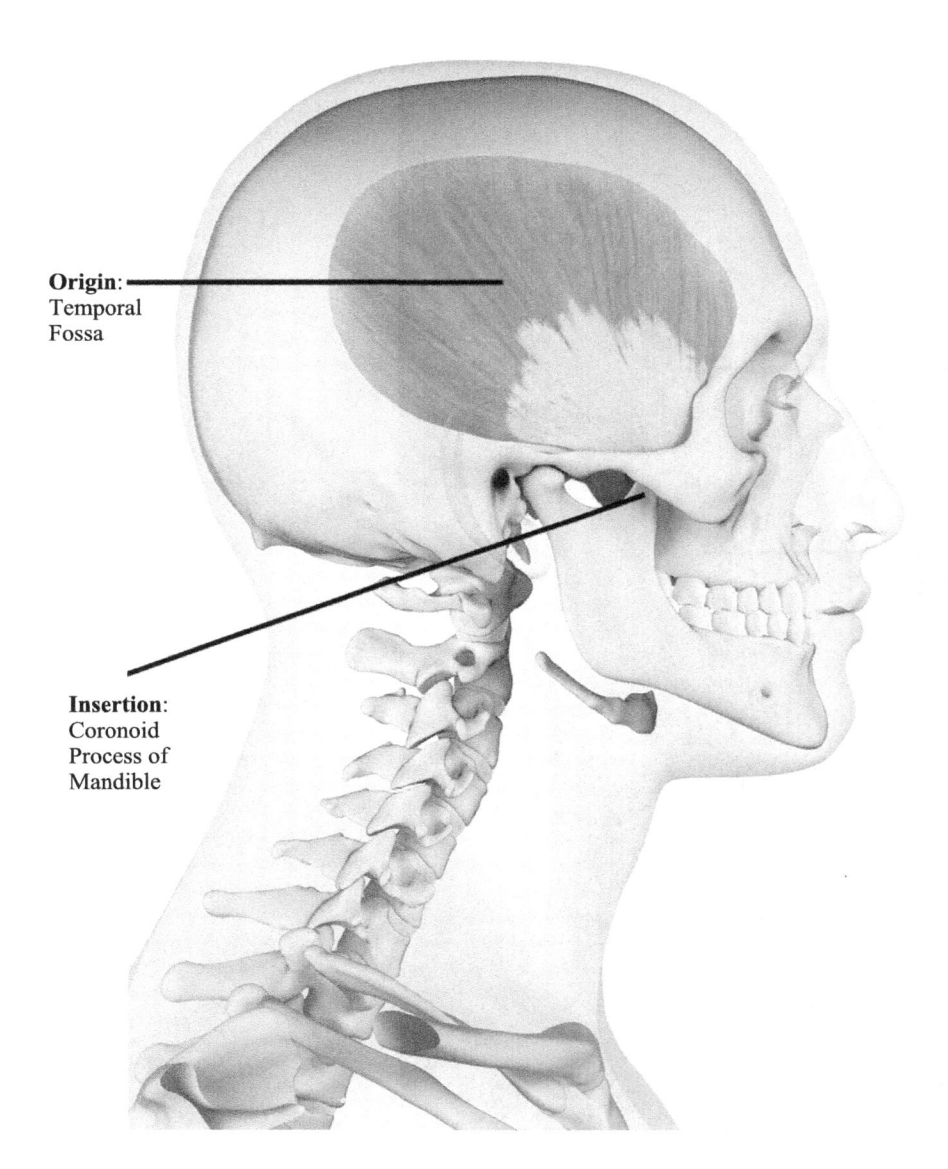

Origin: Temporal Fossa

Insertion: Coronoid Process of Mandible

Mandible Elevation

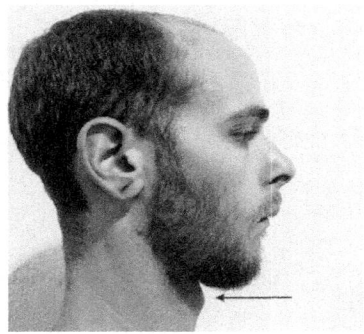

Jaw Retraction

Origin: Temporal Fossa
Insertion: Coronoid Process of Mandible
Action(s): Elevation, Retraction of Mandible
Innervation: Facial Nerve
Synergist: Masseter
Antagonist: Lateral Pterygoid

Muscles of the Neck

Muscles to Know:

Levator Scapulae
Scalenes
Splenius Capitis
Sternocleidomastoid

Terms to Know:

Skalenos: Uneven
Stern/o: Sternum
Cleid/o: Clavicle
Mast/o: Breast
-oid: Resembling
Splenion: Bandage
Capitis: Head

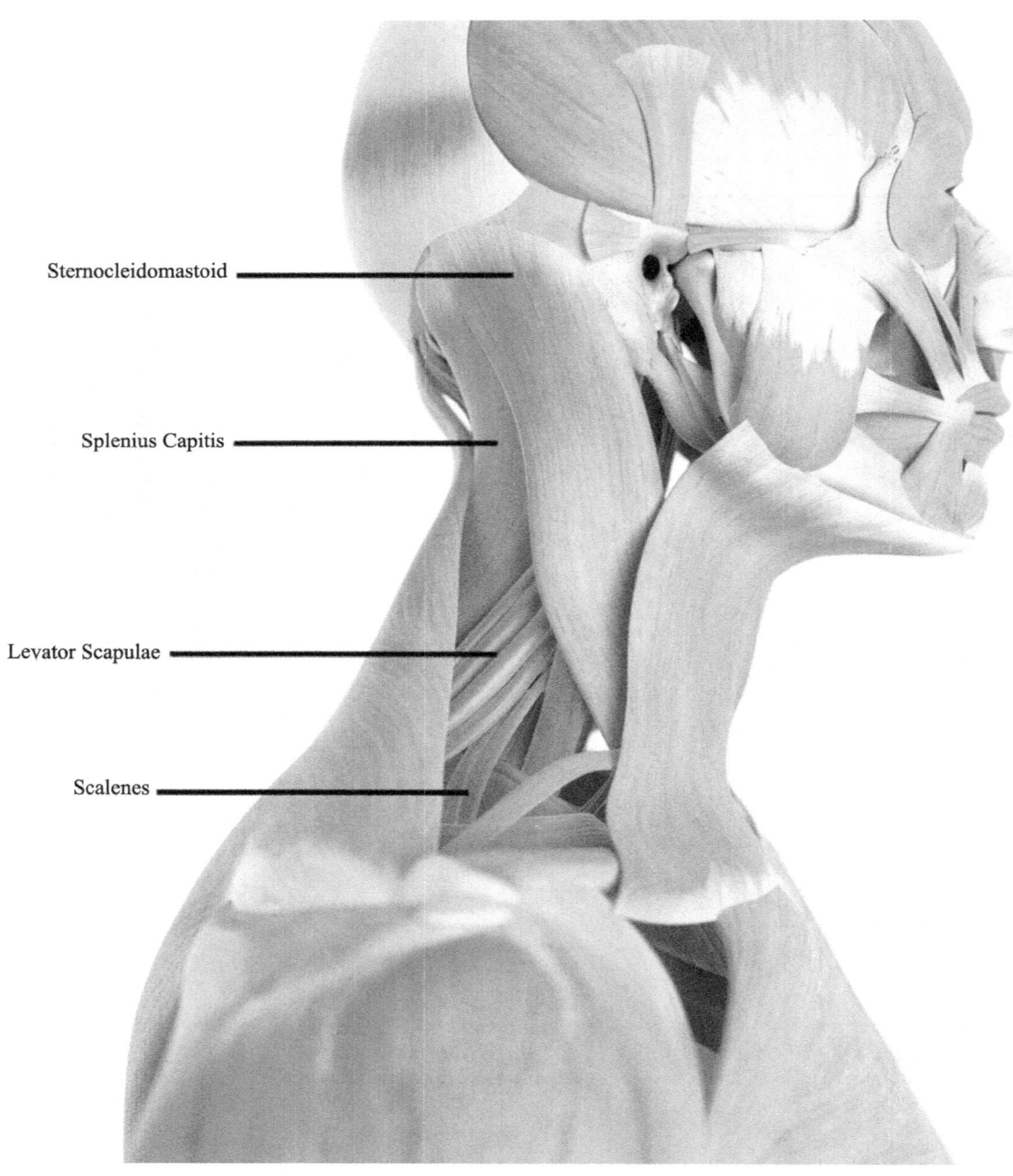

Sternocleidomastoid

Splenius Capitis

Levator Scapulae

Scalenes

Lateral

Levator Scapulae

Levator Scapulae is a muscle of the posterior neck, named after its action(elevation), and insertion(scapula).

Levator Scapulae originates on the Transverse Processes of C1-C4, and inserts onto the Superior Angle of the Scapula.

Levator Scapulae is one of the prime movers of scapular elevation, such as shrugging the shoulders. It also may slightly downwardly rotate the scapula.

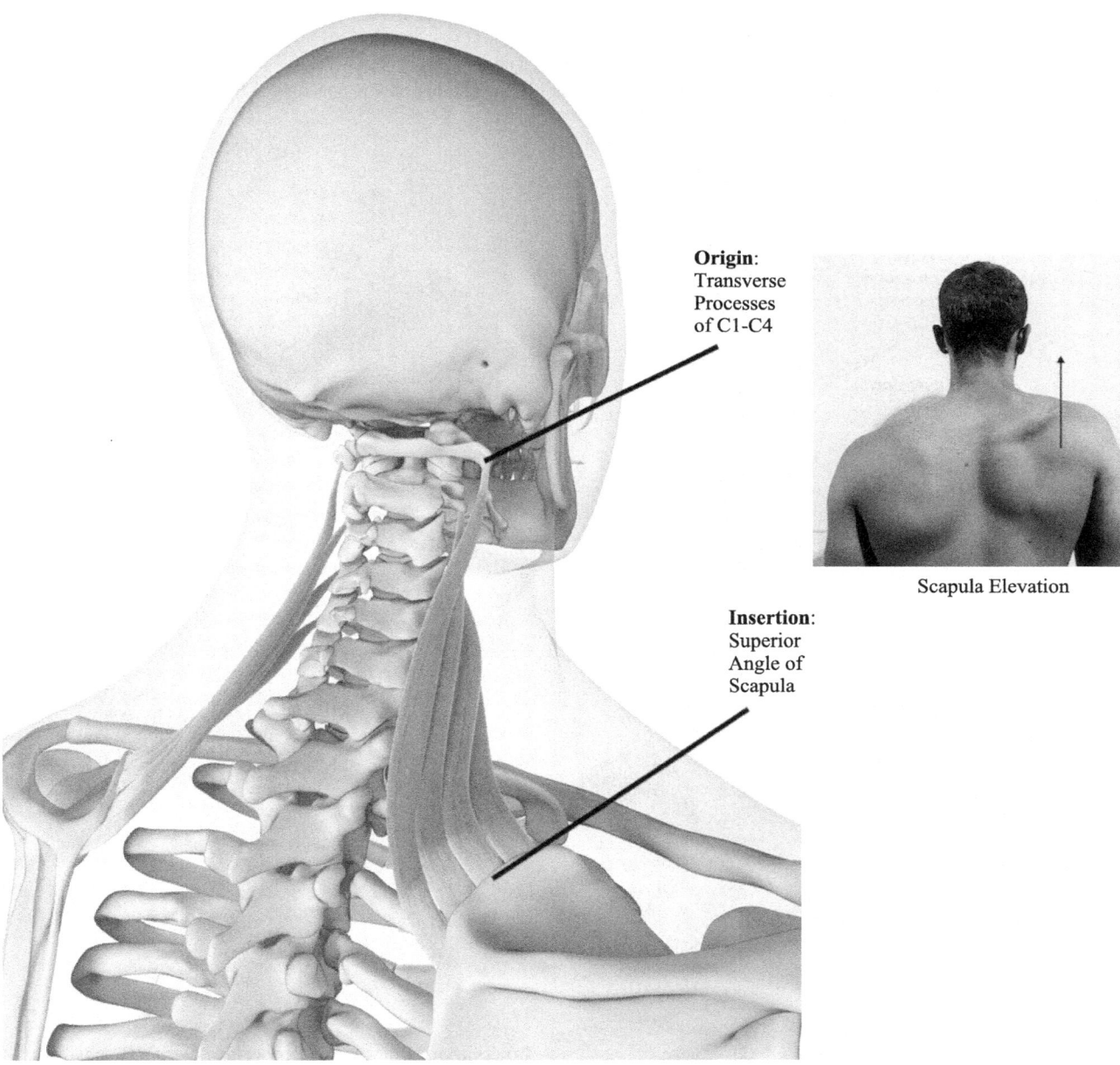

Origin: Transverse Processes of C1-C4

Insertion: Superior Angle of Scapula

Scapula Elevation

Origin: Transverse Processes of C1-C4
Insertion: Superior Angle of Scapula
Action(s): Elevation of Scapula
Innervation: Dorsal Scapular Nerve
Synergist: Upper Trapezius
Antagonist: Lower Trapezius, Serratus Anterior

Scalenes

The Scalenes are muscles of the anterior neck. The Scalenes are split into three parts: Anterior Scalene, Middle Scalene, and Posterior Scalene. The name "scalene" comes from the Greek word "skalenos", which means uneven. All three Scalene muscles are a different size.

The Scalenes originate on the Transverse Processes of C1-C7, and insert onto Ribs 1 and 2.

Unilaterally the scalenes laterally flex the cervical vertebrae, bringing the ear to the shoulder. The Scalenes also elevate the ribs. Bilaterally, the scalenes bring the neck into flexion.

The Scalenes are neurovascular entrappers. Conditions such as Thoracic Outlet Syndrome, where the Brachial plexus, Subclavian artery, and Subclavian vein are compressed, can be caused by hypertonic Scalenes. This condition may result in loss of sensation in the upper limb and reduced blood flow.

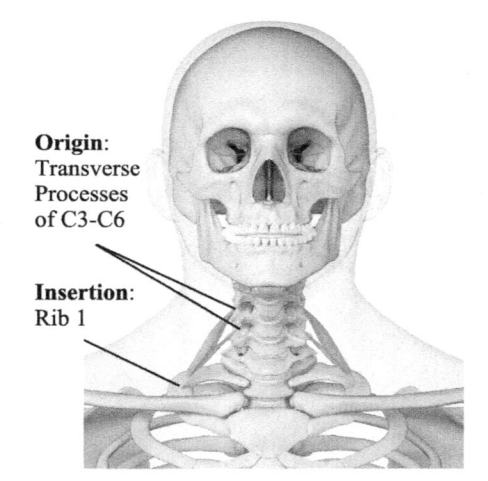

Origin: Transverse Processes of C3-C6
Insertion: Rib 1

Anterior Scalene

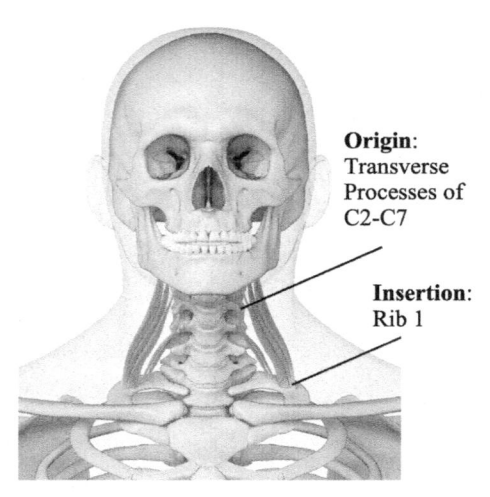

Origin: Transverse Processes of C2-C7
Insertion: Rib 1

Middle Scalene

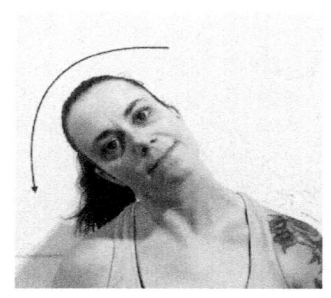

Neck Lateral Flexion

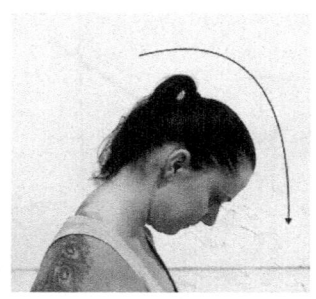

Neck Flexion

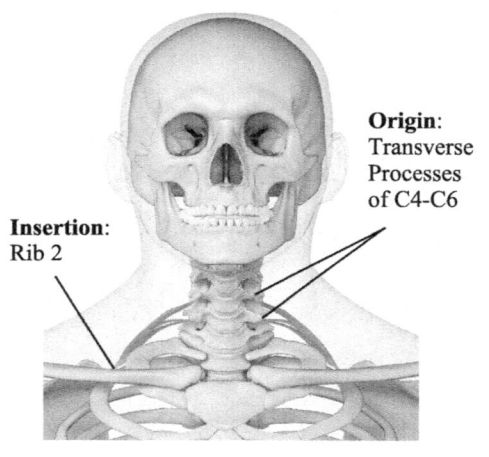

Origin: Transverse Processes of C4-C6
Insertion: Rib 2

Posterior Scalene

Origin: Transverse Processes of C1-C7
Insertion: Ribs 1 and 2
Action(s): Unilaterally: Lateral Flexion of Cervical Vertebrae; Elevation of Ribs
Innervation: Branches of Cervical Plexus and Brachial Plexus
Synergist: Sternocleidomastoid
Antagonist: Spinalis Cervicis, Splenius Capitis

Splenius Capitis

Splenius Capitis is a muscle of the posterior neck, named after its appearance("splenius" derives from the Greek word "splenion", which means "bandage"), and its insertion("capitis" refers to the head).

Splenius Capitis originates on the Spinous Processes of C7-T3. Splenius Capitis inserts onto the Mastoid Process of the Temporal bone, and the Occipital bone.

Unilaterally, the Splenius Capitis will laterally flex the neck, and rotate the Cervical vertebrae to the same side. Bilaterally, Splenius Capitis assists in extension of the head/neck.

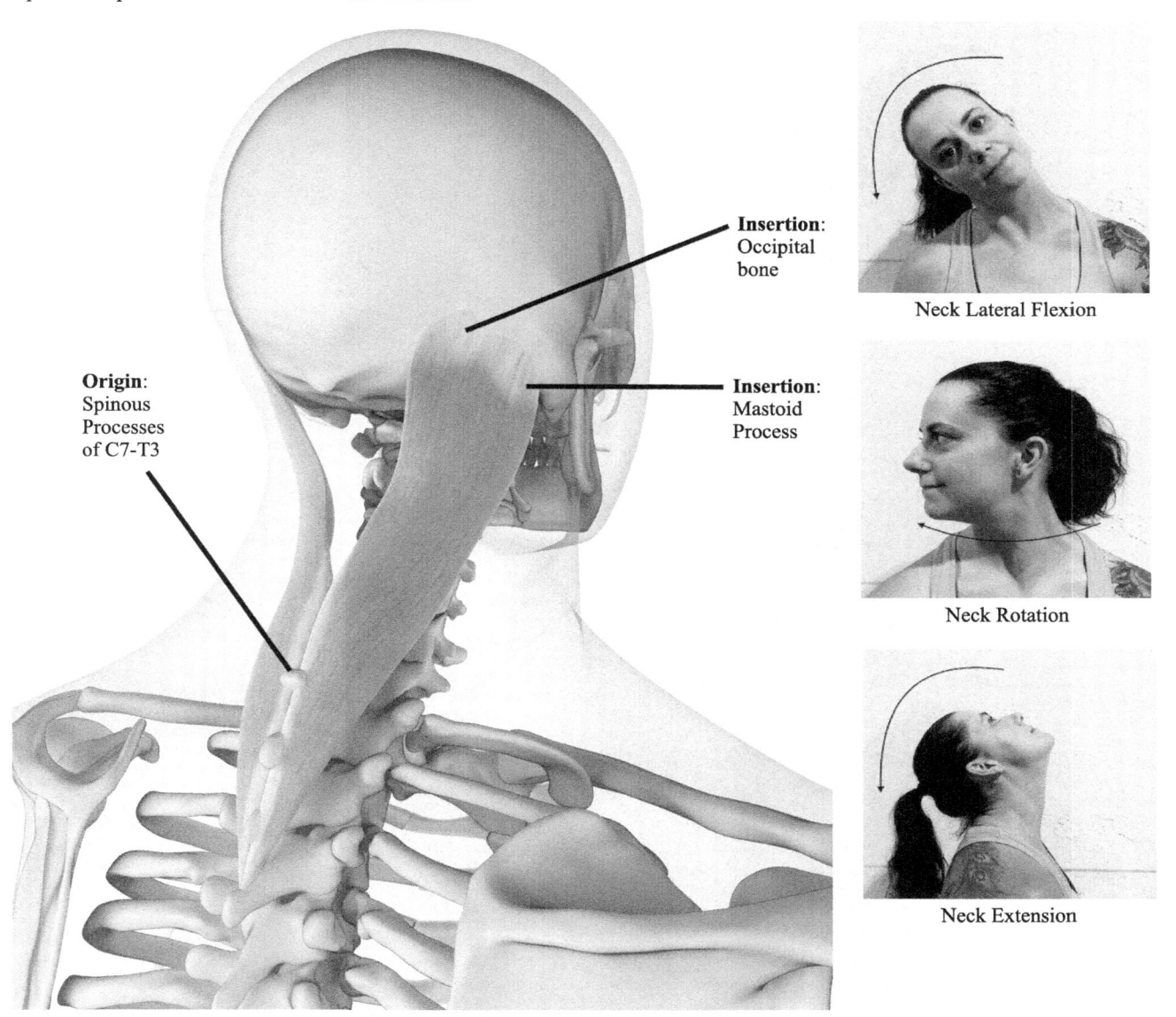

Origin: Spinous Processes of C7-T3

Insertion: Occipital bone

Insertion: Mastoid Process

Neck Lateral Flexion

Neck Rotation

Neck Extension

Origin: Spinous Processes of C7-T3
Insertion: Mastoid Process of Temporal bone, Occipital bone
Action(s): Unilaterally: Lateral Flexion, Rotation of Cervical Vertebrae to same side; Bilaterally: Extension of Head
Innervation: Dorsal Primary Rami of Spinal Nerves C2-C6
Synergist: Spinalis Cervicis
Antagonist: Sternocleidomastoid

Sternocleidomastoid

Sternocleidomastoid is a muscle of the anterior neck, named after its origins(Sternum, Clavicle) and insertion(Mastoid Process). This muscle may also be known as "Sternomastoid".

Sternocleidomastoid has numerous actions. Unilaterally, it rotates the cervical vertebrae to the opposite side of the contracting muscle. It also laterally flexes the cervical vertebrae to the same side of the contracting muscle. Bilaterally, it flexes the cervical vertebrae, allowing the chin to come to the chest.

Sternocleidomastoid establishes the borders of the anterior triangle of the neck, creating a V shape.

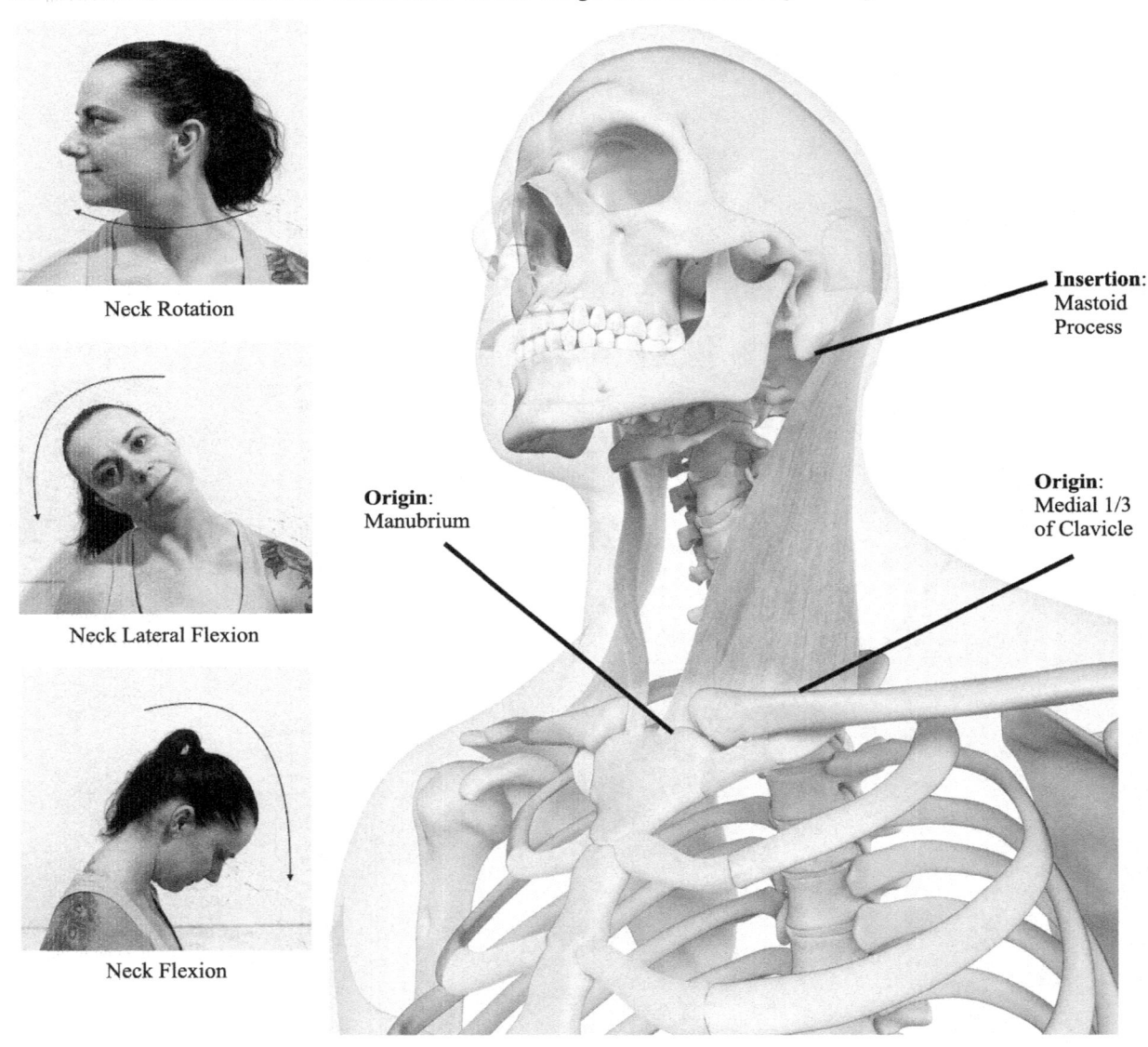

Neck Rotation

Neck Lateral Flexion

Neck Flexion

Insertion: Mastoid Process

Origin: Manubrium

Origin: Medial 1/3 of Clavicle

Origin: Manubrium, Medial Third of Clavicle
Insertion: Mastoid Process of Temporal bone
Action(s): Unilaterally: Rotation of Cervical Vertebrae to opposite side, Lateral Flexion of Cervical Vertebrae to same side; Bilaterally: Flexion of Cervical Vertebrae

Innervation: Accessory Nerve
Synergist: Scalenes
Antagonist: Splenius Capitis, Trapezius

Muscles of the Back

Muscles to Know:

Infraspinatus
Latissimus Dorsi
Longissimus
Multifidus
Quadratus Lumborum
Rhomboids
Rotatores
Spinalis
Subscapularis
Supraspinatus
Teres Major
Teres Minor
Trapezius

Terms to Know:

Infra-: Below
Latissimus: Wide
Dorsi: Back
Quadr/o: Four
Lumb/o: Lumbar
Sub-: Under
Supra-: Above
Teres: Round and Long

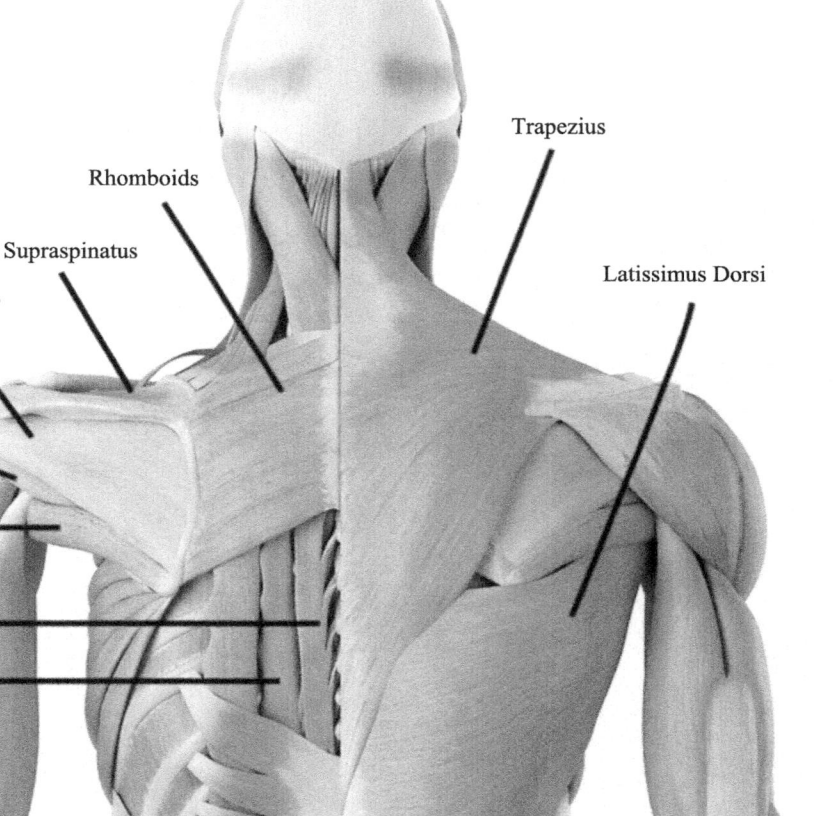

Rhomboids
Supraspinatus
Infraspinatus
Teres Minor
Teres Major
Spinalis
Longissimus
Trapezius
Latissimus Dorsi

Not Pictured: Multifidus, Rotatores, Quadratus Lumborum, Subscapularis

Infraspinatus

Infraspinatus is a muscle of the back, named after its location(inferior to the Spine of Scapula).

Infraspinatus is a member of the rotator cuff muscle group, along with Supraspinatus, Teres Minor, and Subscapularis. Infraspinatus originates on the Infraspinous Fossa, located on the posterior surface of the Scapula. Infraspinatus inserts onto the Greater Tubercle(sometimes also known as the Greater Tuberosity) of the Humerus.

Infraspinatus is primarily responsible for lateral rotation, extension, and horizontal abduction of the shoulder. Infraspinatus and Teres Minor have the same actions.

*Easy to Remember: To remember the muscles of the rotator cuff, think "**SITS**"!*
This stands for:
Supraspinatus
Infraspinatus
Teres Minor
Subscapularis

Shoulder Lateral Rotation

Shoulder Horizontal Abduction

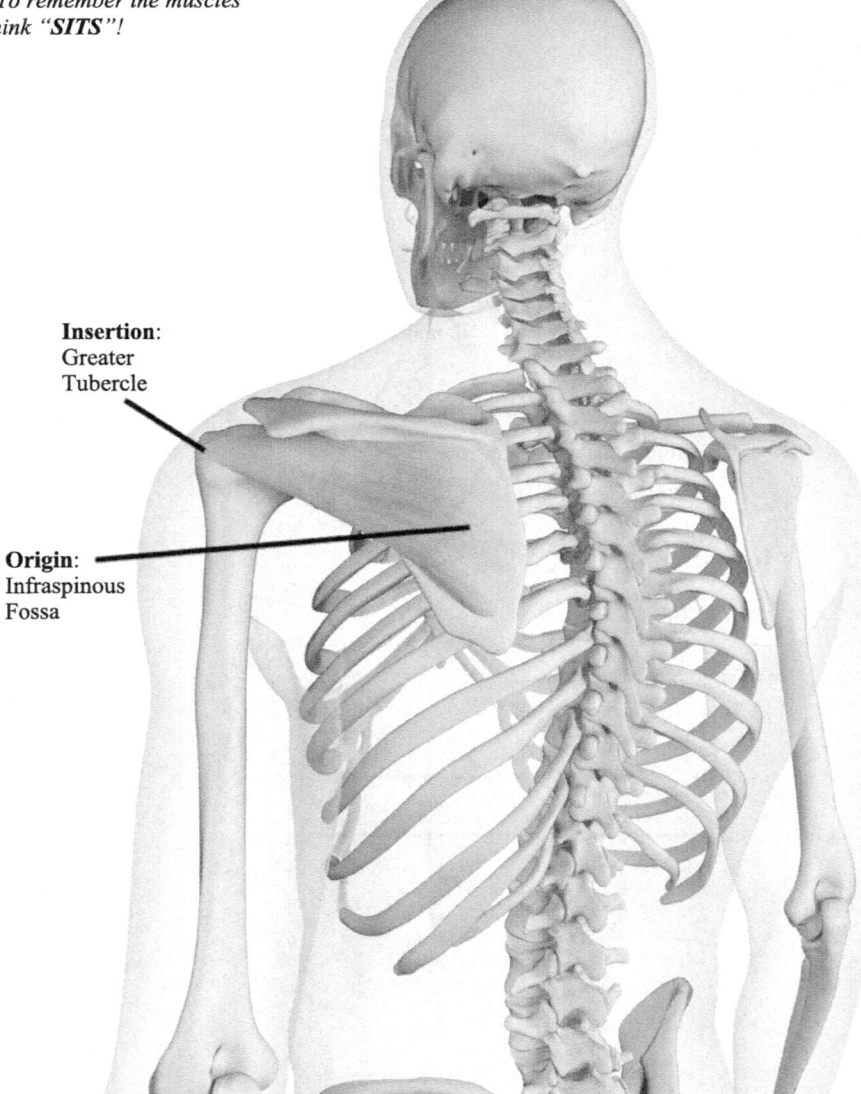

Insertion: Greater Tubercle

Origin: Infraspinous Fossa

Origin: Infraspinous Fossa
Insertion: Greater Tubercle of Humerus
Action(s): Lateral Rotation, Horizontal Abduction of Shoulder

Innervation: Suprascapular Nerve
Synergist: Teres Minor, Latissimus Dorsi, Posterior Deltoid
Antagonist: Anterior Deltoid, Subscapularis, Pectoralis Major

Latissimus Dorsi

Latissimus Dorsi is a muscle of the back, named after its size("Latissimus" means "wide") and location("Dorsi" refers to the back). Latissimus Dorsi is the widest muscle in the body.

Latissimus Dorsi originates on the Iliac Crest, Thoracolumbar Aponeurosis, and the Spinous Processes of T7-T12. Latissimus Dorsi inserts onto the Medial Lip of the Intertubercular Groove(also may be known as the Bicipital Groove).

Latissimus Dorsi is the muscle primarily responsible for performing adduction of the shoulder. If a person were to perform pull-up exercises, it would be Latissimus Dorsi contracting strongest. Latissimus Dorsi also medially rotates and extends the shoulder. Latissimus Dorsi, Teres Major, and Subscapularis all perform the same actions. When the insertion is fixed in place, Latissimus Dorsi may elevate the hip.

Latissimus Dorsi is often referred to as the "Swimmer's Muscle" due to its actions, which are used when swimming.

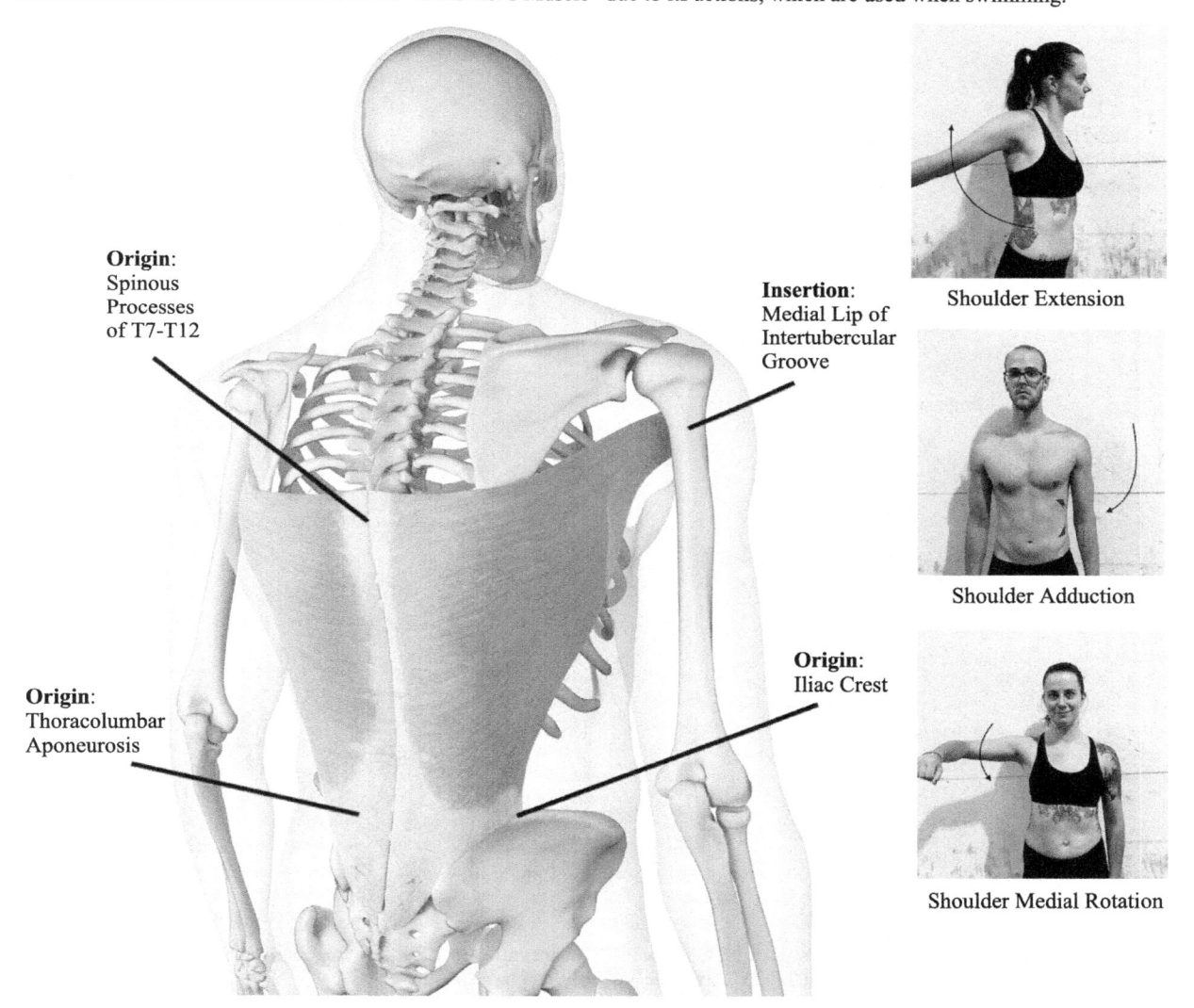

Origin: Spinous Processes of T7-T12

Origin: Thoracolumbar Aponeurosis

Insertion: Medial Lip of Intertubercular Groove

Origin: Iliac Crest

Shoulder Extension

Shoulder Adduction

Shoulder Medial Rotation

Origin: Iliac Crest, Thoracolumbar Aponeurosis, Spinous Processes of T7-T12
Insertion: Medial lip of Intertubercular Groove
Action(s): Extension, Adduction, Medial Rotation of Shoulder
Innervation: Thoracodorsal Nerve
Synergist: Teres Major, Subscapularis
Antagonist: Pectoralis Major, Coracobrachialis

Longissimus

Longissimus is a group of three muscles, Longissimus Cervicis, Longissimus Capitis, and Longissimus Thoracis, which are all part of the Erector Spinae muscle group. Each muscle is named after the region of the body it is located on or attaches to.

Longissimus Thoracis originates on the Transverse Processes of L1-L5, the Iliac Crest, and the Sacrum. Longissimus Cervicis originates on the Transverse Processes of T1-T5. Longissimus Capitis originates on the Articular Surfaces of C4-C7.

Longissimus Thoracis inserts onto the Transverse Processes of T1-T12. Longissimus Cervicis inserts onto the Transverse Processes of C2-C6. Longissimus Capitis inserts onto the Mastoid Process.

Unilaterally, the Longissimus laterally flexes the trunk.
Bilaterally, Longissimus extends the trunk.

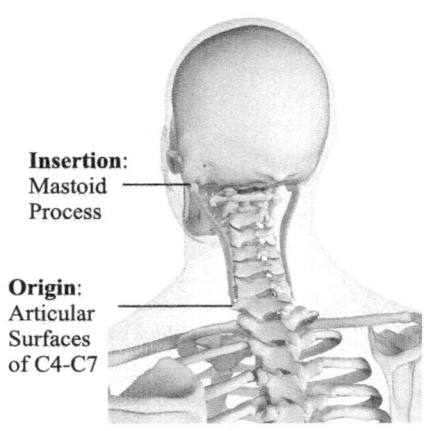

Insertion: Mastoid Process
Origin: Articular Surfaces of C4-C7

Longissimus Capitis

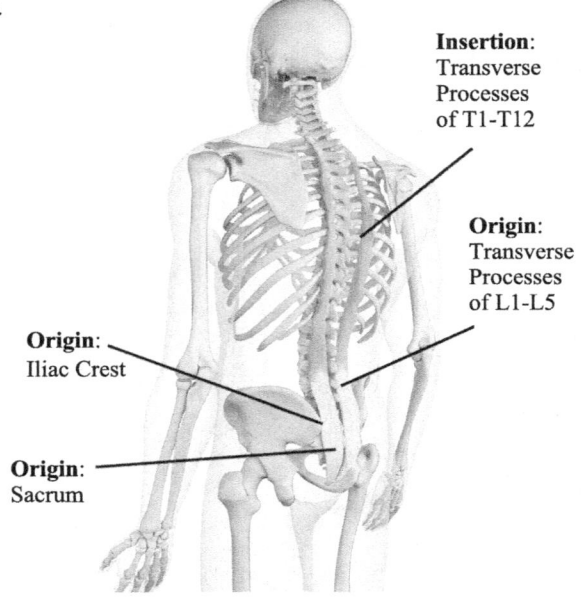

Insertion: Transverse Processes of C2-C6
Origin: Transverse Processes of T1-T5

Longissimus Cervicis

Insertion: Transverse Processes of T1-T12
Origin: Transverse Processes of L1-L5
Origin: Iliac Crest
Origin: Sacrum

Longissimus Thoracis

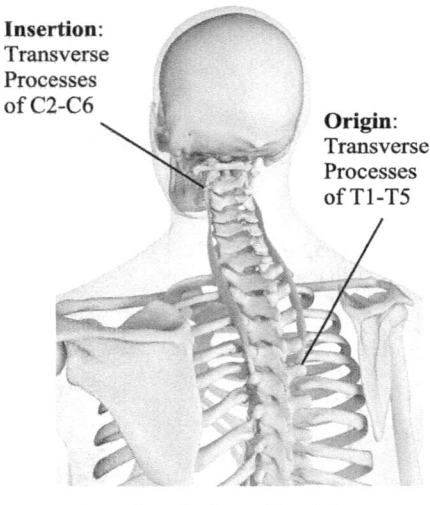

Trunk Lateral Flexion    Trunk Extension

Origin: Transverse and Spinous Processes of L1-L5, Iliac Crest, Sacrum, Transverse Processes of T1-T5, Articular Surfaces of C4-C7
Insertion: Transverse Processes of T1-T12, Transverse Processes of C2-C6, Mastoid Process
Action(s): Unilaterally: Lateral Flexion of Trunk; Bilaterally: Extension of Trunk

Innervation: Dorsal Primary Rami of T1-L5
Synergist: Spinalis
Antagonist: Rectus Abdominis

Multifidus

Multifidus is a muscle of the back, often grouped together with other multifidus muscles to create the Multifidi.

The Multifidi as a group originate on the Posterior Surface of the Sacrum, the Posterior Superior Iliac Spine(PSIS), Mamillary Processes of L1-L5, the Transverse Processes of T1-T12, and the Articular Processes of C4-C7. The Multifidi insert on the Transverse Processes of C2-L5, spanning essentially the entire vertebral column.

Unilaterally, the Multifidi will laterally flex the trunk, and rotate the trunk. Bilaterally, the Multifidi extend the trunk.

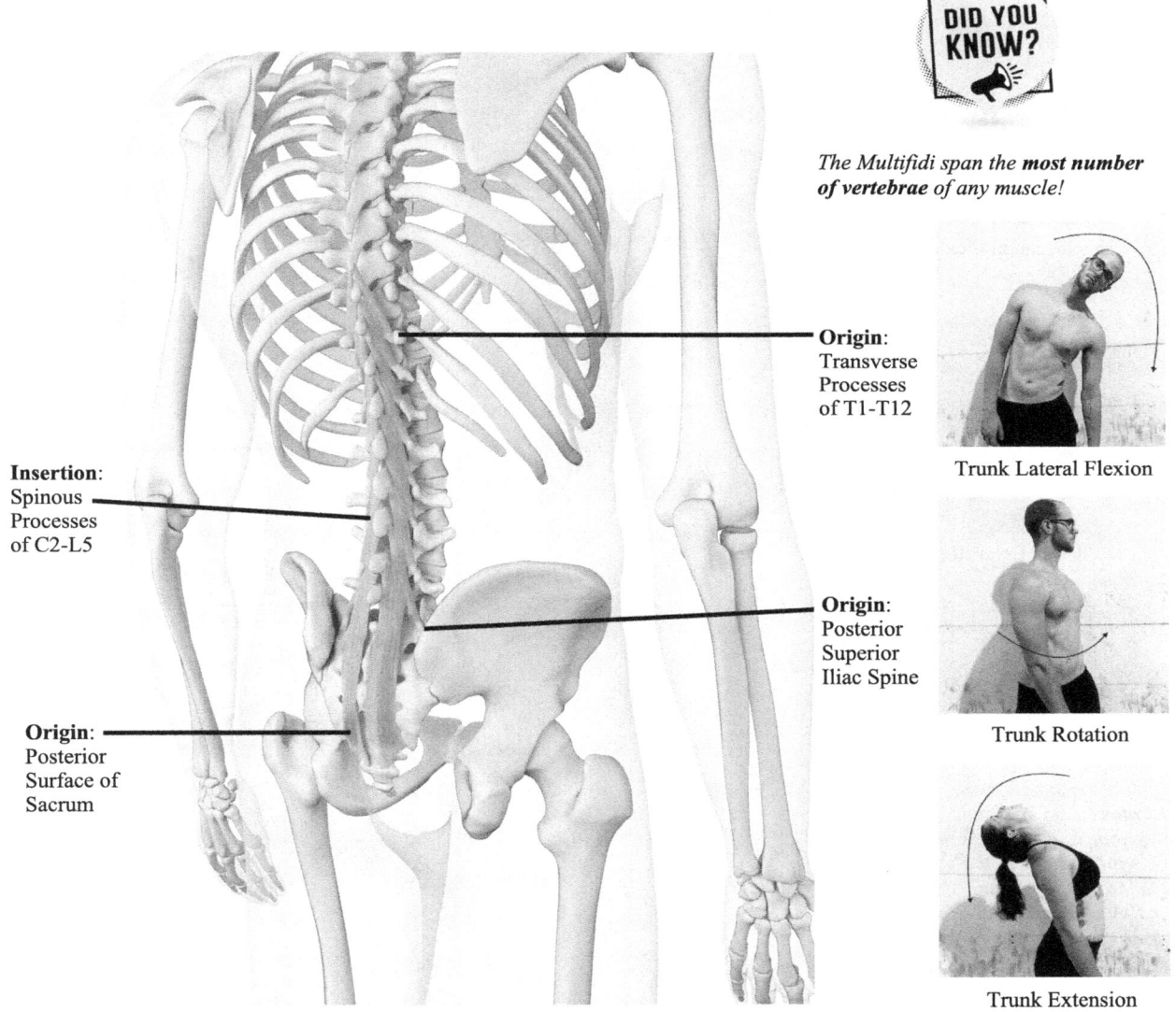

DID YOU KNOW?

*The Multifidi span the **most number of vertebrae** of any muscle!*

Origin: Transverse Processes of T1-T12

Insertion: Spinous Processes of C2-L5

Origin: Posterior Superior Iliac Spine

Origin: Posterior Surface of Sacrum

Trunk Lateral Flexion

Trunk Rotation

Trunk Extension

Origin: Posterior surface of Sacrum, Posterior Superior Iliac Spine, Mamillary Processes of L1-L5, Transverse Processes T1-T12, Articular Processes of C4-C7
Insertion: Spinous Processes of C2-L5
Action(s): Unilaterally: Lateral Flexion of Trunk, Rotation of Trunk; Bilaterally: Extension of Trunk
Innervation: Dorsal Rami of Spinal Nerves
Synergist: Longissimus, Spinalis
Antagonist: Rectus Abdominis

Quadratus Lumborum

Quadratus Lumborum is a muscle of the lower back, named after its shape(four sides), and its location(in the lumbar region).

Quadratus Lumborum originates on the Iliac Crest, and inserts onto the 12th Rib, and the Transverse Processes of L1-L4.

Quadratus Lumborum, unilaterally, will assist in lateral flexion of the trunk. Bilaterally, it will assist in extension of the trunk.

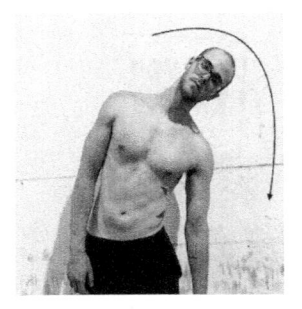

Trunk Lateral Flexion

Trunk Extension

DID YOU KNOW?

*If a person suffers from **Lordosis**(also known as Swayback), it may be caused by **hypertonicity** in the Quadratus Lumborum, pulling the pelvis **anteriorly**, thus increasing the curvature of the lumbar vertebrae!*

Insertion: 12th Rib

Origin: Iliac Crest

Insertion: Transverse Processes of L1-L4

Origin: Iliac Crest
Insertion: 12th Rib, Transverse Processes of L1-L4
Action(s): Unilaterally: Lateral Flexion of Trunk; Bilaterally: Extension of Trunk
Innervation: Ventral Primary Rami of T12-L3
Synergist: Longissimus, Spinalis
Antagonist: Rectus Abdominis

Rhomboids

The Rhomboids(Rhomboid Major and Rhomboid Minor) are two muscles located on the back. They are named after their shape(rhombus).

Rhomboid Major originates on the Spinous Processes of T3-T5. Rhomboid Minor originates on the Spinous Processes of C7-T2. Together, the Rhomboids insert onto the Medial/Vertebral Border of the Scapula.

When the Rhomboids contract, they pull the Scapula towards the vertebrae. This action is known as retraction/adduction. Two primary antagonists to the Rhomboids are Serratus Anterior and Pectoralis Minor. Both of these muscles protract/abduct the Scapula.

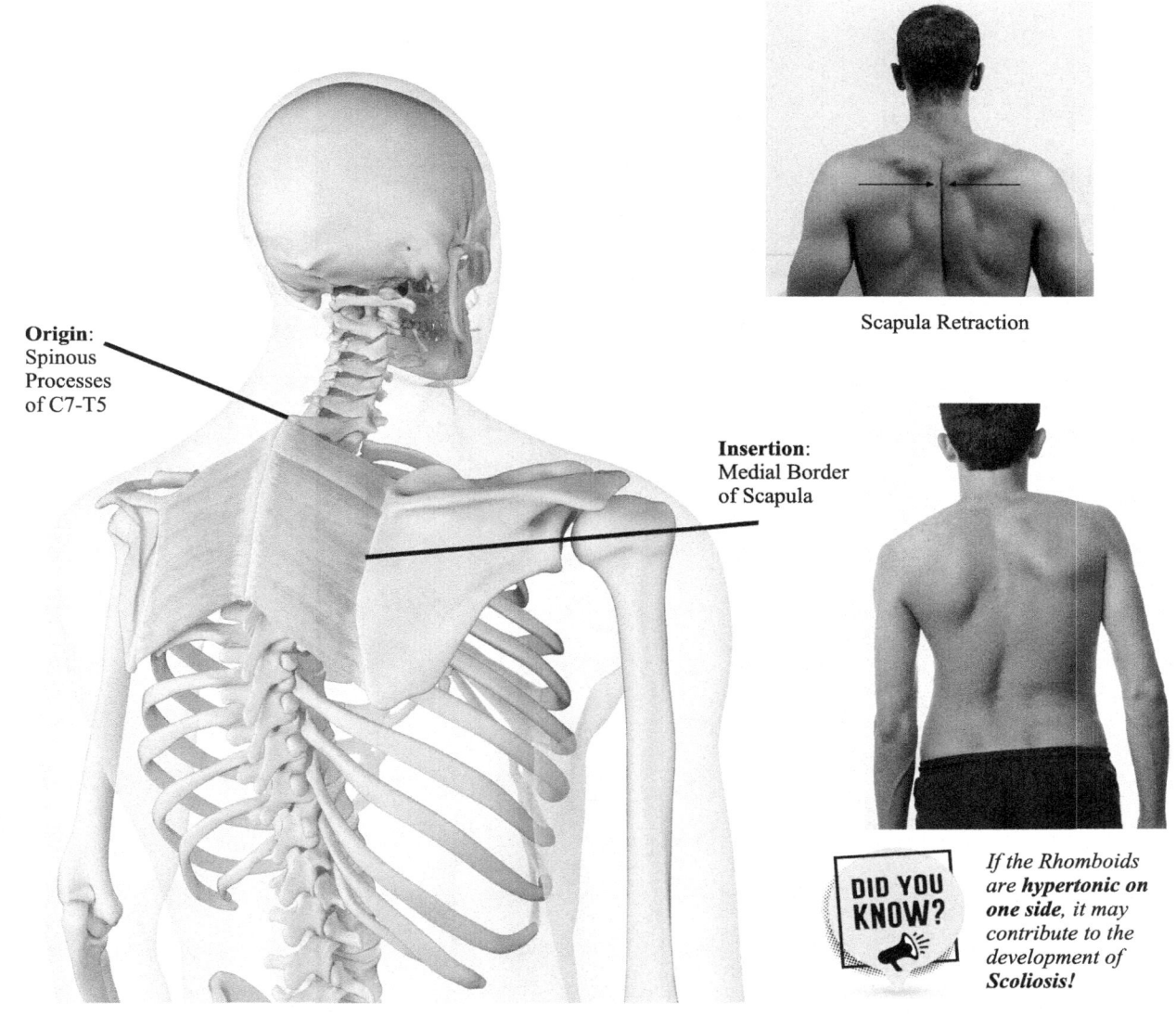

Origin: Spinous Processes of C7-T5

Insertion: Medial Border of Scapula

Scapula Retraction

*If the Rhomboids are **hypertonic on one side**, it may contribute to the development of **Scoliosis!***

Origin: Rhomboid Minor: Spinous processes of C7-T2; Rhomboid Major: Spinous processes of T3-T5
Insertion: Medial/vertebral border of scapula
Action(s): Retraction/adduction of scapula
Innervation: Dorsal Scapular Nerve C5
Synergist: Middle Trapezius
Antagonist: Serratus Anterior, Pectoralis Minor

Rotatores

The Rotatores are a group of muscles that span the entire vertebral column. They are named after their action.

The Rotatores originate on the Transverse Processes of C1-L5, and insert onto the Spinous Processes of the vertebrae just superior. An example, the Rotator muscle that originates on the Transverse Process of C2 would insert onto the Spinous Process of C1.

Unilaterally, the Rotatores will rotate the trunk to the opposite side. Bilaterally, the Rotatores assist in extension of the trunk.

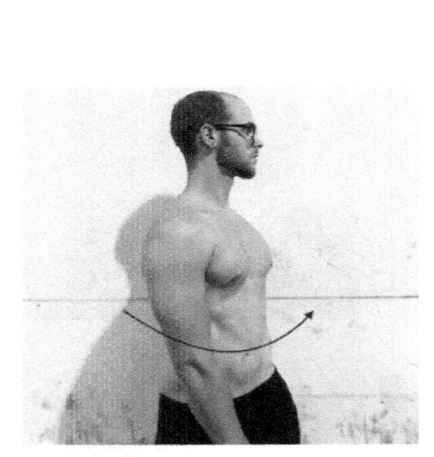

Trunk Rotation

Trunk Extension

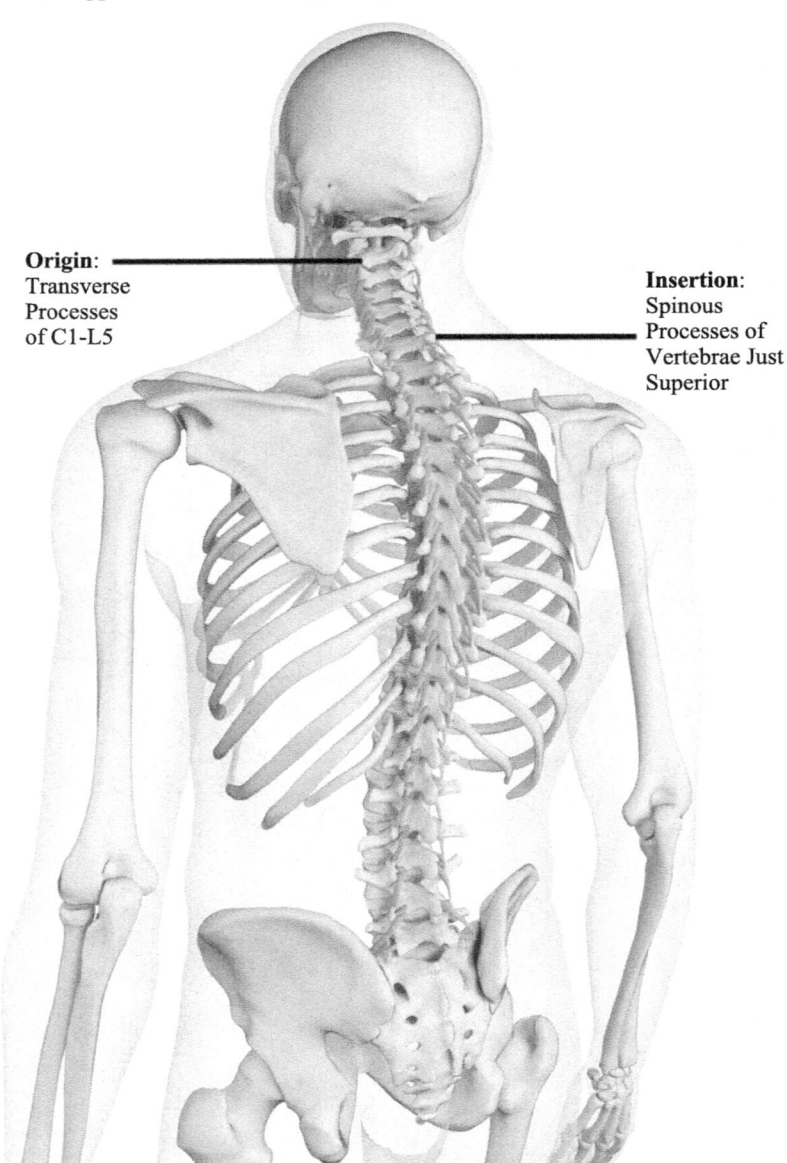

Origin: Transverse Processes of C1-L5

Insertion: Spinous Processes of Vertebrae Just Superior

Origin: Transverse Processes of C1-L5
Insertion: Spinous Processes of Vertebrae just superior
Action(s): Unilaterally: Rotate Trunk to opposite side; Bilaterally: Extension of Trunk

Innervation: Dorsal Primary Rami of Spinal Nerves C1-T12
Synergist: Spinalis, Longissimus
Antagonist: Rectus Abdominis

Spinalis

Spinalis is a group of two muscles, both located on the back. Each muscle is named after its location: Spinalis Thoracis(in the Thoracic region), Spinalis Cervicis(in the Cervical region).

Spinalis Thoracis originates on the Spinous Processes of T11-L2. There may be slight variation of the origin, however, ranging from T10-L3. Spinalis Cervicis originates on the Nuchal Ligament, and Spinous Process of C7. Spinalis Thoracis inserts onto the Spinous Processes of T3-T8. Spinalis Cervicis inserts onto the Spinous Process of C2.

Unilaterally, the Spinalis muscles laterally flex and rotate the trunk to the same side. Bilaterally, they work with other muscles such as Longissimus to extend the trunk.

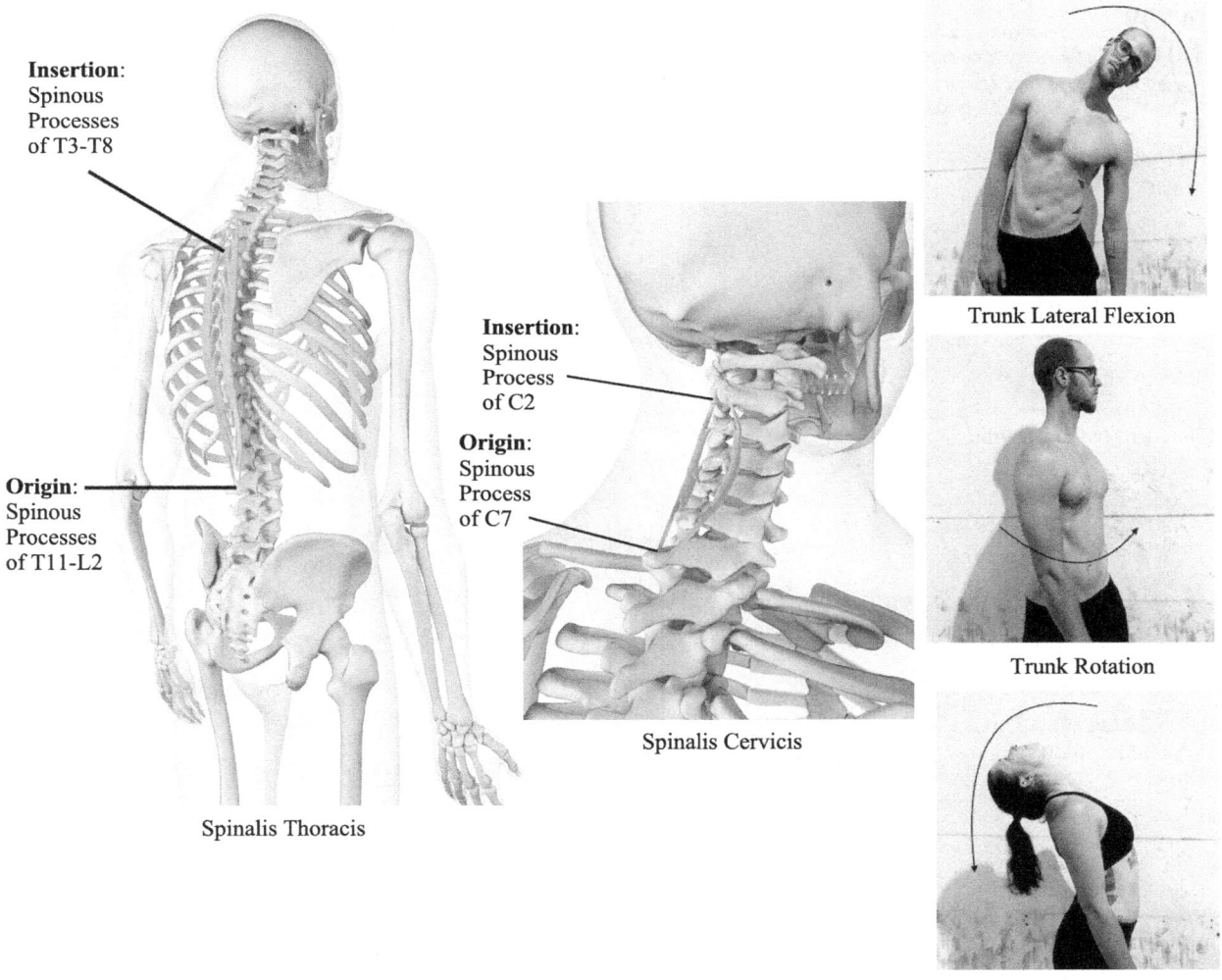

Insertion: Spinous Processes of T3-T8

Origin: Spinous Processes of T11-L2

Spinalis Thoracis

Insertion: Spinous Process of C2

Origin: Spinous Process of C7

Spinalis Cervicis

Trunk Lateral Flexion

Trunk Rotation

Trunk Extension

Origin: Spinalis Thoracis: Spinous Processes of T11-L2; Spinalis Cervicis: Nuchal Ligament, Spinous Process of C7
Insertion: Spinalis Thoracis: Spinous Processes of T3-T8; Spinalis Cervicis: Spinous Process of C2
Action(s): Unilaterally: Flex and Rotate Spine to the same side; Bilaterally: Extend the Trunk

Innervation: Dorsal Rami of Cervical and Thoracic Spinal Nerves
Synergist: Longissimus
Antagonist: Rectus Abdominis

Subscapularis

Subscapularis is a muscle of the back, named after it's location(under the scapula).

Subscapularis originates on the Subscapular Fossa, located on the anterior surface of the scapula. Subscapularis inserts onto the Lesser Tubercle(sometimes also called the Lesser Tuberosity of the Humerus). It is part of the rotator cuff muscle group, along with Infraspinatus, Teres Minor, and Supraspinatus.

Subscapularis is a synergist to Latissimus Dorsi, performing the same actions on the shoulder. These actions are adduction, extension, and medial rotation.

DID YOU KNOW? *If a person is affected by* **Adhesive Capsulitis** *(Frozen Shoulder), there may be* **hypertonicity** *in the Subscapularis, reducing range-of-motion during actions such as shoulder flexion!*

Origin: Subscapular Fossa

Insertion: Lesser Tubercle

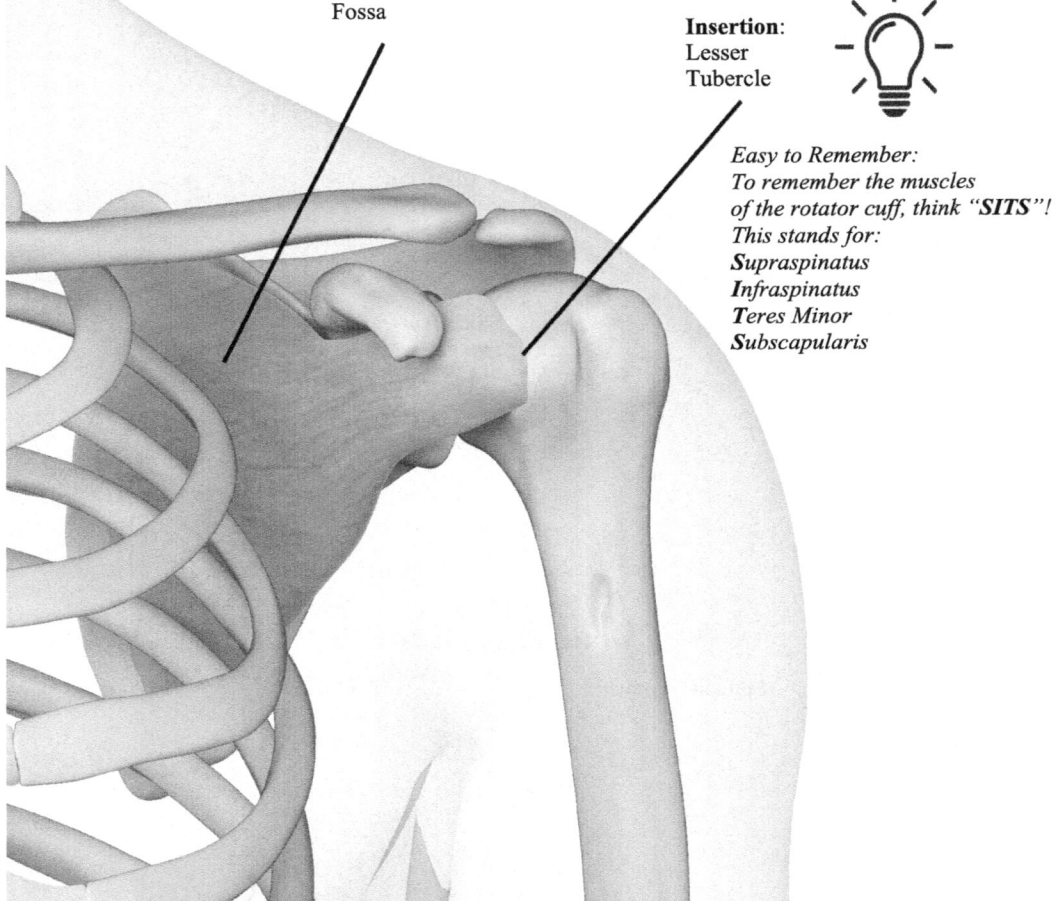

Easy to Remember:
To remember the muscles of the rotator cuff, think **"SITS"**!
This stands for:
Supraspinatus
Infraspinatus
Teres Minor
Subscapularis

Shoulder Medial Rotation

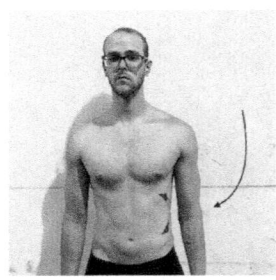

Shoulder Adduction

Shoulder Extension

Origin: Subscapular Fossa
Insertion: Lesser Tubercle of Humerus
Action(s): Medial Rotation, Adduction, Extension of the Shoulder

Innervation: Upper and Lower Subscapular Nerves
Synergist: Latissimus Dorsi, Teres Major
Antagonist: Pectoralis Major, Coracobrachialis

Supraspinatus

Supraspinatus is a muscle of the back, named after it's location(superior to the Spine of the Scapula).

Supraspinatus originates on the Supraspinous Fossa, just above the Spine of the Scapula. Supraspinatus inserts onto the Greater Tubercle(sometimes called the Greater Tuberosity of the Humerus). It is part of the rotator cuff muscle group, along with Infraspinatus, Teres Minor, and Subscapularis.

Supraspinatus has one primary action: abduction of the shoulder. It is a synergist to the Deltoid in performing this action. Supraspinatus also helps hold the humerus in place against the Glenoid Fossa, providing stability to the shoulder joint.

Most commonly, if a person suffers from a torn rotator cuff, it likely involves the Supraspinatus more than other muscles. A torn rotator cuff might require surgery to repair, depending on the severity.

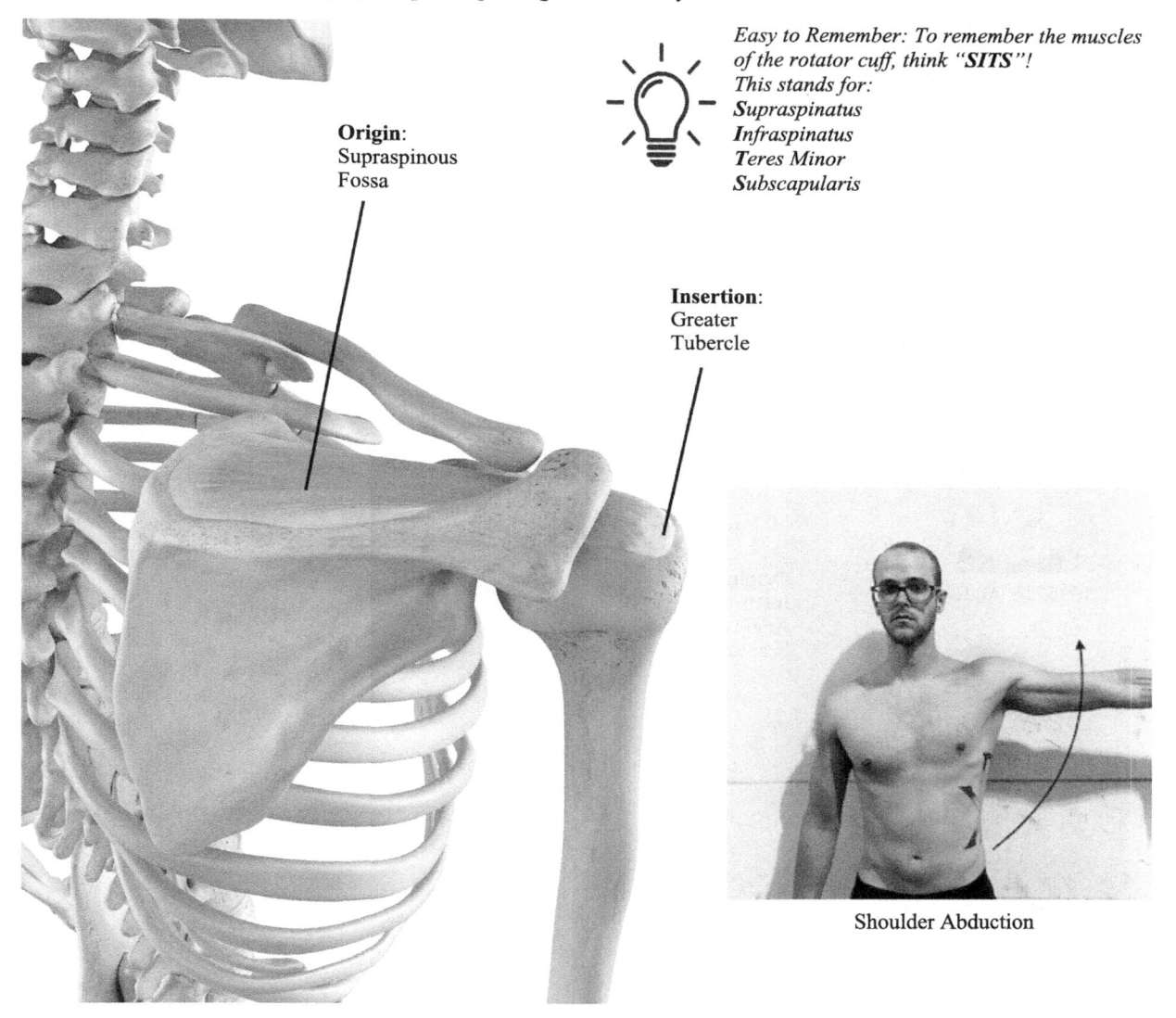

Origin: Supraspinous Fossa

Insertion: Greater Tubercle

*Easy to Remember: To remember the muscles of the rotator cuff, think "**SITS**"!*
This stands for:
Supraspinatus
Infraspinatus
Teres Minor
Subscapularis

Shoulder Abduction

Origin: Supraspinous Fossa
Insertion: Greater Tubercle of Humerus
Action(s): Abduction of Shoulder

Innervation: Suprascapular Nerve
Synergist: Deltoid
Antagonist: Latissimus Dorsi, Teres Major

Teres Major

Teres Major is a muscle of the back. The name "Teres" means "round and long". Teres Major has a long, round shape.

Teres Major originates on the Inferior Angle of the Scapula, and inserts onto the Medial Lip of the Intertubercular Groove. It shares its insertion with Latissimus Dorsi.

Teres Major and Latissimus Dorsi both perform the same actions: medial rotation, extension, and adduction of the shoulder.

Shoulder Medial Rotation

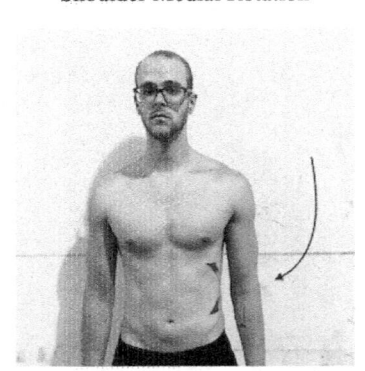

Shoulder Adduction

Shoulder Extension

Insertion: Medial Lip of Intertubercular Groove

Origin: Inferior Angle of Scapula

Origin: Inferior Angle of Scapula
Insertion: Medial Lip of Intertubercular Groove
Action(s): Medial Rotation, Adduction, Extension of Shoulder

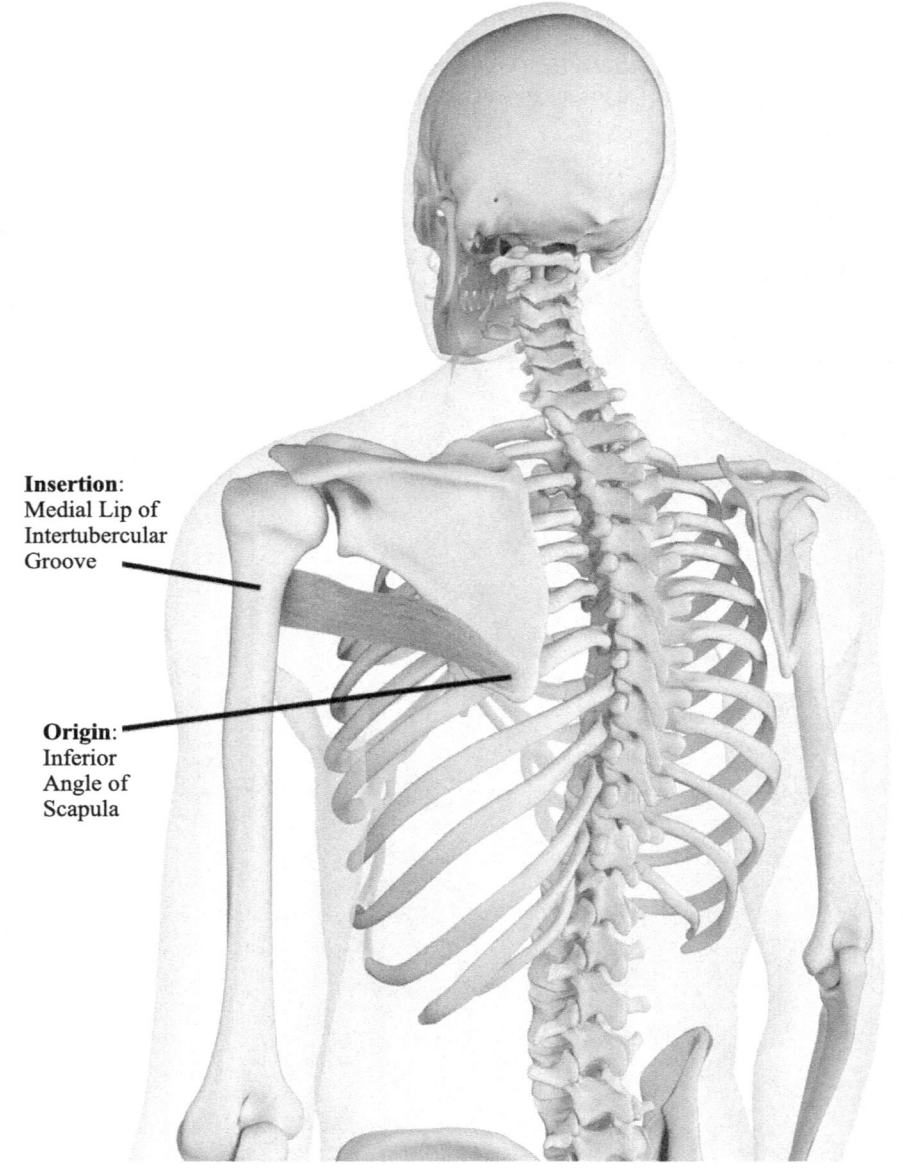

Innervation: Lower Subscapular Nerve
Synergist: Latissimus Dorsi, Subscapularis
Antagonist: Pectoralis Major, Coracobrachialis

Teres Minor

Teres Minor is a muscle of the back. The word "Teres" means "round and long". Teres Minor has a long, round shape.

Teres Minor originates on the Lateral/Axillary Border of the Scapula. The term "Axillary" refers to the armpit, which Teres Minor is located next to. Teres Minor inserts onto the Greater Tubercle(sometimes known as the Greater Tuberosity) of the humerus. Teres Minor is a member of the rotator cuff muscle group, along with Infraspinatus, Subscapularis, and Supraspinatus.

Teres Minor and Infraspinatus are located immediately next to one another, and sometimes may even fuse together. These muscles perform the same actions: lateral rotation, extension, and horizontal abduction of the shoulder.

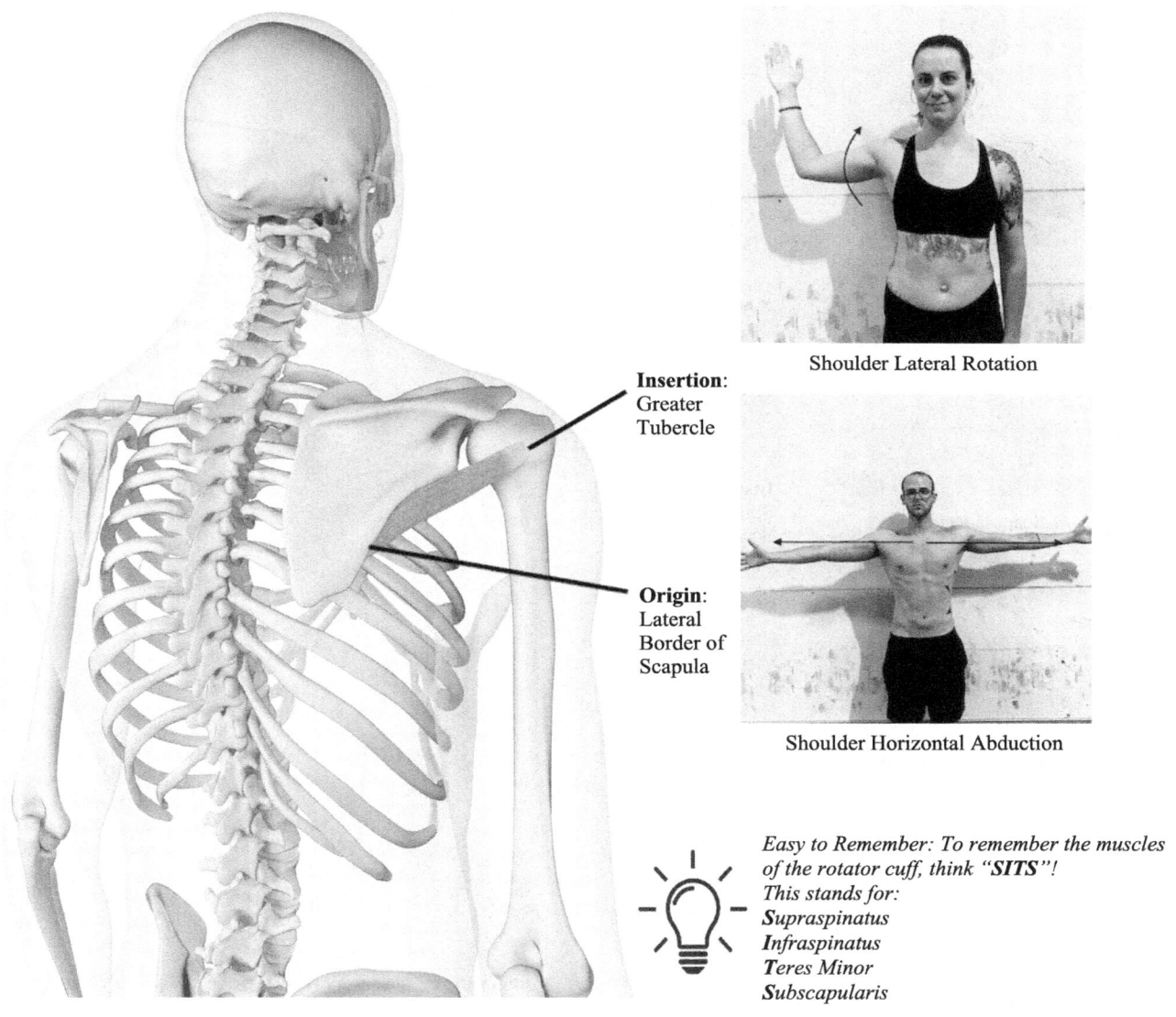

Insertion: Greater Tubercle

Origin: Lateral Border of Scapula

Shoulder Lateral Rotation

Shoulder Horizontal Abduction

Easy to Remember: To remember the muscles of the rotator cuff, think "SITS"! This stands for:
Supraspinatus
Infraspinatus
Teres Minor
Subscapularis

Origin: Lateral/Axillary Border of Scapula
Insertion: Greater Tubercle of Humerus
Action(s): Lateral Rotation, Horizontal Abduction of Shoulder

Innervation: Axillary Nerve
Synergist: Infraspinatus
Antagonist: Pectoralis Major

Trapezius

Trapezius is a large muscle of the back, named after its shape (trapezoid). Trapezius is the most superficial muscle of the back.

Trapezius originates on the External Occipital Protuberance of the occipital bone, and the Spinous Processes of T1-T12. Trapezius inserts on the Acromion Process, the Spine of the Scapula, and the Lateral 1/3 of the Clavicle.

The Trapezius can be divided into three sections: Upper Trapezius, Middle Trapezius, and Lower Trapezius. When contracting, Upper Trapezius assists in elevation of the scapula. When contracting, Middle Trapezius assists in retraction/adduction of the scapula. When contracting, Lower Trapezius depresses the scapula.

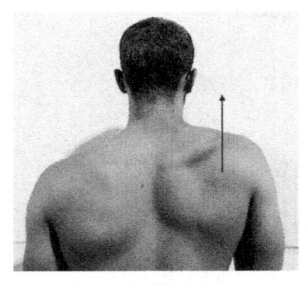

Scapula Elevation

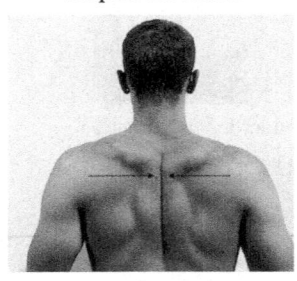

Scapula Retraction

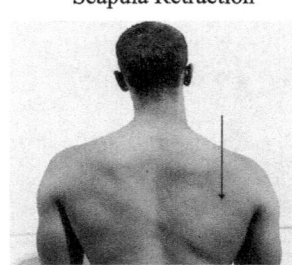

Scapula Depression

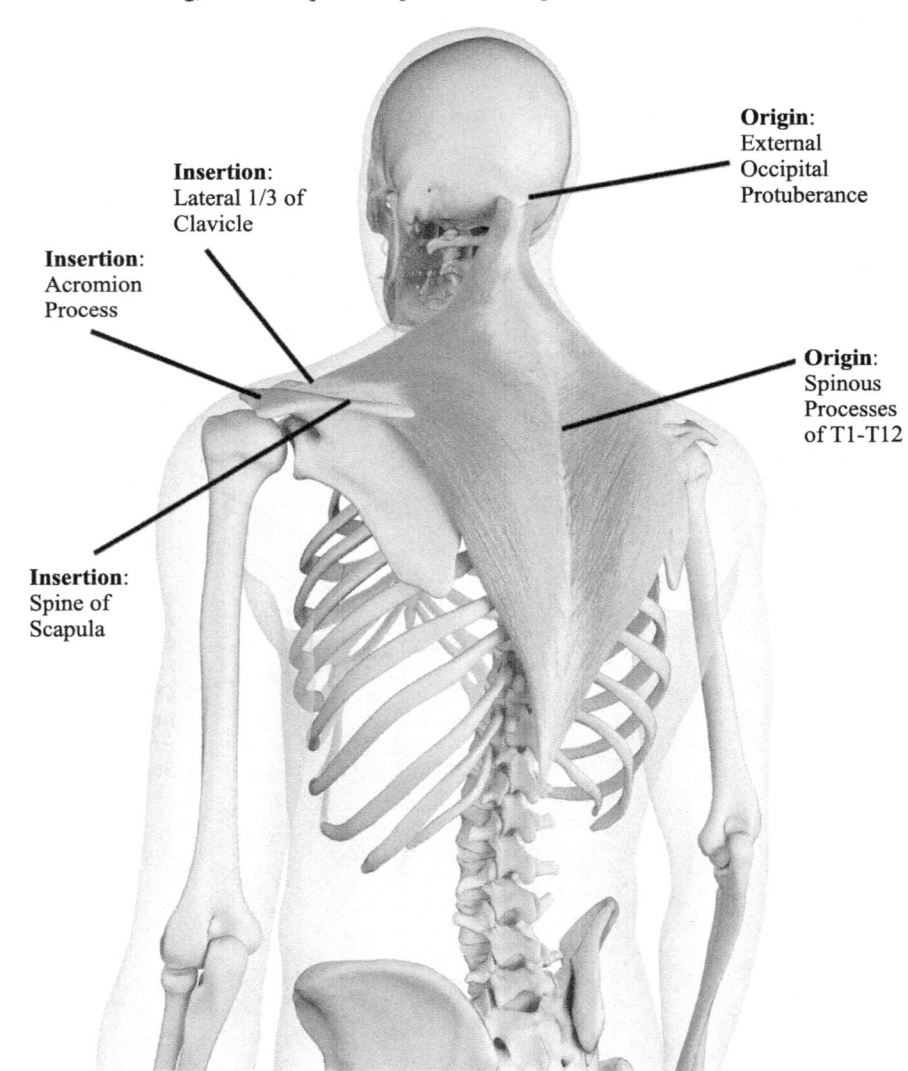

Origin: External Occipital Protuberance

Origin: Spinous Processes of T1-T12

Insertion: Lateral 1/3 of Clavicle

Insertion: Acromion Process

Insertion: Spine of Scapula

Origin: External Occipital Protuberance, Spinous Processes of T1-T12
Insertion: Lateral 1/3 of Clavicle, Acromion Process, Spine of Scapula
Action(s): Elevation, Retraction/Adduction, Depression of Scapula

Innervation: Accessory Nerve, Cervical Nerves C3 and C4
Synergist: Levator Scapulae(elevation), Rhomboids(retraction), Serratus Anterior(depression)
Antagonist: Serratus Anterior(elevation), Pectoralis Minor(retraction), Levator Scapulae(depression)

Kinesiology 251

Muscles of the Chest

Muscles to Know:

Pectoralis Major
Pectoralis Minor
Serratus Anterior

Terms to Know:

Pector/o: Chest
Serratus: Finely Notched Edge

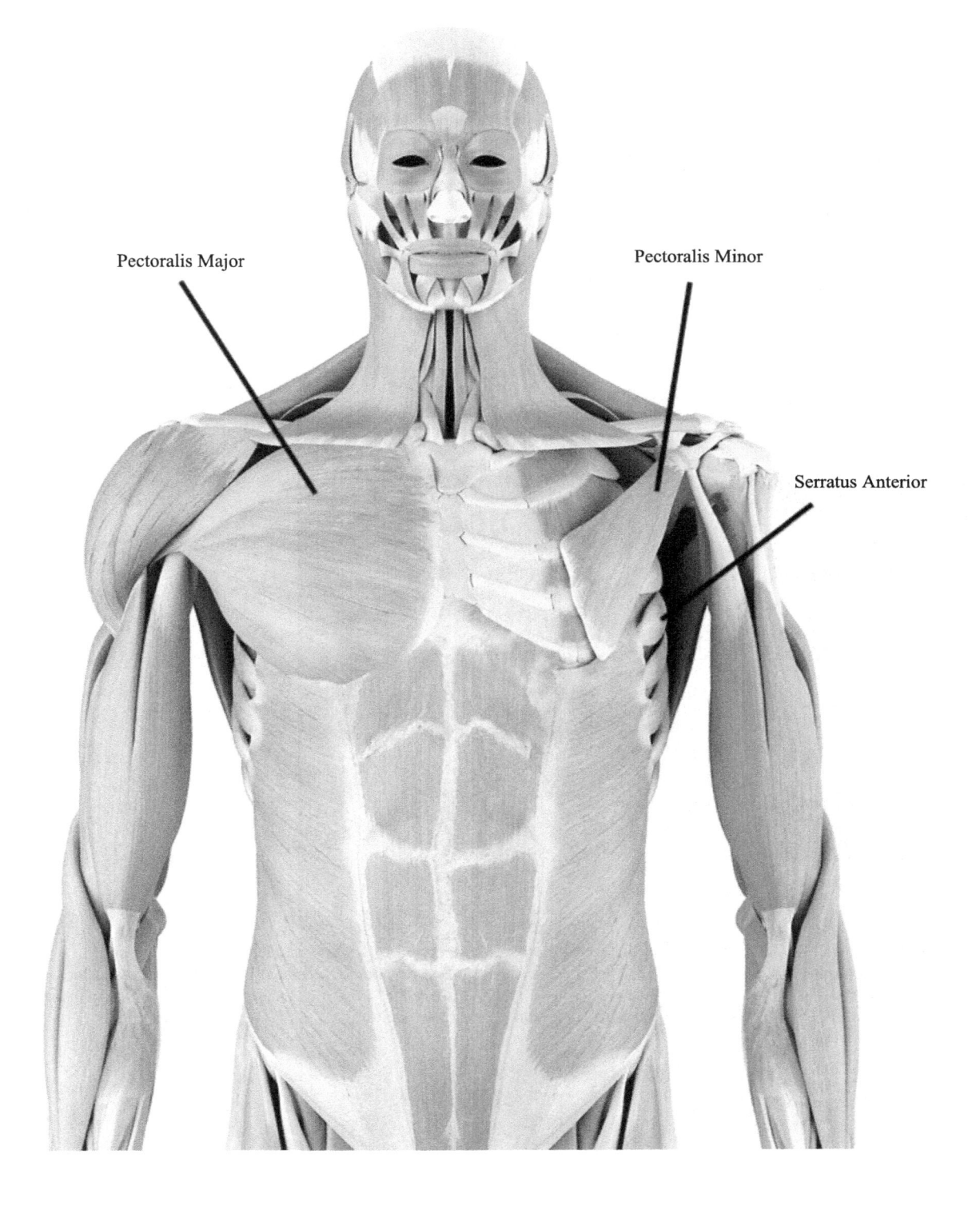

Pectoralis Major

Pectoralis Minor

Serratus Anterior

Pectoralis Major

Pectoralis Major is a large muscle of the chest. The term "pector/o" means "breast" or "chest".

Pectoralis Major originates on the Medial Half of the Clavicle, the Anterior Surface of the Sternum, and the Costal Cartilage of Ribs 1-6. Pectoralis Major inserts onto the Lateral Lip of the Intertubercular Groove.

When contracting, the Pectoralis Major has multiple actions: flexion, medial rotation, and horizontal adduction of the shoulder. Pectoralis Major also performs extension of the shoulder when the shoulder is already flexed, making it an antagonist to itself.

Shoulder Flexion

Shoulder Medial Rotation

Shoulder Horizontal Adduction

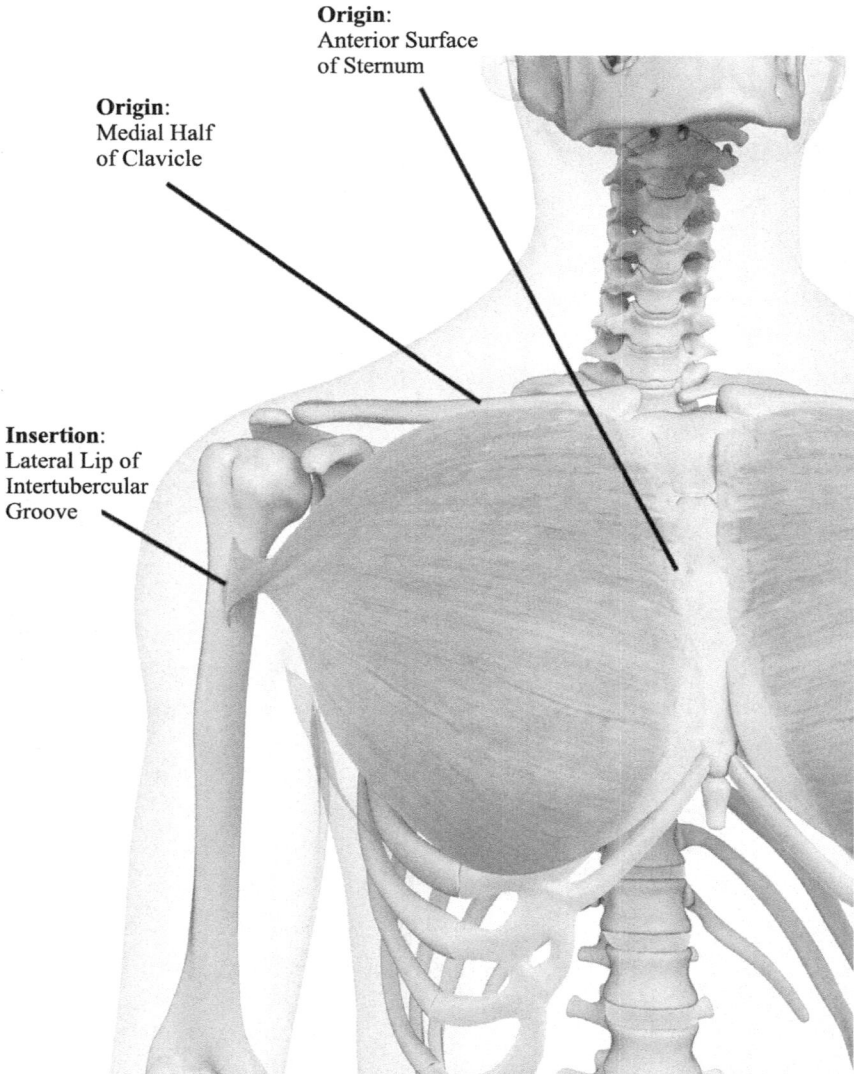

Origin: Anterior Surface of Sternum
Origin: Medial Half of Clavicle
Insertion: Lateral Lip of Intertubercular Groove

Origin: Medial Half of Clavicle, Anterior Surface of Sternum, Costal Cartilage 1-6
Insertion: Lateral Lip of Intertubercular Groove
Action(s): Flexion, Medial Rotation, Horizontal Adduction, Extension of Shoulder
Innervation: Lateral and Medial Pectoral Nerves
Synergist: Coracobrachialis, Biceps Brachii, Anterior Deltoid
Antagonist: Latissimus Dorsi, Teres Major, Subscapularis, Posterior Deltoid

Pectoralis Minor

Pectoralis Minor is a muscle of the chest, lying deep to the Pectoralis Major.

Pectoralis Minor originates on the Anterior Surface of Ribs 3-5. Pectoralis Minor inserts onto the Coracoid Process.

When Pectoralis Minor contracts, it protracts/abducts the scapula. Along with Serratus Anterior, it is an antagonist to the Rhomboids.

Pectoralis Minor is often associated with Thoracic Outlet Syndrome. When hypertonic, Pectoralis Minor may compress the Brachial plexus, Subclavian artery, and Subclavian nerve, which may cause a lack of sensation in the upper limb, or restrict blood supply.

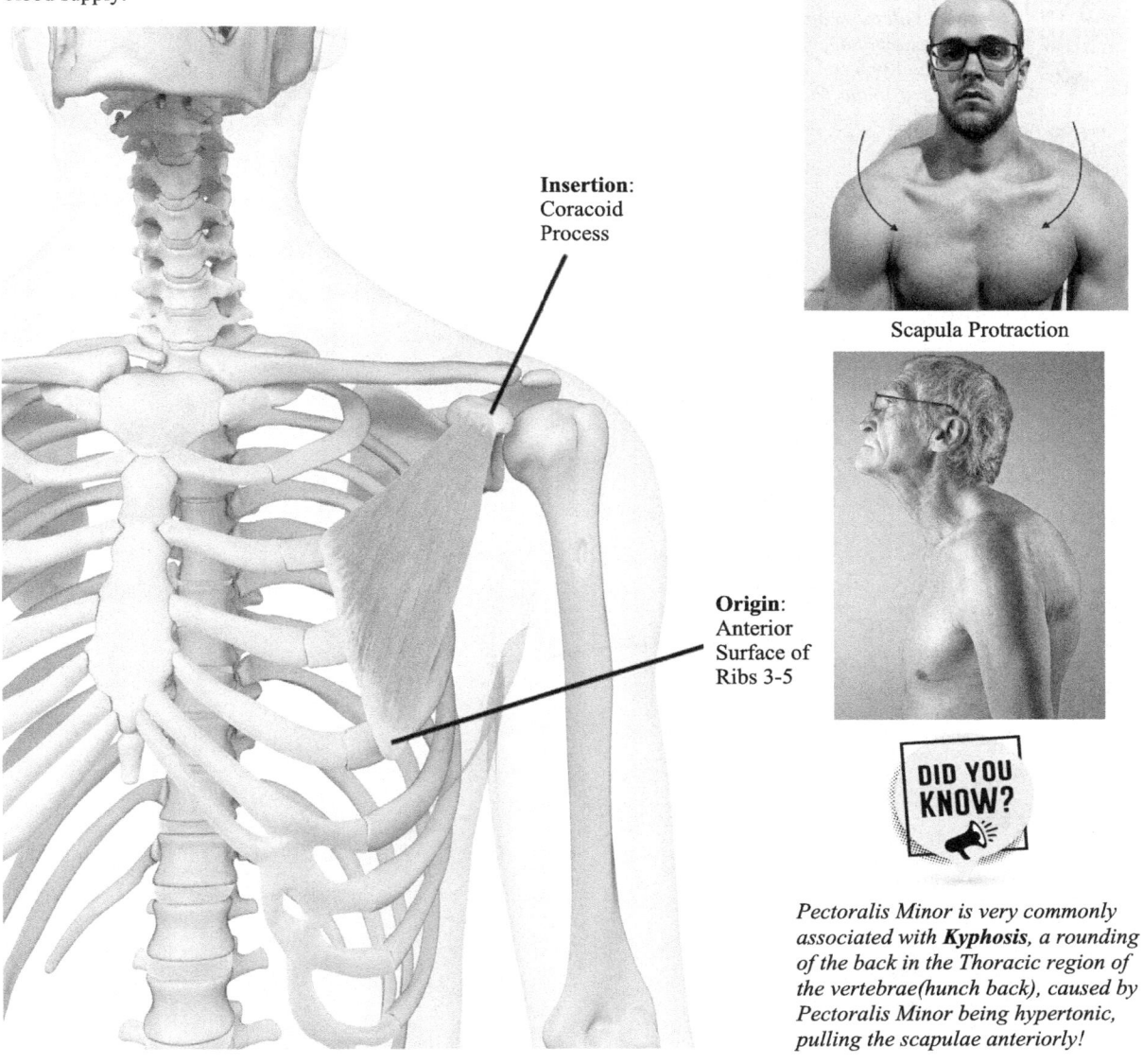

Insertion: Coracoid Process

Origin: Anterior Surface of Ribs 3-5

Scapula Protraction

DID YOU KNOW?

*Pectoralis Minor is very commonly associated with **Kyphosis**, a rounding of the back in the Thoracic region of the vertebrae(hunch back), caused by Pectoralis Minor being hypertonic, pulling the scapulae anteriorly!*

Origin: Anterior Surface of Ribs 3-5
Insertion: Coracoid Process of Scapula
Action(s): Protraction/Abduction of Scapula

Innervation: Medial Pectoral Nerve
Synergist: Serratus Anterior
Antagonist: Rhomboids

Serratus Anterior

Serratus Anterior is a muscle of the chest, named after its appearance. "Serratus" means "finely notched edge", such as a serrated knife.

Serratus Anterior originates on the Anterior Surface of Ribs 1-8. Serratus Anterior inserts onto the Anterior Surface of the Medial/Vertebral Border of the Scapula.

When Serratus Anterior contracts, it moves the scapula anteriorly, producing protraction/abduction. Serratus Anterior also may assist in depression of the scapula.

DID YOU KNOW? *If Serratus Anterior is hypertonic, it may pull the scapulae too far into protraction/abduction, which would produce **Kyphosis**, a rounding of the vertebrae in the Thoracic region!*

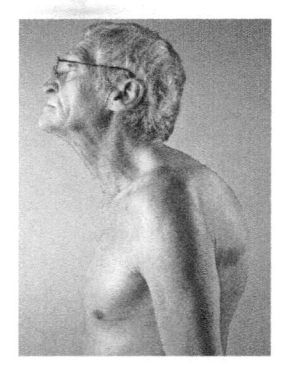

Scapula Protraction

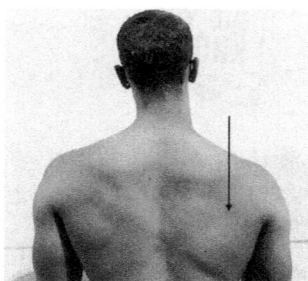

Scapula Depression

Insertion: Medial Border of Scapula

Origin: Anterior Surface of Ribs 1-8

Origin: Anterior Surface of Ribs 1-8
Insertion: Medial/Vertebral Border of Scapula
Action(s): Protraction/Abduction, Depression of Scapula

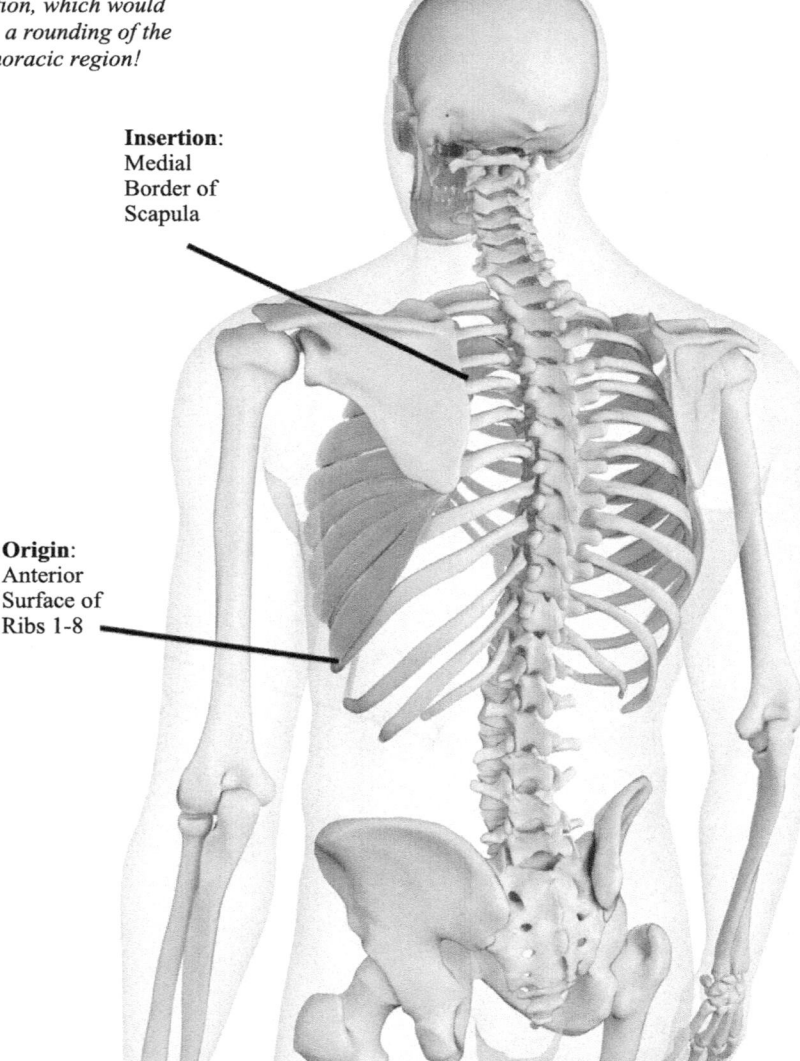

Innervation: Long Thoracic Nerve
Synergist: Pectoralis Minor, Lower Trapezius
Antagonist: Rhomboids, Levator Scapulae

Muscles of the Abdomen

Muscles to Know:

Diaphragm
Rectus Abdominis

Terms to Know:

Diaphragma: Barrier
Rectus: Straight

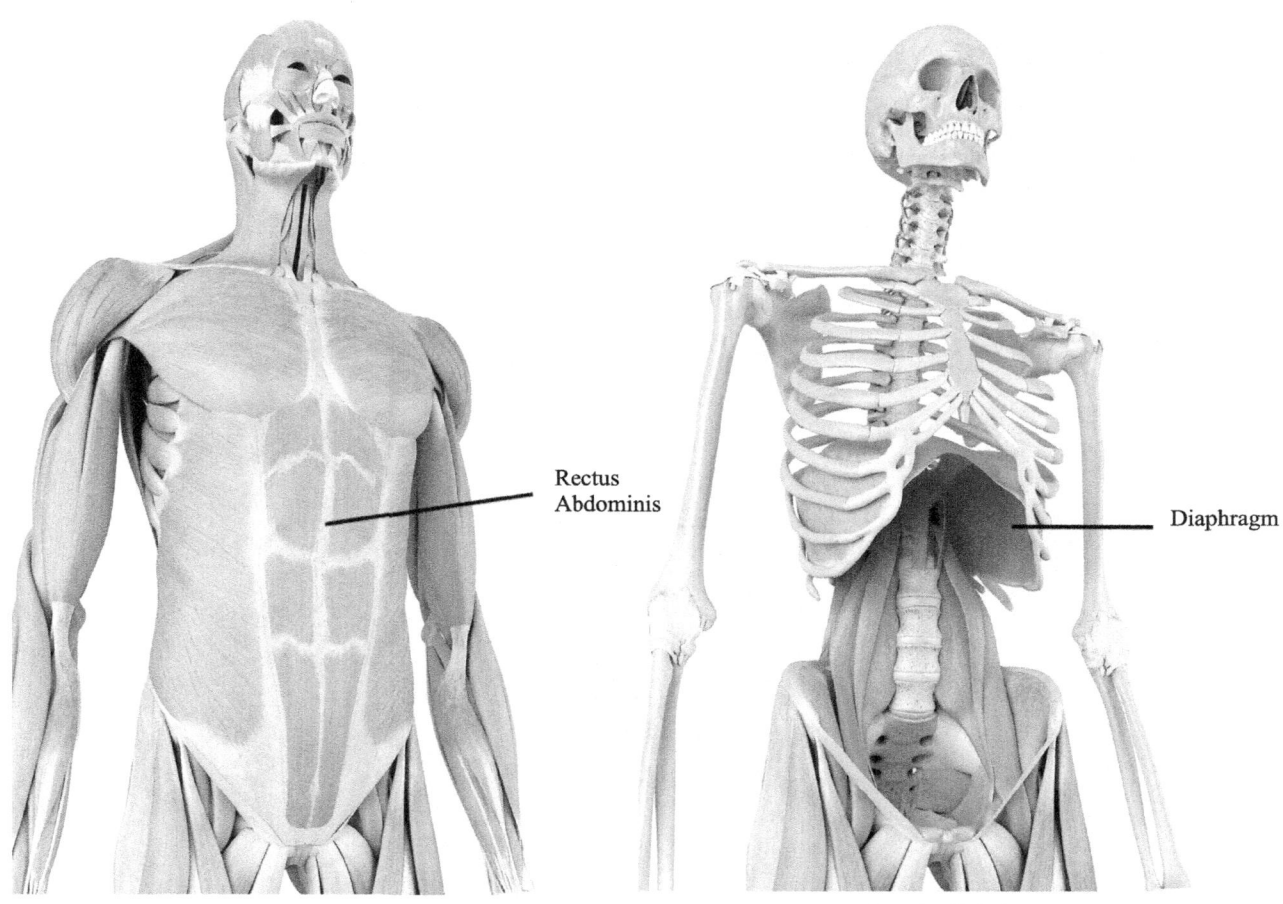

— Rectus Abdominis

— Diaphragm

Anterior

Anterior (Deep)

Diaphragm

The Diaphragm is a muscle of the abdomen, named after one of its actions("diaphragma" means "barrier" in Greek).

The Diaphragm is located between the abdomen and thorax, separating the two body cavities. The Diaphragm originates on the sternum, xiphoid process, inferior six ribs, and L1-L3. The Diaphragm inserts onto a broad sheet of tendon known as the Central Tendon.

The Diaphragm is responsible for inhalation. When the Diaphragm contracts, it moves inferiorly, which creates a vacuum in the thorax, allowing air to move into the lungs. When the Diaphragm relaxes, the muscle moves superiorly into the chest, pushing air out of the lungs. The Central Tendon anchors the Diaphragm in place while breathing.

Several structures actually pass through the Diaphragm, including the esophagus, inferior vena cava, thoracic duct, and aorta. Because of these openings, the Diaphragm is prone to herniation. For example, a hiatal hernia is when part of the stomach ascends upwards through the opening of the Diaphragm the esophagus passes through.

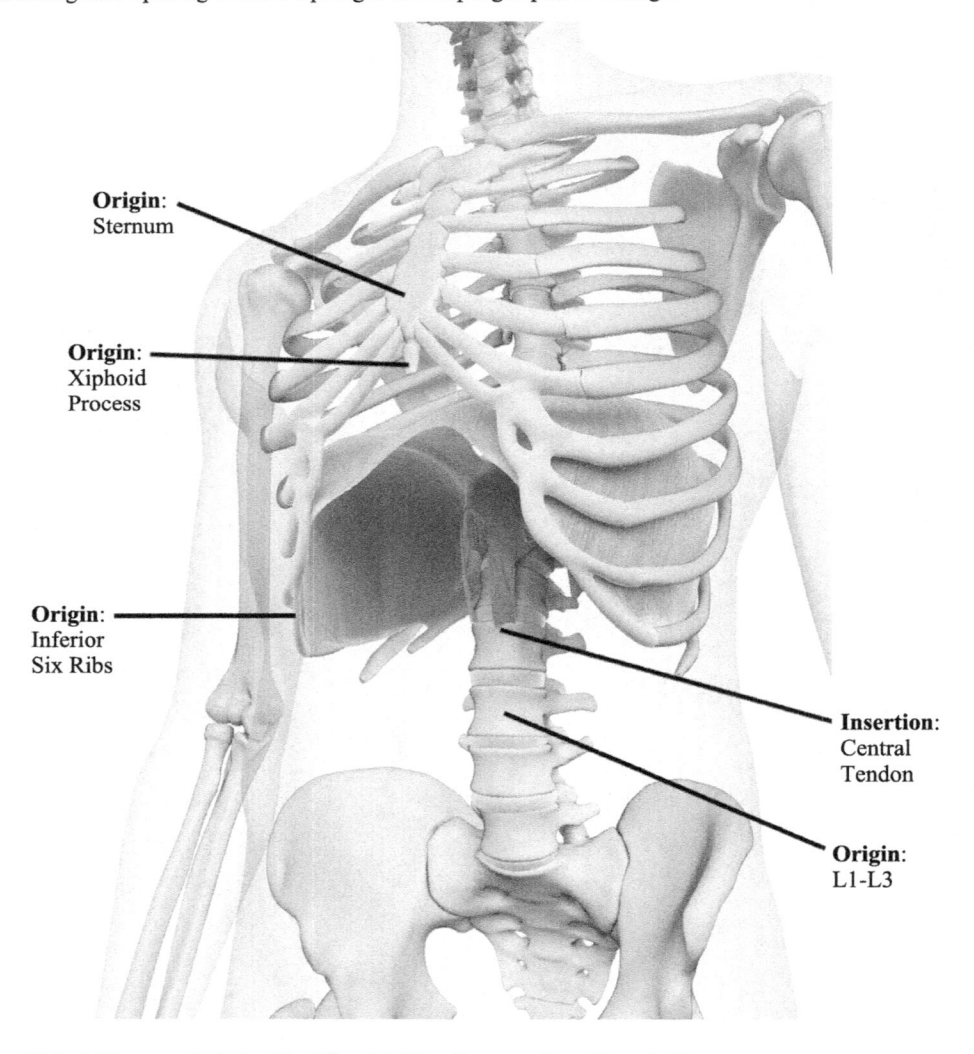

Origin: Sternum, Xiphoid Process, Inferior Six Ribs, L1-L3
Insertion: Central Tendon
Action(s): Inhalation
Innervation: Phrenic Nerve
Synergist: External Intercostals
Antagonist: Internal Intercostals

Rectus Abdominis

Rectus Abdominis is a muscle of the abdomen. Rectus Abdominis is the most superficial muscle of the abdomen.

Rectus Abdominis originates on the Pubic Symphysis and the Pubic Crest. Rectus Abdominis inserts onto the Xiphoid Process of the Sternum and the Costal Cartilage of Ribs 5-7.

When Rectus Abdominis contracts, is allows the trunk to flex.

Insertion: Xiphoid Process

Insertion: Costal Cartilage of Ribs 5-7

Trunk Flexion

DID YOU KNOW?

*If Rectus Abdominis is **too weak**, it may lead to a condition known as **Lordosis**, or Swayback. This causes an increased **anterior tilt** to the pelvis and Lumbar vertebrae. Strengthening of the Rectus Abdominis may help return the pelvis and vertebrae to their natural state!*

Origin: Pubic Crest

Origin: Pubic Symphysis

Origin: Pubic Symphysis, Pubic Crest
Insertion: Xiphoid Process, Costal Cartilage of Ribs 5-7
Action(s): Flexion of Trunk

Innervation: Anterior Primary Rami T7-T12
Synergist: External Obliques, Internal Obliques
Antagonist: Spinalis, Longissimus

Muscles of the Arm

Muscles to Know:

Biceps Brachii
Brachialis
Coracobrachialis
Deltoid
Triceps Brachii

Terms to Know:

Bi-: Two
-cep: Head
Brachi/o: Arm
Corac/o: Crow-like
Tri-: Three

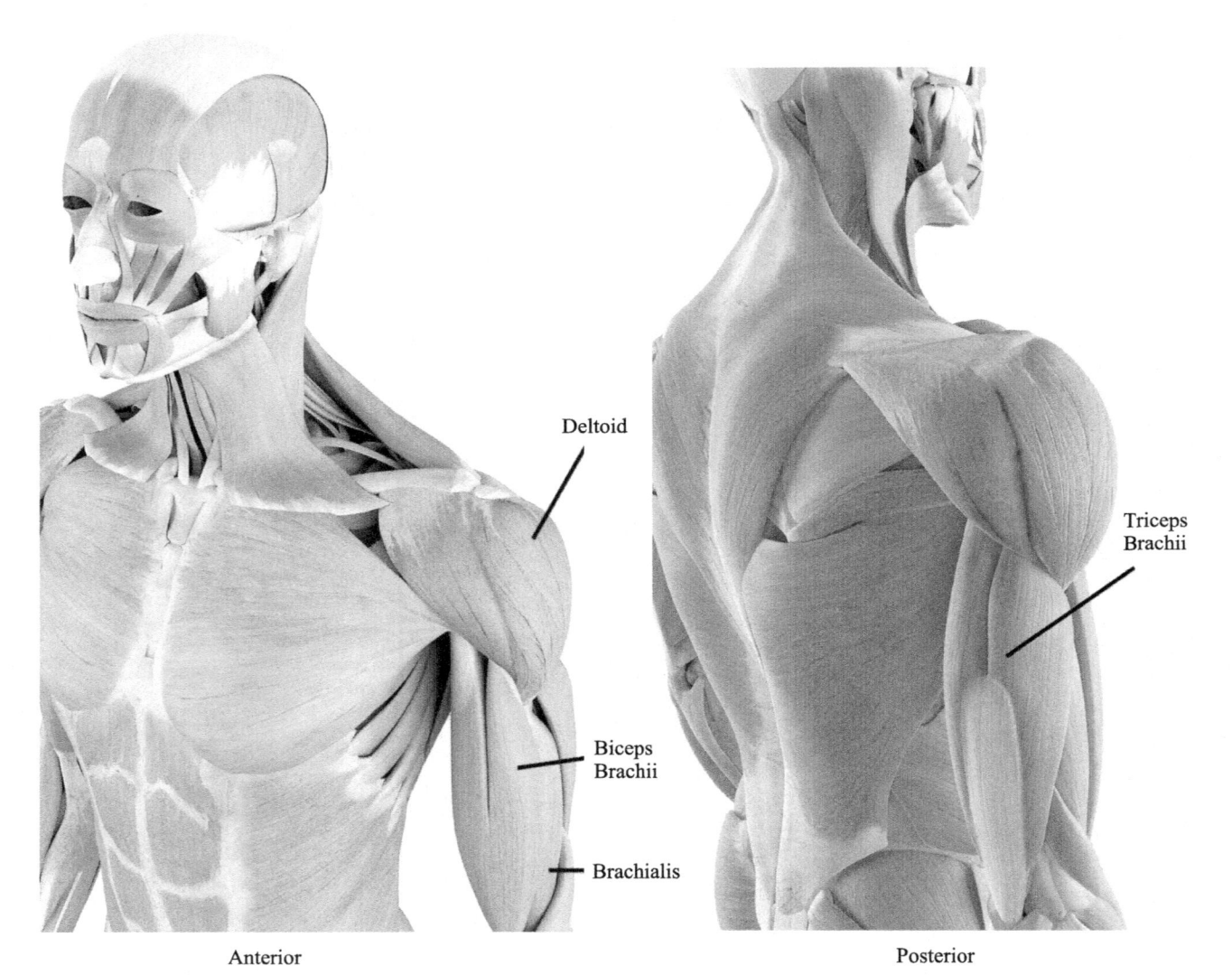

- Deltoid
- Biceps Brachii
- Brachialis
- Triceps Brachii

Anterior

Posterior

Not Pictured: Coracobrachialis

Biceps Brachii

Biceps Brachii is a muscle of the arm. The term "Biceps" means "two heads", and "Brachii" refers to the arm.

Biceps Brachii has two heads. The Short Head of the Biceps Brachii originates on the Coracoid Process. The Long Head of the Biceps Brachii originates on the Supraglenoid Tubercle. Both heads join together in the arm, and together insert onto the Radial Tuberosity.

When Biceps Brachii contracts, it helps produce flexion of the shoulder, flexion of the elbow, and supination of the forearm. Biceps Brachii is the prime mover of supination.

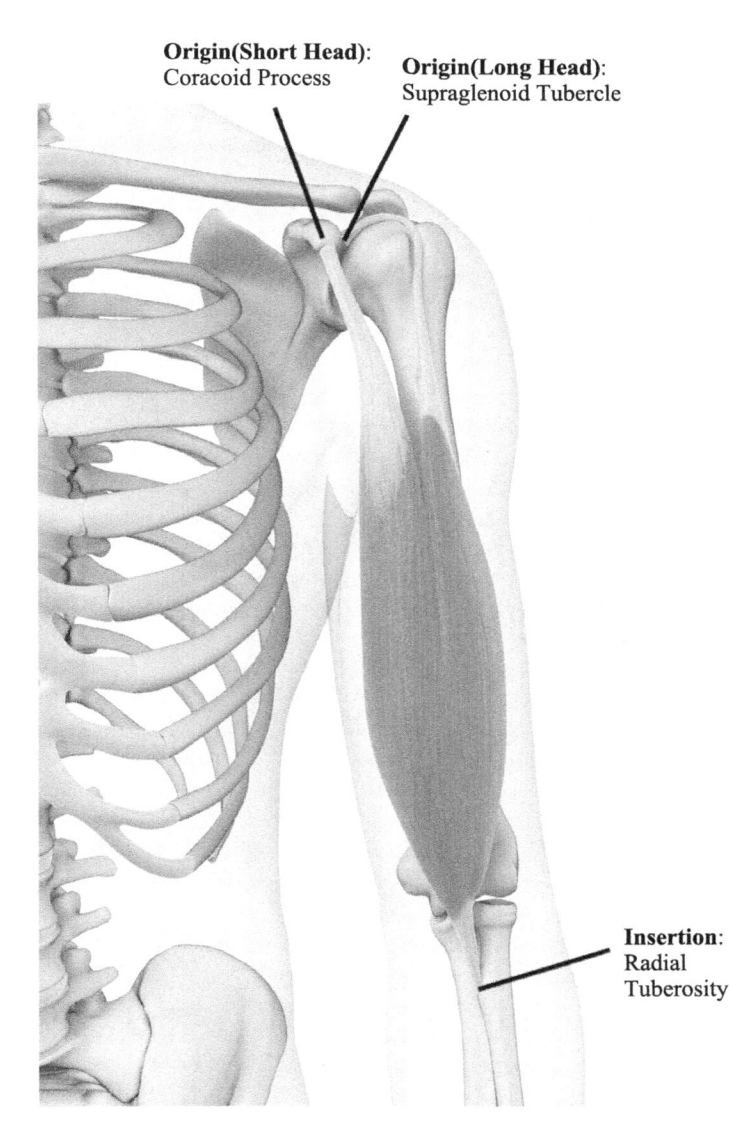

Origin(Short Head): Coracoid Process
Origin(Long Head): Supraglenoid Tubercle
Insertion: Radial Tuberosity

Shoulder Flexion

Elbow Flexion

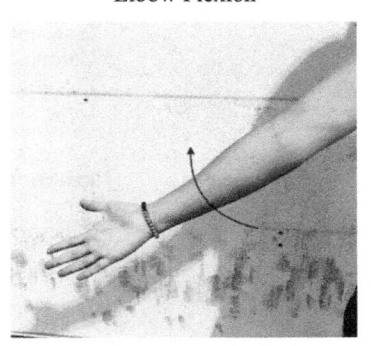

Forearm Supination

Origin: Long Head: Supraglenoid Tubercle; Short Head: Coracoid Process
Insertion: Radial Tuberosity
Action(s): Flexion of Shoulder, Flexion of Elbow, Supination of Forearm

Innervation: Musculocutaneous Nerve
Synergist: Pectoralis Major, Brachialis, Supinator
Antagonist: Triceps Brachii, Pronator Teres

Brachialis

Brachialis is a muscle of the arm. It is named after it's location, the "brachial" region.

Brachialis originates on the Anterior Distal Shaft of the Humerus, and inserts onto both the Coronoid Process of the Ulna, and the Ulnar Tuberosity.

Brachialis is a powerful muscle. It is the prime mover of elbow flexion. It is located deep to the Biceps Brachii. When Brachialis contracts, it pushes the Biceps Brachii up, allowing Biceps Brachii to be more visible during this action.

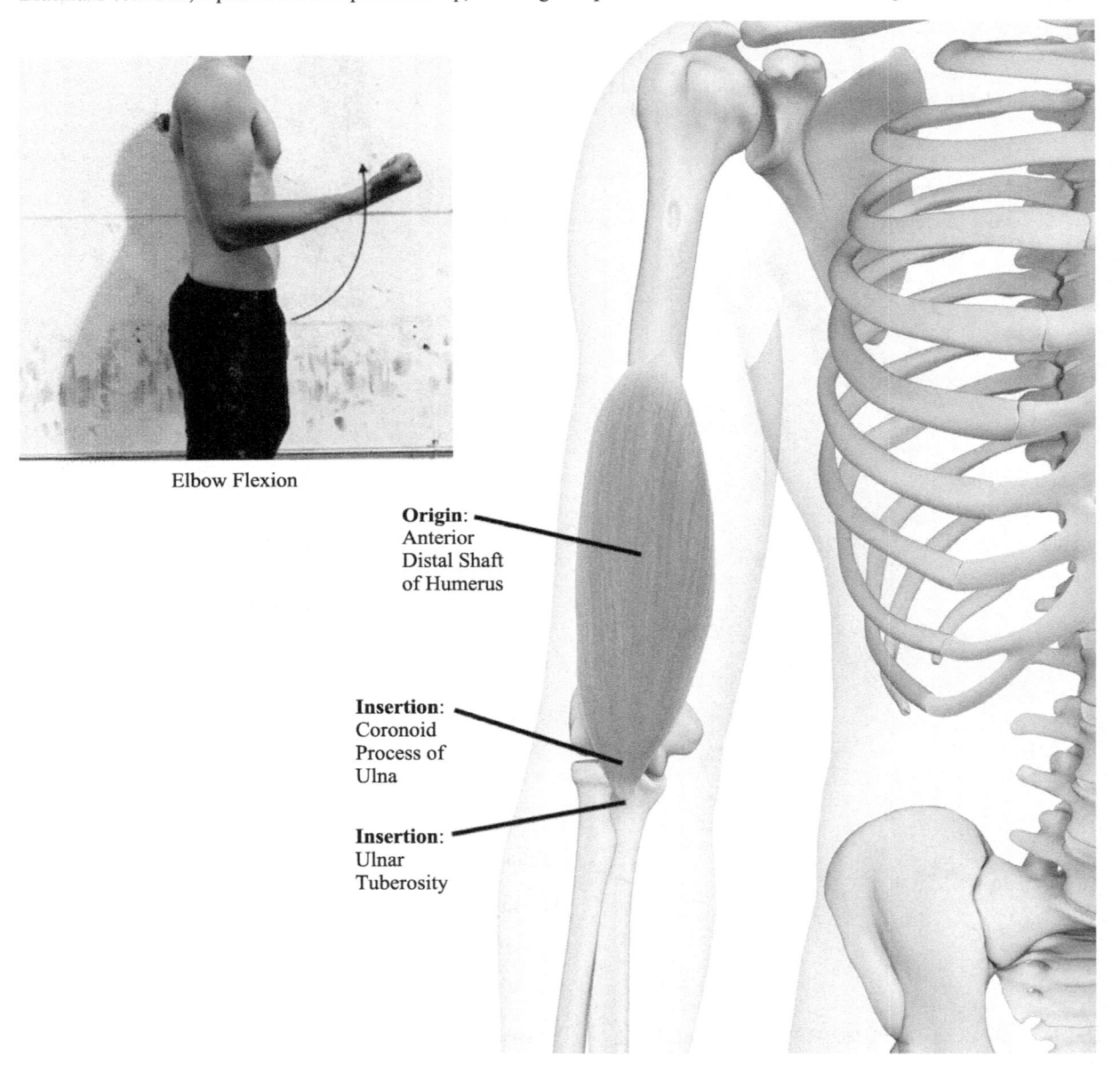

Elbow Flexion

Origin: Anterior Distal Shaft of Humerus

Insertion: Coronoid Process of Ulna

Insertion: Ulnar Tuberosity

Origin: Anterior Distal Shaft of Humerus
Insertion: Coronoid Process and Ulnar Tuberosity
Action(s): Flexion of Elbow

Innervation: Musculocutaneous Nerve
Synergist: Biceps Brachii
Antagonist: Triceps Brachii

Coracobrachialis

Coracobrachialis is a muscle of the arm, named after it's origin and location.

Coracobrachialis originates on the Coracoid Process, and inserts onto the Medial Proximal Shaft of the Humerus.

Coracobrachialis is primarily a synergist to Pectoralis Major. When Coracobrachialis contracts, it flexes and horizontally adducts the shoulder.

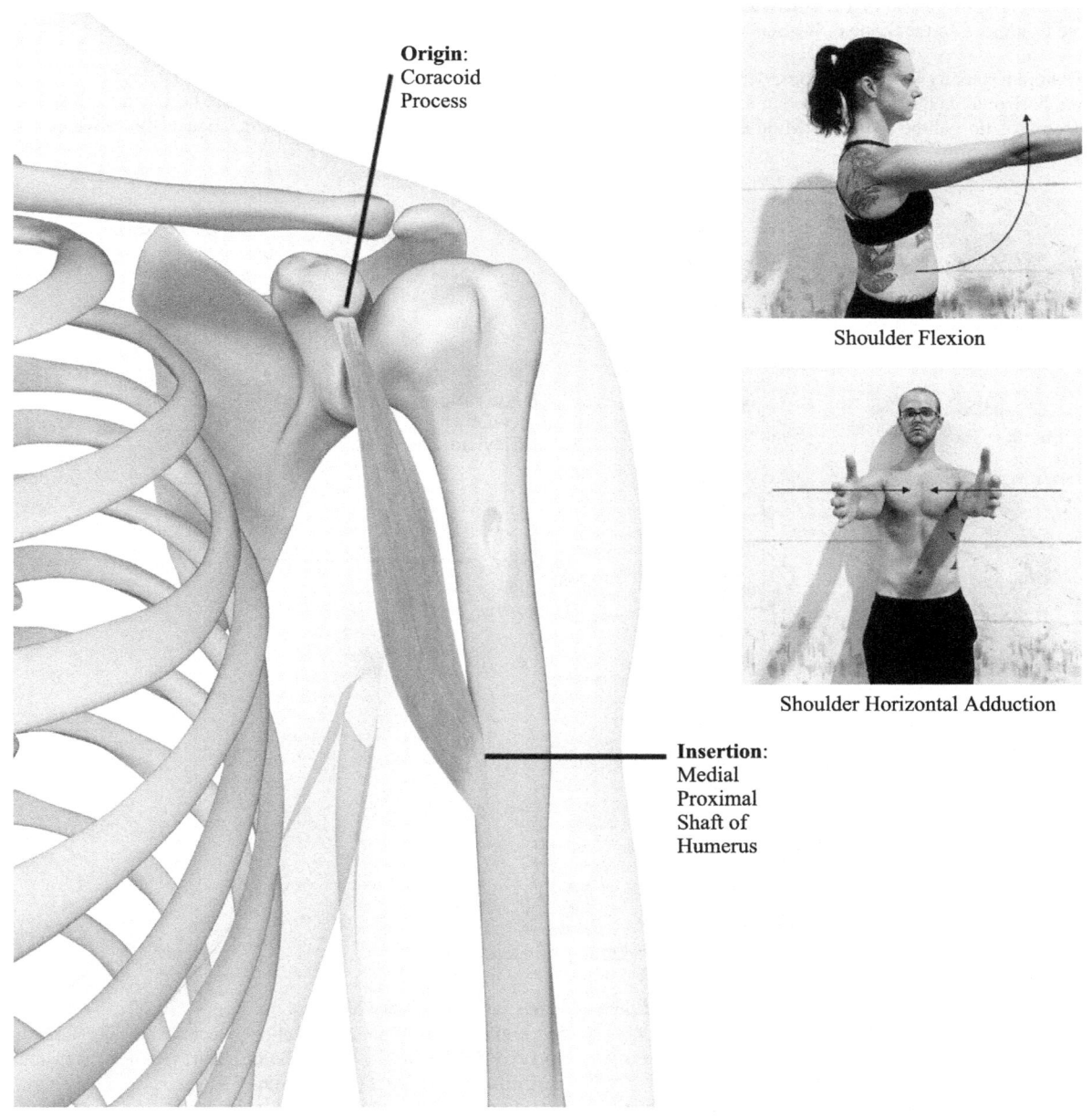

Origin: Coracoid Process

Insertion: Medial Proximal Shaft of Humerus

Shoulder Flexion

Shoulder Horizontal Adduction

Origin: Coracoid Process
Insertion: Medial Proximal Shaft of Humerus
Action(s): Flexion, Horizontal Adduction of Shoulder
Innervation: Musculocutaneous Nerve
Synergist: Pectoralis Major, Biceps Brachii
Antagonist: Infraspinatus, Teres Minor

Deltoid

Deltoid is a muscle of the arm/shoulder, named after the Greek letter "delta", which is shaped like an equilateral triangle(all sides are the same length).

Deltoid has three different portions that make up the muscle: Anterior Deltoid, Middle Deltoid, and Posterior Deltoid. All three combined create the Deltoid muscle.

Anterior Deltoid originates on the lateral third of the clavicle. Middle Deltoid originates on the Acromion Process. Posterior Deltoid originates on the Spine of the Scapula. All three join together distally and insert onto the Deltoid Tuberosity.

The Deltoid has many different actions, depending on which fibers of the muscle are contracting. Anterior Deltoid assists in flexion, horizontal adduction, and medial rotation of the shoulder. Posterior Deltoid assists in extension, horizontal abduction, and lateral rotation of the shoulder. Middle Deltoid, in conjunction with the two other Deltoid fibers, abducts the shoulder.

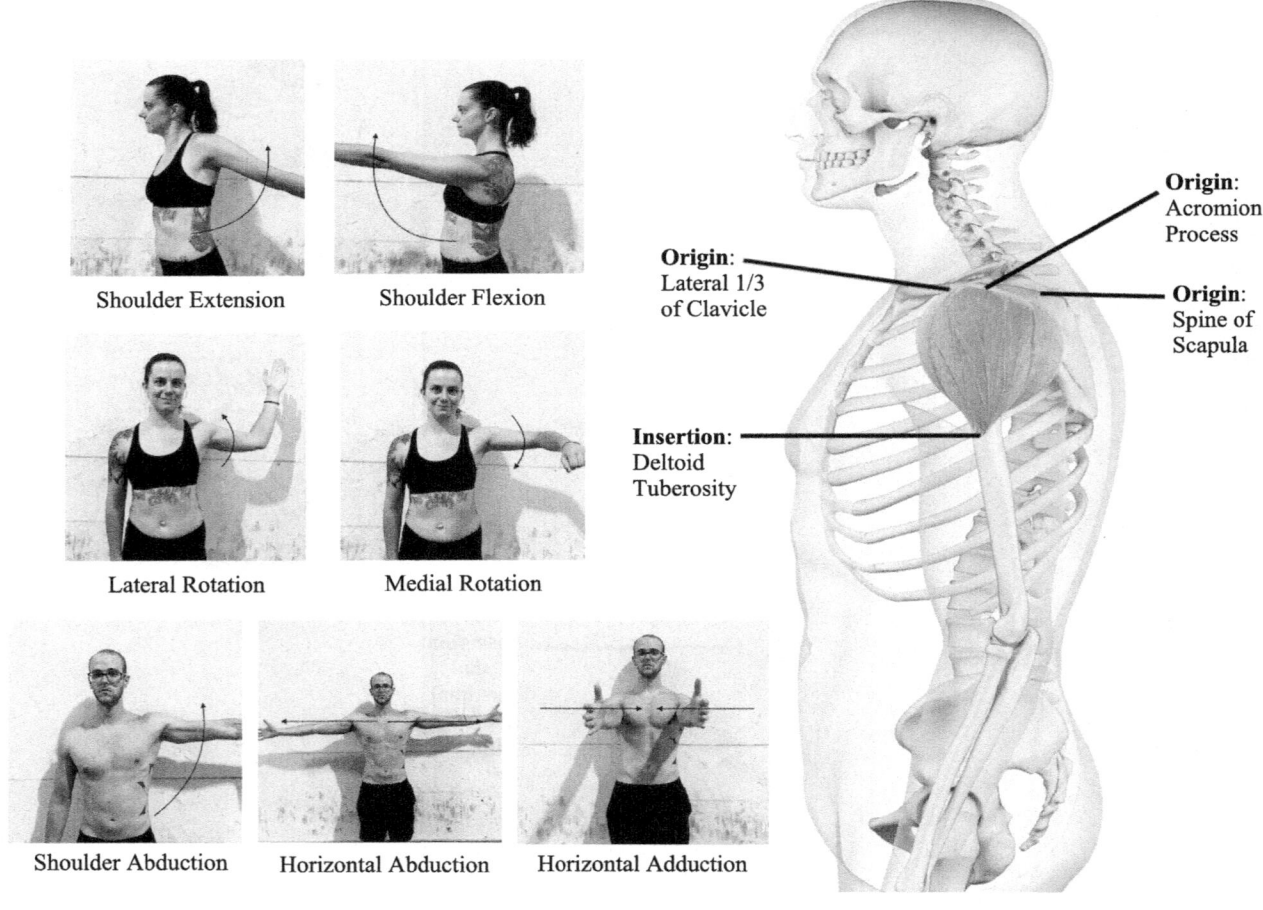

Shoulder Extension   Shoulder Flexion

Lateral Rotation   Medial Rotation

Shoulder Abduction   Horizontal Abduction   Horizontal Adduction

Origin: Acromion Process
Origin: Lateral 1/3 of Clavicle
Origin: Spine of Scapula
Insertion: Deltoid Tuberosity

Origin: Anterior Deltoid: Lateral Third of Clavicle; Middle Deltoid: Acromion Process; Posterior Deltoid: Spine of Scapula
Insertion: Deltoid Tuberosity
Action(s): Abduction, Medial Rotation, Lateral Rotation, Horizontal Adduction, Horizontal Abduction, Flexion, Extension of Shoulder

Innervation: Axillary Nerve
Synergist: Supraspinatus(abduction), Pectoralis Major(flexion, horizontal adduction, medial rotation), Infraspinatus(extension, horizontal abduction, lateral rotation)
Antagonist: Latissimus Dorsi(abduction), Infraspinatus(flexion, horizontal adduction, medial rotation), Pectoralis Major(extension, horizontal abduction, lateral rotation)

Triceps Brachii

Triceps Brachii is a muscle of the posterior arm. The name "Triceps" means "three heads", and "Brachii" refers to the arm.

Triceps Brachii has three heads. The Long Head originates on the Infraglenoid Tubercle of the Humerus. The Medial Head originates on the Posterior Shaft of the Humerus, on the medial side. The Lateral Head originates on the Posterior Shaft of the Humerus, on the lateral side. All three heads join together and insert on the Olecranon Process.

When Triceps Brachii contracts, it extends the shoulder and extends the elbow.

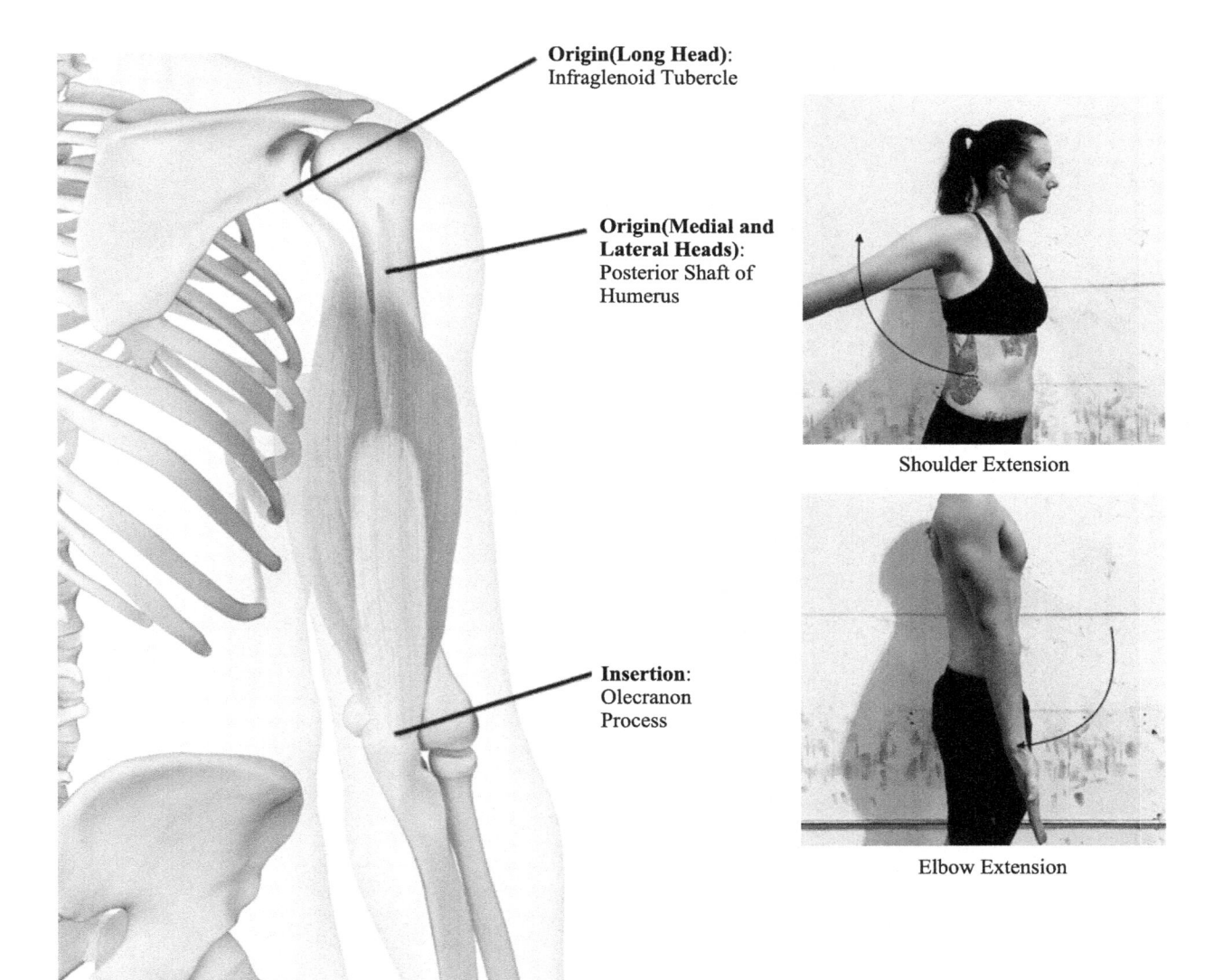

Origin(Long Head): Infraglenoid Tubercle

Origin(Medial and Lateral Heads): Posterior Shaft of Humerus

Insertion: Olecranon Process

Shoulder Extension

Elbow Extension

Origin: Long Head: Infraglenoid tubercle; Medial Head: Posterior Shaft of Humerus; Lateral Head: Posterior Shaft of Humerus
Insertion: Olecranon Process
Action(s): Extension of Shoulder, Extension of Elbow

Innervation: Radial Nerve
Synergist: Latissimus Dorsi, Anconeus
Antagonist: Pectoralis Major, Biceps Brachii

Muscles of the Forearm

Muscles to Know:

Anconeus
Brachioradialis
Pronator Teres

Terms to Know:

Agkon: Elbow
Brachi/o: Arm
Teres: Round and Long

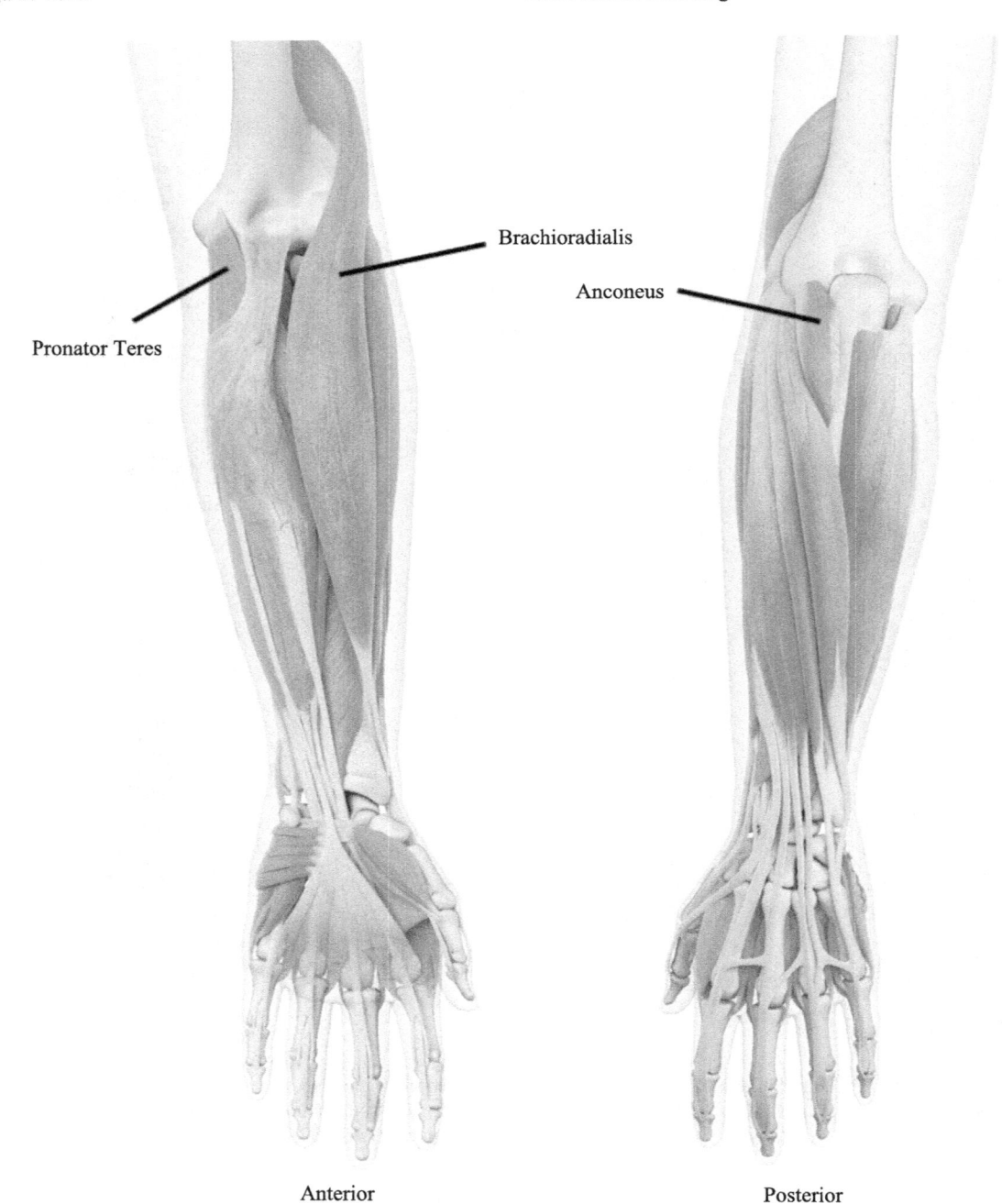

Pronator Teres — Brachioradialis

Anconeus

Anterior

Posterior

Anconeus

Anconeus is a muscle of the forearm. Its name derives from the Greek "agkon", which means "elbow".

Anconeus originates on the Lateral Epicondyle of the Humerus, and inserts onto the Olecranon Process.

Anconeus is primarily only a synergist to the Triceps Brachii, assisting to perform elbow extension.

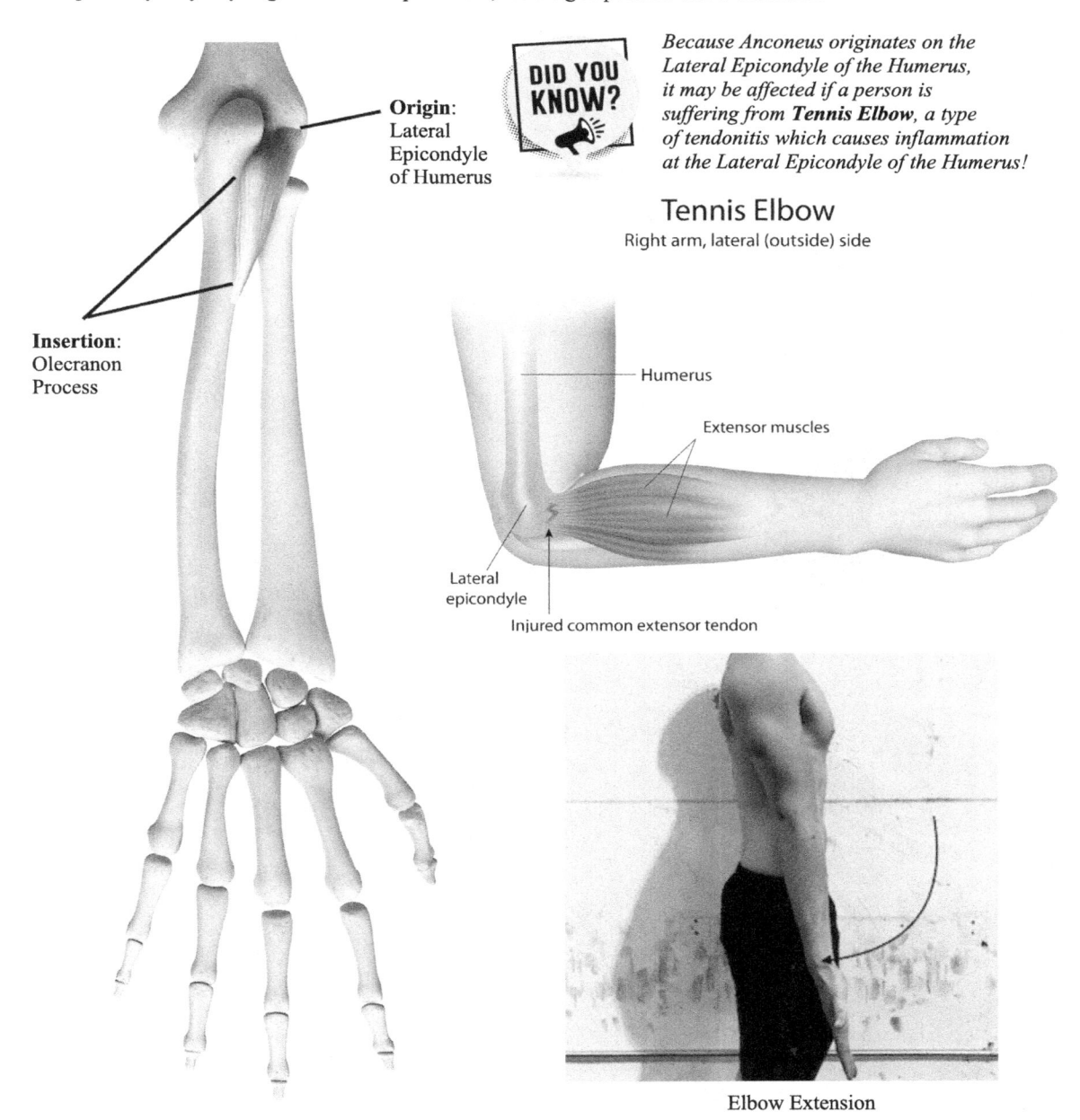

Origin: Lateral Epicondyle of Humerus

Insertion: Olecranon Process

*Because Anconeus originates on the Lateral Epicondyle of the Humerus, it may be affected if a person is suffering from **Tennis Elbow**, a type of tendonitis which causes inflammation at the Lateral Epicondyle of the Humerus!*

Tennis Elbow
Right arm, lateral (outside) side

- Humerus
- Extensor muscles
- Lateral epicondyle
- Injured common extensor tendon

Elbow Extension

Origin: Lateral Epicondyle of Humerus
Insertion: Olecranon Process
Action(s): Extension of Elbow

Innervation: Radial Nerve
Synergist: Triceps Brachii
Antagonist: Brachialis

Brachioradialis

Brachioradialis is a muscle of the forearm, named after its location and insertion. "Brachio" refers to the arm, and "radialis" refers to the radius.

Brachioradialis originates on the Lateral Supracondylar Ridge of the humerus, the ridge just superior to the Lateral Epicondyle. Brachioradialis inserts onto the Styloid Process of the radius.

Brachioradialis primarily performs flexion of the elbow with the hand in the neutral position(neither in pronation or supination).

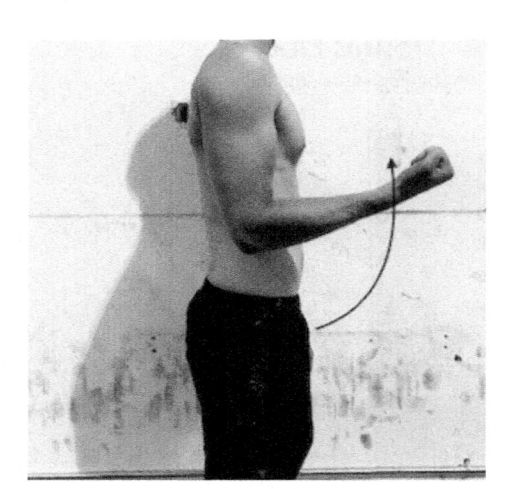

Elbow Flexion

Origin: Lateral Supracondylar Ridge

Insertion: Styloid Process of Radius

Origin: Lateral Supracondylar Ridge of Humerus
Insertion: Styloid Process of Radius
Action(s): Flexion of Elbow

Innervation: Radial Nerve
Synergist: Biceps Brachii
Antagonist: Triceps Brachii

Pronator Teres

Pronator Teres is a muscle of the forearm, named for its action and shape ("Teres" means "round and long". Pronator Teres has a long, round shape).

Pronator Teres originates on the Medial Epicondyle of the humerus and the Coronoid Process of the ulna. Pronator Teres inserts onto the Middle of the Lateral Surface of the radius.

Pronator Teres, as the name suggests, is the strongest pronator of the forearm. Because Pronator Teres crosses the elbow joint, it also assists in flexion of the elbow.

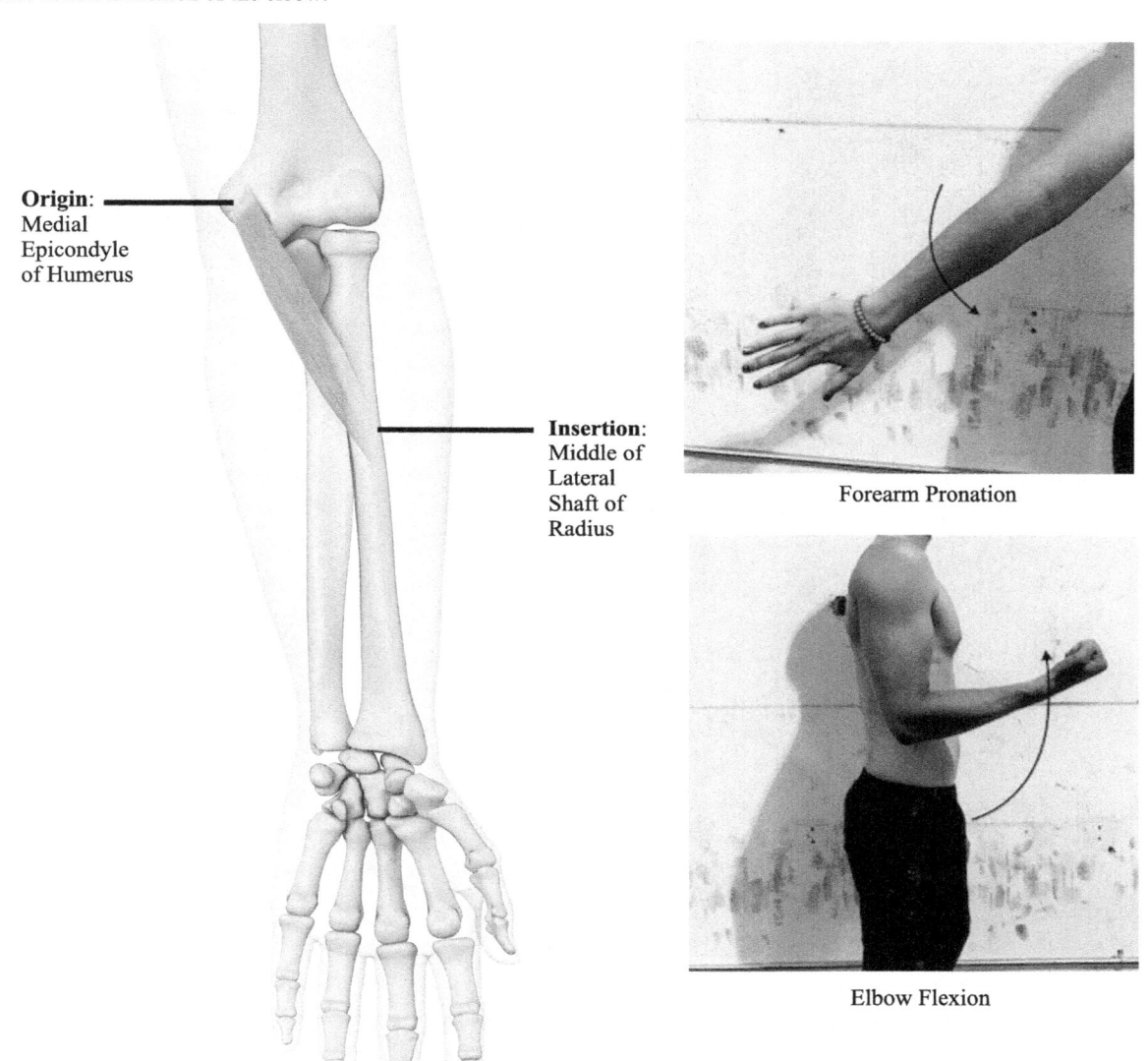

Origin: Medial Epicondyle of Humerus

Insertion: Middle of Lateral Shaft of Radius

Forearm Pronation

Elbow Flexion

Origin: Medial Epicondyle of Humerus, Coronoid Process of Ulna
Insertion: Middle of Lateral Surface of Radius
Action(s): Pronation of Forearm, Flexion of Elbow

Innervation: Median Nerve
Synergist: Pronator Quadratus, Brachialis
Antagonist: Biceps Brachii, Triceps Brachii

Muscles of the Pelvis

Muscles to Know:

Gluteus Maximus
Iliacus
Piriformis
Psoas Major

Terms to Know:

Iliac: Ilium
Pirum: Pear
Psoa: Loin Region

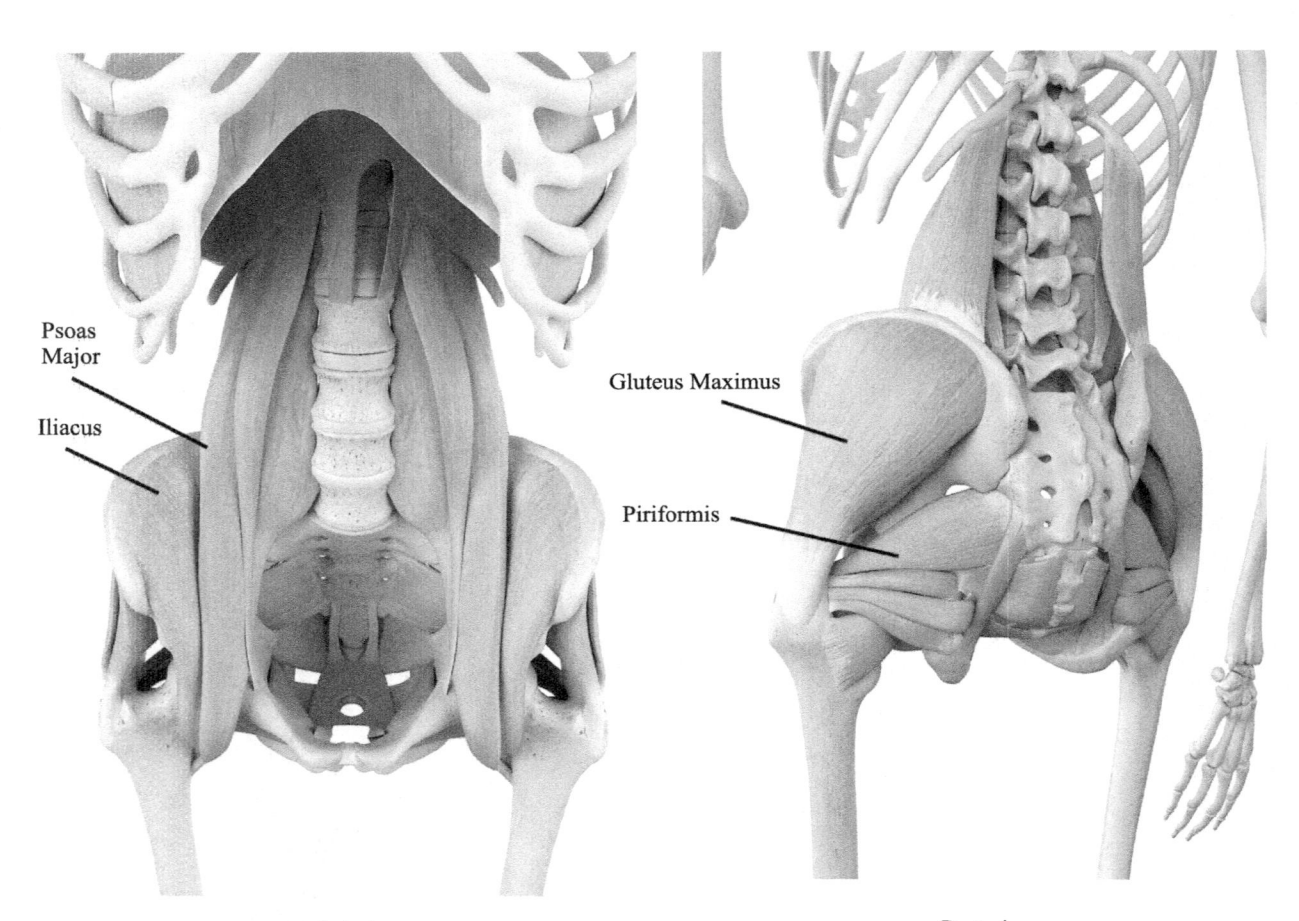

Psoas Major
Iliacus

Gluteus Maximus
Piriformis

Anterior

Posterior

Gluteus Maximus

Gluteus Maximus is a muscle of the pelvis, named for its location and size.

Gluteus Maximus originates on the Posterior Iliac Crest, the Posterior Sacrum and Coccyx, and the Sacrotuberous Ligament. Gluteus Maximus inserts partially onto the Gluteal Tuberosity, and into the Iliotibial Band.

Gluteus Maximus is primarily responsible for assisting in extension of the hip, and abduction of the hip.

Gluteus Maximus is the most superficial of the gluteus muscle group.

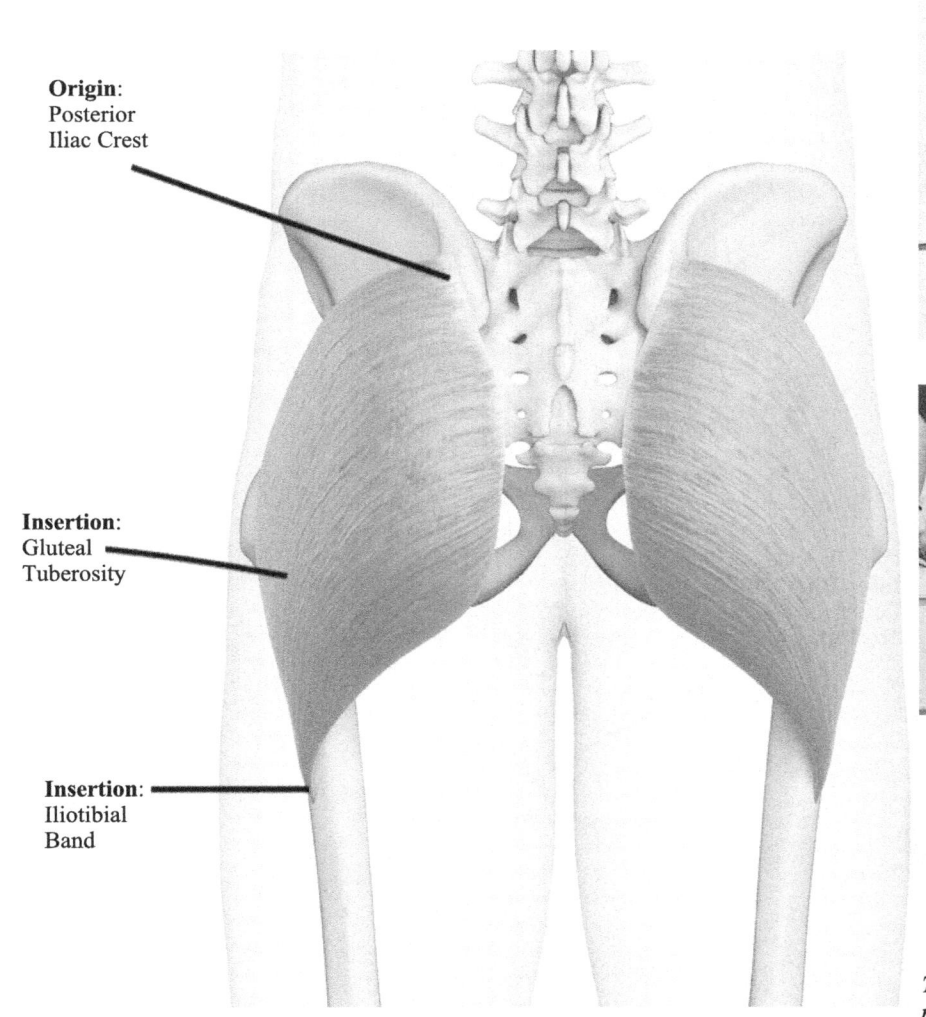

Origin: Posterior Iliac Crest

Insertion: Gluteal Tuberosity

Insertion: Iliotibial Band

Hip Extension

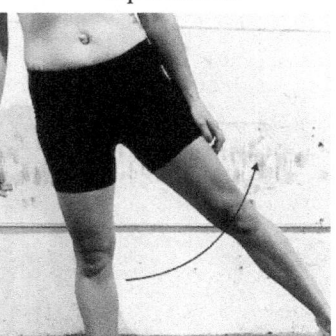

Hip Abduction

DID YOU KNOW?

*The Gluteus Maximus is the **largest** muscle in the human body!*

Origin: Posterior Iliac Crest, Posterior Sacrum and Coccyx, Sacrotuberous Ligament
Insertion: Gluteal Tuberosity, Iliotibial Band
Action(s): Extension, Abduction of Hip
Innervation: Inferior Gluteal Nerve
Synergist: Hamstrings, Piriformis
Antagonist: Rectus Femoris, Adductor Magnus

Iliacus

Iliacus is a muscle of the pelvis, named for its origin.

Iliacus originates in the Iliac Fossa, and crosses the hip joint to insert onto the Lesser Trochanter.

Iliacus is one of the prime movers of hip flexion. It is often joined with the Psoas Major, which also aids in hip flexion, to make a single muscle named the Iliopsoas.

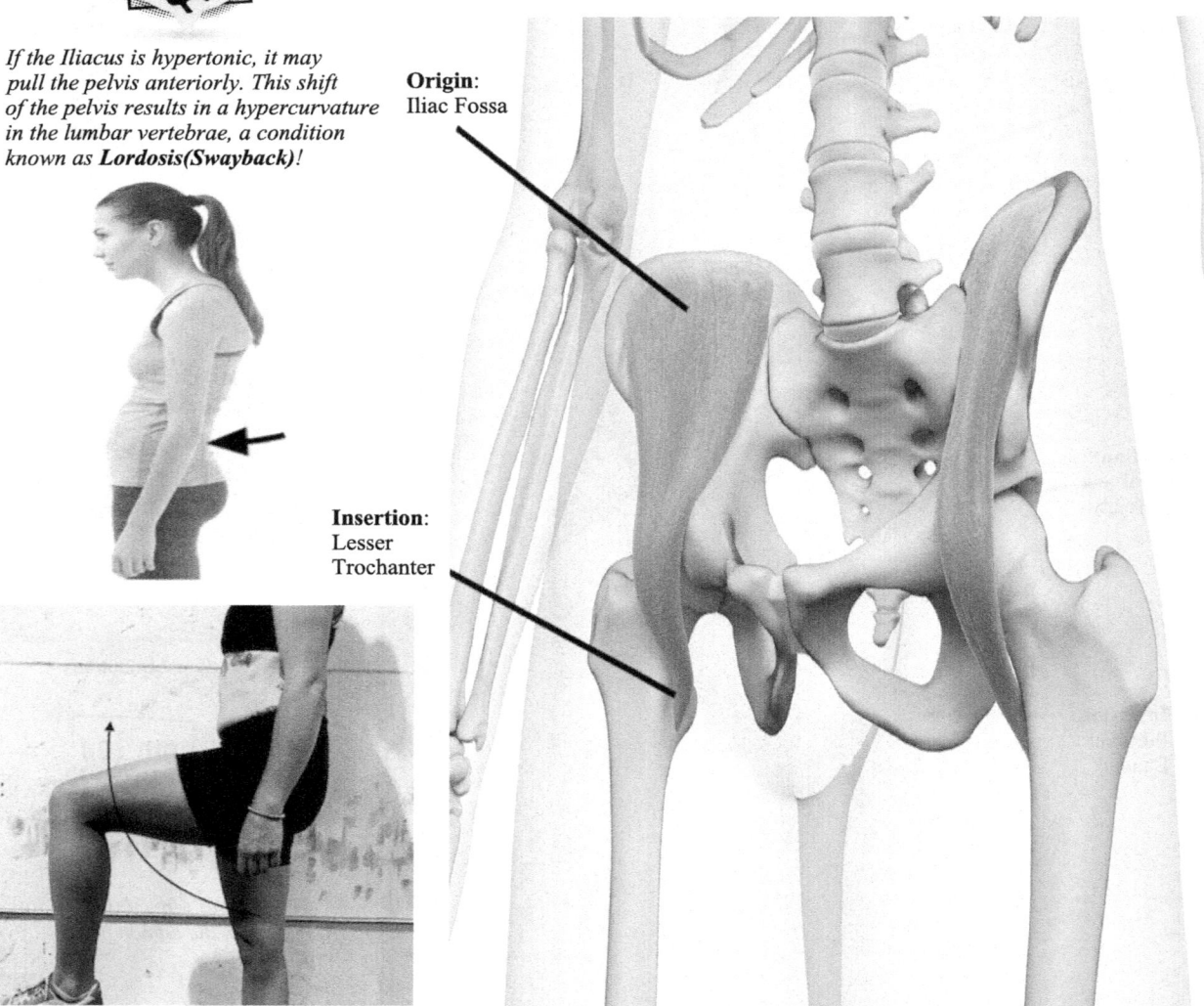

*If the Iliacus is hypertonic, it may pull the pelvis anteriorly. This shift of the pelvis results in a hypercurvature in the lumbar vertebrae, a condition known as **Lordosis(Swayback)**!*

Origin: Iliac Fossa

Insertion: Lesser Trochanter

Hip Flexion

Origin: Iliac Fossa
Insertion: Lesser Trochanter
Action(s): Flexion of Hip

Innervation: Femoral Nerve
Synergist: Psoas Major
Antagonist: Hamstrings

Piriformis

Piriformis is a muscle of the pelvis, named for its shape ("piri" refers to "pirum", which means "pear" in Latin. Piriformis is shaped like a pear).

Piriformis originates on the Anterior Surface of the Sacrum, and inserts onto the Greater Trochanter.

Piriformis works with the Gluteus Maximus to perform abduction and lateral rotation of the hip.

Piriformis is part of the Deep Six muscle group.

When hypertonic, Piriformis may place substantial pressure on the Sciatic Nerve, which passes by, and sometimes through, the muscle itself. This is a form of Sciatica known as Piriformis Syndrome. This can result in pain in the hip, posterior thigh, posterior leg, and plantar surface of the foot.

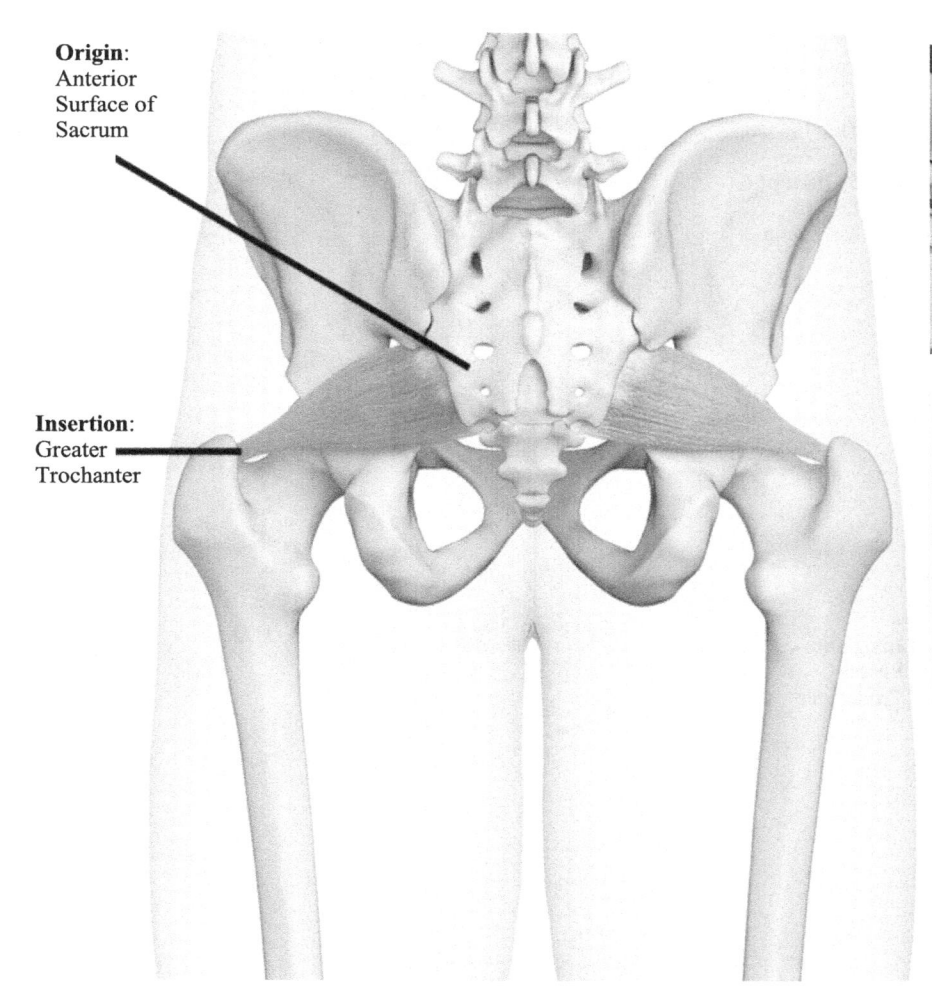

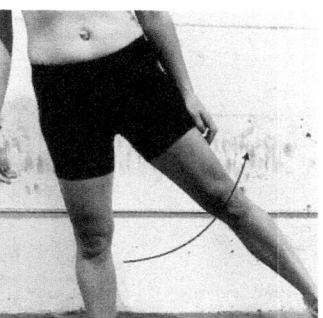

Origin: Anterior Surface of Sacrum

Insertion: Greater Trochanter

Hip Abduction

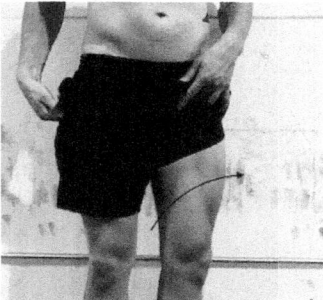

Hip Lateral Rotation

Origin: Anterior Surface of Sacrum
Insertion: Greater Trochanter
Action(s): Abduction, Lateral Rotation of Hip

Innervation: Piriformis Nerve
Synergist: Gluteus Maximus, Sartorius
Antagonist: Adductor Magnus, Pectineus

Psoas Major

Psoas Major is a muscle of the abdomen and pelvis, named for its location("psoas" comes from the Greek word "psoa", which means "loin region") and size.

Psoas Major originates on the Anterior Surface of the Lumbar Vertebrae. Psoas Major inserts onto the Lesser Trochanter.

Psoas Major is responsible for flexion of the hip, along with Iliacus. Psoas Major often joins with Iliacus to form one muscle known as the Iliopsoas.

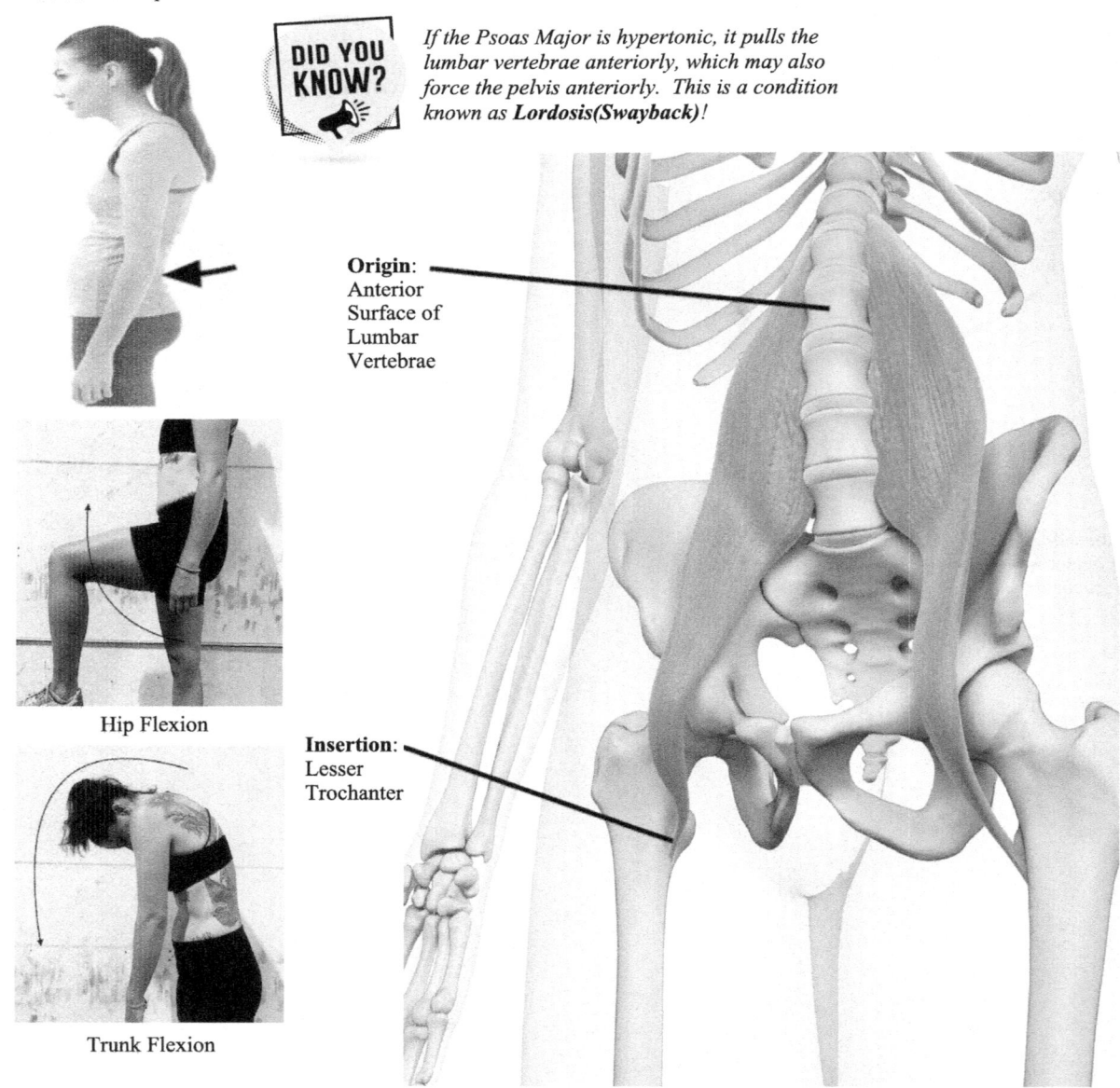

DID YOU KNOW? *If the Psoas Major is hypertonic, it pulls the lumbar vertebrae anteriorly, which may also force the pelvis anteriorly. This is a condition known as **Lordosis(Swayback)**!*

Origin: Anterior Surface of Lumbar Vertebrae

Insertion: Lesser Trochanter

Hip Flexion

Trunk Flexion

Origin: Anterior Surface of Lumbar Vertebrae
Insertion: Lesser Trochanter
Action(s): Flexion of Hip, Flexion of Trunk

Innervation: Lumbar Plexus
Synergist: Iliacus, Rectus Abdominis
Antagonist: Hamstrings, Spinalis

Muscles of the Thigh

Muscles to Know:

Adductor Magnus
Biceps Femoris
Gracilis
Rectus Femoris
Sartorius
Semimembranosus
Semitendinosus
Tensor Fasciae Latae

Terms to Know:

Magnus: Great
Bi-: Two
-cep: Head
Gracilis: Slender
Rectus: Straight
Sartor: Tailor
Semi-: Half
Membranosus: Skin
Tendere: To Stretch
Fasciae: Band
Latae: Side

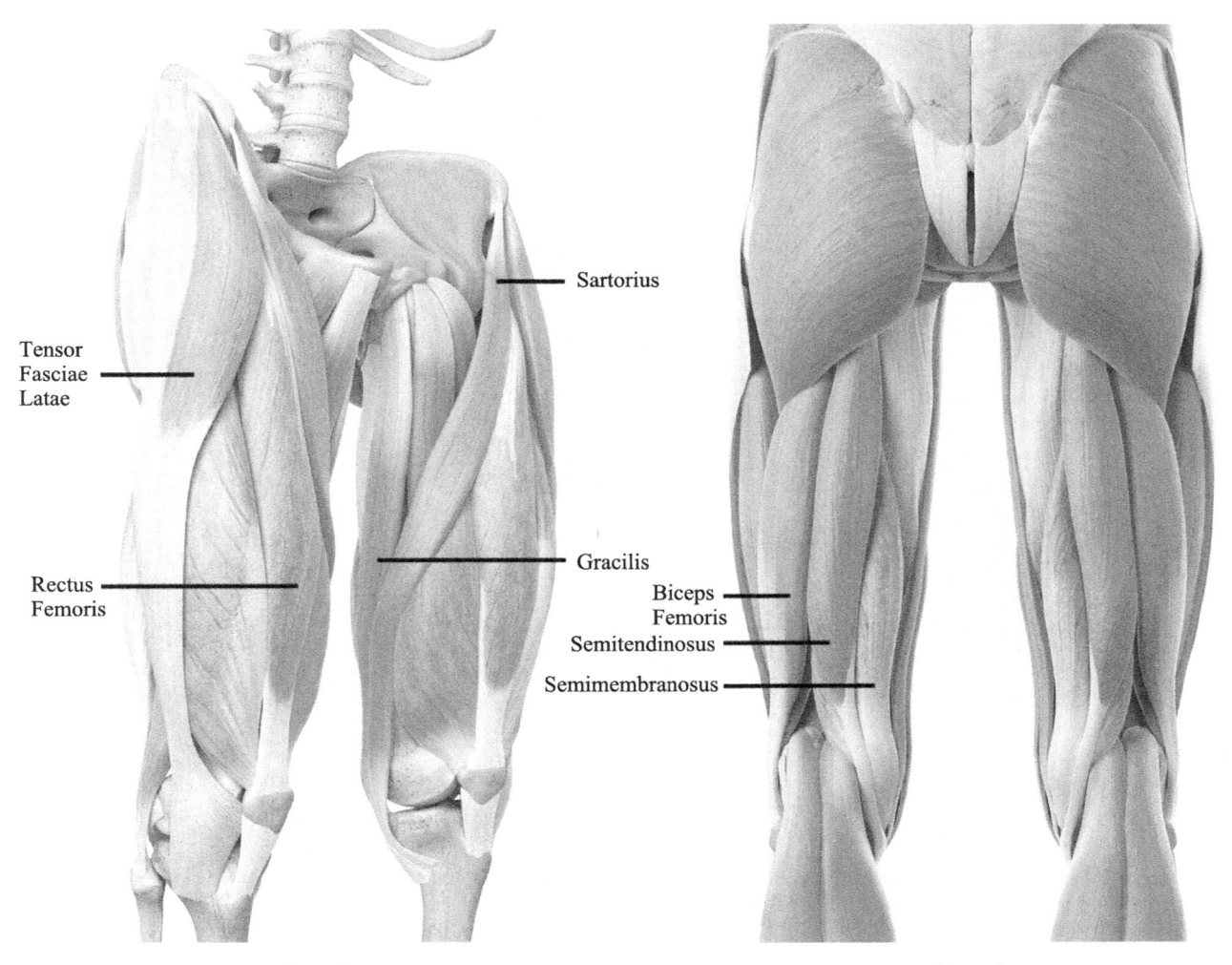

Anterior

- Tensor Fasciae Latae
- Sartorius
- Rectus Femoris
- Gracilis

Posterior

- Biceps Femoris
- Semitendinosus
- Semimembranosus

Not Pictured: Adductor Magnus

Adductor Magnus

Adductor Magnus is a muscle of the thigh, named after its action(adduction) and size("Magnus" means "great" in Latin).

Adductor Magnus has multiple origins. It originates on the Inferior Ramus of the Pubis and Ischial Tuberosity. Adductor Magnus inserts onto the Medial Lip of the Linea Aspera, and the Adductor Tubercle.

Adductor Magnus is an antagonist to itself. It can flex and extend the hip. It also, as the name implies, adducts the hip.

Adductor Magnus is the largest muscle of the Adductor muscle group, which also consists of Adductor Longus, Adductor Brevis, Gracilis, and Pectineus.

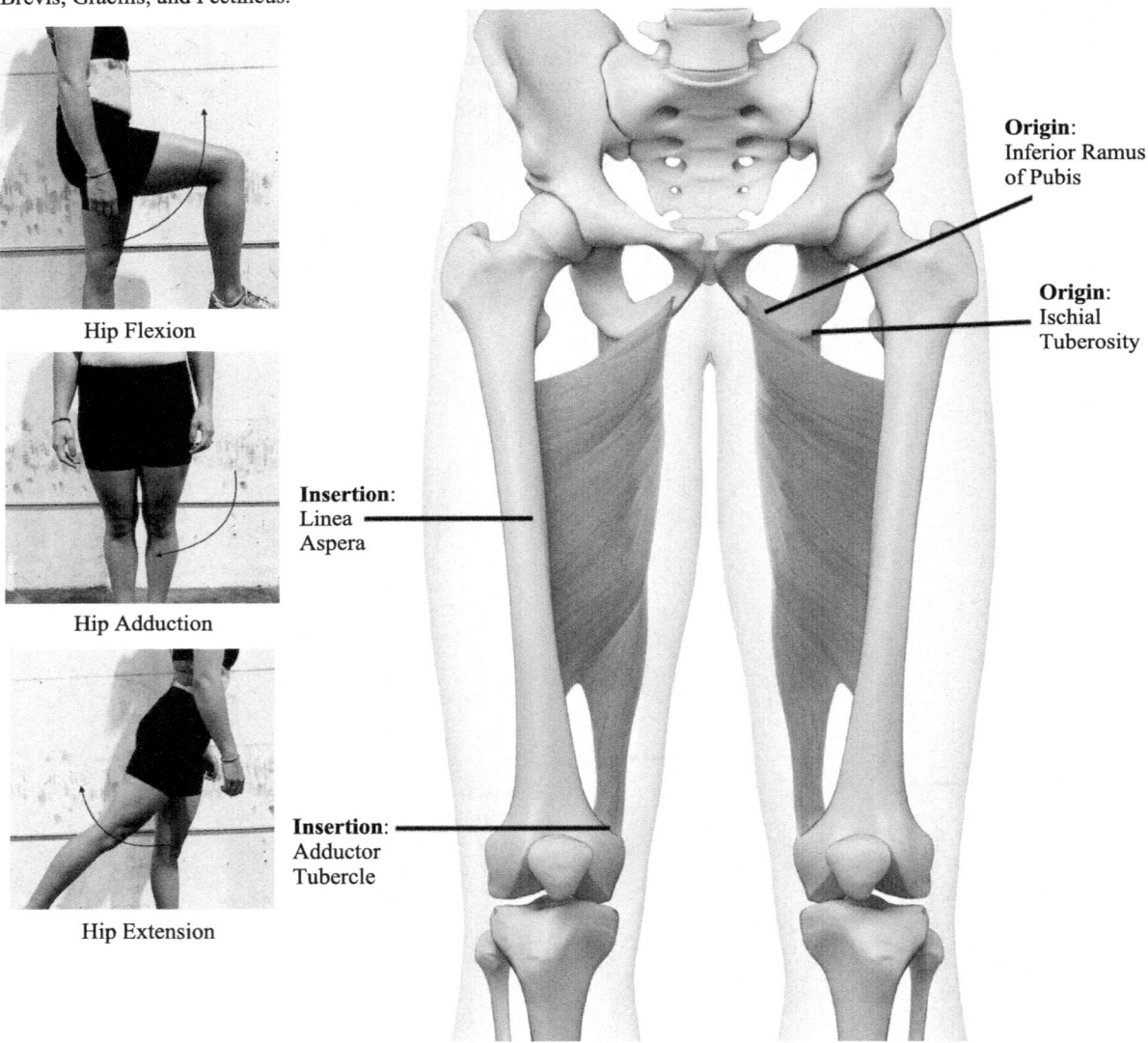

Hip Flexion

Hip Adduction

Hip Extension

Origin: Inferior Ramus of Pubis
Origin: Ischial Tuberosity
Insertion: Linea Aspera
Insertion: Adductor Tubercle

Origin: Inferior Ramus of Pubis, Ischial Tuberosity
Insertion: Linea Aspera, Adductor Tubercle
Action(s): Adduction, Flexion, Extension of Hip

Innervation: Obturator Nerve, Sciatic Nerve(Tibial branch)
Synergist: Adductor Longus(adduction), Iliacus(flexion), Gluteus Maximus(extension)
Antagonist: Piriformis(adduction), Hamstrings(flexion), Rectus Femoris(extension)

Biceps Femoris

Biceps Femoris is a muscle of the posterior thigh, named after the number of heads it has("Biceps" means "two heads") and its location(femur).

Biceps Femoris has two origins: The Long Head of Biceps Femoris originates on the Ischial Tuberosity. The Short Head of Biceps Femoris originates on the Lateral Lip of the Linea Aspera, on the distal end of the femur. Biceps Femoris inserts onto the Head of the Fibula.

Biceps Femoris crosses the hip and the knee. When it contracts, it extends the hip, and flexes the knee.

Biceps Femoris is a member of the Hamstrings muscle group. It is the most lateral Hamstring muscle, the only Hamstring muscle that attaches to the fibula.

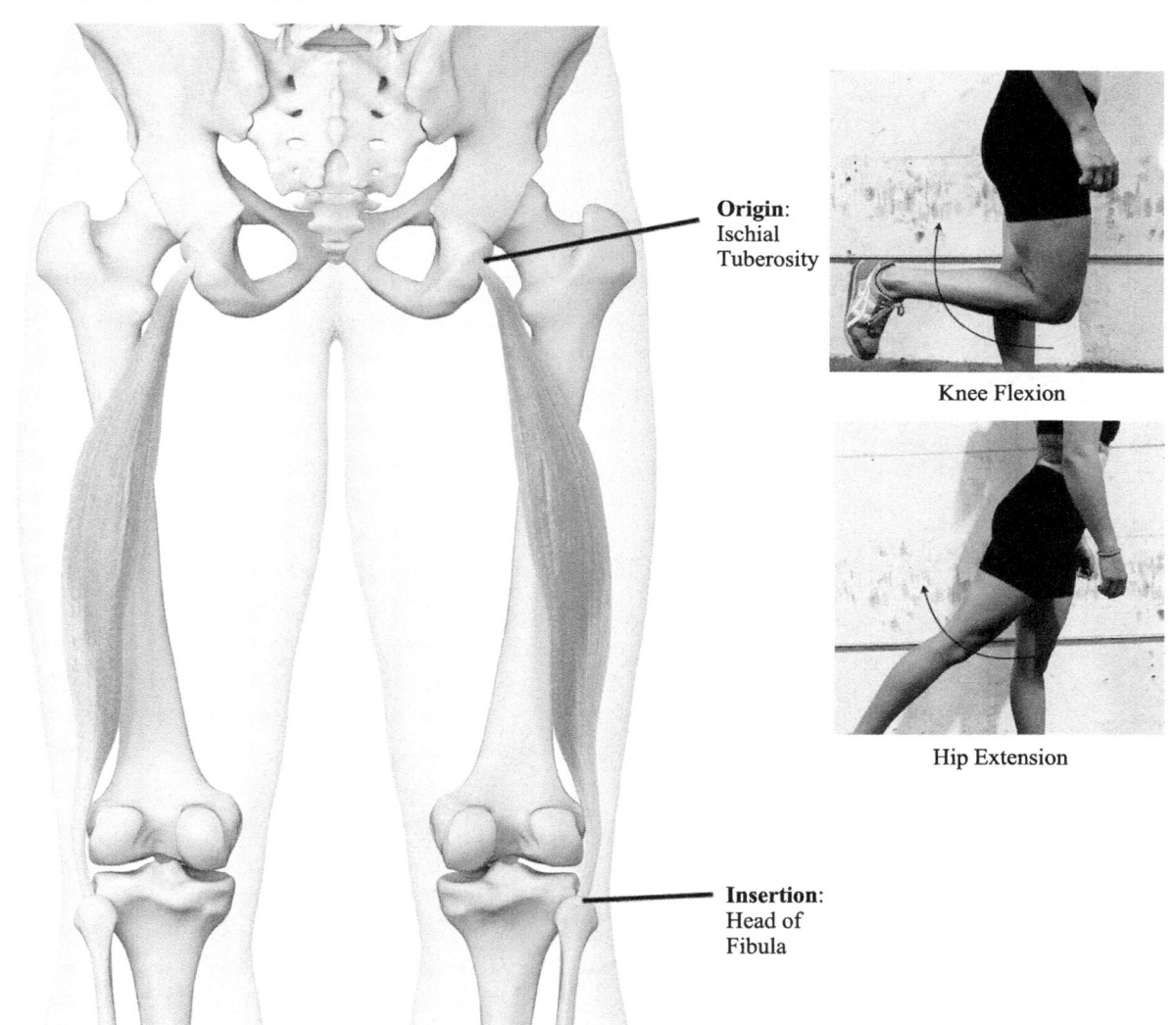

Origin: Ischial Tuberosity

Knee Flexion

Hip Extension

Insertion: Head of Fibula

Origin: Long Head: Ischial Tuberosity; Short Head: Lateral Lip of Linea Aspera
Insertion: Head of Fibula
Action(s): Extension of Hip, Flexion of Knee

Innervation: Sciatic Nerve(Tibial branch)
Synergist: Semimembranosus, Semitendinosus
Antagonist: Rectus Femoris

Gracilis

Gracilis is a muscle of the medial thigh. The word "Gracilis" means "slender" in Latin. The Gracilis is a thin, slender, long muscle.

Gracilis originates on the Inferior Ramus of the Pubis. Gracilis inserts onto the Pes Anserinus, located on the Medial Proximal Shaft of the Tibia. "Pes" means "foot", "anserinus" means "goose". The Pes Anserinus resembles a goose foot.

Gracilis performs adduction and flexion of the hip. Gracilis also crosses the knee, and will assist in flexion of the knee.

Gracilis is a member of the Adductor muscle group, and is the most medial muscle of the group. The Gracilis is the only Adductor muscle that crosses two joints. All the other Adductor muscles(Adductor Magnus, Adductor Longus, Adductor Brevis, Pectineus) only cross the hip.

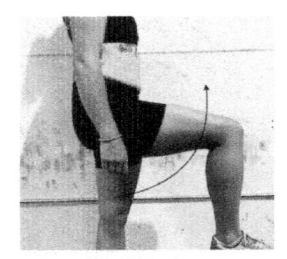

Hip Flexion

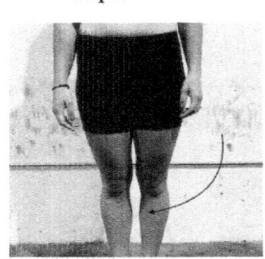

Hip Adduction

Knee Flexion

To remember the muscles that insert on the Pes Anserinus, just think "SGT Goosefoot":
Sartorius
Gracilis
Semitendinosus

Origin: Inferior Ramus of Pubis

Insertion: Pes Anserinus

Origin: Inferior Ramus of Pubis
Insertion: Pes Anserinus
Action(s): Adduction, Flexion of Hip, Flexion of Knee

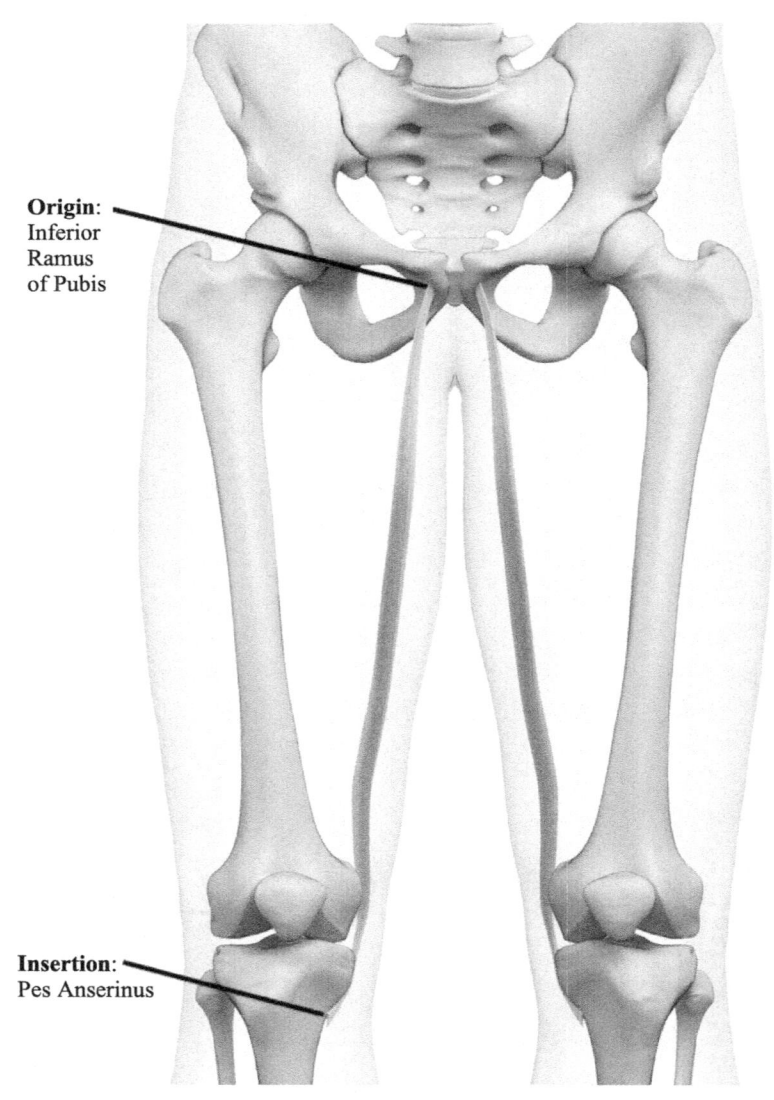

Innervation: Obturator Nerve
Synergist: Adductor Magnus, Gastrocnemius
Antagonist: Gluteus Maximus, Hamstrings, Rectus Femoris

Rectus Femoris

Rectus Femoris is a muscle of the thigh, named after its function("rectus" in Latin means "straight", referring to ones ability to stand straight) and location.

Rectus Femoris originates on the Anterior Inferior Iliac Spine(AIIS), and inserts onto the Tibial Tuberosity.

Rectus Femoris is the prime mover of both hip flexion and knee extension.

Rectus Femoris is the most anterior muscle of the Quadriceps muscle group.

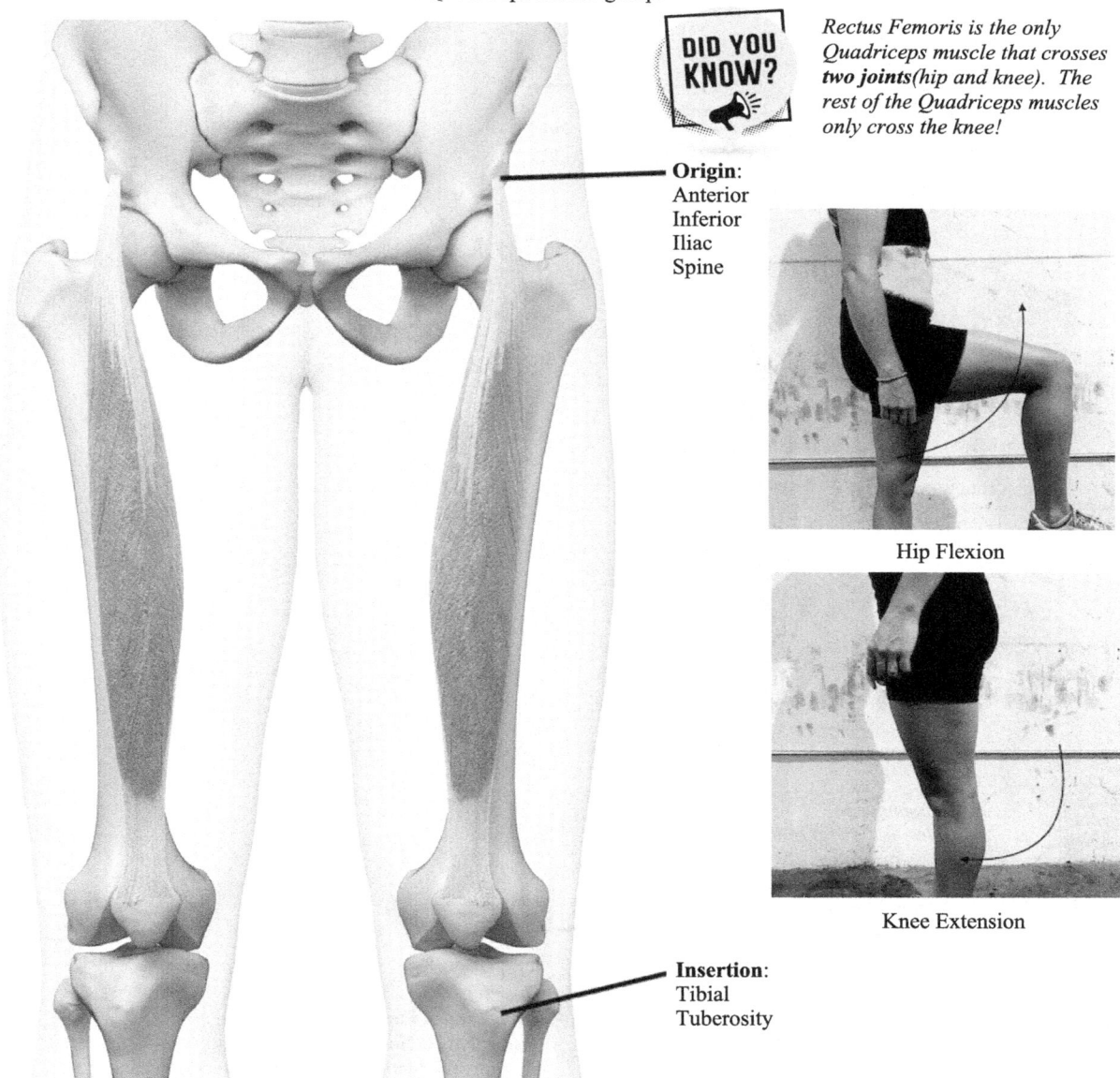

DID YOU KNOW? *Rectus Femoris is the only Quadriceps muscle that crosses **two joints**(hip and knee). The rest of the Quadriceps muscles only cross the knee!*

Origin: Anterior Inferior Iliac Spine

Hip Flexion

Knee Extension

Insertion: Tibial Tuberosity

Origin: Anterior Inferior Iliac Spine
Insertion: Tibial Tuberosity
Action(s): Flexion of Hip, Extension of Knee
Innervation: Femoral Nerve
Synergist: Sartorius, Vastus Lateralis
Antagonist: Hamstrings

Sartorius

Sartorius is a muscle of the thigh, named for its action ("sartor" is Latin for "tailor". It is named as such due to the actions of the muscle, which are the position a tailor places their leg into while working).

Sartorius originates on the Anterior Superior Iliac Spine(ASIS), and inserts onto the Pes Anserinus, located just medial to the Tibial Tuberosity. "Pes" means "foot", "anserinus" means "goose". The Pes Anserinus resembles a goose foot in appearance.

Sartorius is responsible for flexion and lateral rotation of the hip, and flexion of the knee.

DID YOU KNOW?

*Sartorius is the **longest** muscle in the human body!*

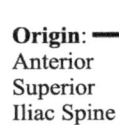

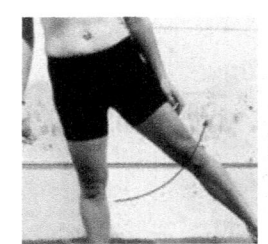

Hip Abduction

Hip Flexion

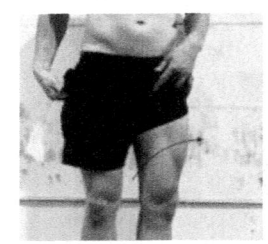

Hip Lateral Rotation

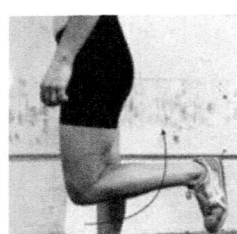

Knee Flexion

To remember the muscles that insert on the Pes Anserinus, just think "SGT Goosefoot":
Sartorius
Gracilis
Semitendinosus

Origin: Anterior Superior Iliac Spine

Insertion: Pes Anserinus

Origin: Anterior Superior Iliac Spine
Insertion: Pes Anserinus
Action(s): Flexion, Abduction, Lateral Rotation of Hip, Flexion of Knee

Innervation: Femoral Nerve
Synergist: Rectus Femoris(hip flexion), Gluteus Maximus(abduction), Piriformis(lateral rotation), Gastrocnemius(knee flexion)
Antagonist: Biceps Femoris(hip flexion), Adductor Magnus(abduction), Pectineus(lateral rotation), Rectus Femoris(knee flexion)

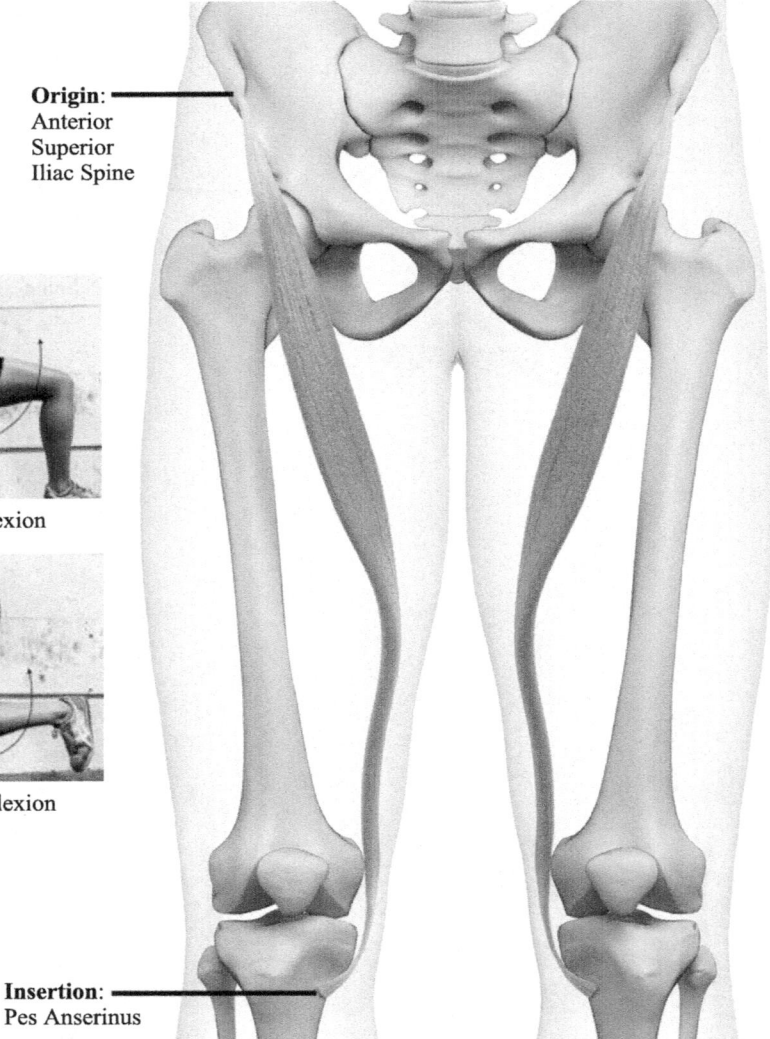

Semimembranosus

Semimembranosus is a muscle of the thigh, named after its appearance("semi" means "half", "membranosus" means "skin". Semimembranosus is about half muscle, half membranous tendon).

Semimembranosus originates on the Ischial Tuberosity, and inserts onto the Posterior Medial Condyle of the Tibia.

Semimembranosus is one muscle responsible for extension of the hip, and flexion of the knee, along with Semitendinosus and Biceps Femoris.

Semimembranosus is a member of the Hamstring muscle group, located on the posterior thigh. Semimembranosus is the most medial of the Hamstring muscles.

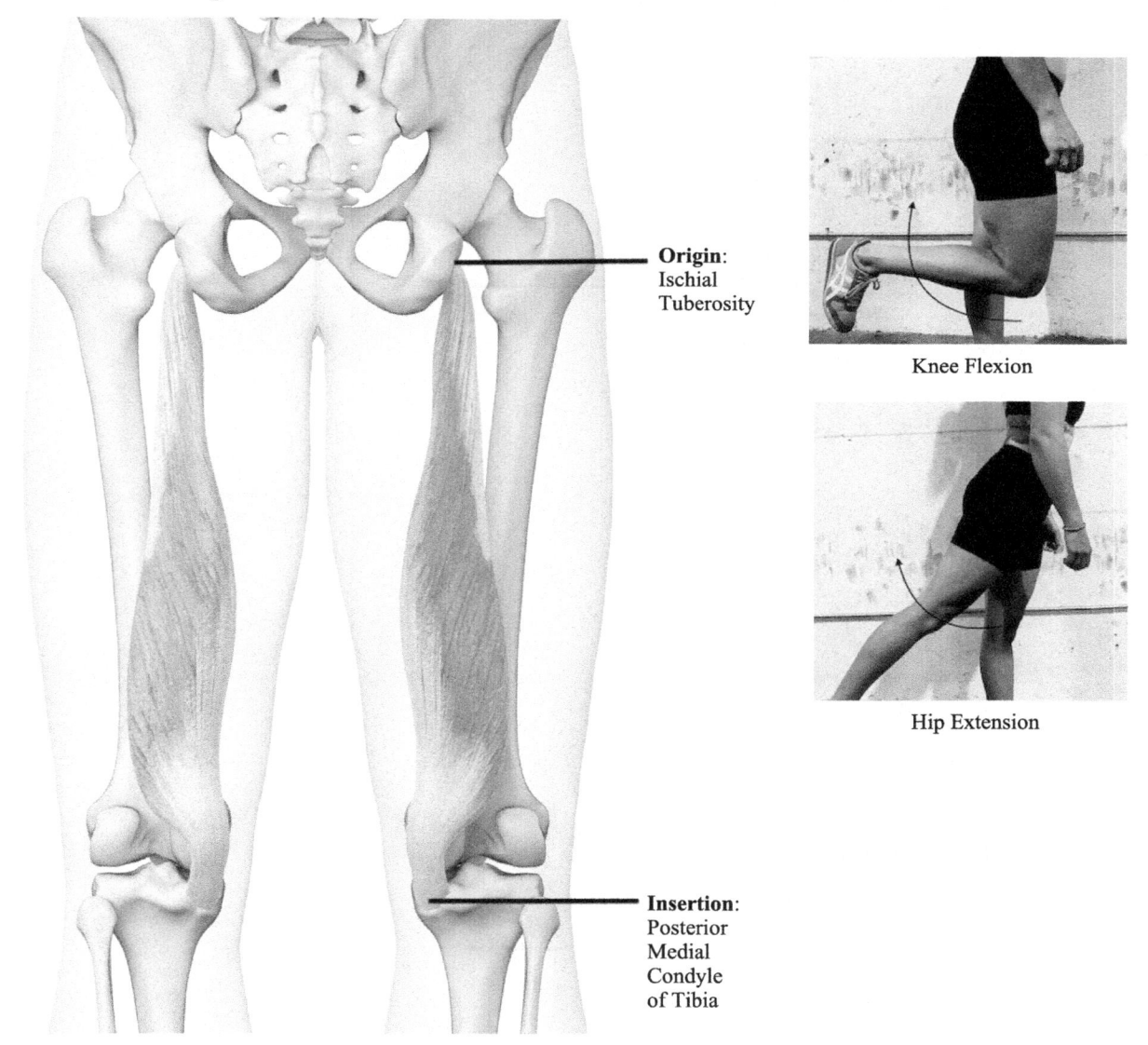

Origin: Ischial Tuberosity

Insertion: Posterior Medial Condyle of Tibia

Knee Flexion

Hip Extension

Origin: Ischial Tuberosity
Insertion: Posterior Medial Condyle of Tibia
Action(s): Extension of Hip, Flexion of Knee

Innervation: Sciatic Nerve(Peroneal branch)
Synergist: Semitendinosus
Antagonist: Rectus Femoris

Semitendinosus

Semitendinosus is a muscle of the thigh, named for its appearance("semi" means "half", "tendinosus" refers to the Latin word "tendere", which means "to stretch").

Semitendinosus originates on the Ischial Tuberosity, and inserts onto the Pes Anserinus, located just medial to the Tibial Tuberosity. "Pes" means "foot", "anserinus" means "goose". The Pes Anserinus resembles a goose foot in appearance.

Semitendinosus is one muscle responsible for extending the hip and flexing the knee, along with Semimembranosus and Biceps Femoris.

Semitendinosus is a member of the Hamstring muscle group, located on the posterior thigh. Semitendinosus sits atop Semimembranosus, and is the intermediate Hamstring muscle.

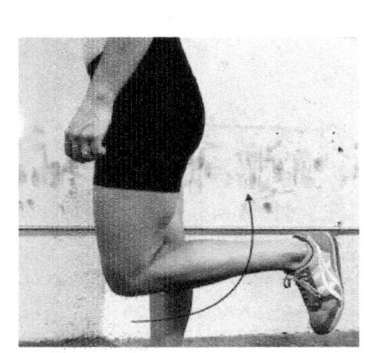

Knee Flexion

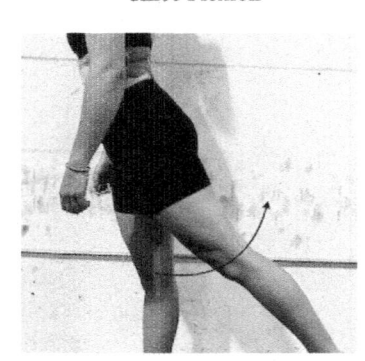

Hip Extension

Origin: Ischial Tuberosity

To remember the muscles that insert on the Pes Anserinus, just think "SGT Goosefoot":
Sartorius
Gracilis
Semitendinosus

Origin: Ischial Tuberosity
Insertion: Pes Anserinus
Action(s): Extension of Hip, Flexion of Knee

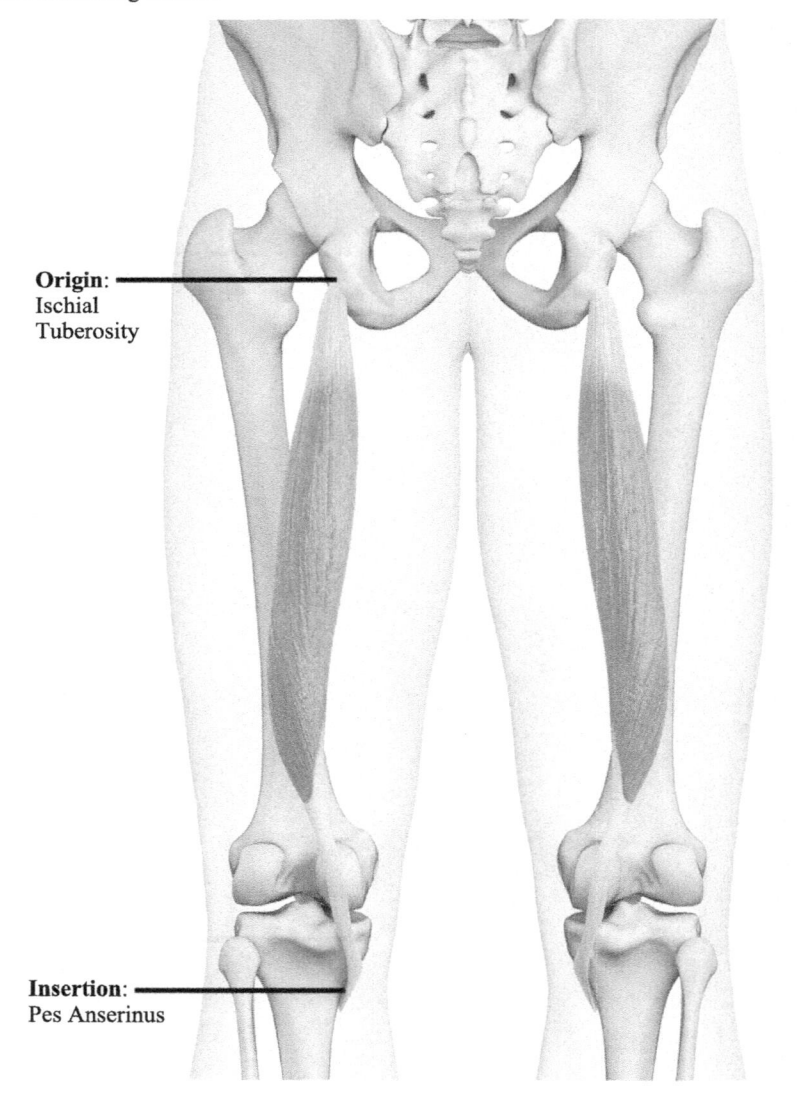

Insertion: Pes Anserinus

Innervation: Sciatic Nerve(Peroneal branch)
Synergist: Biceps Femoris
Antagonist: Rectus Femoris

Tensor Fasciae Latae

Tensor Fasciae Latae is a muscle of the thigh, named after its appearance("tensor" comes from the Latin "tensere", which means "to stretch". "Fasciae" is Latin for "band". "Latae" is Latin for "side", such as the term "lateral").

Tensor Fasciae Latae originates on the Anterior Superior Iliac Spine(ASIS) and the Iliac Crest. Tensor Fasciae Latae inserts into the Iliotibial Tract(also known as the IT Band).

Tensor Fasciae Latae is a synergist in hip flexion.

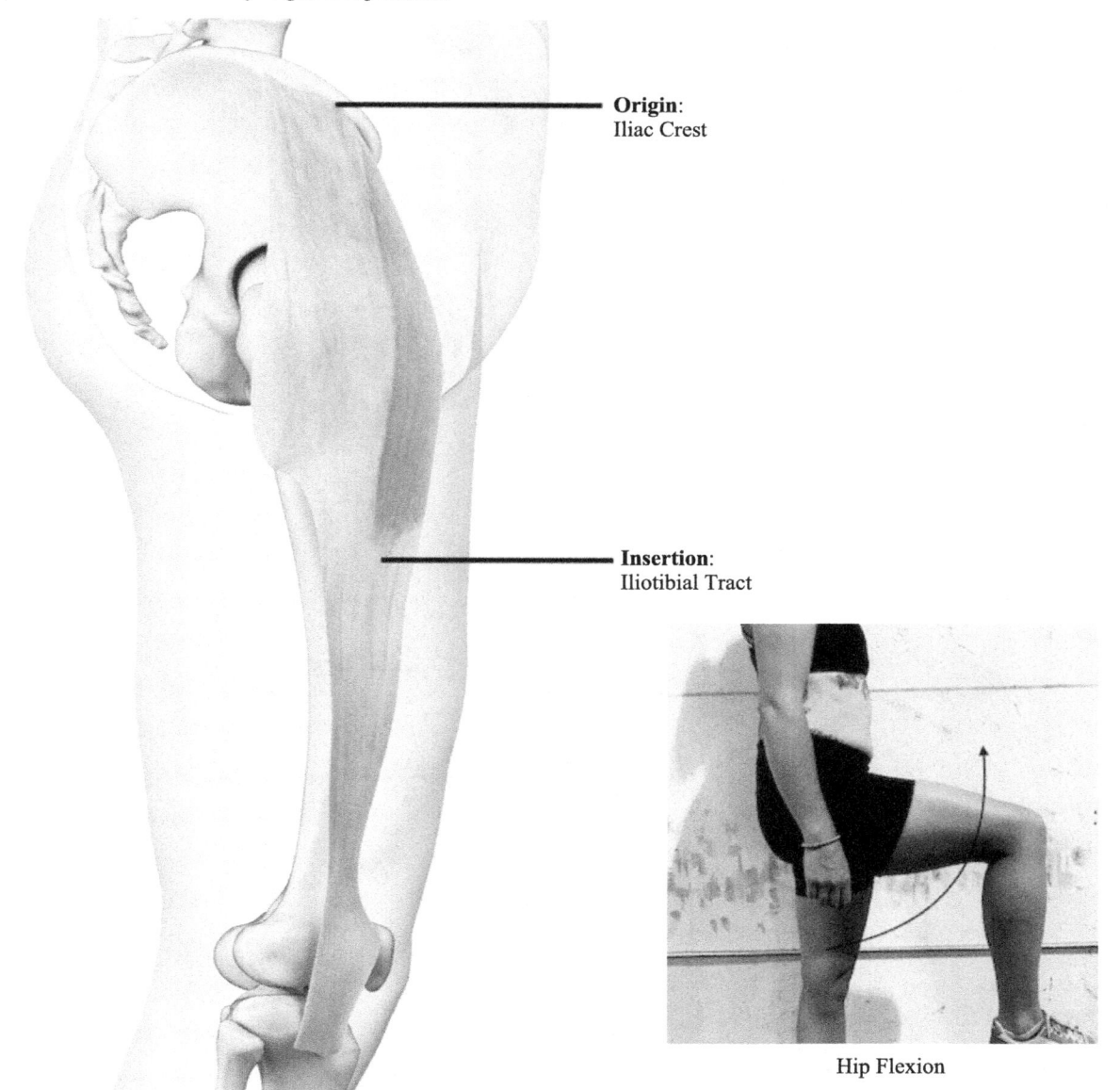

Origin: Iliac Crest

Insertion: Iliotibial Tract

Hip Flexion

Origin: Anterior Superior Iliac Spine, Iliac Crest
Insertion: Iliotibial Tract
Action(s): Flexion of Hip

Innervation: Superior Gluteal Nerve
Synergist: Rectus Femoris
Antagonist: Hamstrings

Muscles of the Leg

Muscles to Know:

Gastrocnemius
Peroneus Longus
Plantaris
Soleus
Tibialis Anterior
Tibialis Posterior

Terms to Know:

Gastr/o: Stomach
Kneme: Leg
Longus: Long

- Gastrocnemius
- Tibialis Anterior
- Soleus
- Peroneus Longus

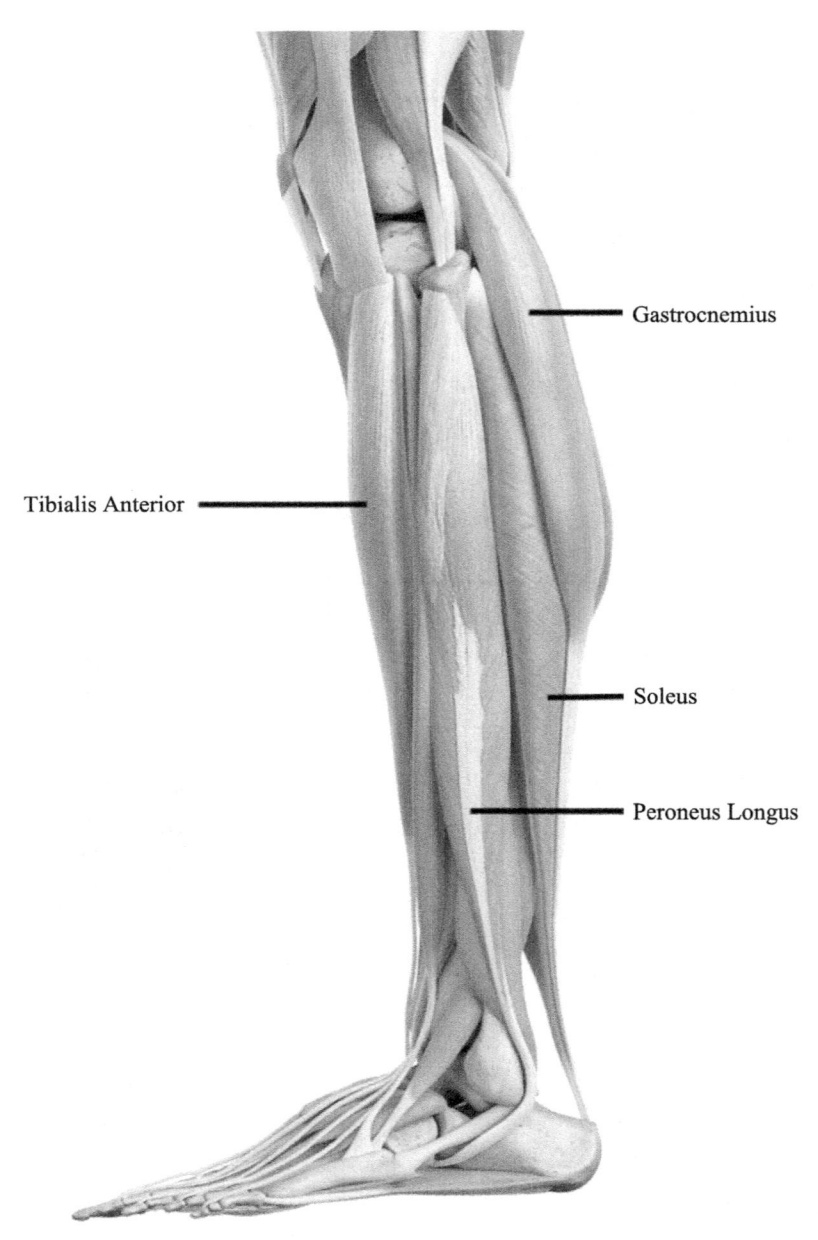

Lateral

Not Pictured: Tibialis Posterior, Plantaris

Gastrocnemius

Gastrocnemius is a muscle of the posterior leg. Its name means stomach(gastro) of the leg(kneme), from Greek origin.

Gastrocnemius originates on the Medial and Lateral Epicondyles of the Femur on the posterior side. The two muscle bellies join together at the Calcaneal Tendon, and insert at the Calcaneus. Another name for the Calcaneal Tendon is "Achilles Tendon", so named after the Greek legend of Achilles.

Gastrocnemius, when contracted, assists the Hamstrings in performing flexion of the knee. Gastrocnemius is the prime mover of plantarflexion.

A primary synergist to Gastrocnemius is the Soleus, the muscle deep to the Gastrocnemius. Soleus joins with the Gastrocnemius at the Calcaneal Tendon, and assists in plantarflexion.

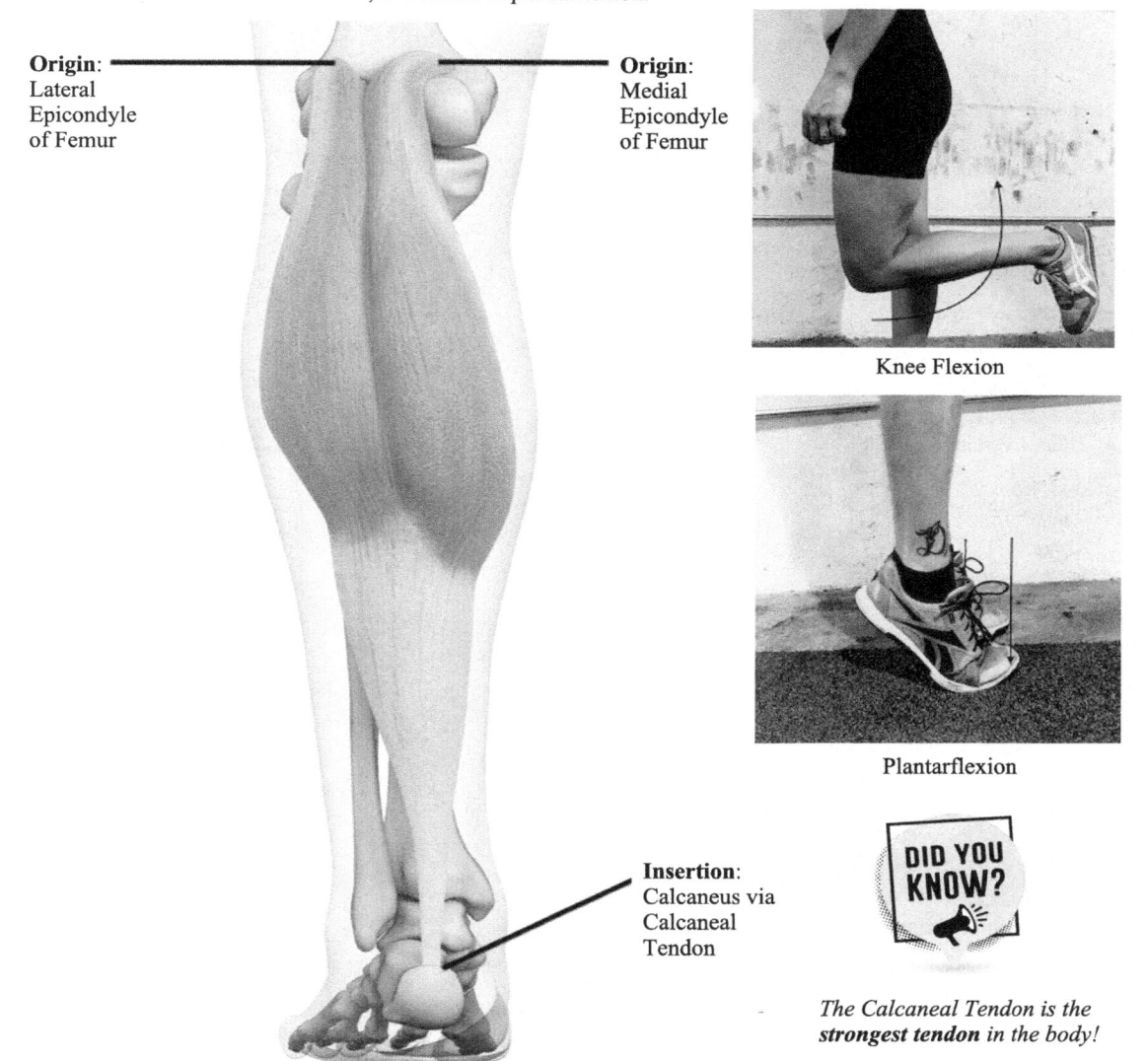

Origin: Lateral Epicondyle of Femur

Origin: Medial Epicondyle of Femur

Knee Flexion

Plantarflexion

Insertion: Calcaneus via Calcaneal Tendon

DID YOU KNOW?
*The Calcaneal Tendon is the **strongest tendon** in the body!*

Origin: Medial and Lateral Epicondyles on Posterior Femur
Insertion: Calcaneus via Calcaneal Tendon
Action(s): Flexion of Knee, Plantarflexion
Innervation: Tibial Nerve
Synergist: Hamstrings, Soleus
Antagonist: Rectus Femoris, Tibialis Anterior

Peroneus Longus

Peroneus Longus is a muscle of the lateral leg, named after its origin("perone" means "fibula" and the two are interchangeable) and length.

Peroneus Longus originates on the Proximal Lateral Shaft of the Fibula, and the Head of the Fibula. It wraps beneath the Lateral Malleolus and onto the plantar surface of the foot, inserting onto the Base of the 1st Metatarsal and Cuneiform I(also known as the Medial Cuneiform).

When Peroneus Longus contracts, is is the prime mover of eversion/pronation of the foot. It also assists the Gastrocnemius and Soleus in performing plantarflexion.

Foot Eversion/Pronation

Plantarflexion

Origin: Head of Fibula

Origin: Proximal Lateral Shaft of Fibula

Insertion: Base of 1st Metatarsal and Cuneiform I

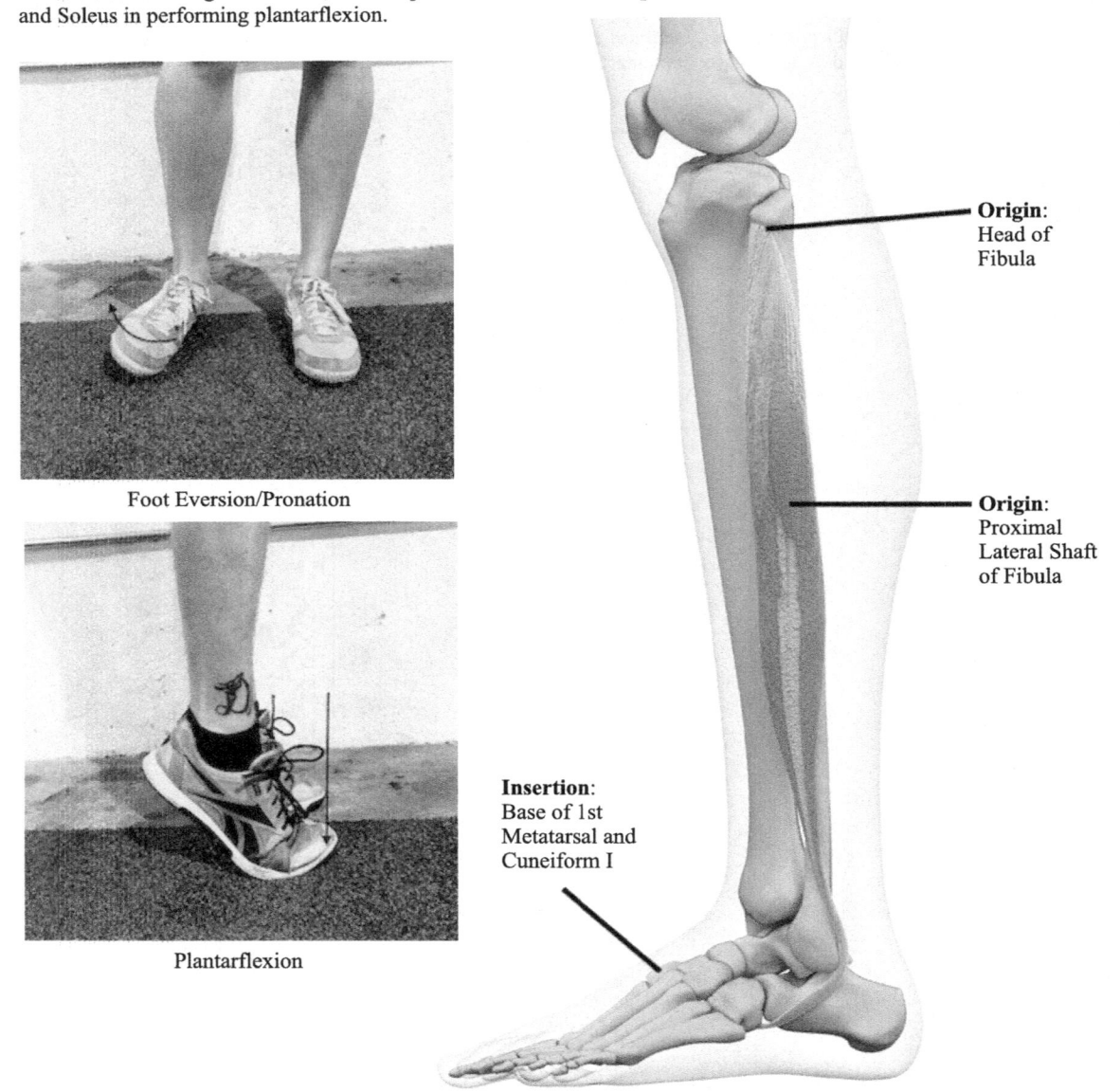

Origin: Head of Fibula, Proximal Shaft of Fibula
Insertion: Base of 1st Metatarsal, Cuneiform I
Action(s): Plantarflexion, Eversion/Pronation of Foot
Innervation: Superficial Peroneal Nerve
Synergist: Peroneus Brevis
Antagonist: Tibialis Anterior

Plantaris

Plantaris is a muscle of the posterior leg, named after its action(plantarflexion).

Plantaris originates on the Lateral Supracondylar Ridge of the Femur, just above the Lateral Epicondyle. It crosses the knee and ankle, inserting onto the calcaneus.

Plantaris is a synergist in all of its actions. At the knee, it assists the Hamstrings and Gastrocnemius in flexion. At the ankle, it assists Gastrocnemius and Soleus in plantarflexion.

If a person injures the Plantaris, they may be diagnosed with a condition known as Tennis Leg, a straining of not just the Plantaris, but the other calf muscles.

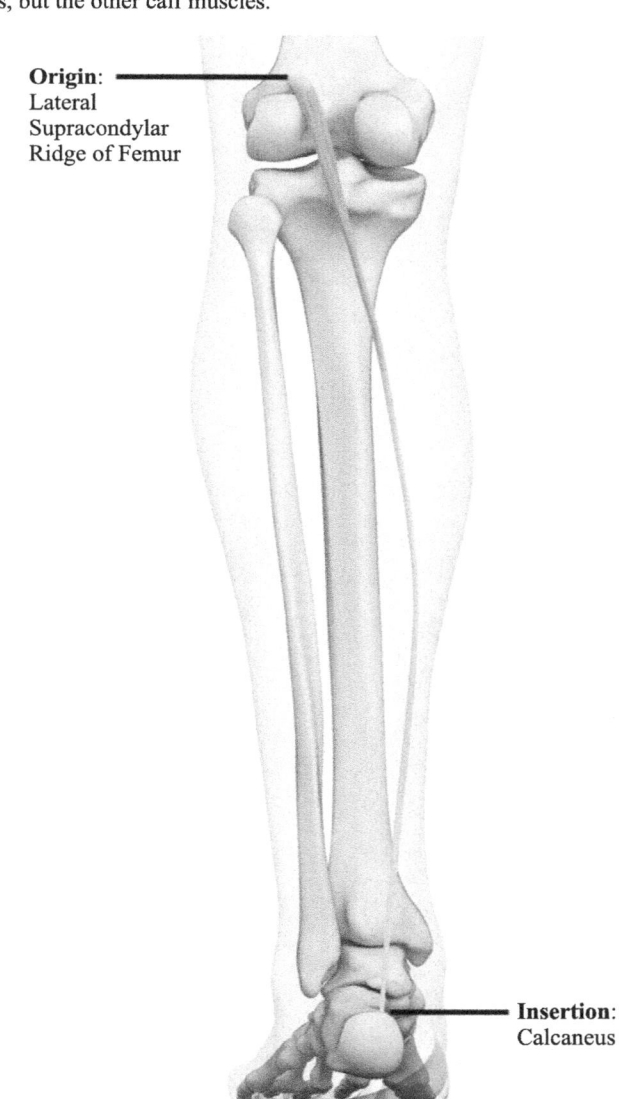

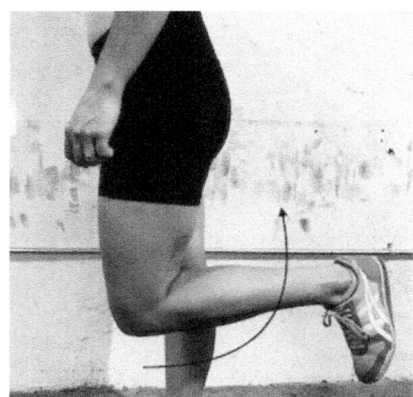

Origin: Lateral Supracondylar Ridge of Femur

Insertion: Calcaneus

Knee Flexion

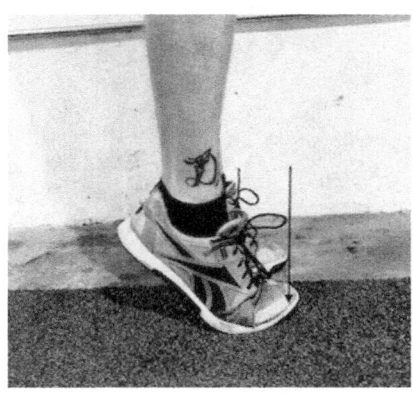

Plantarflexion

*The **longest tendon** in the body attaches the Plantaris to the calcaneus!*

Origin: Lateral Supracondylar Ridge of Femur
Insertion: Calcaneus
Action(s): Flexion of Knee, Plantarflexion

Innervation: Tibial Nerve
Synergist: Gastrocnemius
Antagonist: Tibialis Anterior

Soleus

Soleus is a muscle of the posterior leg, named after its appearance(resembles a sole fish in shape).

Soleus originates on the Soleal Line, a ridge located on the Posterior Proximal Surface of the Tibia, and the Head of the Fibula. Soleus joins with the Gastrocnemius at the calcaneal tendon, inserting onto the calcaneus.

Soleus is primarily a synergist to the Gastrocnemius, performing plantarflexion.

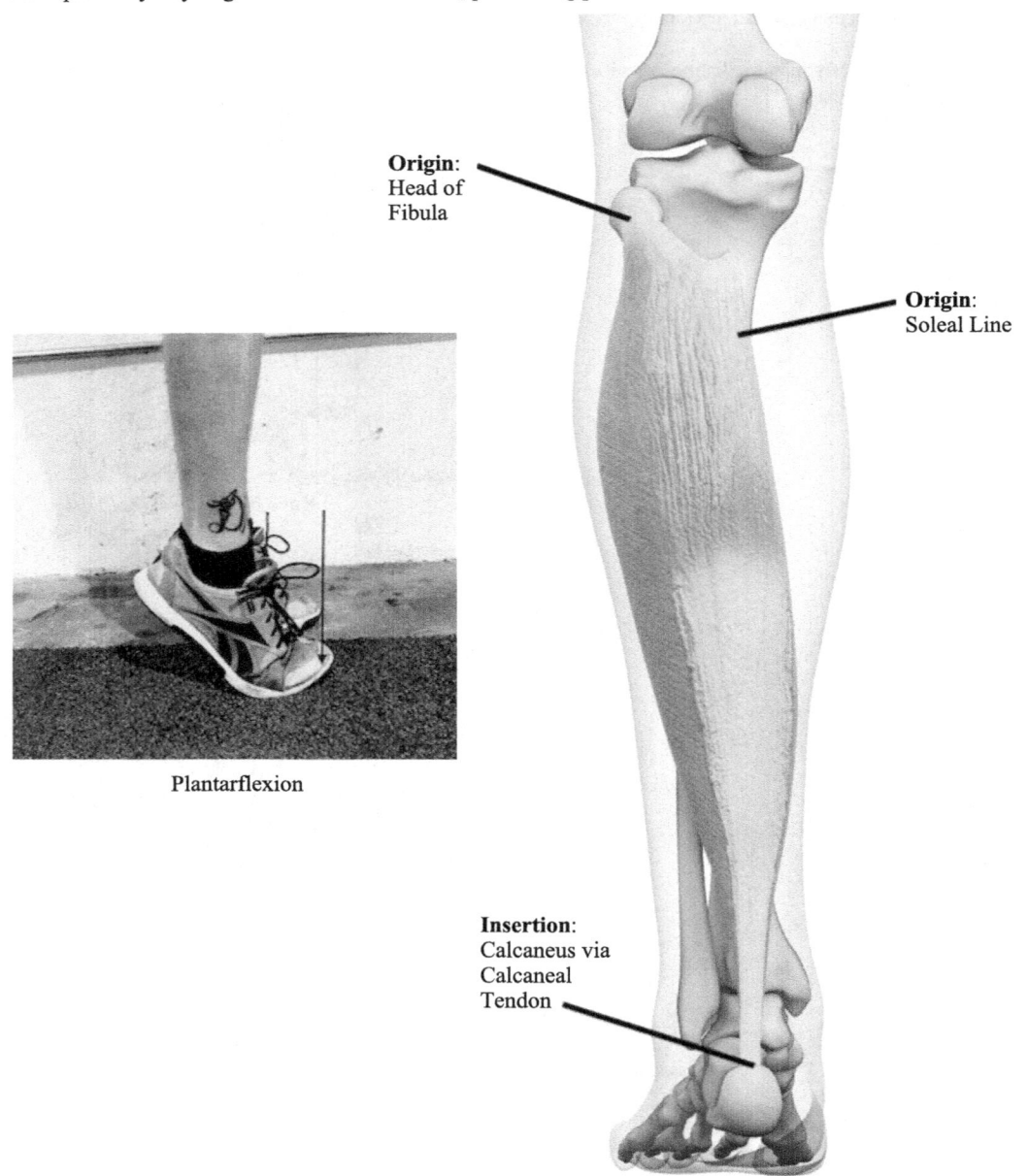

Origin: Head of Fibula

Origin: Soleal Line

Insertion: Calcaneus via Calcaneal Tendon

Plantarflexion

Origin: Soleal Line, Head of Fibula
Insertion: Calcaneus via Calcaneal Tendon
Action(s): Plantarflexion

Innervation: Tibial Nerve
Synergist: Gastrocnemius
Antagonist: Tibialis Anterior

Tibialis Anterior

Tibialis Anterior is a muscle of the anterior leg, named after its origin(Tibia) and location(Anterior).

Tibialis Anterior originates on the Lateral Proximal Shaft of the Tibia, beside the fibula. Tibialis Anterior wraps onto the medial plantar surface of the foot, inserting onto the Base of the 1st Metatarsal, and Cuneiform I(also known as the Medial Cuneiform). It shares its insertion with Peroneus Longus, its direct antagonist.

Tibialis Anterior is the prime mover of inversion/supination of the foot, pulling the soles of the feet in towards the midline when the muscle contracts. It is also the prime mover of dorsiflexion, pulling the foot up.

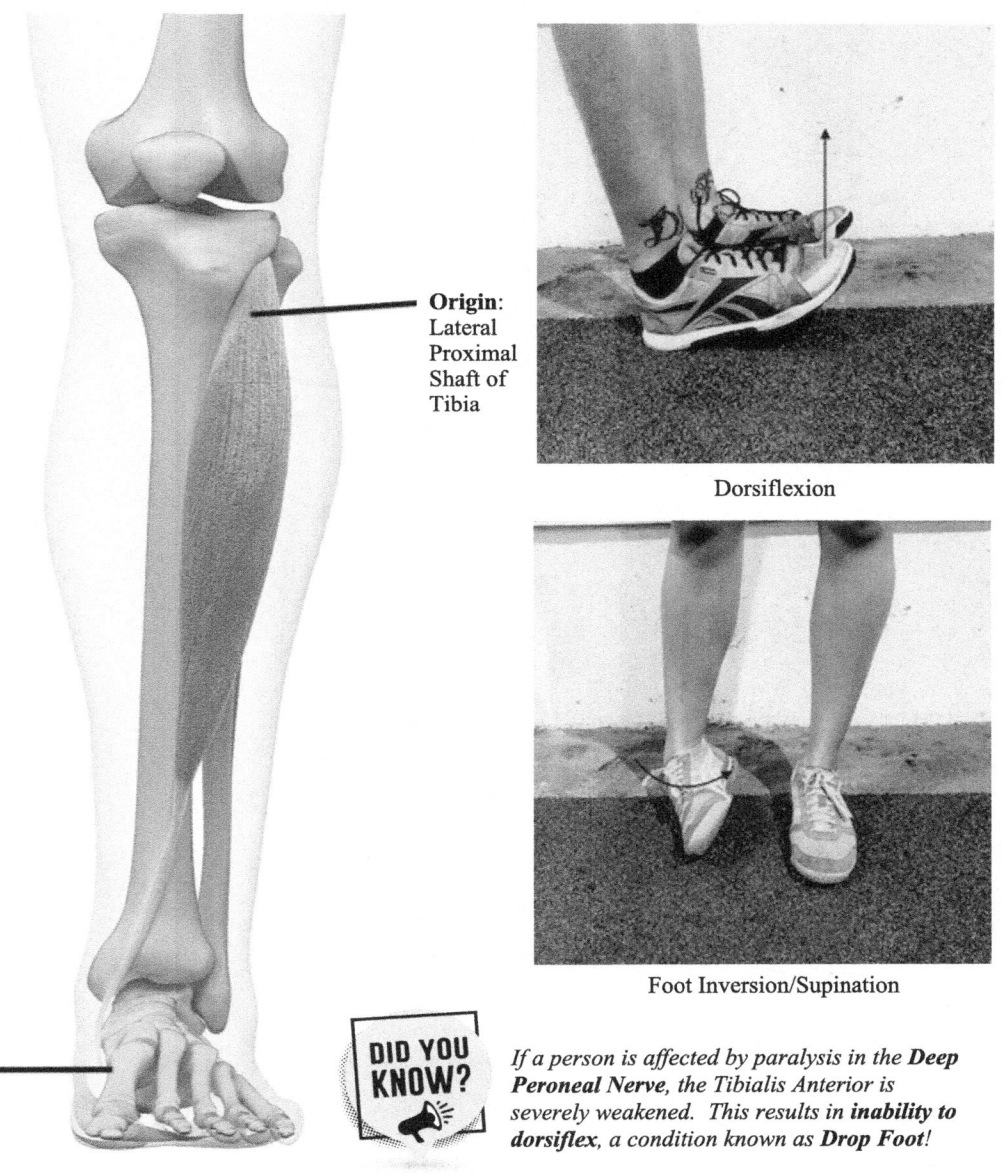

Origin: Lateral Proximal Shaft of Tibia

Dorsiflexion

Foot Inversion/Supination

Insertion: Base of 1st Metatarsal, Cuneiform I

DID YOU KNOW? *If a person is affected by paralysis in the **Deep Peroneal Nerve**, the Tibialis Anterior is severely weakened. This results in **inability to dorsiflex**, a condition known as **Drop Foot**!*

Origin: Lateral Proximal Shaft of Tibia
Insertion: Base of 1st Metatarsal, Cuneiform I
Action(s): Dorsiflexion, Inversion/Supination of Foot

Innervation: Deep Peroneal Nerve
Synergist: Extensor Digitorum Longus, Tibialis Posterior
Antagonist: Peroneus Longus

Tibialis Posterior

Tibialis Posterior is a muscle of the posterior leg, named after its location(on the posterior tibia).

Tibialis Posterior originates on the Posterior Proximal Shaft of the Tibia and Fibula. It crosses the ankle and runs into the plantar surface of the foot, inserting onto the Navicular, Cuneiform I(also called the Medial Cuneiform), and Metatarsals 2-4.

Tibialis Posterior is primarily a synergist, assisting Tibialis Anterior in inversion/supination of the foot, and assisting Gastrocnemius and Soleus in plantarflexing the ankle.

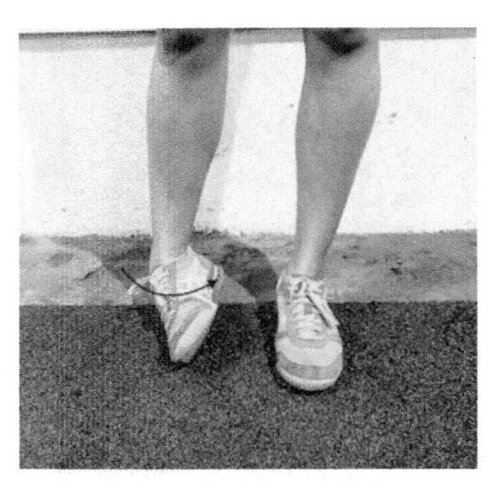

Foot Inversion/Supination

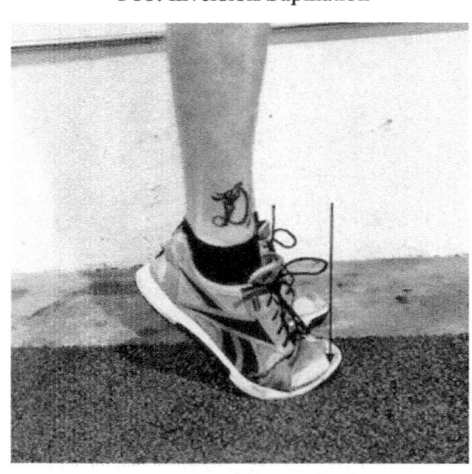

Plantarflexion

Origin: Posterior Proximal Shaft of Tibia

Origin: Posterior Proximal Shaft of Fibula

Insertion: Navicular, Cuneiform I, Metatarsals 2-4

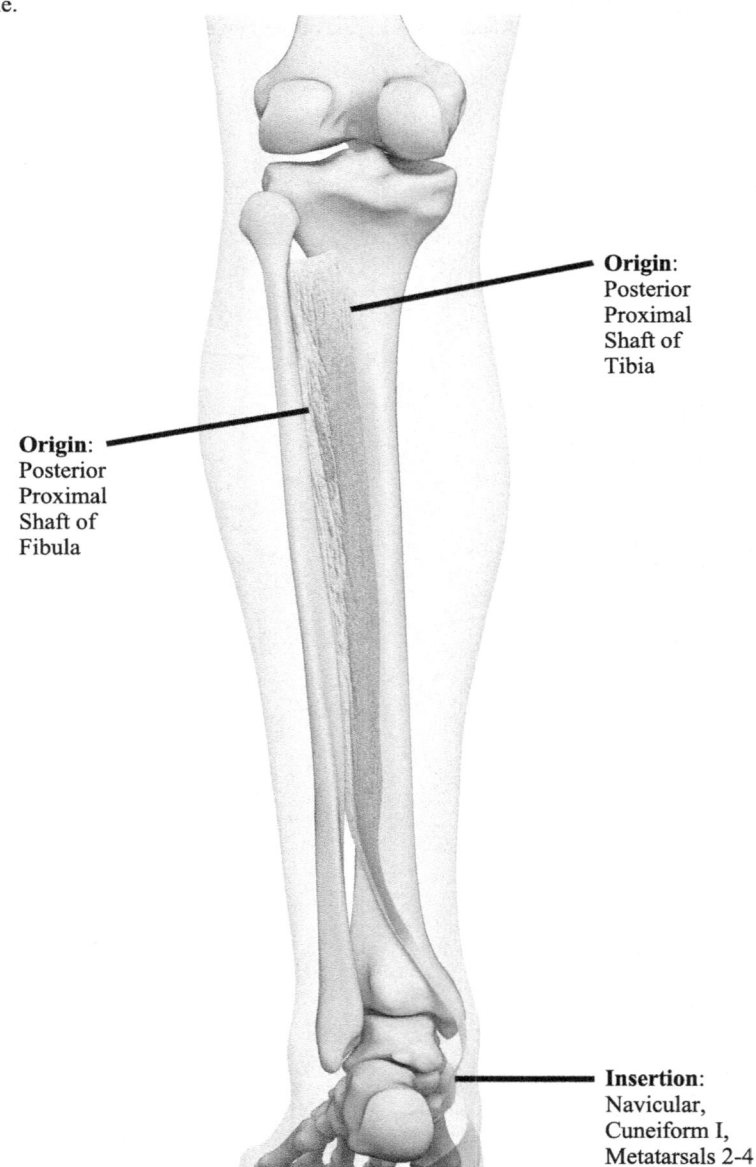

Origin: Posterior Proximal Shaft of Tibia and Fibula
Insertion: Navicular, Cuneiform I, Metatarsals 2-4
Action(s): Inversion of Foot, Plantarflexion

Innervation: Tibial Nerve
Synergist: Tibialis Anterior, Gastrocnemius
Antagonist: Peroneus Longus, Extensor Digitorum Longus

Kinesiology Matching

_____: Action performed by Brachialis

_____: Insertion of Brachioradialis

_____: Muscle that inserts on the Mastoid Process of the Temporal Bone

_____: Insertion of Gracilis

_____: Origin of Temporalis

_____: Action shared by Tibialis Anterior and Tibialis Posterior

_____: Muscle inserting onto the Radial Tuberosity

_____: Prime mover of shoulder abduction

_____: Insertion of Rectus Abdominis

_____: Muscle inserting onto the Pes Anserinus

_____: Origin of Sartorius

_____: Muscles responsible for retracting/adducting the scapula

_____: Action performed by the Biceps Brachii, in which it is the prime mover

_____: Bipennate muscle that crosses the hip and knee on the anterior thigh

_____: Origin of Infraspinatus

_____: Insertion of the Quadriceps

_____: Action performed by the Latissimus Dorsi

_____: Muscle originating in the Supraspinous Fossa

_____: Primary action performed by the Pectoralis Major

_____: Action of the Hamstrings and Gastrocnemius

A: Biceps Brachii
B: Anterior Superior Iliac Spine
C: Elbow Flexion
D: Supraspinatus
E: Deltoid
F: Pes Anserinus
G: Knee Flexion
H: Shoulder Adduction
I: Rectus Femoris
J: Tibial Tuberosity

K: Sartorius
L: Styloid Process of Radius
M: Temporal Fossa
N: Sternocleidomastoid
O: Horizontal Adduction of the Shoulder
P: Rhomboids
Q: Infraspinous Fossa
R: Xiphoid Process
S: Supination
T: Inversion

Answer Key on Page 312

Kinesiology

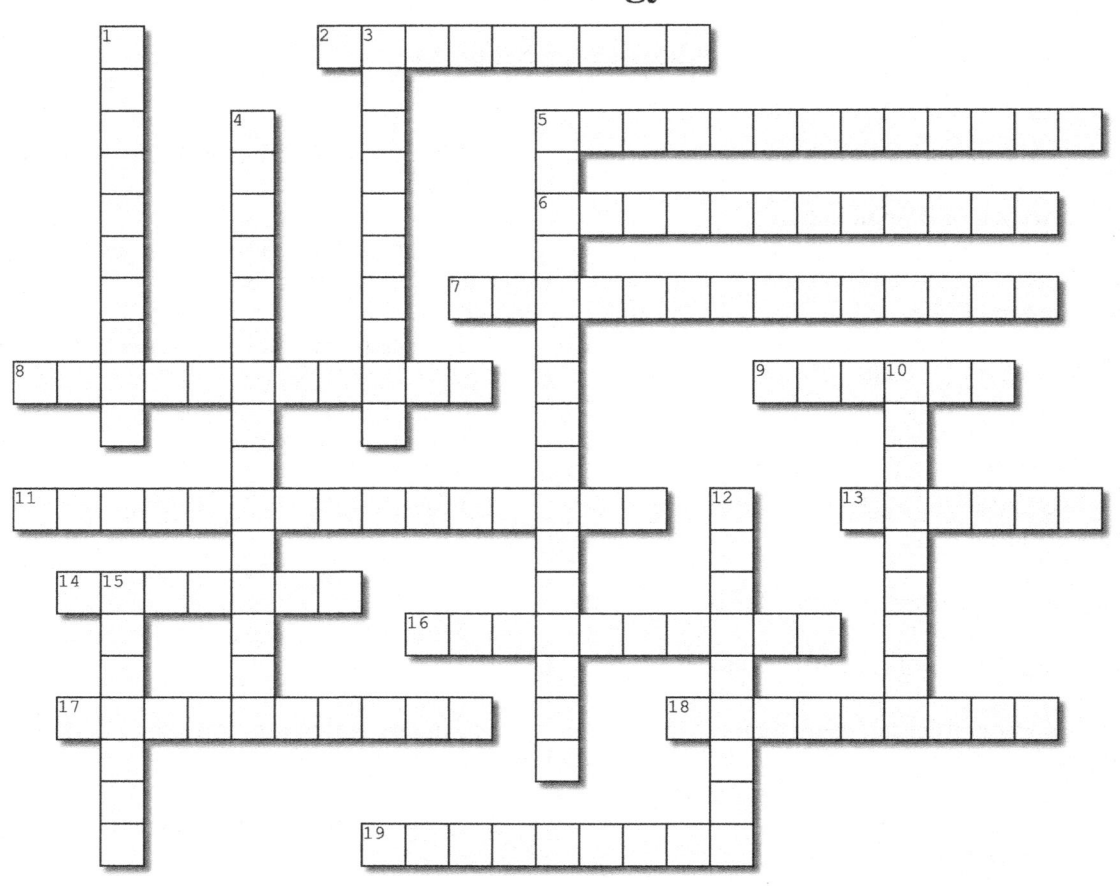

Across
2. Primary action of the Deltoid
5. Muscle originating on the Anterior Inferior Iliac Spine
6. Action Tibialis Anterior performs on the ankle
7. Action Gastrocnemius performs on the ankle
8. Action of the Pectoralis Minor on the scapula
9. Synergist to Gastrocnemius when moving the ankle
11. Origin of the Coracobrachialis
13. Type of rotation Subscapularis performs at the shoulder joint
14. Primary action of Iliopsoas on the hip
16. Antagonists to the Quadriceps when moving the hip
17. Synergist to Latissimus Dorsi
18. Strongest tendon in the body
19. Muscle originating on the Anterior Superior Iliac Spine

Down
1. Action of the Rhomboids on the scapula
3. Strongest flexor of the elbow
4. Muscle primarily responsible for flexion of the trunk
5. Insertion of Biceps Brachii
10. Action of Triceps Brachii on the elbow
12. The longest tendon in the body attaches to this muscle
15. Type of rotation Infraspinatus performs on the shoulder joint

Answer Key on Page 313

Kinesiology 291

Label the numbered muscles on a separate piece of paper

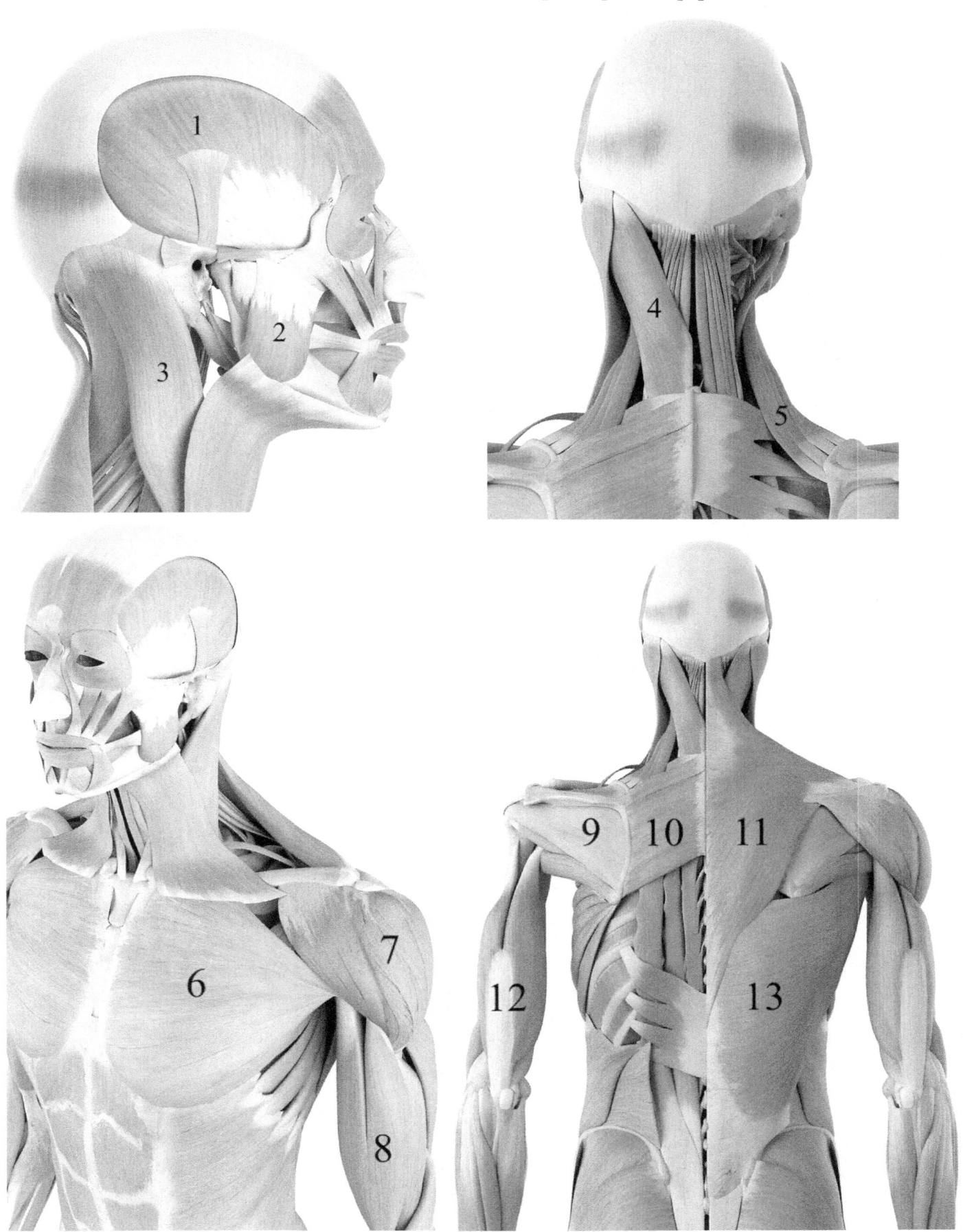

292 Kinesiology

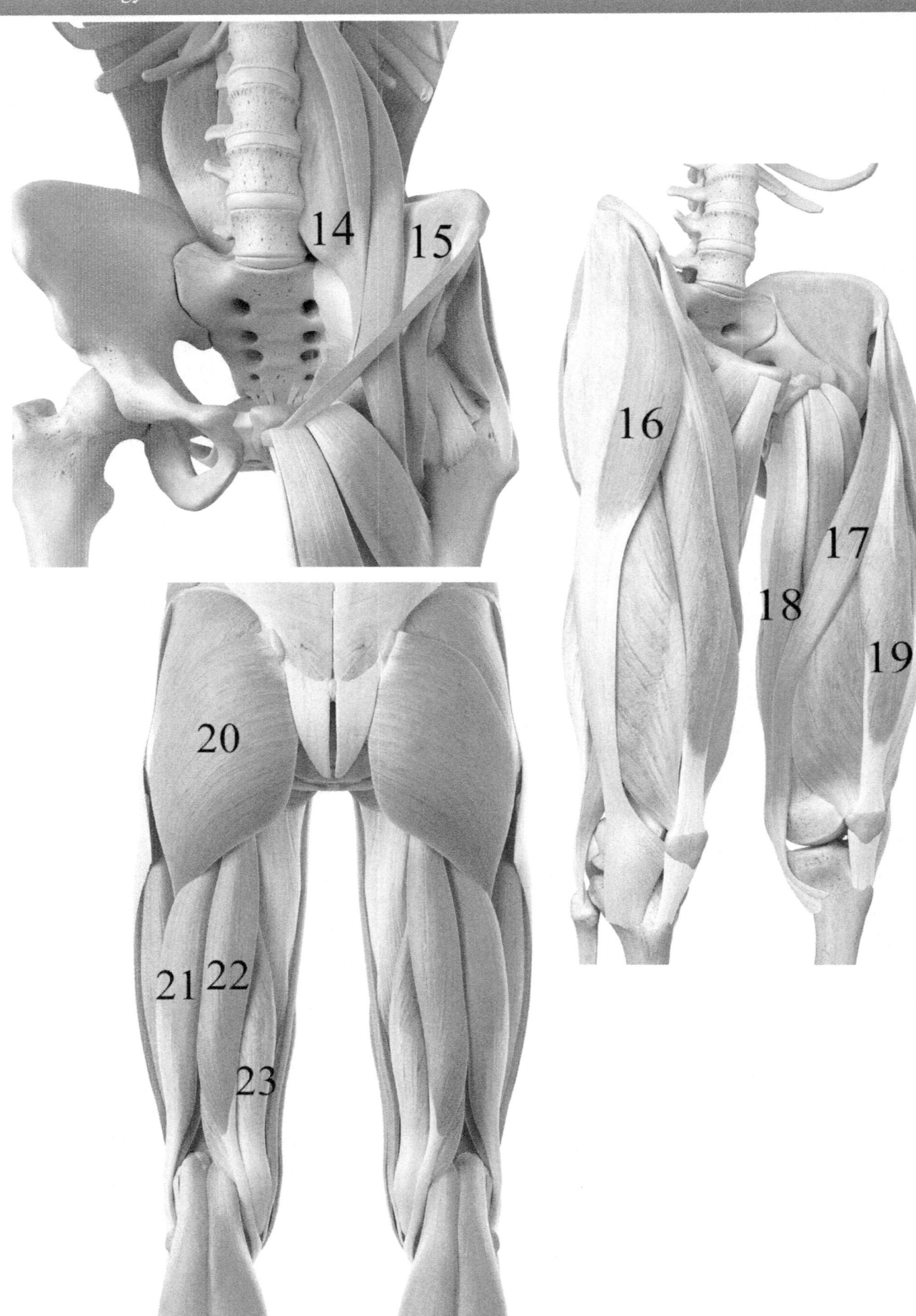

Kinesiology 293

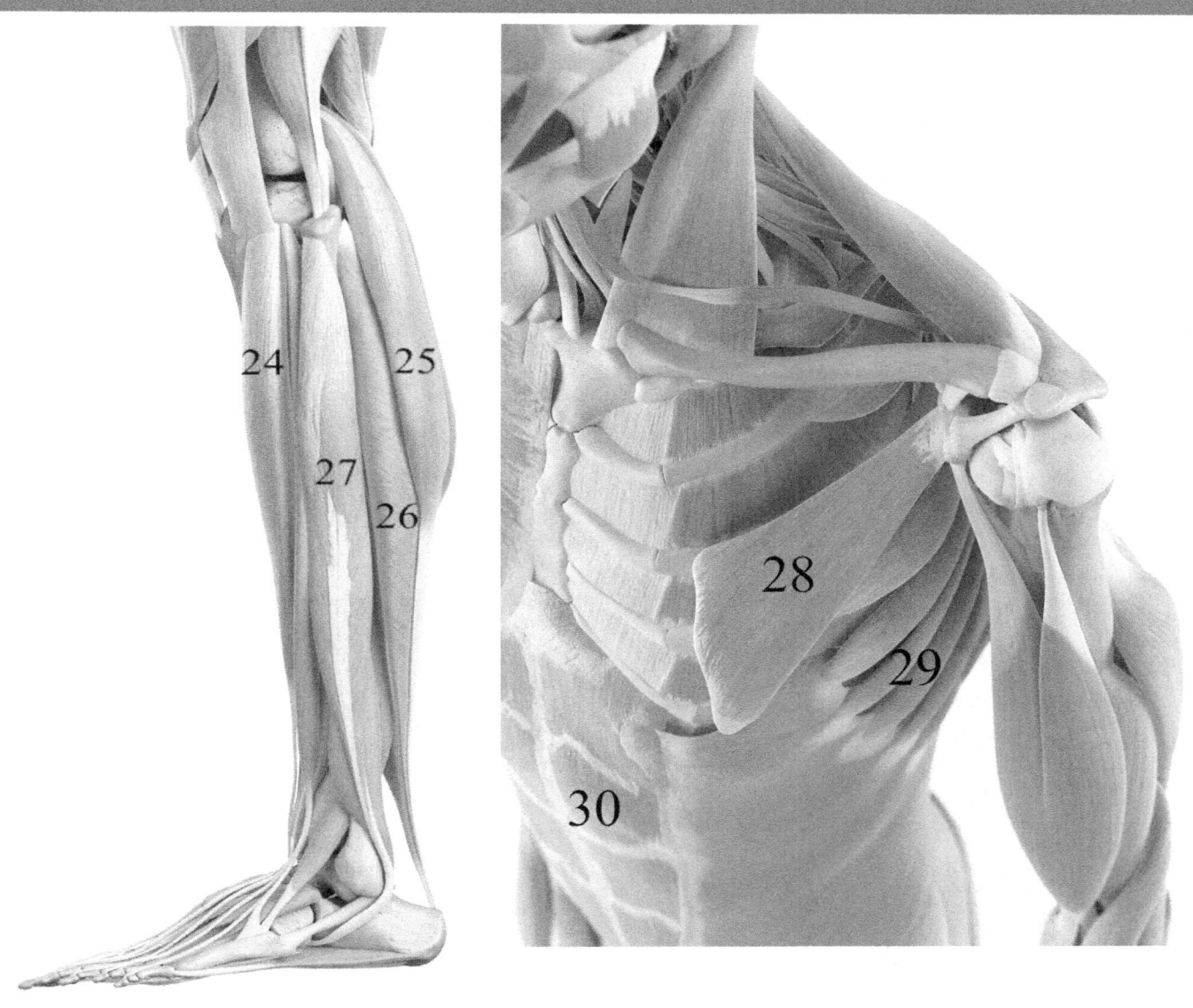

Answer Key on Page 313

Kinesiology Practice Exam

1. Most medial muscle of the erector spinae muscle group
A. Longissimus
B. Semispinalis
C. Spinalis
D. Iliocostalis

2. Insertion of the adductor longus
A. Lesser trochanter
B. Pectineal line
C. Linea aspera
D. Greater trochanter

3. Elbow extension and shoulder extension is performed by the following muscle
A. Triceps brachii
B. Biceps brachii
C. Coracobrachialis
D. Anconeus

4. Part of the scapula serratus anterior inserts onto
A. Medial border
B. Lateral border
C. Spine
D. Inferior angle

5. Muscle originating in the subscapular fossa
A. Pectoralis Minor
B. Supraspinatus
C. Infraspinatus
D. Subscapularis

6. Large bony structures located at the proximal end of the humerus
A. Trochlea and capitulum
B. Medial and lateral epicondyles
C. Deltoid tuberosity and olecranon fossa
D. Greater and lesser tubercles

7. An antagonist to the biceps brachii is
A. Coracobrachialis
B. Brachialis
C. Pronator Teres
D. Supinator

8. Adductor magnus has a common origination site with which muscle group
A. Wrist flexors
B. Quadriceps
C. Rotator cuff
D. Hamstrings

9. All of the following are located on the femur except
A. Medial condyle
B. Greater trochanter
C. Linea alba
D. Adductor tubercle

10. The second cervical vertebrae is also known as
A. Atlas
B. Axis
C. Occiput
D. Temporal

11. Muscle originating on the spinous processes of T7-L5, the iliac crest, and lumbar aponeurosis
A. Quadratus lumborum
B. Latissimus dorsi
C. Spinalis
D. Psoas major

12. Which fiber of the deltoid originates on the acromion process of the scapula
A. Inferior deltoid
B. Anterior deltoid
C. Posterior deltoid
D. Middle deltoid

13. Shoulder flexion, elbow flexion, and forearm supination are all performed by which muscle
A. Brachialis
B. Coracobrachialis
C. Brachioradialis
D. Biceps Brachii

14. Which of the following is a hinge joint
A. Knee
B. Hip
C. Shoulder
D. Wrist

15. Muscle inserting onto the medial lip of the linea aspera and adductor tubercle of the femur
A. Adductor longus
B. Adductor magnus
C. Adductor brevis
D. Gracilis

16. The linea aspera is located on which side of the femur
A. Anterior
B. Posterior
C. Medial
D. Lateral

17. The following muscle inserts onto the lateral lip of the intertubercular groove
A. Pectoralis minor
B. Pectoralis major
C. Latissimus dorsi
D. Teres major

18. The origin of teres minor
A. Lateral border of the scapula
B. Medial border of the scapula
C. Spine of the scapula
D. Inferior angle of the scapula

19. Origin of the rectus femoris
A. Anterior Superior Iliac Spine
B. Anterior Inferior Iliac Spine
C. Ischial tuberosity
D. Body of the pubis

20. Which two structures form the hip joint
A. Head of femur and obturator foramen
B. Head of femur and acetabulum
C. Head of humerus and glenoid fossa
D. Head of humerus and acromion process

21. Contraction of the middle fibers of the trapezius result in
A. Retraction
B. Protraction
C. Elevation
D. Depression

22. The coronal suture connects the following bones of the cranium
A. Occipital and parietal
B. Parietal and parietal
C. Parietal and frontal
D. Temporal and parietal

23. The interphalangeal joints can perform which actions
A. Adduction and abduction
B. Rotation
C. Flexion and extension
D. Protraction and retraction

24. Brachioradialis inserts onto which part of the radius
A. Styloid process
B. Radial tuberosity
C. Head
D. Interosseous border

25. A massage therapist is working on the lateral side of the forearm. The bone they are working on top of is the
A. Radius
B. Ulna
C. Humerus
D. Fibula

26. Muscles originating on the spinous processes of C7-T5
A. Levator scapulae
B. Serratus anterior
C. Trapezius
D. Rhomboids

27. The socket of the hip is also called the
A. Ischial tuberosity
B. Obturator foramen
C. Acetabulum
D. Iliac crest

28. Primary muscle a massage therapist palpates on the lateral edge of the leg
A. Soleus
B. Tibialis anterior
C. Peroneus longus
D. Gastrocnemius

29. The ankle joint is comprised of which two bones
A. Tibia and talus
B. Tibia and fibula
C. Talus and calcaneus
D. Talus and fibula

30. Origin of pectoralis minor
A. Coracoid process
B. Ribs 3-5
C. Ribs 1-3
D. Sternum

31. Extension of the thumb can be accomplished by contraction of which muscle
A. Extensor pollicis longus
B. Flexor pollicis longus
C. Extensor hallucis longus
D. Flexor hallucis longus

32. The saddle joint is located where
A. Elbow
B. Thumb
C. Knee
D. Ankle

33. Structure located on the lateral distal end of the humerus
A. Medial epicondyle
B. Greater tubercle
C. Lateral epicondyle
D. Trochlea

34. Antagonist to the rhomboids, responsible for abduction of the scapula
A. Latissimus dorsi
B. Pectoralis major
C. Trapezius
D. Serratus anterior

35. Proximal attachment of coracobrachialis
A. Coracoid process
B. Coronoid process
C. Medial proximal shaft of humerus
D. Radial tuberosity

36. Joint located between the occiput and first cervical vertebrae, responsible for flexion and extension of the head
A. Atlantoaxial
B. Atlantooccipital
C. Occipitofrontalis
D. Occipitoaxial

37. Three of the four rotator cuff muscles insert onto the greater tubercle of the humerus. The only one that does not is
A. Teres Minor
B. Supraspinatus
C. Infraspinatus
D. Subscapularis

38. Which of the following muscles crosses the glenohumeral joint
A. Pectoralis minor
B. Trapezius
C. Coracobrachialis
D. Brachialis

39. Distal attachment of the peroneus longus
A. Head of the fibula
B. Tuberosity of the fifth metatarsal
C. Base of first metatarsal
D. Lateral condyle of the tibia

40. Synergist to the hamstrings while flexing the knee
A. Gastrocnemius
B. Soleus
C. Tibialis anterior
D. Rectus femoris

41. A concentric contraction of this muscle causes the hip to extend and the knee to flex
A. Gastrocnemius
B. Rectus femoris
C. Biceps brachii
D. Semitendinosus

42. Structure located immediately distal to the coronoid process of the ulna
A. Ulnar tuberosity
B. Coronoid fossa
C. Olecranon fossa
D. Styloid process

43. If a client were to resist the actions of the pectineus, how would they move their body
A. Adduction and flexion of the hip
B. Abduction and extension of the hip
C. Abduction and flexion of the hip
D. Adduction and extension of the hip

44. Muscle originating on the sternum and clavicle, responsible for neck flexion and unilateral head rotation to the opposite side
A. Levator scapulae
B. Sternocleidomastoid
C. Scalenes
D. Pectoralis major

45. The capitulum articulates with
A. Head of the radius
B. Tibial plateau
C. Coracoid process
D. Greater trochanter

46. Which muscle originates on the sternum, ribs, and medial half of the clavicle
A. Teres minor
B. Pectoralis minor
C. Anterior deltoid
D. Pectoralis major

47. What are the two actions performed by the rectus femoris
A. Hip flexion, knee flexion
B. Hip extension, knee extension
C. Hip flexion, knee extension
D. Hip extension, knee flexion

48. Where does the biceps brachii insert?
A. Ulnar Tuberosity
B. Radial Process
C. Coronoid Process
D. Radial Tuberosity

49. Muscle originating on the medial epicondyle of the humerus
A. Brachioradialis
B. Biceps brachii
C. Brachialis
D. Pronator teres

50. Triceps brachii is innervated by the following nerve
A. Ulnar
B. Radial
C. Musculocutaneous
D. Median

Answer Key on Page 314

Critical Thinking

Critical Thinking

In this section, you will need to utilize your critical thinking skills to determine the right or wrong response to each of these given scenarios. No massage session is exactly the same, and things may happen during a session that range from unethical to illegal. Knowing when to spot problems is incredibly useful in any stage of a massage therapist's career!

NOTE: These are NOT scenarios you will see on your exam. These are designed to prepare you for these TYPES of questions as they may be presented on the exam.

1. Mrs Clean?

Katie is a newly licensed massage therapist, working in a day spa. Today, she is seeing a client for a basic Swedish massage. The client, a regular at the spa, is very nice and polite, respectful of the rules and regulations set forth not just from the spa, but from Katie herself.

The massage goes off without a hitch. Katie works on all of the client's trouble spots, performs some stretches, explains the reasons for her techniques as she goes through the massage whenever the client has a question.

Katie finishes the massage by working on the client's face. The session ends, and the client is extremely happy with Katie's massage. After giving the client instructions for getting off the table and where to go afterwards, Katie opens the door and leaves the room. Katie immediately goes to the rest room and washes her hands. Katie grabs a small cup of water to offer to her client. The client emerges from the massage room, drinks the water, and thanks Katie for the fantastic massage.

After dropping off the client in the changing area, Katie returns to her massage room. She takes the sheets off the table, sprays the table, bolsters, and head rest with a soap and water mixture. After wiping the table off, she then sprays the table with isopropyl alcohol to make sure everything is clean and ready for the next client. Katie gathers the dirty linens. Katie opens the door, disposes of the dirty linens, and is ready for her next client.

Katie meets her next client in the spa waiting area, greets the client, and shakes the client's hand. Katie takes the client in to the massage room to begin the session.

What did Katie do wrong?

2. Extremely Confident(ial)

Brandon is a long-time massage therapist, owning his own massage establishment for over ten years. Brandon has seen hundreds of different clients, but has a solid regular client base. He is usually booked all week, with only one or two available appointments every week.

A regular client of Brandon's, named Stan, comes in for his weekly massage appointment. The massage is the same massage Brandon always does for Stan, working on all his areas of concern, paying extra attention to his hamstrings because he runs marathons and his thighs tighten up quite a bit during training. He even lets Brandon know he is running a marathon later that week! The session ends, and Stan leaves as happy as ever, feeling great.

Brandon works Tuesday through Saturday. It is now Saturday evening, and Brandon has just finished his last appointment for the week. To help himself relax, Brandon walks to a hole in the wall bar a couple blocks from his massage establishment. He takes a seat at the bar and orders a brewski. He looks to his right, and sees Stan sitting further down the bar with a couple friends.

Brandon grabs his beer and walks over to Stan, greeting him warmly. They shake hands, and Stan introduces Brandon to his friends. After greeting Stan's friends, Brandon turns to Stan and asks about the marathon Stan had just run. Stan tells him he finished in about three hours. Brandon asks how Stan's hamstrings are feeling, and if massage helped him feel better while running. Stan claims the massage did help.

What did Brandon do wrong?

3. Cracking Me Up

Johnny works in a Chiropractic office as the only massage therapist on staff. He's been working here for over a year, and really enjoys the work. It's a steady job and pays well, and he really enjoys the clientele he gets to work with.

Johnny greets his next client with a very professional demeanor, shaking the client's hand and introducing himself. He brings the client back to the massage room, performs the pre-massage interview and assessment, and instructs the client how he'd like the client on the table. He leaves the room and the client gets on the table as instructed.

Johnny enters the room and begins the massage. While the client is prone, Johnny works on the back. The client enjoys the work on the back, as the client does a lot of manual labor and is constantly lifting heavy objects.

The client seems to be experiencing a small amount of discomfort whenever Johnny massages one specific area in the low back. Johnny asks if the client is all right, and the client says yes, just that it's a little uncomfortable in the area. The client states it feels as if a bone is out of place and needs to be popped back in.

Johnny thinks about this for a second, and remembers watching his boss perform spinal manipulation. Johnny offers to pop the client's back, thinking this could help alleviate the client's pain. The client agrees, and Johnny pushes on the client's back, trying to force the back to pop. He succeeds, and the back does pop. The client thanks Johnny for helping him with his pain. Johnny resumes the massage to completion.

What did Johnny do wrong?

4. New Boot Goofin'

Steph is a massage therapist working for a mountain resort. It is winter time, so it is extremely busy, and the ski slopes are packed. Steph sees many different clients, most of whom she never gets the opportunity to massage again.

A client comes in for a massage scheduled with Steph. Steph greets the client as usual and brings the client back to her massage room. Steph begins the massage, and the client seems to be enjoying it.

During the course of the massage, the client and Steph begin chatting. The client tells Steph that she is in town to ski, but forgot her ski boots at home, and does not want to buy a brand new pair just for this one trip. Steph remembers, she has a couple used pairs of ski boots she never uses any more that she'd be willing to part with. Steph offers to sell the client her used ski boots. The client becomes excited and agrees to buy the boots.

After the session ends, the client and Steph make arrangements to meet at the resort's coffee shop to make the transaction. Later that day they meet at the coffee shop, and the client pays Steph for her used ski boots.

What did Steph do wrong?

5. I Think I Love You

Amber, a massage therapist of six years, has built up a regular clientele base and typically sees the same people at least once every two weeks or so. There is one client in particular she enjoys working on, named James.

James is a good looking man, only a couple years older than Amber. Their personalities mesh, they always have great conversations when he comes in for a massage, and James never misses an appointment. They get along so well, in fact, Amber wonders what might happen if she asks James out on a date.

James comes in for his weekly appointment. Amber has been thinking about James a lot lately, and becomes flustered when she sees him. She brings him in to the massage room, he gets on the table, and the session begins.

The massage is perfectly professional, with no boundaries being crossed by either party. The conversation is delightful as usual. After the massage, Amber meets James outside the massage room with his standard cup of water. James pays for the massage, and books another appointment in one week.

Nervous, Amber stops James before he walks out the door. She states that they've been seeing each other for quite a while and have really gotten to know each other well. She continues, asking James if he'd be interested in going out to dinner with her later that week. James smiles and agrees, and they set up a date.

What did Amber do wrong?

6. Five Finger Discount

Jonah has just been hired as a massage therapist at a local membership-based massage establishment. It is his first massage job, and he's excited to begin his career.

Jonah meets all of his fellow co-workers, and feels right at home at his job. Anxiously, he walks to the waiting area and greets his client. He brings his client to the massage room, instructs the client on how he'd like them on the table, then he leaves. The client gets on the table.

Jonah forgets that he left his massage oil and holster in the break room. He walks down the hall to the employee break room, opens the door, and spots a fellow male co-worker looking in a female co-worker's purse. His co-worker looks up, sees Jonah, and immediately looks away from the purse. He makes quick small talk with Jonah, then leaves the break room, all without Jonah taking his eyes off of him. Jonah grabs his massage oil and holster and leaves the break room, heading back to perform his first massage.

Jonah suspects his co-worker of trying to steal from their other co-workers.

What should Jonah do?

7. Blurred Lines

Charlie is performing a massage on a female client he's never met before. She seems normal, and seems to receive massage quite often. The client complains to Charlie of pain in her low back and glute area.

During the massage, Charlie performs massage on the client, making sure to work on her lower back. The client states that Charlie can work lower, but Charlie states he is already working at the edge of the sheet and cannot work any lower than this.

In an effort to get Charlie to work lower, the client pulls the sheet down further, exposing more of her lower back, but also her underwear.

What should Charlie do?

8. The Bad Touch

Sasha brings a client in for a massage at the local day spa she works at. She has never met the man before, but he seems pleasant.

She begins the massage, working on his back. While working on the trapezius, the client begins making moaning sounds. This is a little strange to Sasha, but nothing she hasn't heard before. Suddenly, she feels the client's hand touch her thigh, and move up towards her buttocks.

What should Sasha do?

9. Flipping Out

Skylar is a young, active teenager involved in gymnastics. She recently had a big meet out of town and her mom booked an appointment for her to receive massage. When Skylar comes in her mom fills out the needed paperwork. The therapist notices that Skylar has some small pustular looking lesions on her skin around her mouth that have dried, forming a honey color crust. The therapist asks about the area and Skylar says it started recently and the area sometimes itches and even burns a little.

What pathologic condition may Skylar be experiencing?

What is it and what are the most common causes?

Is this condition contagious?

Is it safe for Skylar to receive a massage?

What considerations or protocols may the therapist need to make or follow?

10. Harder, Better, Faster, Stronger

Deshaun has decided to get into shape and start lifting weights. After consulting with a personal trainer and doing research on the internet, he determines which exercises to perform to build the muscles he'd like to be larger. During his first visit to the gym, he wants to impress all of the other gym patrons, so he grabs a 45 pound plate in one hand, and carries it across the gym and back. He switches hands, and repeats the process, holding the plate by his side and walking from one end to the gym and back. The next day, Deshaun experiences muscle soreness, and is not able to move certain areas as effectively as before. The next day, the pain has mostly subsided, and Deshaun is able to move the areas again.

What muscle or muscles is Deshaun likely experiencing pain in?

What action was being performed by the side holding the plate to keep it in place?

What type of muscle contraction was performed as Deshaun held the plate in place?

What medical condition has Deshaun suffered, and are there any precautions a massage therapist should take in regards to it?

11. You Were Cold As Ice

Tracey makes an appointment to get a massage for her birthday. She doesn't get them frequently and is seeing a massage therapist she has never seen before. When she arrives, she fills out the intake form and gives it to the therapist. She has checked off the box that indicates that she experiences numbness. The therapist asks Tracey where she experiences the numbness, how often, and if there is any associated pain. The therapist discovers that the numbness is in Tracey's hands. Tracey says her fingers will turn sort of white or lighter in color, then the numbness and pins and needle feeling starts, then they turn a grayish blue color which has a stinging or throbbing feeling, and then it turns back to normal color and sensation. Today, she is not experiencing any of those symptoms. Other than that, Tracey has indicated no other health concerns and just wants to relax for today's session.

What pathologic condition might Tracey be experiencing?

Is massage safe for Tracey?

What considerations may you need to make while Tracey is on the table?

What is the medical name for the white or lighter color called that Tracey experiences?

What is the medical term for "pins and needles"?

What is the medical name for the grayish-blue color that Tracey experiences?

12. A-OK

Dan is a car mechanic and is coming in to the clinic for a massage. His wife booked his massage appointment because he has been complaining of many aches and pains, and she thought it would help. His therapist asks questions about his areas of concern, and all sound like normal muscular issues. Dan does mention that he has been having pain at the base of his right thumb, which is his dominant hand. The pain always gets worse as his work day progresses and is fairly sore at the moment. The therapist asks Dan to grasp his thumb with his four fingers and adduct the wrist. There is a sharp, intense pain at the distal end of the radius at the thumb side of the wrist.

What condition is Dan likely experiencing?

Is massage indicated or contraindicated for this condition?

What is the therapist's next step?

13. Pain in the Neck

Paige comes in to seek massage therapy for the first time. She complains of pain in her neck and in between her scapulae. While she is filling out her intake form, her therapists takes note that she sits with an increased thoracic curve, protracted scapulae, internally rotated shoulders, and a forward head posture. In the interview process the therapist asks some basic questions and discovers that the pain has gotten worse over time and comes and goes. Paige is a student who often sits for long hours in front of a computer as well as works on a computer at her job. The pain comes and goes but is normally worse at the end of the day. Paige finally went to see her doctor and they recommended she seek the help of a massage therapist.

What condition is likely present?

Is it safe for Paige to receive a massage?

What muscles might the therapist find that are short and tight?

What muscles might the therapist find that are stretched and weak?

Is there anything that the therapist would need to be cautious of?

What self-care recommendations should the therapist recommend Paige do?

14. Bowl Me Over

Barold loves to bowl. However, it has been a while since he's bowled. He grabs his ball, shoes, and hits the town ready to destroy some pins. He arrives at the bowling alley and sets up shop on a lane with a couple budskis. Barold is pumped to be back at the alley with all his friends. It is finally Barold's turn to bowl, and he grabs his bowling ball, and steps up to the lane. He sends the ball rolling down the lane, and hits a perfect strike. He openly weeps and smiles, as he is so overcome with joy.

When Barold rolls the ball, what action is his shoulder performing?

What action are Barold's fingers performing while he is holding the ball?

What muscles are contracting when Barold rolls the ball down the lane?

What muscle is contracting when Barold smiles?

15. Step By Step

Natalie seeks out massage treatment for pain and discomfort in her feet. Both seem to hurt as of recently but she says the right side is slightly worse. Her therapist asks some basic questions and discovers Natalie started a new job about a month and a half ago where she is on her feet much more than she used to be. The pain had a fast onset about a week ago and seems to be a burning and aching pain in the arch of the foot and the worst pain is felt when she pushes off of her step, especially when walking up the stairs at her apartment. The pain is the most intense near the heel when she wakes up in the morning and starts walking. Natalie went to see her doctor and they recommended she seek the help of a massage therapist.

What condition is likely present?

Is receiving massage safe for Natalie?

What muscles would the therapist want to work on to treat the condition?

Is there anything the therapist needs to be cautious of?

What is a typical cause of this condition?

What self-care recommendations should the therapist recommend Natalie do at home?

16. The Wanderer

Shawn is a touring musician, traveling the country playing concerts almost every night. He plays the guitar and sings, and has been building a steady fan base since beginning producing music five years ago. He arrives for his latest concert, sets up his merch stand, and greets the concert-goers as they arrive. When each concert-goer approaches Shawn, he extends his hand out and firmly shakes their hand. Eventually, it is time for Shawn to begin his concert. He steps on stage, takes a seat on the stool, sets the guitar in his lap, and begins singing and playing.

What muscles are responsible for putting the hand and forearm into position to shake hands?

What action are Shawn's digits performing when he holds the guitar and places his fingers on the frets?

What is the structure responsible for helping Shawn produce the sound that lets him sing?

What bony landmark is Shawn sitting on while performing, and what muscle group originates on this landmark?

17. We Got a Little Ol' Convoy

Dave, a long distance truck driver, has had a lot of lower back discomfort recently. He visits his doctor and explains he has been experiencing pain and weakness in his lower back, especially when standing, and the doctor recommends Dave see a massage therapist to help with muscular discomfort. Dave makes an appointment and during the intake the therapist asks Dave to stand up to assess Dave's posture and gait. The therapist notices Dave's abdomen seems to be sticking out anteriorly, and his pelvis is tilted anteriorly as well.

What condition could Dave be experiencing?

What muscles may be short and tight?

What muscles may be stretched and weakened?

Is massage indicated or contraindicated?

What special considerations may the therapist need to make?

What self-care recommendations should the therapist suggest to Dave?

18. Pump Up The Jam

Amanda and her husband have gotten a baby sitter for the evening, and are going on a date. They have made plans to visit the nicest, fanciest, most luxurious French restaurant west of the Mississippi. Amanda's husband dresses in his best suit, complete with a red neck tie(power knotted, of course). Amanda applies makeup, throws on a lovely halter-style backless cocktail dress, and she looks absolutely stunning. The one thing missing from her ensemble, however, is her shoes. Amanda grabs a pair of four inch open toed pumps. Real fancy high heeled stuff. She puts the shoes on, looks herself over in a mirror, spritzes herself with her most expensive perfume, and is ready to go.

What position is Amanda's ankle in when she is standing in her high heel shoes?

What muscles are contracted that allow this action to be performed?

What muscle is being stretched while Amanda is wearing her high heel shoes?

Amanda's husband is wearing a neck tie. The tie is placed around which region of the vertebral column?

The tie is tied at the origin of which muscle? This muscle is responsible for turning the head to the opposite side, and flexion of the head.

19. Thumbs Down

Doug is a licensed massage therapist who has been in practice for nine years. Through the years he has noticed pain in his thumbs on and off. The pain has gotten much worse and more frequent over the past two years. Doug assumed it was just from over-use and ignored it. Doug received massage as often as he could for his normal body aches, and would ask for focus on his hands and forearms. Doug had increased his hours at work over the past few years, and he noticed the discomfort turned into pain and visible inflammation. Now, Doug often has trouble making it through a full day of work, and has had to drop down to four days of work a week instead of five. He is also considering taking less clients due to the pain he experiences in his thumb.

What condition is Doug likely experiencing?

Is massage indicated for this condition?

What are some things Doug should do to help manage the condition?

20. Two Steaks, Four Potatoes

Robert has been working all day at the local paint shop. He's exhausted, beat, pooped, whatever you want to call it. He did not receive a long enough lunch break during the day, so he is starving. He jumps in his truck and heads to a chain Texas themed restaurant for some delicious dinner. The hostess seats him, asks what he'd like to drink, and he says "Soda pop would be lovely, thank you." The waitress returns, and after skimming through the menu, Robert decides on what to eat. "Hey. I'll have... two steaks.. and four potatoes.. and a bucket of peanuts.." Robert says, obviously exhausted. The waitress takes his order, and a few minutes later, she brings Robert his food. At this point, he is so tired, he is practically unconscious at the table. The delicious smell of the steaks and potatoes riles him awake, and he quickly devours the meal.

What muscles are responsible for helping Robert chew his food?

When Robert swallows the food, what structure stops food from entering the larynx, preventing choking?

Smooth muscle in the digestive tract helps to move food through the body. This process is known as what?

Steak is made of muscle. What is the contractile unit of a muscle known as?

21. World Class Athlete

Ellie is an avid gym-goer, who loves exercise of all kinds. She loves to run, lift weights, and play sports. After a great session at the gym performing cardiovascular exercises, Ellie heads in to the locker room and jumps in the shower. This is typical, as Ellie doesn't particularly enjoy smelling like sweat and body odor after a workout. She finishes the shower, quickly dries as best she can, gets dressed, and leaves the gym. Several days pass, and while getting dressed in the morning, Ellie notices some redness and irritation between her toes. She examines further, and notices skin peeling in the area. The area slightly itches as well.

What medical condition has Ellie likely contracted, and what type of infection is it?

What kind of medication is used to combat this infection?

If the infection spreads to the nails, what is it called?

Running increases heart rate. What is an irregular heart rhythm?

Heat, such as hot water from a shower, has what affect on blood vessels?

22. Holiday Cancelled

Nick is a delivery man, who is used to carrying heavy loads of cargo. One cold and bitter evening, he places packages into his delivery satchel, and throws it over his back. Suddenly, Nick feels an intense pain in his low back. He sets his satchel on the ground to try and alleviate the pain, but the damage is already done. Nick's low back muscles begin to spasm. With such intense pain, Nick is forced to take the night off of work. The next day, Nick has difficulty moving his trunk, and is experiencing pain radiating down his posterior thigh and leg.

What medical condition may Nick have experienced?

How can this medical condition affect the spinal nerves emerging from the spinal cord?

Pain radiating down the posterior thigh and leg may be an indication of what condition?

What region of the vertebral column has experienced trauma?

Nick enjoys snacking on cookies and a whole milk during his breaks at work. What hormone stimulates the production of milk?

If Nick were to stay in the cold too long, his body temperature may drop to unsafe levels. What is this condition known as?

23. Give Me a Quarterback

Ross is a professional football player, who plays on the offensive line. Game day has arrived, and Ross is eagerly awaiting the start of the game. The game begins, he grabs his helmet, puts it on, and runs out onto the field for the first play. The quarterback calls out the play in the huddle, and they all line up for the play. The center snaps the ball to the quarterback, who hands it off to the running back. The play calls for Ross to make a key block on a linebacker to let the running back gain as many yards as possible. Ross finds the linebacker he's assigned to block and absolutely levels him, sending him flying backwards a few yards. The running back runs past the linebacker who is now flat on his back, and finds nothing but open field ahead of him. He runs the ball for a 75 yard touchdown! The team is excited, especially Ross, who runs down the field to celebrate with his running back and other teammates. Knowing that the running back would not have scored the touchdown without Ross, everyone hoists Ross onto their shoulders in celebration. Ross is the happiest offensive lineman in the world!

Helmets are used to protect the head and brain from injury. What injury can occur when there is a blow to the head that may result in loss of consciousness?

What bones in the skull produce a natural helmet for the body, providing protection for the brain?

The quarterback has to tell the other players what the play will be. What structure in the throat is responsible for producing sound used for speech?

After being blocked by Ross, the linebacker finds himself lying flat on his back. What body position is the linebacker in?

The running back sprints down the field as he approaches the end zone. What actions are the running back's ankles performing as he runs?

When celebrating, Ross sits on other players' shoulders. What is the scientific name of the shoulder joint, and what kind of synovial joint is it?

24. My Neck, My Back

Brianna is a student who is busy studying for the MBLEx. In conjunction with purchasing a brand new copy of the MBLEx Test Prep study guide, she also uses all the online resources the MBLEx Test Prep study guide offers(located on page 3). Brianna sits at her desk, with her laptop in front of her, clicking and typing away. She knows that if she studies hard, she'll do a great job on the exam and pass with flying colors. As the night wears on, she becomes more tired, and begins leaning forward in her chair closer to the computer. Her head and neck are more anterior than normal, and her shoulders become rounded. Eventually, she calls it a night and stops studying, opting for the comfort of her bed.

Which cranial nerve is responsible for sight?

Which bones in the fingers are used on the keys when typing?

What curvature does the cervical vertebrae have, and what can happen to this curvature if Brianna does not correct this posture?

Rounding of the shoulders may result in which condition?

Which hormone regulates the body's circadian rhythm, also known as the wake/sleep cycle, and which gland produces it?

25. Tricky

Owen has grown up near the mountains, and always finds time to hit the slopes and get some snowboarding in when there is fresh snow. One morning, Owen heads to the ski resort, having packed all of his necessary equipment. He parks, grabs his stuff, and heads up the mountain on the ski lift. He reaches the top, and begins his descent down the mountain on his snowboard. Quickly he realizes that he has forgotten a layer of clothing to cover his face. He's hit with cold wind and snow as he works his way down the mountain. Once he reaches the bottom, his face stings from the sensation. He heads back to his car, finds his mask, and puts it on. To help warm himself further, he grabs a hot chocolate from a snack vendor and guzzles it.

If Owen's face were exposed to the cold for an extended period of time, what may form in the soft tissues of his face, and what is that condition known as?

Pain is detected by which sensory receptor?

What path does the hot chocolate take on its way through Owen's digestive tract, ending at the stomach?

Snowboarding is typically performed at higher altitudes. What does the body consume less of at higher altitudes, and what condition is this similar to in regards to systemic function?

26. The Compliant Gait

Harry likes being alone, and is an avid hiker. The time comes for his morning hike through the dark woods of the Pacific Northwest. Harry steps out of his abode located deep in the forest, and inhales the fresh morning air. He spots his typical walking trail, and makes his way towards it. He's walked this trail many times, and really enjoys how serene and quiet it is. After a mile or so, Harry notices footsteps behind him, maybe 50 yards or so. There usually aren't others on the trail, and this worries Harry slightly. Not willing to take any chances, Harry makes his way off the path and hides behind a tree. A few minutes pass, and two people walk by, examining Harry's footprints. They remark how large his footprints are, and seem extremely excited about them. Harry thinks this is rather odd, and remains hidden amongst the foliage. The people take photographs of Harry's footprints, and keep walking until they are out of sight and can no longer be heard. Harry is confused.

Assessing a person's walking pattern is known as what?

What muscle is responsible for inhalation?

Hip flexion plays an important role in walking. What are four muscles that perform flexion of the hip?

How many phalangeal bones are in each foot?

What type of protein produces hair?

27. Whip It Good

Carl has just left work and is ready to head home and see his beloved family. He hops in his car and hits the road. Carl is known to be a safe driver, obeying all traffic laws, being courteous on the road, and being as defensive as possible while behind the wheel. Unfortunately, this does not apply to others on the road! Carl approaches a red light and stops, waiting patiently for the light to change to green. Unbeknownst to him, another driver approaching the light is not paying attention to the road, instead fiddling with their cell phone in an attempt to start the next thrilling episode of the MBLEx Test Prep Podcast. The driver fails to see the red light until it's too late. The driver slams on the brakes, but there is not enough time to stop, and the car hits Carl's vehicle from behind. Because Carl was not anticipating the impact, he did not have time to brace himself for the collision. Carl's head is thrown back and then forward in a rapid motion. A few moments pass, and Carl assesses the situation, and climbs out of the car.

What injury did Carl likely sustain?

Is this injury a contraindication for massage, and if so, what kind of contraindication?

Traffic collisions and sports are the most common ways people tear the strongest ligament in the knee responsible for holding the tibia and femur together. What is this ligament?

A seatbelt is buckled near the hip joint. What is the scientific name of the hip joint, and what kind of synovial joint is it?

In a traffic collision, contusions may occur. What is a contusion, is a contusion contraindicated, and if so, what kind kind of contraindication is it?

28. Say Goodnight?

Colin has been working hard trying to balance his home life and his work life. Colin works in a high-stress environment, in which deadlines are firm and the bosses are uncompromising. After work, he's tasked with paying bills, cleaning the house, and tending to his children. The amount of stress Colin deals with on a daily basis is extensive, and Colin notices it taking an effect on his physical and mental well-being. At night, Colin is unable to get much sleep. What little sleep he gets isn't helpful in recovery, and he often wakes more tired than when he went to bed. He has begun increasing intake of carbohydrates and caffeine to increase his energy during the day. After an especially stressful day at work, Colin's wife suggests he receive a massage to help with the stress.

When the body is placed under stress, which division of the autonomic nervous system is activated?

What hormones specifically are released in a stress response, and what are effects of these hormones on the body?

What condition might Colin have that results in a lack of sleep?

Is this condition contraindicated for massage, and if so, what kind of contraindication is it? If not, what techniques and other elements should be utilized to help Colin?

Increased consumption of carbohydrates and caffeine may lead to which health complications?

29. Kickin' Back

Lacey's back has been killing her for a few days. She works in a nursery and helps move heavy loads of soil, plant flowers, and landscaping. She decides the best way to help with her back pain is to get a massage. She sets up an appointment for the next day, hoping to have work performed mainly on her back. The day of her appointment arrives, and she heads in to the spa. She greets her massage therapist, and makes her way back to the massage room. The massage begins, and the therapist notices some inflammation and tenderness next to the vertebrae. This is where Lacey is experiencing pain, and the pain radiates around the area and even in to other areas of the body. The massage therapist tells Lacey she knows a chiropractor that is really good and can fit Lacey in. Lacey gets the number from the massage therapist after the appointment. The massage therapist says she appreciates Lacey calling the chiropractor, and to mention the massage therapist by name, because the chiropractor pays a referral fee of $10 per referral.

Lifting and twisting in the vertebrae may result in which injury?

Which muscle group is located just lateral to the vertebrae?

To help prevent injuries at work, what should Lacey practice? What can a massage therapist do to prevent injuries at work?

The massage therapist referring someone to a specific chiropractor in exchange for monetary compensation is known as what?

Is the previous question considered a violation of ethics? Why or why not?

30. Quit Bugging Me

Pierre is a photographer in Montreal, who specializes in wedding photography. He also loves outdoor weddings, because it allows him to use natural lighting to capture the beauty of the occasion. Pierre arrives for his latest wedding shoot and photographs the ceremony perfectly. The ceremony finishes, and it's time for photographs in a more private setting with just the bride and groom. He takes them into a grassy field, which has a great natural golden tone to work with. Pierre asks his models to pose, and they oblige, and Pierre takes some amazing photos for their collection. The wedding reception goes just as well, and Pierre considers the day a success. Pierre heads home, removes his clothes to prepare for a shower, and notices a small insect burying itself into the skin near his ankle.

What insect is likely attached to Pierre?

What type of infection, and subsequent medical condition, can the insect spread to Pierre?

What kind of rash may a person experience around the bite location?

Certain people may be allergic to tall grass. What may the body produce in response to allergens, which cause blood vessels to dilate?

Sunlight exposure causes the skin to produce what nutrient?

31. A Vicious Cycle

Cathy is a huge fan of cycling, and makes sure she gets out and rides her bicycle every day or two. One morning, Cathy jumps on her bicycle and hits the road, heading to work. Cathy rides in the bicycle lane as much as possible, but once in a while she has to enter in to traffic. Cathy obeys traffic laws, and actually rides at a relatively high rate of speed, keeping pace with most cars on the road. Cathy approaches a stop light and stops behind a car, resting one leg on the asphalt. Cathy takes a deep breath, then reaches for her water bottle. She brings the water bottle to her mouth and squeezes it, sending water spraying out into her mouth. She takes another quick drink of water, and puts the water bottle back on her bicycle's body, just in time for the light to change colors. She begins riding again as traffic moves with her.

What are the primary actions performed by the hip when a person is riding a bicycle?

What are the primary actions performed by the knee when a person is riding a bicycle?

Riding a bicycle, along with many other exercises, can increase the production of what substance, used to decrease body temperature?

Exercise can temporarily increase blood pressure. In a blood pressure reading of 130/85, what does the higher number represent, and what is specifically being measured that determines the number given?

What number does water measure as on a pH scale?

32. Stop Wine-ing

Ashley is an outgoing woman who loves to go to the local watering hole with her friends. One night, she meets up with several of her friends, and they all take a seat around a large circular table. A waitress comes by to take their orders, and Ashley decides she's in the mood for a glass of Willamette Valley Vineyards Whole Cluster Pinot Noir(it's delicious, trust me). The drinks arrive, and Ashley pounds her glass of wine, pointing out how delicious it is to all her friends. She decides to order another, and she really pounds that one too! Ashley is feeling a little buzzed, but it's nothing she hasn't been able to handle before. She decides "YOLO" and orders ANOTHER glass of wine! Halfway through the third glass, Ashley begins feeling a headache starting. She polishes off the wine, and soon, the headache gets much, much worse. She has difficulty focusing on vision, light bothers her, sharp noises make the pain worse. She decides she has to leave and go home to recover. Her friends order her a ride-share, and she makes it home safely, but she feels even worse when she gets home than she did before she left. She makes it in to her house, turns off all the lights, jumps in bed, and tries to ride out whatever pain she's experiencing.

What medical condition is Ashley likely experiencing?

What are triggers that may contribute to this condition occurring?

What structures in the body are specifically causing Ashley to experience pain?

Wine contains alcohol, which increases the production of what substance in the body?

When a person is seated in a chair, what position are the hips in?

33. Lost at Sea

Julius slowly opens his eyes to the lapping of waves on the beach. He has no idea where he is, or how he got there. The last thing he remembers is being on an airplane somewhere over the Pacific ocean, and the oxygen masks suddenly dropping from the ceiling. Julius stands up and takes his surroundings into account. He appears to be on a deserted island, with nobody else in sight. The sun is beating down on Julius, so he removes his shirt and places it on his head to help himself cool down. He begins walking along the beach to search for anything, whether it be other people, a way off the island, or even just food and water. The island is small, there is a small amount of vegetation, and things aren't looking good for Julius.

The ocean contains a high concentration of which substance, an extremely important electrolyte in the body?

Excessive exposure to sunlight over a short period may result in what?

Excessive exposure to sunlight over a long period of time, in some cases years, may result in the development of what?

Medications that are designed to lower body temperature in cases such as fever are known as?

What are the three stages of "injury" a person may experience if their body temperature is too high for too long?

34. Found at Sea

Weeks pass, and Julius has found a way to survive. He's developed a way to catch rain fall, and has been eating nuts, roots, and insects he's found. He's even figured out how to catch fish! However, Julius is not willing to stay on the island his entire life, and is determined to find a way off and back to civilization. He builds himself a raft using a home-made hammer and tying pieces of driftwood together. Finally the day arrives where he plans on setting sail. He pushes the raft out into the water and climbs on. The wind blows the raft past the breakers, and Julius is now at sea, anxious to be rescued.

Two days go by, and Julius has begun running short on his supplies. Just as Julius begins feeling as if the end is near, he spots a shimmering light in the horizon. A ship! He signals to the ship using a piece of metal he found on the island, hoping they spot it. Luckily for Julius, they spot him, and turn towards him! Julius openly celebrates as the ship nears. His excitement can't be contained as the ship gets ever closer, and he jumps in the ocean and swims towards it. He's finally pulled aboard, and is saved!

Julius uses a hammer. What muscle is primarily responsible for performing the action of hammering?

What muscles perform extension of the hip, the primary action used when pushing an object?

What muscle is known as the "swimmer's muscle" due to its actions, which are performed when a person swims?

What specific actions do the "swimmer's muscle" perform?

35. Sorry 'Bout That One

Jenny works at as medical receptionist and is constantly on the telephone, often holding the phone to her ear with her shoulder. After several months of this, she decides enough is enough, and she needs to get a massage. She stops in to a chain massage establishment after work and books herself a massage for right then. She takes a seat in the waiting area, and the massage therapist, Becky, introduces herself and takes Jenny back to the massage room. Becky asks Jenny what brings her in for the appointment, and Jenny states that she has pain in her neck from her job. Becky asks Jenny to rotate and laterally flex her head/neck. After performing these brief exercises, Becky instructs Jenny to get on the table, under the top sheet. Jenny obliges after Becky leaves the room. Becky returns a moment later, and the massage begins. Becky asks Jenny if there were any areas she wants massaged specifically, and Jenny says she doesn't know, but she trusts Becky to do whatever because

Becky knows what she's doing. Becky begins massaging the back, and Jenny lets out a deep sigh, then immediately apologizes, thinking her breathing has upset Becky in some way. Becky assures Jenny that everything is fine. Jenny then apologizes for apologizing! Finally, Becky is able to get Jenny to relax and enjoy the massage.

Holding a phone with the shoulder and ear produces what type of muscle contraction to be performed?

What muscle, which is part of the anterior triangle of the neck, may be strained from performing this action excessively?

Becky asking Jenny to rotate and laterally flex her head/neck is part of what aspect of the massage session?

Jenny lies under the top sheet on the massage table. This is known as what, and what is the primary reason for this?

Jenny deferring to Becky on preferred areas to be massaged due to Becky's perceived expertise, and apologizing for coughing may be a sign of what occurring?

Answer Keys

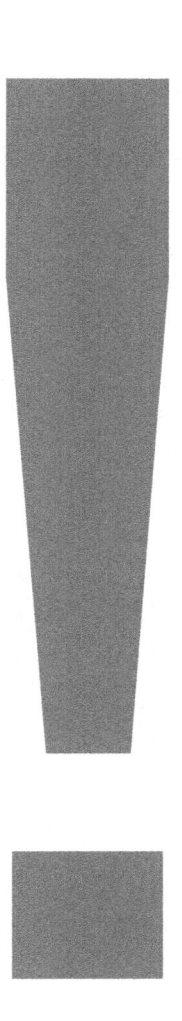

Matching Answer Key

Massage Matching(p 32):

K	G
H	I
M	O
E	T
R	N
L	S
D	C
A	F
Q	B
J	P

Word Root Matching(p 44):

R	H
M	A
G	D
J	E
K	T
L	S
P	I
Q	F
C	O
B	N

Prefix Matching(p 44):

S	D
C	K
P	I
B	M
O	E
A	H
J	N
R	Q
T	L
G	F

Suffix Matching(p 44):

M	I
L	C
R	Q
S	K
O	J
A	D
P	F
H	T
B	E
G	N

Anatomy Matching(p 89):

C	P
K	N
E	A
T	H
O	S
D	J
M	F
L	G
B	I
Q	R

Pathology Matching(p 199):

D	R
P	B
G	I
O	M
A	L
N	H
T	C
J	F
S	K
E	Q

Kinesiology Matching(p 289):

C	P
L	S
N	I
F	Q
M	J
T	H
A	D
E	O
R	G
K	
B	

Medical Terminology Breaking Down/Building(p 45):

Breaking Down:
1. Artery/hard/condition
2. Renal pelvis/kidney/inflammation
3. Brain/inflammation
4. Lymph/swelling
5. Excessive/thyroid/condition
6. Bile/bladder/inflammation
7. Liver/inflammation
8. Vein/inflammation
9. Twisted/neck
10. Skin/plant/condition
11. Extremity/ irregular enlargement
12. Muscle/heart/blood flow obstruction
13. Not/sleep
14. Nerve/pain
15. Tendon/synovial/inflammation

Building:
1. An/emia
2. Athero/scler/osis
3. Gastr/itis
4. Melan/oma
5. Fibro/my/algia
6. Osteo/arthr/itis
7. Cyst/itis
8. A/pnea
9. Onycho/myc/osis
10. Dermat/itis
11. Hyper/tension
12. Ar/rhythmia
13. Leuk/emia
14. Kyph/osis
15. Cellul/itis

Answer Keys

Massage Therapy (p 33)

Anatomy and Physiology (p 90)

Pathology (p 200)

Kinesiology (p 290)

Kinesiology Muscle Labeling (p 291)

1. Temporalis
2. Masseter
3. Sternocleidomastoid
4. Splenius Capitis
5. Levator Scapulae
6. Pectoralis Major
7. Deltoid
8. Biceps Brachii
9. Infraspinatus
10. Rhomboids
11. Trapezius
12. Triceps Brachii
13. Latissimus Dorsi
14. Psoas Major
15. Iliacus
16. Tensor Fascia Lata
17. Sartorius
18. Gracilis
19. Rectus Femoris
20. Gluteus Maximus
21. Biceps Femoris
22. Semitendinosus
23. Semimembranosus
24. Tibialis Anterior
25. Gastrocnemius
26. Soleus
27. Peroneus Longus
28. Pectoralis Minor
29. Serratus Anterior
30. Rectus Abdominis

Individual Subject Practice Test Answer Keys

Massage Therapy (p 34)		Medical Terminology (p 46)		Anatomy and Physiology (p 91)		Pathology (p 201)		Kinesiology (p 294)	
01. C	26. A	01. A	26. B	01. C	26. C	01. C	26. C	01. C	26. D
02. D	27. C	02. D	27. D	02. B	27. C	02. C	27. A	02. C	27. C
03. B	28. A	03. C	28. A	03. A	28. D	03. C	28. D	03. A	28. C
04. D	29. A	04. A	29. B	04. B	29. A	04. A	29. C	04. A	29. A
05. A	30. D	05. B	30. C	05. D	30. C	05. B	30. D	05. D	30. B
06. A	31. A	06. A	31. C	06. A	31. D	06. D	31. A	06. D	31. A
07. C	32. B	07. C	32. A	07. C	32. C	07. B	32. C	07. C	32. B
08. B	33. C	08. B	33. D	08. A	33. A	08. A	33. B	08. D	33. C
09. C	34. D	09. D	34. B	09. A	34. D	09. C	34. A	09. C	34. D
10. C	35. A	10. D	35. A	10. D	35. B	10. C	35. D	10. B	35. A
11. C	36. B	11. C	36. D	11. D	36. B	11. A	36. C	11. B	36. B
12. D	37. A	12. A	37. B	12. B	37. A	12. D	37. D	12. D	37. D
13. B	38. C	13. C	38. B	13. A	38. C	13. A	38. A	13. D	38. C
14. D	39. B	14. B	39. C	14. D	39. D	14. B	39. B	14. A	39. C
15. A	40. C	15. A	40. B	15. A	40. D	15. C	40. A	15. B	40. A
16. D	41. C	16. C	41. D	16. D	41. C	16. B	41. D	16. B	41. D
17. A	42. A	17. D	42. A	17. B	42. C	17. B	42. A	17. B	42. A
18. B	43. D	18. C	43. C	18. B	43. B	18. C	43. C	18. A	43. B
19. B	44. C	19. A	44. B	19. A	44. C	19. D	44. C	19. B	44. B
20. D	45. B	20. C	45. C	20. A	45. A	20. C	45. C	20. B	45. A
21. C	46. A	21. B	46. A	21. A	46. B	21. A	46. C	21. A	46. D
22. D	47. A	22. B	47. B	22. D	47. D	22. B	47. A	22. C	47. C
23. A	48. A	23. A	48. D	23. C	48. B	23. D	48. B	23. C	48. D
24. B	49. D	24. C	49. C	24. C	49. C	24. A	49. C	24. A	49. D
25. B	50. A	25. D	50. A	25. B	50. A	25. B	50. A	25. A	50. B

For detailed answer explanations, watch the videos at mblextestprep.com/resources.html

Critical Thinking Answers

1. Katie forgot to clean the door handle! The client, who had not washed their hand, opened the door. This contaminated the door handle. Katie cleaned the table, bolsters, and head rest perfectly, but her hand became contaminated when she grabbed the door handle without cleaning it first. She then shook the hand of her next client, which resulted in cross-contamination. Make sure you clean anything the client touches!

2. Brandon has violated confidentiality. Anything the client states during the massage is to be kept confidential, and should only be discussed with the client in a massage setting. By asking Stan about the marathon and the work on his hamstrings in a public setting, he has violated the confidentiality established with Stan.

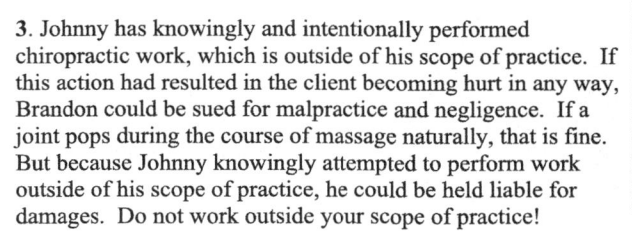

3. Johnny has knowingly and intentionally performed chiropractic work, which is outside of his scope of practice. If this action had resulted in the client becoming hurt in any way, Brandon could be sued for malpractice and negligence. If a joint pops during the course of massage naturally, that is fine. But because Johnny knowingly attempted to perform work outside of his scope of practice, he could be held liable for damages. Do not work outside your scope of practice!

4. Steph has committed a violation of ethics. The client is seeing Steph for a massage, and nothing more. Attempting to solicit a client anything that is not directly massage related is a violation of ethics, and should not be done. Instead, Steph should have recommended the client go to a vendor that sells used ski boots.

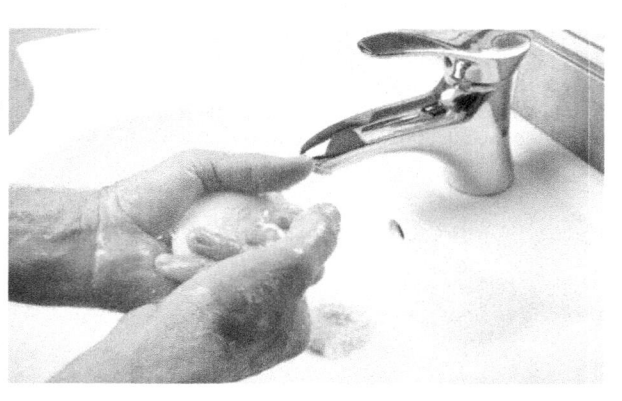

5. Amber is crossing in to counter-transference and dual relationships. If a massage therapist begins feeling any sort of attraction towards a client, they should end the business relationship before it becomes a problem. If the therapist is working for someone, they should notify their employer of the situation so the client can be booked with another therapist. If the client wishes to date a client, the therapist needs to make sure they are no longer that therapist's client.

6. Jonah has likely witnessed a theft in progress. Jonah should report the potential theft to his employer. Jonah should not approach or confront the co-worker suspected of stealing. Doing so could create many issues between co-workers if there is no proof of any wrong doing, an altercation could ensue, etc. If any issue arises between co-workers, the issue should be brought to the attention of the employer.

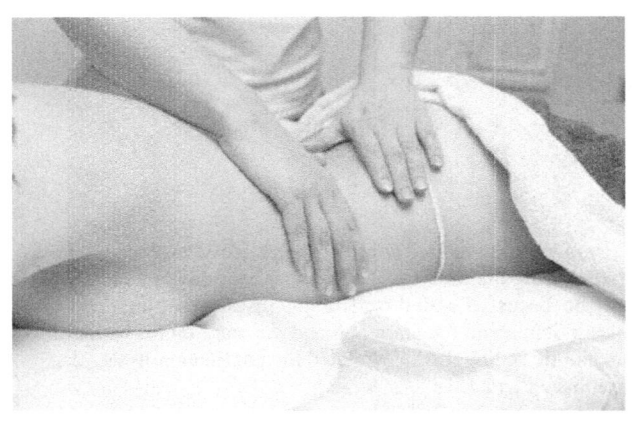

7. The client has violated Charlie's boundaries. Boundaries set limitations on where the massage therapist works, and are set by both the therapist and client. When Charlie sets the drape, the boundary is established, and Charlie is non-verbally telling the client that there will be no massage past this point on the back. By pulling the sheet down, the client has violated Charlie's boundaries. Charlie should explain to the client that the sheet is setting the boundary, and needs to stay where it is. If the client insists on the sheet being lowered, Charlie may tell the client that the session will end.

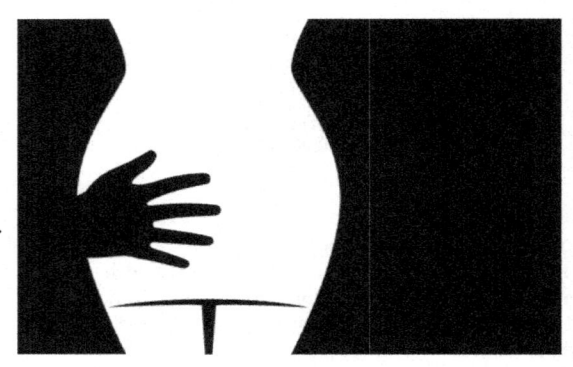

8. Sasha should immediately leave the massage room and report the incident to the employer. The client should be escorted off the property and barred from returning. This type of incident, in which a massage therapist is physically assaulted, can happen to anyone, and should never be tolerated. Side note, this exact circumstance happened to me once! Like I said, it can happen to anyone!

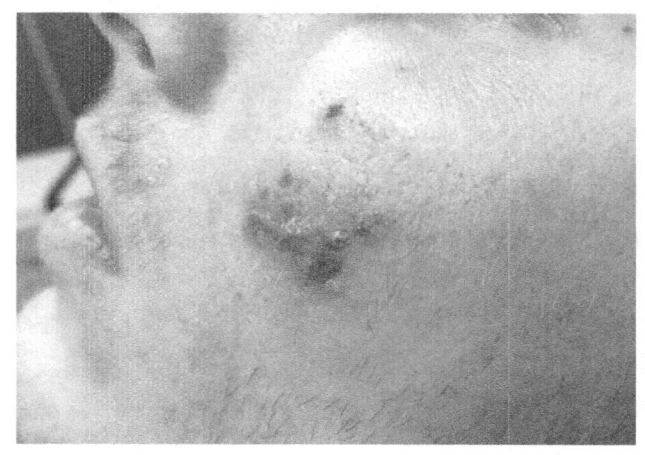

9. **What pathologic condition may Skylar be experiencing?**
Impetigo.

What is it and what are the most common causes?
Impetigo is a bacterial infection that is more common in children than adults. Most commonly the cause is staphylococci or streptococci bacteria.

Is this condition contagious?
Yes, it is highly contagious. It can be spread by direct contact with the client or through contaminated objects like the linens.

Is it safe for the therapist to give Skylar a massage?
No. It is a highly contagious infection therefore an absolute contraindication.

What recommendations could the therapist make to Skylar and her mother?
The therapist should recommend that she follow up with a doctor for diagnosis. If it is in fact impetigo, topical or oral antibiotics may be used to kill the bacteria. After the use of the antibiotic medication, Skylar should be able to return for her massage. Healing time should take about a week after the start of medication.

Answer Keys   317

10. What muscle or muscles is Deshaun likely experiencing pain in?
Levator scapulae and upper fibers of the trapezius.

What action was being performed by the side holding the plate to keep it in place?
Scapular elevation.

What type of muscle contraction was performed as Deshaun held the plate in place?
Levator scapulae and upper fibers of the trapezius were performing an isometric contraction, in which there is tension in the muscle, but the length of the muscle remains constant.

What medical condition has Deshaun suffered, and are there any precautions a massage therapist should take in regards to it?
Deshaun has suffered a grade 1 muscle strain, and is experiencing delayed onset muscle soreness. In the immediate acute stage, the massage therapist should avoid the area, but in the post-acute stage, massage may be performed to help speed healing by bringing more blood into the area.

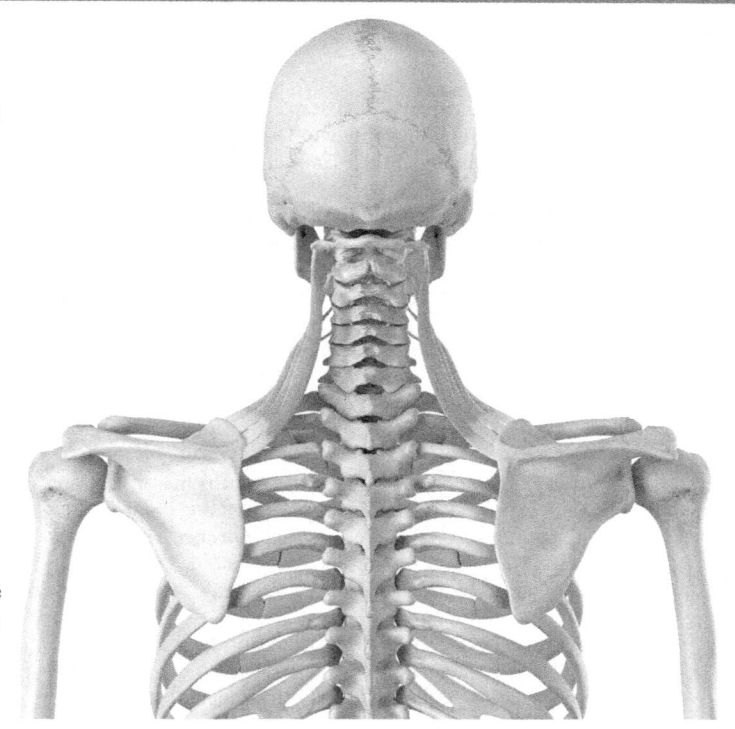

11. What pathologic condition might Tracey be experiencing?
Raynaud's Disease.

Is massage safe for Tracey?
Yes. Between attacks or episodes massage is indicated and may help improve circulation. Be sure to have an extra blanket or table warmer if need be and keep her covered when possible.

What considerations may you need to make while Tracey is on the table?
If she starts to have an attack or episode during the massage session, a warm towel may be applied if available.

Are there any contraindications to this pathological condition?
Cryotherapy.

What is the medical name for the white or lighter color called that Tracey experiences?
Pallor.

What is the medical term for "pins and needles"?
Paresthesia.

What is the medical name for the grayish blue color that Tracey experiences?
Cyanosis.

12. What condition is Dan likely experiencing?
De Quervain's Tenosynovitis.

Is massage indicated or contraindicated for this condition?
Massage is a local contraindication in the acute stage because it may increase inflammation and pain associated with this condition. Cryotherapy may be performed to decrease inflammation.

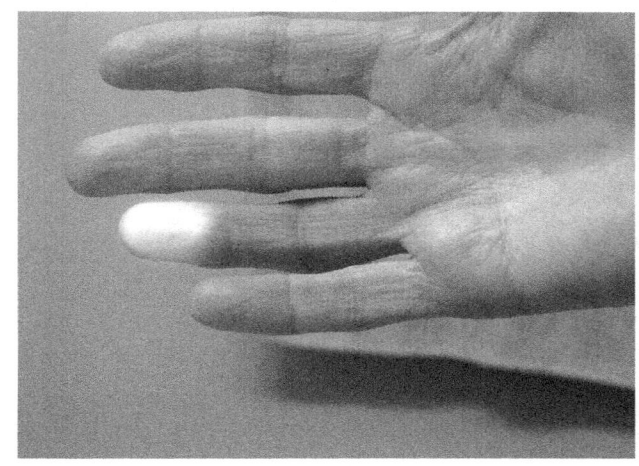

What is the therapist's next step?
The therapist should recommend Dan follow up with his doctor for diagnosis and treatment, and document this recommendation under the Plan section of SOAP notes.

13. What condition is likely present?
Kyphosis, a hyper-curvature of the thoracic vertebrae.

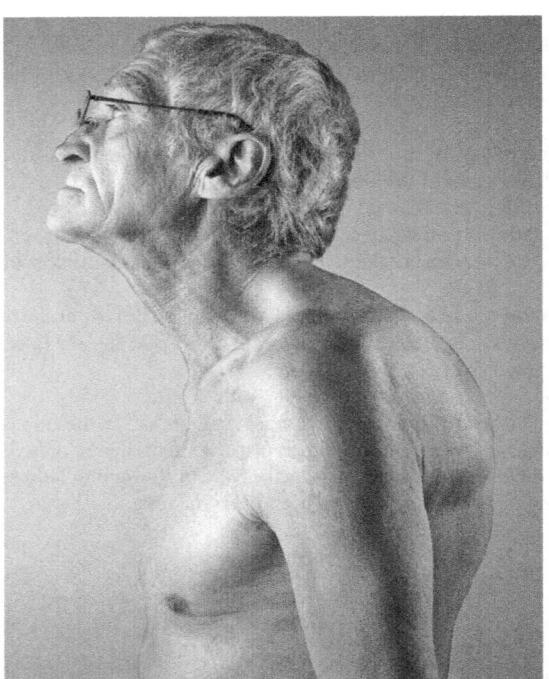

Is it safe for Paige to receive a massage?
As long as there is a doctor's clearance and Paige doesn't have an underlying condition that needs to be considered, massage is indicated.

What muscles might the therapist find that are short and tight?
Medial Rotation of the Shoulder: Pectoralis major, anterior deltoid, subscapularis, teres major, latissimus dorsi.
Protraction of Scapulae: Serratus anterior, pectoralis minor.
Forward Head Posture: Sternocleidomastoid, scalenes.
Upper Cervical Extension: Upper trapezius, levator scapulae.

What muscles might the therapist find that are stretched and weak?
Medial rotation of the shoulder: Infraspinatus, posterior deltoid, teres minor.
Protraction of Scapula: Middle trapezius, rhomboid major.
Forward Head Posture: Longissimus capitis, longissimus cervicis.
Upper Cervical Extension: Suprahyoids, infrahyoids, thoracic erector spinae.

Is there anything that the therapist would need to be cautious of?
Endangerment sites in the neck and axilla, treatment duration and pressure, and positioning.

What self-care recommendations should the therapist recommend Paige do?
Demonstrate to the client proper posture in the seated position.
Encourage the client to take regular breaks from the computer and stretch and move around throughout the day. Demonstrate all stretches for the client to do to stretch those short and tight muscles. Stretches should be slow and gentle and not be forced, and should be held between 15-30 seconds and done multiple times throughout the day.

14. When Barold rolls the ball, what action is his shoulder performing?
His shoulder first performs extension to bring the ball back, and then flexion to bring the ball forward.

What action are Barold's fingers performing while he is holding the ball?
Flexion.

What muscles are contracting when Barold rolls the ball down the lane?
When the shoulder is extended, the triceps brachii, latissimus dorsi, teres major, subscapularis, and posterior deltoid all contract. When the shoulder is flexed, biceps brachii, coracobrachialis, pectoralis major, and anterior deltoid all contract.

What muscle is contracting when Barold smiles?
Buccinator.

15. What condition is likely present?
Plantarfasciitis.

Is receiving massage safe for Natalie?
As long as there is a doctor's clearance and Natalie doesn't have an injury that's in the acute stage where the pain is too intense to tolerate massage, massage is indicated.

What muscles would the therapist want to work on to treat the condition?
Working muscles that would be short and tight with the condition are ideal. Plantarflexors and everters of the ankle include the gastrocnemius, soleus, peroneus longus and brevis, extensor digitorum longus, tibialis posterior, flexor digitorum longus and flexor hallucis longus. All muscles of the lower leg should be assessed. However, the therapist should pay special attention to address these muscles along their full length.

Is there anything the therapist needs to be cautious of?
The amount of pressure being used during treatment.

What is a typical cause of this condition?
Over-use.

What self-care recommendations should the therapist recommend Natalie to do at home?
Try to rest as much as possible to try to give the tissues time to heal.
Elevate the heel and apply ice to the area to reduce inflammation (can even use a frozen water bottle rolled along the bottom of the foot).
Be diligent to stretch the plantar flexors before activity.
Wear shoes with a good arch support.

16. What muscles are responsible for putting the hand and forearm into position to shake hands?
The biceps brachii begins the process of supination, which puts the hand into neutral position. Brachioradialis flexes the elbow with the hand in neutral position, when it is neither supinated nor pronated.

What action are Shawn's digits performing when he holds the guitar and places his fingers on the frets?
The digits are performing flexion in order to hold the neck of the guitar, or to hold the guitar pick.

What is the structure responsible for helping Shawn produce the sound that lets him sing?
Sound is produced in the larynx.

What bony landmark is Shawn sitting on while performing, and what muscle group originates on this landmark?
Shawn is sitting on the ischial tuberosity. The muscle group that originates on the ischial tuberosity is the hamstrings.

17. What condition could Dave be experiencing?
Lordosis.

What muscles may be short and tight?
Psoas major, iliacus, rectus femoris, latissimus dorsi, and quadratus lumborum. Psoas major will pull the lumbar vertebrae anteriorly, increasing the lordotic curve. Iliacus and rectus femoris will pull the pelvis into an anterior tilt, further exaggerating the lordotic curvature. On the back, latissimus dorsi and quadratus lumborum will also contribute towards pulling the pelvis into an anterior tilt.

What muscles may be stretched and weakened?
Rectus abdominis and the hamstrings. When rectus abdominis is weakened and stretched out, it is unable to properly pull the pelvis from the pubis, and other muscles such as iliacus are then able to force the pelvis into an anterior tilt. The hamstrings work similarly, pulling the pelvis into a posterior tilt at the ischial tuberosity, where they originate. If the hamstrings are weak, other muscles will pull the pelvis into an anterior tilt, and the hamstrings will become stretched.

Is massage indicated or contraindicated?
Massage therapy is indicated.

What special considerations may the therapist need to make?
Positioning and bolstering the client for comfort is important. When supine, the therapist may need to place a larger bolster than normal under the knees to keep the hip flexors, such as iliacus and rectus femoris, from fully lengthening. This can help reduce pressure felt in the lumbar spine. When prone, a bolster under the anterior superior iliac spines may help reduce the anterior pelvic tilt, and placing a bolster under the ankles may reduce any stress or pressure felt in the lower back by placing the hips into slight flexion.

What self-care recommendations should the therapist suggest to Dave?
Self-care should be performed throughout the day. Dave should take regular breaks, and should be instructed on proper standing, sitting, and body mechanics. Stretches may be demonstrated for Dave to perform to loosen tight contributing muscles, and exercises to strengthen weak muscles such as the rectus abdominis and hamstrings may be recommended. These suggestions should be documented under the Plan section of SOAP notes.

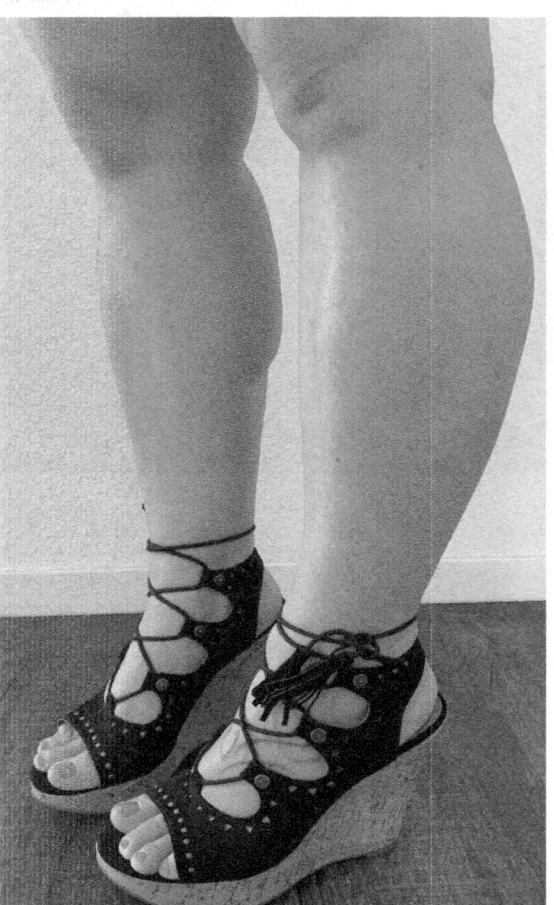

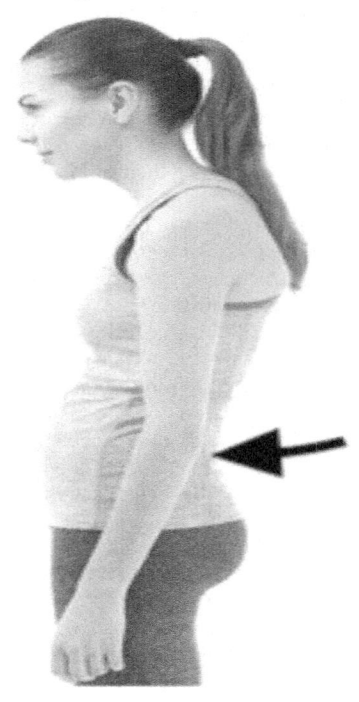

18. What position is Amanda's ankle in when she is standing in her high heel shoes?
Amanda's ankle is in plantarflexion while she is wearing her high heel shoes.

What muscles are contracted that allow this action to be performed?
Gastrocnemius, soleus, and peroneus longus are all contracted, as they all perform plantarflexion.

What muscle is being stretched while Amanda is wearing her high heel shoes?
Tibialis anterior is being stretched, as it performs dorsiflexion.

Amanda's husband is wearing a neck tie. The tie is placed around which region of the vertebral column?
Cervical vertebrae.

The tie is tied at the origin of which muscle? This muscle is responsible for turning the head to the opposite side, and flexion of the head.
Sternocleidomastoid.

Answer Keys   321

19. What condition is Doug likely experiencing?
Osteoarthritis.

What joint is most likely involved?
The carpometacarpal joint of the thumb, also called the saddle joint.

Is massage indicated for this condition?
In the acute stage, massage is a local contraindication. In the post-acute stage, it may be beneficial to increase blood flow to the area, and stimulate synovial fluid production.

What are some things Doug should do to help manage the condition?
Doug should visit a doctor for diagnosis and treatment. Doug should stop using his thumb to perform massage, and wear a brace for his thumb that helps stabilize the saddle joint.

20. What muscles are responsible for helping Robert chew his food?
Masseter is responsible for elevating the mandible, which compresses the food between the teeth. Buccinator compresses the cheeks, moving the food in towards the teeth, allowing the food to be properly masticated.

When Robert swallows the food, what structure stops food from entering the larynx, preventing choking?
The epiglottis rests atop the larynx when food or drink is swallowed, preventing choking.

Smooth muscle in the digestive tract helps to move food through the body. This process is known as what?
Peristalsis.

Steak is made of muscle. What is the contractile unit of a muscle known as?
The contractile unit of a muscle is known as a sarcomere.

21. What medical condition has Ellie likely contracted, and what type of infection is it?
Ellie has likely contracted athlete's foot, which is a fungal infection.

What kind of medication is used to combat this infection?
Antifungal medication, typically in a topical ointment.

If the infection spreads to the nails, what is it called?
Onychomycosis. "Onych/o" means "nail", "myc/o" means "fungus", "-osis" means "condition".

Running increases heart rate. What is an irregular heart rhythm?
Arrhythmia.

Heat, such as hot water from a shower, has what affect on blood vessels?
Heat causes blood vessels to dilate.

22. What medical condition may Nick have experienced?
Nick has likely experienced a herniated disc in the lumbar region.

How can this medical condition affect the spinal nerves emerging from the spinal cord?
A herniated disc may place pressure on nerves emerging from the spinal cord.

Pain radiating down the posterior thigh and leg may be an indication of what condition?
Most commonly sciatica, but may also be caused by piriformis syndrome.

What region of the vertebral column has experienced trauma?
Lumbar.

Nick enjoys snacking on cookies and a whole milk during his breaks at work. What hormone stimulates the production of milk?
Milk production is stimulated by prolactin, which is secreted by the pituitary gland.

If Nick were to stay in the cold too long, his body temperature may drop to unsafe levels. What is this condition known as?
Hypothermia.

23. Helmets are used to protect the head and brain from injury. What injury can occur when there is a blow to the head that may result in loss of consciousness?
A blow to the head with potential loss of consciousness is known as a concussion.

What bones in the skull produce a natural helmet for the body, providing protection for the brain?
The bones of the cranium: the frontal, temporal, parietal, and occipital bones.

The quarterback has to tell the other players what the play will be. What structure in the throat is responsible for producing sound used for speech?
The larynx, also known as the voice box.

After being blocked by Ross, the linebacker finds himself lying flat on his back. What body position is the linebacker in?
The linebacker is in the supine position.

The running back sprints down the field as he approaches the end zone. What actions are the running back's ankles performing as he runs?
Plantarflexion and dorsiflexion.

When celebrating, Ross sits on other players' shoulders. What is the scientific name of the shoulder joint, and what kind of synovial joint is it?
The shoulder joint is also known as the glenohumeral joint(where the glenoid fossa joins with the humerus), and it is a ball-and-socket joint.

24. Which cranial nerve is responsible for sight?
The optic nerve.

Which bones in the fingers are used on the keys when typing?
The distal phalanges.

What curvature does the cervical vertebrae have, and what can happen to this curvature if Brianna does not correct this posture?
The cervical vertebrae has a lordotic curvature. If the posture is not corrected, the cervical curvature can straighten, which stretches the posterior neck muscles.

Rounding of the shoulders may result in which condition?
Kyphosis.

Which hormone regulates the body's circadian rhythm, also known as the wake/sleep cycle, and which gland produces it?
Melatonin, which is produced by the pineal gland.

25. If Owen's face were exposed to the cold for an extended period of time, what may form in the soft tissues of his face, and what is that condition known as?
Ice crystals may form, which can damage tissue if present over an extended period. This is known as frostbite.

Pain is detected by which sensory receptor?
Nociceptors.

What path does the hot chocolate take on its way through Owen's digestive tract, ending at the stomach?
Hot chocolate enters into the oral cavity. When it is swallowed, it enters the pharynx. From the pharynx, it moves into the esophagus, and then empties from the esophagus into the stomach.

Snowboarding is typically performed at higher altitudes. What does the body consume less of at higher altitudes, and what condition is this similar to in regards to systemic function?
The body is not able to consume as much oxygen at higher altitudes due to less oxygen being present in the atmosphere. When the body isn't able to consume adequate oxygen, it is similar to anemia.

26. Assessing a person's walking pattern is known as what?
Gait analysis.

What muscle is responsible for inhalation?
The diaphragm.

Hip flexion plays an important role in walking. What are four muscles that perform flexion of the hip?
Hip flexion is performed by rectus femoris, sartorius, iliacus, and psoas major.

How many phalangeal bones are in each foot?
There are 14 phalangeal bones in each foot.

What type of protein produces hair?
Hair is produced by keratin.

27. What injury did Carl likely sustain?
Carl likely experienced whiplash.

Is this injury a contraindication for massage, and if so, what kind of contraindication?
In the acute stage, whiplash is a local contraindication for massage.

Traffic collisions and sports are the most common ways people tear the strongest ligament in the knee responsible for holding the tibia and femur together. What is this ligament?
While there are several ligaments that hold the tibia and femur together, the anterior cruciate ligament is the strongest of these, and is more prone to tearing due to sports or traffic collisions.

A seatbelt is buckled near the hip joint. What is the scientific name of the hip joint, and what kind of synovial joint is it?
The hip joint, where the femur and pelvis come together, is known as the iliofemoral or coxal joint. This joint is a ball-and-socket joint.

In a traffic collision, contusions may occur. What is a contusion, is a contusion contraindicated, and if so, what kind kind of contraindication is it?
A contusion is a form of internal bleeding caused by damage to blood vessels, which most commonly presents in the skin. A contusion is also known as a bruise. A contusion is a local contraindication due to the possible presence of blood clots in the area.

28. When the body is placed under stress, which division of the autonomic nervous system is activated?
The sympathetic response is activated when the body is under stress. This response is also known as "fight-or-flight".

What hormones specifically are released in a stress response, and what are effects of these hormones on the body?
The primary hormones released when in a stress response are epinephrine and norepinephrine. These hormones help to elevate heart rate, blood pressure, and blood sugar.

What condition might Colin have that results in a lack of sleep?
Colin may be experiencing insomnia.

Is this condition contraindicated for massage, and if so, what kind of contraindication is it? If not, what techniques and other elements should be utilized to help Colin?
Insomnia is not contraindicated for massage. A person who suffers from insomnia should receive a lighter, more relaxing massage to help calm the body and help it rest. Massage may also reduce stress hormones in the body, which can allow Colin to potentially have restful sleep. Essential oils may also be helpful, specifically oils that have a calming effect such as lavender.

Increased consumption of carbohydrates and caffeine may lead to which health complications?
Diabetes may result with excessive consumption of carbohydrates. Excessive caffeine may lead to the development of hypertension.

29. Lifting and twisting in the vertebrae may result in which injury?
This can cause a herniated disc.

Which muscle group is located just lateral to the vertebrae?
The erector spinae muscle group is located just lateral to the vertebrae.

To help prevent injuries at work, what should Lacey practice? What can a massage therapist do to prevent injuries at work?
Lacey should practice proper body mechanics. The massage therapist should also practice body mechanics, including keeping the back straight, not locking joints, having the knees slightly flexed, and keeping the massage table at the proper height.

The massage therapist referring someone to a specific chiropractor in exchange for monetary compensation is known as what?
This is known as a kickback.

Is the previous question considered a violation of ethics? Why or why not?
Kickbacks in healthcare are considered a violation of ethics. This creates a situation where a client may be referred to someone who is not the best fit for their healthcare needs, all in the hopes of getting some form of monetary compensation. This can compromise the care the client is receiving. Instead, a list of potential referrals should be offered, and there should be no compensation given to the massage therapist for any referral.

30. What insect is likely attached to Pierre?
There is likely a deer tick feasting on Pierre's blood.

What type of infection, and subsequent medical condition, can the insect spread to Pierre?
Ticks may cause a person to contract a bacterial infection. This infection can result in the development of Lyme disease.

What kind of rash may a person experience around the bite location?
The rash is known as a bullseye rash, because it is in a circular manner with a lighter area around the site of the bite and a darker area in the more peripheral area of infection.

Certain people may be allergic to tall grass. What may the body produce in response to allergens, which cause blood vessels to dilate?
Histamines are responsible for dilating blood vessels, allowing more blood and interstitial fluid to enter in to an area.

Sunlight exposure causes the skin to produce what nutrient?
Vitamin D.

31. What are the primary actions performed by the hip when a person is riding a bicycle?
While riding a bicycle, the hip mainly performs flexion and extension.

What are the primary actions performed by the knee when a person is riding a bicycle?
While riding a bicycle, the knee mainly performs flexion and extension.

Riding a bicycle, along with many other exercises, can increase the production of what substance, used to decrease body temperature?
Sweat is produced by sudoriferous glands. Sweat evaporates off the skin, which helps cool the body and lower body temperature.

Exercise can temporarily increase blood pressure. In a blood pressure reading of 130/85, what does the higher number represent, and what is specifically being measured that determines the number given?
The higher number presented in a blood pressure reading is the systolic pressure. This number represents the pressure felt in the walls of arteries as blood passes through them, or when the heart beats.

What number does water measure as on a pH scale?
Water is considered neutral, neither acidic nor alkaline, and therefore is 7 on a pH scale. If a substance is higher than 7, it is considered alkaline, such as blood(7.4). If a substance is lower than 7 on a pH scale, it is acidic, such as coffee(5).

32. What medical condition is Ashley likely experiencing?
Ashley is likely experiencing a migraine headache.

What are triggers that may contribute to this condition occurring?
Triggers vary from person to person, but common triggers include smoke, stress, nitrates, or in this case, tyramine. Tyramine is a substance that can be found in wine, aged cheese, and cured meats.

What structures in the body are specifically causing Ashley to experience pain?
Extracranial blood vessels are dilating and placing pressure on the meninges, which is causing the intense pain.

Wine contains alcohol, which increases the production of what substance in the body?
Alcohol is a form of diuretic, which causes the body to produce more urine.

When a person is seated in a chair, what position are the hips in?
The hips are in flexion when a person is seated in a chair.

33. The ocean contains a high concentration of which substance, an extremely important electrolyte in the body?
Sodium chloride, or salt.

Excessive exposure to sunlight over a short period may result in what?
The most common form of first degree burn, a sunburn.

Excessive exposure to sunlight over a long period of time, in some cases years, may result in the development of what?
Excessive sun exposure may result in the development of cancers such as basal cell carcinoma, squamous cell carcinoma, and malignant melanoma.

Medications that are designed to lower body temperature in cases such as fever are known as?
Antipyretics.

What are the three stages of "injury" a person may experience if their body temperature is too high for too long?
Heat cramps, heat exhaustion, and heat stroke.

34. Julius uses a hammer. What muscle is primarily responsible for performing the action of hammering?
Brachioradialis, which flexes the elbow with the hand in neutral position.

What muscles perform extension of the hip, the primary action used when pushing an object?
Semimembranosus, semitendinosus, biceps femoris, and gluteus maximus all perform extension of the hip.

What muscle is known as the "swimmer's muscle" due to its actions, which are performed when a person swims?
Latissimus dorsi.

What specific actions do the "swimmer's muscle" perform?
Latissimus dorsi performs extension, medial rotation, and adduction of the shoulder.

35. Holding a phone with the shoulder and ear produces what type of muscle contraction to be performed?
The sustained holding of the phone with the ear and shoulder produces an isometric contraction of the muscles involved in performing this action.

What muscle, which is part of the anterior triangle of the neck, may be strained from performing this action excessively?
Sternocleidomastoid, which rotates the head to the opposite side and laterally flexes the head/neck.

Becky asking Jenny to rotate and laterally flex her head/neck is part of what aspect of the massage session?
Assessment. Becky is asking Jenny to perform range-of-motion to help determine what restrictions in movement Jenny may be experiencing, which can help Becky form an effective treatment.

Jenny lies under the top sheet on the massage table. This is known as what, and what is the primary reason for this?
This is known as draping, which is used to establish boundaries between the therapist and the client.

Jenny deferring to Becky on preferred areas to be massaged due to Becky's perceived expertise, and apologizing for coughing may be a sign of what occurring?
This may be a sign of transference, in which a client views the massage therapist similarly to a person in their personal or early life. In this case, Jenny views Becky as an authority figure, and is looking for approval and guidance from Becky in regards to her massage treatment. This can happen when there is a power differential between the client and therapist.

Greatness is setting ambitious goals that your former self would have thought impossible, and trying to get a little better every day.

- Tim Ferriss

Practice Tests

Welcome to the full length practice test section of the book! This is one of the most important parts of the study guide. This is where you get to finally put your knowledge to use and see what you know, what you don't know, what you need to study more of, and most importantly, using your test-taking techniques!

Just be aware: THESE ARE NOT THE EXACT SAME QUESTIONS YOU WILL SEE ON THE MBLEx. I DO NOT WORK FOR, NOR HAVE ANY ASSOCIATION WITH THE FSMTB OR HAVE ANY INSIGHT INTO THE QUESTIONS ASKED ON THE EXAM. These questions were created by me, and only me!

These questions test you on the material you MAY see on the exam! There are even questions in these practice tests covering information not seen in this study guide. Just like the MBLEx, you will have questions on things you've never seen or learned before. This is where your test-taking techniques come in! Practice answering questions on things you've never learned before and it can help you do the exact same thing on the MBLEx! If you're tested on information you've never seen before, look it up! Learn about that information, and if that information comes up on the MBLEx, you'll be even more prepared!

What I always recommend my students do while taking their exams is, if they have access to a piece of paper, write down as many test-taking techniques as they can remember before trying to answer any questions. This way, while they're taking the MBLEx, they can look at their test-taking techniques and remind themselves to do them. Write things down like: Take your time, don't change answers, identify key words, eliminate answers, stay relaxed, and read the entire question.

On the MBLEx, you may have questions giving you scenarios involving clients, therapists, coworkers, etc, and it expects you to deconstruct the situation and give the appropriate answer. With regards to ethical questions like these, I've mostly left them out of the practice exams. I'd rather test you on more difficult information than something that should be common sense. The easiest way to approach any ethical question is simple. Just ask yourself, "If I wanted to keep my job or license, what would I do?" It can't get much easier than that!

For a reminder of your test-taking techniques, visit page 4.

For more practice tests, go online to: **http://www.mblextestprep.com/resources.html**

Make a photocopy of this page for use with each practice test! When you take the MBLEx, replicate this page on your own scratch paper provided by the testing center and put it to use!

Test Taking Tips:
Read the entire question.
Read all of the answers.
Identify key words.
Eliminate answers.
Take your time.
Don't change answers.
Breathe and stay relaxed.

Important Information Found For Reference:

Additional Notes:

Illustrations:

Practice Test 1

1. Plan information is
A. Information the client shares about themselves
B. Measurable information visible to the massage therapist
C. Medical conditions the client has been assessed with
D. Recommendations for future massage sessions

2. If a client experiences lower back pain due to a hypertonic psoas major while in the supine position, a bolster should be placed
A. Under the knees
B. Under the ankles
C. Between the legs
D. Under the hips

3. Most common form of arthritis
A. Rheumatoid arthritis
B. Gouty arthritis
C. Osteoarthritis
D. Periostitis

4. Elbow extension and shoulder extension is performed by the following muscle
A. Triceps brachii
B. Biceps brachii
C. Coracobrachialis
D. Anconeus

5. The sympathetic nervous system is also referred to as
A. Housekeeping
B. Rest and digest
C. Fight or flight
D. Central

6. The longest vein in the body, located on the medial aspect of the leg and thigh
A. Great saphenous
B. Femoral
C. External iliac
D. Brachial

7. Cryotherapy treatment used for an acute strain or sprain
A. PPALM
B. SOAP
C. PRICE
D. CAR

8. Technique primarily used to work on trigger points
A. Wringing
B. Ischemic compression
C. Cross-fiber friction
D. Myofascial release

9. Primary function of a gland
A. Secretion
B. Protection
C. Absorption
D. Contraction

10. Branching muscle tissue is also called
A. Smooth
B. Skeletal
C. Cardiac
D. Striated

11. Mastication is more commonly known as
A. Chewing
B. Swallowing
C. Sneezing
D. Defecating

12. Part of the scapula serratus anterior inserts onto
A. Medial border
B. Lateral border
C. Spine
D. Inferior angle

13. The leading cause of lung, oral, and esophageal cancer
A. Industrial dust
B. Cigarette smoking
C. Asbestos
D. Cystic fibrosis

14. The most common substance used in body scrubs
A. Salt
B. Sugar
C. Ground coffee
D. Powdered milk

15. Stoppage of range of motion due to trauma to an area
A. Soft end feel
B. Hard end feel
C. Empty end feel
D. Nervous end feel

16. Goals are
A. Measurable or attainable accomplishments
B. A generalized statement about the purpose of a business
C. The theme of a business
D. Business plans detailing projected income

17. Growth hormone, prolactin, and follicle-stimulating hormone are all produced by the
A. Thalamus
B. Pituitary
C. Testes
D. Thyroid

18. All of the following are contagious conditions except
A. Mononucleosis
B. Hepatitis A
C. Psoriasis
D. Osteomyelitis

19. Antiarrhythmics
A. Medication that controls rate of heart contraction
B. Medication that reduces the amount on inflammation in an area
C. Medication that controls the cholesterol levels in the blood
D. Medication that controls urine output

20. How many muscles attach to the scapula
A. 10
B. 16
C. 11
D. 14

21. A certification is obtained via
A. Passing a jurisprudence exam
B. Paying a fee to a jurisdiction licensing agency
C. Obtaining liability insurance to protect against malpractice
D. Completing educational requirements in a school setting

22. Synergist to the hamstrings while flexing the knee
A. Gastrocnemius
B. Soleus
C. Tibialis anterior
D. Rectus femoris

23. A concentric contraction of this muscle causes the hip to extend and the knee to flex
A. Gastrocnemius
B. Rectus femoris
C. Biceps brachii
D. Semitendinosus

24. A client comes in for a massage, complaining of pain in the right upper trapezius and neck. The first thing a massage therapist should do in this situation is
A. Ask the client if they are taking any medications for the pain
B. Ask the client to perform range-of-motion on the affected area
C. Palpate the area to locate any adhesions present
D. Determine any causes of the pain

25. There are seven vertebrae in which region of the vertebral column
A. Thoracic
B. Cervical
C. Lumbar
D. Coccygeal

26. An active stretch
A. Client stretches into resistance without the help of a massage therapist
B. Client stretches into resistance with the assistance of a massage therapist
C. Massage therapist stretches the client into resistance with assistance from the client
D. Massage therapist stretches the client into resistance without assistance from the client

27. Erythrocytes
A. Carry oxygen and carbon dioxide throughout the body
B. Are also called neutrophils and perform phagocytosis
C. Produce thrombi at an area of trauma
D. Allow transport of blood cells throughout the body

28. Peristalsis is controlled by which of the following types of muscle
A. Cardiac
B. Skeletal
C. Smooth
D. Striated

29. Vitamin D is produced in the following organ
A. Liver
B. Skin
C. Pancreas
D. Spleen

30. Structural realignment therapy working on muscles and fascia over the course of ten sessions
A. Rolfing
B. Trager method
C. Feldenkrais
D. Myofascial release

31. Massage results in increased production of
A. Cortisol
B. Blood cells
C. Pathogens
D. Water retention

32. Part of the respiratory passage that divides into the left and right bronchus
A. Larynx
B. Pharynx
C. Trachea
D. Epiglottis

33. Information the client shares about themselves is documented under which section of SOAP notes
A. Objective
B. Subjective
C. Assessment
D. Plan

34. A massage therapist should wash their hands
A. Only after using the restroom
B. Before each massage
C. After each massage
D. Before and after each massage

35. Phlebitis
A. Swelling of veins as a result of valve incompetence, causing blood to flow backwards
B. Inflammation of a vein due to trauma to a vein
C. Swelling of a vein due to excessive lymph fluid in a limb
D. Inflammation of an artery due to immobility as a result of surgery

36. Dilation of blood vessels during the inflammatory stage is controlled by
A. Histamines
B. Leukocytes
C. Neutrophils
D. Fibrosis

37. Psoriasis
A. Inflammation of skin resulting in skin coming into contact with an irritant
B. Autoimmune disorder resulting in thick, dry, silvery patches of skin
C. Blockage of sebaceous glands, resulting in pustules
D. Skin irritation caused by exposure to cold, affecting blood vessels and hair follicles

38. Observable information the massage therapist can physically see is documented under what category in SOAP notes
A. Subjective
B. Objective
C. Assessment
D. Plan

39. Keeping a client covered while performing a massage
A. Bolstering
B. Draping
C. Covering
D. Wrapping

40. Amount that may be reported as gift tax per client per year
A. $200
B. $100
C. $25
D. $75

41. Cells in the peripheral nervous system can perform an action that cells in the central nervous system generally cannot. What is this action
A. Die
B. Regenerate
C. Produce neurotransmitters
D. Communicate with one another

42. Structure located directly inferior to the coronoid process of the ulna
A. Ulnar tuberosity
B. Coronoid fossa
C. Olecranon fossa
D. Styloid process

43. The esophagus passes through the following structure on its way to the stomach
A. Peritoneum
B. Liver
C. Pericardium
D. Diaphragm

44. Liabilities are
A. Large companies free to operate independently
B. Possessions owned by a business
C. Raising the price of a product for sale
D. Debts owed to a person or business

45. Percussion strokes, used to loosen phlegm in the respiratory tract and activate muscle spindle cells
A. Petrissage
B. Effleurage
C. Friction
D. Tapotement

46. The functional unit of tissue is called
A. Cell
B. Nerve
C. Blood
D. Muscle

47. A patient with severe bradycardia would most likely need a pacemaker implanted into their body to regulate
A. Embolism formation
B. Lipid accumulation
C. Heart rhythm
D. Phlebitis

48. Body temperature below 90 degrees results in
A. Hypothermia
B. Heat stroke
C. Heat cramps
D. Frostbite

49. If a client were to resist the actions of the pectineus, how would they move their body
A. Adduction and flexion of the hip
B. Abduction and extension of the hip
C. Abduction and flexion of the hip
D. Adduction and extension of the hip

50. Adhesive capsulitis
A. Adhesions forming in the liver, causing decreased bile production and blood detoxification
B. Joint capsule surrounding the glenohumeral joint adhering to the head of the humerus, reducing movement
C. Tearing of fascia along the medial tibia, causing increased pain upon walking
D. Autoimmune disorder causing degeneration of myelin sheaths in the central nervous system, resulting in scarring of an axon

51. Most superior portion of the sternum
A. Costal cartilage
B. Body
C. Xiphoid process
D. Manubrium

52. Stimulation of tsubo points to stimulate nerves and increase circulation
A. Shiatsu
B. Reflexology
C. Amma
D. Ayurveda

53. Holding and carrying a heavy item in one hand requires which type of contraction of the upper fibers of the trapezius
A. Isotonic
B. Concentric
C. Isometric
D. Eccentric

54. What personal information is usually listed on a W2
A. The independent contractor's full name and address
B. The employee's full name, address, and complete social security number
C. The name of the business owner and their home address
D. The amount the business made and royalties paid out to the contracted associate

55. All of the following carry blood away from the heart except
A. Capillaries
B. Arteries
C. Arterioles
D. Veins

56. Protein fiber that gives bone its strength
A. Cartilage
B. Elastin
C. Collagen
D. Periosteum

57. An end feel is
A. Also known as a foot massage
B. A very light massage stroke performed at the end of a massage
C. Stoppage of range of motion due to factors such as muscle, bone, or an injury
D. A passive joint mobilization performed by a massage therapist

58. An injury that tears skin, producing jagged edges
A. Laceration
B. Incision
C. Puncture
D. Abrasion

59. When reading blood pressure, the lower number represents
A. Diastolic pressure
B. Systolic pressure
C. Venous pressure
D. Pulmonary pressure

60. Muscle originating on the sternum and clavicle, responsible for neck flexion and unilateral head rotation to the opposite side
A. Levator scapulae
B. Sternocleidomastoid
C. Scalenes
D. Pectoralis major

61. The adrenal glands are located atop which organs
A. Large intestine
B. Small intestine
C. Kidneys
D. Ureters

62. Dopamine is an example of a
A. Neurotransmitter
B. Synapse
C. Neuron
D. Dendrite

63. A client who suffers from psoriasis schedules a massage. An appropriate treatment modification would be
A. Performing vigorous friction on the patches to exfoliate dead skin
B. Avoiding the affected patches to not worsen them
C. Working on the dry patches if pain is not present
D. Reschedule the massage as psoriasis is contagious

64. A vertebral curvature positioned anteriorly is called
A. Lordotic
B. Kyphotic
C. Scoliotic
D. Amniotic

65. A license is obtained by a massage therapist in order to
A. Perform massage services but not receive monetary compensation
B. Perform massage services and receive monetary compensation
C. Protect the massage therapist against malpractice lawsuits
D. Perform diagnoses and prognoses

66. Amoxicillin and methicillin are forms of
A. Macrolides
B. Penicillin
C. Cephalosporins
D. Tetracyclines

67. The cardiac sphincter is located in which body system
A. Urinary
B. Cardiovascular
C. Nervous
D. Digestive

68. Bone found in the region of the forearm
A. Radius
B. Humerus
C. Fibula
D. Hamate

69. The capitulum articulates with
A. Head of the radius
B. Tibial plateau
C. Coracoid process
D. Greater trochanter

70. Which muscle originates on the sternum, ribs, and medial half of the clavicle
A. Teres minor
B. Pectoralis minor
C. Anterior deltoid
D. Pectoralis major

71. Water is absorbed by the
A. Large intestine
B. Pancreas
C. Esophagus
D. Liver

72. Which of the following is an example of an exocrine gland
A. Hypothalamus
B. Thymus
C. Adrenal
D. Sudoriferous

73. The rectus femoris is biarticular. What are the two actions performed by this muscle
A. Hip flexion, knee flexion
B. Hip extension, knee extension
C. Hip flexion, knee extension
D. Hip extension, knee flexion

74. Where does the biceps brachii insert
A. Ulnar Tuberosity
B. Radial Process
C. Coronoid Process
D. Radial Tuberosity

75. Gliding movements are performed with
A. Petrissage
B. Effleurage
C. Tapotement
D. Friction

76. Contraindications for hydrotherapy include all of the following except
A. Contagious conditions
B. Hypertension
C. Acne
D. Skin rash

77. Tendons
A. Connect ligaments to muscles to prevent friction
B. Connect bones to bones to provide stability
C. Connect muscles to muscles to allow synergists
D. Connect bones and muscles to allow movement

78. Massage may have all of the following psychological effects except
A. Increased relaxation
B. Decreased stress
C. Increased stress
D. Increased energy

79. Rectus femoris has what shape
A. Bipennate
B. Circular
C. Convergent
D. Spiral

80. The pineal gland is located
A. In the neck
B. In the chest
C. In the abdomen
D. In the skull

81. Bronchial tubes branch out into smaller tubes called
A. Larynx
B. Alveoli
C. Trachea
D. Bronchioles

82. Drug used to treat acute asthma
A. Bronchodilator
B. Expectorant
C. Decongestant
D. Anticoagulant

83. Blood passes from the right atrium through the tricuspid valve into the
A. Left ventricle
B. Left atrium
C. Right ventricle
D. Pulmonary artery

84. Muscle originating on the medial lip of the linea aspera
A. Vastus medialis
B. Vastus lateralis
C. Semimembranosus
D. Semitendinosus

85. Muscle primarily responsible for supination of the forearm
A. Biceps brachii
B. Triceps brachii
C. Brachioradialis
D. Brachialis

86. Balancing electrolyte and acid levels in the body is regulated by
A. Stomach
B. Bladder
C. Large intestine
D. Kidneys

87. Vibration of air produces speech, which is the responsibility of
A. Larynx
B. Pharynx
C. Trachea
D. Epiglottis

88. Most superior portion of the tibia
A. Soleal line
B. Tibial tuberosity
C. Medial malleolus
D. Tibial plateau

89. Epinephrine and norepinephrine are produced by which glands
A. Adrenal
B. Pituitary
C. Pineal
D. Ovaries

90. Virus resulting in the development of warts
A. Herpes simplex
B. Human papilloma virus
C. Epstein-Barr virus
D. Urticaria

91. Application of hot and cold on the skin results in the blood vessels
A. Breaking down and building up
B. Constricting and closing
C. Dilating and opening
D. Dilating and constricting

92. ABMP and AMTA offer
A. Business plans
B. Massage licensure
C. Massage certification
D. Liability insurance

93. Stimulating massage strokes include all of the following except
A. Friction
B. Effleurage
C. Tapotement
D. Vibration

94. Type of cell broken down inside the spleen
A. Osteocyte
B. Leukocyte
C. Thrombocyte
D. Erythrocyte

95. Vein running from the medial surface of the foot to the inguinal region
A. Great saphenous vein
B. Femoral vein
C. Obturator vein
D. Superficial tibial vein

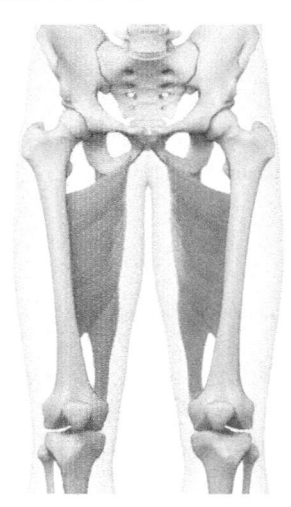

96. What action does this muscle perform
A. Adduction
B. Retraction
C. Protraction
D. Abduction

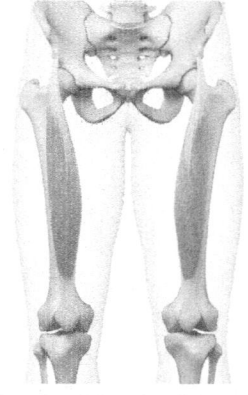

97. If a client complains of straining of this muscle, what action may be affected
A. Knee flexion
B. Hip flexion
C. Shoulder extension
D. Hip extension

98. While performing the following action, what position is the shoulder in
A. Flexion
B. Abduction
C. Lateral Rotation
D. Horizontal Adduction

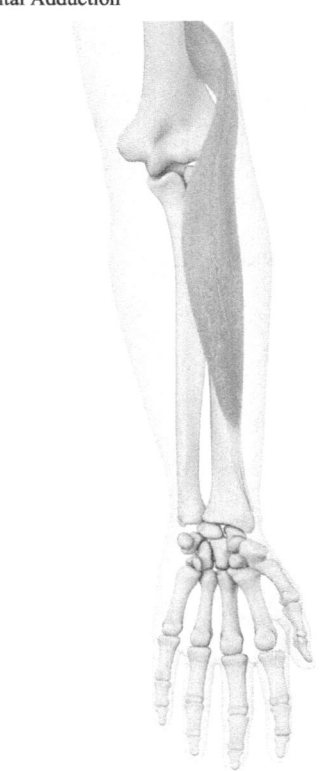

99. The primary function of the following muscle on the elbow
A. Pronation
B. Extension
C. Supination
D. Flexion

100. Hypertonicity of the iliacus, associated with psoas major, may result in
A. Lordosis
B. Scoliosis
C. Ankylosing Spondylitis
D. Kyphosis

Practice Test 2

1. Insertion of pectoralis major
A. Deltoid tuberosity
B. Medial lip of intertubercular groove
C. Lateral lip of intertubercular groove
D. Acromion process

2. The elbow joint performs the following actions
A. Flexion and extension
B. Adduction and abduction
C. Medial and lateral rotation
D. Protraction and retraction

3. Tissue specializing in protection, absorption, and secretion
A. Muscular
B. Connective
C. Nervous
D. Epithelial

4. Keeping client information private and protected
A. Self-disclosure
B. Assurance
C. Confidentiality
D. Closed-ended

5. Phenol, bleach, and alcohol are all examples of
A. Disinfectants
B. Soap
C. Hand sanitizers
D. Oil removers

6. Heat creation is produced by which type of muscle tissue
A. Smooth
B. Cardiac
C. Skeletal
D. Adipose

7. Autoimmune disorder affecting myelin sheaths in the central nervous system
A. Multiple sclerosis
B. Myasthenia gravis
C. Parkinson's disease
D. Alzheimer's disease

8. After a massage, the massage therapist notifies the client of stretches that the therapist thinks might help with a client's range-of-motion. This information would be documented under which section of SOAP notes
A. Subjective
B. Objective
C. Assessment
D. Plan

9. The primary goal of a massage performed after a sporting event is
A. Move metabolic waste out of tissues
B. Increase circulation
C. Stimulate muscle fibers
D. Break up adhesions between tissues

10. Distal attachment of what muscle is located at the tibial tuberosity
A. Biceps Femoris
B. Rectus Femoris
C. Sartorius
D. Tibialis Anterior

11. Insertion of levator scapulae
A. Superior angle of scapula
B. Transverse processes of C1-C4
C. Spinous processes of C5-T1
D. Inferior angle of scapula

12. Nociceptors detect
A. Pain
B. Temperature
C. Chemical concentration
D. Body position

13. The glenohumeral joint is considered what kind of synovial joint
A. Hinge
B. Pivot
C. Gliding
D. Ball-and-socket

14. Autoimmune disorder resulting in increased epithelial production, producing thick scaly patches of skin
A. Psoriasis
B. Rosacea
C. Wart
D. Lupus

15. Ibuprofen is an example of
A. Non-steroidal anti-inflammatory drug
B. Statin
C. Bronchodilator
D. Expectorant

16. Herpes simplex is a
A. Bacteria
B. Virus
C. Fungus
D. Parasite

17. Anatomical law stating bone adapts to load under which it is placed
A. Davis' Law
B. Wolff's Law
C. Johnson's Law
D. Merlino's Law

18. Mammary glands produce what substance
A. Oil
B. Sweat
C. Milk
D. Testosterone

19. The thoracic and sacral vertebrae are curved in which way
A. Lordotic
B. Kyphotic
C. Scoliotic
D. Amniotic

20. Movement of the limbs is controlled by which type of muscle tissue
A. Cardiac
B. Skeletal
C. Smooth
D. Hyaline

21. An asset is
A. Nontaxable income
B. A weakness in a company's business model
C. A business with no liabilities
D. A possession of a business

22. All of the following companies provide liability insurance for massage therapists except
A. NCBTMB
B. ABMP
C. AMTA
D. NAMT

23. There are how many pairs of spinal nerves in the peripheral nervous system
A. 24
B. 12
C. 18
D. 31

24. Epiphyses are covered in the following
A. Elastic cartilage
B. Periosteum
C. Hyaline cartilage
D. Mesentery

25. The thoracic vertebrae contains how many bones
A. Twelve
B. Seven
C. Five
D. Eleven

26. Technique used to treat adhesions found between fascia and muscles
A. Rolfing
B. Myofascial release
C. Deep tissue
D. Osteosymmetry

27. The descending order of the small intestine is
A. Duodenum, ileum, jejunum
B. Ileum, jejunum, duodenum
C. Duodenum, jejunum, ileum
D. Jejunum, duodenum, ileum

28. If systolic pressure measures 140 or higher, a person may be diagnosed with
A. Hypotension
B. Hypertension
C. Hyperemia
D. Myocardial infarction

29. A podiatrist is a doctor that specializes in the
A. Ears
B. Mouth
C. Feet
D. Bladder

30. Plantarflexion and dorsiflexion take place at which joint
A. Tibiofemoral
B. Talocalcaneal
C. Talotibial
D. Tibiofibular

31. Motor axons carry nerve impulses
A. Towards the cerebellum
B. Towards the brain
C. Away from the brain
D. Away from muscle

32. Certain leukocytes perform phagocytosis, which is when cells perform what action
A. Eat substances
B. Absorb nutrients
C. Move from an area of high concentration to an area of low concentration
D. Transportation of oxygen and carbon dioxide

33. Insertion of the adductor magnus
A. Inferior ramus of the pubis
B. Ischial tuberosity
C. Lateral epicondyle of the femur
D. Medial lip of linea aspera and adductor tubercle

34. Lateral curvature of the thoracic vertebrae
A. Swayback
B. Dowager's hump
C. Scoliosis
D. Bamboo spine

35. Fungal infection affecting the epidermis, resulting in a circular rash
A. Cordyceps
B. Athlete's foot
C. Ringworm
D. Whitlow

36. Irregular heart beat
A. Myocardial infarction
B. Heart murmur
C. Arrhythmia
D. Angina pectoris

37. The cervical vertebrae contains how many bones
A. Twelve
B. Seven
C. Five
D. One

38. Serous membranes
A. Secrete synovial fluid into a joint cavity to lubricate a joint
B. Are filled with interstitial fluid to fight disease
C. Separate organs to prevent friction
D. Surround fasciculi in muscle tissue

39. Muscle originating on the anterior surface of the sacrum
A. Psoas major
B. Pectineus
C. Sartorius
D. Piriformis

40. The styloid process of the ulna lies where in relation to the olecranon process
A. Posterior
B. Proximal
C. Anterior
D. Distal

41. Business expenses include all of the following except
A. Massages
B. Advertising
C. Electricity
D. Credit card fees

42. Slightly bent knees, straight back, and limp wrists are all examples of
A. Proper massage modalities
B. Improper body mechanics
C. Proper body mechanics
D. Improper massage modalities

43. The pyloric sphincter is located between which two structures
A. Stomach and small intestine
B. Stomach and esophagus
C. Pancreas and small intestine
D. Small intestine and large intestine

44. Involuntary painful contraction of a muscle caused by lack of oxygen or dehydration
A. Cramp
B. Spasm
C. Twitch
D. Strain

45. Ulceration may occur in the fingers and toes in severe cases of
A. Emphysema
B. Cyanosis
C. Raynaud's syndrome
D. Paraplegia

46. A synapse is
A. Where two or more neurons meet
B. Where the brain meets the cerebellum
C. Where a dendrite meets a cell body
D. Where a nerve cell body meets an axon

47. Stance in which the feet are placed parallel to the table
A. Warrior
B. Horse
C. Archer
D. Swimmer

48. An employee receives the following tax form detailing income and tax information
A. W-2
B. 1040
C. Schedule K1
D. 1099

49. The rest and digest response is also known as
A. Peripheral
B. Sympathetic
C. Parasympathetic
D. Fight or flight

50. If a client is unable to withstand any amount of pressure during a massage, a treatment the therapist might recommend would be
A. Reiki
B. Rolfing
C. Myofascial release
D. Lymphatic drainage

51. Storage of urine is found in the
A. Kidneys
B. Gallbladder
C. Bladder
D. Urethra

52. The inguinal region is located near which part of the body
A. Elbow
B. Knee
C. Shoulder
D. Hip

53. All of the following are located on the ilium except
A. Ischial spine
B. Anterior superior iliac spine
C. Anterior inferior iliac spine
D. Iliac fossa

54. Gastrocnemius takes what action on the ankle when contracted
A. Dorsiflexes
B. Plantarflexes
C. Inverts
D. Everts

55. Nerve running deep to the flexor retinaculum of the wrist, which may be compressed, resulting in loss of sensation in the hand
A. Radial
B. Ulnar
C. Median
D. Tibial

56. Contraction of hepatitis B is most likely due to exposure to
A. Blood
B. Feces
C. Saliva
D. Semen

57. Substance produced by the liver which aids in the digestion of lipids
A. Bile
B. Vitamin A
C. Insulin
D. Glucagon

58. Superficial muscle to the vastus intermedius
A. Rectus femoris
B. Vastus lateralis
C. Vastus medialis
D. Pectineus

59. Hypotension is also referred to as
A. Low blood pressure
B. High blood pressure
C. Arrhythmia
D. Varicose veins

60. Massage has the following effect on blood vessels
A. Constriction
B. Dilation
C. Toning
D. Formation

61. An electroencephalogram measures
A. Muscle contractions
B. Heart rhythm
C. Blood pressure
D. Brain wave activity

62. The "I" in PRICE stands for
A. Immersion
B. Ice
C. Inflammation
D. Increase

63. Hormone responsible for increasing heart rate and moving blood from digestive organs into the muscles
A. Aldosterone
B. Oxytocin
C. Growth hormone
D. Norepinephrine

64. Basal cell carcinoma is what type of tumor
A. Idiopathic
B. Malignant
C. Benign
D. Lymphatic

65. The study of the cause of disease
A. Oncology
B. Etiology
C. Radiology
D. Idiopathology

66. Periosteum
A. Surrounds the heart
B. Surrounds the epiphysis of a long bone
C. Covers articular surface of bones to prevent friction
D. Surrounds the shaft of long bones

67. Over-production in melanocytes results in a tumor known as
A. Sarcoma
B. Carcinoma
C. Melanoma
D. Lymphoma

68. The pancreas empties its secretions into the duodenum and they mix with
A. Feces
B. Bolus
C. Chyme
D. Water

69. In a herniated disc, the nucleus pulposus protrudes through the
A. Annulus fibrosis
B. Vertebral body
C. Intervertebral facet
D. Sacral foramina

70. Hawaiian massage similar to Swedish massage, utilizing rhythmic massage strokes that flow freely up and down the body
A. Watsu
B. Thai Massage
C. Amma
D. Lomi Lomi

71. Muscle inserting on the pes anserinus
A. Gracilis
B. Semimembranosus
C. Rectus femoris
D. Biceps femoris

72. Cartilage found surrounding the glenoid fossa which aids in structural support of the shoulder joint
A. Labrum
B. Coracoid process
C. Bicipital tendon
D. Acetabulum

73. Expectorants help in
A. Thinning mucous
B. Draining sinuses
C. Blocking histamines
D. Dilating respiratory passages

74. Cranial nerve VII is involved in
A. Bell's palsy
B. Cerebral palsy
C. Trigeminal neuralgia
D. Hemotaxis

75. Proprioceptive neuromuscular facilitation utilizes what specific kind of contraction before the secondary stretch
A. Eccentric
B. Isotonic
C. Isometric
D. Concentric

76. A massage license from one jurisdiction being recognized as valid in another jurisdiction
A. Reciprocity
B. Certification
C. Liability
D. Malpractice

77. Function of insulin
A. Digestion of protein
B. Absorption of glucose
C. Absorption of lipids
D. Elimination of wastes

78. Aged red blood cells are destroyed in the following organ
A. Liver
B. Stomach
C. Pancreas
D. Spleen

79. A bolster is placed between the legs and arms and under the head in which position
A. Slightly elevated
B. Supine
C. Prone
D. Side-lying

80. Swedish massage is based on the Western principals of
A. Anatomy and physiology
B. Energy
C. Life force
D. Chi

81. Migraine headaches are also known as
A. Trigeminal headaches
B. Muscular tension headaches
C. Glycemic headaches
D. Vascular headaches

82. Each of the following are contagious conditions except
A. Mononucleosis
B. Ringworm
C. Meningitis
D. Lupus

83. Type of metal vital in the formation of hemoglobin
A. Tin
B. Aluminum
C. Iron
D. Steel

84. Penicillin is a form of
A. Antiviral
B. Anti-inflammatory
C. Antibiotic
D. Antifungal

85. All of the following are parts of the ulna except
A. Trochlea
B. Olecranon process
C. Coronoid process
D. Styloid process

86. The pylorus is found at the exit of what organ
A. Small intestine
B. Stomach
C. Large intestine
D. Esophagus

87. A client experiences acute pain during shoulder abduction. Which muscle is most likely involved
A. Teres minor
B. Infraspinatus
C. Deltoid
D. Coracobrachialis

88. The sagittal suture is located between which two cranial bones
A. Occipital and parietal
B. Parietal bones
C. Parietal and frontal
D. Temporal and parietal

89. Rolfing aligns major body segments, known as
A. Structural realignment
B. Somatic holding pattern
C. Mentastics
D. Balance of body and mind

90. Stretch technique in which a muscle is stretched to resistance, followed by an isometric contraction by the client, then the muscle stretched further after the contraction
A. Active static stretch
B. Proprioceptive neuromuscular facilitation
C. Strain counter-strain
D. Myofascial release

91. Lungs and kidneys are both examples of
A. Paired organs
B. Digestive organs
C. Respiratory organs
D. Urinary organs

92. Cartilage found covering the surface of articulating bones
A. Dense
B. Elastic
C. Hyaline
D. Loose

93. Angina pectoris, hypertension, and migraines may all be treated with
A. Vasodilators
B. Antihistamines
C. Beta-blockers
D. Corticosteroids

94. Hookworm, ascariasis, and pinworm are all forms of
A. Parasite
B. Virus
C. Bacteria
D. Fungus

95. A set of guiding moral principles is known as
A. Regulations
B. Scope of practice
C. Ethics
D. Reputation

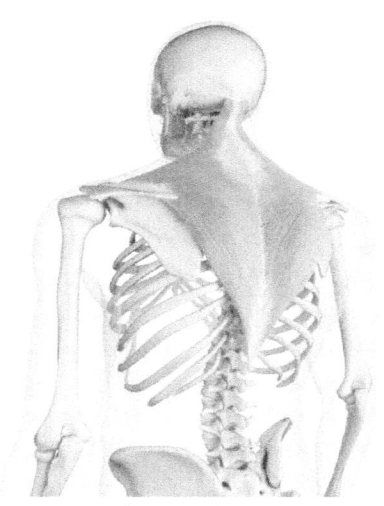

96. Actions of the following muscle
A. Elevation, retraction, depression
B. Medial rotation, protraction, abduction
C. Depression, flexion
D. Flexion, protraction, extension

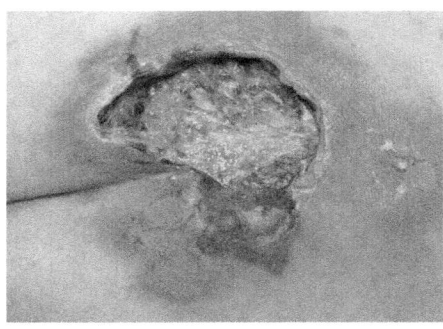

97. Name the following condition
A. Cellulitis
B. Herpes Simplex
C. Decubitus Ulcer
D. Impetigo

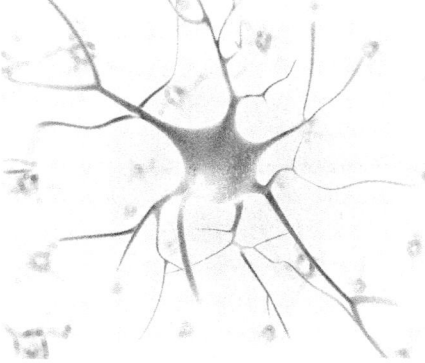

98. This type of cell is known as
A. Basophil
B. Erythrocyte
C. Neuron
D. Nociceptor

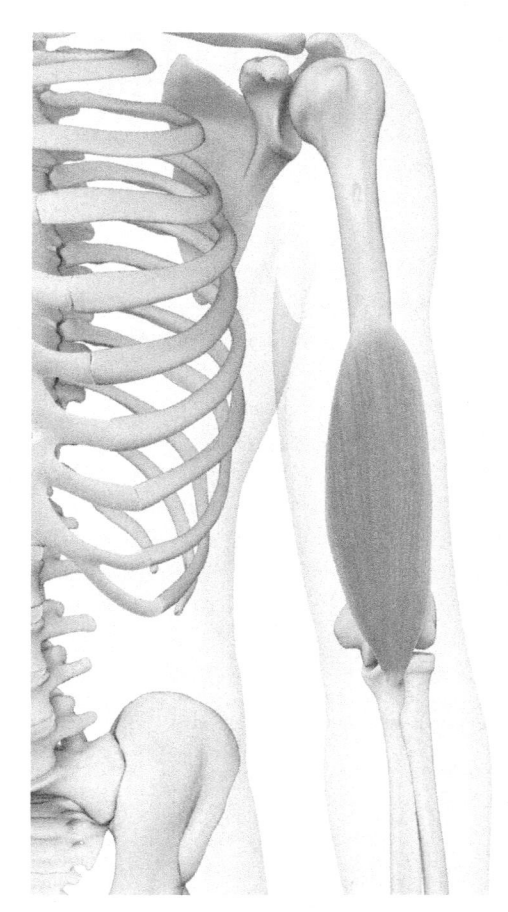

99. Synergist to the following muscle
A. Anconeus
B. Biceps Brachii
C. Coracobrachialis
D. Supraspinatus

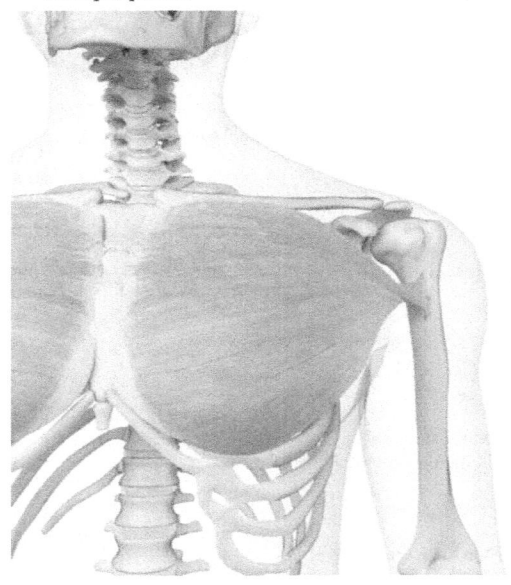

100. Insertion of the following muscle
A. Lateral lip of the intertubercular groove
B. Greater tubercle
C. Medial lip of the intertubercular groove
D. Lesser trochanter

Practice Test 3

1. The thyroid produces the following hormone
A. Insulin
B. Calcitonin
C. Testosterone
D. Progesterone

2. Cryotherapy treatment used for an acute strain or sprain
A. PPALM
B. SOAP
C. PRICE
D. CAR

3. The pituitary gland produces all of the following hormones except
A. Growth hormone
B. Testosterone
C. Follicle stimulating hormone
D. Prolactin

4. Perirenal fat is found surrounding the
A. Rectum
B. Bladder
C. Liver
D. Kidneys

5. Elbow extension and shoulder extension is performed by the following muscle
A. Triceps brachii
B. Biceps brachii
C. Coracobrachialis
D. Anconeus

6. Part of the scapula that serratus anterior inserts onto
A. Medial border
B. Lateral border
C. Spine
D. Inferior angle

7. Medication prescribed to fight off bacterial infections
A. Anti-inflammatory
B. Antivenoms
C. Antipyretics
D. Antibiotics

8. Adductor magnus has a common origination site with which muscle group
A. Wrist flexors
B. Quadriceps
C. Rotator cuff
D. Hamstrings

9. T-lymphocytes are produced by which gland
A. Thymus
B. Thalamus
C. Pituitary
D. Pineal

10. Goals are
A. Measurable or attainable accomplishments
B. A generalized statement about the purpose of a business
C. The theme of a business
D. Business plans detailing projected income

11. A glove should be worn by the massage therapist if
A. The client has an open wound on the back
B. The client has an open wound on the arm
C. The massage therapist has an open wound on the leg
D. The massage therapist has an open wound on the hand

12. The most common site of sprain
A. Shoulder
B. Knee
C. Elbow
D. Ankle

13. Nausea, vomiting, and fatigue with yellowing of the skin may be the result of
A. Hepatitis
B. Food poisoning
C. Diarrhea
D. Meningitis

14. Another name for a leukocyte is
A. Thrombocyte
B. Red blood cell
C. Platelet
D. White blood cell

15. A dermatologist is a doctor who specializes in the
A. Heart
B. Kidneys
C. Skin
D. Brain

16. If a massage therapist begins to feel sexual attraction towards a client, what should the massage therapist do
A. Act upon these urges
B. Do nothing
C. Tell the client
D. Recommend the client see another therapist

17. A client with Bell's palsy would be referred to which doctor
A. Cardiologist
B. Neurologist
C. Rheumatologist
D. Dermatologist

18. There are seven vertebrae in which region of the vertebral column
A. Thoracic
B. Cervical
C. Lumbar
D. Coccygeal

19. Erythrocytes
A. Carry oxygen and carbon dioxide throughout the body
B. Are also called neutrophils and perform phagocytosis
C. Produce thrombi at an area of trauma
D. Allow transport of blood cells throughout the body

20. Technique primarily used to work on trigger points
A. Wringing
B. Ischemic compression
C. Cross-fiber friction
D. Myofascial release

21. HIPAA ensures client information remains
A. Confidential
B. In the government's possession
C. With the client's spouse
D. Unimportant

22. Muscle originating on the spinous processes of T7-L5, the iliac crest, and lumbar aponeurosis
A. Quadratus lumborum
B. Latissimus dorsi
C. Spinalis
D. Psoas major

23. The ethmoid bone is found in which part of the face
A. Eye socket
B. Nose
C. Cheek
D. Ear canal

24. Absorption of nutrients primarily takes place in what part of the small intestine
A. Jejunum
B. Ileum
C. Duodenum
D. Cecum

25. Information the client shares about themselves is documented under which section of SOAP notes
A. Objective
B. Subjective
C. Assessment
D. Plan

26. If a person were to fall forward, landing on their outstretched arms, the shoulder joint could most likely become dislocated in which direction
A. Medially
B. Anteriorly
C. Distally
D. Posteriorly

27. The second cervical vertebrae is also called the
A. Occiput
B. Atlas
C. Axis
D. Dens

28. Areas of the body in which caution is advised during massage of a pregnant client include all of the following except
A. Face
B. Abdomen
C. Ankles
D. Lumbar

29. Rheumatoid arthritis is what type of disorder
A. Sarcoma
B. Viral
C. Bacterial
D. Autoimmune

30. The most fatal form of tumor is
A. Cystic
B. Benign
C. Malignant
D. Gangrenous

31. Cilia contain glands that secrete
A. Sebum
B. Mucous
C. Sweat
D. Ear wax

32. Perception of your own body parts and position of your body
A. Integration
B. Proprioception
C. Reflexes
D. Nociceptor

33. In a client with herpes simplex, exposure to sunlight, stress, or hormonal changes may result in the development of
A. Impetigo
B. Decubitus ulcers
C. Cold sores
D. Acne

34. Massage stroke directed toward the heart used to increase circulation, transition between strokes, and apply massage lubricant
A. Friction
B. Petrissage
C. Effleurage
D. Vibration

35. A pre-event sports massage requires the following kinds of strokes to be performed
A. Relaxing
B. Invigorating
C. Slow
D. Sedative

36. Which type of gland is found in the skin
A. Adrenal
B. Mammary
C. Pineal
D. Sebaceous

37. The alimentary canal
A. Is also known as the circulatory system
B. Contains the brain and spinal cord
C. Consists of the mouth, esophagus, stomach, and intestines
D. Brings blood from the heart to the lungs and back to the heart

38. A trigger point that results in pain only when being palpated
A. Acute
B. Active
C. Passive
D. Latent

39. An antipyretic is a type of medication responsible for
A. Eliminating increased glucose
B. Decreasing inflammation
C. Destroying bacteria
D. Lowering fever

40. Protein found inside of red blood cells, responsible for transporting oxygen and carbon dioxide throughout the body
A. Mitochondria
B. Hemoglobin
C. Hemophilia
D. Leukocyte

41. The vagus nerve controls which autonomic nervous system
A. Fight or flight
B. Sympathetic
C. Autonomic
D. Parasympathetic

42. An upper respiratory tract infection may result in
A. Acute bronchitis
B. Emphysema
C. Asthma
D. Pleurisy

43. An aura stroke is a massage stroke in which
A. The hands are pressed firmly into the body
B. The hands are touching the body very lightly
C. The hands are held just above the body
D. The hands are placed on the body without substantial pressure

44. Hair is made of which type of tissue
A. Muscular
B. Connective
C. Epithelial
D. Nervous

45. A resistive joint movement
A. Client moves the joint without the assistance of a massage therapist
B. A client moves the joint with the assistance of a massage therapist
C. A client resists a movement being performed by a massage therapist
D. A massage therapist moves a client's joint without the help of the client

46. Essential oil commonly used to aid in relaxation of smooth muscles in the respiratory tract
A. Eucalyptus
B. Grapefruit
C. Lemongrass
D. Peppermint

47. All of the following are located on the femur except
A. Medial condyle
B. Greater trochanter
C. Linea alba
D. Adductor tubercle

48. Origin of pectoralis minor
A. Coracoid process
B. Ribs 3-5
C. Ribs 1-3
D. Sternum

49. The most distal structure on the tibia
A. Lateral condyle
B. Lateral malleolus
C. Medial condyle
D. Medial malleolus

50. Release of urine from the bladder is controlled by which nervous system
A. Sympathetic
B. Parasympathetic
C. Fight or flight
D. Autonomic

51. Pain felt at the lateral epicondyle of the humerus is associated with
A. Tennis elbow
B. Golfer's elbow
C. Carpal tunnel syndrome
D. Synovitis

52. Another term for a blood clot within a blood vessel
A. Thrombus
B. Embolus
C. Aneurysm
D. Fibrin

53. Hyper-curvature in the thoracic region
A. Swayback
B. Dowager's hump
C. Scoliosis
D. Bamboo spine

54. A disease that has an unknown cause is known as
A. Pathological
B. Carcinogenic
C. Etiologic
D. Idiopathic

55. A constant ringing in the ear is known as
A. Tinnitus
B. Acromegaly
C. Pinocytosis
D. Vertigo

56. Eversion of the foot is also known as
A. Pronation
B. Supination
C. Plantarflexion
D. Dorsiflexion

57. The condyles of the femur articulate with which structures on the tibia
A. Tuberosities
B. Malleoli
C. Head
D. Condyles

58. Protection from malpractice lawsuits is gained by obtaining
A. Limited Liability Corporation
B. Massage certification
C. Licensure
D. Professional liability insurance

59. A soft end feel is felt at the end of a range of motion due to
A. Tight muscle
B. Bone
C. Injuries
D. Inflammation

60. The most abundant form of connective tissue found in the body
A. Fascia
B. Bone
C. Cartilage
D. Blood

61. Allergic reactions in the body may be controlled with use of
A. Vasodilators
B. Statins
C. Antihistamines
D. Beta-blockers

62. Dilation of a small portion of an artery, caused by a weakened arterial wall
A. Embolism
B. Aneurysm
C. Thrombus
D. Murmur

63. During the fight or flight response, what body function shuts down
A. Movement
B. Circulation
C. Respiration
D. Digestion

64. An independent contractor is responsible for filing which tax form
A. Schedule K1
B. W2
C. 1099
D. Schedule C

65. Nociceptors detect which sensation
A. Temperature
B. Pain
C. Light pressure
D. Deep pressure

66. A massage therapist bringing their own unresolved issues into the therapeutic relationship
A. Self-disclosure
B. Transference
C. Counter-transference
D. Ethics

67. The femur connects to the tibia via the
A. Anterior cruciate ligament
B. Meniscus
C. Articular cartilage
D. Interosseous membrane

68. Normal cells growing uncontrollably results in
A. Inflammation
B. Cyst
C. Cancer
D. Edema

69. Compression of the following nerve by the transverse carpal ligament results in carpal tunnel syndrome
A. Median
B. Ulnar
C. Radial
D. Musculocutaneous

70. Inflammation of a tendon and its surrounding sheath is known as
A. Tendonitis
B. Carpal Tunnel Syndrome
C. Sprain
D. Tenosynovitis

71. Slow heart rhythm
A. Bradycardia
B. Tachycardia
C. Atrial fibrillation
D. Myocarditis

72. Lateral rotation of the shoulder is performed by which two rotator cuff muscles
A. Supraspinatus, Infraspinatus
B. Infraspinatus, Teres Major
C. Teres Minor, Infraspinatus
D. Supraspinatus, Subscapularis

73. Pressure felt as blood passes through an artery
A. Diastolic
B. Systolic
C. Venous
D. Cardiac

74. Nerve responsible for facial expression
A. Cranial nerve VII
B. Cranial nerve V
C. Cranial nerve I
D. Cranial nerve X

75. Decreasing the angle of a joint
A. Extension
B. Flexion
C. Rotation
D. Abduction

76. Bile aids in the digestion of
A. Lipids
B. Glucose
C. Carbohydrates
D. Protein

77. With a client lying supine, a bolster should be placed
A. Between the legs and arms, and under the head
B. Under the ankles and neck
C. Under the knees
D. Under the head only

78. Ability to perform services legally according to occupational standards and licensing
A. Certification
B. Scope of practice
C. Reciprocity
D. Regulations

79. Cryotherapy is used to reduce
A. Inflammation
B. Frostbite
C. Hypoxia
D. Edema

80. A contusion is also known as
A. Bruise
B. Wart
C. Fracture
D. Hives

81. Chris, who has recently suffered from a heart attack, has requested a massage. The proper course a massage therapist should take is
A. Reschedule the massage until medical clearance has been provided from the client's physician
B. Perform the massage to promote circulation
C. Perform the massage and use a cold compress to lower blood pressure
D. Perform the massage while avoiding shaking or trembling actions

82. The lungs
A. Exchange oxygen and carbon monoxide in the blood
B. Exchange sodium and potassium in the blood
C. Exchange oxygen and carbon dioxide in the blood
D. Exchange nitrogen and carbon monoxide in the blood

83. The largest lymph vessel in the body
A. Thoracic duct
B. Subclavian vein
C. Superior vena cava
D. Aorta

84. Basal cell carcinoma
A. Most common, most serious, fastest growing form of skin cancer
B. Least common, most serious, fastest growing form of skin cancer
C. Most common, least serious, slowest growing form of skin cancer
D. Least common, least serious, slowest growing form of skin cancer

85. Digestive enzyme located in the stomach that aids in breaking down food into usable parts for absorption
A. Insulin
B. Bile
C. Bilirubin
D. Pepsin

86. A disease that is present at birth is known as
A. Hereditary
B. Acquired
C. Congenital
D. Autoimmune

87. Tapotement
A. Light gliding strokes towards the heart, used to increase circulation and apply lubricant
B. Strokes that move across tissue, used to break up adhesions
C. Kneading strokes, used to release adhesions and increase circulation
D. Percussion strokes, used to stimulate muscle spindle cells

88. Urine flows from the kidneys through the ureters on its way to the
A. Urethra
B. Bladder
C. Bloodstream
D. Liver

89. The deltoid is an antagonist to itself. What does this mean?
A. It has actions that aren't connected
B. It has two of the same actions
C. It has actions that are similar
D. It has two opposing actions

90. Form of compression in which a muscle fiber is compressed between the thumb and fingers
A. Pincer compression
B. Transverse compression
C. Cross-fiber compression
D. Longitudinal compression

91. Which of the following is a function of connective tissue
A. Absorb nutrients
B. Hold structures together
C. Sensory input
D. Regulation of hormones

92. Tinea is a form of
A. Virus
B. Fungus
C. Bacteria
D. Parasite

93. Depletion of water content in the body results in
A. Hypothermia
B. Hydronephrosis
C. Dehydration
D. Frostbite

346 Practice Test 3

94. Name of the joint found between the atlas and axis
A. Spinous joint
B. Atlantooccipital
C. Occipitotemporal
D. Atlantoaxial

95. The long head of the biceps brachii originates where
A. Supraglenoid tubercle
B. Infraglenoid tubercle
C. Coracoid process
D. Radial tuberosity

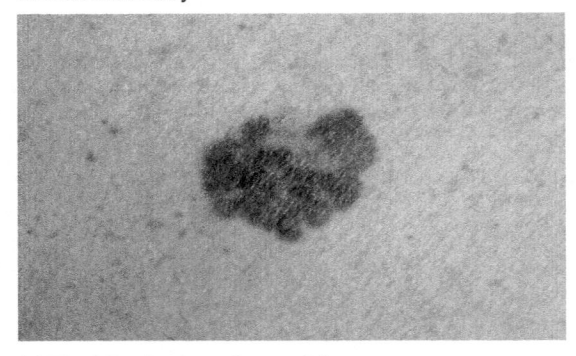

96. The following type of cancer is known as
A. Basal Cell Carcinoma
B. Malignant Melanoma
C. Squamous Cell Carcinoma
D. Kaposi's Sarcoma

97. Law which states that bone density and strength will increase as a result of increased load on a bone
A. Newton's Law
B. Hilton's Law
C. Davis's Law
D. Wolff's Law

98. The origin of the teres minor is
A. Lateral Border
B. Greater Tubercle
C. Intertubercular Groove
D. Inferior Angle

99. With reference to the above image, which muscle group is being stretched
A. Hamstrings
B. Adductors
C. Quadriceps
D. Calf

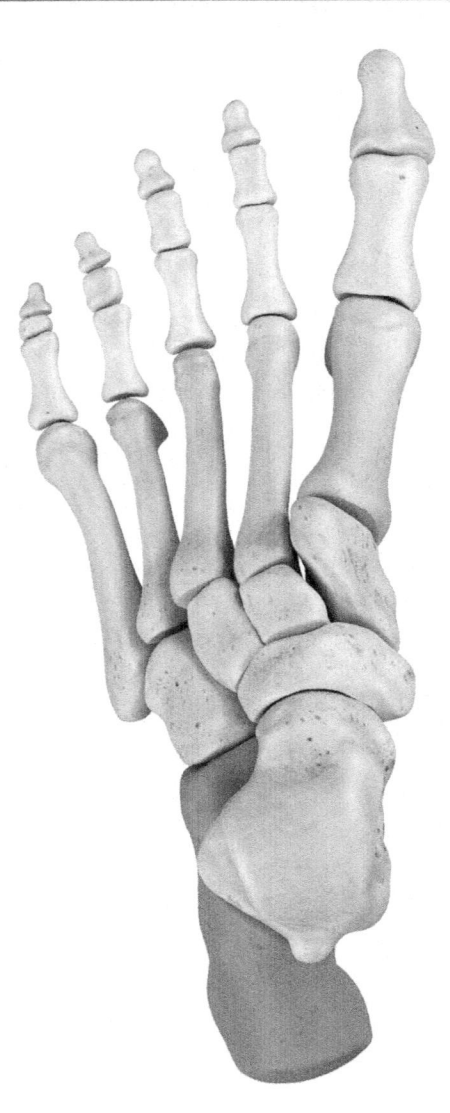

100. Name the bone highlighted in the image
A. Calcaneus
B. Talus
C. Cuboid
D. Hamate

Practice Test 4

1. The knee is considered which type of synovial joint
A. Ellipsoid
B. Pivot
C. Ball and socket
D. Hinge

2. A trigger point that causes pain without palpation
A. Acute
B. Latent
C. Active
D. Chronic

3. Sebaceous glands produce what substance
A. Oil
B. Sweat
C. Milk
D. Epinephrine

4. Tendon attaching the gastrocnemius to the calcaneus
A. Tibial
B. Calcaneal
C. Gastroc
D. Patellar

5. A rheumatologist is a doctor that specializes in
A. Connective tissue
B. Stomach
C. Kidneys
D. Urinary bladder

6. Complete rupture of a ligament
A. Grade 3 strain
B. Grade 3 sprain
C. Grade 2 strain
D. Grade 2 sprain

7. The smallest type of blood vessel
A. Capillary
B. Artery
C. Vein
D. Arteriole

8. Gait analysis is observation and interpretation of a person's
A. Walking pattern
B. Somatic holding pattern
C. Sitting pattern
D. Range of motion

9. All of the following are local contraindications except
A. Herniated disc
B. Grade 2 sprain
C. Trigeminal neuralgia
D. Acute osteoarthritis

10. Shearing of the anterior cruciate ligament most commonly results from force placed on the femur, causing it to move too far in which direction
A. Posteriorly
B. Medially
C. Anteriorly
D. Laterally

11. Another term for inversion of the foot is
A. Supination
B. Pronation
C. Dorsiflexion
D. Plantarflexion

12. The thoracic body cavity
A. Contains the liver, stomach, small intestine, large intestine, pancreas, spleen, and gallbladder
B. Is separated from the dorsal body cavity via the diaphragm
C. Contains the lungs, heart, and major blood vessels
D. Holds the spleen against the stomach to prevent rupture of the spleen

13. Which of the following is not a part of the axial skeleton
A. Sacrum
B. Ribs
C. Skull
D. Clavicle

14. Objective information is
A. Information the client shares about themselves
B. Measurable information visible to the massage therapist
C. Medical conditions the client has been assessed with
D. Recommendations for future massage sessions

15. Tennis elbow is also known as
A. Olecranon bursitis
B. Medial epicondylitis
C. Tuberculitis
D. Lateral epicondylitis

16. Tearing of a muscle is considered a
A. Sprain
B. Strain
C. Contracture
D. Subluxation

17. The first cervical vertebrae is also known as
A. Atlas
B. Axis
C. Occiput
D. Temporal

18. Which of the following massage strokes is best in aiding lung decongestion
A. Tapotement
B. Effleurage
C. Friction
D. Petrissage

19. Changes in temperature can be detected by
A. Chemoreceptors
B. Thermoreceptors
C. Nociceptors
D. Baroreceptors

20. Nephrons are responsible for reabsorption of
A. Staphylococci
B. Urea
C. Vitamins
D. Lactic acid

21. If diastolic pressure measures 90 or higher, a person may be diagnosed with
A. Myocardial infarction
B. Hypotension
C. Hyperemia
D. Hypertension

22. Follicle-stimulating hormone, produced by the pituitary gland, affects what other structure in the body
A. Ovaries
B. Thymus
C. Pancreas
D. Thyroid

23. An accountant may handle all of the following except
A. Bookkeeping
B. Taxes
C. Accounting
D. Advertising

24. A blockage of a blood vessel may result in
A. Arrhythmia
B. Phlebitis
C. Ischemia
D. Hypotension

25. The origin of gracilis is found at what body region
A. Inguinal
B. Popliteal
C. Cubital
D. Antecubital

26. Extension is
A. Moving a structure toward the midline
B. Decreasing the angle of a joint
C. Increasing the angle of a joint
D. Taking a structure away from the midline

27. A cancer spreading from one location in the body to another makes it
A. Asymptomatic
B. Benign
C. Malignant
D. Asymmetrical

28. Which type of gland plays an important role in maintaining body temperature
A. Pineal
B. Sebaceous
C. Sudoriferous
D. Adrenal

29. Which of the following is not a characteristic of muscle tissue
A. Extensibility
B. Protectability
C. Contractility
D. Elasticity

30. A client demonstrating range of motion is an example of which joint movement
A. Active
B. Assistive
C. Passive
D. Resistive

31. Flexion of the lumbar vertebrae can be accomplished by contraction of the following muscle
A. Rectus abdominis
B. Iliacus
C. Quadratus lumborum
D. Latissimus dorsi

32. Which of the following is not a function of connective tissue
A. Insulating the body
B. Protection
C. Separating tissues
D. Hormone release

33. Tearing of the fascia on the bottom of the foot
A. Flat feet
B. Plantar warts
C. Plantarfasciitis
D. Bunion

34. Antagonist to the quadriceps, responsible for hip extension and knee flexion
A. Calf
B. Adductors
C. Rotators
D. Hamstrings

35. Sympathetic nervous system
A. Is voluntary and increases heart rate and blood pressure
B. Is involuntary and increases heart rate and blood pressure
C. Is involuntary and decreases heart rate and blood pressure
D. Is voluntary and decreases heart rate and blood pressure

36. The three types of muscle tissue are
A. Striated, dense, cardiac
B. Skeletal, cardiac, epithelial
C. Epithelial, smooth, branching
D. Skeletal, cardiac, smooth

37. A person trembling during fine motor movements is a sign of
A. Alzheimer's disease
B. Parkinson's disease
C. Anemia
D. Bell's palsy

38. Anatomical law that states a nerve that innervates a muscle will also innervate surrounding tissues
A. Campbell's Law
B. Davis' Law
C. Wolff's Law
D. Hilton's Law

39. All of the following muscles insert onto the scapula except
A. Rhomboids
B. Supraspinatus
C. Serratus anterior
D. Pectoralis minor

40. Hemoglobin is a substance made of iron, located where
A. Erythrocytes
B. Leukocytes
C. Lymph
D. Thrombocytes

41. A client complains of numbness and tingling sensations in the arm. The limb is extremely difficult to use and very weak. It feels colder to the touch than other areas, and even exhibits a slightly bluish tint. The most likely condition causing these symptoms is
A. Myocardial infarction
B. Bell's palsy
C. Myasthenia gravis
D. Thoracic outlet syndrome

42. Stretching of the quadriceps muscle group is achieved by moving the body in what ways
A. Knee extension, hip flexion
B. Knee extension, hip extension
C. Knee flexion, hip flexion
D. Knee flexion, hip extension

43. Action of psoas major on the hip
A. Medial rotation
B. Extension
C. Flexion
D. Lateral rotation

44. Multiple sclerosis is what type of disorder
A. Bacterial
B. Autoimmune
C. Viral
D. Ulcerative

45. There are how many bones in the ankle
A. Eight
B. Two
C. Seven
D. Five

46. The largest part of the brain is also known as
A. Cerebellum
B. Cerebrum
C. Spinal cord
D. Diencephalon

47. Actions of the tibialis anterior
A. Supination and plantarflexion
B. Pronation and plantarflexion
C. Supination and dorsiflexion
D. Pronation and dorsiflexion

48. Massage stroke best utilized to sedate an area
A. Petrissage
B. Vibration
C. Friction
D. Tapotement

49. A massage therapist solicits a product to a client not related to a massage session or treatment. This could be a violation of
A. Ethics
B. Scope of Practice
C. Licensure
D. Reciprocity

50. Anatomical law which states soft tissue will change length under specific amounts of load or tension
A. Davis' Law
B. Hilton's Law
C. Campbell's Law
D. Wolff's Law

51. Insertion of supraspinatus
A. Greater Tubercle
B. Lesser Tubercle
C. Supraspinous Fossa
D. Infraspinous Fossa

52. An increased amount of interstitial fluid in an area results in
A. Aneurysm
B. Inflammation
C. Edema
D. Thrombus

53. Dead white blood cells in a localized area will form
A. Pus
B. Wart
C. Mole
D. Cancer

54. Blood passes from the right atrium into which chamber
A. Left ventricle
B. Left atrium
C. Right ventricle
D. Aorta

55. Circumduction is
A. Moving a structure around the circumference of a joint
B. Bringing a structure closer to the midline
C. Rotating a structure laterally
D. Flexing a joint

56. Another name for thrombocytes is
A. Red blood cells
B. Platelets
C. White blood cells
D. Plasma

57. The sheet or towel used to cover a client while performing a massage
A. Top cover
B. Full sheet
C. Diaper
D. Full towel

58. Streptococcal infection which enters the body through wounds, resulting in infection of the skin and surrounding tissues
A. Cold sore
B. Boil
C. Rosacea
D. Cellulitis

59. Another name for cardiac muscle is
A. Smooth
B. Striated
C. Non-striated
D. Branching

60. During the course of a massage, the massage therapist notices a pre-existing contusion on the client's leg. The massage therapist should
A. Avoid the contusion, notify the client where the contusion is located, and document the contusion in SOAP notes
B. Work over the contusion to help break up potential blood clots that may have formed during the course of healing
C. Apply a cold compress to the affected contusion to reduce blood flow to the contusion
D. Reschedule the massage until the contusion has resolved

61. The aorta carries blood to the liver via the
A. Carotid artery
B. Renal artery
C. Hepatic artery
D. Pulmonary artery

62. The longest tendon in the body connects to which muscle
A. Gastrocnemius
B. Biceps Brachii
C. Semimembranosus
D. Plantaris

63. Primary muscle involved in adhesive capsulitis which tightens and restricts range-of-motion
A. Pectoralis major
B. Supraspinatus
C. Subscapularis
D. Trapezius

64. An active assistive stretch
A. Client stretches into resistance without the help of a massage therapist
B. Client stretches into resistance with the assistance of a massage therapist
C. The client stretches the massage therapist into resistance
D. Massage therapist stretches the client into resistance without assistance from the client

65. Glands are made of which type of tissue
A. Nervous
B. Connective
C. Muscular
D. Epithelial

66. Muscles inserting onto the medial border of the scapula, responsible for adduction of the scapula
A. Serratus anterior
B. Rhomboids
C. Upper fibers of the trapezius
D. Latissimus dorsi

67. Attack of the epithelial cells of the skin by the body's immune system results in
A. Rosacea
B. Acne
C. Psoriasis
D. Systemic lupus

68. Which of the following describes a fossa
A. Articulation
B. Small protrusion
C. Large protrusion
D. Shallow depression

69. Autoimmune disorder in which the immune system attacks the inner linings of the digestive tract, possibly causing ulcers and scarring
A. Crohn's Disease
B. Diverticulosis
C. Pyelonephritis
D. Gastroesophageal Reflux Disease

70. The nucleus pulposus is located in
A. Stratum germinativum
B. Vertebral bodies
C. Squamous epithelium
D. Intervertebral discs

71. Upon dilation of blood vessels in the inflammatory response, the following type of cell moves into the location to destroy bacteria and debris
A. Leukocytes
B. Thrombocytes
C. Erythrocytes
D. Osteoclasts

72. Actions of the hamstring muscle group
A. Hip extension, knee flexion
B. Knee extension, hip flexion
C. Knee flexion, hip flexion
D. Knee extension, hip extension

73. Abrupt stoppage of range of motion due to structures such as bone
A. Soft end feel
B. Hard end feel
C. Empty end feel
D. Nervous end feel

74. The four types of tissue found in the body
A. Muscular, smooth, skeletal, cardiac
B. Epithelial, connective, nervous, muscular
C. Epithelial, skeletal, connective, nervous
D. Connective, epithelial, nervous, smooth

75. Most common form of arthritis
A. Rheumatoid arthritis
B. Gouty arthritis
C. Osteoarthritis
D. Periostitis

76. The region of the body found at the back of the knee is known as
A. Popliteal
B. Crural
C. Inguinal
D. Antecubital

77. Which of the following massage strokes is best in increasing venous circulation
A. Tapotement
B. Friction
C. Effleurage
D. Petrissage

78. A system of movements performed in specific ways to achieve certain results is known as
A. Stroke
B. Process
C. Modality
D. Treatment

79. An ophthalmoscope is used to view the inside of a person's
A. Eyeball
B. Large intestine
C. Mouth
D. Ear

80. Bacterial infection that affects the kidneys, usually occurring acutely
A. Uremia
B. Kidney stones
C. Pyelonephritis
D. Cystitis

81. Muscle inserting into the fascia of the upper chest
A. Sternocleidomastoid
B. Platysma
C. Pectoralis major
D. Subclavius

82. The most common form of papilloma
A. Wart
B. Acne
C. Psoriasis
D. Cyst

83. Alveoli are located at the ends of
A. Pulmonary veins
B. Bronchial tubes
C. Bronchioles
D. Trachea

84. Chronic inflammation located at the tibial tuberosity, caused by over-use of the quadriceps
A. Osgood-Schlatter disease
B. Graves' disease
C. Raynaud's disease
D. Knock-knee

85. The glenohumeral joint is made by combining the head of the humerus with which structure on the scapula
A. Supraglenoid tubercle
B. Acromion process
C. Coracoid process
D. Glenoid fossa

86. Sartorius attaches proximally to what structure of the pelvis
A. Anterior superior iliac spine
B. Anterior inferior iliac spine
C. Ischial tuberosity
D. Superior ramus of pubis

87. A question asked that is used when seeking a yes or no response
A. Open-ended
B. Close-ended
C. Confidential
D. Tactful

88. Connective tissue holding bones together
A. Tendon
B. Ligament
C. Cartilage
D. Periosteum

89. The trigeminal nerve is which numbered cranial nerve
A. X
B. VII
C. V
D. III

90. A red-ringed rash is found in
A. Tinea pedis
B. Ringworm
C. Shingles
D. Psoriasis

91. An assessment is performed
A. Only before and after a massage
B. Only before a massage
C. Only after a massage
D. Before, during, and after the massage

92. Melanin
A. Provides pigmentation to the skin
B. Allows protection by producing a thickened area of skin
C. Waterproofs the skin
D. Allows absorption of water into the skin

93. A short general statement detailing the goal of a business
A. Public image
B. Purpose
C. Mission statement
D. Business plan

94. A doctor that specializes in the feet is known as a
A. Podiatrist
B. Oncologist
C. Radiologist
D. Rheumatologist

95. The outer most membrane of a serous membrane is called
A. Peritoneal membrane
B. Visceral serous membrane
C. Temporal serous membrane
D. Parietal serous membrane

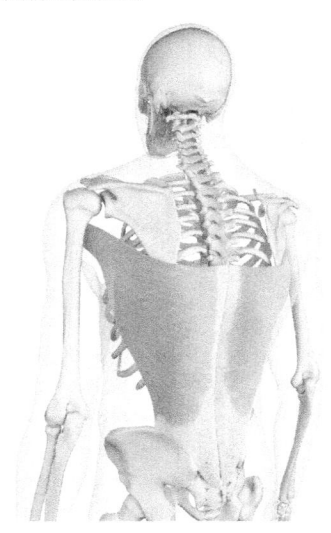

96. Primary actions of the muscle pictured
A. Extension, abduction, lateral rotation
B. Flexion, abduction, lateral rotation
C. Extension, adduction, medial rotation
D. Flexion, adduction, lateral rotation

97. A step backwards psychologically when faced with stress is known as
A. Repression
B. Denial
C. Displacement
D. Regression

98. If a massage therapist begins to feel sexually attracted to a client, what should the best course of action be
A. No longer book appointments with the client
B. Ignore the feelings because they are natural
C. Act on the feelings
D. Ask the client out on a date

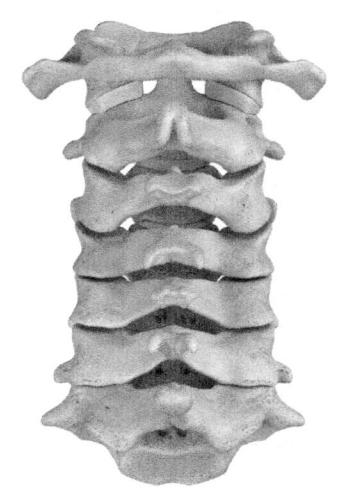

99. There are seven vertebrae in which region of the vertebral column, pictured above
A. Thoracic
B. Lumbar
C. Cervical
D. Sacral

100. Carrying a heavy bucket with one hand for an extended period of time may result in soreness in the following muscle, the result of an isometric contraction
A. Levator scapulae
B. Rectus abdominis
C. Sternocleidomastoid
D. Scalenes

Practice Test 5

1. Reiki originated in
A. Japan
B. China
C. India
D. America

2. Massage strokes directed towards the heart are called
A. Centrifugal
B. Centripetal
C. Chucking
D. Superficial

3. Muscle group primarily responsible for extension of the hip and flexion of the knee
A. Glutes
B. Quadriceps
C. Adductors
D. Hamstrings

4. High altitudes can cause altitude sickness, a common form of
A. Hypoxia
B. Hypothermia
C. Hyperplasia
D. Frostbite

5. The definition of physiology is
A. Studying movement
B. Studying the structure of the body
C. Studying the cause of disease
D. Studying the function of the body

6. Structure bringing air into the lungs
A. Epiglottis
B. Pharynx
C. Trachea
D. Uvula

7. A body out of vertical alignment might most benefit from the following treatment
A. Swedish massage
B. Lymphatic drainage
C. Rolfing
D. Thai massage

8. Self-disclosure
A. The client sharing feelings and emotions during a massage session
B. The massage therapist sharing their feelings and emotions during a massage session
C. A massage therapist disclosing their scope of practice
D. A client viewing a massage therapist as they would a significant person in their early life

9. The lesser trochanter is positioned where in relation to the greater trochanter
A. Lateral
B. Medial
C. Anterior
D. Posterior

10. A lack of erythrocytes in the body results in
A. Myocardial infarction
B. Raynaud's syndrome
C. Anemia
D. Decreased immune response

11. Excessive alcohol consumption may result in
A. Nephritis
B. Cirrhosis
C. Gastritis
D. Diverticulitis

12. Tachycardia, a form of arrhythmia, results in
A. Slow heart beat
B. Rapid heart beat
C. Heart murmur
D. Angina pectoris

13. A sitz bath is a bath in which the client immerses their body up to
A. The knees
B. The chest
C. The neck
D. The hips

14. The ovaries produce
A. Luteinizing hormone
B. Testosterone
C. Progesterone
D. Melatonin

15. The radiocarpal joint is considered which type of synovial joint
A. Hinge
B. Ball and socket
C. Condyloid
D. Pivot

16. Infection caused by bacteria or virus that causes inflammation of the meninges, resulting in vomiting, headache, and fever
A. Osteomyelitis
B. Meningitis
C. Impetigo
D. Encephalitis

17. Jasmine, sandalwood, and grapefruit are all examples of
A. Massage table materials
B. Gemstones
C. Essential oils
D. Perfumes

18. An empty end feel is felt at the end of a range of motion due to
A. Tight muscle
B. Bone
C. Trauma to a joint
D. Resistance

19. The inferior five pairs of ribs are also called
A. True ribs
B. False ribs
C. Superior ribs
D. Inferior ribs

20. Abduction of the scapula can be accomplished by contraction of which muscle
A. Serratus anterior
B. Rhomboids
C. Latissimus dorsi
D. Trapezius

21. The cerebellum is formed by which type of tissue
A. Connective
B. Nervous
C. Epithelial
D. Muscular

22. Which part of a long bone is the diaphysis
A. Shaft
B. End
C. Articular surface
D. Growth plate

23. A massage table, chair, and music source are located in
A. Massage room
B. Business area
C. Changing room
D. Bathroom

24. Lymphatic drainage massage involves light strokes and
A. Application of heat
B. Deep strokes
C. Tapotement
D. Pumping actions

25. All of the following are local contraindications except
A. Raynaud's syndrome
B. Phlebitis
C. Fracture
D. Acne

26. The atlantooccipital joint is responsible for producing which two actions on the head
A. Lateral deviation
B. Rotation
C. Flexion and extension
D. Adduction and abduction

27. Plane joint connecting the scapula to the clavicle
A. Sternoclavicular
B. Acromioclavicular
C. Atlantooccipital
D. Atlantoaxial

28. The lumbar region contains how many vertebrae
A. Seven
B. Twelve
C. Five
D. One

29. Transference
A. Keeping a client's information private and protected
B. The massage therapist bringing their own unresolved issues into the therapeutic relationship
C. The client viewing a massage therapist similarly to a significant person in their early life
D. Relocating from one office to another

30. Which type of muscle tissue is controlled voluntarily
A. Epithelial
B. Cardiac
C. Smooth
D. Skeletal

31. Polarity therapy helps clients to balance
A. Mind and soul
B. Hips and shoulders
C. Knees and ankles
D. Body and mind

32. Pain is detected by
A. Photoreceptors
B. Baroreceptors
C. Mechanoreceptors
D. Nociceptors

33. A furuncle is a
A. Bacterial infection of hair follicles
B. Bacterial infection of mucous membranes
C. Viral infection of mucous membranes
D. Bacterial infection of bone

34. Primary action of the pronator teres
A. Elbow extension
B. Supination
C. Elbow flexion
D. Pronation

35. Gentle, rhythmic massage strokes may be
A. Centrifugal
B. Stimulating
C. Sedative
D. Deep

36. The pattern or design of a massage treatment is known as
A. Deliberation
B. Process
C. Sequence
D. Contact

37. Sebaceous glands connect to
A. Arrector pili
B. Hair follicles
C. Skin openings
D. Kidneys

38. Muscle inserting on the pes anserinus, responsible for flexing and externally rotating the hip, and flexing the knee
A. Gracilis
B. Sartorius
C. Semitendinosus
D. Biceps femoris

39. Massage technique targeting reflex points on the hands, feet, and ears to stimulate organs and tissue throughout the body
A. Mentastics
B. Reiki
C. Trager method
D. Reflexology

40. Sprain
A. Tearing of cartilage
B. Tearing of a tendon
C. Over-stretching of a muscle
D. Over-stretching of a ligament

41. Muscle primarily responsible for elevation of the scapula
A. Middle fibers of trapezius
B. Supraspinatus
C. Levator scapulae
D. Sternocleidomastoid

42. Etiology
A. Study of movement
B. Study of cause of disease
C. Study of tumors
D. Study of tissue

43. Vein found in the region of the arm
A. Femoral vein
B. Brachial vein
C. Great saphenous vein
D. Axillary vein

44. Medications given to help control hypertension are known as
A. Statins
B. Antihistamines
C. Chemotherapy
D. Nitrates

45. Stance used to perform massage strokes such as petrissage, friction, and tapotement
A. Archer
B. Horse
C. Bow
D. Swimmer

46. Medial and lateral rotation can be performed at which of the following joints
A. Hip
B. Elbow
C. Ankle
D. Wrist

47. Physical effects of massage therapy are called
A. Emotional effects
B. Mechanical effects
C. Reflex effects
D. Sensory effects

48. The epiglottis
A. Allows food to move from the mouth into the pharynx
B. Allows food to move from the pharynx into the esophagus
C. Prevents food from moving from the pharynx into the nasal sinus
D. Prevents food and liquid from moving into the larynx upon swallowing

49. Exocrine glands secrete their substances where
A. Onto a surface
B. Into the blood
C. Onto the brain
D. Into endocrine glands

50. Suggestions for future treatments by the massage therapist would be documented under which section of SOAP notes
A. Subjective
B. Objective
C. Assessment
D. Plan

51. A massage therapist is working on the lateral side of the forearm. The bone they are working on top of is the
A. Radius
B. Ulna
C. Humerus
D. Fibula

52. An injury to the adductor magnus muscle would make which movements more difficult to perform
A. Hip flexion, abduction, and extension
B. Hip flexion, adduction, and extension
C. Hip extension, abduction, and medial rotation
D. Hip flexion, abduction, and medial rotation

53. All of the following are forms of parasites except
A. Ringworm
B. Tapeworm
C. Hookworm
D. Pinworm

54. The small intestine
A. Breaks down food into usable parts for absorption
B. Absorbs water from feces and eliminates waste
C. Absorbs nutrients from chyme into the blood
D. Transports food from the mouth to the stomach

55. Over-stretching of veins resulting from excessive pressure
A. Arteriosclerosis
B. Phlebitis
C. Edema
D. Varicose veins

56. Good body mechanics are important to
A. Perform a shorter massage
B. Prevent injuries to the therapist
C. Massage the head and neck
D. Prevent injuries to the client

57. All of the following muscles extend the shoulder except
A. Teres major
B. Latissimus dorsi
C. Supraspinatus
D. Subscapularis

58. Mononucleosis, warts, and cold sores are all caused by
A. Fungus
B. Bacteria
C. Virus
D. Parasite

59. Aromatherapy affects which portion of the brain
A. Limbic System
B. Midbrain
C. Occipital Lobe
D. Pons

60. Periosteum is a form of which type of tissue
A. Nervous
B. Connective
C. Epithelial
D. Muscular

61. The hip joint is also known as
A. Coaxal joint
B. Tibiofemoral joint
C. Talocrural joint
D. Glenohumeral joint

62. Anemia results in
A. Varicose veins
B. Myocardial infarction
C. Lack of oxygen traveling through the body
D. Increased lipid content in the blood

63. Glucagon is a digestive enzyme produced by the pancreas responsible for
A. Decreasing glucose levels in the blood
B. Increasing glucose levels in the blood
C. Increasing potassium levels in the blood
D. Decreasing potassium levels in the blood

64. Movement of a joint through the entire extent of its action is known as
A. Stretching
B. Range of motion
C. Traction
D. Active movement

65. Antagonist to sartorius with regards to knee flexion
A. Biceps femoris
B. Rectus femoris
C. Semitendinosus
D. Semimembranosus

66. Dilation of blood vessels during the inflammatory stage is controlled by
A. Histamines
B. Leukocytes
C. Neutrophils
D. Fibrosis

67. Psoriasis
A. Inflammation of skin resulting in skin coming into contact with an irritant
B. Autoimmune disorder resulting in thick, dry, silvery patches of skin
C. Blockage of sebaceous glands, resulting in pustules
D. Skin irritation caused by exposure to cold, affecting blood vessels and hair follicles

68. The left ventricle is located directly inferior to
A. Bicuspid valve
B. Tricuspid valve
C. Right atrium
D. Right ventricle

69. Proximal attachment of the short head of biceps brachii
A. Coracoid process
B. Supraglenoid tubercle
C. Infraglenoid tubercle
D. Coronoid process

70. Contrast baths utilize
A. Warm and lukewarm water
B. Hot and cold water
C. Hot and warm water
D. Cold water and ice

71. The medial epicondyle of the humerus is the origination site of which muscle group
A. Adductors
B. Wrist extensors
C. Wrist flexors
D. Abductors

72. An antagonist to the biceps brachii is
A. Coracobrachialis
B. Brachialis
C. Pronator Teres
D. Pectoralis Major

73. The floating ribs are considered
A. A local contraindication
B. An absolute contraindication
C. An endangerment site
D. Not a contraindication

74. The fight or flight response is also known as
A. Sympathetic
B. Parasympathetic
C. Autonomic
D. Peripheral

75. Medical conditions the client has been assessed with are documented on which section of SOAP notes
A. Subjective
B. Objective
C. Assessment
D. Plan

76. Muscle responsible for external rotation and extension of the shoulder
A. Subscapularis
B. Supraspinatus
C. Infraspinatus
D. Latissimus Dorsi

77. The ulna is positioned where in relation to the radius
A. Proximal
B. Lateral
C. Medial
D. Distal

78. Paralysis of the lower limbs
A. Quadriplegia
B. Hemiplegia
C. Paraplegia
D. Triplegia

79. The jejunum is responsible for
A. Absorption of nutrients into the blood stream
B. Digestion and excretion of waste
C. Filtration of electrolytes into the kidneys
D. Mastication of food in the alimentary canal

80. A client is looking for structural realignment therapy. The type of massage they are requesting is
A. Myofascial release
B. Feldenkrais
C. Rolfing
D. Sports massage

81. Muscle located on the lateral side of the leg, responsible for pronation and plantarflexion of the foot
A. Tibialis anterior
B. Peroneus longus
C. Gastrocnemius
D. Soleus

82. Another name for a nerve cell
A. Neuron
B. Axon
C. Neuroglia
D. Brain

83. The "R" in PRICE stands for
A. Rest
B. Resist
C. Reflex
D. Regain

84. Paralysis of one half of the face, caused by stimulation of the Herpes Simplex virus, which affects the Facial nerve
A. Graves' disease
B. Cerebral palsy
C. Trigeminal neuralgia
D. Bell's palsy

85. The skeletal system
A. Absorbs substances into the blood stream
B. Connects tissues together
C. Protects organs and creates blood cells
D. Circulates blood throughout the body

86. Friction
A. Light gliding strokes towards the heart, used to increase circulation and apply lubricant
B. Strokes that move across tissue, used to break up adhesions
C. Kneading strokes, used to release adhesions and increase circulation
D. Percussion strokes, used to stimulate muscle spindle cells

87. Muscle originating on the temporal bone, inserting onto the coronoid process of the mandible
A. Pterygoid
B. Buccinator
C. Masseter
D. Temporalis

88. A client notifies a massage therapist that they have a small area of skin affected by cellulitis. The appropriate response by the massage therapist would be
A. Apply heat to the affected area to allow increased circulation to enter the area
B. Work on the affected area to help break up fat deposits under the skin
C. Avoid the affected area but continue massaging the rest of the body
D. Reschedule the massage until the cellulitis has completely cleared up

89. All of the following are structures that pass through the diaphragm except
A. Inferior vena cava
B. Esophagus
C. Abdominal aorta
D. Stomach

90. Deltoid and supraspinatus share a common action. That action is
A. Extension of the shoulder
B. Abduction of the shoulder
C. Flexion of the shoulder
D. Adduction of the shoulder

91. Long gliding stroke in which the hands are held just above the body, not touching
A. Nerve stroke
B. Effleurage
C. Aura stroke
D. Feather stroke

92. Urea and ammonia are filtered from the blood by the
A. Large intestine
B. Bladder
C. Kidneys
D. Spleen

93. Arteriosclerosis
A. Hardening of the walls of the arteries
B. Fatty plaque buildup in the arteries
C. Bulging of an arterial wall
D. Inflammation of a vein

94. The three muscles that attach to the coracoid process
A. Long head of biceps brachii, coracobrachialis, pectoralis major
B. Coracobrachialis, brachialis, pectoralis minor
C. Short head of biceps brachii, coracobrachialis, pectoralis minor
D. Short head of biceps femoris, coracobrachialis, pectoralis minor

95. Using the same linen between two separate clients is known as
A. Common sheet
B. Same linen
C. Common towel
D. Same towel

96. Increasing the temperature in a room may be useful in treating the following condition
A. Rosacea
B. Psoriasis
C. Carpal Tunnel Syndrome
D. Raynaud's Disease

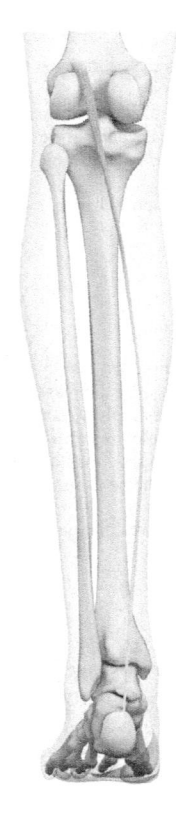

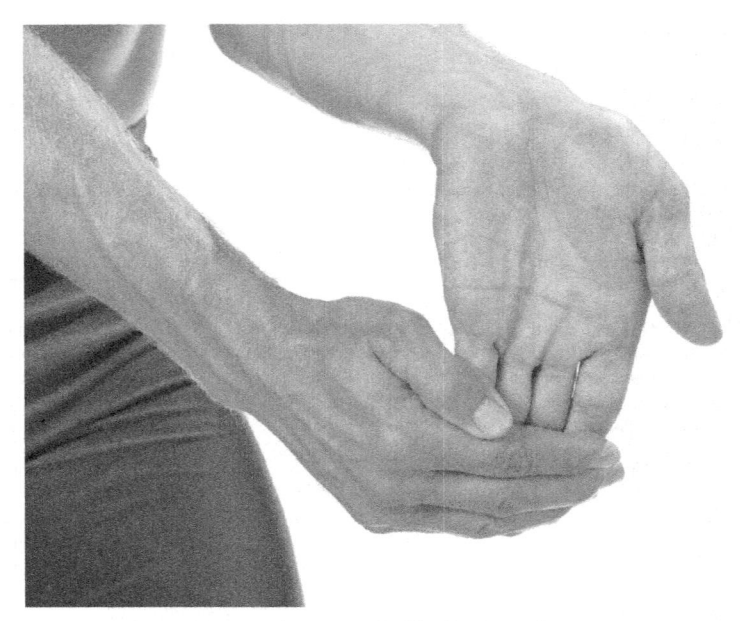

100. The muscle group being stretched in this picture is
A. Elbow extensors
B. Wrist flexors
C. Elbow flexors
D. Wrist extensors

97. The longest tendon in the body connects to the following muscle, pictured above
A. Soleus
B. Tibialis Posterior
C. Plantaris
D. Peroneus Longus

98. Draping establishes
A. Scope of practice
B. Ethics
C. Boundaries
D. Liabilities

99. If a client presents with trigeminal neuralgia, the best modification to the massage table would be
A. Remove the head rest and have client lie with their head turned to the side, or supine
B. Elevate the right hip with bolsters
C. Only position the client in a semi-reclined position
D. Have the client place both arms across the chest to relax the platysma

Full Practice Test Answer Keys

Practice Test 1		**Practice Test 2**		**Practice Test 3**		**Practice Test 4**		**Practice Test 5**	
01. D	51. D	01. C	51. C	01. B	51. A	01. D	51. A	01. A	51. A
02. A	52. A	02. A	52. D	02. C	52. A	02. C	52. C	02. B	52. B
03. C	53. C	03. D	53. A	03. B	53. B	03. A	53. A	03. D	53. C
04. A	54. B	04. C	54. B	04. D	54. D	04. B	54. C	04. A	54. C
05. C	55. D	05. A	55. C	05. A	55. A	05. A	55. A	05. D	55. D
06. A	56. C	06. C	56. A	06. A	56. A	06. B	56. B	06. C	56. B
07. C	57. C	07. A	57. A	07. D	57. D	07. A	57. A	07. C	57. C
08. B	58. A	08. D	58. A	08. D	58. D	08. A	58. D	08. A	58. C
09. A	59. A	09. A	59. A	09. A	59. A	09. C	59. D	09. B	59. A
10. C	60. B	10. B	60. B	10. A	60. D	10. C	60. A	10. C	60. B
11. A	61. C	11. A	61. D	11. D	61. C	11. A	61. C	11. B	61. A
12. A	62. A	12. A	62. B	12. D	62. B	12. C	62. D	12. B	62. C
13. B	63. C	13. D	63. D	13. A	63. D	13. D	63. C	13. D	63. B
14. A	64. A	14. A	64. B	14. D	64. C	14. B	64. B	14. C	64. B
15. C	65. B	15. A	65. B	15. C	65. B	15. D	65. D	15. C	65. B
16. A	66. B	16. B	66. D	16. D	66. C	16. B	66. B	16. B	66. A
17. B	67. D	17. B	67. C	17. B	67. A	17. A	67. C	17. C	67. B
18. C	68. A	18. C	68. C	18. B	68. C	18. A	68. D	18. C	68. A
19. A	69. A	19. B	69. A	19. A	69. A	19. B	69. A	19. B	69. A
20. B	70. D	20. B	70. D	20. B	70. D	20. C	70. D	20. A	70. B
21. D	71. A	21. D	71. A	21. A	71. A	21. D	71. A	21. B	71. C
22. A	72. D	22. A	72. A	22. B	72. C	22. A	72. A	22. A	72. C
23. D	73. C	23. D	73. A	23. A	73. B	23. D	73. B	23. A	73. C
24. D	74. D	24. C	74. A	24. A	74. A	24. C	74. B	24. D	74. A
25. B	75. B	25. A	75. C	25. B	75. B	25. A	75. C	25. A	75. C
26. A	76. C	26. B	76. A	26. B	76. A	26. C	76. C	26. C	76. C
27. A	77. D	27. C	77. B	27. C	77. C	27. C	77. C	27. B	77. C
28. C	78. C	28. B	78. D	28. A	78. B	28. C	78. C	28. C	78. C
29. B	79. A	29. C	79. D	29. D	79. A	29. B	79. A	29. C	79. A
30. A	80. D	30. C	80. A	30. C	80. A	30. A	80. C	30. D	80. C
31. B	81. D	31. C	81. D	31. B	81. A	31. A	81. B	31. D	81. B
32. C	82. A	32. A	82. D	32. B	82. C	32. D	82. A	32. D	82. A
33. B	83. C	33. D	83. C	33. C	83. A	33. C	83. C	33. A	83. A
34. D	84. A	34. C	84. C	34. C	84. C	34. D	84. A	34. D	84. D
35. B	85. A	35. C	85. A	35. B	85. D	35. B	85. D	35. C	85. C
36. A	86. D	36. C	86. B	36. D	86. C	36. D	86. A	36. C	86. B
37. B	87. A	37. B	87. C	37. C	87. D	37. B	87. B	37. B	87. D
38. B	88. D	38. C	88. B	38. D	88. B	38. D	88. B	38. B	88. C
39. B	89. A	39. D	89. A	39. D	89. D	39. B	89. C	39. D	89. D
40. C	90. B	40. D	90. B	40. B	90. A	40. A	90. B	40. D	90. B
41. B	91. D	41. A	91. A	41. D	91. B	41. D	91. D	41. C	91. C
42. A	92. D	42. C	92. C	42. A	92. B	42. D	92. A	42. B	92. C
43. D	93. B	43. A	93. C	43. C	93. C	43. C	93. C	43. B	93. A
44. D	94. D	44. A	94. A	44. C	94. D	44. B	94. A	44. A	94. C
45. D	95. A	45. C	95. C	45. C	95. A	45. C	95. D	45. B	95. C
46. A	96. A	46. A	96. A	46. A	96. B	46. B	96. C	46. A	96. D
47. C	97. B	47. C	97. C	47. C	97. D	47. C	97. D	47. B	97. C
48. A	98. D	48. A	98. C	48. B	98. A	48. B	98. A	48. D	98. C
49. B	99. D	49. C	99. B	49. D	99. C	49. A	99. C	49. A	99. A
50. B	100. A	50. A	100. A	50. B	100. A	50. A	100. A	50. D	100. B

References

This study guide was created with assistance from the following resources:

Tappan's Handbook of Massage Therapy: Blending Art with Science(6th Edition), 2015 – Patricia J. Benjamin, PhD

30 Second Anatomy: The 50 Most Important Structures and Systems in the Human Body, Each Explained in Half a Minute, 2013 – Gabrielle M. Finn, Judith Barbaro-Brown

Anatomica: The Complete Home Medical Reference, 2010 – Ken Ashwell

Mosby's Pathology for Massage Therapists(3rd Edition), 2013 – Susan Salvo

The Four Hour Chef: The Simple Path to Cooking Like a Pro, Learn Anything, and Living the Good Life, 2013 – Timothy Ferriss

Gray's Anatomy – Henry Gray

Essentials of Anatomy and Physiology(4th Edition), 2002 – Rod Seeley, Trent Stephens, Philip Tate

Introducing Medical Terminology Specialties: A Medical Specialties Approach with Patient Records, 2003 – Regina Masters, Barbara Gylys

Exploring Medical Language: A Student-Directed Approach(5th Edition), 2002 – Myrna LaFleur Brooks

Basic Clinical Massage Therapy: Integrating Anatomy and Treatment, 2003 – James H. Clay, David M. Pounds

Milady's Theory and Practice of Therapeutic Massage, 1999 – Mark F. Beck

Recommended Reading

The Obstacle is the Way: The Timeless Art of Turning Trials into Triumph, 2014 – Ryan Holiday

Ego is the Enemy, 2016 – Ryan Holiday

Outliers: The Story of Success, 2008 – Malcolm Gladwell

Tools of Titans, 2016 – Timothy Ferriss

Index

A

Abdomen	52
Abducens Nerve	71
Abduction	67
Abrasion	145
Absolute Contraindication	13
Accessory Nerve	71
Accounts Payable	28
Accounts Receivable	28
Acetabulum	224
Acetylcholine	65
Acne	134
Acquired Disease	96
Acromegaly	129
Acromial End(Clavicle)	220
Acromion Process	218
Actin	65
Action Potential	65
Active Joint Movement	9
Active Assistive Movement	9
Active Listening	30
Addison's Disease	129
Adduction	67
Adductor Magnus	274
Adductor Tubercle	225
Adhesive Capsulitis	151
Adrenal Glands	62
AED	107
Afferent	69
Agonist	67
AIDS	147
Allergy	147
Alveoli	75
Alzheimer's Disease	157
Amphiarthrotic	77
Analgesics	105
Anatomy	50
Anconeus	265
Anemia	112
Aneurysm	113
Ankle	86
Ankylosing Spondylitis	168
Anorexia Nervosa	189
Antacids	105
Antagonist	68
Anterior	50
Anterior Inferior Iliac Spine	224
Anterior Superior Iliac Spine	224
Antibiotics	105
Antibodies	102
Anticoagulants	105
Antifungals	105
Antihistamines	105
Anti-inflammatory Agents	105
Antipyretics	105
Antivirals	105
Anxiety Disorders	189
Aorta	57
Apnea	163
Appendicular Skeleton	79
Arachnoid	70
Aromatherapy	22
Arrhythmia	113
Arteries	58
Arteriosclerosis	114
Arthroscopy	107
Assessment	11
Assessment(SOAP)	17
Assisted Stretch	9
Asthma	163
Asthma Attack	197
Atherosclerosis	114
Athlete's Foot	134
Autoimmune Disease	96
Autonomic Nervous System	73
Avulsion	145
Axial Skeleton	79
Axillary Nerve	71
Axon	54

B

Ball-and-Socket Joint	79
Basal Cell Carcinoma	183
Bell's Palsy	157
Beta Blockers	105
Biceps Brachii	259
Biceps Femoris	275
Bicuspid Valve	57
Blast Cells	55
Blood	55
Blood Vessels	58
Body Language	30
Body Mechanics	20
Body of Sternum	220
Boil	135
Bolster	19
Bone Graft	107
Boundaries	29
Bow/Archer Stance	21
Brachial Plexus	71
Brachialis	260
Brachioradialis	266
Brain	69
Brain Stem	69
Breast Cancer	183
Bronchi	75
Bronchitis	164
Bronchodilators	105
Buccinator	229
Bulimia	190
Bunion	168
Burns	135
Bursitis	169
Business Plan	27

C

Calcaneus	86
Calcitonin	62
Cancer	182
Capillaries	58
Capitate	84
Capitulum	221
Cardiac Muscle	54
Cardiac Sphincter	61
Cardiopulmonary Resuscitation	195
Cardiovascular System	57
Carpal Tunnel Syndrome	158
Carpals	84
CAT Scan	108
Catheter	107
Cell	52
Cellulitis	136
Central Body Region	52
Central Nervous System	69
Centrifuge	107
Cerebellum	69
Cerebral Vascular Accident	196
Cerebrum	69
Certification	27
Cervical Plexus	71
Cervical Vertebrae	81
Cervix	74
Chair	18
Chemotherapy	107
Choking	195
Cholecystitis	121
Circular(Muscle shape)	66
Circumduction	67
Cirrhosis	121
Clast Cells	55
Clavicle	82
Close-Ended Question	30
Common Peroneal Nerve	72
Compression Device	108
Concentric Contraction	66
Concussion	197
Condyloid Joint	79
Confidentiality	29
Congenital Disease	96
Conjunctivitis	193
Connective Tissue	54
Contrast Bath	22
Contusion	137
Convergent(Muscle shape)	66
Coracobrachialis	261
Coracoid Process	218
Coronal Suture	77
Coronoid Process	222
Counter-Transference	30
Cranial Nerves	71
Craniosacral Therapy	22
Crohn's Disease	122
Cryotherapy	108
Cuboid	86
Cuneiforms	86
Cushing's Disease	130
Cystitis	179
Cytoplasm	52

D

Davis's Law	68
Decongestants	105
Decubitus Ulcer	137
Deep	50
Deep Peroneal Nerve	72
Deep Tissue	22
Deep Vein Thrombosis	115
Deficiency Disease	96
Deltoid	262
Deltoid Tuberosity	221
Dementia	191
Dendrite	54
Denial	31
Depression(action)	67
Depression(disorder)	191
De Quervain's Tenosynovitis	151
Dermatitis	138
Diabetes Mellitus	130
Diabetic Ketoacidosis	196
Dialysis	108
Diaphragm	256
Diaphysis	77
Diarthrotic	77
Digestive System	59
Directional Terms	50
Disease	96
Dislocation	169
Displacement	31
Distal	50
Diuretics	105
Diverticulitis	123
Diverticulosis	123
Dopamine	62
Dorsiflexion	67
Draping	19
Dura Mater	70

E

Eccentric Contraction	67
Echocardiogram	108
Efferent	69
Effleurage	8
Electrocardiogram	109
Electromyography	109
Elevation	67
Ellipsoid Joint	79
Emphysema	165
Empty End Feel	10
Encephalitis	159
End Feel	10
Endangerment Site	13
Endocrine System	62
Epididymis	74
Epidural	109
Epiglottis	75
Epinephrine	62
Epiphysis	77
Epithelial Tissue	53
Erythrocyte	55
Esophageal Sphincter	61
Esophagus	59
Estrogen	62
Ethics	29
Ethmoid Bone	80
Eversion	67
Expectorants	105
External Occipital Protuberance	216
Extension	67

F

Facial Nerve	71
Fallopian Tube	74
False Ribs	82
Female Reproductive System	74
Femoral Nerve	72
Femur	85
Fibromyalgia	152
Fibula	86
Financial Plan	27
First Aid	195
Fixator	68
Flat Bone	76
Flexion	67
Floating Ribs	82
Follicle-Stimulating Hormone	62
Foot	87
Forearm	84
Fracture	170
Friction	8
Frontal Bone	80
Frontal/Coronal Plane	51
Frontal Lobe	69
Frostbite	197
Furuncle	135

G

Gallbladder	59

Gastritis	124	Ilium	83	Liver	59	**N**			
Gastrocnemius	283	Immunity	101	Local Anesthetics	106				
Gastroenteritis	124	Impetigo	139	Local Contraindication	13	Nails	63		
General Anesthetics	105	Incision	145	Lomi Lomi	22	Nasal Bone	80		
General Liability Insurance	27	Independent Contractor	28	Long Bone	76	Navicular	86		
GERD	125	Infectious Disease	97	Longissimus	240	Nephron	88		
Gift Tax	29	Inferior	50	Lordosis	172	Nerve Stroke	8		
Glenoid Fossa	218	Inferior Angle	218	Lower Limb	52	Nervous System	69		
Gliding Joint	79	Inferior Articular Process	217	Lubricant	18	Nervous Tissue	54		
Glossopharangeal Nerve	71	Inferior Ramus of Pubis	224	Lumbar Vertebrae	81	Neuromuscular Junction	65		
Gluteal Tuberosity	225	Inferior Vena Cava	57	Lumbosacral Plexus	71	Neuron	54		
Gluteus Maximus	269	Inflammation	103	Lunate	84	Nociceptors	63		
Goiter	131	Influenza	166	Lung	75	Non-Hodgkin's Lymphoma	187		
Golfer's Elbow	152	Informed Consent	14	Lung Cancer	185	Norepinephrine	62		
Golgi Apparatus	52	Infraglenoid Tubercle	219	Lupus Erythematosus	148	Nose	75		
Golgi Tendon Organ	67	Infraspinatus	238	Lyme Disease	173	Nucleolus	52		
Gout	171	Infraspinous Fossa	219	Lymph	64	Nucleus	52		
Gracilis	276	Insomnia	192	Lymph Node	64				
Graves' Disease	132	Insulin	106	Lymph Vessels	64	**O**			
Greater Trochanter	225	Insulin Shock	196	Lymphatic Drainage	22				
Greater Tubercle	221	Intake Form	14	Lymphatic System	64	Objective(SOAP)	17		
Growth Hormone	62	Integumentary System	63	Lymphedema	149	Observation(SOAP)	17		
		Intertubercular Groove	221	Lysosome	52	Obturator Foramen	224		
H		Inversion	67			Obturator Nerve	72		
		Irregular Bone	76	**M**		Occipital Bone	80		
Hair	63	Ischial Tuberosity	224			Occipital Lobe	69		
Hamate	84	Ischium	83	Magnetic Resonance Imaging	110	Oculomotor Nerve	71		
Hand	85	Isometric Contraction	66	Male Reproductive System	74	Olecranon Fossa	221		
Hard End Feel	10	Isotonic Contraction	66	Malignant Melanoma	186	Olecranon Process	222		
Head(Femur)	225			Mammogram	110	Olfactory Nerve	71		
Head(Fibula)	226	**J**		Mandible	80	Onychomycosis	140		
Head(Humerus)	221			Manubrium	220	Open-Ended Question	30		
Head(Radius)	222	Joint	77	Market Analysis	28	Opposition	67		
Head(Ulna)	222	Joint Capsule	78	Massage Table	18	Optic Nerve	71		
Heart	57			Masseter	230	Organelle	52		
Heart Murmur	116	**K**		Mastoid Process	216	Osgood-Schlatter Disease	174		
Heat Cramps	197			Maxilla	80	Osteoarthritis	174		
Heat Exhaustion	197	Keratin	63	Mechanical Effects	8	Osteoporosis	175		
Heat Stroke	197	Kidney	88	Medial	50	Ovaries	62		
Hemoglobin	55	Kidney Stones	179	Medial Border of Scapula	218				
Hepatitis	125	Kyphosis	172	Medial Condyle(Femur)	225	**P**			
Hereditary Disease	97			Medial Condyle(Tibia)	226				
Hernia	126	**L**		Medial Epicondyle(Femur)	225	Pacemaker	110		
Herniated Disc	171			Medial Epicondyle(Humerus)	221	Pacinian Corpuscles	63		
Herpes Simplex	139	Labrum	77	Medial Malleolus	226	Pancreas	59		
Hilton's Law	69	Laceration	145	Median Nerve	71	Pancreatic Islets	62		
Hinge Joint	79	Lacrimal Bone	80	Medical History	14	Pancreatitis	127		
HIPAA	14	Lambdoid Suture	77	Medulla Oblongata	69	Parallel(Muscle shape)	66		
Hodgkin's Lymphoma	184	Large Intestine	59	Meissner's Corpuscles	63	Parasympathetic Response	73		
Homeostasis	50	Larynx	75	Melatonin	62	Parietal Bone	80		
Homeostatic Mechanisms	50	Lateral	50	Meninges	70	Parietal Lobe	69		
Hook of Hamate	223	Lateral Border of Scapula	219	Meningitis	159	Parkinson's Disease	160		
Hormones	62	Lateral Condyle(Femur)	225	Mesentery	60	Partnership	28		
Horse/Warrior Stance	21	Lateral Condyle(Tibia)	226	Metacarpals	85	Passive Movement	9		
Hot Stone	22	Lateral Deviation	67	Metaphysis	77	Passive Listening	30		
Hot Stone Warmer	19	Lateral Epicondyle(Femur)	225	Metatarsals	87	Pectoral Girdle	82		
Hot Towel Cabinet	19	Lateral Epicondyle(Humerus)	221	Midbrain	69	Pectoralis Major	252		
Humerus	83	Lateral Malleolus	226	Midsagittal Plane	51	Pectoralis Minor	253		
Hyaline Cartilage	77	Lateral Supracondylar Ridge	221	Migraine Headaches	117	Pelvic Girdle	83		
Hydrocollator	19	Latissimus Dorsi	239	Mission Statement	27	Pelvis	52		
Hydrotherapy	22	Laxatives	106	Mitochondria	52	Penis	74		
Hypertension	116	Left Atrium	57	Mitosis	52	Pennate(Muscle shape)	66		
Hyperthyroidism	132	Left Ventricle	57	Mouth	59	Pericardium	56		
Hyperventilation	197	Leg	86	Multifidus	241	Peripheral Nervous System	71		
Hypoglossal Nerve	71	Lesser Trochanter	225	Multiple Sclerosis	160	Peristalsis	59		
Hypothalamus	62	Lesser Tubercle	221	Muscle Contraction	66	Peritoneum	56		
Hypothermia	197	Leukemia	184	Muscle Cramp	153	Peroneus Longus	284		
		Leukocyte	55	Muscle Spindles	67	Personal Hygiene	21		
I		Levator Scapulae	233	Muscular System	65	Pes Anserinus	226		
		Lice	140	Muscular Tissue	53	Petrissage	8		
Idiopathic Disease	97	License	27	Musculocutaneous Nerve	71	pH Scale	88		
Ileocecal Sphincter	61	Ligaments	77	Myocardial Infarction	117	Phagocytosis	102		
Iliac Crest	224	Linea Aspera	225	Myofascial Release	23	Phalanges(Foot)	87		
Iliac Fossa	224	Linens	19	Myosin	65	Phalanges(Hand)	85		
Iliacus	270	Lithotripsy	109			Pharyngitis	128		

Pharynx	59	Ribosome	52	Sternocleidomastoid	236	TMJ Dysfunction	178
Phlebitis	118	Right Atrium	57	Sternum	220	Torticollis	155
Phrenic Nerve	71	Right Ventricle	57	Steroids	106	Trachea	75
Physiology	50	Ringworm	142	Stomach	59	Transference	30
Pia Mater	70	Rolfing	23	Strain	153	Transverse/Horizontal Plane	51
Pineal Gland	62	Rotation	67	Strep Throat	128	Transverse Process	217
Piriformis	271	Rotatores	244	Stretch	9	Trapezium	74
Pisiform	84	Rule of 9's	198	Styloid Process(Fibula)	226	Trapezius	250
Pitting Edema	149			Styloid Process(Radius)	222	Trapezoid	74
Pituitary Gland	62	**S**		Styloid Process(Ulna)	222	Triceps Brachii	263
Pivot Joint	79			Subjective(SOAP)	17	Tricuspid Valve	57
Plan(SOAP)	17	S Corporation	28	Subpoena	27	Trigeminal Nerve	71
Plane Joint	79	Sacrum	81	Subscapular Fossa	218	Trigeminal Neuralgia	162
Plantarflexion	67	Saddle Joint	79	Subscapularis	246	Triquetrum	84
Plantaris	285	Sagittal Plane	51	Sudoriferous Glands	63	Trochlea	221
Plasma	55	Sagittal Suture	77	Superficial	50	Trochlear Nerve	71
Pneumonia	166	Sarcomere	65	Superficial Peroneal Nerve	72	Tropomyosin	65
PNF	9	Sartorius	278	Superior	50	True Ribs	82
Poisoning	198	Scabies	142	Superior Angle	218	Trunk	52
Pons	69	Scalenes	234	Superior Articular Process	217	Tuberosity of 5th Metatarsal	227
Posterior	50	Scaphoid	84	Superior Nuchal Line	216	Tuina	23
Power Differential	30	Scapula(Anterior)	218	Superior Ramus of Pubis	224		
Pregnancy Massage	23	Scapula(Posterior)	219	Superior Vena Cava	57	**U**	
PRICE	198	Scar	104	Supination	67		
Prime Mover	67	Schedule C	29	Supine(Bolster)	20	Ulna	84
Professional Liability Insurance	27	Schedule K-1	29	Suppositories	106	Ulnar Nerve	71
Profit and Loss Statement	29	Sciatic Nerve	72	Supraglenoid Tubercle	218	Ulnar Tuberosity	222
Progesterone	67	Sciatica	161	Supraspinatus	247	Ultrasound	111
Projection	31	Scoliosis	176	Supraspinous Fossa	219	Unassisted Stretch	9
Prolactin	62	Scope of Practice	29	Swedish Massage	23	Upper Limb	52
Pronation	67	Sebaceous Cyst	143	Sympathetic Response	73	Ureters	88
Pronator Teres	267	Sebaceous Glands	63	Synarthrotic	77	Urethra	88
Prone(Bolster)	20	Sedatives	106	Syncope	196	Urethritis	181
Proprioceptor	67	Seizure	196	Synergist	68	Urinary Bladder	88
Prostate	74	Self Disclosure	30	Synovial Fluid	78	Urinary System	88
Protraction	67	Semimembranosus	279	Synovial Membrane	78	Urticaria	144
Proximal	50	Semi-reclined(Bolster)	20			Uterus	74
Psoas Major	272	Semitendinosus	280	**T**		Universal Precautions	195
Psoriasis	141	Sensory Receptors	63				
Psychological Disease	100	Serous Membrane	56	T-lymphocytes	64	**V**	
Pubic Symphysis	224	Serratus Anterior	254	Talus	86		
Pubis	83	Sesamoid Bone	76	Tapotement	8	Vaccines	106
Pulmonary Arteries	57	Shingles	143	Tarsals	86	Vagina	74
Pulmonary Veins	57	Shock	196	Temporal Bone	80	Vagus Nerve	71
Puncture	145	Short Bone	76	Temporal Fossa	216	Varicose Veins	119
Pyelonephritis	180	Side-lying(Bolster)	20	Temporal Lobe	69	Vas Deferens	74
Pyloric Sphincter	61	Sinusitis	167	Temporalis	231	Veins	58
		Skeletal Muscle	54	Tendonitis	154	Vertebral Body	217
Q		Skeletal System	76	Tendons	78	Vertigo	194
		Skin	63	Tennis Elbow	154	Vestibulocochlear Nerve	71
Quadratus Lumborum	242	Skin Graft	110	Tenosynovitis	155	Vibration	8
		Skull	80	Tensor Fasciae Latae	281	Vichy Shower	22
R		Small Intestine	59	Teres Major	248	Vomer Bone	80
		Smooth Endoplasmic Reticulum	52	Teres Minor	249		
Radial Nerve	71	Smooth Muscle	54	Testes	62	**W**	
Radial Tuberosity	222	SOAP Notes	17	Testosterone	62		
Radiation Therapy	110	Soft End Feel	10	Thai Massage	23	W-2	28
Radius	84	Sole Proprietorship	28	Therapeutic Relationship	30	Wart	144
Raynaud's Syndrome	119	Soleus	286	Thigh	85	Wolff's Law	86
Reciprocity	27	Spermatozoa	74	Thoracic Duct	64	Wounds	145
Rectus Abdominis	257	Sphenoid Bone	80	Thoracic Outlet Syndrome	162	Wrist	84
Rectus Femoris	277	Sphygmomanometer	111	Thoracic Vertebrae	81		
Reflexive Effects	8	Spinal Cord	69	Thorax	52	**X**	
Reflexology	23	Spinal Nerves	71	Thrombocyte	55		
Regression	31	Spinalis	245	Thymus	64	X-Ray	111
Reiki	23	Spine of Scapula	219	Thyroid	62	Xiphoid Process	220
Renal Failure	180	Spinous Process	217	Tibia	86		
Repression	31	Spleen	64	Tibial Nerve	72	**Z**	
Reproductive System	74	Splenius Capitis	235	Tibial Plateau	226		
Resistive Joint Movement	9	Sports Massage	23	Tibial Tuberosity	226	Zygomatic Arch	216
Respiratory System	75	Sprain	177	Tibialis Anterior	287	Zygomatic Bone	80
Retraction	67	Squamous Cell Carcinoma	187	Tibialis Posterior	288		
Rheumatoid Arthritis	176	Squamous Suture	77	Tinnitus	193	**0-9**	
Rhomboids	243	Statins	106	Tissue	53		
Rib Cage	82	Sternal End(Clavicle)	220	Tissue Repair	103	1099	29

Also Available!

Kinesiology Made Easy - A Quick Guide to Musculoskeletal Anatomy gives everyone looking to learn about the structures of the body all the important information needed! From origins and insertions, to actions and innervations, bony landmarks, nerves, and reviews of the Skeletal, Nervous, and Muscular systems, Kinesiology Made Easy makes learning Kinesiology, well, easy!

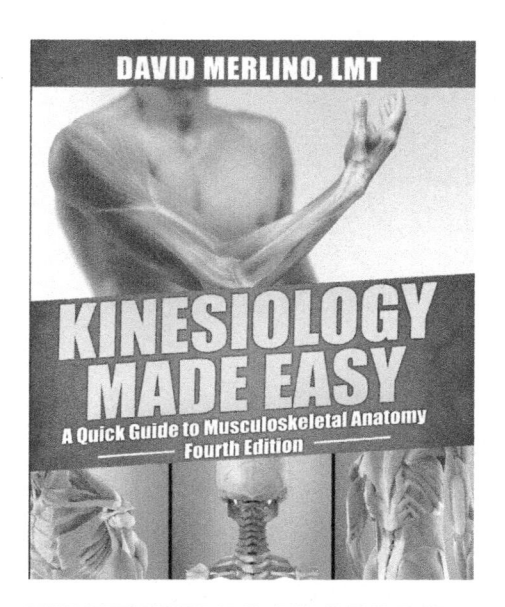

Prepare to pass your MBLEx with this book, containing 10 practice exams, 1000 test questions, study skills, test-taking techniques, and tips on how to reduce test anxiety!

Other MBLEx practice exam books only contain two or three exams. **MBLEx Test Prep - 10 MBLEx Practice Tests and Flashcards**, as the name says, contains 10! This book gives the most value for the price, and is sure to help refine your test-taking ability, drastically increasing your chances of passing the MBLEx!

Included in the book are pre-made flashcards that you only need to cut out! Grab the scissors and put these flashcards to use while saving time and money in the process!

Pathology for Massage Therapy, Second Edition is the most up-to-date, easiest to utilize pathology textbook in circulation! Going in-depth on the body systems, medical terminology, diseases, symptoms, treatments, and contraindications, Pathology for Massage Therapy is an excellent resource for the classroom and for massage therapists looking to stay current on diseases they may encounter!

Made in the USA
Las Vegas, NV
18 October 2021